Introduction to Econometrics

Introduction to
Econometrics

THIRD EDITION

Christopher Dougherty
London School of Economics

OXFORD
UNIVERSITY PRESS

OXFORD
UNIVERSITY PRESS

Great Clarendon Street, Oxford OX2 6DP

Oxford University Press is a department of the University of Oxford.
It furthers the University's objective of excellence in research, scholarship,
and education by publishing worldwide in

Oxford New York

Auckland Cape Town Dar es Salaam Hong Kong Karachi
Kuala Lumpur Madrid Melbourne Mexico City Nairobi
New Delhi Shanghai Taipei Toronto

With offices in

Argentina Austria Brazil Chile Czech Republic France Greece
Guatemala Hungary Italy Japan Poland Portugal Singapore
South Korea Switzerland Thailand Turkey Ukraine Vietnam

Oxford is a registered trade mark of Oxford University Press
in the UK and in certain other countries

Published in the United States
by Oxford University Press Inc., New York

British Library Cataloguing in Publication Data
Data available

Library of Congress Cataloging in Publication Data
Dougherty, Christopher.
Introduction to econometrics / Christopher Dougherty.—3rd ed.
p. cm.
ISBN-13: 978–0–19–928096–4
1. Econometrics. I. Title.
HB139.D69 2006
330.01′5195—dc22   2006033141

Typeset by Newgen Imaging Systems (P) Ltd., Chennai, India
Printed in Great Britain
on acid-free paper by
Ashford Colour Press Ltd, Gosport, Hants

ISBN 978–0–19–928096–4

5 7 9 10 8 6

Preface

Introduction to Econometrics

This is a textbook for a year-long undergraduate course in econometrics. It is intended to fill a need that has been generated by the changing profile of the typical econometrics student. Econometrics courses often used to be optional for economics majors, but now they are becoming compulsory. Several factors are responsible. Perhaps the most important is the recognition that an understanding of empirical research techniques is not just a desirable but an essential part of the basic training of an economist, and that courses limited to applied statistics are inadequate for this purpose. No doubt this has been reinforced by the fact that graduate-level courses in econometrics have become increasingly ambitious, with the consequence that a lack of exposure to econometrics at an undergraduate level is now a handicap in gaining admission to the leading graduate schools. There are also supply side factors. The wave that has lifted econometrics to prominence in economics teaching comes on the heels of another that did the same for mathematics and statistics. Without this prior improvement in quantitative training, the shift of econometrics to the core of the economics curriculum would not have been possible.

As a consequence of this development, students on econometrics courses are more varied in their capabilities than ever before. No longer are they a self-selected minority of mathematical high-fliers. The typical student now is a regular economics major who has taken basic, but not advanced, courses in calculus and statistics. The democratization of econometrics has created a need for a broader range of textbooks than before, particularly for the wider audience. The mathematical elite has for many years been served by a number of accomplished texts. The wider audience has been less well served. This new edition continues to be chiefly addressed to it.

Objectives of the text

The text is intended to provide a framework for a year's instruction with the depth and breadth of coverage that would enable the student to continue with the subject at the graduate level. It is therefore ambitious in terms of theory and proofs, given the constraints imposed by the nature of its target audience and not making use of linear algebra.

A primary concern has been not to overwhelm the student with information. This is not a reference work. It is hoped that the student will find the text readable and that in the course of a year he or she would comfortably be able to traverse its contents. For the same reason the mathematical demands on the student have been kept to a minimum. For nearly everyone, there is a limit to the rate at which formal mathematical analysis can be digested. If this limit is exceeded, the student spends much mental energy grappling with the technicalities rather than the substance, impeding the development of a unified understanding of the subject.

Although its emphasis is on theory, the text is intended to provide substantial hands-on practical experience in the form of regression exercises using a computer. In particular, the Educational Attainment and Earnings Function data provide opportunities for 50 cross-sectional exercises spread through the first ten chapters of the text. Students start with a simple model and gradually develop it into a more sophisticated one as their knowledge of econometric theory grows. It is hoped that seeing how the specification of their models improves will motivate students and help sustain their interest. The Demand Functions data set, with its 15 time series exercises, is intended to provide a similar experience in the remaining chapters. Further data sets have been provided for specialist applications.

Changes to this edition

The main changes to this edition are the inclusion of a chapter on panel data models, a more detailed treatment of the regression model assumptions, a change of notation for the estimators of the regression coefficients, the updating of the main data sets, and an extension of the Review chapter on statistics.

The change of notation involves the replacement of sample covariances and variances in the expressions for regression coefficients by conventional Σ expressions. The previous use of sample covariances and variances did simplify the analysis of the properties of the regression estimators and it has not been abandoned lightly. One reason for making the change was the difficulty of keeping sample concepts separate from population concepts with similar notation. Another was to improve backwards compatibility with the statistics course that should be a prerequisite. Such courses typically provide an introduction to regression analysis using Σ expressions.

The extension to the Review chapter gives improved coverage of consistency and asymptotics, topics that typically receive very little attention in introductory statistics courses.

Additional resources

The online resource centre

http://www.oup.co/best.textbooks/economics/dougherty3e/

offers the following resources for instructors and students:

- PowerPoint slideshows that offer a graphical treatment of most of the topics in the text. Narrative boxes provide an explanation of the slides.
- Links to data sets and manuals.
- Instructor's manuals for the text and data sets, detailing the exercises and their solutions.
- A student area that provides answers to the starred exercises in the text and offers additional exercises.

It is hoped that the provision of these materials will not only be helpful for the study of econometrics but also make it satisfying and pleasurable.

Christopher Dougherty
July 2006

Contents

13   Introduction to Nonstationary Time Series

14   Introduction to Panel Data Models

Review: Random Variables, Sampling, and Estimation

R.1 Introduction

A course in basic statistical theory is a non-negotiable prerequisite for any serious course in econometrics. The reason for this is that econometrics courses have two objectives. One is to show how various quantitative techniques can be used to fit models given suitable data. This is relatively easy. The other is to develop an understanding of the statistical properties of these techniques and hence an understanding of why they work satisfactorily in certain contexts and not in others. This is much more demanding and it does require a good basic knowledge of statistical theory. If you have not taken a statistics course, you should lay this text aside, take one, and return to econometrics afterwards.

What you need from a statistics course

Basic statistics courses tend to be service courses catering to students from many disciplines with a wide variety of priorities and interests. For this reason, they usually cover some topics that are of little relevance to future students of econometrics and they give too much weight to others. Apart from the core theory on sampling, estimation, and inference, the topics that are relevant to business studies or psychology are quite different from those relevant to econometrics. Here is a checklist of topics that are required as a foundation for econometrics.

Descriptive statistics: Frequency distributions and their graphical representations, including histograms (but not stem-and-leaf displays); line plots; measures of location and variation (mean, median, mode, variance, and standard deviation). This is everyday material that should not present any intellectual challenge.

Probability: Sample space, events, relative frequencies, and the notion of probability; marginal and conditional probability distributions. For our purposes, a quite simple understanding of these ideas will suffice. Bayes' theorem is not necessary.

Random variables, probability distributions, and expectations: This material needs attention. However, there is no need to undertake a comprehensive survey of all the different types of probability distribution that are dear to the hearts of statisticians. It is absolutely essential that you understand the properties of the normal distribution, and marginally desirable that you understand those of the binomial distribution. Other distributions you can ignore.

Sampling: For sampling, simple random sampling is enough. There is no need to spend time on stratification or clustering, although you should be familiar with these topics if you ever undertake a survey to raise data. You do not need to cover the topic of sampling without replacement.

Estimation: The distinction between an estimator and an estimate is very important. You will need to know about unbiasedness in relation to estimators, variance, and the estimation of variance.

Statistical inference: A sound understanding of the principles of statistical inference is essential. When it comes to statistical inference you will need to know about Type I and Type II errors, to understand what is meant by a significance test, and to understand the logic behind using a one-sided test in preference to a two-sided test. You will need to know how to perform t tests and F tests, but there is no need to be familiar with the mathematical definitions of the t and F distributions. You will need to know what is meant by a confidence interval. It is sufficient to apply these concepts to the testing of hypotheses relating to sample means. There is no need to spend time on testing hypotheses relating to differences in sample means, or to hypotheses relating to sample proportions.

Analysis of variance: It is helpful to know about this topic, but it should not be given priority.

After covering these topics, a basic statistics course is likely to embark upon an introduction to regression analysis, the pretext being that many statistics students will never take a course in econometrics and it is useful for them to have some exposure to the topic. This may be so, but for our purposes it is premature and duplicative.

This review is not a substitute for a statistics course. Instead, as its title suggests, it is intended to provide an opportunity to review and reinforce statistical concepts that are particularly important in econometric analysis. The only material that may not be familiar is the discussion of the asymptotic properties of estimators (their properties when samples become very large), an area of great importance to us and one that often receives little or no attention in basic statistics courses. This review does not cover hypothesis testing. The principles of hypothesis testing are discussed in the context of the regression model but, if you have never encountered this topic, you should at this point be taking a statistics course, postponing your studies of econometrics.

R.2 Discrete random variables and expectations

Discrete random variables

A simple notion of probability is adequate for the purposes of this text. We shall begin with discrete random variables. A random variable is any variable whose value cannot be predicted exactly. A **discrete random variable** is one that has a specific set of possible values. An example is the total score when two dice are thrown. An example of a random variable that is not discrete is the temperature in a room. It can take any one of a continuing range of values and is an example of a **continuous random variable**. We shall come to these later in this review.

Continuing with the example of the two dice, suppose that one of them is green and the other red. When they are thrown, there are 36 possible experimental **outcomes**, since the green one can be any of the numbers from 1 to 6 and the red one likewise. The random variable defined as their sum, which we will denote X, can taken only one of 11 **values**—the numbers from 2 to 12. The relationship between the experimental outcomes and the values of this random variable is illustrated in Figure R.1.

Assuming that the dice are fair, we can use Figure R.1 to work out the probability of the occurrence of each value of X. Since there are 36 different combinations of the dice, each outcome has probability 1/36. {Green $= 1$, red $= 1$} is the only combination that gives a total of 2, so the probability of $X = 2$ is 1/36. To obtain $X = 7$, we would need {green $= 1$, red $= 6$} or {green $= 2$, red $= 5$} or {green $= 3$, red $= 4$} or {green $= 4$, red $= 3$} or {green $= 5$, red $= 2$} or {green $= 6$, red $= 1$}. In this case six of the possible outcomes would do, so the probability of throwing 7 is 6/36. All the probabilities are given in Table R.1. If you add all the probabilities together, you get exactly 1. This is because it is 100 percent certain that the value must be one of the numbers from 2 to 12.

red green	1	2	3	4	5	6
1	2	3	4	5	6	7
2	3	4	5	6	7	8
3	4	5	6	7	8	9
4	5	6	7	8	9	10
5	6	7	8	9	10	11
6	7	8	9	10	11	12

Figure R.1 Outcomes in the example with two dice

Table R.1 Frequencies and probability distribution, example with two dice

Value of X	2	3	4	5	6	7	8	9	10	11	12
Frequency	1	2	3	4	5	6	5	4	3	2	1
Probability	1/36	2/36	3/36	4/36	5/36	6/36	5/36	4/36	3/36	2/36	1/36

The set of all possible values of a random variable is described as the **population** from which it is drawn. In this case, the population is the set of numbers from 2 to 12.

Expected values of random variables

The **expected value** (sometimes described as **expectation**) of a discrete random variable is the weighted average of all its possible values, taking the probability of each outcome as its weight. You calculate it by multiplying each possible value of the random variable by its probability and adding. In mathematical terms, if the random variable is denoted X, its expected value is denoted $E(X)$.

Let us suppose that X can take n particular values $x_1, x_2, \ldots, x_n$ and that the probability of x_i is p_i. Then

$$E(X) = x_1 p_1 + \cdots + x_n p_n = \sum_{i=1}^{n} x_i p_i. \qquad (R.1)$$

(Appendix R.1 provides an explanation of Σ notation for those who would like to review its use.)

In the case of the two dice, the values x_1 to x_n were the numbers 2 to 12: $x_1 = 2$, $x_2 = 3, \ldots, x_{11} = 12$, and $p_1 = 1/36$, $p_2 = 2/36, \ldots, p_{11} = 1/36$. The easiest and neatest way to calculate an expected value is to use a spreadsheet. The left half of Table R.2 shows the working in abstract. The right half shows the working for the present example. As you can see from the table, the expected value is equal to 7.

Before going any further, let us consider an even simpler example of a random variable, the number obtained when you throw just one die. There are six possible outcomes: $x_1 = 1$, $x_2 = 2$, $x_3 = 3$, $x_4 = 4$, $x_5 = 5$, $x_6 = 6$. Each has

Table R.2 Expected value of X, example with two dice

X	p	Xp	X	p	Xp
x_1	p_1	$x_1 p_1$	2	1/36	2/36
x_2	p_2	$x_2 p_2$	3	2/36	6/36
x_3	p_3	$x_3 p_3$	4	3/36	12/36
...	...	...	5	4/36	20/36
...	...	...	6	5/36	30/36
...	...	...	7	6/36	42/36
...	...	...	8	5/36	40/36
...	...	...	9	4/36	36/36
...	...	...	10	3/36	30/36
...	...	...	11	2/36	22/36
x_n	p_n	$x_n p_n$	12	1/36	12/36
Total		$E(X) = \sum_{i=1}^{n} x_i p_i$			$252/36 = 7$

probability 1/6. Using these data to compute the expected value, you find that it is equal to 3.5. Thus in this case the expected value of the random variable is a number you could not obtain at all.

The expected value of a random variable is frequently described as its **population mean**. In the case of a random variable X, the population mean is often denoted by μ_X, or just μ, if there is no ambiguity.

Expected values of functions of discrete random variables

Let $g(X)$ be any function of X. Then $E\{g(X)\}$, the expected value of $g(X)$, is given by

$$E\{g(X)\} = g(x_1)p_1 + \cdots + g(x_n)p_n = \sum_{i=1}^{n} g(x_i)p_i \qquad (R.2)$$

where the summation is taken over all possible values of X.

The left half of Table R.3 illustrates the calculation of the expected value of a function of X. Suppose that X can take the n different values x_1 to x_n, with associated probabilities p_1 to p_n. In the first column, you write down all the values that X can take. In the second, you write down the corresponding probabilities. In the third, you calculate the value of the function for the corresponding value of X. In the fourth, you multiply columns 2 and 3. The answer is given by the total of column 4.

The right half of Table R.3 shows the calculation of the expected value of X^2 for the example with two dice. You might be tempted to think that this is

Table R.3 Expected value of $g(X)$, example with two dice

\multicolumn{4}{Expected value of $g(X)$}			\multicolumn{4}{Expected value of X^2}			
X	p	$g(X)$	$g(X)p$	X	p	X^2	X^2p
x_1	p_1	$g(x_1)$	$g(x_1)p_1$	2	1/36	4	0.11
x_2	p_2	$g(x_2)$	$g(x_2)p_2$	3	2/36	9	0.50
x_3	p_3	$g(x_3)$	$g(x_3)p_3$	4	3/36	16	1.33
...	...	...	...	5	4/36	25	2.78
...	...	...	...	6	5/36	36	5.00
...	...	...	...	7	6/36	49	8.17
...	...	...	...	8	5/36	64	8.89
...	...	...	...	9	4/36	81	9.00
...	...	...	...	10	3/36	100	8.83
...	...	...	...	11	2/36	121	6.72
x_n	p_n	$g(x_n)$	$g(x_n)p_n$	12	1/36	144	4.00
Total			$E\{g(X)\} = \sum_{i=1}^{n} g(x_i)p_i$				54.83

equal to μ_X^2, but this is not correct. $E(X^2)$ is 54.83. The expected value of X was shown in Table R.2 to be equal to 7. Thus it is not true that $E(X^2)$ is equal to μ_X^2, which means that you have to be careful to distinguish between $E(X^2)$ and $[E(X)]^2$ (the latter being $E(X)$ multiplied by $E(X)$: that is, μ_X^2).

Expected value rules

There are three rules that we are going to use over and over again. They are virtually self-evident, and they are equally valid for discrete and continuous random variables.

Expected value rule 1 The expected value of the sum of several variables is equal to the sum of their expected values. For example, if you have three random variables X, Y, and Z,

$$E(X + Y + Z) = E(X) + E(Y) + E(Z). \tag{R.3}$$

Expected value rule 2 If you multiply a random variable by a constant, you multiply its expected value by the same constant. If X is a random variable and b is a constant,

$$E(bX) = bE(X). \tag{R.4}$$

Expected value rule 3 The expected value of a constant is that constant. For example, if b is a constant,

$$E(b) = b. \tag{R.5}$$

The proof of rule 2 is left as an exercise (Exercise R.5). The proof of rule 3 is trivial in that it follows from the definition of a constant. Although the proof of rule 1 is quite easy, we will omit it here.

Putting the three rules together, you can simplify more complicated expressions. For example, suppose you wish to calculate $E(Y)$, where

$$Y = b_1 + b_2 X \tag{R.6}$$

and b_1 and b_2 are constants. Then,

$$
\begin{aligned}
E(Y) &= E(b_1 + b_2 X) \\
&= E(b_1) + E(b_2 X) \quad \text{using rule 1} \\
&= b_1 + b_2 E(X) \quad\quad \text{using rules 2 and 3.}
\end{aligned} \tag{R.7}
$$

Therefore, instead of calculating $E(Y)$ directly, you could calculate $E(X)$ and obtain $E(Y)$ from equation (R.7).

Population variance of a discrete random variable

In this text there is only one function of X in which we shall take much interest, and that is its **population variance**, var(X), a useful measure of the dispersion of its probability distribution. It is defined as the expected value of the square of the difference between X and its mean, that is, of $(X - \mu_X)^2$, where μ_X is the population mean. In equations it is usually denoted σ_X^2, with the subscript being dropped when it is obvious that it is referring to a particular variable:

$$\text{var}(X) = \sigma_X^2 = E\left\{(X - \mu_X)^2\right\}$$

$$= (x_1 - \mu_X)^2 p_1 + \cdots + (x_n - \mu_X)^2 p_n = \sum_{i=1}^{n}(x_i - \mu_X)^2 p_i. \qquad (R.8)$$

From σ_X^2 one obtains σ_X, the standard deviation, an equally popular measure of the dispersion of the probability distribution; the standard deviation of a random variable is the square root of its variance.

We will illustrate the calculation of population variance with the example of the two dice. Since $\mu_X = E(X) = 7$, $(X - \mu_X)^2$ is $(X - 7)^2$ in this case. We shall calculate the expected value of $(X - 7)^2$ in Table R.4 using Table R.3 as a pattern. An extra column, $(X - \mu_X)$, has been introduced as a step in the calculation of $(X - \mu_X)^2$. By summing the last column in Table R.4, one finds that σ_X^2 is equal to 5.83. Hence σ_X, the standard deviation, is equal to $\sqrt{5.83}$, which is 2.41.

One particular use of the expected value rules that is quite important is to show that the population variance of a random variable can be written

$$\sigma_X^2 = E\left(X^2\right) - \mu_X^2, \qquad (R.9)$$

an expression that is sometimes more convenient than the original definition. The proof is a good example of the use of the expected value rules.

Table R.4 Population variance of X, example with two dice

X	p	$X - \mu_X$	$(X - \mu_X)^2$	$(X - \mu_X)^2 p$
2	1/36	−5	25	0.69
3	2/36	−4	16	0.89
4	3/36	−3	9	0.75
5	4/36	−2	4	0.44
6	5/36	−1	1	0.14
7	6/36	0	0	0.00
8	5/36	1	1	0.14
9	4/36	2	4	0.44
10	3/36	3	9	0.75
11	2/36	4	16	0.89
12	1/36	5	25	0.69
Total				5.83

From its definition,

$$\sigma_X^2 = E\left\{(X - \mu_X)^2\right\}$$

$$= E\left(X^2 - 2\mu_X X + \mu_X^2\right)$$

$$= E\left(X^2\right) + E\left(-2\mu_X X\right) + E\left(\mu_X^2\right)$$

$$= E\left(X^2\right) - 2\mu_X E\left(X\right) + \mu_X^2$$

$$= E\left(X^2\right) - 2\mu_X^2 + \mu_X^2$$

$$= E\left(X^2\right) - \mu_X^2. \tag{R.10}$$

Thus, if you wish to calculate the population variance of X, you can calculate the expected value of X^2 and subtract μ_X^2.

Fixed and random components of a random variable

Instead of regarding a random variable as a single entity, it is often possible and convenient to break it down into a fixed component and a pure random component, the fixed component always being the population mean. If X is a random variable and μ_X its population mean, one may make the following decomposition:

$$X = \mu_X + u, \tag{R.11}$$

where u is what will be called the pure random component (in the context of regression analysis, it is usually described as the disturbance term).

You could of course look at it the other way and say that the random component, u, is defined to be the difference between X and μ_X:

$$u = X - \mu_X. \tag{R.12}$$

It follows from its definition that the expected value of u is zero. From equation (R.12),

$$E(u_i) = E(X_i - \mu_X) = E(X_i) + E(-\mu_X) = \mu_X - \mu_X = 0. \tag{R.13}$$

Since all the variation in X is due to u, it is not surprising that the population variance of X is equal to the population variance of u. This is easy to prove. By definition,

$$\sigma_X^2 = E\left\{(X - \mu_X)^2\right\} = E(u^2) \tag{R.14}$$

and

$$\sigma_u^2 = E\left\{(u - \text{mean of } u)^2\right\}$$
$$= E\left\{(u - 0)^2\right\} = E(u^2). \tag{R.15}$$

Hence σ^2 can equivalently be defined to be the variance of X or u.

To summarize, if X is a random variable defined by (R.11), where μ_X is a fixed number and u is a random component, with mean zero and population variance σ^2, then X has population mean μ_X and population variance σ^2.

Exercises

R.1 A random variable X is defined to be the difference between the higher value and the lower value when two dice are thrown. If they have the same value, X is defined to be zero. Find the probability distribution for X.

R.2* A random variable X is defined to be the larger of the two values when two dice are thrown, or the value if the values are the same. Find the probability distribution for X. [*Note*: Answers to exercises marked with an asterisk are provided in the *Study Guide*.]

R.3 Find the expected value of X in Exercise R.1.

R.4* Find the expected value of X in Exercise R.2.

R.5 If X is a random variable with mean μ_X, and λ is a constant, prove that the expected value of λX is $\lambda\mu_X$.

R.6 Calculate $E(X^2)$ for X defined in Exercise R.1.

R.7* Calculate $E(X^2)$ for X defined in Exercise R.2.

R.8 Let X be the total when two dice are thrown. Calculate the possible values of Y, where Y is given by

$$Y = 2X + 3$$

and hence calculate $E(Y)$. Show that this is equal to $2E(X) + 3$.

R.9 Calculate the population variance and the standard deviation of X as defined in Exercise R.1, using the definition given by equation (R.8).

R.10* Calculate the population variance and the standard deviation of X as defined in Exercise R.2, using the definition given by equation (R.8.).

R.11 Using equation (R.9), find the variance of the random variable X defined in Exercise R.1 and show that the answer is the same as that obtained in

Exercise R.9. (*Note*: You have already calculated μ_X in Exercise R.3 and $E(X^2)$ in Exercise R.6.)

R.12* Using equation (R.9), find the variance of the random variable X defined in Exercise R.2 and show that the answer is the same as that obtained in Exercise R.10. (*Note*: You have already calculated μ_X in Exercise R.4 and $E(X^2)$ in Exercise R.7.)

R.3 Continuous random variables

Probability density

Discrete random variables are very easy to handle in that, by definition, they can take only a finite set of values. Each of these values has a 'packet' of probability associated with it, the sum of the probabilities being equal to 1. This is illustrated in Figure R.2 for the example with two dice. X can take values from 2 to 12 and the associated probabilities are as shown. If you know the size of these packets, you can calculate the population mean and variance in a straightforward fashion.

However, the analysis in this text usually deals with continuous random variables, which can take an infinite number of values. The discussion will be illustrated with the example of the temperature in a room. For the sake of argument, we will assume that this varies within the limits of 55 to 75°F, and initially we will suppose that it is equally likely to be anywhere within this range.

Since there are an infinite number of different values that the temperature can take, it is useless trying to divide the probability into little packets and we have to adopt a different approach. Instead, we talk about the probability of the random variable lying within a given interval, and we represent the probability graphically as an area within the interval. For example, in the present case,

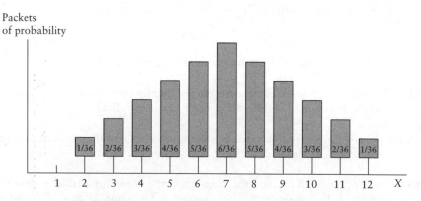

Figure R.2 Discrete probabilities (example with two dice)

the probability of X lying in the interval 59–60°F is 0.05 since this range is one-twentieth of the complete range 55–75°F. Figure R.3 shows the rectangle depicting the probability of X lying in this interval. Since its area is 0.05 and its base is one, its height must be 0.05. The same is true for all the other one-degree intervals in the range that X can take.

Having found the height at all points in the range, we can answer such questions as, What is the probability that the temperature lies between 65 and 70°F? The answer is given by the area in the interval 65–70°F, represented by the shaded area in Figure R.4. The base of the shaded area is 5, and its height is 0.05, so the area is 0.25. The probability is a quarter, which is obvious anyway in that 65–70°F is a quarter of the whole range.

The height at any point is formally described as the probability density at that point, and, if it can be written as a function of the random variable, it is known as the **probability density function**. In this case, it is given by $f(X)$, where X is the temperature and

$$f(X) = 0.05 \quad \text{for } 55 \le X \le 75$$
$$f(X) = 0 \qquad \text{for } X < 55 \text{ or } X > 75. \qquad \text{(R.16)}$$

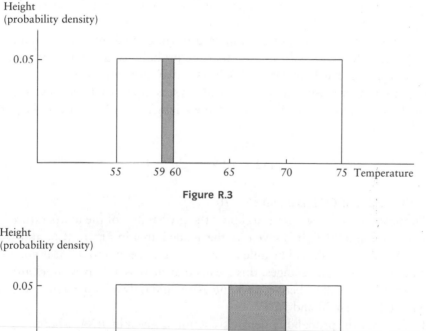

Figure R.3

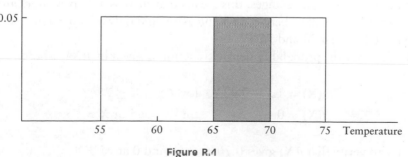

Figure R.4

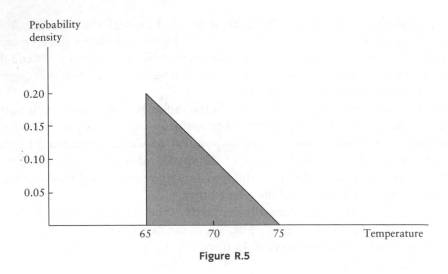

Figure R.5

The foregoing example was particularly simple to handle because the probability density function was constant over the range of possible values of X. Next we will consider an example in which the function is not constant, because not all temperatures are equally likely. We will suppose that the central heating and air conditioning have been fixed so that the temperature never falls below 65°F, and that on hot days the temperature will exceed this, with a maximum of 75°F as before. We will suppose that the probability is greatest at 65°F and that it decreases evenly to zero at 75°F, as shown in Figure R.5.

The total area within the range, as always, is equal to 1, because the total probability is equal to 1. The area of the triangle is 1/2 × base × height, so one has

$$1/2 \times 10 \times \text{height} = 1 \tag{R.17}$$

and the height at 65°F is equal to 0.20.

Suppose again that we want to know the probability of the temperature lying between 65 and 70°F. It is given by the shaded area in Figure R.6, and with a little geometry you should be able to verify that it is equal to 0.75. If you prefer to talk in terms of percentages, this means that there is a 75 percent chance that the temperature will lie between 65 and 70°F, and only a 25 percent chance that it will lie between 70 and 75°F.

In this case the probability density function is given by $f(X)$, where

$$f(X) = 1.5 - 0.02X \quad \text{for } 65 \le X \le 75$$
$$f(X) = 0 \qquad\qquad \text{for } X < 65 \text{ or } X > 75. \tag{R.18}$$

(You can verify that $f(X)$ gives 0.20 at 65°F and 0 at 75°F.)

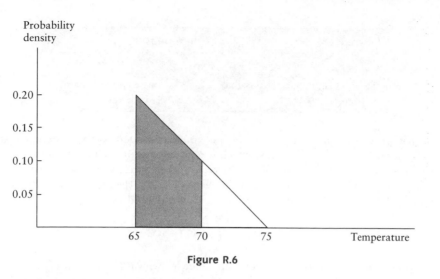

Figure R.6

If you want to calculate probabilities for more complicated, curved functions, simple geometry will not do. In general you have to use integral calculus or refer to specialized tables, if they exist. Fortunately, specialized probability tables do exist for all the functions that are going to interest us in practice. Integral calculus is also used in the definitions of the expected value and variance of a continuous random variable. These have much the same meaning for continuous random variables that they have for discrete ones (formal definitions are given in Box R.1), and the expected value rules work in exactly the same way.

BOX R.1   Expected value and variance of a continuous random variable

The definition of the expected value of a continuous random variable is very similar to that for a discrete random variable:

$$E(X) = \int Xf(X)dX$$

where $f(X)$ is the probability density function of X, with the integration being performed over the interval for which $f(X)$ is defined.

In both cases the different possible values of X are weighted by the probability attached to them. In the case of the discrete random variable, the summation is done on a packet-by-packet basis over all the possible values of X. In the continuous case, it is of course done on a continuous basis, integrating replacing summation, and the probability density function $f(X)$ replacing the packets of probability p_i. However, the principle is the same.

In the section on discrete random variables, it was shown how to calculate the expected value of a function of X, $g(X)$. You make a list of all the different values that $g(X)$ can take, weight each of them by the corresponding probability, and sum.

Discrete	Continuous
$E(X) = \sum_{i=1}^{n} x_i p_i$	$E(X) = \int X f(X) dX$
(Summation over all possible discrete values)	(Integration over the range for which $f(X)$ is defined)

The process is exactly the same for a continuous random variable, except that it is done on a continuous basis, which means summation by integration instead of $\sum$ summation. In the case of the discrete random variable, $E[g(X)]$ is equal to $\sum_{i=1}^{n} g(x_i) p_i$ with the summation taken over $x_1, \ldots, x_n$, the set of specific discrete values that X can take. In the continuous case, it is defined by

$$E[g(X)] = \int g(X) f(X) dx,$$

with the integration taken over the whole range for which $f(X)$ is defined.

As in the case of discrete random variables, there is only one function in which we have an interest, the population variance, defined as the expected value of $(X - \mu_X)^2$, where $\mu_X \doteq E(X)$ is the population mean. To calculate the variance, you have to sum $(X - \mu_X)^2$, weighted by the appropriate probability, over all the possible values of X. In the case of a continuous random variable, this means that you have to evaluate

$$\sigma_X^2 = E\left\{(X - \mu_X)^2\right\} = \int (X - \mu_X)^2 f(X) dX.$$

It is instructive to compare this with equation (R.8), the parallel expression for a discrete random variable:

$$\sigma_X^2 = E\left\{(X - \mu_X)^2\right\} = \sum_{i=1}^{n} (X_i - \mu_X)^2 p_i.$$

As before, when you have evaluated the population variance, you can calculate the standard deviation, σ_X, by taking its square root.

R.4   Population covariance, covariance and variance rules, and correlation

Covariance

We come now to some concepts relating to two random variables. The first is covariance. If we have two random variables, X and Y, their **population covariance**, cov(X, Y), usually written σ_{XY} in equations, is defined to be the expected value of the product of their deviations from their means:

$$\text{cov}(X, Y) = \sigma_{XY} = E\left\{(X - \mu_X)(Y - \mu_Y)\right\} \tag{R.19}$$

where μ_X and μ_Y are the population means of X and Y, respectively. It is a measure of association, but not as useful as correlation, to be discussed shortly. We are mostly interested in covariance as an ingredient in some of our analysis of the properties of estimators.

Independence of random variables

Two random variables X and Y are said to be **independent** if $E[g(X)h(Y)]$ is equal to $E[g(X)]\,E[h(Y)]$ for any functions $g(X)$ and $h(Y)$. In particular, if X and Y are independent, $E(XY)$ is equal to $E(X)E(Y)$. If X and Y are independent, their population covariance is zero, since then

$$E\{(X - \mu_X)\,(Y - \mu_Y)\} = E\,(X - \mu_X)\,E\,(Y - \mu_Y) = 0 \times 0 \qquad \text{(R.20)}$$

by virtue of the fact that $E(X)$ and $E(Y)$ are equal to μ_X and μ_Y, respectively.

Covariance rules

There are some rules that follow in a perfectly straightforward way from the definition of covariance, and since they are going to be used frequently in later chapters it is worthwhile establishing them immediately:

Covariance rule 1   If $Y = V + W$, $\text{cov}(X, Y) = \text{cov}(X, V) + \text{cov}(X, W)$.

Covariance rule 2   If $Y = bZ$, where b is a constant and Z is a variable, $\text{cov}(X, Y) = b\text{cov}(X, Z)$.

Covariance rule 3   If $Y = b$, where b is a constant, $\text{cov}(X, Y) = 0$.

Proof of covariance rule 1

Since $Y = V + W$, $\mu_Y = \mu_V + \mu_W$ by virtue of expected value rule 1. Hence

$$\begin{aligned}
\text{cov}(X, Y) &= E\{(X - \mu_X)\,(Y - \mu_Y)\} \\
&= E\{(X - \mu_X)\,([V + W] - [\mu_V + \mu_W])\} \\
&= E\{(X - \mu_X)\,(V - \mu_V) + (X - \mu_X)\,(W - \mu_W)\} \\
&= \text{cov}(X, V) + \text{cov}(X, W). \qquad \text{(R.21)}
\end{aligned}$$

Proof of covariance rule 2

If $Y = bZ$, $\mu_Y = b\mu_Z$. Hence

$$\begin{aligned}
\text{cov}(X, Y) &= E\{(X - \mu_X)(Y - \mu_Y)\} \\
&= E\{(X - \mu_X)(bZ - b\mu_Z)\} \\
&= bE\{(X - \mu_X)(Z - \mu_Z)\} \\
&= b\text{cov}(X, Z). \qquad \text{(R.22)}
\end{aligned}$$

Proof of covariance rule 3

This is trivial. If $Y = b, \mu_Y = b$ and

$$
\begin{aligned}
\mathrm{cov}(X, Y) &= E\{(X - \mu_X)(Y - \mu_Y)\} \\
&= E\{(X - \mu_X)(b - b)\} \\
&= E\{0\} = 0.
\end{aligned}
\tag{R.23}
$$

Further developments

With these basic rules, you can simplify much more complicated covariance expressions. For example, if a variable Y is equal to the sum of three variables U, V, and W,

$$
\begin{aligned}
\mathrm{cov}(X, Y) &= \mathrm{cov}(X, [U + V + W]) \\
&= \mathrm{cov}(X, U) + \mathrm{cov}(X, [V + W])
\end{aligned}
\tag{R.24}
$$

using rule 1 and breaking up Y into two parts, U and $V + W$. Hence

$$
\mathrm{cov}(X, Y) = \mathrm{cov}(X, U) + \mathrm{cov}(X, V) + \mathrm{cov}(X, W)
\tag{R.25}
$$

using rule 1 again.

Another example: If $Y = b_1 + b_2 Z$, where b_1 and b_2 are constants and Z is a variable,

$$
\begin{aligned}
\mathrm{cov}(X, Y) &= \mathrm{cov}(X, [b_1 + b_2 Z]) & \\
&= \mathrm{cov}(X, b_1) + \mathrm{cov}(X, b_2 Z) & \text{using rule 1} \\
&= 0 + \mathrm{cov}(X, b_2 Z) & \text{using rule 3} \\
&= b_2 \mathrm{cov}(X, Z) & \text{using rule 2.}
\end{aligned}
\tag{R.26}
$$

Variance rules

There are some straightforward rules for variances that are counterparts of those for covariance:

Variance rule 1   If $Y = V + W$, $\mathrm{var}(Y) = \mathrm{var}(V) + \mathrm{var}(W) + 2\mathrm{cov}(V, W)$.

Variance rule 2   If $Y = bZ$, where b is a constant, $\mathrm{var}(Y) = b^2 \mathrm{var}(Z)$.

Variance rule 3   If $Y = b$, where b is a constant, $\mathrm{var}(Y) = 0$.

Variance rule 4   If $Y = V + b$, where b is a constant, $\mathrm{var}(Y) = \mathrm{var}(V)$.

First, note that the variance of a variable X can be thought of as the covariance of X with itself:

$$
\begin{aligned}
\mathrm{var}(X) &= E\{(X - \mu_X)^2\} \\
&= E\{(X - \mu_X)(X - \mu_X)\} \\
&= \mathrm{cov}(X, X).
\end{aligned}
\tag{R.27}
$$

In view of this equivalence, we can make use of the covariance rules to establish the variance rules.

Proof of variance rule 1

If $Y = V + W$,

$$\text{var}(Y) = \text{cov}(Y, Y) = \text{cov}(Y, [V + W])$$
$$= \text{cov}(Y, V) + \text{cov}(Y, W) \quad \text{using covariance rule 1}$$
$$= \text{cov}([V + W], V) + \text{cov}([V + W], W)$$
$$= \text{cov}(V, V) + \text{cov}(W, V) + \text{cov}(V, W)$$
$$+ \text{cov}(W, W) \quad \text{using covariance rule 1 again}$$
$$= \text{var}(V) + \text{var}(W) + 2\text{cov}(V, W). \tag{R.28}$$

Proof of variance rule 2

If $Y = bZ$, where b is a constant, using covariance rule 2 twice,

$$\text{var}(Y) = \text{cov}(Y, Y) = \text{cov}(bZ, Y) = b\text{cov}(Z, Y)$$
$$= b\text{cov}(Z, bZ) = b^2\text{cov}(Z, Z) = b^2\text{var}(Z). \tag{R.29}$$

Proof of variance rule 3

If $Y = b$, where b is a constant, using covariance rule 3,

$$\text{var}(Y) = \text{cov}(b, b) = 0. \tag{R.30}$$

This is trivial. If Y is a constant, its expected value is the same constant and $(Y - \mu_Y) = 0$. Hence $\text{var}(Y) = 0$.

Proof of variance rule 4

If $Y = V + b$, where V is a variable and b is a constant, using variance rule 1,

$$\text{var}(Y) = \text{var}(V + b) = \text{var}(V) + \text{var}(b) + 2\text{cov}(V, b)$$
$$= \text{var}(V). \tag{R.31}$$

Correlation

As a measure of association between two variables X and Y, $\text{cov}(X, Y)$ is unsatisfactory because it depends on the units of measurement of X and Y. It is the expected value of the product of the deviation of X from its population mean and the deviation of Y from its population mean, $E\{(X - \mu_X)(Y - \mu_Y)\}$. The first deviation is measured in units of X and the second in units of Y. Change the units of measurement and you change the covariance. A better measure is the **population correlation coefficient** because it is dimensionless and therefore invariant to changes in the units of measure. It is traditionally denoted ρ, the

Greek letter that is the equivalent of 'r', and pronounced 'row', as in 'row a boat'. For variables X and Y it is defined by

$$\rho_{XY} = \frac{\sigma_{XY}}{\sqrt{\sigma_X^2 \sigma_Y^2}}. \qquad (R.32)$$

The numerator possesses the units of measurement of both X and Y. The variances of X and Y in the denominator possess the squared units of measurement of those variables. However, once the square root has been taken into account, the units of measurement are the same as those of the numerator, and the expression as a whole is unit free. It is left as an exercise that replacing X or Y by a linear function of itself (which is what happens when one changes units) has no effect on the correlation.

If X and Y are independent, ρ_{XY} will be equal to zero because σ_{XY} will be zero. If there is a positive association between them, σ_{XY}, and hence ρ_{XY}, will be positive. If there is an exact positive linear relationship, ρ_{XY} will assume its maximum value of 1. Similarly, if there is a negative relationship, ρ_{XY} will be negative, with minimum value of -1. Proofs are again left as exercises.

Exercises

R.13* Let ρ_{HT} be the correlation between humidity, H, and temperature measured in degrees Fahrenheit, F. Demonstrate that the correlation coefficient is unaffected if temperature is instead measured in degrees Celsius, C. *Note*: $C = 5/9(F - 32)$.

R.14 Suppose a variable Y is an exact linear function of X:

$$Y = \lambda + \mu X$$

where λ and μ are constants. Demonstrate that the correlation between X and Y is equal to 1 or -1, according to the sign of μ.

R.5 Sampling and estimators

So far we have assumed that we have exact information about the random variable under discussion, in particular that we know the probability distribution, in the case of a discrete random variable, or the probability density function, in the case of a continuous variable. With this information it is possible to work out the population mean and variance, and any other population characteristics in which we might be interested.

Now in practice, except for artificially simple random variables such as the numbers on thrown dice, you do not know the exact probability distribution or density function. It follows that you do not know the population mean or variance. However, you would like to obtain an estimate of them or some other population characteristic.

The procedure is always the same. You take a sample of observations and derive an estimate of the population characteristic using some appropriate formula. It is important to be very clear conceptually about what this involves and we will take it one step at a time.

Sampling

We will suppose that we have a random variable X with unknown population mean μ_X and that we take a sample of n observations with the intention of obtaining an estimate of μ_X. We need to make a distinction between the way we think about the sample *before* it has actually been taken and *after* we have taken it. Before we take the sample we will refer to it as the set of quantities $\{X_1, X_2, \ldots, X_n\}$. Let us focus on the first observation, X_1. Before we take the sample, we do not know what the value of X_1 will be. All we know is that it will be generated randomly from the distribution for X. It is itself, therefore, a random variable. Being generated randomly from the distribution for X means that its potential distribution, before the sample is generated, is that of X. The same is true for all the other observations in the sample, when we are thinking about their potential distribution before the sample is generated. So we are now thinking about the variable on two levels: the X variable that is the subject of attention, and the X_i components in a potential sample.

Once the sample has been generated, of course, the observations are just specific numbers. A statistician would refer to this as a realization and would denote it as $\{x_1, x_2, \ldots, x_n\}$, the lower case indicating that the values are now specific numbers.

Estimators

An **estimator** is a general rule, usually just a formula, for estimating an unknown population parameter given the sample of data. It is defined in terms of the $\{X_1, X_2, \ldots, X_n\}$. Once we have obtained a specific sample $\{x_1, x_2, \ldots, x_n\}$ we use it to obtain a specific number that we describe as the **estimate**. To repeat, the estimator is a formula, whereas the estimate is a number. If we take repeated samples, the estimator will be the same, but the estimate will vary from sample to sample.

An estimator is a special case of a random variable. This is because it is a combination of the $\{X_1, X_2, \ldots, X_n\}$ and, since the $\{X_1, X_2, \ldots, X_n\}$ are random quantities, a combination of them must also be a random variable.

The sample mean $\overline{X}$, the usual estimator of the population mean, provides a simple example since it is just the average of the X_i in the sample:

$$\overline{X} = \frac{1}{n}(X_1 + X_2 + \cdots + X_n) = \frac{1}{n}\sum_{i=1}^{n} X_i. \tag{R.33}$$

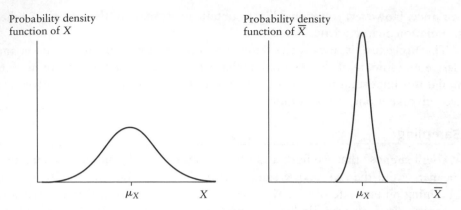

Probability density function of X

Probability density function of $\overline{X}$

Figure R.7 Comparison of the probability density functions of a single observation and the mean of a sample

The probability density functions of both X and $\overline{X}$ have been drawn in the same diagram in Figure R.7. By way of illustration, X is assumed to have a normal distribution. You will see that the distributions of both X and $\overline{X}$ are symmetrical about μ_X. The difference between them is that the distribution for $\overline{X}$ is narrower and taller. $\overline{X}$ tends to be closer to μ_X than a single observation on X because it is an average. Some of the X_i in the sample will be greater than the population mean, some will be smaller, and the positive deviations and the negative deviations will to some extent cancel each other out when the average is taken. We will demonstrate that if the distribution of X has variance σ_X^2, the sample mean has variance σ_X^2/n:

$$\sigma_{\overline{X}}^2 = \text{var}\left\{\frac{1}{n}(X_1 + \cdots + X_n)\right\}$$

$$= \frac{1}{n^2}\text{var}(X_1 + \cdots + X_n)$$

$$= \frac{1}{n^2}\{\text{var}(X_1) + \cdots + \text{var}(X_n)\}$$

$$= \frac{1}{n^2}\left(\sigma_X^2 + \cdots + \sigma_X^2\right)$$

$$= \frac{1}{n^2}\left(n\sigma_X^2\right) = \frac{\sigma_X^2}{n}. \tag{R.34}$$

It may be helpful to have some further explanation of equation (R.34). There are some important conceptual issues at stake that are crucial to an understanding of basic statistical theory. We will go through the equation line by line.

The first line simply explains what is meant by $\sigma_{\overline{X}}^2$.

The second uses variance rule 2 to take the factor $1/n$ out of the expression. The factor must be squared when it is taken out, as shown in the derivation of the rule in Section R.4.

The third and fourth lines are the ones that sometimes give rise to trouble. The third line reads as

$$\text{var}(X_1 + \cdots + X_n) = \text{var}(X_1) + \cdots + \text{var}(X_n). \qquad (R.35)$$

This uses variance rule 1. There are no population covariance terms on the right side of the equation because the observations are assumed to be generated independently. The fourth line reads as

$$\text{var}(X_i) = \sigma_X^2 \quad \text{for all } i. \qquad (R.36)$$

What is going on? X has a specific value in observation i, so how can it have a population variance?

The key to this is quite simple. We need to make a distinction between the *potential* distribution of the observations, and the sample mean, *before* the sample is generated, and the *actual* outcome *after* the sample has been generated. We will refer to these as the *beforehand* and *afterwards* concepts.

To make matters concrete, we will suppose that X has a normal distribution with population mean 5 and variance 1, and that there are 10 observations in the sample.

The first line of Table R.5 (Sample 1) shows the result of randomly drawing numbers for X_1 to X_{10} from this distribution. The sample mean is 5.04. The numbers that appear in this line are *afterwards* in the sense just defined. The remaining 19 rows are the same as the first, but with different sets of randomly generated numbers. Taken individually, they should also be viewed as *afterwards*.

Next we will focus on the observation X_1. Looking at its values in the 20 samples, we obtain an insight into its *potential* distribution. We see that its average value is 4.95 and its estimated variance (see Section R.7) is 1.11. This is not a surprise, because X_1 has been generated randomly from a normal distribution with population mean 5 and population variance 1. The same is true for all the other X observations. In each case their average over the 20 samples is approximately 5, and their variances are approximately 1, and the approximations would have been closer to the population values if we had had more samples. This is what we are referring to when we write

$$\frac{1}{n^2}(\sigma_{X_1}^2 + \cdots + \sigma_{X_n}^2) = \frac{1}{n^2}(\sigma_X^2 + \cdots + \sigma_X^2) \qquad (R.37)$$

in equation (R.34). We are saying that the variance of the *potential* distribution of X_1, before a sample is generated, is σ_X^2, because X_1 is drawn randomly from the distribution for X. The same is true for all the other observations.

Of course, we are not interested in the distributions of the individual observations, but in the distribution of the estimator, in this case $\overline{X}$. What we are

Table R.5

sample	X_1	X_2	X_3	X_4	X_5	X_6	X_7	X_8	X_9	X_{10}	$\overline{X}$
1	6.25	4.35	5.30	6.44	4.63	3.13	5.97	5.21	3.88	5.28	5.04
2	3.81	5.19	4.49	5.51	4.41	4.39	5.43	4.75	5.39	5.63	4.90
3	5.65	4.88	6.86	6.42	6.98	4.50	4.92	7.04	5.32	5.77	5.83
4	5.78	4.15	3.99	5.86	6.27	6.32	3.80	4.78	3.67	4.83	4.95
5	2.92	5.48	5.07	4.75	4.73	5.09	5.50	4.46	3.50	4.76	4.63
6	4.82	3.01	5.59	5.02	5.37	4.06	6.04	5.21	6.17	4.59	4.99
7	5.84	4.30	4.69	3.82	5.21	5.74	6.05	7.29	3.77	5.13	5.18
8	5.13	5.02	5.35	4.03	4.90	5.42	4.90	4.21	4.41	5.50	4.89
9	4.13	5.16	5.85	6.11	7.12	5.77	3.91	6.30	3.88	2.81	5.10
10	5.21	4.91	4.01	4.45	5.75	3.20	3.84	3.93	4.08	3.88	4.33
11	7.32	3.96	2.75	5.69	4.60	7.90	3.61	5.88	5.47	3.34	5.05
12	6.52	5.51	5.34	5.47	4.51	5.72	2.78	4.40	4.55	4.80	4.96
13	4.71	5.06	6.22	5.99	4.62	5.00	5.38	3.56	3.90	5.35	4.98
14	4.59	4.54	4.63	4.84	6.38	5.62	4.75	5.86	4.57	4.64	5.04
15	5.13	4.99	7.36	4.60	3.85	5.26	6.13	5.26	5.83	4.83	5.32
16	4.26	4.99	4.49	4.48	4.76	3.77	5.49	5.31	6.66	6.44	5.07
17	4.07	5.55	4.26	5.07	4.96	4.38	5.85	5.51	4.21	5.12	4.90
18	3.83	5.14	5.69	5.24	3.41	4.24	5.00	4.99	5.40	4.09	4.70
19	4.38	5.54	3.70	5.06	5.59	4.00	5.16	4.64	6.25	6.03	5.03
20	4.74	4.45	4.69	5.67	5.51	3.84	5.14	4.89	4.16	4.89	4.80
mean	4.95	4.81	5.02	5.23	5.18	4.87	4.98	5.17	4.75	4.89	4.98
estimated variance	1.11	0.43	1.19	0.64	0.98	1.33	0.89	0.96	0.99	0.77	0.09

saying is that the variance of the potential distribution of $\overline{X}$, before the sample is generated, is σ_X^2/n.

R.6 Unbiasedness and efficiency

Much of the analysis in later chapters will be concerned with three properties of estimators: unbiasedness, efficiency, and consistency. The first two, treated in this section, relate to finite sample analysis: analysis where the samples have finite number of observations. Consistency, a property that relates to analysis when the sample size tends to infinity, is treated in the next section.

Unbiasedness

Since estimators are random variables, it follows that only by coincidence will an estimate be exactly equal to the population characteristic. Generally there will be some degree of error, which will be small or large, positive or negative, according to the pure random components of the values of X in the sample.

Although this must be accepted, it is nevertheless desirable that the estimator should be accurate on average in the long run, to put it intuitively. To put it technically, we should like the expected value of the estimator to be equal to the population characteristic. If this is true, the estimator is said to be **unbiased**. If it is not, the estimator is said to be **biased**, and the difference between its expected value and the population characteristic is described as the **bias**.

Let us start with the sample mean. Is it an unbiased estimator of the population mean? Is $E(\overline{X})$ equal to μ_X? Yes, it is:

$$E\left(\overline{X}\right) = E\left\{\frac{1}{n}(X_1 + \cdots + X_n)\right\} = \frac{1}{n}E(X_1 + \cdots + X_n)$$

$$= \frac{1}{n}\{E(X_1) + \cdots + E(X_n)\}$$

$$= \frac{1}{n}(\mu_X + \cdots + \mu_X) = \frac{1}{n}(n\mu_X) = \mu_X. \qquad \text{(R.38)}$$

Note that when we make the step

$$\frac{1}{n}\{E(X_1) + \cdots + E(X_n)\} = \frac{1}{n}(\mu_X + \cdots + \mu_X) \qquad \text{(R.39)}$$

we are referring to the fact that the potential distribution of each X_i has population mean μ_X. In the language of Section R.5, we are dealing with beforehand concepts.

We have shown that the sample mean is an unbiased estimator of the population mean μ_X. However, it is not the only unbiased estimator that we could construct. To keep the analysis simple, suppose that we have a sample of just two observations, X_1 and X_2. Any weighted average of the observations X_1 and X_2 will be an unbiased estimator, provided that the weights add up to 1. To see this, suppose we construct a generalized estimator:

$$Z = \lambda_1 X_1 + \lambda_2 X_2. \qquad \text{(R.40)}$$

The expected value of Z is given by

$$E(Z) = E(\lambda_1 X_1 + \lambda_2 X_2) = E(\lambda_1 X_1) + E(\lambda_2 X_2)$$

$$= \lambda_1 E(X_1) + \lambda_2 E(X_2) = \lambda_1 \mu_X + \lambda_2 \mu_X$$

$$= (\lambda_1 + \lambda_2)\mu_X. \qquad \text{(R.41)}$$

If λ_1 and λ_2 add up to 1, we have $E(Z) = \mu_X$, and Z is an unbiased estimator of μ_X.

Thus, in principle, we have an infinite number of unbiased estimators. How do we choose among them? Why do we always in fact use the sample average, with $\lambda_1 = \lambda_2 = 0.5$? Perhaps you think that it would be unfair to give the observations different weights, or that asymmetry should be avoided on principle? However, we are not concerned with fairness, or with symmetry for its own sake. There is a more compelling reason: efficiency.

Efficiency

Unbiasedness is one desirable feature of an estimator, but it is not the only one. Another important consideration is its reliability. We want the estimator to have as high a probability as possible of giving a close estimate of the population characteristic, which means that we want its probability density function to be as concentrated as possible around the true value. One way of summarizing this is to say that we want its population variance to be as small as possible.

Suppose that we have two estimators of the population mean, that they are calculated using the same information, that they are both unbiased, and that their probability density functions are as shown in Figure R.8. Since the probability density function for estimator B is more highly concentrated than that for estimator A, it is more likely to give an accurate estimate. It is therefore said to be more **efficient,** to use the technical term.

Note carefully that the definition says 'more likely'. Even though estimator B is more efficient, that does not mean that it will always give the more accurate estimate. Sometimes it will have a bad day, and estimator A will have a good day, and A will be closer to the true value. But as a matter of probability, B will tend to be more accurate than A.

It is rather like the issue of whether you should fasten your seat belt when driving a vehicle. A large number of surveys in different countries have shown that you are much less likely to be killed or seriously injured in a road accident if you wear a seat belt, but there are always the odd occasions when individuals not wearing belts have miraculously escaped when they might have been killed, had they been strapped in. The surveys do not deny this. They simply conclude that the odds are on the side of belting up. Similarly, the odds are on the side of the efficient estimator.

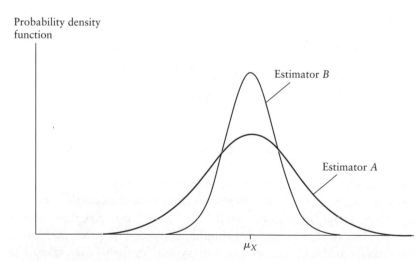

Figure R.8 Efficient and inefficient estimators

We have said that we want the variance of an estimator to be as small as possible, and that the efficient estimator is the one with the smallest variance. We shall now investigate the variance of the generalized estimator of the population mean and show that it is minimized when the two observations are given equal weight.

The population variance of the generalized estimator is given by

$$
\begin{aligned}
\sigma_Z^2 &= \mathrm{var}\,(\lambda_1 X_1 + \lambda_2 X_2) \\
&= \mathrm{var}\,(\lambda_1 X_1) + \mathrm{var}\,(\lambda_2 X_2) + 2\mathrm{cov}\,(\lambda_1 X_1, \lambda_2 X_2) \\
&= \lambda_1^2 \sigma_{X_1}^2 + \lambda_2^2 \sigma_{X_2}^2 + 2\lambda_1 \lambda_2 \sigma_{X_1 X_2} \\
&= (\lambda_1^2 + \lambda_2^2)\sigma_X^2.
\end{aligned}
\tag{R.42}
$$

We are assuming that X_1 and X_2 are generated independently and hence that $\sigma_{X_1 X_2}$ is zero.

Now, we have already seen that λ_1 and λ_2 must add up to 1 if the estimator is to be unbiased. Hence for unbiasedness, $\lambda_2 = 1 - \lambda_1$ and

$$
\lambda_1^2 + \lambda_2^2 = \lambda_1^2 + (1 - \lambda_1)^2 = 2\lambda_1^2 - 2\lambda_1 + 1.
\tag{R.43}
$$

Since we want to choose λ_1 in such a way that the variance is minimized, we want to choose it to minimize $(2\lambda_1^2 - 2\lambda_1 + 1)$. You could solve this problem graphically or by using the differential calculus. The first-order condition is

$$
4\lambda_1 - 2 = 0.
\tag{R.44}
$$

Thus the minimum value is reached when λ_1 is equal to 0.5. Hence λ_2 is also equal to 0.5. (We should check the second derivative. This is equal to 4, which is positive, confirming that we have found a minimum rather than a maximum.)

We have thus shown that the sample average has the smallest variance of estimators of this kind. This means that it has the most concentrated probability distribution around the true mean, and hence that (in a probabilistic sense) it is the most accurate. To use the correct terminology, of the set of unbiased estimators, it is the most efficient. Of course, we have shown this only for the case where the sample consists of just two observations, but the conclusions are valid for samples of any size, provided that the observations are independent of one another.

Two final points. First, efficiency is a *comparative* concept. You should use the term only when comparing alternative estimators. You should not use it to summarize changes in the variance of a single estimator. In particular, as we shall see in Section R.8, the variance of an estimator generally decreases as the sample size increases, but it would be wrong to say that the estimator is becoming more efficient. You must reserve the term for comparisons of *different* estimators. Second, you can compare the efficiency of alternative estimators only if they are using the same information: for example, the same set of observations on a number of random variables. If the estimators use different information, one may well have a smaller variance, but it would not be correct to describe it as being more efficient.

Conflicts between unbiasedness and minimum variance

We have seen in this review that it is desirable that an estimator be unbiased and that it have the smallest possible variance. These are two quite different criteria and occasionally they conflict with each other. It sometimes happens that one can construct two estimators of a population characteristic, one of which is unbiased (*A* in Figure R.9), the other being biased but having smaller variance (*B*).

A will be better in the sense that it is unbiased, but *B* is better in the sense that its estimates are always close to the true value. How do you choose between them?

It will depend on the circumstances. If you are not bothered by errors, provided that in the long run they cancel out, you should probably choose *A*. On the other hand, if you can tolerate small errors, but not large ones, you should choose *B*.

Technically speaking, it depends on your **loss function**, the cost to you of an error as a function of its size. It is usual to choose the estimator that yields the smallest expected loss, which is found by weighting the loss function by the probability density function. (If you are risk averse, you may wish to take the variance of the loss into account as well.)

A common example of a loss function, illustrated by the quadratic curve in Figure R.10, is the square of the error. The expected value of this, known as the

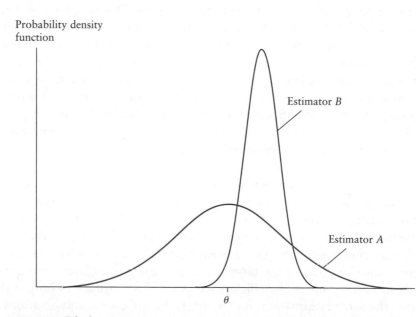

Figure R.9 Which estimator is to be preferred? *A* is unbiased but *B* has smaller variance

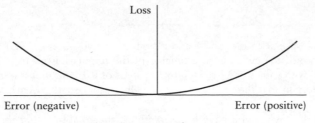

Figure R.10 Loss function

mean square error (MSE), has the simple decomposition

$$\text{MSE of estimator} = \text{variance of estimator} + \text{bias}^2. \qquad (R.45)$$

To show this, suppose that you are using an estimator Z to estimate an unknown population parameter θ. Let the expected value of Z be μ_Z. This will be equal to θ only if Z is an unbiased estimator. In general there will be a bias, given by $(\mu_Z - \theta)$. The variance of Z is equal to $E\{(Z - \mu_Z)^2\}$. The MSE of Z can be decomposed as follows:

$$E\{(Z - \theta)^2\} = E\{([Z - \mu_Z] + [\mu_Z - \theta])^2\}$$
$$= E\{(Z - \mu_Z)^2 + 2(Z - \mu_Z)(\mu_Z - \theta) + (\mu_Z - \theta)^2\}$$
$$= E\{(Z - \mu_Z)^2\} + 2(\mu_Z - \theta)E(Z - \mu_Z) + E\{(\mu_Z - \theta)^2\}. $$
$$(R.46)$$

The first term is the population variance of Z. The second term is zero because

$$E(Z - \mu_Z) = E(Z) + E(-\mu_Z) = \mu_Z - \mu_Z = 0. \qquad (R.47)$$

The expected value of the third term is $(\mu_Z - \theta)^2$, the bias squared, since both μ_Z and θ are constants. Hence we have shown that the MSE of the estimator is equal to the sum of its population variance and the square of its bias.

In Figure R.9, estimator A has no bias component, but it has a much larger variance component than B and therefore could be inferior by this criterion.

The MSE is often used to generalize the concept of efficiency to cover comparisons of biased as well as unbiased estimators. However, in this text, comparisons of efficiency will mostly be confined to unbiased estimators.

Exercises

R.15 For the special case $\sigma^2 = 1$ and a sample of two observations, calculate the variance of the generalized estimator of the population mean using equation (R.43) with values of λ_1 from 0 to 1 at steps of 0.1, and plot it in a diagram. Is it important that the weights λ_1 and λ_2 should be exactly equal?

R.16* Show that, when you have n observations, the condition that the generalized estimator $(\lambda_1 X_1 + \cdots + \lambda_n X_n)$ should be an unbiased estimator of μ_X is $\lambda_1 + \cdots + \lambda_n = 1$.

R.17 Give examples of applications where you might (1) prefer an estimator of type A, (2) prefer one of type B, in Figure R.9.

R.18 Draw a loss function for getting to an airport later (or earlier) than the official check-in time.

R.19* In general, the variance of the distribution of an estimator decreases when the sample size is increased. Is it correct to describe the estimator as becoming more efficient?

R.20 If you have two estimators of an unknown population parameter, is the one with the smaller variance necessarily more efficient?

R.7   Estimators of variance, covariance, and correlation

The concepts of population variance and covariance were defined in Sections R.2 and R.4. For a random variable X, the population variance σ_X^2 is

$$\text{var}(X) = \sigma_X^2 = E\left\{(X - \mu_X)^2\right\}. \tag{R.48}$$

Given a sample of n observations, the usual estimator of σ_X^2 is the sum of the squared deviations around the sample mean divided by $n-1$, typically denoted s_X^2:

$$s_X^2 = \frac{1}{n-1} \sum_{i=1}^{n} \left(X_i - \overline{X}\right)^2. \tag{R.49}$$

Since the population variance is the expected value of the squared deviation of X about its mean, it makes intuitive sense to use the average of the sample squared deviations as an estimator. But why divide by $n - 1$ rather than by n? The reason is that the sample mean is by definition in the middle of the sample, while the unknown population mean is not, except by coincidence. As a consequence, the sum of the squared deviations from the sample mean tends to be slightly smaller than the sum of the squared deviations from the population mean. As a consequence, a simple average of the squared sample deviations is a downwards biased estimator of the population variance. However, the bias can be shown to be a factor of $(n-1)/n$. Thus one can allow for the bias by dividing the sum of the squared deviations by $n-1$ instead of n. A formal proof of the unbiasedness of s_X^2 is given in Appendix R.2.

A similar adjustment has to be made when estimating a population covariance. For two random variables X and Y the population covariance σ_{XY} is

$$\text{cov}(X, Y) = \sigma_{XY} = E\{(X - \mu_X)(Y - \mu_Y)\}. \qquad (R.50)$$

An unbiased estimator of σ_{XY} is given by the sum of the products of the deviations around the sample means divided by $n-1$, typically denoted s_{XY}:

$$s_{XY} = \frac{1}{n-1} \sum_{i=1}^{n} \left(X_i - \overline{X}\right)\left(Y_i - \overline{Y}\right). \qquad (R.51)$$

Again, for a formal proof of the unbiasedness of s_{XY}, see Appendix R.2.

The population correlation coefficient ρ_{XY} was defined in Section R.4 as

$$\rho_{XY} = \frac{\sigma_{XY}}{\sqrt{\sigma_X^2 \sigma_Y^2}}. \qquad (R.52)$$

The sample correlation coefficient, r_{XY} is obtained from this by replacing σ_{XY}, σ_X^2, and σ_Y^2 by their estimators:

$$r_{XY} = \frac{s_{XY}}{\sqrt{s_X^2 s_Y^2}} = \frac{\frac{1}{n-1}\sum\left(X - \overline{X}\right)\left(Y - \overline{Y}\right)}{\sqrt{\frac{1}{n-1}\sum\left(X - \overline{X}\right)^2 \frac{1}{n-1}\sum\left(Y - \overline{Y}\right)^2}}$$

$$= \frac{\sum\left(X - \overline{X}\right)\left(Y - \overline{Y}\right)}{\sqrt{\sum\left(X - \overline{X}\right)^2 \sum\left(Y - \overline{Y}\right)^2}}. \qquad (R.53)$$

R.8 Asymptotic properties of estimators

The asymptotic properties of estimators are their properties as the number of observations in a sample becomes very large and tends to infinity. We shall be concerned with the concepts of probability limits and consistency and the central limit theorem. These topics are usually mentioned in standard statistics texts, but with no great seriousness of purpose, and generally without an explanation of why they are relevant and useful. The reason is that most standard introductory statistics courses cater to a wide variety of students, most of whom will never have any use for the asymptotic properties of estimators. However, asymptotic properties lie at the heart of much econometric analysis, and so for students of econometrics they are important.

Probability limits

We will start with an abstract definition of a **probability limit** and then illustrate it with a simple example. A sequence of random variables X_n is said to converge in probability to a constant a if

$$\lim_{n \to \infty} P\big(|X_n - a| > \varepsilon\big) \to 0 \qquad (\text{R}.54)$$

for any positive ε, however small. The constant a is described as the probability limit of the sequence, usually abbreviated as **plim**:

$$\text{plim}\, X_n = a. \qquad (\text{R}.55)$$

We will take as our example the mean of a sample of observations, $\overline{X}$, generated from a random variable X with unknown population mean μ_X and population variance σ_X^2. We will investigate how $\overline{X}$ behaves as the sample size n becomes large. For convenience we shall assume that X has a normal distribution, but this does not affect the analysis. If X has a normal distribution with mean μ_X, $\overline{X}$ will also have a normal distribution with mean μ_X, the difference being that the distribution for $\overline{X}$ will have variance σ_X^2/n, as we saw in Section R.5.

As n increases, the variance decreases. This is illustrated in Figure R.11. We are assuming that X has mean 100 and standard deviation 50. If the sample size is 4, the standard deviation of $\overline{X}$, $\sigma_X/\sqrt{n}$, is equal to $50/\sqrt{4} = 25$. If the sample size is 25, the standard deviation is 10. If it is 100, the standard deviation is 5.

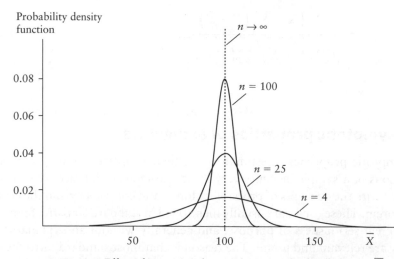

Figure R.11 Effect of increasing the sample size on the distribution of $\overline{X}$

Figure R.11 shows the corresponding probability density functions. The larger the sample size, the narrower and taller will be the probability density function of $\overline{X}$. As n tends to infinity, the probability density function will collapse to a vertical spike located at $\overline{X} = \mu_X$. Formally,

$$\lim_{n \to \infty} P\left(\left|\overline{X} - \mu_X\right| > \varepsilon\right) \to 0 \qquad (R.56)$$

meaning that the probability of $\overline{X}$ differing from μ_X by any finite amount, however small, tends to zero as n becomes large. Hence we can say

$$\operatorname{plim} \overline{X} = \mu_X. \qquad (R.57)$$

Consistency

An estimator of a population characteristic is said to be **consistent** if it satisfies two conditions:

1. it possesses a probability limit, and so its distribution collapses to a spike as the sample size becomes large, and
2. the spike is located at the true value of the population characteristic.

The sample mean $\overline{X}$ in our example satisfies both conditions and so it is a consistent estimator of μ_X. Most standard estimators in simple applications satisfy the first condition because their variances tend to zero as the sample size becomes large. The only issue then is whether the distribution collapses to a spike at the true value of the population characteristic.

A sufficient condition for consistency is that the estimator should be unbiased and that its variance should tend to zero as n becomes large. It is easy to see why this is a sufficient condition. If the estimator is unbiased for a finite sample, it must stay unbiased as the sample size becomes large. Meanwhile, if the variance of its distribution is decreasing, its distribution must collapse to a spike. Since the estimator remains unbiased, this spike must be located at the true value. The sample mean is an example of an estimator that satisfies this sufficient condition.

However, the condition is only sufficient, not necessary. It is possible for a biased estimator to be consistent, if the bias vanishes as the sample size becomes large. This is illustrated in principle in Figure R.12. The estimator is biased upwards for finite samples, but nevertheless it is consistent because its distribution collapses to a spike at the true value. To return to our example, consider

$$Z = \frac{1}{n+1} \sum_{i=1}^{n} X_i. \qquad (R.58)$$

This is biased downwards because

$$E\left(Z\right) = \frac{n}{n+1} \mu_X. \qquad (R.59)$$

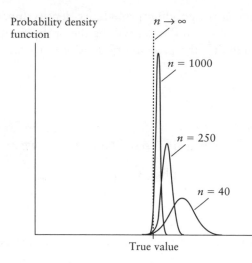

Figure R.12 Estimator that is consistent despite being biased in finite samples

However, the bias will disappear asymptotically because $n/(n+1)$ will tend to 1. The distribution is said to be asymptotically unbiased because the expectation tends to the true value as the sample size becomes large. The variance of the estimator is given by

$$\text{var}(Z) = \frac{n}{(n+1)^2}\sigma_X^2 \tag{R.60}$$

which tends to zero as n becomes large. Thus, Z is consistent because its distribution collapses to a spike at the true value.

An estimator is described as **inconsistent** if its distribution collapses at a point other than the true value. It is also described as inconsistent if its distribution fails to collapse as the sample size becomes large. See Exercise R.22 for a simple example.

Why is consistency of interest?

In practice we deal with finite samples, not infinite ones. So why should we be interested in whether an estimator is consistent? Is this not just an abstract, academic exercise?

One reason is that estimators of the type shown in Figure R.12 are quite common in regression analysis, as we shall see later in this text. Sometimes it is impossible to find an estimator that is unbiased for small samples. If you can find one that is at least consistent, that may be better than having no estimate at all, especially if you are able to assess the direction of the bias in finite samples.

A second reason is that often we are unable to say anything at all about the expectation of an estimator. The expected value rules are weak analytical instruments that can be applied in relatively simple contexts. In particular, the multiplicative rule $E\{g(X)h(Y)\} = E\{g(X)\}\ E\{h(Y)\}$ applies only when X and Y are independent, and in most situations of interest this will not be the case. By contrast, we have a much more powerful set of rules for plims. The first three are the counterparts of those for expectations. The remainder are new.

Plim rule 1 The plim of the sum of several variables is equal to the sum of their plims. For example, if you have three random variables X, Y, and Z, each possessing a plim,

$$\text{plim}(X + Y + Z) = \text{plim}X + \text{plim}Y + \text{plim}Z. \qquad (R.61)$$

Plim rule 2 If you multiply a random variable possessing a plim by a constant, you multiply its plim by the same constant. If X is a random variable and b is a constant,

$$\text{plim } bX = b \text{ plim } X. \qquad (R.62)$$

Plim rule 3 The plim of a constant is that constant. For example, if b is a constant,

$$\text{plim } b = b. \qquad (R.63)$$

Plim rule 4 The plim of a product is the product of the plims, if they exist. For example, if $Z = XY$, and if X and Y both possess plims,

$$\text{plim } Z = (\text{plim } X)(\text{plim } Y). \qquad (R.64)$$

Plim rule 5 The plim of a ratio is the ratio of the plims, if they exist. For example, if $Z = X/Y$, and if X and Y both possess plims, and plim Y is not equal to zero,

$$\text{plim } Z = \frac{\text{plim } X}{\text{plim } Y}. \qquad (R.65)$$

Plim rule 6 The plim of a function of a variable is equal to the function of the plim of the variable, provided that the variable possesses a plim and provided that the function is continuous at that point,

$$\text{plim } f(X) = f(\text{plim } X). \qquad (R.66)$$

To illustrate how the plim rules can lead us to conclusions when the expected value rules do not, consider the following example. Suppose that you know that a variable Y is a constant multiple of another variable Z:

$$Y = \lambda Z. \qquad (R.67)$$

Z is generated randomly from a fixed distribution with population mean μ_Z and variance σ_Z^2. λ is unknown and we wish to estimate it. We have a sample of n observations. Y is measured accurately but Z is measured with random error w with population mean zero and constant variance σ_w^2. Thus, in the sample we have observations on X, where

$$X = Z + w \qquad (R.68)$$

rather than Z. One estimator of λ (not necessarily the best) is $\dfrac{\sum Y_i}{\sum X_i}$. Given (R.67) and (R.68),

$$\frac{\sum\limits_{i=1}^{n} Y_i}{\sum\limits_{i=1}^{n} X_i} = \frac{\sum\limits_{i=1}^{n} \lambda Z_i}{\sum\limits_{i=1}^{n} (Z_i + w_i)} = \frac{\lambda \sum\limits_{i=1}^{n} Z_i}{\sum\limits_{i=1}^{n} Z_i + \sum\limits_{i=1}^{n} w_i}$$

$$= \lambda - \lambda \frac{\sum\limits_{i=1}^{n} w_i}{\sum\limits_{i=1}^{n} Z_i + \sum\limits_{i=1}^{n} w_i} = \lambda - \lambda \frac{\overline{w}}{\overline{Z} + \overline{w}}. \qquad (R.69)$$

Hence we have decomposed the estimator into the true value, λ, and an error term. To investigate whether the estimator is biased or unbiased, we need to take the expectation of the error term. But we cannot do this. The random quantity $\overline{w}$ appears in both the numerator and the denominator and the expected value rules are too weak to allow us to investigate the expectation analytically. However, we know that a sample mean tends to a population mean as the sample size tends to infinity, and so plim $\overline{w}$ is zero and plim $\overline{Z}$ is μ_Z. Since the plims exist,

$$\text{plim} \left\{ \frac{\sum\limits_{i=1}^{n} Y_i}{\sum\limits_{i=1}^{n} X_i} \right\} = \lambda - \lambda \frac{\text{plim}\,\overline{w}}{\text{plim}\,\overline{Z} + \text{plim}\,\overline{w}} = \lambda - \frac{0}{\mu_Z + 0} = \lambda. \qquad (R.70)$$

Thus, we are able to show that the estimator is consistent, despite the fact that we cannot say anything about its finite sample properties.

This subsection started out by asking why we are interested in consistency. As a first approximation, the answer is that if we can show that an estimator is consistent, then we may be optimistic about its finite sample properties, whereas is the estimator is inconsistent, we know that for finite samples it will definitely be biased. However, there are reasons for being cautious about preferring consistent estimators to inconsistent ones. First, a consistent estimator may also be biased for finite samples. Second, we are usually also interested in variances. If a consistent estimator has a larger variance than an inconsistent one, the latter might be preferable if judged by the mean square error or similar criterion that allows a trade-off between bias and variance. How can you resolve these issues? Mathematically they are intractable, otherwise we would not have resorted to large sample analysis in the first place.

Simulations

The answer is to conduct a **simulation experiment,** directly investigating the distributions of estimators under controlled conditions. We will do this for the

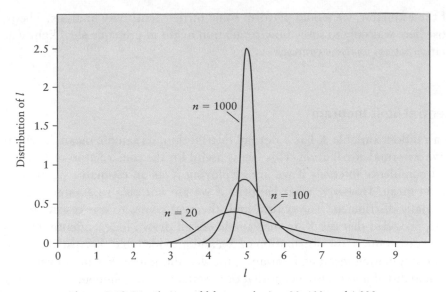

Figure R.13 Distribution of l for sample sizes 20, 100, and 1,000

example in the previous subsection. We will generate Z as a random variable with a normal distribution with mean 1 and variance 0.25. We will set λ equal to 5, so the value of Y in any observation is 5 times the value of Z. We will generate the measurement error as a normally distributed random variable with zero mean and unit variance. The value of X in any observation is equal to the value of Z plus this measurement error. We will start by taking samples of size 20. The value of l, the estimator of λ, for the sample is $\sum Y_i \Big/ \sum X_i$. We calculate the estimator for one million samples and plot the distribution of l. This is shown in Figure R.13. The figure also shows the distributions of l for sample sizes 100 and 1,000, in both cases for one million samples.

We can see that the variance of the distribution diminishes as the sample size increases and it is reasonable to suppose that if the sample size became very large the distribution would collapse to a spike at the true value, 5. For $n = 20$, the distribution is positively skewed. Its mode is 4.65 and its mean 5.33. When the sample size is increased to 100, the mode is 4.94 and the mean 5.05. When it is increased to 1,000, the mode is 4.99 and the mean 5.005. Thus, although there is some element of bias for a sample of 20 observations, it has mostly disappeared for samples of 100 observations and the estimator is virtually unbiased for samples of size 1,000.

Of course, these conclusions are valid only for the particular way in which Z, Y, and X have been generated. If we had had a different mean for Z, different standard deviations for Z and the measurement error, or a different value of λ, we might have found different results for the attenuation of the bias as a function of the sample size. If we were serious about investigating the properties of the estimator, we would perform some further sensitivity analysis. The purpose here was only to show how simulation might in principle shed light where mathematical analysis cannot.

Central limit theorem

If a random variable X has a normal distribution, its sample mean $\overline{X}$ will also have a normal distribution. This fact is useful for the construction of t statistics and confidence intervals if we are employing $\overline{X}$ as an estimator of the population mean. However, what happens if we are *not* able to assume that X is normally distributed? The **central limit theorem** comes to our rescue. It states that, provided that the X_i in the sample are all drawn independently from the same distribution (the distribution of X), and provided that this distribution has finite population mean and variance, the distribution of $\overline{X}$ will converge on a normal distribution. This means that our t statistics and confidence intervals will be approximately valid after all, provided that the sample size is large enough. Actually, there are multiple central limit theorems. Others allow us to weaken our assumptions concerning the distributions of the X_i. For a discussion of a technical point, see Box R.2.

How big does the sample have to be for the approximation to a normal distribution to be good? This depends on the distribution of X and is usually best determined through simulation. Figure R.14 shows the distribution of $\overline{X}$ for the case where the X has a uniform distribution with range -0.5 to 0.5, for

---

BOX R.2   Central limit theorem

The simple version of the central limit theorem presented here assumes that the sample X_i are i.i.d. with population mean μ_X and variance σ_X^2, 'i.i.d.' being a common abbreviation for identically and independently distributed. Under this assumption $\overline{X}$ will have population mean μ_X and variance σ_X^2 / n. We now have a conceptual difficulty. If n becomes very large, the distribution of $\overline{X}$ will collapse to a spike. How, then, can we say that in large samples it converges to a normal distribution?

To avoid this problem, the central limit theorem is applied to $\sqrt{n}\left(\overline{X} - \mu_X\right)$. If X is i.i.d. with population mean μ_X and variance σ_X^2, this will have population mean 0 and variance σ_X^2. Neither of these is affected by changes in the sample size, and so it is meaningful to say that the distribution of $\sqrt{n}\left(\overline{X} - \mu_X\right)$ will converge to a normal distribution with mean 0 and variance σ_X^2. The central limit theorem proves this.

In practice, of course, our statistic is $\overline{X}$, not $\sqrt{n}\left(\overline{X} - \mu_X\right)$, and what we have in mind is the distribution of $\overline{X}$ approximating a normal distribution with mean μ_X and variance σ_X^2 / n before it collapses to a spike at μ_X.

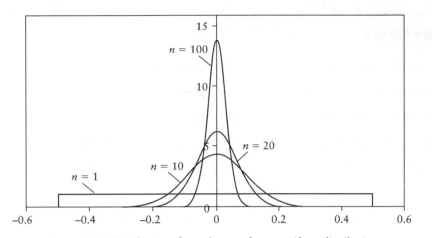

Figure R.14 Distribution of sample mean from a uniform distribution

one million samples. (A uniform distribution is one in which all values over a finite range are equally likely.) For a sample of 1, the distribution is the uniform distribution itself, and so is a horizontal line. The figure also shows the distribution of the sample mean for sample sizes 10, 20, and 100. It can be seen that the mean has a distribution very close to a normal distribution even when the sample size is only 10, and for larger sample sizes the approximation is even better. If X had a different distribution, the sample size required for a good approximation would be different, but even with quite extreme distributions the convergence is quite rapid, allowing us to perform significance tests and construct confidence intervals.

Exercises

R.21 A random variable X has unknown population mean μ_X and population variance σ_X^2. A sample of n observations $\{X_1, \ldots, X_n\}$ is generated. The average of the odd-numbered observations is used to estimate μ_X. Determine whether this estimator is consistent.

R.22* A random variable X has unknown population mean μ_X and population variance σ_X^2. A sample of n observations $\{X_1, \ldots, X_n\}$ is generated. Show that

$$Z = \frac{1}{2}X_1 + \frac{1}{4}X_2 + \frac{1}{8}X_3 + \cdots + \frac{1}{2^{n-1}}X_{n-1} + \frac{1}{2^{n-1}}X_n$$

is an unbiased estimator of μ_X. Show that the variance of Z does not tend to zero as n tends to infinity and that therefore Z is an inconsistent estimator, despite being unbiased.

Key terms

asymptotic properties	outcome
bias, biased	plim
central limit theorem	population
consistent, consistency	population correlation coefficient
continuous random variable	population covariance
discrete random variable	population mean
efficient, efficiency	population variance
estimate	probability density function
estimator	probability limit
inconsistent, inconsistency	simulation experiment
independence	unbiased
loss function	value
mean square error	

Appendix R.1: Σ notation: a review

Σ notation provides a quick way of writing the sum of a series of similar terms. Anyone reading this text ought to be familiar with it, but here is a brief review for those who need a reminder. We will begin with an example. Suppose that the output of a sawmill, measured in tons, in month i is q_i, with q_1 being the gross output in January, q_2 being the gross output in February, etc. Let output for the year be denoted Z. Then

$$Z = q_1 + q_2 + q_3 + q_4 + q_5 + q_6 + q_7 + q_8 + q_9 + q_{10} + q_{11} + q_{12}.$$

Obviously, there is no need to write down all 12 terms when defining Z. Sometimes you will see it simplified to

$$Z = q_1 + \cdots + q_{12},$$

it being understood that the missing terms are included in the summation.

Σ notation allows you to write down this summary in a tidy symbolic form:

$$Z = \sum_{i=1}^{12} q_i.$$

The expression to the right of the Σ sign tells us what kind of term is going to be summed, in this case, terms of type q_i. Underneath the Σ sign is written the subscript that is going to alter in the summation, in this case i, and its starting point, in this case 1. Hence we know that the first term will be q_1. The equality sign reinforces the fact that i should be set equal to 1 for the first term. Above the Σ sign is written the last value of i, in this case 12, so we know that the last term is q_{12}. It is automatically understood that all the terms between q_1 and q_{12} will also be included in the summation, and so we have effectively rewritten the second definition of Z.

Suppose that the average price per ton of the output of the mill in month i is p_i. The value of output in month i will be p_iq_i, and the total value during the year will be V, where V is given by

$$V = p_1q_1 + \cdots + p_{12}q_{12}.$$

We are now summing terms of type p_iq_i with the subscript i running from 1 to 12, and using Σ notation this may be written as

$$V = \sum_{i=1}^{12} p_iq_i.$$

If c_i is the total cost of operating the mill in month i, profit in month i will be $(p_iq_i - c_i)$, and hence the total profit over the year, P, will be given by

$$P = (p_1q_1 - c_1) + \cdots + (p_{12}q_{12} - c_{12}),$$

which may be summarized as

$$P = \sum_{i=1}^{12} (p_iq_i - c_i).$$

Note that the profit expression could also have been written as total revenue minus total costs:

$$P = (p_1q_1 + \cdots + p_{12}q_{12}) - (c_1 + \cdots + c_{12}),$$

and this can be summarized in Σ notation as

$$P = \sum_{i=1}^{12} p_iq_i - \sum_{i=1}^{12} c_i.$$

If the price of output is constant during the year at level p, the expression for the value of annual output can be simplified:

$$V = pq_1 + \cdots + pq_{12} = p(q_1 + \cdots + q_{12}) = p\sum_{i=1}^{12} q_i.$$

Hence

$$\sum_{i=1}^{12} pq_i = p \sum_{i=1}^{12} q_i.$$

If the output in each month is constant at level q, the expression for annual output can also be simplified:

$$Z = q_1 + \cdots + q_{12} = q + \cdots + q = 12q.$$

Hence, in this case,

$$\sum_{i=1}^{12} q_i = 12q.$$

We have illustrated three rules, which can be stated formally:

Σ *Rule* 1   (illustrated by the decomposition of profit into total revenue minus total cost)

$$\sum_{i=1}^{n} (x_i + y_i) = \sum_{i=1}^{n} x_i + \sum_{i=1}^{n} y_i.$$

Σ *Rule* 2   (illustrated by the expression for V when the price was constant)

$$\sum_{i=1}^{n} ax_i = a \sum_{i=1}^{n} x_i \quad \text{(if } a \text{ is a constant)}.$$

Σ *Rule* 3   (illustrated by the expression for Z when quantity was constant)

$$\sum_{i=1}^{n} a = na \quad \text{(if } a \text{ is a constant)}.$$

Often it is obvious from the context what are the initial and final values of the summation. In such cases $\sum_{i=1}^{n} x_i$ is often simplified to $\sum x_i$. Furthermore, it is often equally obvious what subscript is being changed, and the expression is simplified to just $\sum x$.

Appendix R.2: Unbiased estimators of the population covariance and variance

We will start with the estimator of the population covariance. The proof of the unbiasedness of the estimator of population variance follows immediately if one treats variances as special cases of covariances.

The estimator of the population covariance of X and Y is

$$s_{XY} = \frac{1}{n-1} \sum_{i=1}^{n} \left(X_i - \overline{X}\right)\left(Y_i - \overline{Y}\right).$$

Rewrite it as

$$s_{XY} = \frac{1}{n-1} \sum_{i=1}^{n} \left(X_i - \mu_X + \mu_X - \overline{X}\right)\left(Y_i - \mu_Y + \mu_Y - \overline{Y}\right).$$

Then

$$s_{XY} = \frac{1}{n-1} \sum_{i=1}^{n} (X_i - \mu_X)(Y_i - \mu_Y) + \frac{1}{n-1} \sum_{i=1}^{n} (X_i - \mu_X)\left(\mu_Y - \overline{Y}\right)$$

$$+ \frac{1}{n-1} \sum_{i=1}^{n} \left(\mu_X - \overline{X}\right)\left(Y_i - \mu_Y\right) + \frac{1}{n-1} \sum_{i=1}^{n} \left(\mu_X - \overline{X}\right)\left(\mu_Y - \overline{Y}\right).$$

In the second term $\left(\mu_Y - \overline{Y}\right)$ is a common factor and can be taken out of the expression. Similarly, in the third term $\left(\mu_X - \overline{X}\right)$ is a common factor and can be taken out. The summation in the fourth term consists of n identical products $\left(\mu_X - \overline{X}\right)\left(\mu_Y - \overline{Y}\right)$ and is thus equal to $n\left(\mu_X - \overline{X}\right)\left(\mu_Y - \overline{Y}\right)$. Hence

$$s_{XY} = \frac{1}{n-1} \sum_{i=1}^{n} (X_i - \mu_X)(Y_i - \mu_Y) + \frac{1}{n-1}\left(\mu_Y - \overline{Y}\right)\sum_{i=1}^{n}(X_i - \mu_X)$$

$$+ \frac{1}{n-1}\left(\mu_X - \overline{X}\right)\sum_{i=1}^{n}(Y_i - \mu_Y) + \frac{n}{n-1}\left(\mu_X - \overline{X}\right)\left(\mu_Y - \overline{Y}\right).$$

Now

$$\sum_{i=1}^{n}(X_i - \mu_X) = \sum_{i=1}^{n} X_i - n\mu_X = n\left(\overline{X} - \mu_X\right)$$

and similarly

$$\sum_{i=1}^{n}(Y_i - \mu_Y) = \sum_{i=1}^{n} Y_i - n\mu_Y = n\left(\overline{Y} - \mu_Y\right).$$

Hence

$$s_{XY} = \frac{1}{n-1} \sum_{i=1}^{n} (X_i - \mu_X)(Y_i - \mu_Y) + \frac{n}{n-1}\left(\mu_Y - \overline{Y}\right)\left(\overline{X} - \mu_X\right)$$

$$+ \frac{n}{n-1}\left(\mu_X - \overline{X}\right)\left(\overline{Y} - \mu_Y\right) + \frac{n}{n-1}\left(\mu_X - \overline{X}\right)\left(\mu_Y - \overline{Y}\right)$$

$$= \frac{1}{n-1} \sum_{i=1}^{n} (X_i - \mu_X)(Y_i - \mu_Y) - \frac{n}{n-1} \left(\overline{X} - \mu_X\right)\left(\overline{Y} - \mu_Y\right)$$

$$- \frac{n}{n-1} \left(\overline{X} - \mu_X\right)\left(\overline{Y} - \mu_Y\right) + \frac{n}{n-1} \left(\overline{X} - \mu_X\right)\left(\overline{Y} - \mu_Y\right)$$

$$= \frac{1}{n-1} \sum_{i=1}^{n} (X_i - \mu_X)(Y_i - \mu_Y) - \frac{n}{n-1} \left(\overline{X} - \mu_X\right)\left(\overline{Y} - \mu_Y\right).$$

Now

$$\left(\overline{X} - \mu_X\right) = \frac{1}{n} \sum_{i=1}^{n} (X_i - \mu_X) \quad \text{and} \quad \left(\overline{Y} - \mu_Y\right) = \frac{1}{n} \sum_{j=1}^{n} (Y_j - \mu_Y).$$

Hence

$$s_{XY} = \frac{1}{n-1} \sum_{i=1}^{n} (X_i - \mu_X)(Y_i - \mu_Y) - \frac{n}{n-1} \frac{1}{n} \sum_{i=1}^{n} (X_i - \mu_X) \frac{1}{n} \sum_{j=1}^{n} (Y_j - \mu_Y)$$

$$= \frac{1}{n-1} \sum_{i=1}^{n} (X_i - \mu_X)(Y_i - \mu_Y) - \frac{1}{n(n-1)} \sum_{i=1}^{n} \sum_{j=1}^{n} (X_i - \mu_X)(Y_j - \mu_Y).$$

By definition, the expected value of any component $(X_i - \mu_X)(Y_j - \mu_Y)$ is the population covariance σ_{XY} when j is the same as i. There are n such components in the first term of s_{XY} and n in the second. (There are also $n(n-1)$ components $(X_i - \mu_X)(Y_j - \mu_Y)$ in the second term with j different from i. These have expected value zero.) Hence

$$E(s_{XY}) = \frac{1}{n-1} n\sigma_{XY} - \frac{1}{n(n-1)} n\sigma_{XY} = \frac{n-1}{n-1} \sigma_{XY} = \sigma_{XY}$$

and so s_{XY} is an unbiased estimator of their population covariance.

In the special case where Y is the same as X, s_{XY} is s_X^2 and σ_{XY} is σ_X^2. Hence we have also proved that s_X^2 is an unbiased estimator of its population variance.

Simple Regression Analysis

This chapter shows how a hypothetical linear relationship between two variables can be quantified using appropriate data. The principle of least squares regression analysis is explained, and expressions for the coefficients are derived.

1.1 The simple linear model

The correlation coefficient may indicate that two variables are associated with one another, but it does not give any idea of the kind of relationship involved. We will now take the investigation a step further in those cases for which we are willing to hypothesize that one variable, usually known as the **dependent variable**, is determined by other variables, usually known as **explanatory variables, independent variables**, or **regressors**. The hypothesized mathematical relationship linking them is known as the **regression model**. If there is only one regressor, as will be assumed in this chapter and the next, it is described as a **simple regression model**. If there are two or more regressors, it is described as a **multiple regression model**.

It must be stated immediately that one would not expect to find an exact relationship between any two economic variables, unless it is true as a matter of definition. In textbook expositions of economic theory, the usual way of dealing with this awkward fact is to write down the relationship as if it were exact and to warn the reader that it is really only an approximation. In statistical analysis, however, one generally acknowledges the fact that the relationship is not exact by explicitly including in it a random factor known as the **disturbance term**.

We shall start with the simple regression model:

$$Y_i = \beta_1 + \beta_2 X_i + u_i. \tag{1.1}$$

Y_i, the value of the dependent variable in observation i, has two components: (1) the nonrandom component $\beta_1 + \beta_2 X_i$, where β_1 and β_2 are fixed quantities known as the **parameters** of the equation and X_i is the value of the explanatory variable is observation i, and (2) the disturbance term, u_i.

Figure 1.1 illustrates how these two components combine to determine Y. X_1, X_2, X_3, and X_4 are four hypothetical values of the explanatory variable. If the relationship between Y and X were exact, the corresponding values of Y would

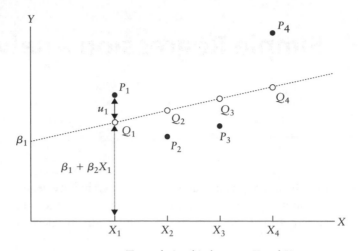

Figure 1.1 True relationship between Y and X

be represented by the points Q_1–Q_4 on the line. The disturbance term causes the actual values of Y to be different. In the diagram, the disturbance term has been assumed to be positive in the first and fourth observations and negative in the other two, with the result that, if one plots the actual values of Y against the values of X, one obtains the points P_1–P_4.

It must be emphasized that in practice the P points are all one can see of Figure 1.1. The actual values of β_1 and β_2, and hence the location of the Q points, are unknown, as are the values of the disturbance term in the observations. The task of regression analysis is to obtain estimates of β_1 and β_2, and hence an estimate of the location of the line, given the P points.

Why does the disturbance term exist? There are several reasons.

1. *Omission of explanatory variables*: The relationship between Y and X is almost certain to be a simplification. In reality there will be other factors affecting Y that have been left out of equation (1.1), and their influence will cause the points to lie off the line. It often happens that there are variables that you would like to include in the regression equation but cannot because you are unable to measure them. For example, later on in this chapter we will fit an earnings function relating hourly earnings to years of schooling. We know very well that schooling is not the only determinant of earnings and eventually we will improve the model by including other variables, such as years of work experience. However, even the best specified earnings function accounts for at most half of the variation in earnings. Many other factors affect the chances of obtaining a good job, such as the unmeasurable attributes of an individual, and even pure luck in the sense of the individual finding a job that is a good match for his or her attributes. All of these other factors contribute to the disturbance term.

2. *Aggregation of variables*: In many cases, the relationship is an attempt to summarize in aggregate a number of microeconomic relationships. For example,

the aggregate consumption function is an attempt to summarize a set of individual expenditure decisions. Since the individual relationships are likely to have different parameters, any attempt to relate aggregate expenditure to aggregate income can only be an approximation. The discrepancy is attributed to the disturbance term.

3. *Model misspecification*: The model may be misspecified in terms of its structure. Just to give one of the many possible examples, if the relationship refers to time series data, the value of Y may depend not on the actual value of X but on the value that had been anticipated in the previous period. If the anticipated and actual values are closely related, there will appear to be a relationship between Y and X, but it will only be an approximation, and again the disturbance term will pick up the discrepancy.

4. *Functional misspecification*: The functional relationship between Y and X may be misspecified mathematically. For example, the true relationship may be nonlinear instead of linear. We will consider the fitting of nonlinear relationships in Chapter 4. Obviously, one should try to avoid this problem by using an appropriate mathematical specification, but even the most sophisticated specification is likely to be only an approximation, and the discrepancy contributes to the disturbance term.

5. *Measurement error*: If the measurement of one or more of the variables in the relationship is subject to error, the observed values will not appear to conform to an exact relationship, and the discrepancy contributes to the disturbance term.

The disturbance term is the collective outcome of all these factors. Obviously, if you were concerned only with measuring the effect of X on Y, it would be much more convenient if the disturbance term did not exist. Were it not for its presence, the P points in Figure 1.1 would coincide with the Q points, you would know that every change in Y from observation to observation was due to a change in X, and you would be able to calculate β_1 and β_2 exactly. However, in fact, part of each change in Y is due to a change in u, and this makes life more difficult. For this reason, u is sometimes described as 'noise'.

1.2 Least squares regression

Suppose that you are given the four observations on X and Y represented in Figure 1.1 and you are asked to obtain estimates of the values of β_1 and β_2 in equation (1.1). As a rough approximation, you could do this by plotting the four P points and drawing a line to fit them as best you can. This has been done in Figure 1.2. The intersection of the line with the Y-axis provides an estimate of the intercept β_1, which will be denoted b_1, and the slope provides an estimate of

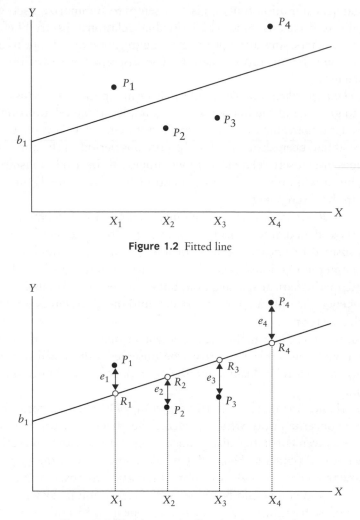

Figure 1.2 Fitted line

Figure 1.3 Fitted regression line showing residuals

the slope coefficient β_2, which will be denoted b_2. The line, known as the **fitted model**, will be written

$$\hat{Y}_i = b_1 + b_2 X_i \qquad (1.2)$$

the caret mark over Y indicating that it is the **fitted value** of Y corresponding to X, not the actual value. In Figure 1.3, the fitted points are represented by the points R_1–R_4.

One thing that should be accepted from the beginning is that you can never discover the true values of β_1 and β_2, however much care you take in drawing the line. b_1 and b_2 are only estimates, and they may be good or bad. Once in a while your estimates may be absolutely accurate, but this can only be by coincidence, and even then you will have no way of knowing that you have hit the target exactly.

This remains the case even when you use more sophisticated techniques. Drawing a regression line by eye is all very well, but it leaves a lot to subjective judgment. Furthermore, as will become obvious, it is not even possible when you have a variable Y depending on two or more explanatory variables instead of only one. The question arises, is there a way of calculating good estimates of β_1 and β_2 algebraically?

The first step is to define what is known as a **residual** for each observation. This is the difference between the actual value of Y in any observation and the fitted value given by the regression line: that is, the vertical distance between P_i and R_i in observation i. It will be denoted e_i:

$$e_i = Y_i - \hat{Y}_i. \tag{1.3}$$

The residuals for the four observations are shown in Figure 1.3. Substituting (1.2) into (1.3), we obtain

$$e_i = Y_i - b_1 - b_2 X_i \tag{1.4}$$

and hence the residual in each observation depends on our choice of b_1 and b_2. Obviously, we wish to fit the regression line, that is, choose b_1 and b_2, in such a way as to make the residuals as small as possible. Equally obviously, a line that fits some observations well will fit others badly and vice versa. We need to devise a criterion of fit that takes account of the size of all the residuals simultaneously.

There are a number of possible criteria, some of which work better than others. It is useless minimizing the sum of the residuals, for example. The sum will automatically be equal to zero if you make $b_1 = \overline{Y}$ and $b_2 = 0$, obtaining the horizontal line $Y = \overline{Y}$. The positive residuals will then exactly balance the negative ones but, other than this, the line will not fit the observations.

One way of overcoming the problem is to minimize RSS, the **residual sum of squares** (sum of the squares of the residuals). For Figure 1.3,

$$RSS = e_1^2 + e_2^2 + e_3^2 + e_4^2. \tag{1.5}$$

The smaller one can make RSS, the better is the fit, according to this criterion. If one could reduce RSS to zero, one would have a perfect fit, for this would imply that all the residuals are equal to zero. The line would go through all the points, but of course in general the disturbance term makes this impossible.

There are other quite reasonable solutions, but the **least squares criterion** yields estimates of b_1 and b_2 that are unbiased and the most efficient of their type, provided that certain conditions are satisfied. For this reason, the least squares technique is far and away the most popular in uncomplicated applications of regression analysis. The form used here is usually referred to as **ordinary least squares** and abbreviated **OLS**. Variants designed to cope with particular problems will be discussed later in the text.

1.3   Least squares regression: two examples

Example 1

First, a very simple example indeed, with only two observations, just to show the mechanics working. Y is observed to be equal to 3 when X is equal to 1; Y is equal to 5 when X is equal to 2, as shown in Figure 1.4.

We shall assume that the true model is

$$Y_i = \beta_1 + \beta_2 X_i + u_i \tag{1.6}$$

and we shall estimate the coefficients b_1 and b_2 of the equation

$$\hat{Y}_i = b_1 + b_2 X_i. \tag{1.7}$$

Obviously, when there are only two observations, we can obtain a perfect fit by drawing the regression line through the two points, but we shall pretend that we have not realized this. Instead we shall arrive at this conclusion by using the regression technique.

When X is equal to 1, $\hat{Y}$ is equal to $(b_1 + b_2)$, according to the regression line. When X is equal to 2, $\hat{Y}$ is equal to $(b_1 + 2b_2)$. Therefore, we can set up Table 1.1. So the residual for the first observation, e_1, which is given by $(Y_1 - \hat{Y}_1)$, is equal to $(3 - b_1 - b_2)$, and e_2, given by $(Y_2 - \hat{Y}_2)$, is equal to $(5 - b_1 - 2b_2)$. Hence

$$\begin{aligned} RSS &= (3 - b_1 - b_2)^2 + (5 - b_1 - 2b_2)^2 \\ &= 9 + b_1^2 + b_2^2 - 6b_1 - 6b_2 + 2b_1 b_2 \\ &\quad + 25 + b_1^2 + 4b_2^2 - 10b_1 - 20b_2 + 4b_1 b_2 \\ &= 34 + 2b_1^2 + 5b_2^2 - 16b_1 - 26b_2 + 6b_1 b_2. \end{aligned} \tag{1.8}$$

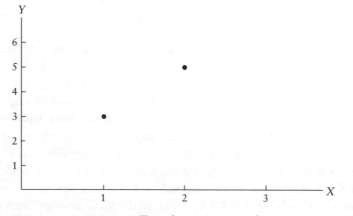

Figure 1.4 Two-observation example

Table 1.1 Two-observation example

X	Y	$\hat{Y}$	e
1	3	$b_1 + b_2$	$3 - b_1 - b_2$
2	5	$b_1 + 2b_2$	$5 - b_1 - 2b_2$

Now we want to choose b_1 and b_2 to minimize RSS. To do this, we use the calculus and find the values of b_1 and b_2 that satisfy

$$\frac{\partial RSS}{\partial b_1} = 0 \quad \text{and} \quad \frac{\partial RSS}{\partial b_2} = 0. \tag{1.9}$$

Taking partial differentials,

$$\frac{\partial RSS}{\partial b_1} = 4b_1 + 6b_2 - 16 \tag{1.10}$$

and

$$\frac{\partial RSS}{\partial b_2} = 10b_2 + 6b_1 - 26 \tag{1.11}$$

and so we have

$$2b_1 + 3b_2 - 8 = 0 \tag{1.12}$$

and

$$3b_1 + 5b_2 - 13 = 0. \tag{1.13}$$

Solving these two equations, we obtain $b_1 = 1$ and $b_2 = 2$, and hence the regression equation

$$\hat{Y}_i = 1 + 2X_i. \tag{1.14}$$

Just to check that we have come to the right conclusion, we shall calculate the residuals:

$$e_1 = 3 - b_1 - b_2 = 3 - 1 - 2 = 0 \tag{1.15}$$
$$e_2 = 5 - b_1 - 2b_2 = 5 - 1 - 4 = 0. \tag{1.16}$$

Thus both the residuals are zero, implying that the line passes exactly through both points, which of course we knew from the beginning.

Example 2

We shall take the example in the previous section and add a third observation: Y is equal to 6 when X is equal to 3. The three observations, shown in Figure 1.5,

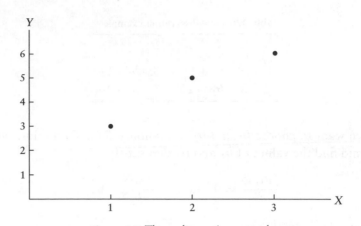

Figure 1.5 Three-observation example

Table 1.2 Three-observation example

X	Y	$\hat{Y}$	e
1	3	$b_1 + b_2$	$3 - b_1 - b_2$
2	5	$b_1 + 2b_2$	$5 - b_1 - 2b_2$
3	6	$b_1 + 3b_2$	$6 - b_1 - 3b_2$

do not lie on a straight line, so it is impossible to obtain a perfect fit. We will use least squares regression analysis to calculate the position of the line.

We start with the standard equation

$$\hat{Y}_i = b_1 + b_2 X_i. \tag{1.17}$$

For values of X equal to 1, 2, and 3, this gives fitted values of Y equal to (b_1+b_2), $(b_1 + 2b_2)$, and $(b_1 + 3b_2)$, respectively, and one has Table 1.2. Hence

$$
\begin{aligned}
RSS &= (3 - b_1 - b_2)^2 + (5 - b_1 - 2b_2)^2 + (6 - b_1 - 3b_2)^2 \\
&= 9 + b_1^2 + b_2^2 - 6b_1 - 6b_2 + 2b_1 b_2 \\
&\quad + 25 + b_1^2 + 4b_2^2 - 10b_1 - 20b_2 + 4b_1 b_2 \\
&\quad + 36 + b_1^2 + 9b_2^2 - 12b_1 - 36b_2 + 6b_1 b_2 \\
&= 70 + 3b_1^2 + 14b_2^2 - 28b_1 - 62b_2 + 12b_1 b_2.
\end{aligned}
\tag{1.18}
$$

The first-order conditions $\dfrac{\partial RSS}{\partial b_1} = 0$ and $\dfrac{\partial RSS}{\partial b_2} = 0$ give us

$$6b_1 + 12b_2 - 28 = 0 \tag{1.19}$$

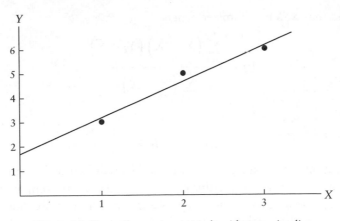

Figure 1.6 Three-observation example with regression line

and

$$12b_1 + 28b_2 - 62 = 0 \,. \tag{1.20}$$

Solving these two equations, one obtains $b_1 = 1.67$ and $b_2 = 1.50$. The regression equation is therefore

$$\hat{Y}_i = 1.67 + 1.50X_i \,. \tag{1.21}$$

The three points and the regression line are shown in Figure 1.6.

1.4 Least squares regression with one explanatory variable

We shall now consider the general case where there are n observations on two variables X and Y and, supposing Y to depend on X, we will fit the equation

$$\hat{Y}_i = b_1 + b_2X_i \,. \tag{1.22}$$

The fitted value of the dependent variable in observation i, $\hat{Y}_i$, will be $(b_1 + b_2X_i)$, and the residual e_i will be $(Y_i - b_1 - b_2X_i)$. We wish to choose b_1 and b_2 so as to minimize the residual sum of the squares, RSS, given by

$$RSS = e_1^2 + \cdots + e_n^2 = \sum_{i=1}^{n} e_i^2 \,. \tag{1.23}$$

We will find that *RSS* is minimized when

$$b_2 = \frac{\sum_{i=1}^{n} \left(X_i - \overline{X} \right) \left(Y_i - \overline{Y} \right)}{\sum_{i=1}^{n} \left(X_i - \overline{X} \right)^2} \tag{1.24}$$

and

$$b_1 = \overline{Y} - b_2 \overline{X}. \tag{1.25}$$

The derivation of the expressions for b_1 and b_2 will follow the same procedure as the derivation in the two preceding examples, and you can compare the general version with the examples at each step. We will begin by expressing the square of the residual in observation i in terms of b_1, b_2, and the data on X and Y:

$$e_i^2 = \left(Y_i - \hat{Y}_i \right)^2 = \left(Y_i - b_1 - b_2 X_i \right)^2$$

$$= Y_i^2 + b_1^2 + b_2^2 X_i^2 - 2 b_1 Y_i - 2 b_2 X_i Y_i + 2 b_1 b_2 X_i. \tag{1.26}$$

Summing over all the n observations, we can write *RSS* as

$$RSS = \left(Y_1 - b_1 - b_2 X_1 \right)^2 + \cdots + \left(Y_n - b_1 - b_2 X_n \right)^2$$

$$= Y_1^2 + b_1^2 + b_2^2 X_1^2 - 2 b_1 Y_1 - 2 b_2 X_1 Y_1 + 2 b_1 b_2 X_1$$

$$+ \cdots$$

$$+ Y_n^2 + b_1^2 + b_2^2 X_n^2 - 2 b_1 Y_n - 2 b_2 X_n Y_n + 2 b_1 b_2 X_n$$

$$= \sum_{i=1}^{n} Y_i^2 + n b_1^2 + b_2^2 \sum_{i=1}^{n} X_i^2 - 2 b_1 \sum_{i=1}^{n} Y_i - 2 b_2 \sum_{i=1}^{n} X_i Y_i + 2 b_1 b_2 \sum_{i=1}^{n} X_i. \tag{1.27}$$

Note that *RSS* is effectively a quadratic expression in b_1 and b_2, with numerical coefficients determined by the data on X and Y in the sample. We can influence the size of *RSS* only through our choice of b_1 and b_2. The data on X and Y, which determine the locations of the observations in the scatter diagram, are fixed once we have taken the sample. The equation is the generalized version of equations (1.8) and (1.18) in the two examples.

The first-order conditions for a minimum, $\dfrac{\partial RSS}{\partial b_1} = 0$ and $\dfrac{\partial RSS}{\partial b_2} = 0$, yield the following equations:

$$2 n b_1 - 2 \sum_{i=1}^{n} Y_i + 2 b_2 \sum_{i=1}^{n} X_i = 0 \tag{1.28}$$

$$2 b_2 \sum_{i=1}^{n} X_i^2 - 2 \sum_{i=1}^{n} X_i Y_i + 2 b_1 \sum_{i=1}^{n} X_i = 0. \tag{1.29}$$

These equations are known as the normal equations for the regression coefficients and are the generalized versions of (1.12) and (1.13) in the first example, and (1.19) and (1.20) in the second. Equation (1.28) allows us to write b_1 in terms of $\overline{Y}$, $\overline{X}$, and the as yet unknown b_2. Noting that $\overline{X} = \frac{1}{n}\sum X_i$ and $\overline{Y} = \frac{1}{n}\sum Y_i$, (1.28) may be rewritten

$$2nb_1 - 2n\overline{Y} + 2b_2n\overline{X} = 0 \tag{1.30}$$

and hence

$$b_1 = \overline{Y} - b_2\overline{X}. \tag{1.31}$$

Substituting for b_1 in (1.29), and again noting that $\sum_{i=1}^{n} X_i = n\overline{X}$, we obtain

$$2b_2 \sum_{i=1}^{n} X_i^2 - 2\sum_{i=1}^{n} X_i Y_i + 2(\overline{Y} - b_2\overline{X})n\overline{X} = 0. \tag{1.32}$$

Separating the terms involving b_2 and not involving b_2 on opposite sides of the equation, we have

$$2b_2 \left(\sum_{i=1}^{n} X_i^2 \quad n\overline{X}^2 \right) - 2\sum_{i=1}^{n} X_i Y_i - 2n\overline{X}\,\overline{Y}. \tag{1.33}$$

Hence

$$b_2 = \frac{\sum\limits_{i=1}^{n} X_i Y_i - n\overline{X}\,\overline{Y}}{\sum\limits_{i=1}^{n} X_i^2 - n\overline{X}^2}. \tag{1.34}$$

An alternative form that we shall prefer is

$$b_2 = \frac{\sum\limits_{i=1}^{n} \left(X_i - \overline{X} \right)\left(Y_i - \overline{Y} \right)}{\sum\limits_{i=1}^{n} \left(X_i - \overline{X} \right)^2}. \tag{1.35}$$

To see the equivalence, note that

$$\sum_{i=1}^{n} \left(X_i - \overline{X} \right)\left(Y_i - \overline{Y} \right) = \sum_{i=1}^{n} X_i Y_i - \sum_{i=1}^{n} X_i\overline{Y} - \sum_{i=1}^{n} \overline{X}Y_i + \sum_{i=1}^{n} \overline{X}\,\overline{Y}$$

$$= \sum_{i=1}^{n} X_i Y_i - \overline{Y}\sum_{i=1}^{n} X_i - \overline{X}\sum_{i=1}^{n} Y_i + n\overline{X}\,\overline{Y}$$

$$= \sum_{i=1}^{n} X_i Y_i - \overline{Y}\left(n\overline{X}\right) - \overline{X}\left(n\overline{Y}\right) + n\overline{X}\,\overline{Y}$$

$$= \sum_{i=1}^{n} X_i Y_i - n\overline{X}\,\overline{Y}. \tag{1.36}$$

Similarly,

$$\sum_{i=1}^{n} \left(X_i - \overline{X}\right)^2 = \sum_{i=1}^{n} X_i^2 - n\overline{X}^2. \tag{1.37}$$

Just put X instead of Y in (1.36). Having found b_2 from (1.35), you find b_1 from (1.31). Those who know about the second-order conditions will have no difficulty confirming that we have minimized *RSS*.

In the second numerical example in Section 1.3, $\overline{Y} = 4.67$, $\overline{X} = 2.00$, $\sum\left(X_i - \overline{X}\right)\left(Y_i - \overline{Y}\right) = 3.00$, and $\sum\left(X_i - \overline{X}\right)^2 = 2.00$, so

$$b_2 = 3.00/2.00 = 1.50 \tag{1.38}$$

and

$$b_1 = \overline{Y} - b_2\overline{X} = 4.67 - 1.50 \times 2.00 = 1.67, \tag{1.39}$$

which confirms the original calculation.

1.5 Two decompositions of the dependent variable

In the preceding pages we have encountered two ways of decomposing the value of the dependent variable in a regression model. They are going to be used throughout the text, so it is important that they be understood properly and that they be kept apart conceptually.

The first decomposition relates to the process by which the values of Y are generated:

$$Y_i = \beta_1 + \beta_2 X_i + u_i. \tag{1.40}$$

In observation i, Y_i is generated as the sum of two components, the nonstochastic component, $\beta_1 + \beta_2 X_i$, and the disturbance term u_i. This decomposition is purely theoretical. We will use it in the analysis of the properties of the regression estimators. It is illustrated in Figure 1.7a, where QT is the nonstochastic component of Y and PQ is the disturbance term.

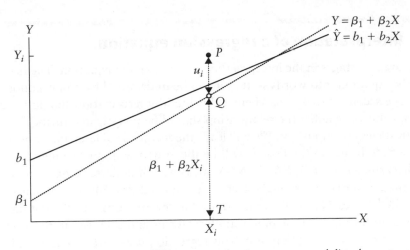

Figure 1.7a Decomposition of Y into nonstochastic component and disturbance term

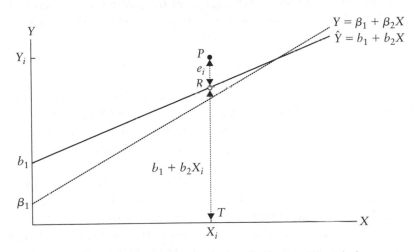

Figure 1.7b Decomposition of Y into fitted value and residual

The other decomposition relates to the regression line:

$$Y_i = \hat{Y}_i + e_i$$
$$= b_1 + b_2 X_i + e_i. \tag{1.41}$$

Once we have chosen the values of b_1 and b_2, each value of Y is split into the fitted value, $\hat{Y}_i$, and the residual, e_i. This decomposition is operational, but it is to some extent arbitrary because it depends on our criterion for determining b_1 and b_2, and it will inevitably be affected by the particular values taken by the disturbance term in the observations in the sample. It is illustrated in Figure 1.7b, where RT is the fitted value and PR is the residual.

1.6 Interpretation of a regression equation

There are two stages in the interpretation of a regression equation. The first is to turn the equation into words so that it can be understood by a noneconometrician. The second is to decide whether this literal interpretation should be taken at face value or whether the relationship should be investigated further.

Both stages are important. We will leave the second until later and concentrate for the time being on the first. It will be illustrated with an earnings function, hourly earnings in 2002, *EARNINGS*, measured in dollars, being regressed on schooling, *S*, measured as highest grade completed, for 540 respondents from the United States National Longitudinal Survey of Youth 1979, the data set that is used for many of the practical illustrations and exercises in this text. See Appendix B for a description of it. This regression uses *EAEF* Data Set 21. The Stata output for the regression is shown in Table 1.3. The scatter diagram and regression line are shown in Figure 1.8.

For the time being, ignore everything except the column headed 'coef.' in the bottom half of the table. This gives the estimates of the coefficient of *S* and the constant, and thus the following fitted equation:

$$\widehat{EARNINGS} = -13.93 + 2.46\,S. \tag{1.42}$$

Interpreting it literally, the slope coefficient indicates that, as *S* increases by one unit (of *S*), *EARNINGS* increases by 2.46 units (of *EARNINGS*). Since *S* is measured in years, and *EARNINGS* is measured in dollars per hour, the coefficient of *S* implies that hourly earnings increase by $2.46 for every extra year of schooling.

What about the constant term? Strictly speaking, it indicates the predicted level of *EARNINGS* when $S = 0$. Sometimes the constant will have a clear meaning, but sometimes not. If the sample values of the explanatory variable are a long way from zero, extrapolating the regression line back to zero may be dangerous. Even if the regression line gives a good fit for the sample of observations, there

Table 1.3

```
. reg EARNINGS S

    Source       SS         df       MS              Number of obs =     540
                                                     F(1, 538)     =  112.15
     Model   19321.5589      1    19321.5589         Prob > F      =  0.0000
  Residual   92688.6722    538    172.283777         R-squared     =  0.1725
                                                     Adj R-squared =  0.1710
     Total   112010.231    539    207.811189         Root MSE      =  13.126


  EARNINGS       Coef.   Std. Err.        t    P>|t|    [95% Conf.  Interval]

         S    2.455321    .2318512    10.59    0.000    1.999876    2.910765
     _cons   -13.93347   3.219851     -4.33    0.000   -20.25849   -7.608444
```

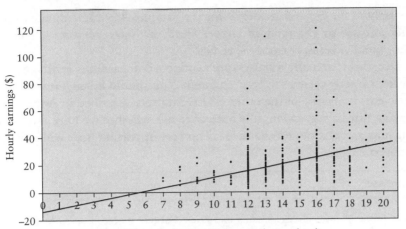

Figure 1.8 A simple earnings function

BOX 1.1   Interpretation of a linear regression equation

This is a foolproof way of interpreting the coefficients of a linear regression

$$\hat{Y}_i = b_1 + b_2 X_i$$

when Y and X are variables with straightforward natural units (not logarithms or other functions).

The first step is to say that a one-unit increase in X (measured in units of X) will cause a b_2 unit increase in Y (measured in units of Y). The second step is to check to see what the units of X and Y actually are, and to replace the word 'unit' with the actual unit of measurement. The third step is to see whether the result could be expressed in a better way, without altering its substance.

The constant, b_1, gives the predicted value of Y (in units of Y) for X equal to 0. It may or may not have a plausible meaning, depending on the context.

---

is no guarantee that it will continue to do so when extrapolated to the left or to the right.

In this case, a literal interpretation of the constant would lead to the nonsensical conclusion that an individual with no schooling would have hourly earnings of −$13.93. In this data set, no individual had less than seven years of schooling, so it is not surprising that extrapolation to zero leads to trouble.

Box 1.1 gives a general guide to interpreting regression equations when the variables are measured in natural units.

It is important to keep three things in mind when interpreting a regression equation. First, b_1 is only an estimate of β_1 and b_2 is only an estimate of β_2, so the interpretation is really only an estimate. Second, the regression equation refers only to the general tendency for the sample. Any individual case will be further affected by the random factor. Third, the interpretation is conditional on the equation being correctly specified.

In fact, this is actually a naïve specification of an earnings function. We will reconsider it several times in later chapters. You should be undertaking parallel experiments using one of the other *EAEF* data sets described in Appendix B.

Having fitted a regression, it is natural to ask whether we have any means of telling how accurate our estimates are. This very important issue will be discussed in the next chapter.

Exercises

Note: Some of the exercises in this and later chapters require you to fit regressions using one of the *EAEF* data sets. See Appendix B for details.

1.1 The table shows the average rates of growth of real GDP, g, and employment, e, for 25 OECD countries for the period 1988–97. The regression output shows the result of regressing e on g. Provide an interpretation of the coefficients.

Average rates of employment growth and real GDP growth(%), 1988–97					
	Employment	GDP		Employment	GDP
Australia	1.68	3.04	Korea	2.57	7.73
Austria	0.65	2.55	Luxembourg	3.02	5.64
Belgium	0.34	2.16	Netherlands	1.88	2.86
Canada	1.17	2.03	New Zealand	0.91	2.01
Denmark	0.02	2.02	Norway	0.36	2.98
Finland	−1.06	1.78	Portugal	0.33	2.79
France	0.28	2.08	Spain	0.89	2.60
Germany	0.08	2.71	Sweden	−0.94	1.17
Greece	0.87	2.08	Switzerland	0.79	1.15
Iceland	−0.13	1.54	Turkey	2.02	4.18
Ireland	2.16	6.40	United Kingdom	0.66	1.97
Italy	−0.30	1.68	United States	1.53	2.46
Japan	1.06	2.81			

```
. reg e g

     Source         SS        df        MS              Number of obs =      25
---------------------------------------------           F(1,23)       =   33.10
      Model 14.5753023         1   14.5753023           Prob > F      =  0.0000
   Residual 10.1266731        23   .440290135           R-squared     =  0.5900
---------------------------------------------           Adj R-squared =  0.5722
      Total 24.7019754        24   1.02924898           Root MSE      =  .66354

---------------------------------------------------------------------------------
        e      Coef.  Std. Err.        t  P>|t|    [95% Conf.   Interval]
---------------------------------------------------------------------------------
        g    .489737  .0851184      5.75  0.000     .3136561     .6658179
    _cons  −.5458912  .2740387     −1.99  0.058    −1.112784     .0210011
```

1.2 In Exercise 1.1, $\bar{e} = 0.83$, $\bar{g} = 2.82$, $\sum (e - \bar{e})(g - \bar{g}) = 29.76$, and $\sum (g - \bar{g})^2 = 60.77$. Calculate the regression coefficients and check that they are the same as in the regression output.

1.3 Does educational attainment depend on intellectual ability? In the United States, as in most countries, there is a positive correlation between educational attainment and cognitive ability. S (highest grade completed by 2002) is the number of years of schooling of the respondent. $ASVABC$ is a composite measure of numerical and verbal ability with mean 50 and standard deviation 10 (both approximately; for further details of the measure, see Appendix B). Perform a regression of S on $ASVABC$ and interpret the regression results. Comment on the value of R^2.

1.4 Do earnings depend on education? Using your $EAEF$ data set, fit an earnings function parallel to that discussed in Section 1.6, regressing $EARNINGS$ on S, and give an interpretation of the coefficients. Comment on the value of R^2.

1.5* The output shows the result of regressing the weight of the respondent in 1985, measured in pounds, on his or her height, measured in inches, using $EAEF$ Data Set 21. Provide an interpretation of the coefficients.

```
. reg WEIGHT85 HEIGHT
    Source        SS         df        MS                Number of obs  =      540
--------------------------------------------            F(1,538)       =   355.97
    Model    261111.383        1    261111.383          Prob > F       =   0.0000
 Residual    394632.365      538    733.517407          R-squared      =   0.3982
--------------------------------------------            Adj R-squared  =   0.3971
    Total    655743.748      539    1216.59322          Root MSE       =   27.084

------------------------------------------------------------------------------
 WEIGHT85      Coef.    Std. Err.        t    P>|t|    [95% Conf. Interval]
------------------------------------------------------------------------------
   HEIGHT    5.192973    .275238      18.87   0.000     4.6523     5.733646
    _cons   -194.6815   18.6629       10.43   0.000   -231.3426  -158.0204
------------------------------------------------------------------------------
```

1.6 Two individuals fit earnings functions relating $EARNINGS$ to S as defined in Section 1.6, using $EAEF$ Data Set 21. The first individual does it correctly and obtains the result found in Section 1.6:

$$\widehat{EARNINGS} = -13.93 + 2.46S.$$

The second individual makes a mistake and regresses S on $EARNINGS$, obtaining the following result:

$$\hat{S} = 12.29 + 0.070\,EARNINGS.$$

From this result the second individual derives

$$\widehat{EARNINGS} = -175.57 + 14.29S.$$

Explain why this equation is different from that fitted by the first individual.

1.7* Derive, with a proof, the slope coefficient that would have been obtained in Exercise 1.5 if weight and height had been measured in metric units. (*Note*: one pound is 454 grams, and one inch is 2.54 cm.)

1.8* A researcher has data on the aggregate expenditure on services, Y, and aggregate disposable personal income, X, both measured in $ billion at constant prices, for each of the US states and fits the equation

$$Y_i = \beta_1 + \beta_2 X_i + u_i.$$

The researcher initially fits the equation using OLS regression analysis. However, suspecting that tax evasion causes both Y and X to be substantially underestimated, the researcher adopts two alternative methods of compensating for the under-reporting:

1. The researcher adds $90 billion to the data for Y in each state and $200 billion to the data for X.

2. The researcher increases the figures for both Y and X in each state by 10 percent.

Evaluate the impact of the adjustments on the regression results.

1.9* A researcher has international cross-sectional data on aggregate wages, W, aggregate profits, P, and aggregate income, Y, for a sample of n countries. By definition,

$$Y_i = W_i + P_i.$$

The regressions

$$\hat{W}_i = a_1 + a_2 Y_i$$

$$\hat{P}_i = b_1 + b_2 Y_i$$

are fitted using OLS regression analysis. Show that the regression coefficients will automatically satisfy the following equations:

$$a_2 + b_2 = 1$$

$$a_1 + b_1 = 0.$$

Explain intuitively why this should be so.

1.10* Derive from first principles the least squares estimator of β_2 in the model

$$Y_i = \beta_2 X_i + u_i.$$

1.11 Derive from first principles the least squares estimator of β_1 in the even more primitive model

$$Y_i = \beta_1 + u_i.$$

(In other words, Y consists simply of a constant plus a disturbance term. First define *RSS* and then differentiate.)

1.12 Explain mathematically and intuitively what would happen if you tried to fit a regression equation when all the values of the explanatory variable in the sample are the same.

1.7   Goodness of fit: R^2

The aim of regression analysis is to explain the behavior of the dependent variable Y. In any given sample, Y is relatively low in some observations and relatively high in others. We want to know why. The variations in Y in any sample can be summarized by $\sum \left(Y_i - \overline{Y} \right)^2$, the sum of the squared deviations about its sample mean. We should like to be able to account for the size of this statistic.

We have seen that we can split the value of Y_i in each observation into two components, $\hat{Y}_i$ and e_i, after running a regression:

$$Y_i = \hat{Y}_i + e_i. \tag{1.43}$$

We can use this to decompose $\sum \left(Y_i - \overline{Y} \right)^2$:

$$\sum_{i=1}^{n} \left(Y_i - \overline{Y} \right)^2 = \sum_{i=1}^{n} \left(\left[\hat{Y}_i + e_i \right] - \left[\overline{\hat{Y}} + \overline{e} \right] \right)^2 = \sum_{i=1}^{n} \left(\left[\hat{Y}_i - \overline{Y} \right] + e_i \right)^2. \tag{1.44}$$

In the second step we have used the results $\overline{e} = 0$ and $\overline{\hat{Y}} = \overline{Y}$ demonstrated in Box 1.2. Hence

$$\sum_{i=1}^{n} \left(Y_i - \overline{Y} \right)^2 = \sum_{i=1}^{n} \left(\hat{Y}_i - \overline{Y} \right)^2 + \sum_{i=1}^{n} e_i^2 + 2 \sum_{i=1}^{n} \left(\left[\hat{Y}_i - \overline{Y} \right] e_i \right)$$

$$= \sum_{i=1}^{n} \left(\hat{Y}_i - \overline{Y} \right)^2 + \sum_{i=1}^{n} e_i^2 + 2 \sum_{i=1}^{n} \hat{Y}_i e_i - 2 \overline{Y} \sum_{i=1}^{n} e_i. \tag{1.45}$$

Now $\sum \hat{Y}_i e_i = 0$, as demonstrated in Box 1.2, and $\sum e_i = n\overline{e} = 0$. Hence

$$\sum_{i=1}^{n} \left(Y_i - \overline{Y} \right)^2 = \sum_{i=1}^{n} \left(\hat{Y}_i - \overline{Y} \right)^2 + \sum_{i=1}^{n} e_i^2. \tag{1.46}$$

Thus we have the decomposition

$$TSS = ESS + RSS \tag{1.47}$$

where TSS, the **total sum of squares**, is given by the left side of the equation and ESS, the **'explained' sum of squares**, and RSS, the **residual ('unexplained') sum** of squares, are the two terms on the right side. [*Note:* The words *explained* and *unexplained* have been put in quotation marks because the explanation may

---

BOX 1.2   Four useful results relating to OLS regressions

$$(1)\ \overline{e} = 0, \quad (2)\ \overline{\hat{Y}} = \overline{Y}, \quad (3)\ \sum_{i=1}^{n} X_i e_i = 0, \quad (4)\ \sum_{i=1}^{n} \hat{Y}_i e_i = 0.$$

Proof of (1)

$$e_i = Y_i - \hat{Y}_i = Y_i - b_1 - b_2 X_i$$

so

$$\sum_{i=1}^{n} e_i = \sum_{i=1}^{n} Y_i - nb_1 - b_2 \sum_{i=1}^{n} X_i.$$

Dividing by n,

$$\overline{e} = \overline{Y} - b_1 - b_2 \overline{X}$$
$$= \overline{Y} - (\overline{Y} - b_2 \overline{X}) - b_2 \overline{X} = 0.$$

Proof of (2)

$$e_i = Y_i - \hat{Y}_i$$

so

$$\sum_{i=1}^{n} e_i = \sum_{i=1}^{n} Y_i - \sum_{i=1}^{n} \hat{Y}_i.$$

Dividing by n,

$$\overline{e} = \overline{Y} - \overline{\hat{Y}}.$$

But $\overline{e} = 0$, so $\overline{\hat{Y}} = \overline{Y}$.

Proof of (3)

$$\sum_{i=1}^{n} X_i e_i = \sum_{i=1}^{n} X_i (Y_i - b_1 - b_2 X_i) = \sum_{i=1}^{n} X_i Y_i - b_1 \sum_{i=1}^{n} X_i - b_2 \sum_{i=1}^{n} X_i^2 = 0.$$

The final step uses equation (1.29).

Proof of (4)

$$\sum_{i=1}^{n} \hat{Y}_i e_i = \sum_{i=1}^{n} (b_1 + b_2 X_i) e_i = b_1 \sum_{i=1}^{n} e_i + b_2 \sum_{i=1}^{n} X_i e_i = 0$$

$\sum e_i = 0$ since $\overline{e} = 0$ and $\sum X_i e_i = 0$ from (3).

in fact be false. Y might really depend on some other variable Z, and X might be acting as a proxy for Z (more about this later). It would be safer to use the expression *apparently explained* instead of *explained*.]

In view of (1.46), $\sum \left(\hat{Y}_i - \overline{Y}\right)^2 / \sum \left(\hat{Y}_i - \overline{Y}\right)^2$ is the proportion of the total sum of squares explained by the regression line. This proportion is known as the **coefficient of determination** or, more usually, R^2:

$$R^2 = \frac{\sum_{i=1}^{n} \left(\hat{Y}_i - \overline{Y}\right)^2}{\sum_{i=1}^{n} \left(Y_i - \overline{Y}\right)^2}. \tag{1.48}$$

Regression output always includes R^2 and may also present the underlying analysis of variance. Table 1.4 reproduces the Stata earnings function output in Table 1.3. The column heading 'SS' stands for sums of squares. *ESS*, here described as the 'model' sum of squares, is 19,322. *TSS* is 112,010. Dividing *ESS* by *TSS*, we have $R^2 = 19,322/112010 = 0.1725$, as stated in the top right quarter of the output. The low R^2 is partly attributable to the fact that important variables, such as work experience, are missing from the model. It is also partly attributable to the fact that unobservable characteristics are important in determining earnings, R^2 seldom being much above 0.5 even in a well-specified model.

The maximum value of R^2 is 1. This occurs when the regression line fits the observations exactly, so that $\hat{Y}_i = Y_i$ in all observations and all the residuals are zero. Then $\sum \left(\hat{Y}_i - \overline{Y}\right)^2 = \sum \left(Y_i - \overline{Y}\right)^2$, $\sum e_i^2 = 0$, and one has a perfect fit. If there is no apparent relationship between the values of Y and X in the sample, R^2 will be close to zero.

Other things being equal, one would like R^2 to be as high as possible. In particular, we would like the coefficients b_1 and b_2 to be chosen in such a way as to maximize R^2. Does this conflict with our criterion that b_1 and b_2 should be chosen to minimize the sum of the squares of the residuals? No, they are easily

Table 1.4

```
. reg EARNINGS S

    Source        SS         df        MS                Number of obs =      540
                                                         F(1,538)      =   112.15
     Model    19321.5589     1     19321.5589            Prob > F      =   0.0000
  Residual    92688.6722    538    172.283777            R-squared     =   0.1725
                                                         Adj R-squared =   0.1710
     Total   112010.231     539    207.811189            Root MSE      =   13.126


 EARNINGS       Coef.    Std. Err.          t    P>|t|    [95% Conf.   Interval]

        S     2.455321   .2318512       10.59    0.000    1.999876    2.910765
    _cons   -13.93347    3.219851       -4.33    0.000   -20.25849   -7.608444
```

shown to be equivalent criteria. In view of (1.46) we can rewrite R^2 as

$$R^2 = 1 - \frac{\sum\limits_{i=1}^{n} e_i^2}{\sum\limits_{i=1}^{n} \left(Y_i - \overline{Y}\right)^2} \tag{1.49}$$

and so the values of b_1 and b_2 that minimize the residual sum of squares automatically maximize R^2.

Note that the four useful results in Box 1.2 depend on the model including an intercept (see Exercise 1.17). If there is no intercept, the decomposition (1.46) is invalid and the two definitions of R^2 in equations (1.48) and (1.49) are no longer equivalent. Any definition of R^2 in this case may be misleading and should be treated with caution.

Example of how R^2 is calculated

R^2 is always calculated by the computer as part of the regression output, so this example is for illustration only. We shall use the primitive three-observation example described in Section 1.3, where the regression line

$$\hat{Y}_i = 1.6667 + 1.5000 X_i \tag{1.50}$$

was fitted to the observations on X and Y in Table 1.5. The table also shows $\hat{Y}_i$ and e_i for each observation. $\sum \left(Y_i - \overline{Y}\right)^2 = 4.6667$, $\sum \left(\hat{Y}_i - \overline{Y}\right)^2 = 4.5000$, and $\sum e_i^2 = 0.1667$. From these figures, we can calculate R^2 using either (1.48) or (1.49):

$$R^2 = \frac{\sum\limits_{i=1}^{n} \left(\hat{Y}_i - \overline{Y}\right)^2}{\sum\limits_{i=1}^{n} \left(Y_i - \overline{Y}\right)^2} = \frac{4.5000}{4.6667} = 0.96 \tag{1.51}$$

$$R^2 = 1 - \frac{\sum\limits_{i=1}^{n} e_i^2}{\sum\limits_{i=1}^{n} \left(Y_i - \overline{Y}\right)^2} = 1 - \frac{0.1667}{4.6667} = 0.96. \tag{1.52}$$

Table 1.5 Analysis of variance in the three-observation example

Observation	X	Y	$\hat{Y}$	e	$Y - \overline{Y}$	$\hat{Y} - \overline{\hat{Y}}$	$(Y - \overline{Y})^2$	$(\hat{Y} - \overline{\hat{Y}})^2$	e^2
1	1	3	3.1667	−0.1667	−1.6667	−1.5	2.7778	2.25	0.0278
2	2	5	4.6667	0.3333	0.3333	0.0	0.1111	0.00	0.1111
3	3	6	6.1667	−0.1667	1.3333	1.5	1.7778	2.25	0.0278
Total	6	14	14				4.6667	4.50	0.1667
Mean	2	4.6667	4.6667						

Alternative interpretation of R^2

It should be intuitively obvious that, the better is the fit achieved by the regression equation, the higher should be the correlation coefficient for the actual and predicted values of Y. We will show that R^2 is in fact equal to the square of this correlation coefficient, which we will denote

$$r_{Y,\hat{Y}} = \frac{\sum\limits_{i=1}^{n} \left(Y_i - \overline{Y} \right)\left(\hat{Y}_i - \overline{Y} \right)}{\sqrt{\sum\limits_{i=1}^{n} \left(Y_i - \overline{Y} \right)^2 \sum\limits_{i=1}^{n} \left(\hat{Y}_i - \overline{Y} \right)^2}}. \tag{1.53}$$

Now

$$\sum_{i=1}^{n} \left(Y_i - \overline{Y} \right)\left(\hat{Y}_i - \overline{Y} \right) = \sum_{i=1}^{n} \left(\left[\hat{Y}_i + e_i \right] - \left[\overline{Y} + \overline{e} \right] \right)\left(\hat{Y}_i - \overline{Y} \right)$$

$$= \sum_{i=1}^{n} \left(\left[\hat{Y}_i - \overline{Y} \right] + e_i \right)\left(\hat{Y}_i - \overline{Y} \right)$$

$$= \sum_{i=1}^{n} \left(\hat{Y}_i - \overline{Y} \right)^2 + \sum_{i=1}^{n} e_i \hat{Y}_i - \overline{Y} \sum_{i=1}^{n} e_i$$

$$= \sum_{i=1}^{n} \left(\hat{Y}_i - \overline{Y} \right)^2. \tag{1.54}$$

In the second line we have used $\overline{e} = 0$ and in the fourth we have used $\sum \hat{Y}_i e_i = 0$, as demonstrated in Box 1.2. In the fourth line we have also used $\sum e_i = n\overline{e} = 0$. Hence,

$$r_{Y,\hat{Y}} = \frac{\sum\limits_{i=1}^{n} \left(\hat{Y}_i - \overline{Y} \right)^2}{\sqrt{\sum\limits_{i=1}^{n} \left(Y_i - \overline{Y} \right)^2 \sum\limits_{i=1}^{n} \left(\hat{Y}_i - \overline{Y} \right)^2}} = \sqrt{\frac{\sum\limits_{i=1}^{n} \left(\hat{Y}_i - \overline{Y} \right)^2}{\sum\limits_{i=1}^{n} \left(Y_i - \overline{Y} \right)^2}} = \sqrt{R^2}. \tag{1.55}$$

Key terms

coefficient of determination

dependent variable

disturbance term

explained sum of squares (*ESS*)

explanatory variable

fitted model

fitted value	regression model
independent variable	regressor
least squares criterion	residual
multiple regression model	residual sum of squares (*RSS*)
ordinary least squares (OLS)	simple regression model
parameter	total sum of squares (*TSS*)
R^2	

Exercises

1.13 Using the data in Table 1.5, calculate the correlation between Y and $\hat{Y}$ and verify that its square is equal to the value of R^2.

1.14 What was the value of R^2 in the educational attainment regression fitted by you in Exercise 1.3? Comment on it.

1.15 What was the value of R^2 in the earnings function fitted by you in Exercise 1.4? Comment on it.

1.16* The output shows the result of regressing weight in 2002 on height, using *EAEF* Data Set 21. In 2002 the respondents were aged 37–44. Explain why R^2 is lower than in the regression reported in Exercise 1.5.

```
. reg WEIGHT02 HEIGHT

    Source         SS        df        MS              Number of obs =     540
------------------------------------------            F(1,538)      = 216.95
    Model    311260.383       1    311260.383          Prob > F      = 0.0000
  Residual   771880.527     538    1434.72217          R-squared     = 0.2874
------------------------------------------            Adj R-squared = 0.2860
    Total    1083140.91     539    2009.53787          Root MSE      = 37.878

------------------------------------------------------------------------------
  WEIGHT02      Coef.   Std. Err.       t     P>|t|    [95% Conf. Interval]
------------------------------------------------------------------------------
    HEIGHT    5.669766   .3849347    14.73    0.000     4.913606    6.425925
     _cons   -199.6832   26.10105    -7.65    0.000    -250.9556   -148.4107
------------------------------------------------------------------------------
```

1.17* The useful results in Box 1.2 are in general no longer valid if the model does not contain an intercept. Demonstrate, in particular, that $\bar{e}$ will not in general be equal to zero.

2 Properties of the Regression Coefficients and Hypothesis Testing

With the aid of regression analysis we can obtain estimates of the parameters of a relationship. However, they are only *estimates*. The next question to ask is, how reliable are they? What are their properties? We will investigate these questions in this chapter. Both the way that we ask these questions, and their answers, depend upon the assumptions that we are making relating to the regression model, and these in turn depend upon the nature of the data that we are using.

2.1 Types of data and regression model

We shall be applying our regression techniques to three kinds of data: cross-sectional, time series, and panel. **Cross-sectional data** consist of observations relating to units of observation at one moment in time. The units of observation may be individuals, households, enterprises, countries, or any set of elements that are sufficiently similar in nature to allow one reasonably to use them to explore hypothetical relationships. **Time series data** consist of repeated observations through time on the same entities, usually with fixed intervals between the observations. Examples within a macroeconomic context would be quarterly data on gross domestic product, consumption, the money supply, and interest rates. **Panel data,** which can be thought of as combining the features of cross-sectional data and time series data, consist of repeated observations on the same elements through time. An example is the US National Longitudinal Survey of Youth used to illustrate the interpretation of a regression in Section 1.6. This consists of observations on the same individuals from 1979 to the present, interviews having been conducted annually until 1994 and every two years since then.

Following the treatment in Davidson (2000), we will consider three types of regression model:

Model A (for regressions using cross-sectional data): the regressors (explanatory variables) are **nonstochastic**. This means that their values in the observations in a sample do not have stochastic (random) components. See Box 2.1 for a brief further discussion.

BOX 2.1 **Nonstochastic regressors**

For the first part of this text, until Chapter 8, we will assume that the regressors (explanatory variables) in the model do not have stochastic components. This is to simplify the analysis. In fact, it is not easy to think of truly nonstochastic variables, other than time, so the following example is a little artificial. Suppose that we are relating earnings to schooling, S, in terms of highest grade completed. Suppose that we know from the national census that 1 percent of the population have $S = 8$, 3 percent have $S = 9$, 5 percent have $S = 10$, 7 percent have $S = 11$, 43 percent have $S = 12$ (graduation from high school), and so on. Suppose that we have decided to undertake a survey with sample size 1,000 and we want the sample to match the population as far as possible. We might then select what is known as a stratified random sample, designed so that it includes 10 individuals with $S = 8$, 30 individuals with $S = 9$, and so on. The values of S in the sample would then be predetermined and therefore nonstochastic. In large surveys drawn in such a way as to be representative of the population as a whole, such as the National Longitudinal Survey of Youth, schooling and other demographic variables probably approximate this condition quite well. In Chapter 8 we will acknowledge the restrictiveness of this assumption and replace it with the assumption that the values of the regressors are drawn from defined populations.

Model B (also for regressions using cross-sectional data): the values of the regressors are drawn randomly and independently from defined populations.
Model C (for regressions using time series data): the values of the regressors may exhibit persistence over time. The meaning of 'persistent over time' will be explained when we come to time series regressions in Chapters 11–13.
Regressions with panel data will be treated as an extension of Model B.

Most of this text will be concerned with regressions using cross-sectional data, that is, Models A and B. The reason for this is that regressions with time series data potentially involve complex technical issues that are best avoided initially.

We will start with Model A. We will do this purely for analytical convenience. It enables us to conduct the discussion of regression analysis within the relatively straightforward framework of what is known as the Classical Linear Regression Model. We will replace it in Chapter 8 by the weaker and more realistic assumption, appropriate for regressions with cross-sectional data, that the variables are randomly drawn from defined populations.

2.2 Assumptions for regression models with nonstochastic regressors

To examine the properties of the regression model we need to make some assumptions. In particular, for Model A, we will make the following six assumptions.

A.1 *The model is linear in parameters and correctly specified.*

$$Y = \beta_1 + \beta_2 X + u. \tag{2.1}$$

'Linear in parameters' means that each term on the right side includes a β as a simple factor and there is no built-in relationship among the βs. An example of a model that is not linear in parameters is

$$Y = \beta_1 X^{\beta_2} + u. \tag{2.2}$$

We will defer a discussion of issues relating to linearity and nonlinearity to Chapter 4.

A.2 *There is some variation in the regressor in the sample.*

Obviously, if X is constant in the sample, it cannot account for any of the variation in Y. If we tried to regress Y on X, when X is constant, we would find that we would not be able to compute the regression coefficients. X_i would be equal to $\overline{X}$ for all i and hence both the numerator and the denominator of

$$b_2 = \frac{\sum\limits_{i=1}^{n} \left(X_i - \overline{X} \right) \left(Y_i - \overline{Y} \right)}{\sum\limits_{i=1}^{n} \left(X_i - \overline{X} \right)^2} \tag{2.3}$$

would be equal to zero. Since we would not be able to compute b_2, we would not be able to obtain b_1 either.

A.3 *The disturbance term has zero expectation.*

$$E(u_i) = 0 \quad \text{for all } i. \tag{2.4}$$

We assume that the expected value of the disturbance term in any observation should be zero. Sometimes the disturbance term will be positive, sometimes negative, but it should not have a systematic tendency in either direction.

Actually, if an intercept is included in the regression equation, it is usually reasonable to assume that this condition is satisfied automatically since the role of the intercept is to pick up any systematic but constant tendency in Y not accounted for by the explanatory variables included in the regression equation. To put this mathematically, suppose that our regression model is

$$Y_i = \beta_1 + \beta_2 X_i + u_i \tag{2.5}$$

and

$$E(u_i) = \mu_u \tag{2.6}$$

where $\mu_u \neq 0$. Define

$$v_i = u_i - \mu_u. \tag{2.7}$$

Then, using (2.7) to substitute for u_i in (2.5), one has

$$Y_i = \beta_1 + \beta_2 X_i + v_i + \mu_u$$
$$= \beta_1' + \beta_2 X_i + v_i \qquad (2.8)$$

where $\beta_1' = \beta_1 + \mu_u$. The disturbance term in the respecified model now satisfies the condition because

$$E(v_i) = E(u_i - \mu_u) = E(u_i) - E(\mu_u) = \mu_u - \mu_u = 0. \qquad (2.9)$$

The price that we pay is that the interpretation of the intercept has changed. It has absorbed the nonzero component of the disturbance term in addition to whatever had previously been responsible for it. Usually this does not matter because we are seldom interested in the intercept in a regression model.

A.4 *The disturbance term is homoscedastic.*

We assume that the disturbance term is **homoscedastic**, meaning that its value in each observation is drawn from a distribution with constant population variance. In the language of the section on sampling and estimators in the Review chapter, this is a 'beforehand' concept, where we are thinking about the potential distribution of the disturbance term before the sample is actually generated. Once we have generated the sample, the disturbance term will turn out to be greater in some observations, and smaller in others, but there should not be any a priori reason for it to be more erratic in some observations than in others. Denoting the potential variance of the disturbance term in observation i $\sigma_{u_i}^2$, the assumption is

$$\sigma_{u_i}^2 = \sigma_u^2 \quad \text{for all } i. \qquad (2.10)$$

Since $E(u_i) = 0$, the population variance of u_i is equal to $E(u_i^2)$, so the condition can also be written

$$E(u_i^2) = \sigma_u^2 \quad \text{for all } i. \qquad (2.11)$$

σ_u, of course, is unknown. One of the tasks of regression analysis is to estimate the standard deviation of the disturbance term.

   If this assumption is not satisfied, the OLS regression coefficients will be inefficient, and you should be able to obtain more reliable results by using a modification of the regression technique. This will be discussed in Chapter 7.

A.5 *The values of the disturbance term have independent distributions.*

$$u_i \text{ is distributed independently of } u_j \text{ for all } j \neq i. \qquad (2.12)$$

We assume that the disturbance term is not subject to **autocorrelation**, meaning that there should be no systematic association between its values in any two observations. For example, just because the disturbance term is large and positive in one observation, there should be no tendency for it to be large and positive in the next (or large and negative, for that matter, or small and positive, or small and negative). The values of the disturbance term should be absolutely independent of one another.

The assumption implies that $\sigma_{u_i u_j}$, the population covariance between u_i and u_j, is zero, because

$$\sigma_{u_i u_j} = E\left\{(u_i - \mu_u)(u_j - \mu_u)\right\} = E(u_i u_j)$$
$$= E(u_i)E(u_j) = 0. \tag{2.13}$$

(Note that the population means of u_i and u_j are both zero, by virtue of Assumption A.3, and that $E(u_i u_j)$ can be decomposed as $E(u_i)E(u_j)$ if u_i and u_j are generated independently—see the Review chapter.)

If this assumption is not satisfied, OLS will again give inefficient estimates. Chapter 12 discusses the problems that arise and ways of getting around them. Violations of this assumption are in any case rare with cross-sectional data.

With these assumptions we will show in this chapter that the OLS estimators of the coefficients are BLUE: best (most efficient) linear (function of the observations on Y) unbiased estimators and that the sum of the squares of the residuals divided by the number of degrees of freedom provides an unbiased estimator of σ_u^2.

A.6 *The disturbance term has a normal distribution.*

We usually assume that the disturbance term has a normal distribution. You should know all about the normal distribution from your introductory statistics course. If u is normally distributed, so will be the regression coefficients, and this will be useful to us later in the chapter when we come to the business of performing t tests and F tests of hypotheses and constructing confidence intervals for β_1 and β_2 using the regression results.

The justification for the assumption depends on the **central limit theorem.** In essence, this states that, if a random variable is the composite result of the effects of a large number of other random variables, it will have an approximately normal distribution even if its components do not, provided that none of them is dominant. The disturbance term u is composed of a number of factors not appearing explicitly in the regression equation so, even if we know nothing about the distribution of these factors (or even their identity), we are usually entitled to assume that the disturbance term is normally distributed.

2.3 The random components of the regression coefficients

A least squares regression coefficient is a special form of random variable whose properties depend on those of the disturbance term in the equation. This will be demonstrated first theoretically and then by means of a controlled experiment.

Throughout the discussion we shall continue to work with the simple regression model where Y depends on a nonstochastic variable X according to the relationship

$$Y_i = \beta_1 + \beta_2 X_i + u_i \qquad (2.14)$$

and we are fitting the regression equation

$$\hat{Y}_i = b_1 + b_2 X_i \qquad (2.15)$$

given a sample of n observations.

First, note that Y_i has two components. It has a nonrandom component $(\beta_1 + \beta_2 X_i)$, which owes nothing to the laws of chance (β_1 and β_2 may be unknown, but nevertheless they are fixed constants), and it has the random component u_i.

This implies that, when we calculate b_2 according to the formula

$$b_2 = \frac{\sum\limits_{i=1}^{n} \left(X_i - \overline{X} \right) \left(Y_i - \overline{Y} \right)}{\sum\limits_{i=1}^{n} \left(X_i - \overline{X} \right)^2} \qquad (2.16)$$

b_2 also has a random component. $\sum \left(X_i - \overline{X} \right) \left(Y_i - \overline{Y} \right)$ depends on the values of Y, and the values of Y depend on the values of u. If the values of the disturbance term had been different in the n observations, we would have obtained different values of Y, hence of $\sum \left(X_i - \overline{X} \right) \left(Y_i - \overline{Y} \right)$, and hence of b_2.

We can in theory decompose b_2 into its nonrandom and random components. In view of (2.14),

$$\sum_{i=1}^{n} \left(X_i - \overline{X} \right) \left(Y_i - \overline{Y} \right) = \sum_{i=1}^{n} \left(X_i - \overline{X} \right) \left([\beta_1 + \beta_2 X_i + u_i] - [\beta_1 + \beta_2 \overline{X} + \overline{u}] \right)$$

$$= \sum_{i=1}^{n} \left(X_i - \overline{X} \right) \left(\beta_2 [X_i - \overline{X}] + [u_i - \overline{u}] \right)$$

$$= \beta_2 \sum_{i=1}^{n} \left(X_i - \overline{X} \right)^2 + \sum_{i=1}^{n} \left(X_i - \overline{X} \right) (u_i - \overline{u}). \qquad (2.17)$$

Hence

$$b_2 = \frac{\sum\limits_{i=1}^{n}\left(X_i - \overline{X}\right)\left(Y_i - \overline{Y}\right)}{\sum\limits_{i=1}^{n}\left(X_i - \overline{X}\right)^2} = \frac{\beta_2 \sum\limits_{i=1}^{n}\left(X_i - \overline{X}\right)^2 + \sum\limits_{i=1}^{n}\left(X_i - \overline{X}\right)\left(u_i - \overline{u}\right)}{\sum\limits_{i=1}^{n}\left(X_i - \overline{X}\right)^2}$$

$$= \beta_2 + \frac{\sum\limits_{i=1}^{n}\left(X_i - \overline{X}\right)\left(u_i - \overline{u}\right)}{\sum\limits_{i=1}^{n}\left(X_i - \overline{X}\right)^2}. \tag{2.18}$$

Thus, we have shown that the regression coefficient b_2 obtained from any sample consists of (1) a fixed component, equal to the true value, β_2, and (2) a random component dependent the values of the disturbance term in the sample. The random component is responsible for the variations of b_2 around its fixed component β_2. If we wish, we can express this decomposition more tidily:

$$\sum\limits_{i=1}^{n}\left(X_i - \overline{X}\right)\left(u_i - \overline{u}\right) = \sum\limits_{i-1}^{n}\left(X_i - \overline{X}\right)u_i - \overline{u}\sum\limits_{i=1}^{n}\left(X_i - \overline{X}\right)$$

$$= \sum\limits_{i=1}^{n}\left(X_i - \overline{X}\right)u_i - \overline{u}\sum\limits_{i=1}^{n}X_i + n\overline{u}\,\overline{X}$$

$$= \sum\limits_{i=1}^{n}\left(X_i - \overline{X}\right)u_i \tag{2.19}$$

since $\sum\limits_{i=1}^{n}X_i = n\overline{X}$. Hence

$$b_2 = \beta_2 + \frac{\sum\limits_{i=1}^{n}\left(X_i - \overline{X}\right)u_i}{\sum\limits_{i=1}^{n}\left(X_i - \overline{X}\right)^2} = \beta_2 + \sum\limits_{i=1}^{n}\left\{\frac{\left(X_i - \overline{X}\right)}{\sum\limits_{i=1}^{n}\left(X_i - \overline{X}\right)^2}\right\}u_i - \beta_2 + \sum\limits_{i=1}^{n}a_i u_i \tag{2.20}$$

where

$$a_i = \frac{\left(X_i - \overline{X}\right)}{\sum\limits_{i=1}^{n}\left(X_i - \overline{X}\right)^2}. \tag{2.21}$$

Thus, we have shown that b_2 is equal to the true value, β_2, plus a linear combination of the values of the disturbance term in all the observations in the sample. There is a slight awkwardness in the definition of a_i and it

BOX 2.2   **Proofs of three properties of the** a_i **coefficients**

Proof that $\sum a_i = 0$

$$\sum a_i = \sum_{i=1}^{n} \left(\frac{X_i - \overline{X}}{\sum_{j=1}^{n} \left(X_j - \overline{X} \right)^2} \right) = \frac{1}{\sum_{j=1}^{n} \left(X_j - \overline{X} \right)^2} \sum_{i=1}^{n} \left(X_i - \overline{X} \right) = 0$$

since

$$\sum_{i=1}^{n} \left(X_i - \overline{X} \right) = \sum_{i=1}^{n} X_i - n\overline{X} = n\overline{X} - n\overline{X} = 0$$

using $\overline{X} = \frac{1}{n} \sum X_i$.

Proof that $\sum a_i^2 = \dfrac{1}{\sum_{i=1}^{n} \left(X_i - \overline{X} \right)^2}$

$$\sum_{i=1}^{n} a_i^2 = \sum_{i=1}^{n} \left(\frac{X_i - \overline{X}}{\sum_{j=1}^{n} \left(X_j - \overline{X} \right)^2} \right)^2 = \frac{1}{\left(\sum_{j=1}^{n} \left(X_j - \overline{X} \right)^2 \right)^2} \sum_{i=1}^{n} \left(X_i - \overline{X} \right)^2$$

$$= \frac{1}{\sum_{i=1}^{n} \left(X_i - \overline{X} \right)^2}.$$

Proof that $\sum a_i X_i = 1$ First note that

$$\sum_{i=1}^{n} \left(X_i - \overline{X} \right)^2 = \sum_{i=1}^{n} \left(X_i - \overline{X} \right)\left(X_i - \overline{X} \right) = \sum_{i=1}^{n} \left(X_i - \overline{X} \right) X_i - \sum_{i=1}^{n} \left(X_i - \overline{X} \right) \overline{X}$$

$$= \sum_{i=1}^{n} \left(X_i - \overline{X} \right) X_i - \overline{X} \sum_{i=1}^{n} \left(X_i - \overline{X} \right) = \sum_{i=1}^{n} \left(X_i - \overline{X} \right) X_i$$

since $\sum \left(X_i - \overline{X} \right) = 0$ (see above). Then, using the above equation in reverse,

$$\sum_{i=1}^{n} a_i X_i = \sum_{i=1}^{n} \frac{\left(X_i - \overline{X} \right) X_i}{\sum_{j=1}^{n} \left(X_j - \overline{X} \right)^2} = \frac{1}{\sum_{j=1}^{n} \left(X_j - \overline{X} \right)^2} \sum_{i=1}^{n} \left(X_i - \overline{X} \right) X_i$$

$$= \frac{\sum_{i=1}^{n} \left(X_i - \overline{X} \right)^2}{\sum_{j=1}^{n} \left(X_j - \overline{X} \right)^2} = 1.$$

is as well to deal with it before mathematicians start getting excited. The numerator changes as i changes and is different for each observation. However, the denominator is the sum of the squared deviations for the whole sample and is not dependent on i. So we are using i in two different senses in the definition. To avoid any ambiguity, we will use a different index for the summation and write the denominator $\sum_{j=1}^{n} \left(X_j - \overline{X} \right)^2$. It still means the same thing. We could avoid the problem entirely by writing the denominator as $\left(X_1 - \overline{X} \right)^2 + \cdots + \left(X_n - \overline{X} \right)^2$, but this would be clumsy.

We will note for future reference three properties of the a_i coefficients:

$$\sum_{i=1}^{n} a_i = 0, \quad \sum_{i=1}^{n} a_i^2 = \frac{1}{\sum_{j=1}^{n} \left(X_j - \overline{X} \right)^2}, \quad \text{and} \quad \sum_{i=1}^{n} a_i X_i = 1. \quad (2.22)$$

Proofs are supplied in Box 2.2.

In a similar manner, one may also show that b_1 has a fixed component equal to the true value, β_1, plus a random component that is a linear combination of the values of the disturbance term. This is left as an exercise.

Note that you are not able to make these decompositions in practice because you do not know the true values of β_1 and β_2 or the actual values of u in the sample. We are interested in them because they enable us to say something about the theoretical properties of b_1 and b_2, given certain assumptions.

Exercise

2.1* Demonstrate that $b_1 = \beta_1 + \sum c_i u_i$, where $c_i = \frac{1}{n} - a_i \overline{X}$ and a_i is defined in equation (2.21).

2.4 A Monte Carlo experiment

Nobody seems to know for certain how the Monte Carlo experiment got its name. Probably it has something to do with the famous casino, as a symbol of the laws of chance.

The basic concept will be explained by means of an analogy. Suppose you have trained a dog to find truffles for you. These fungi grow wild in the ground in France and Italy and are considered to be delicious. They are expensive because they are hard to find, and a good truffle dog is highly valued. The question is, how do you know if your dog is any good at truffle hunting? It may find them from time to time, but for all you know it may miss a lot as well. If you were really interested, you could evaluate your dog by taking a piece of land, burying truffles in several places, letting the dog loose, and seeing how many it located. By means of this controlled experiment, you would have a direct measure of its success rate.

What has this got to do with regression analysis? The problem is that we never know the true values of β_1 and β_2 (otherwise, why should we use regression analysis to estimate them?), so we have no means of telling whether the technique is giving us good or bad estimates. A Monte Carlo experiment is an artificial, controlled experiment that allows us to check.

The simplest possible Monte Carlo experiment has three parts. First,

1. you choose the true values of β_1 and β_2,
2. you choose the value of X in each observation, and
3. you use some random number generating process to provide the random factor u in each observation.

Second, you *generate* the value of Y in each observation, using the relationship (2.1) and the values of β_1, β_2, X and u. Third, using only the values of Y thus generated and the data for X, you use regression analysis to obtain estimates b_1 and b_2. You can then see if b_1 is a good estimator of β_1 and if b_2 is a good estimator of β_2, and this will give you some idea of whether the regression technique is working properly.

In the first two steps, you are preparing a challenge for the regression technique. You are in complete control of the model that you are constructing and you *know* the true values of the parameters because you yourself have determined them. In the third step, you see whether the regression technique can meet your challenge and provide good estimates of β_1 and β_2 using only the data on Y and X. Note that the inclusion of a stochastic term in the generation of Y is responsible for the element of challenge. If you did not include it, the observations would lie exactly on the straight line (2.1), and it would be a trivial matter to determine the exact values of β_1 and β_2 from the data on Y and X.

Quite arbitrarily, let us put β_1 equal to 2 and β_2 equal to 0.5, so the true relationship is

$$Y_i = 2 + 0.5X_i + u_i. \tag{2.23}$$

To keep things simple, we will assume that we have 20 observations and that the values of X go from 1 to 20. For u, the disturbance term, we will use random numbers drawn from a normally distributed population with zero mean and unit variance. We will need a set of 20 and will denote them rn_1 to rn_{20}. u_1, the disturbance term in the first observation, is simply equal to rn_1, u_2 to rn_2, etc.

Table 2.1

X	u	Y	X	u	Y
1	−0.59	1.91	11	1.59	9.09
2	−0.24	2.76	12	−0.92	7.08
3	−0.83	2.67	13	−0.71	7.79
4	0.03	4.03	14	−0.25	8.75
5	−0.38	4.12	15	1.69	11.19
6	−2.19	2.81	16	0.15	10.15
7	1.03	6.53	17	0.02	10.52
8	0.24	6.24	18	−0.11	10.89
9	2.53	9.03	19	−0.91	10.59
10	−0.13	6.87	20	1.42	13.42

Given the values of X_i and u_i in each observation, it is possible to calculate the value of Y_i using (2.23), and this is done in Table 2.1.

If you now regress Y on X, you obtain

$$\hat{Y}_i = 1.63 + 0.54X_i. \tag{2.24}$$

In this case b_1 is an underestimate of β_1 (1.63 as opposed to 2.00) and b_2 is a slight overestimate of β_2 (0.54 as opposed to 0.50). The discrepancies are caused by the collective effects of the disturbance terms in the 20 observations.

Of course, one sample such as this is hardly enough to allow us to evaluate the regression technique. It gave quite good results, but perhaps this was a fluke. To check further, we will repeat the experiment, keeping the *same* true equation (2.23) and the *same* values of X, but using a *new* set of random numbers for the disturbance term drawn from the same distribution (zero mean and unit variance). From these, and the values of X, we generate a new set of values for Y.

To save space, the table giving the new values of u and Y is omitted. The result when the new values of Y are regressed on X is

$$\hat{Y}_i = 2.52 + 0.48X_i. \tag{2.25}$$

This second sample also produced good results. Now b_1 is an overestimate of β_1 and b_2 is a slight underestimate of β_2. Table 2.2 gives the estimates b_1 and b_2 for 10 samples, using a different set of random numbers for the disturbance term in each case.

You can see that, although you sometimes get overestimates and sometimes underestimates, on the whole b_1 and b_2 are clustered around the true values of 2.00 and 0.50, respectively. And there are more good estimates than bad ones. Taking b_2, for example, if you repeated the experiment a very large number of times and constructed a frequency table, you would obtain an approximation to the probability density function shown in Figure 2.1. It is a normal distribution with mean 0.50 and standard deviation 0.0388.

Table 2.2

Sample	b_1	b_2
1	1.63	0.54
2	2.52	0.48
3	2.13	0.45
4	2.14	0.50
5	1.71	0.56
6	1.81	0.51
7	1.72	0.56
8	3.18	0.41
9	1.26	0.58
10	1.94	0.52

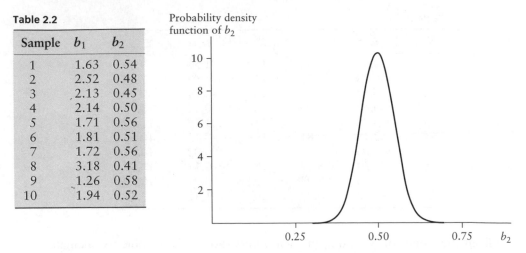

Figure 2.1 Distribution of b_2 in the Monte Carlo experiment

It has been asserted that the discrepancies between the regression coefficients and the true values of the parameters are caused by the disturbance term u. A consequence of this is that the bigger is the random element, the less accurate will be the estimate, in general.

This will be illustrated with a second set of samples related to the first. We shall use the same values for β_1 and β_2 as before, and the same values of X, and the same source of random numbers for the disturbance term, but we will now make the disturbance term in each observation, which will be denoted u', equal to twice the random number drawn: $u'_1 = 2rn_1$, $u'_2 = 2rn_2$, etc. In fact, we will use exactly the same sample of random numbers as before, but double them. Corresponding to Table 2.1, we now have Table 2.3.

Regressing Y on X, we now obtain the equation

$$\hat{Y}_i = 1.26 + 0.58X_i. \tag{2.26}$$

This is less accurate than its counterpart, equation (2.24).

Table 2.4 gives the results for all 10 samples, putting $u' = 2rn$. We will call this set of samples II and the original set, summarized in Table 2.2, I. Comparing Tables 2.2 and 2.4, you can see that the values of b_1 and b_2 are much more erratic in the latter, although there is still no systematic tendency either to underestimate or to overestimate.

Detailed inspection reveals an important feature. In Set I, the value of b_2 in sample 1 was 0.54, an overestimate of 0.04. In Set II, the value of b_2 in sample 1 was 0.58, an overestimate of 0.08, exactly twice as much as before. The same is true for each of the other nine samples, and also for the regression coefficient b_1 in each sample. Doubling the disturbance term in each observation causes a doubling of the errors in the regression coefficients.

Table 2.3

X	u	Y	X	u	Y
1	−1.18	1.32	11	3.18	10.68
2	−0.48	2.52	12	−1.84	6.16
3	−1.66	1.84	13	−1.42	7.08
4	0.06	3.94	14	−0.50	8.50
5	−0.76	3.74	15	3.38	12.88
6	−4.38	0.62	16	0.30	10.30
7	2.06	7.56	17	0.04	10.54
8	0.48	6.48	18	−0.22	10.78
9	5.06	11.56	19	−1.82	9.68
10	−0.26	6.74	20	2.84	14.84

Table 2.4

Sample	b_1	b_2
1	1.26	0.58
2	3.05	0.45
3	2.26	0.39
4	2.28	0.50
5	1.42	0.61
6	1.61	0.52
7	1.44	0.63
8	4.37	0.33
9	0.52	0.65
10	1.88	0.55

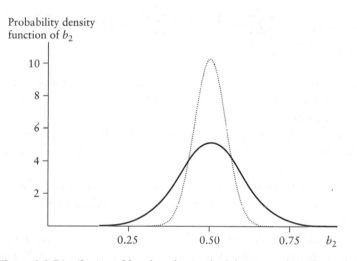

Figure 2.2 Distribution of b_2 when the standard deviation of u is doubled

This result follows directly from the decomposition of b_2 given by (2.20). In Set I the error component of b_2 is given by $\sum a_i u_i$. In Set II it is given by $\sum a_i u_i'$, and

$$\sum_{i=1}^{n} a_i u_i' = \sum_{i=1}^{n} a_i 2u_i = 2 \sum_{i=1}^{n} a_i u_i. \qquad (2.27)$$

The increase in inaccuracy is reflected in the probability density function for b_2 in Set II, shown as the solid curve in Figure 2.2. This is still distributed around the true value, 0.50, but, if you compare it with that for Set I, the dotted curve, you will see that it is flatter and wider. Doubling the values of u has caused a doubling of the standard deviation of the distribution.

2.5 Unbiasedness of the regression coefficients

We saw in Section 2.3 that the slope coefficient b_2 could be decomposed as

$$b_2 = \beta_2 + \sum_{i=1}^{n} a_i u_i \tag{2.28}$$

where

$$a_i = \frac{(X_i - \overline{X})}{\sum_{j=1}^{n} (X_j - \overline{X})^2}. \tag{2.29}$$

It follows that b_2 is an unbiased estimator of β_2 if X is nonstochastic, for

$$E\left(b_2\right) = E\left(\beta_2\right) + E\left\{\sum_{i=1}^{n} a_i u_i\right\} = \beta_2 + \sum_{i=1}^{n} E\left(a_i u_i\right) = \beta_2 + \sum_{i=1}^{n} a_i E\left(u_i\right) = \beta_2 \tag{2.30}$$

since $E\left(u_i\right) = 0$ for all i. Since we are assuming that the values of X are non-stochastic, the a_i coefficients are also nonstochastic and hence $E\left(a_i u_i\right) = a_i E\left(u_i\right)$.

Unless the random factor in the n observations happens to cancel out exactly, which can happen only by coincidence, b_2 will be different from β_2 for any given sample, but in view of (2.30) there will be no systematic tendency for it to be either higher or lower.

Likewise, it can be shown that b_1 is an unbiased estimator of β_1. This is left as an exercise. Of course in any given sample the random factor will cause b_1 to differ from β_1.

It is important to realize that the OLS estimators of the parameters are not the only unbiased estimators. We will give an example of another. We continue to assume that the true relationship between Y and X is given by

$$Y_i = \beta_1 + \beta_2 X_i + u_i. \tag{2.31}$$

Someone who had never heard of regression analysis, on seeing a scatter diagram of a sample of observations, might be tempted to obtain an estimate of the slope merely by joining the first and the last observations, and by dividing the increase in the height by the horizontal distance between them, as in Figure 2.3. The estimator b_2 would then be given by

$$b_2 = \frac{Y_n - Y_1}{X_n - X_1}. \tag{2.32}$$

We will investigate whether it is biased or unbiased. Applying (2.31) to the first and last observations, we have

$$Y_1 = \beta_1 + \beta_2 X_1 + u_1 \tag{2.33}$$

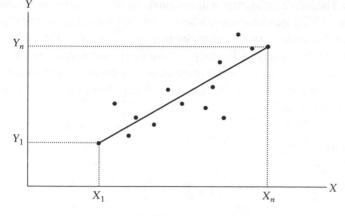

Figure 2.3 Naïve estimation of b_2

and

$$Y_n = \beta_1 + \beta_2 X_n + u_n. \tag{2.34}$$

Hence

$$b_2 = \frac{\beta_2 X_n + u_n - \beta_2 X_1 - u_1}{X_n - X_1}$$

$$= \beta_2 + \frac{u_n - u_1}{X_n - X_1}. \tag{2.35}$$

Thus, we have decomposed this naïve estimator into two components, the true value and an error term. This decomposition is parallel to that for the OLS estimator in Section 2.3, but the error term is different. The expected value of the estimator is given by

$$E(b_2) = E(\beta_2) + E\left[\frac{u_n - u_1}{X_n - X_1}\right]$$

$$= \beta_2 + \frac{1}{X_n - X_1} E(u_n - u_1) \tag{2.36}$$

since β_2 is a constant and X_1 and X_n are nonstochastic. If Assumption A.3 is satisfied,

$$E(u_n - u_1) = E(u_n) - E(u_1) = 0. \tag{2.37}$$

Therefore, despite being naïve, this estimator is unbiased.

This is not by any means the only estimator besides OLS that is unbiased. You could derive one by joining any two arbitrarily selected observations, and in fact the possibilities are infinite if you are willing to consider less naïve procedures.

It is intuitively easy to see that we would not prefer a naïve estimator such as (2.32) to OLS. Unlike OLS, which takes account of every observation, it employs only the first and the last and is wasting most of the information in the sample. The naïve estimator will be sensitive to the value of the disturbance term u in those two observations, whereas the OLS estimator combines all the values of the disturbance term and takes greater advantage of the possibility that to some extent they cancel each other out. More rigorously, it can be shown that the population variance of the naïve estimator is greater than that of the OLS estimator, and that the naïve estimator is therefore less efficient. We will discuss efficiency in Section 2.7.

Exercises

2.2* Using the decomposition in Exercise 2.1, demonstrate that b_1 is an unbiased estimator of β_1.

2.3 An investigator correctly believes that the relationship between two variables X and Y is given by

$$Y_i = \beta_1 + \beta_2 X_i + u_i.$$

Given a sample of n observations, the investigator estimates β_2 by calculating it as the average value of Y divided by the average value of X. Discuss the properties of this estimator. What difference would it make if it could be assumed that $\beta_1 = 0$?

2.4* An investigator correctly believes that the relationship between two variables X and Y is given by

$$Y_i = \beta_1 + \beta_2 X_i + u_i.$$

Given a sample of observations on Y, X and a third variable Z (which is not a determinant of Y), the investigator estimates β_2 as

$$\frac{\sum\limits_{i=1}^{n} \left(Z_i - \overline{Z}\right)\left(Y_i - \overline{Y}\right)}{\sum\limits_{i=1}^{n} \left(Z_i - \overline{Z}\right)\left(X_i - \overline{X}\right)}.$$

Demonstrate that this estimator is unbiased.

2.6 Precision of the regression coefficients

Now we shall consider $\sigma_{b_1}^2$ and $\sigma_{b_2}^2$, the population variances of b_1 and b_2 about their population means. These are given by the following expressions:

$$\sigma_{b_1}^2 = \sigma_u^2 \left(\frac{1}{n} + \frac{\overline{X}^2}{\sum\limits_{i=1}^{n} \left(X_i - \overline{X}\right)^2} \right) \quad \text{and} \quad \sigma_{b_2}^2 = \frac{\sigma_u^2}{\sum\limits_{i=1}^{n} \left(X_i - \overline{X}\right)^2}. \tag{2.38}$$

See Box 2.3 for a proof of the expression for $\sigma_{b_2}^2$. The proof of the expression for $\sigma_{b_1}^2$ follows similar lines and is left as an exercise.

BOX 2.3   Proof of the expression for the population variance of b_2

By definition

$$\sigma_{b_2}^2 = E\left\{(b_2 - E(b_2))^2\right\} = E\left\{(b_2 - \beta_2)^2\right\}$$

since we have shown that $E(b_2) = \beta_2$. We have seen that

$$b_2 = \beta_2 + \sum_{i=1}^{n} a_i u_i$$

where

$$a_i = \frac{(X_i - \overline{X})}{\sum\limits_{j=1}^{n} \left(X_j - \overline{X}\right)^2}.$$

Hence

$$\sigma_{b_2}^2 = E\left\{\left(\sum_{i=1}^{n} a_i u_i\right)^2\right\}.$$

Expanding the quadratic,

$$\sigma_{b_2}^2 = E\left\{\sum_{i=1}^{n} a_i^2 u_i^2 + \sum_{i=1}^{n}\sum_{j\neq i} a_i a_j u_i u_j\right\}$$

$$= \sum_{i=1}^{n} a_i^2 E\left(u_i^2\right) + \sum_{i=1}^{n}\sum_{j\neq i} a_i a_j E\left(u_i u_j\right).$$

Now by virtue of Assumption A.4, $E\left(u_i^2\right) = \sigma_u^2$ and, by virtue of Assumption A.5, $E\left(u_i u_j\right) = 0$ for $j \neq i$, so

$$\sigma_{b_2}^2 = \sum_{i=1}^{n} a_i^2 \sigma_u^2 = \sigma_u^2 \sum_{i=1}^{n} a_i^2 = \frac{\sigma_u^2}{\sum\limits_{i=1}^{n} \left(X_i - \overline{X}\right)^2}$$

using the second of the properties of the a_i coefficients proved in Box 2.2.

We will focus on the implications of the expression for $\sigma_{b_2}^2$. Clearly, the larger is $\sum \left(X_i - \overline{X} \right)^2$, the smaller is the variance of b_2. However, the size of $\sum \left(X_i - \overline{X} \right)^2$ depends on two factors: the number of observations, and the size of the deviations of X_i about its sample mean. To discriminate between them, it is convenient to define the mean square deviation of X, MSD(X):

$$\text{MSD}(X) = \frac{1}{n} \sum_{i=1}^{n} \left(X_i - \overline{X} \right)^2. \tag{2.39}$$

Using this to rewrite $\sigma_{b_2}^2$ as

$$\sigma_{b_2}^2 = \frac{\sigma_u^2}{n\text{MSD}(X)} \tag{2.40}$$

it is then obvious that the variance of b_2 is inversely proportional to the number of observations in the sample, holding the mean square deviation constant. This makes good sense. The more information you have, the more accurate your estimates are likely to be.

It is also obvious that the variance of b_2 is proportional to the variance of the disturbance term. The bigger the variance of the random factor in the relationship, the worse the estimates of the parameters are likely to be, other things being equal. This is illustrated graphically in Figures 2.4a and 2.4b. In both diagrams

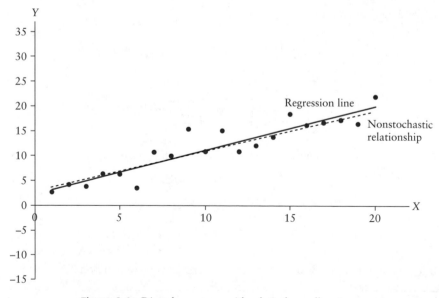

Figure 2.4a Disturbance term with relatively small variance

the nonstochastic component of the relationship between Y and X, depicted by the dotted line, is given by

$$Y_i = 3.0 + 0.8X_i. \tag{2.41}$$

There are 20 observations, with the values of X being the integers from 1 to 20. The same random numbers are used to generate the values of the disturbance term, but those in the Figure 2.4b have been multiplied by a factor of 5. As a consequence, the regression line, depicted by the solid line, is a much poorer approximation to the nonstochastic relationship in Figure 2.4b than in Figure 2.4a.

From (2.40) it can be seen mathematically that the variance of b_2 is inversely related to the mean square deviation of X. What is the reason for this? Remember that (1) the regression coefficients are calculated on the assumption that the observed variations in Y are due to variations in X, but (2) they are in reality *partly* due to variations in X and *partly* to variations in u. The smaller the variations in X, as summarized by the mean square deviation, the greater is likely to be the relative influence of the random factor in determining the variations in Y and the more likely is regression analysis to give inaccurate estimates. This is illustrated by Figures 2.5a and 2.5b. The nonstochastic component of the relationship is given by (2.41), and the disturbance terms are identical. In Figure 2.5a the values of X are the integers from 1 to 20. In Figure 2.5b, the values of X are the numbers $9.1, 9.2, \ldots, 10.9, 11$. In Figure 2.5a, the variations in X are responsible for most of the variations in Y and the relationship between the two variables can be determined relatively accurately. However, in Figure 2.5b, the variations in X are so small that their influence is overwhelmed by the

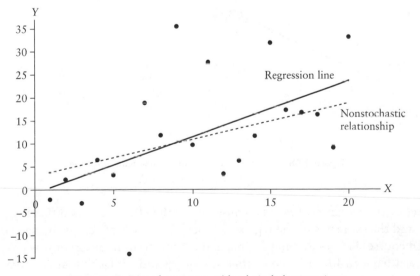

Figure 2.4b Disturbance term with relatively large variance

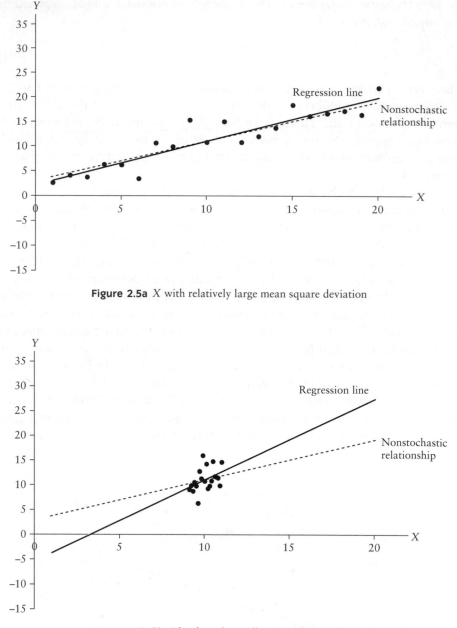

Figure 2.5a X with relatively large mean square deviation

Figure 2.5b X with relatively small mean square deviation

effect of the variance of u. As a consequence the effect of X is difficult to pick out and the estimates of the regression coefficients will be relatively inaccurate.

Of course, Figures 2.4 and 2.5 make the same point in different ways. As can be seen from (2.40), it is the *relative* size of σ_u^2 and MSD(X) that is important, rather than the *actual* size of either.

In practice, one cannot calculate the population variances of either b_1 or b_2 because σ_u^2 is unknown. However, we can derive an estimator of σ_u^2 from the residuals. Clearly the scatter of the residuals around the regression line will reflect the unseen scatter of u about the line $Y_i = \beta_1 + \beta_2 X_i$, although in general the residual and the value of the disturbance term in any given observation are not equal to one another. One measure of the scatter of the residuals is their mean square deviation, MSD(e), defined by

$$ \text{MSD}(e) = \frac{1}{n} \sum_{i=1}^{n} (e_i - \bar{e})^2 = \frac{1}{n} \sum_{i=1}^{n} e_i^2 \tag{2.42} $$

(remember that $\bar{e} = 0$, from Box 1.2). Intuitively this should provide a guide to σ_u^2.

Before going any further, ask yourself the following question. Which line is likely to be closer to the points representing the sample of observations on X and Y, the true line $Y_i = \beta_1 + \beta_2 X_i$ or the regression line $\hat{Y}_i = b_1 + b_2 X_i$? The answer is the regression line, because by definition it is drawn in such a way as to minimize the sum of the squares of the distances between it and the observations. Hence the spread of the residuals will tend to be smaller than the spread of the values of u, and MSD(e) will tend to underestimate σ_u^2. Indeed, it can be shown that the expected value of MSD(e), when there is just one explanatory variable, is $\frac{n-2}{n}\sigma_u^2$. However, it follows that, if one defines s_u^2 by

$$ s_u^2 = \frac{n}{n-2}\text{MSD}(e) = \frac{n}{n-2}\frac{1}{n}\sum_{i=1}^{n} e_i^2 = \frac{1}{n-2}\sum_{i=1}^{n} e_i^2 \tag{2.43} $$

then s_u^2 will be an unbiased estimator of σ_u^2.

Using (2.38) and (2.43), one can obtain estimates of the population variances of b_1 and b_2 and, by taking square roots, estimates of their standard deviations. Rather than talk about the estimate of the standard deviation of the probability density function of a regression coefficient, which is a bit cumbersome, one uses the term **standard error of a regression coefficient**, which in this text will frequently be abbreviated to s.e. For simple regression analysis, therefore, one has

$$ \text{s.e.}(b_1) = \sqrt{s_u^2 \left(\frac{1}{n} + \frac{\overline{X}^2}{\sum_{i=1}^{n} \left(X_i - \overline{X} \right)^2} \right)} \quad \text{and} \quad \text{s.e.}(b_2) = \sqrt{\frac{s_u^2}{\sum_{i=1}^{n} \left(X_i - \overline{X} \right)^2}}. \tag{2.44} $$

The standard errors of the regression coefficients are automatically calculated as part of the computer output.

These relationships will be illustrated with the Monte Carlo experiment described in Section 2.4. In Set I, u was determined by random numbers drawn

Table 2.5

Sample	$s.e.(b_2)$	Sample	$s.e.(b_2)$
1	0.043	6	0.044
2	0.041	7	0.039
3	0.038	8	0.040
4	0.035	9	0.033
5	0.027	10	0.033

from a population with zero mean and unit variance, so $\sigma_u^2 = 1$. X was the set of numbers from 1 to 20, whose mean is 10.5. With a little arithmetic one can show that $\sum \left(X_i - \overline{X} \right)^2 = 665$. Hence

$$\sigma_{b_1}^2 = \sigma_u^2 \left(\frac{1}{n} + \frac{\overline{X}^2}{\sum_{i=1}^{n} \left(X_i - \overline{X} \right)^2} \right) = \frac{1}{20} + \frac{10.5^2}{665} = 0.2158 \qquad (2.45)$$

and

$$\sigma_{b_2}^2 = \frac{\sigma_u^2}{\sum_{i=1}^{n} \left(X_i - \overline{X} \right)^2} = \frac{1}{665} = 0.001504. \qquad (2.46)$$

Therefore, the true standard deviation of b_2 is $\sqrt{0.001504} = 0.0388$. What did the computer make of it in the 10 samples in Set I? It had to calculate the standard error using (2.44), with the results shown in Table 2.5 in the 10 samples. As you can see, most of the estimates are quite good.

One fundamental point must be emphasized. The standard error gives only a general guide to the likely accuracy of a regression coefficient. It enables you to obtain some idea of the width, or narrowness, of its probability density function as represented in Figure 2.1, but it does *not* tell you whether your regression estimate comes from the middle of the function, and is therefore accurate, or from the tails, and is therefore relatively inaccurate.

The higher the variance of the disturbance term, the higher the sample variance of the residuals is likely to be, and hence the higher will be the standard errors of the coefficients in the regression equation, reflecting the risk that the coefficients are inaccurate. However, it is only a *risk*. It is possible that in any particular sample the effects of the disturbance term in the different observations will cancel each other out and the regression coefficients will be accurate after all. The trouble is that in general there is no way of telling whether you happen to be in this fortunate position or not.

Exercises

Where performance on a game of skill is measured numerically, the improvement that comes with practice is called a learning curve. This is especially obvious with some arcade-type games. The first time players try a new one, they are likely to score very little. With more attempts, their scores should gradually improve as they become accustomed to the game, although obviously there will be variations caused by the luck factor. Suppose that their scores are determined by the learning curve

$$Y_i = 500 + 100X_i + u_i,$$

where Y is the score, X is the number of times that they have played before, and u is a disturbance term.

The table gives the results of the first 20 games of a new player: X automatically goes from 0 to 19; u was set equal to 400 times the numbers generated by a normally distributed random variable with zero mean and unit variance; and Y was determined by X and u according to the learning curve.

Regressing Y on X, one obtains the equation (standard errors in parentheses)

$$\hat{Y} = 369 + 116.8X.$$
$$(190) \quad (17.1)$$

Observation	X	u	Y
1	0	236	264
2	1	−96	504
3	2	−332	368
4	3	12	812
5	4	−152	748
6	5	−876	124
7	6	412	1,512
8	7	96	1,296
9	8	1,012	2,312
10	9	−52	1,348
11	10	636	2,136
12	11	−368	1,232
13	12	−284	1,416
14	13	−100	1,700
15	14	676	2,576
16	15	60	2,060
17	16	8	2,108
18	17	−44	2,156
19	18	−364	1,936
20	19	568	2,968

2.5 Why is the constant in this equation not equal to 500 and the coefficient of X not equal to 100?

2.6 What is the meaning of the standard errors?

2.7 The experiment is repeated with nine other new players (the disturbance term being generated by 400 times a different set of 20 random numbers in each case), and the regression results for all ten players are shown in the table. Why do the constant, the coefficient of X, and the standard errors vary from sample to sample?

Player	Constant	Standard error of constant	Coefficient of X	Standard error of coefficient of X
1	369	190	116.8	17.1
2	699	184	90.1	16.5
3	531	169	78.5	15.2
4	555	158	99.5	14.2
5	407	120	122.6	10.8
6	427	194	104.3	17.5
7	412	175	123.8	15.8
8	613	192	95.8	17.3
9	234	146	130.1	13.1
10	485	146	109.6	13.1

2.8 $\sum \left(X_i - \overline{X}\right)^2 = 665$ and $\sigma_u^2 = 160{,}000$. Using equation (2.38), show that the standard deviation of the probability density function of the coefficient of X is equal to 15.5. Are the standard errors in the table good estimates of this standard deviation?

2.9* Using the decomposition of b_1 obtained in Exercise 2.1, derive the expression for $\sigma_{b_1}^2$ given in equation (2.38).

2.7 The Gauss–Markov theorem

In the Review chapter, we considered estimators of the unknown population mean μ_X of a random variable X, given a sample of observations. Although we instinctively use the sample mean $\overline{X}$ as our estimator, we saw that it was only one of an infinite number of possible unbiased estimators of μ_X. The reason that the sample mean is preferred to any other estimator is that, under certain assumptions, it is the most efficient.

Similar considerations apply to regression coefficients. The **Gauss–Markov theorem** states that, provided that the assumptions in Section 2.2 are satisfied, the OLS estimators are BLUE: best (most efficient) linear (combinations of the Y_i) unbiased estimators of the regression parameters. We will demonstrate this for the slope coefficient b_2.

To see the linearity property, note that

$$\sum_{i=1}^{n}\left(X_i-\overline{X}\right)\left(Y_i-\overline{Y}\right) = \sum_{i=1}^{n}\left(X_i-\overline{X}\right)Y_i - \sum_{i=1}^{n}\left(X_i-\overline{X}\right)\overline{Y}$$

$$= \sum_{i=1}^{n}\left(X_i-\overline{X}\right)Y_i - \overline{Y}\sum_{i=1}^{n}\left(X_i-\overline{X}\right)$$

$$= \sum_{i=1}^{n}\left(X_i-\overline{X}\right)Y_i - \overline{Y}\left\{\sum_{i=1}^{n}X_i - n\overline{X}\right\}$$

$$= \sum_{i=1}^{n}\left(X_i-\overline{X}\right)Y_i. \qquad (2.47)$$

Then

$$b_2 = \frac{\sum_{i=1}^{n}\left(X_i-\overline{X}\right)\left(Y_i-\overline{Y}\right)}{\sum_{j-1}^{n}\left(X_j-\overline{X}\right)^2} = \frac{\sum_{i=1}^{n}\left(X_i-\overline{X}\right)Y_i}{\sum_{j=1}^{n}\left(X_j-\overline{X}\right)^2} = \sum_{i=1}^{n}\frac{\left(X_i-\overline{X}\right)}{\sum_{i=1}^{n}\left(X_j-\overline{X}\right)^2}Y_i = \sum_{i=1}^{n}a_iY_i$$

$$(2.48)$$

where the a_i are as defined as before.

We will demonstrate the efficiency property. Consider any other unbiased estimator

$$\tilde{b}_2 = \sum_{i=1}^{n}g_iY_i \qquad (2.49)$$

that is a linear function of the Y_i. We will show that it has a larger variance unless $g_i = a_i$ for all i. For $\tilde{b}_2$ to be unbiased, we need $E\left(\tilde{b}_2\right) = \beta_2$.

$$\tilde{b}_2 = \sum_{i=1}^{n}g_iY_i = \sum_{i=1}^{n}g_i\left(\beta_1+\beta_2X_i+u_i\right) = \sum_{i=1}^{n}\beta_1g_i + \sum_{i=1}^{n}\beta_2g_iX_i + \sum_{i=1}^{n}g_iu_i.$$

$$(2.50)$$

Hence

$$E\left(\tilde{b}_2\right) = \beta_1\sum_{i=1}^{n}g_i + \beta_2\sum_{i=1}^{n}g_iX_i + E\left\{\sum_{i=1}^{n}g_iu_i\right\}. \qquad (2.51)$$

The first two terms on the right side are nonstochastic and are therefore unaffected by taking expectations. Now

$$E\left\{\sum_{i=1}^{n}g_iu_i\right\} = \sum_{i=1}^{n}E\left(g_iu_i\right) = \sum_{i=1}^{n}g_iE\left(u_i\right) = 0. \qquad (2.52)$$

The first step used the first expected value rule. Thus

$$E\left(\tilde{b}_2\right) = \beta_1 \sum_{i=1}^{n} g_i + \beta_2 \sum_{i=1}^{n} g_i X_i. \tag{2.53}$$

Hence for $E\left(\tilde{b}_2\right) = \beta_2$, the g_i must satisfy $\sum g_i = 0$ and $\sum g_i X_i = 1$. The variance of $\tilde{b}_2$ is given by

$$\sigma_{\tilde{b}_2}^2 = E\left\{\left(\tilde{b}_2 - E\left(\tilde{b}_2\right)\right)^2\right\} = E\left\{\sum_{i=1}^{n} (g_i u_i)^2\right\} = \sigma_u^2 \sum_{i=1}^{n} g_i^2. \tag{2.54}$$

The last step is exactly parallel to the proof that $E\left\{\sum (a_i u_i)^2\right\} = \sigma_u^2 \sum a_i^2$ in Box 2.3. Let

$$h_i = g_i - a_i. \tag{2.55}$$

Writing $g_i = a_i + h_i$, the first condition for the unbiasedness of $\tilde{b}_2$ becomes

$$\sum_{i=1}^{n} g_i = \sum_{i=1}^{n} (a_i + h_i) = 0. \tag{2.56}$$

Since $\sum a_i = 0$ (see Box 2.2), this implies $\sum h_i = 0$. The second condition for the unbiasedness of $\tilde{b}_2$ becomes

$$\sum_{i=1}^{n} g_i X_i = \sum_{i=1}^{n} (a_i + h_i) X_i = \sum_{i=1}^{n} a_i X_i + \sum_{i=1}^{n} h_i X_i = 1. \tag{2.57}$$

Since $\sum a_i X_i = 1$ (see Box 2.2 again), this implies $\sum h_i X_i = 0$. The variance of $\tilde{b}_2$ becomes

$$\sigma_{\tilde{b}_2}^2 = \sigma_u^2 \sum_{i=1}^{n} g_i^2 = \sigma_u^2 \sum_{i=1}^{n} (a_i + h_i)^2 = \sigma_u^2 \left\{\sum_{i=1}^{n} a_i^2 + \sum_{i=1}^{n} h_i^2 + 2\sum_{i=1}^{n} a_i h_i\right\}. \tag{2.58}$$

Now

$$\sum_{i=1}^{n} a_i h_i = \sum_{i=1}^{n} \frac{\left(X_i - \overline{X}\right) h_i}{\sum_{j=1}^{n} \left(X_j - \overline{X}\right)^2}$$

$$= \frac{1}{\sum_{j=1}^{n} \left(X_j - \overline{X}\right)^2} \left\{\sum_{i=1}^{n} h_i X_i - \overline{X} \sum_{i=1}^{n} h_i\right\}. \tag{2.59}$$

This is zero because, as we have seen, the conditions for unbiasedness of $\tilde{b}_2$ require $\sum h_i = 0$ and $\sum h_i X_i = 0$. Hence

$$\sigma_{\tilde{b}_2}^2 = \sigma_u^2 \left\{ \sum_{i=1}^{n} a_i^2 + \sum_{i=1}^{n} h_i^2 \right\}. \tag{2.60}$$

This must be greater than $\sigma_u^2 \sum a_i^2$, the variance of the OLS estimator b_2, unless $h_i = 0$ for all i, in which case $\tilde{b}_2$ is the same as b_2.

Exercises

Note: For each of the following exercises, it may be assumed that the true model is

$$Y_i = \beta_1 + \beta_2 X_i + u_i.$$

2.10 In Section 2.5 it was demonstrated that the naïve estimator of the slope coefficient

$$b_2 = \frac{Y_n - Y_1}{X_n - X_1}$$

is unbiased. It can be shown that its variance is given by

$$\frac{\sigma_u^2}{\left(X_1 - \overline{X}\right)^2 + \left(X_n - \overline{X}\right)^2 - 0.5\left(X_1 + X_n - 2\overline{X}\right)^2}.$$

Use this information to verify that the estimator is less efficient than the OLS estimator.

2.11* It can be shown that the variance of the estimator of the slope coefficient in Exercise 2.4,

$$\frac{\sum\limits_{i=1}^{n}\left(Z_i - \overline{Z}\right)\left(Y_i - \overline{Y}\right)}{\sum\limits_{i=1}^{n}\left(Z_i - \overline{Z}\right)\left(X_i - \overline{X}\right)}$$

is given by

$$\sigma_{b_2}^2 = \frac{\sigma_u^2}{\sum\limits_{i=1}^{n}\left(X_i - \overline{X}\right)^2} \times \frac{1}{r_{XZ}^2}$$

where r_{XZ} is the correlation between X and Z. What are the implications for the efficiency of the estimator?

2.12 Can one come to any conclusions concerning the efficiency of the estimator in Exercise 2.3, for the case $\beta_1 = 0$?

2.8   Testing hypotheses relating to the regression coefficients

Which comes first, theoretical hypothesizing or empirical research? This is a bit like asking which came first, the chicken or the egg. In practice, theorizing and experimentation feed on each other, and questions of this type cannot be answered. For this reason, we will approach the topic of hypothesis testing from both directions. On the one hand, we may suppose that the theory has come first and that the purpose of the experiment is to evaluate its plausibility. This will lead to the execution of significance tests. Alternatively, we may perform the experiment first and then consider what theoretical hypotheses would be consistent with the results. This will lead to the construction of confidence intervals.

You will already have encountered the logic underlying significance tests and confidence intervals in an introductory statistics course. You will thus be familiar with most of the concepts in the following applications to regression analysis. There is, however, one topic that may be new: the use of one-sided tests. Such tests are used very frequently in regression analysis. Indeed, they are, or they ought to be, more common than the traditional textbook two-sided tests. It is therefore important that you understand the rationale for their use, and this involves a sequence of small analytical steps. None of this should present any difficulty, but be warned that, if you attempt to use a short cut or, worse, try to reduce the whole business to the mechanical use of a few formulae, you will be asking for trouble.

Formulation of a null hypothesis

We will start by assuming that the theory precedes the experiment and that you have some hypothetical relationship in your mind. For example, you may believe that the percentage rate of price inflation in an economy, p, depends on the percentage rate of wage inflation, w, according to the linear equation

$$p = \beta_1 + \beta_2 w + u \tag{2.61}$$

where β_1 and β_2 are parameters and u is a disturbance term. You might further hypothesize that, apart from the effects of the disturbance term, price inflation is equal to wage inflation. Under these circumstances, you would say that the hypothesis that you are going to test, known as your **null hypothesis** and denoted H_0, is that β_2 is equal to 1. We also define an **alternative hypothesis**, denoted H_1, which represents your conclusion if the experimental test indicates that H_0 is false. In the present case, H_1 is simply that β_2 is not equal to 1. The two hypotheses are stated using the notation

$$H_0: \beta_2 = 1$$
$$H_1: \beta_2 \neq 1.$$

In this particular case, if we really believe that price inflation is equal to wage inflation, we are trying to establish the credibility of H_0 by subjecting it to the strictest possible test and hoping that it emerges unscathed. In practice, however, it is more usual to set up a null hypothesis and attack it with the objective of establishing the alternative hypothesis as the correct conclusion. For example, consider the simple earnings function

$$EARNINGS = \beta_1 + \beta_2 S + u \qquad (2.62)$$

where $EARNINGS$ is hourly earnings in dollars and S is years of schooling. On very reasonable theoretical grounds, you expect earnings to be dependent on schooling, but your theory is not strong enough to enable you to specify a particular value for β_2. You can nevertheless establish the dependence of earnings on schooling by the inverse procedure in which you take as your null hypothesis the assertion that earnings does *not* depend on schooling, that is, that β_2 is zero. Your alternative hypothesis is that β_2 is not equal to zero, that is, that schooling *does* affect earnings. If you can reject the null hypothesis, you have established the relationship, at least in general terms. Using the conventional notation, your null and alternative hypotheses are $H_0: \beta_2 = 0$ and $H_1: \beta_2 \neq 0$, respectively.

The following discussion uses the simple regression model

$$Y_i = \beta_1 + \beta_2 X_i + u_i. \qquad (2.63)$$

It will be confined to the slope coefficient, β_2, but exactly the same procedures are applied to the constant term, β_1. We will take the general case, where you have defined a null hypothesis that β_2 is equal to some specific value, say β_2^0, and the alternative hypothesis is that β_2 is not equal to this value ($H_0: \beta_2 = \beta_2^0$, $H_1: \beta_2 \neq \beta_2^0$); you may be attempting to attack or defend the null hypothesis as it suits your purpose. We will take it that the assumptions in Section 2.2 are satisfied.

Developing the implications of a hypothesis

If H_0 is correct, values of b_2 obtained using regression analysis in repeated samples will be distributed with mean β_2^0 and variance $\sigma_u^2 / \sum \left(X_i - \overline{X} \right)^2$. We will now introduce the assumption that u has a normal distribution. If this is the case, b_2 will also be normally distributed, as shown in Figure 2.6. 'sd' in the figure refers to the standard deviation of b_2, that is $\sqrt{\sigma_u^2 / \sum \left(X_i - \overline{X} \right)^2}$. In view of the structure of the normal distribution, most values of b_2 will lie within two standard deviations of β_2^0 (if $H_0: \beta_2 = \beta_2^0$ is true).

Initially, we will assume that we know the standard deviation of the distribution of b_2. This is a most unreasonable assumption, and we will drop it later. In practice we have to estimate it, along with β_1 and β_2, but it will simplify the

Probability density
function of b_2

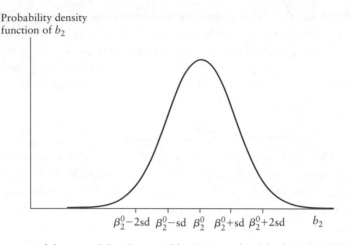

$$\beta_2^0 - 2\text{sd} \quad \beta_2^0 - \text{sd} \quad \beta_2^0 \quad \beta_2^0 + \text{sd} \quad \beta_2^0 + 2\text{sd} \qquad b_2$$

Figure 2.6 Structure of the normal distribution of b_2 in terms of standard deviations about the mean

Probability density
function of b_2

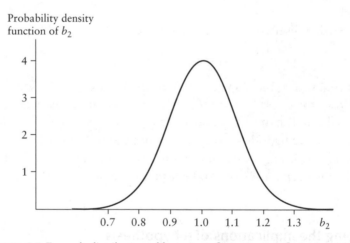

$$0.7 \quad 0.8 \quad 0.9 \quad 1.0 \quad 1.1 \quad 1.2 \quad 1.3 \quad b_2$$

Figure 2.7 Example distribution of b_2 (price inflation/wage inflation model)

discussion if for the time being we suppose that we know it exactly, and hence are in a position to draw Figure 2.6.

We will illustrate this with the price inflation/wage inflation model (2.61). Suppose that for some reason we know that the standard deviation of b_2 is equal to 0.1. Then, if our null hypothesis H_0: $\beta_2 = 1$ is correct, regression estimates would be distributed as shown in Figure 2.7. You can see that, provided that the null hypothesis is correct, the estimates will generally lie between 0.8 and 1.2.

Compatibility, freakiness, and the significance level

Now we come to the crunch. Suppose that we take an actual sample of observations on average rates of price inflation and wage inflation over the past five years for a sample of countries and estimate β_2 using regression analysis. If the estimate is close to 1.0, we should almost certainly be satisfied with the null hypothesis, since it and the sample result are compatible with one another, but suppose, on the other hand, that the estimate is a long way from 1.0. Suppose that it is equal to 0.7. This is three standard deviations below 1.0. If the null hypothesis is correct, the probability of being three standard deviations away from the mean, positive or negative, is only 0.0027, which is very low. You could come to either of two conclusions about this worrisome result:

1. You could continue to maintain that your null hypothesis $H_0: \beta_2 = 1$ is correct, and that the experiment has given a freak result. You concede that the probability of such a low value of b_2 is very small, but nevertheless it does occur 0.27 percent of the time and you reckon that this is one of those times.

2. You could conclude that the hypothesis is contradicted by the regression result. You are not convinced by the explanation in (1) because the probability is so small and you think that a much more likely explanation is that β_2 is not really equal to 1. In other words, you adopt the alternative hypothesis $H_1: \beta_2 \neq 1$ instead.

How do you decide when to choose (1) and when to choose (2)? Obviously, the smaller the probability of obtaining a regression estimate such as the one you have obtained, given your hypothesis, the more likely you are to abandon the hypothesis and choose (2). How small should the probability be before choosing (2)?

There is, and there can be, no definite answer to this question. In most applied work in economics either 5 percent or 1 percent is taken as the critical limit. If 5 percent is taken, the switch to (2) is made when the null hypothesis implies that the probability of obtaining such an extreme value of b_2 is less than 5 percent. The null hypothesis is then said to be rejected at the 5 percent significance level.

This occurs when b_2 is more than 1.96 standard deviations from β_2^0. If you look up the normal distribution table, Table A.1 in Appendix A, you will see that the probability of b_2 being more than 1.96 standard deviations above its mean is 2.5 percent, and similarly the probability of it being more than 1.96 standard deviations below its mean is 2.5 percent. The total probability of it being more than 1.96 standard deviations away is thus 5 percent.

We can summarize this decision rule mathematically by saying that we will reject the null hypothesis if

$$z > 1.96 \quad \text{or} \quad z < -1.96 \qquad\qquad (2.64)$$

where z is the number of standard deviations between the regression estimate and the hypothetical value of β_2:

$$z = \frac{\text{distance between regression estimate and hypothetical value}}{\text{standard deviation of } b_2} = \frac{b_2 - \beta_2^0}{\text{s.d.}(b_2)}. \tag{2.65}$$

The null hypothesis will not be rejected if

$$-1.96 \leq z \leq 1.96. \tag{2.66}$$

This condition can be expressed in terms of b_2 and β_2^0 by substituting for z from (2.65):

$$-1.96 \leq \frac{b_2 - \beta_2^0}{\text{s.d.}(b_2)} \leq 1.96. \tag{2.67}$$

Multiplying through by the standard deviation of b_2, one obtains

$$-1.96 \text{ s.d.}(b_2) \leq b_2 - \beta_2^0 \leq 1.96 \text{ s.d.}(b_2) \tag{2.68}$$

from which one obtains

$$\beta_2^0 - 1.96 \text{ s.d.}(b_2) \leq b_2 \leq \beta_2^0 + 1.96 \text{ s.d.}(b_2). \tag{2.69}$$

Equation (2.69) gives the set of values of b_2 which will not lead to the rejection of a specific null hypothesis $\beta_2 = \beta_2^0$. It is known as the **acceptance region** for b_2, at the 5 percent significance level.

In the case of the price inflation/wage inflation example, where s.d.(b_2) is equal to 0.1, you would reject at the 5 percent level if b_2 lies more than 0.196 above or below the hypothetical mean, that is, above 1.196 or below 0.804. The

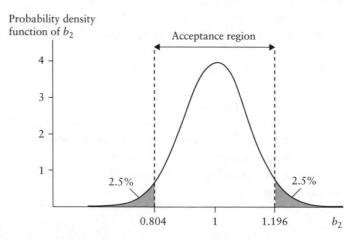

Figure 2.8 Acceptance region for b_2, 5 percent significance level

acceptance region is therefore those values of b_2 from 0.804 to 1.196. This is illustrated by the unshaded area in Figure 2.8.

Similarly, the null hypothesis is said to be rejected at the 1 percent significance level if the hypothesis implies that the probability of obtaining such an extreme value of b_2 is less than 1 percent. This occurs when b_2 is more than 2.58 standard deviations above or below the hypothetical value of β_2, that is, when

$$z > 2.58 \quad \text{or} \quad z < -2.58. \tag{2.70}$$

BOX 2.4   Type I and Type II errors in everyday life

The problem of trying to avoid Type I and Type II errors will already be familiar to everybody. A criminal trial provides a particularly acute example. Taking as the null hypothesis that the defendant is innocent, a Type I error occurs when the jury wrongly decides that the defendant is guilty. A Type II error occurs when the jury wrongly acquits the defendant.

Looking at the normal distribution table again, you will see that the probability of b_2 being more than 2.58 standard deviations above its mean is 0.5 percent, and there is the same probability of it being more than 2.58 standard deviations below it, so the combined probability of such an extreme value is 1 percent. In the case of our example, you would reject the null hypothesis $\beta_2 = 1$ if the regression estimate lay above 1.258 or below 0.742.

You may ask, why do people usually report, or at least consider reporting, the results at both the 5 percent and the 1 percent significance levels? Why not just one? The answer is that they are trying to strike a balance between the risks of making **Type I errors** and **Type II errors**. *A Type I error occurs when you reject a true null hypothesis. A Type II error occurs when you do not reject a false one.*

Obviously, the lower your critical probability, the smaller is the risk of a Type I error. If your significance level is 5 percent, you will reject a true hypothesis 5 percent of the time. If it is 1 percent, you will make a Type I error 1 percent of the time. Thus the 1 percent significance level is safer in this respect. If you reject the hypothesis at this level, you are almost certainly right to do so. For this reason the 1 percent significance level is described as *higher* than the 5 percent.

At the same time, if the null hypothesis happens to be false, the higher your significance level, the wider is your acceptance region, the greater is your chance of not rejecting it, and so the greater is the risk of a Type II error. Thus you are caught between the devil and the deep blue sea. If you insist on a very high significance level, you incur a relatively high risk of a Type II error if the null hypothesis happens to be false. If you choose a low significance level, you run a relatively high risk of making a Type I error if the null hypothesis happens to be true.

Most people take out an insurance policy and perform the test at both these levels, being prepared to quote the results of each. Actually, it is frequently superfluous to quote both results explicitly. Since b_2 has to be more extreme for the hypothesis to be rejected at the 1 percent level than at the 5 percent level, if you reject at the 1 percent level it automatically follows that you reject at the 5 percent level, and there is no need to say so. And if you do not reject at the 5 percent level, it automatically follows that you will not reject at the 1 percent level. The only time when you should quote both results is when you reject the null hypothesis at the 5 percent level but not at the 1 percent level.

t tests

So far we have assumed that the standard deviation of b_2 is known, which is most unlikely in practice. It has to be estimated by the standard error of b_2, given by (2.44). This causes two modifications to the test procedure. First, z is now defined using s.e.(b_2) instead of s.d.(b_2), and it is referred to as the t statistic:

$$t = \frac{b_2 - \beta_2^0}{\text{s.e.}(b_2)}.$$ (2.71)

Second, the critical levels of t depend upon what is known as a t distribution instead of a normal distribution. We will not go into the reasons for this, or even describe the t distribution mathematically. Suffice to say that it is a cousin of the normal distribution, its exact shape depending on the number of degrees of freedom in the regression, and that it approximates the normal distribution increasingly closely as the number of degrees of freedom increases. You will certainly have encountered the t distribution in your introductory statistics course. Table A.2 in Appendix A gives the critical values of t cross-classified by significance level and the number of degrees of freedom.

The estimation of each parameter in a regression equation consumes one degree of freedom in the sample. Hence the number of degrees of freedom is equal to the number of observations in the sample minus the number of parameters estimated. The parameters are the constant (assuming that this is specified in the regression model) and the coefficients of the explanatory variables. In the present case of simple regression analysis, only two parameters, β_1 and β_2, are estimated and hence the number of degrees of freedom is $n - 2$. It should be emphasized that a more general expression will be required when we come to multiple regression analysis.

The critical value of t, which we will denote t_{crit}, replaces the number 1.96 in (2.67). The t test consists of comparing the t statistic with t_{crit}. The condition that a regression estimate should not lead to the rejection of a null hypothesis $H_0: \beta_2 = \beta_2^0$ is

$$-t_{\text{crit}} \leq \frac{b_2 - \beta_2^0}{\text{s.e.}(b_2)} \leq t_{\text{crit}}.$$ (2.72)

Hence we have the decision rule: reject H_0 if $\left|\frac{b_2-\beta_2^0}{\text{s.e.}(b_2)}\right| > t_{\text{crit}}$, do not reject if $\left|\frac{b_2-\beta_2^0}{\text{s.e.}(b_2)}\right| \leq t_{\text{crit}}$, where $\left|\frac{b_2-\beta_2^0}{\text{s.e.}(b_2)}\right|$ is the absolute value (numerical value, neglecting the sign) of t.

Examples

In Section 1.6 hourly earnings were regressed on years of schooling using data from the US National Longitudinal Survey of Youth, with the output shown in Table 2.6. The first two columns give the names of the variables, here just S and the intercept (Stata denotes this as _cons) and the estimates of their coefficients. The third column gives the corresponding standard errors. Let us suppose that one of the purposes of the regression was to confirm our intuition that earnings are affected by education. Accordingly, we set up the null hypothesis $H_0: \beta_2 = 0$ and try to refute it. The corresponding t statistic, using (2.71), is simply the estimate of the coefficient divided by its standard error:

$$t = \frac{b_2 - \beta_2^0}{\text{s.e.}(b_2)} = \frac{b_2 - 0}{\text{s.e.}(b_2)} = \frac{2.4553}{0.2319} = 10.59. \tag{2.73}$$

Since there are 540 observations in the sample and we have estimated two parameters, the number of degrees of freedom is 538. Table A.2 does not give the critical values of t for 538 degrees of freedom, but we know that they must be lower than the corresponding critical values for 500, since the critical value is inversely related to the number of degrees of freedom. The critical value with 500 degrees of freedom at the 5 percent level is 1.965. Hence we can be sure that we would reject H_0 at the 5 percent level with 538 degrees of freedom and we conclude that schooling does affect earnings.

To put this test into words, with 538 degrees of freedom the upper and lower 2.5 percent tails of the t distribution start approximately 1.965 standard deviations above and below its mean of zero. The null hypothesis will not be rejected

Table 2.6

```
. reg EARNINGS S

      Source        SS          df        MS                Number of obs =      540
-------------------------------------------                 F(1,538)      =   112.15
       Model   19321.5589        1    19321.5589            Prob > F      =   0.0000
    Residual   92688.6722      538    172.283777            R-squared     =   0.1725
-------------------------------------------                 Adj R-squared =   0.1710
       Total  112010.231       539    207.811189            Root MSE      =   13.126

---------------------------------------------------------------------------------
    EARNINGS       Coef.    Std. Err.        t    P>|t|     [95% Conf. Interval]
---------------------------------------------------------------------------------
           S    2.455321     .2318512     10.59    0.000     1.999876    2.910765
       _cons   -13.93347     3.219851     -4.33    0.000     20.25849   -7.608444
```

BOX 2.5   Reporting the results of *t* tests

Suppose you have a theoretical relationship

$$Y_i = \beta_1 + \beta_2 X_i + u_i$$

and your null and alternative hypotheses are $H_0: \beta_2 = \beta_2^0, H_1: \beta_2 \neq \beta_2^0$. Given an experimental estimate b_2 of β_2, the acceptance and rejection regions for the hypothesis for the 5 percent and 1 percent significance levels can be represented in general terms by the left part of Figure 2.9.

The right side of the figure gives the same regions for a specific example, the price inflation/wage inflation model, the null hypothesis being that β_2 is equal to 1. The null hypothesis will not be rejected at the 5 percent level if b_2 lies within 2.101 standard errors of 1, that is, in the range 0.79 to 1.21, and it will not be rejected at the 1 percent level if b_2 lies within 2.878 standard deviations of 1, that is, in the range 0.71 to 1.29.

From Figure 2.9, it can be seen that there are three types of decision zone:

1. where b_2 is so far from the hypothetical β_2 that the null hypothesis is rejected at both the 5 percent and the 1 percent levels,

2. where b_2 is far enough from the hypothetical β_2 for the null hypothesis to be rejected at the 5 percent but not the 1 percent level,

3. where b_2 is close enough to the hypothetical β_2 for the null hypothesis not to be rejected at either level.

From the diagram it can be verified that if the null hypothesis is rejected at the 1 percent level, it is automatically rejected at the 5 percent level. Hence in case (1) it is only necessary to report the rejection of the hypothesis at the 1 percent level. To report that it is rejected also at the 5 percent level is superfluous and suggests that you are not aware of this. It would be a bit like reporting that a certain high jumper can clear two meters, and then adding that the athlete can also clear one and a half meters.

In case (3), likewise, you only need to make one statement, in this case that the hypothesis is not rejected at the 5 percent level. It automatically follows that it is not rejected at the 1 percent level, and to add a statement to this effect as well would be like saying that the high jumper cannot clear one and a half meters, and also reporting that the athlete cannot clear two meters either.

Only in case (2) is it necessary (and desirable) to report the results of both tests.

Note that if you find that you can reject the null hypothesis at the 5 percent level, you should not stop there. You have established that the null hypothesis can be rejected at that level, but there remains a 5 percent chance of a Type I error. You should also perform the test at the 1 percent level. If you find that you can reject the null hypothesis at this level, this is the outcome that you should report. The risk of a Type I error is now only 1 percent and your conclusion is much more convincing. This is case (1) above. If you cannot reject at the 1 percent level, you have reached case (2) and you should report the results of both tests.

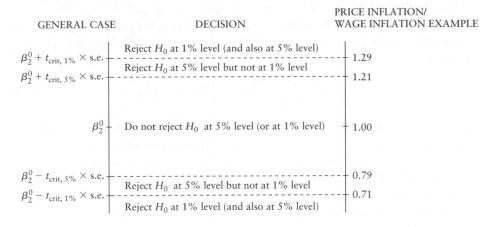

Figure 2.9 Reporting the results of a t test (no need to report conclusions in parentheses)

if the regression coefficient is estimated to lie within 1.965 standard deviations of zero. In this case, however, the discrepancy is equivalent to 10.59 estimated standard deviations and we come to the conclusion that the regression result contradicts the null hypothesis.

Of course, since we are using the 5 percent significance level as the basis for the test, there is in principle a 5 percent risk of a Type I error, if the null hypothesis is true. In this case we could reduce the risk to 1 percent by using the 1 percent significance level instead. The critical value of t at the 1 percent significance level with 500 degrees of freedom is 2.586. Since the t statistic is greater than this, we see that we can easily reject the null hypothesis at this level as well.

Remember that when the 5 percent and 1 percent tests lead to the same conclusion, there is no need to report both, and indeed you would look ignorant if you did. Read carefully Box 2.5 on reporting test results.

This procedure of establishing a relationship between a dependent and an explanatory variable by setting up, and then refuting, a null hypothesis H_0: $\beta_2 = 0$ is used very frequently indeed. Consequently, all serious regression applications automatically print out the t statistic for this special case: that is, the coefficient divided by its standard error. The ratio is often denoted 'the' t statistic. In the regression output, the t statistics for the constant and slope coefficient appear in the middle column.

However, if the null hypothesis specifies some nonzero value of β_2, the more general expression (2.71) has to be used and the t statistic has to be calculated by hand. For example, consider again the price inflation/wage inflation model (2.61) and suppose that the fitted model is (standard errors in parentheses)

$$\hat{p} = -1.21 + 0.82w. \qquad (2.74)$$
$$(0.05) \quad (0.10)$$

If we now investigate the hypothesis that price inflation is equal to wage inflation, our null hypothesis is that the coefficient of w is equal to 1.0. The corresponding t statistic is

$$t = \frac{b_2 - \beta_2^0}{\text{s.e.}(b_2)} = \frac{0.82 - 1.00}{0.10} = -1.80. \qquad (2.75)$$

If there are, say, 20 observations in the sample, the number of degrees of freedom is 18 and the critical value of t at the 5 percent significance level is 2.101. The absolute value of our t statistic is less than this, so on this occasion we do not reject the null hypothesis. The estimate 0.82 is below our hypothesized value 1.00, but not so far below as to exclude the possibility that the null hypothesis is correct. One final note on reporting regression results: some writers place the t statistic in parentheses under a coefficient, instead of the standard error. You should be careful to check, and when you are presenting results yourself, you should make it clear which you are giving.

p values

The fifth column of the output in Table 2.6, headed P > |t|, provides an alternative approach to reporting the significance of regression coefficients. The figures in this column give the **p value** for each coefficient. This is the probability of obtaining the corresponding t statistic as a matter of chance, if the null hypothesis H_0: $\beta_2 = 0$ were true. A p value of less than 0.01 means that the probability is less than 1 percent, which in turn means that the null hypothesis would be rejected at the 1 percent level; a p value between 0.01 and 0.05 means that the null hypothesis would be rejected at the 5 percent, but not the 1 percent level; and a p value of 0.05 or more means that it would not be rejected at the 5 percent level.

BOX 2.6   The reject/fail-to-reject terminology

In this section it has been shown that you should reject the null hypothesis if the absolute value of the t statistic is greater than t_{crit}, and that you fail to reject it otherwise. Why 'fail to reject', which is a clumsy expression? Would it not be better just to say that you accept the hypothesis if the absolute value of the t statistic is less than t_{crit}?

The argument against using the term 'accept' is that you might find yourself 'accepting' several mutually exclusive hypotheses at the same time. For instance, in the price inflation/wage inflation example, you would not reject a null hypothesis H_0: $\beta_2 = 0.9$, or a null hypothesis H_0: $\beta_2 = 0.8$. It is logical to say that you would not reject these null hypotheses, as well as the null hypothesis H_0: $\beta_2 = 1$ discussed in the text, but it makes little sense to say that you simultaneously accept all three hypotheses. In the next section you will see that one can define a whole range of hypotheses which would not be rejected by a given experimental result, so it would be incautious to pick out one as being 'accepted'.

The p value approach is more informative than the 5 percent/1 percent approach, in that it gives the exact probability of a Type I error, if the null hypothesis is true. For example, in the earnings function output in Table 2.6, the p value for the slope coefficient is 0.000, meaning that the probability of obtaining a t statistic as large as 10.59, or larger, as a matter of chance is less than 0.0005 percent. Hence we would reject the null hypothesis that the slope coefficient is zero at the 1 percent level. Indeed we would reject it at the 0.1 percent level—see below. Choice between the p value approach and the 5 percent/1 percent approach appears to be entirely conventional. The medical literature uses p values, but the economics literature generally uses 5 percent/1 percent.

0.1 percent tests

If the t statistic is very high, you should check whether you can reject the null hypothesis at the 0.1 percent level. If you can, you should always report the result of the 0.1 percent test in preference to that of the 1 percent test because it demonstrates that you are able to reject the null hypothesis with an even smaller risk of a Type I error.

Exercises

2.13 Give more examples of everyday instances in which decisions involving possible Type I and Type II errors may arise.

2.14 Before beginning a certain course, 36 students are given an aptitude test. The scores, and the course results (pass/fail) are given below:

student	test score	course result	student	test score	course result	student	test score	course result
1	30	fail	13	26	fail	25	9	fail
2	29	pass	14	43	pass	26	36	pass
3	33	fail	15	43	fail	27	61	pass
4	62	pass	16	68	pass	28	79	fail
5	59	fail	17	63	pass	29	57	fail
6	63	pass	18	42	fail	30	46	pass
7	80	pass	19	51	fail	31	70	fail
8	32	fail	20	45	fail	32	31	pass
9	60	pass	21	22	fail	33	68	pass
10	76	pass	22	30	pass	34	62	pass
11	13	fail	23	40	fail	35	56	pass
12	41	pass	24	26	fail	36	36	pass

Do you think that the aptitude test is useful for selecting students for admission to the course, and if so, how would you determine the pass mark? (Discuss the trade-off between Type I and Type II errors associated with the choice of pass mark.)

2.15 A researcher hypothesizes that years of schooling, S, may be related to the number of siblings (brothers and sisters), *SIBLINGS,* according to the relationship

$$S = \beta_1 + \beta_2 SIBLINGS + u.$$

She is prepared to test the null hypothesis $H_0: \beta_2 = 0$ against the alternative hypothesis $H_1: \beta_2 \neq 0$ at the 5 percent and 1 percent levels. She has a sample of 60 observations. What should she report:

1. if $b_2 = -0.20, \text{s.e.}(b_2) = 0.07$?
2. if $b_2 = -0.12, \text{s.e.}(b_2) = 0.07$?
3. if $b_2 = 0.06, \text{s.e.}(b_2) = 0.07$?
4. if $b_2 = 0.20, \text{s.e.}(b_2) = 0.07$?

2.16* A researcher with a sample of 50 individuals with similar education but differing amounts of training hypothesizes that hourly earnings, *EARNINGS,* may be related to hours of training, *TRAINING,* according to the relationship

$$EARNINGS = \beta_1 + \beta_2 TRAINING + u.$$

He is prepared to test the null hypothesis $H_0: \beta_2 = 0$ against the alternative hypothesis $H_1: \beta_2 \neq 0$ at the 5 percent and 1 percent levels. What should he report:

1. if $b_2 = 0.30, \text{s.e.}(b_2) = 0.12$?
2. if $b_2 = 0.55, \text{s.e.}(b_2) = 0.12$?
3. if $b_2 = 0.10, \text{s.e.}(b_2) = 0.12$?
4. if $b_2 = -0.27, \text{s.e.}(b_2) = 0.12$?

2.17 Perform a t test on the slope coefficient and the intercept of the educational attainment function fitted using your *EAEF* data set, and state your conclusions.

2.18 Perform a t test on the slope coefficient and the intercept of the earnings function fitted using your *EAEF* data set, and state your conclusions.

2.19 In Exercise 1.1, the growth rate of employment was regressed on the growth rate of GDP for a sample of 25 OECD countries. Perform t tests on the slope coefficient and the intercept and state your conclusions.

2.9 Confidence intervals

Thus far we have been assuming that the hypothesis preceded the empirical investigation. This is not necessarily the case. Usually theory and experimentation are interactive, and the earnings function regression provides a typical example. We ran the regression in the first place because economic theory tells us to expect earnings to be affected by schooling. The regression result confirmed this intuition since we rejected the null hypothesis $\beta_2 = 0$, but we were then left with something of a vacuum, since our theory is not strong enough to suggest that the true value of β_2 is equal to some specific number. However, we can now move in the opposite direction and ask ourselves the following question: given our regression result, what hypotheses would be compatible with it?

Obviously a hypothesis $\beta_2 = 2.455$ would be compatible, because then hypothesis and experimental result coincide. Also $\beta_2 = 2.454$ and $\beta_2 = 2.456$ would be compatible, because the difference between hypothesis and experimental result would be so small. The question is, how far can a hypothetical value differ from our experimental result before they become incompatible and we have to reject the null hypothesis?

We can answer this question by exploiting the previous analysis. From (2.72), we can see that regression coefficient b_2 and hypothetical value β_2 are incompatible if either

$$\frac{b_2 - \beta_2}{\text{s.e.}(b_2)} > t_{\text{crit}} \quad \text{or} \quad \frac{b_2 - \beta_2}{\text{s.e.}(b_2)} < -t_{\text{crit}} \tag{2.76}$$

that is, if either

$$b_2 - \beta_2 > \text{s.e.}(b_2) \times t_{\text{crit}} \quad \text{or} \quad b_2 - \beta_2 < -\text{s.e.}(b_2) \times t_{\text{crit}} \tag{2.77}$$

that is, if either

$$b_2 - \text{s.e.}(b_2) \times t_{\text{crit}} > \beta_2 \quad \text{or} \quad b_2 + \text{s.e.}(b_2) \times t_{\text{crit}} < \beta_2. \tag{2.78}$$

It therefore follows that a hypothetical β_2 *is* compatible with the regression result if both

$$b_2 - \text{s.e.}(b_2) \times t_{\text{crit}} \leq \beta_2 \quad \text{and} \quad b_2 + \text{s.e.}(b_2) \times t_{\text{crit}} \geq \beta_2 \tag{2.79}$$

that is, if β_2 satisfies the double inequality

$$b_2 - \text{s.e.}(b_2) \times t_{\text{crit}} \leq \beta_2 \leq b_2 + \text{s.e.}(b_2) \times t_{\text{crit}}. \tag{2.80}$$

Any hypothetical value of β_2 that satisfies (2.80) will therefore automatically be compatible with the estimate b_2, that is, will not be rejected by it. The set of all such values, given by the interval between the lower and upper limits of the inequality, is known as the **confidence interval** for β_2.

Note that the limits of the confidence interval are equidistant from b_2 on either side. Note also that, since the value of t_{crit} depends upon the choice of significance level, the limits will also depend on this choice. If the 5 percent significance level is adopted, the corresponding confidence interval is known as the 95 percent confidence interval. If the 1 percent level is chosen, one obtains the 99 percent confidence interval, and so on.

Since t_{crit} is greater for the 1 percent level than for the 5 percent level, for any given number of degrees of freedom, it follows that the 99 percent interval is wider than the 95 percent interval. It encompasses all the hypothetical values of β_2 in the 95 percent confidence interval and some more on either side as well.

BOX 2.7   A second interpretation of a confidence interval

When you construct a confidence interval, the numbers you calculate for its upper and lower limits contain random components that depend on the values of the disturbance term in the observations in the sample. For example, in inequality (2.80), the upper limit is

$$b_2 + \text{s.e.}(b_2) \times t_{\text{crit}}.$$

Both b_2 and $\text{s.e.}(b_2)$ are partly determined by the values of the disturbance term, and similarly for the lower limit. One hopes that the confidence interval will include the true value of the parameter, but sometimes it will be so distorted by the random element that it will fail to do so.

What is the probability that a confidence interval will capture the true value of the parameter? It can easily be shown, using elementary probability theory, that, in the case of a 95 percent confidence interval, the probability is 95 percent, provided that the model is correctly specified and that the assumptions in Section 2.2 are satisfied. Similarly, in the case of a 99 percent confidence interval, the probability is 99 percent.

The estimated coefficient [for example, b_2 in inequality (2.80)] provides a point estimate of the parameter in question, but of course the probability of the true value being exactly equal to this estimate is infinitesimal. The confidence interval provides what is known as an *interval estimate* of the parameter, that is, a range of values that will include the true value with a high, predetermined probability. It is this interpretation that gives the confidence interval its name (for a detailed and lucid discussion, see Wonnacott and Wonnacott, 1990, Chapter 8).

Example

In the earnings function output in Table 2.6, the coefficient of S was 2.455, its standard error was 0.232, and the critical value of t at the 5 percent significance level was about 1.965. The corresponding 95 percent confidence interval is therefore

$$2.455 - 0.232 \times 1.965 \leq \beta_2 \leq 2.455 + 0.232 \times 1.965 \qquad (2.81)$$

that is,

$$1.999 \leq \beta_2 \leq 2.911. \qquad (2.82)$$

We would therefore reject hypothetical values below 1.999 and above 2.911. Any hypotheses within these limits would not be rejected, given the regression result. This confidence interval actually appears as the final column in the Stata output. However, this is not a standard feature of a regression application, so you usually have to calculate the interval yourself.

Exercises

2.20 Calculate the 99 percent confidence interval for β_2 in the earnings function example in Table 2.6 ($b_2 = 2.455$, s.e.(b_2) $= 0.232$), and explain why it includes some values not included in the 95 percent confidence interval calculated in inequality (2.82).

2.21 Calculate the 95 percent confidence interval for the slope coefficient in the earnings function fitted with your *EAEF* data set.

2.22* Calculate the 95 percent confidence interval for β_2 in the price inflation/wage inflation example:

$$\hat{p} = -1.21 + 0.82w.$$

$$(0.05) \quad (0.10)$$

What can you conclude from this calculation?

2.10 One-sided *t* tests

In our discussion of t tests, we started out with our null hypothesis $H_0: \beta_2 = \beta_2^0$ and tested it to see whether we should reject it or not, given the regression coefficient b_2. If we did reject it, then by implication we accepted the alternative hypothesis $H_1: \beta_2 \neq \beta_2^0$.

Thus far the alternative hypothesis has been merely the negation of the null hypothesis. However, if we are able to be more specific about the alternative hypothesis, we may be able to improve the testing procedure. We will investigate three cases: first, the very special case where there is only one conceivable alternative true value of β_2, which we will denote β_2^1; second, where, if β_2 is not equal to β_2^0, it must be greater than β_2^0; and third, where, if β_2 is not equal to β_2^0, it must be less than β_2^0.

$H_0: \beta_2 = \beta_2^0, H_1: \beta_2 = \beta_2^1$

In this case there are only two possible values of the true coefficient of X, β_2^0 and β_2^1. For the sake of argument we will assume for the time being that β_2^1 is greater than β_2^0.

Suppose that we wish to test H_0 at the 5 percent significance level, and we follow the usual procedure discussed earlier in the chapter. We locate the limits of the upper and lower 2.5 percent tails under the assumption that H_0 is true,

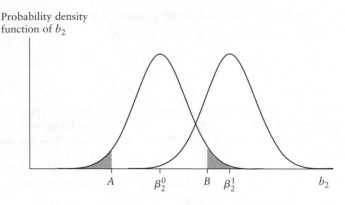

Probability density
function of b_2

Figure 2.10 Distribution of b_2 under H_0 and H_1

indicated by A and B in Figure 2.10, and we reject H_0 if the regression coefficient b_2 lies to the left of A or to the right of B.

Now, if b_2 does lie to the right of B, it is more compatible with H_1 than with H_0; the probability of it lying to the right of B is greater if H_1 is true than if H_0 is true. We should have no hesitation in rejecting H_0. We therefore conclude that H_1 is true.

However, if b_2 lies to the left of A, the test procedure will lead us to a perverse conclusion. It tells us to reject H_0, and therefore conclude that H_1 is true, even though the probability of b_2 lying to the left of A is negligible if H_1 is true. We have not even drawn the probability density function that far for H_1. If such a value of b_2 occurs only once in a million times when H_1 is true, but 2.5 percent of the time when H_0 is true, it is much more logical to assume that H_0 is true. Of course once in a million times you will make a mistake, but the rest of the time you will be right.

Hence we will reject H_0 only if b_2 lies in the upper 2.5 percent tail, that is, to the right of B. We are now performing a **one-sided test**, and we have reduced the probability of making a Type I error to 2.5 percent. Since the significance level is defined to be the probability of making a Type I error, it is now also 2.5 percent.

As we have seen, economists usually prefer 5 percent and 1 percent significance tests, rather than 2.5 percent tests. If you want to perform a 5 percent test, you move B to the left so that you have 5 percent of the probability in the tail and the probability of making a Type I error is increased to 5 percent. (*Question*: why would you deliberately choose to increase the probability of making a Type I error? *Answer*: because at the same time you are reducing the probability of making a Type II error, that is, of not rejecting the null hypothesis when it is false. Most of the time your null hypothesis is that the coefficient is zero, and you are trying to disprove this, demonstrating that the variable in question *does* have an effect. In such a situation, by using a one-sided test, you reduce the risk

Probability density
function of b_2

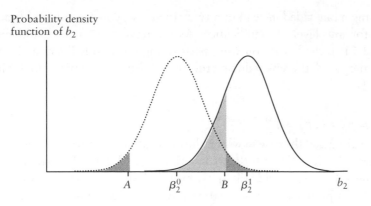

$$A \qquad \beta_2^0 \qquad B \quad \beta_2^1 \qquad\qquad b_2$$

Figure 2.11 Probability of not rejecting H_0 when it is false, two-sided test

of not rejecting a false null hypothesis, while holding the risk of a Type I error at 5 percent.)

If the standard deviation of b_2 is known (most unlikely in practice), so that the distribution is normal, B will be z standard deviations to the right of β_2^0, where z is given by $A(z) = 0.9500$ in Table A.1. The appropriate value of z is 1.64. If the standard deviation is unknown and has been estimated as the standard error of b_2, you have to use a t distribution: you look up the critical value of t in Table A.2 for the appropriate number of degrees of freedom in the column headed 5 percent.

Similarly, if you want to perform a 1 percent test, you move B to the point where the right tail contains 1 percent of the probability. Assuming that you have had to calculate the standard error of b_2 from the sample data, you look up the critical value of t in the column headed 1 percent.

We have assumed in this discussion that β_2^1 is greater than β_2^0. Obviously, if it is less than β_2^0, we should use the same logic to construct a one-sided test, but now we should use the left tail as the rejection region for H_0 and drop the right tail.

The power of a test

In this particular case, we can calculate the probability of making a Type II error, that is, of accepting a false hypothesis. Suppose that we have adopted a false hypothesis H_0: $\beta_2 = \beta_2^0$ and that an alternative hypothesis H_1: $\beta_2 = \beta_2^1$ is in fact true. If we are using a two-sided test, we will fail to reject H_0 if b_2 lies in the interval AB in Figure 2.11. Since H_1 is true, the probability of b_2 lying in that interval is given by the area under the curve for H_1 to the left of B, the lighter shaded area in the figure. If this probability is denoted γ, the **power** of the test, defined to be the probability of not making a Type II error, is $1 - \gamma$. Obviously, you have a trade-off between the power of the test and the significance level. The higher the significance level, the further B will be to the right, and so the larger γ will be, so the lower the power of the test will be.

In using a one-sided instead of a two-sided test, you are able to obtain greater power for any level of significance. As we have seen, you would move B in Figure 2.11 to the left if you were performing a one-sided test at the 5 percent significance level, thereby reducing the probability of accepting H_0 if it happened to be false.

H_0: $\beta_2 = \beta_2^0$, H_1: $\beta_2 > \beta_2^0$

We have discussed the case in which the alternative hypothesis involved a *specific* hypothetical value β_2^1, with β_2^1 greater than β_2^0. Clearly, the logic that led us to use a one-sided test would still apply even if H_1 were more general and merely asserted that $\beta_2^1 > \beta_2^0$, without stating any particular value.

We would still wish to eliminate the left tail from the rejection region because a low value of b_2 is more probable under H_0: $\beta_2 = \beta_2^0$ than under H_1: $\beta_2 > \beta_2^0$, and this would be evidence in support of H_0, not against it. Therefore, we would still prefer a one-sided t test, using the right tail as the rejection region, to a two-sided test. Note that, since β_2^1 is not defined, we now have no way of calculating the power of such a test. However, we can still be sure that, for any given significance level, the power of a one-sided test will be greater than that of the corresponding two-sided test.

H_0: $\beta_2 = \beta_2^0$, H_1: $\beta_2 < \beta_2^0$

Similarly if the alternative hypothesis were H_1: $\beta_2 < \beta_2^0$, we would prefer a one-sided test using the left tail as the rejection region.

Justification of the use of a one-sided test

The use of a one-sided test has to be justified beforehand on the grounds of theory, common sense, or previous experience. When stating the justification, you should be careful not to exclude the possibility that the null hypothesis is true. For example, suppose that you are relating household expenditure on clothing to household income. You would of course expect a significant positive effect, given a large sample. But your justification should not be that, on the basis of theory and common sense, the coefficient should be positive. This is too strong, for it eliminates the null hypothesis of no effect, and there is nothing to test. Instead, you should say that, on the basis of theory and common sense, you would exclude the possibility that income has a *negative* effect. This then leaves the possibility that the effect is zero and the alternative that it is positive.

One-sided tests are important in practice in econometrics. As we have seen, the usual way of establishing that an explanatory variable really does influence a dependent variable is to set up the null hypothesis H_0: $\beta_2 = 0$ and try to refute it. Very frequently, our theory is strong enough to tell us that, if X does influence Y, its effect will be in a given direction. If we have good reason to believe that the effect is not negative, we are in a position to use the alternative hypothesis

H_1: $\beta_2 > 0$ instead of the more general H_1: $\beta_2 \neq 0$. This is an advantage because the critical value of t for rejecting H_0 is lower for the one-sided test, so it is easier to refute the null hypothesis and establish the relationship.

Examples

In the earnings function regression in Table 2.6, there were 538 degrees of freedom and the critical value of t, using the 0.1 percent significance level and a two-sided test, is approximately 3.309. If we take advantage of the fact that it is reasonable to expect schooling not to have a negative effect on earnings, we could use a one-sided test and the critical value is reduced to approximately 3.106. The t statistic is in fact equal to 10.59, so in this case the refinement makes no difference. The estimated coefficient is so large relative to its standard error that we reject the null hypothesis regardless of whether we use a two-sided or a one-sided test, even using a 0.1 percent test.

In the price inflation/wage inflation example, exploiting the possibility of using a one-sided test does make a difference. The null hypothesis was that wage inflation is reflected fully in price inflation and we have H_0: $\beta_2 = 1$. The main reason why the types of inflation may be different is that improvements in productivity may cause price inflation to be lower than wage inflation. Certainly, improvements in productivity will not cause price inflation to be greater than wage inflation and so in this case we are justified in ruling out $\beta_2 > 1$. We are left with H_0: $\beta_2 = 1$ and H_1: $\beta_2 < 1$. Given a regression coefficient 0.82 and a standard error 0.10, the t statistic for the null hypothesis is -1.80. This was not high enough, in absolute terms, to cause H_0 to be rejected at the 5 percent level using a two-sided test (critical value 2.10). However, if we use a one-sided test, as we are entitled to, the critical value falls to 1.73 and we *can* reject the null hypothesis. In other words, we can conclude that price inflation is significantly lower than wage inflation.

Exercises

2.23 Explain whether it would have been possible to perform one-sided tests instead of two-sided tests in Exercise 2.15. If you think that one-sided tests are justified, perform them and state whether the use of a one-sided test makes any difference.

2.24* Explain whether it would have been possible to perform one-sided tests instead of two-sided tests in Exercise 2.16. If you think that one-sided tests are justified, perform them and state whether the use of a one-sided test makes any difference.

2.25 Explain whether it would have been possible to perform one-sided tests instead of two-sided tests in Exercise 2.17. If you think that one-sided tests are justified, perform them and state whether the use of a one-sided test makes any difference.

2.26 Explain whether it would have been possible to perform one-sided tests instead of two-sided tests in Exercise 2.18. If you think that one-sided tests are justified, perform them and state whether the use of a one-sided test makes any difference.

2.11 The *F* test of goodness of fit

Even if there is no relationship between Y and X, in any given sample of observations there may appear to be one, if only a faint one. Only by coincidence will the correlation coefficient and R^2 be *exactly* equal to zero. So how do we know if the value of R^2 for the regression reflects a true relationship or if it has arisen as a matter of chance?

We could in principle adopt the following procedure. Suppose that the regression model is

$$Y_i = \beta_1 + \beta_2 X_i + u_i. \tag{2.83}$$

We take as our null hypothesis that there is no relationship Between Y and X, that is, H_0: $\beta_2 = 0$. We calculate the value that R^2 would exceed 5 percent of the time as a matter of chance. We then take this figure as the critical level of R^2 for a 5 percent significance test. If it is exceeded, we reject the null hypothesis and conclude that $\beta_2 \neq 0$.

Such a test, like the t test on a coefficient, would not be foolproof. Indeed, at the 5 percent significance level, one would risk making a Type I error (rejecting the null hypothesis when it is in fact true) 5 percent of the time. Of course you could cut down on this risk by using a higher significance level, for example, the 1 percent level. The critical level of R^2 would then be that which would be exceeded by chance only 1 percent of the time, so it would be higher than the critical level for the 5 percent test.

How does one find the critical level of R^2 at either significance level? Well, there is a small problem. There is no such thing as a table of critical levels of R^2. The traditional procedure is to use an indirect approach and perform what is known as an *F* test based on analysis of variance.

Suppose that, as in this case, you can decompose the variations in the dependent variable into 'explained' and 'unexplained' components using (1.46):

$$\sum_{i=1}^{n} (Y_i - \overline{Y})^2 = \sum_{i=1}^{n} (\hat{Y}_i - \overline{Y})^2 + \sum_{i=1}^{n} e_i^2. \tag{2.84}$$

(Remember that $\overline{e} = 0$ and that the sample mean of $\hat{Y}$ is equal to the sample mean of Y.)

The left side is *TSS*, the total sum of squares of the values of the dependent variable about its sample mean. The first term on the right side is *ESS*, the explained sum of squares, and the second term is *RSS*, the unexplained, residual sum of squares:

$$TSS = ESS + RSS. \tag{2.85}$$

The *F* statistic for the goodness of fit of a regression is written as the explained sum of squares, per explanatory variable, divided by the residual sum of squares, per degree of freedom remaining:

$$F = \frac{ESS/(k-1)}{RSS/(n-k)} \tag{2.86}$$

where k is the number of parameters in the regression equation (intercept and $k-1$ slope coefficients).

By dividing both the numerator and the denominator of the ratio by TSS, this F statistic may equivalently be expressed in terms of R^2:

$$F = \frac{(ESS/TSS)/(k-1)}{(RSS/TSS)/(n-k)} = \frac{R^2/(k-1)}{(1-R^2)/(n-k)}. \tag{2.87}$$

In the present context, k is 2, so (2.87) becomes

$$F = \frac{R^2}{(1-R^2)/(n-2)}. \tag{2.88}$$

Having calculated F from your value of R^2, you look up F_{crit}, the critical level of F, in the appropriate table. If F is greater than F_{crit}, you reject the null hypothesis and conclude that the 'explanation' of Y is better than is likely to have arisen by chance.

Table A.3 gives the critical levels of F at the 5 percent, 1 percent and 0.1 percent significance levels. In each case the critical level depends on the number of explanatory variables, $k-1$, which is read from along the top of the table, and the number of degrees of freedom, $n-k$, which is read off down the side. In the present context, we are concerned with simple regression analysis, k is 2, and we should use the first column of the table.

In the earnings function example in Table 2.6, R^2 was 0.1725. Since there were 540 observations, the F statistic is equal to $R^2/[(1-R^2)/538] = 0.1725/[0.8275/538] = 112.15$. At the 0.1 percent significance level, the critical level of F for 1 and 500 degrees of freedom (looking at the first column, row 500) is 10.96. The critical value for 1 and 538 degrees of freedom must be lower, so we have no hesitation in rejecting the null hypothesis in this particular example. In other words, the underlying value of R^2 is so high that we reject the suggestion that it could have arisen by chance. In practice the F statistic is always computed for you, along with R^2, so you never actually have to use (2.86) yourself.

Why do we take this indirect approach? Why not publish a table of critical levels of R^2? The answer is that the F table is useful for testing many forms of analysis of variance, of which R^2 is only one. Rather than have a specialized table for each application, it is more convenient (or, at least, it saves a lot of paper) to have just one general table, and make transformations like (2.86) when necessary.

Of course, you could derive critical levels of R^2 if you were sufficiently interested. The critical level of R^2 would be related to the critical level of F by

$$F_{crit} = \frac{R^2_{crit}/(k-1)}{(1-R^2_{crit})/(n-k)} \tag{2.89}$$

which yields

$$R^2_{crit} = \frac{(k-1)F_{crit}}{(k-1)F_{crit} + (n-k)}. \tag{2.90}$$

In the earnings function example, the critical value of F at the 0.1 percent significance level was approximately 10.95. Hence in this case, with $k = 2$,

$$R^2_{crit} = \frac{10.95}{10.95 + 538} = 0.020. \tag{2.91}$$

Although it is low, our R^2 is greater than 0.020, so a direct comparison of R^2 with its critical value confirms the conclusion of the F test that we should reject the null hypothesis.

Exercises

2.27 In Exercise 1.1, in the regression of the rate of growth of employment on the rate of growth of real GDP using a sample of 25 OECD countries, R^2 was 0.5900. Calculate the corresponding F statistic and check that it is equal to 33.10, the value printed in the output. Perform the F test at the 5 percent, 1 percent, and 0.1 percent significance levels. Is it necessary to report the results of the tests at all three levels?

2.28 Calculate the F statistic from the value of R^2 obtained in the earnings function fitted using your *EAEF* data set and check that it is equal to the value printed in the output. Perform an appropriate F test.

2.12 Relationship between the *F* test of goodness of fit and the *t* test on the slope coefficient in simple regression analysis

In the context of simple regression analysis (and *only* simple regression analysis) the F test on R^2 and the two-sided t test on the slope coefficient both have $H_0: \beta_2 = 0$ as the null hypothesis and $H_1 : \beta_2 \neq 0$ as the alternative hypothesis. This gives rise to the possibility that they might lead to different conclusions. Fortunately, they are in fact equivalent. The F statistic is equal to the square of the t statistic, and the critical value of F, at any given significance level, is equal to the square of the critical value of t. Starting with the definition of F in (2.86), and putting $k = 2$,

$$F = \frac{ESS}{RSS/(n-2)} = \frac{\sum_{i=1}^{n}\left(\hat{Y}_i - \overline{Y}\right)^2}{\sum_{i=1}^{n} e_i^2 \Big/ (n-2)} = \frac{\sum_{i=1}^{n}\left([b_1 + b_2 X_i] - [b_1 + b_2 \overline{X}]\right)^2}{s_u^2}$$

$$= \frac{1}{s_u^2}\sum_{i=1}^{n} b_2^2 \left(X_i - \overline{X}\right)^2 = \frac{b_2^2}{s_u^2 \Big/ \sum_{i=1}^{n}\left(X_i - \overline{X}\right)^2} = \frac{b_2^2}{(s.e.(b_2))^2} = t^2. \quad (2.92)$$

The proof that the critical value of F is equal to the critical value of t for a two-sided t test is more complicated and will be omitted. When we come to multiple regression analysis, we will see that the F test and the t tests have different roles and different null hypotheses. However, in simple regression analysis the fact that they are equivalent means that there is no point in performing both. Indeed, you would look ignorant if you did. Obviously, provided that it is justifiable, a one-sided t test would be preferable to either.

Key terms

acceptance region

autocorrelation

central limit theorem

confidence interval

cross-sectional data

F statistic

F test of goodness of fit

Gauss–Markov theorem

homoscedastic disturbance term

hypothesis, alternative

hypothesis, null

Monte Carlo experiment

nonstochastic regressor

p value

panel data

power of a test

significance level

standard error of a regression coefficient

stochastic regressor

t statistic

t test

t test, one-sided

time series data

Type I error

Type II error

Exercises

2.29 Verify that the F statistic in the earnings function regression run by you using your *EAEF* data set is equal to the square of the t statistic for the slope coefficient, and that the critical value of F at the 1 percent significance level is equal to the square of the critical value of t.

2.30 In Exercise 1.6 both researchers obtained values of R^2 equal to 0.17 in their regressions. Was this a coincidence?

3 Multiple Regression Analysis

In this chapter least squares regression analysis is generalized to cover the case in which there are several or many explanatory variables in the regression model, rather than just one. Two new topics are discussed. One is the problem of discriminating between the effects of different explanatory variables, a problem that, when particularly severe, is known as multicollinearity. The other is the evaluation of the joint explanatory power of the independent variables, as opposed to their individual marginal effects.

3.1 Illustration: a model with two explanatory variables

Multiple regression analysis is an extension of simple regression analysis to cover cases in which the dependent variable is hypothesized to depend on more than one explanatory variable. Much of the analysis will be a straightforward extension of the simple regression model, but we will encounter two new problems. First, when evaluating the influence of a given explanatory variable on the dependent variable, we now have to face the problem of discriminating between its effects and the effects of the other explanatory variables. Second, we shall have to tackle the problem of model specification. Frequently a number of variables might be thought to influence the dependent variable; however, they might be irrelevant. We shall have to decide which should be included in the regression equation and which should be excluded. The second problem will be discussed in Chapter 6. In this chapter, we will assume that the model specification is correct. For much of it, we will confine ourselves to the basic case where there are only two explanatory variables.

We will begin by considering an example, the determinants of earnings. We will extend the earlier model to allow for the possibility that earnings are influenced by years of work experience as well as education and assume that the true relationship can be expressed as

$$EARNINGS = \beta_1 + \beta_2 S + \beta_3 EXP + u, \tag{3.1}$$

where $EARNINGS$ is hourly earnings, S is years of schooling (highest grade completed), EXP is years spent working after leaving full-time education, and

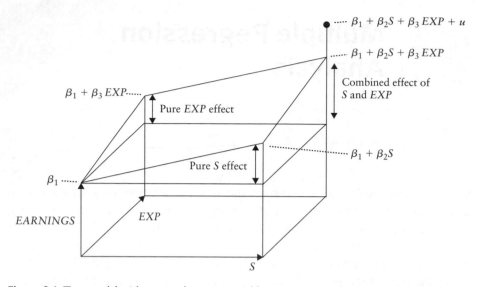

Figure 3.1 True model with two explanatory variables: earnings as a function of schooling and work experience

u is a disturbance term. This model is still of course a great simplification, both in terms of the explanatory variables included in the relationship and in terms of its mathematical specification.

To illustrate the relationship geometrically, one needs a three-dimensional diagram with separate axes for *EARNINGS, S,* and *EXP* as in Figure 3.1. The base of Figure 3.1 shows the axes for S and *EXP,* and, if one neglects the effect of the disturbance term for the moment, the tilted plane above it shows the value of *EARNINGS* corresponding to any (S, EXP) combination, measured by the vertical height of the plane above the base at that point. Since earnings may be expected to increase with both schooling and work experience, the diagram has been drawn on the assumption that β_2 and β_3 are both positive. Literally, the intercept β_1 gives the predicted earnings for zero schooling and zero work experience. However, such an interpretation would be dangerous because there was nobody with no schooling in the NLSY data set. Indeed, very few individuals failed to complete eight years of schooling. Mathematically (3.1) implies that, if *EXP* were zero, for any positive S, earnings would be equal to $\beta_1 + \beta_2 S$, the increase $\beta_2 S$ being marked 'pure S effect' in the figure. Keeping S at zero, the equation implies that for any positive value of *EXP*, earnings would be equal to $\beta_1 + \beta_3 EXP$, the increase $\beta_3 EXP$ being marked 'pure *EXP* effect'. The combined effect of schooling and work experience, $\beta_2 S + \beta_3 EXP$, is also indicated.

We have thus far neglected the disturbance term. If it were not for the presence of this in (3.1), the values of *EARNINGS* in a sample of observations on *EARNINGS, S,* and *EXP* would lie exactly on the tilted plane and it would be a

Table 3.1

```
. reg EARNINGS S EXP

    Source      SS          df        MS              Number of obs =     540
                                                      F(2,537)      =   67.54
     Model  22513.6473       2    11256.8237          Prob > F      = 0.0000
  Residual  89496.5838     537    166.660305          R-squared     = 0.2010
                                                      Adj R-squared = 0.1980
     Total  112010.231     539    207.811189          Root MSE      =  12.91

  EARNINGS     Coef.   Std. Err.         t   P>|t|   [95% Conf. Interval]

         S   2.678125  .2336497      11.46   0.000    2.219146   3.137105
       EXP   .5624326  .1285136       4.38   0.000    .3099816   .8148837
     _cons  -26.48501   4.27251      -6.20   0.000   -34.87789  -18.09213
```

trivial matter to deduce the exact values of β_1, β_2, and β_3 (not trivial geometrically, unless you are a genius at constructing three-dimensional models, but easy enough algebraically).

The disturbance term causes the actual value of earnings to be sometimes above and sometimes below the value indicated by the tilted plane. Consequently, one now has a three-dimensional counterpart to the two-dimensional problem illustrated in Figure 1.2. Instead of locating a line to fit a two-dimensional scatter of points, we now have to locate a plane to fit a three-dimensional scatter. The equation of the fitted plane will be

$$\widehat{EARNINGS} = b_1 + b_2 S + b_3 EXP \qquad (3.2)$$

and its location will depend on the choice of b_1, b_2, and b_3, the estimates of β_1, β_2, and β_3, respectively. Using *EAEF* Data Set 21, we obtain the regression output shown in Table 3.1.

The equation should be interpreted as follows. For every additional grade completed, holding work experience constant, hourly earnings increase by $2.68. For every year of work experience, holding schooling constant, earnings increase by $0.56. The constant has no meaningful interpretation. Literally, it suggests that a respondent with zero years of schooling (no respondent had fewer than six) and no work experience would earn *minus* $26.49 per hour.

3.2 Derivation and interpretation of the multiple regression coefficients

As in the simple regression case, we choose the values of the regression coefficients to make the fit as good as possible in the hope that we will obtain the most satisfactory estimates of the unknown true parameters. As before, our definition of goodness of fit is the minimization of *RSS*, the sum of squares of the

---

BOX 3.1   Whatever happened to X_1?

You may have noticed that X_1 is missing from the general regression model

$$Y_i = \beta_1 + \beta_2 X_{2i} + \cdots + \beta_k X_{ki} + u_i.$$

Why so? The reason is to make the notation consistent with that found in texts using linear algebra (matrix algebra), and your next course in econometrics will almost certainly use such a text. For analysis using linear algebra, it is essential that every term on the right side of the equation should consist of the product of a parameter and a variable. When there is an intercept in the model, as here, the anomaly is dealt with by writing the equation

$$Y_i = \beta_1 X_{1i} + \beta_2 X_{2i} + \cdots + \beta_k X_{ki} + u_i$$

where $X_{1i} = 1$ in every observation. In analysis using ordinary algebra, there is usually no point in introducing X_1 explicitly, and so it has been suppressed. The one occasion in this text where it can help is in the discussion of the dummy variable trap in Section 5.2.

---

residuals:

$$RSS = \sum_{i=1}^{n} e_i^2, \tag{3.3}$$

where e_i is the residual in observation i, the difference between the actual value Y_i in that observation and the value $\hat{Y}_i$ predicted by the regression equation:

$$\hat{Y}_i = b_1 + b_2 X_{2i} + b_3 X_{3i} \tag{3.4}$$

$$e_i = Y_i - \hat{Y}_i = Y_i - b_1 - b_2 X_{2i} - b_3 X_{3i}. \tag{3.5}$$

Note that the X variables now have two subscripts. The first identifies the X variable and the second identifies the observation.

Using (3.5), we can write

$$RSS = \sum_{i=1}^{n} e_i^2 = \sum_{i=1}^{n} (Y_i - b_1 - b_2 X_{2i} - b_3 X_{3i})^2. \tag{3.6}$$

The first-order conditions for a minimum, $\dfrac{\partial RSS}{\partial b_1} = 0, \dfrac{\partial RSS}{\partial b_2} = 0$, and $\dfrac{\partial RSS}{\partial b_3} = 0$, yield the following equations:

$$\frac{\partial RSS}{\partial b_1} = -2 \sum_{i=1}^{n} (Y_i - b_1 - b_2 X_{2i} - b_3 X_{3i}) = 0 \tag{3.7}$$

$$\frac{\partial RSS}{\partial b_2} = -2 \sum_{i=1}^{n} X_{2i}(Y_i - b_1 - b_2 X_{2i} - b_3 X_{3i}) = 0 \tag{3.8}$$

$$\frac{\partial RSS}{\partial b_3} = -2 \sum_{i=1}^{n} X_{3i}(Y_i - b_1 - b_2 X_{2i} - b_3 X_{3i}) = 0. \qquad (3.9)$$

Hence we have three equations in the three unknowns, $b_1, b_2,$ and b_3. The first can easily be rearranged to express b_1 in terms of $b_2, b_3,$ and the data on $Y, X_2,$ and X_3:

$$b_1 = \overline{Y} - b_2 \overline{X}_2 - b_3 \overline{X}_3. \qquad (3.10)$$

Using this expression and the other two equations, with a little work one can obtain the following expression for b_2:

$$b_2 = \frac{\begin{aligned}\sum_{i=1}^{n}(X_{2i} - \overline{X}_2)(Y_i - \overline{Y}) \sum_{i=1}^{n}(X_{3i} - \overline{X}_3)^2 \\ - \sum_{i=1}^{n}(X_{3i} - \overline{X}_3)(Y_i - \overline{Y}) \sum_{i=1}^{n}(X_{2i} - \overline{X}_2)(X_{3i} - \overline{X}_3)\end{aligned}}{\sum_{i=1}^{n}(X_{2i} - \overline{X}_2)^2 \sum_{i=1}^{n}(X_{3i} - \overline{X}_3)^2 - \left(\sum_{i=1}^{n}(X_{2i} - \overline{X}_2)(X_{3i} - \overline{X}_3)\right)^2}. \qquad (3.11)$$

A parallel expression for b_3 can be obtained by interchanging X_2 and X_3 in (3.11).

The intention of this discussion is to press home two basic points. First, the principles behind the derivation of the regression coefficients are the same for multiple regression as for simple regression. Second, the expressions, however, are different, and so you should not try to use expressions derived for simple regression in a multiple regression context.

The general model

In the preceding example, we were dealing with only two explanatory variables. When there are more than two, it is no longer possible to give a geometrical representation of what is going on, but the extension of the algebra is in principle quite straightforward.

We assume that a variable Y depends on $k-1$ explanatory variables $X_2, \ldots, X_k$ according to a true, unknown relationship

$$Y_i = \beta_1 + \beta_2 X_{2i} + \cdots + \beta_k X_{ki} + u_i \qquad (3.12)$$

Given a set of n observations on $Y, X_2, \ldots, X_k$, we use least squares regression analysis to fit the equation

$$\hat{Y}_i = b_1 + b_2 X_{2i} + \cdots + b_k X_{ki}. \qquad (3.13)$$

This again means minimizing the sum of the squares of the residuals, which are given by

$$e_i = Y_i - \hat{Y}_i = Y_i - b_1 - b_2 X_{2i} - \cdots - b_k X_{ki}. \qquad (3.14)$$

Equation (3.14) is the generalization of (3.5). We now choose $b_1, \ldots, b_k$ so as to minimize *RSS*, the sum of the squares of the residuals, $\sum e_i^2$. We obtain k first-order conditions $\dfrac{\partial RSS}{\partial b_1} = 0, \ldots, \dfrac{\partial RSS}{\partial b_k} = 0$, and these provide k equations for solving for the k unknowns. It can readily be shown that the first of these equations yields a counterpart to (3.10) in the case with two explanatory variables:

$$b_1 = \overline{Y} - b_2\overline{X}_2 - \cdots - b_k\overline{X}_k. \tag{3.15}$$

The expressions for $b_2, \ldots, b_k$ become very complicated and the mathematics will not be presented explicitly here. The analysis should be done with matrix algebra.

Interpretation of the multiple regression coefficients

Multiple regression analysis allows one to discriminate between the effects of the explanatory variables, making allowance for the fact that they may be correlated. The regression coefficient of each X variable provides an estimate of its influence on Y, controlling for the effects of all the other X variables.

This can be demonstrated in two ways. One is to show that the estimators are unbiased, if the model is correctly specified and the assumptions relating to the regression model are fulfilled. We shall do this in the next section for the case where there are only two explanatory variables. A second method is to run a simple regression of Y on one of the X variables, having first purged both Y and the X variable of the components that could be accounted for by the other explanatory variables. The estimate of the slope coefficient and its standard error thus obtained are exactly the same as in the multiple regression, a result that is proved by the **Frisch–Waugh–Lovell theorem** (Frisch and Waugh, 1933; Lovell, 1963). It follows that a scatter diagram plotting the purged Y against the purged X variable will provide a valid graphical representation of their relationship that can be obtained in no other way. This result will not be proved but it will be illustrated using the earnings function in Section 3.1:

$$EARNINGS = \beta_1 + \beta_2 S + \beta_3 EXP + u. \tag{3.16}$$

Suppose that we are particularly interested in the relationship between earnings and schooling and that we would like to illustrate it graphically. A straightforward plot of *EARNINGS* on S, as in Figure 1.8, would give a distorted view of the relationship because *EXP* is negatively correlated with S. Among those of similar age, individuals who have spent more time in school will tend to have spent less time working. As a consequence, as S increases, (1) *EARNINGS* will tend to increase, because β_2 is positive; (2) *EXP* will tend to decrease, because S and *EXP* are negatively correlated; and (3) *EARNINGS* will be reduced by the decrease in *EXP* and the fact that β_3 is positive. In other words, the variations in *EARNINGS* will not fully reflect the influence of the variations in *S* because in part they will be undermined by the associated variations in *EXP*. As a consequence, in a simple regression the estimator of β_2 will be biased downwards. We will investigate the bias analytically in Section 6.2.

In this example, there is only one other explanatory variable, *EXP*. To purge *EARNINGS* and *S* of their *EXP* components, we first regress them on *EXP*:

$$EAR\widehat{N}INGS = c_1 + c_2 EXP \tag{3.17}$$

$$\hat{S} = d_1 + d_2 EXP. \tag{3.18}$$

We then subtract the fitted values from the actual values:

$$EEARN = EARNINGS - EAR\widehat{N}INGS \tag{3.19}$$

$$ES = S - \hat{S}. \tag{3.20}$$

The purged variables *EEARN* and *ES* are of course just the residuals from the regressions (3.17) and (3.18). We now regress *EEARN* on *ES* and obtain the output in Table 3.2.

The estimate of the intercept in the regression uses a common convention for fitting very large numbers or very small ones into a field with a predefined number of digits. $e+n$ indicates that the coefficient should be multiplied by 10^n. Similarly $e-n$ indicates that it should be multiplied by 10^{-n}. Thus in this regression the intercept is effectively zero.

You can verify that the coefficient of *ES* is identical to that of *S* in the multiple regression in Section 3.1. Figure 3.2 shows the regression line in a scatter diagram. The dotted line in the figure is the regression line from a simple regression of *EARNINGS* on *S*, shown for comparison. The latter is a little flatter than the true relationship between *EARNINGS* and *S* because it does not control for the effect of *EXP*. In this case, the bias is small because the correlation between

Table 3.2

```
. reg EEARN ES

    Source       SS          df       MS              Number of obs =      540
-------------------------------------------           F(1,538)      =   131.63
     Model   21895.9298       1    21895.9298          Prob > F      =   0.0000
  Residual   89496.5833     538    166.350527          R-squared     =   0.1966
-------------------------------------------           Adj R-squared =   0.1951
     Total   111392.513     539    206.665145          Root MSE      =   12.898

-------------------------------------------------------------------------------
     EEARN       Coef.    Std. Err.         t    P>|t|    [95% Conf. Interval]
-------------------------------------------------------------------------------
        ES    2.678125    .2334325     11.47    0.000     2.219574    3.136676
     _cons    8.10e-09    .5550284      0.00    1.000    -1.090288    1.090288
-------------------------------------------------------------------------------
```

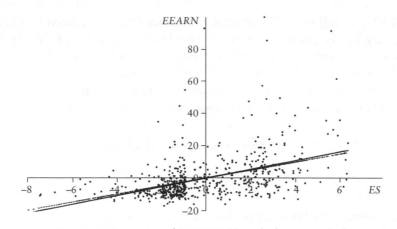

Figure 3.2 Regression of *EARNINGS* residuals on *S* residuals

S and *EXP*, −0.22, is small. Even so, the diagram is valuable because it allows a direct inspection of the relationship between earnings and schooling, controlling for experience. The presence of outliers for large values of *S* suggests that the model is misspecified in some way.

Exercises

3.1 The output is the result of fitting an educational attainment function, regressing *S* on *ASVABC*, *SM*, and *SF*, years of schooling (highest grade completed) of the respondent's mother and father, respectively, using *EAEF* Data Set 21. Give an interpretation of the regression coefficients.

```
. reg S ASVABC SM SF

    Source |       SS       df       MS              Number of obs =     540
-----------+------------------------------           F(3,536)      =  104.30
     Model | 1181.36981       3   393.789935          Prob > F      =  0.0000
  Residual | 2023.61353     536   3.77539837          R-squared     =  0.3686
-----------+------------------------------           Adj R-squared =  0.3651
     Total | 3204.98333     539   5.94616574          Root MSE      =   1.943


         S |      Coef.   Std. Err.        t    P>|t|     [95% Conf. Interval]
-----------+------------------------------------------------------------------
    ASVABC |   .1257087   .0098533      12.76   0.000      .1063528    .1450646
        SM |   .0492424   .0390901       1.26   0.208     -.027546    .1260309
        SF |   .1076825   .0309522       3.48   0.001       .04688    .1684851
     _cons |   5.370631   .4882155      11.00   0.000      4.41158    6.329681
```

3.2 Fit an educational attainment function parallel to that in Exercise 3.1, using your *EAEF* data set. First regress *S* on *ASVABC* and *SM* and interpret the regression results. Repeat the regression using *SF* instead of *SM*, and then again including both *SM* and *SF* as regressors. There is a saying that if you educate a male, you educate an individual, while if you educate a female, you educate a nation. The premise is that the education of a future mother has a future beneficial knock-on effect on the educational attainment of her children. Do your regression results support this view?

3.3 Fit an earnings function parallel to that in Section 3.1, using your *EAEF* data set. Regress *EARNINGS* on *S* and *EXP* and interpret the regression results.

3.4 Using your *EAEF* data set, make a graphical representation of the relationship between *S* and *SM* using the Frisch–Waugh–Lovell technique, assuming that the true model is as in Exercise 3.2. To do this, regress *S* on *ASVABC* and *SF* and save the residuals. Do the same with *SM*. Plot the *S* and *SM* residuals. Also regress the former on the latter, and verify that the slope coefficient is the same as that obtained in Exercise 3.2.

3.5* Explain why the intercept in the regression of *EEARN* on *ES* is equal to zero.

3.3 Properties of the multiple regression coefficients

As in the case of simple regression analysis, the regression coefficients should be thought of as special kinds of random variables whose random components are attributable to the presence of the disturbance term in the model. Each regression coefficient is calculated as a function of the values of *Y* and the explanatory variables in the sample, and *Y* in turn is determined by the explanatory variables and the disturbance term. It follows that the regression coefficients are really determined by the values of the explanatory variables and the disturbance term and that their properties depend critically upon the properties of the latter.

We are continuing to work within the framework of Model A, where the explanatory variables are nonstochastic. We shall make the following six assumptions, which are a restatement of those in Chapter 2 in terms appropriate for the multiple regression model.

A.1 The model is linear in parameters and correctly specified.

$$Y = \beta_1 + \beta_2 X_2 + \cdots + \beta_k X_k + u. \tag{3.21}$$

This is the same as before, except that we have multiple explanatory variables.

A.2 There does not exist an exact linear relationship among the regressors in the sample.

This is the only assumption that requires a new explanation. It will be deferred to Section 3.4 on multicollinearity.

A.3 The disturbance term has zero expectation.

$$E(u_i) = 0 \quad \text{for all } i. \tag{3.22}$$

This is the same as before.

A.4 *The disturbance term is homoscedastic.*

$$\sigma_{u_i}^2 = \sigma_u^2 \quad \text{for all } i. \tag{3.23}$$

This is the same as before.

A.5 *The values of the disturbance term have independent distributions.*

$$u_i \text{ is distributed independently of } u_{i'} \text{ for all } i' \neq i. \tag{3.24}$$

This is the same as before.

A.6 *The disturbance term has a normal distribution.*

This is the same as before.

Note that we are continuing to assume that all of the explanatory variables are nonstochastic.

Unbiasedness

We saw that in the case of the simple regression model

$$b_2 = \beta_2 + \sum_{i=1}^{n} a_i u_i \tag{3.25}$$

where

$$a_i = \frac{X_i - \overline{X}}{\sum_{i=1}^{n} (X_i - \overline{X})^2}. \tag{3.26}$$

Similar relationships obtain in the multiple regression case. The coefficient of X_j can be decomposed as

$$b_j = \beta_j + \sum_{i=1}^{n} a_{ij}^* u_i \tag{3.27}$$

where the a_{ij}^* terms are functions of the data on the explanatory variables in the model. The difference is that the a_{ij}^* terms are more complex than the a_i terms in the simple regression model and the proof of the decomposition likewise more complex. When one makes the transition to matrix algebra, the results are very easily obtained. We shall take them on trust. Taking (3.27) as given, unbiasedness follows as a formality:

$$E(b_j) = \beta_j + E\left\{\sum_{i=1}^{n} a_{ij}^* u_i\right\} = \beta_j + \sum_{i=1}^{n} a_{ij}^* E(u_i) = \beta_j \tag{3.28}$$

applying Assumption A.3.

Efficiency

The Gauss–Markov theorem proves that, for multiple regression analysis, as for simple regression analysis, the ordinary least squares (OLS) technique yields the most efficient linear estimators, in the sense that it is impossible to find other unbiased estimators with lower variances, using the same sample information, provided that the regression model assumptions are satisfied. We will not attempt to prove this theorem since matrix algebra is required.

Precision of the multiple regression coefficients

We will investigate the factors governing the likely precision of the regression coefficients for the case where there are two explanatory variables. Similar considerations apply in the more general case, but with more than two variables the analysis becomes complex and one needs to switch to matrix algebra.

If the true relationship is

$$Y_i = \beta_1 + \beta_2 X_{2i} + \beta_3 X_{3i} + u_i, \tag{3.29}$$

and you fit the regression line

$$\hat{Y}_i = b_1 + b_2 X_{2i} + b_3 X_{3i}, \tag{3.30}$$

using appropriate data, $\sigma_{b_2}^2$, the population variance of the probability distribution of b_2, is given by

$$\sigma_{b_2}^2 = \frac{\sigma_u^2}{\sum\limits_{i=1}^{n}(X_{2i} - \overline{X}_2)^2} \times \frac{1}{1 - r_{X_2 X_3}^2} \tag{3.31}$$

where σ_u^2 is the population variance of u and $r_{X_2 X_3}$ is the correlation between X_2 and X_3. A parallel expression may be obtained for the population variance of b_3, replacing $\sum(X_{2i} - \overline{X}_2)^2$ with $\sum(X_{3i} - \overline{X}_3)^2$. Rewriting this as

$$\sigma_{b_2}^2 = \frac{\sigma_u^2}{n\,\text{MSD}(X_2)} \times \frac{1}{1 - r_{X_2 X_3}^2} \tag{3.32}$$

where $\text{MSD}(X_2)$, the mean square deviation of X_2, is given by $\dfrac{1}{n}\sum(X_{2i} - \overline{X}_2)^2$, we can see that, as in the case of simple regression analysis, it is desirable for n and $\text{MSD}(X_2)$ to be large and for σ_u^2 to be small. However, we now have the further term $(1 - r_{X_2 X_3}^2)$ and clearly it is desirable that the correlation between X_2 and X_3 should be low.

It is easy to give an intuitive explanation of this. The greater the correlation, the harder it is to discriminate between the effects of the explanatory variables on Y, and the less accurate will be the regression estimates. This can be a serious problem and it is discussed in the next section.

The standard deviation of the distribution of b_2 is the square root of the variance. As in the simple regression case, the standard error of b_2 is the estimate of the standard deviation. For this we need to estimate σ_u^2. The sample average of the squared residuals provides a biased estimator:

$$E\left\{\frac{1}{n}\sum_{i=1}^{n}e_i^2\right\} = \frac{n-k}{n}\sigma_u^2 \tag{3.33}$$

where k is the number of parameters in the regression equation. However, we can obtain an unbiased estimator, s_u^2, by dividing by $n-k$, instead of n, thus neutralizing the bias:

$$s_u^2 = \frac{1}{n-k}\sum_{i=1}^{n}e_i^2. \tag{3.34}$$

The standard error is then given by

$$\text{s.e.}(b_2) = \sqrt{\frac{s_u^2}{\sum_{i=1}^{n}(X_{2i}-\overline{X}_{2i})^2} \times \frac{1}{1-r_{X_2,X_3}^2}}. \tag{3.35}$$

The determinants of the standard error will be illustrated by comparing them in earnings functions fitted to two subsamples of the respondents in *EAEF* Data Set 21: those who reported that their wages were set by collective bargaining and the remainder. Regression output for the two subsamples is shown in Tables 3.3 and 3.4. In Stata, subsamples may be selected by adding an 'if' expression to a command. *COLLBARG* is a variable in the data set defined to be 1 for the collective bargaining subsample and 0 for the others. Note that in tests for equality, Stata requires the = sign to be duplicated.

The standard error of the coefficient of S in the first regression is 0.5493, twice as large as that in the second, 0.2604. We will investigate the reasons for the difference. It will be convenient to rewrite (3.35) in such a way as to isolate

Table 3.3

```
. reg EARNINGS S EXP if COLLBARG == 1

      Source       SS         df       MS              Number of obs =      101
                                                        F(2,98)       =     9.72
       Model   3076.31726      2    1538.15863          Prob > F      =   0.0001
    Residual   15501.9762     98     158.18343          R-squared     =   0.1656
                                                        Adj R-squared =   0.1486
       Total   18578.2934    100     185.782934         Root MSE      =   12.577


    EARNINGS       Coef.   Std. Err.          t    P>|t|    [95% Conf. Interval]

           S    2.333846   .5492604        4.25    0.000     1.243857   3.423836
         EXP    .2235095   .3389455        0.66    0.511    -.4491169    .8961358
       _cons   -15.12427   11.38141       -1.33    0.187    -37.71031   7.461779
```

Table 3.4

```
. reg EARNINGS S EXP if COLLBARG == 0

      Source        SS         df        MS              Number of obs =      439
---------------------------------------------            F(2,436)      =    57.77
       Model   19540.1761      2     9770.08805          Prob > F      =   0.0000
    Residual    73741.593    436     169.132094          R-squared     =   0.2095
---------------------------------------------            Adj R-squared =   0.2058
       Total   93281.7691    438     212.972076          Root MSE      =   13.005
--------------------------------------------------------------------------------
    EARNINGS       Coef.   Std. Err.          t    P>|t|    [95% Conf.   Interval]
--------------------------------------------------------------------------------
           S    2.721698    .2604411      10.45    0.000     2.209822    3.233574
         EXP    .6077342    .1400846       4.34    0.000     .3324091    .8830592
       _cons   -28.00805    4.643211      -6.03    0.000    -37.13391   -18.88219
```

the contributions of the various factors:

$$\text{s.e.}(b_2) = s_u \times \frac{1}{\sqrt{n}} \times \frac{1}{\sqrt{\text{MSD}(X_2)}} \times \frac{1}{\sqrt{1 - r^2_{X_2, X_3}}}. \tag{3.36}$$

The first element we need, s_u, can be obtained directly from the regression output. s_u^2 is equal to the sum of the squares of the residuals divided by $n - k$, here $n - 3$:

$$s_u^2 = \frac{1}{n-k} \sum_{i=1}^{n} e_i^2 = \frac{1}{n-k} RSS. \tag{3.37}$$

(Note that $\bar{e} = 0$. This was proved in Box 1.2 in Chapter 1 for the simple regression model, and the proof generalizes easily.) *RSS* is given in the top left quarter of the regression output, as part of the decomposition of the total sum of squares into the explained sum of squares (in the Stata output denoted the model sum of squares) and the residual sum of squares. The value of $n-k$ is given to the right of *RSS*, and the ratio $RSS/(n-k)$ to the right of that. The square root, s_u, is listed as the Root MSE (root mean square error) in the top right quarter of the regression output, 12.577 for the collective bargaining subsample and 13.005 for the regression with the other respondents.

The number of observations, 101 in the first regression and 439 in the second, is also listed in the top right quarter of the regression output. The mean squared deviations of *S*, 6.2325 and 5.6, were calculated as the squares of the standard deviations reported using the Stata 'sum' command, multiplied by $(n - 1)/n$. The correlations between *S* and *ASVABC*, −0.4087 and −0.1784 respectively, were calculated using the Stata 'cor' command. The factors of the components of the standard error in equation (3.36) were then derived and are shown in the lower half of Table 3.5.

It can be seen that, in this example, the reason that the standard error of *S* in the collective bargaining subsample is relatively large is that the number of observations in that subsample is relatively small. The larger correlation coefficient for

Table 3.5 Decomposition of the standard error of S

	s_u	n		MSD(S)	$r_{S,ASVABC}$	s.e.
Component						
Collective bargaining	12.577	101		6.2325	−0.4087	0.5493
Not collective bargaining	13.005	439		5.8666	−0.1784	0.2604
Factor						
Collective bargaining	12.577	0.0995	0.4006	1.0957	0.5493
Not collective bargaining	13.005	0.0477	0.4129	1.0163	0.2603

S and EXP reinforces the difference while the smaller s_u and the larger MSD(S) reduce it, but these are relatively minor factors.

t tests and confidence intervals

t tests on the regression coefficients are performed in the same way as for simple regression analysis. Note that when you are looking up the critical level of t at any given significance level, it will depend on the number of degrees of freedom, $n - k$: the number of observations minus the number of parameters estimated. The confidence intervals are also constructed in exactly the same way as in simple regression analysis, subject to the above comment about the number of degrees of freedom. As can be seen from the regression output, Stata automatically calculates confidence intervals for the coefficients (95 percent by default, other levels if desired), but this is not a standard feature of regression applications.

Exercises

3.6 Perform t tests on the coefficients of the variables in the educational attainment function reported in Exercise 3.1.

3.7 Perform t tests on the coefficients of the variables in the educational attainment and earnings functions fitted by you in Exercises 3.2 and 3.3.

3.8 The following earnings functions were fitted separately for males and females, using *EAEF* Data Set 21 (standard errors in parentheses):

males

$$\widehat{EARNINGS} = -31.5168 + 3.1408\,S + 0.6453 EXP$$
$$(7.8708)\quad(0.3693)\quad(0.2382)$$

females

$$\widehat{EARNINGS} = -17.2028 + 2.0772\,S + 0.3179 EXP.$$
$$(4.5797)\quad(0.2805)\quad(0.1388)$$

Using equation (3.36), explain why the standard errors of the coefficients of S and EXP are greater for the male subsample than for the female subsample, and why the difference in the standard errors is relatively large for EXP.

Further data:

	males	females
s_u	14.278	10.548
n	270	270
$r_{S, EXP}$	−0.4029	−0.0632
MSD(S)	6.6080	5.2573
MSD(EXP)	15.8858	21.4628

3.9* Demonstrate that $\bar{e} = 0$ in multiple regression analysis. (*Note:* The proof is a generalization of the proof for the simple regression model, given in Box 1.2 in Section 1.7.)

3.10 Investigate whether you can extend the determinants of weight model using your *EAEF* data set, taking *WEIGHT02* as the dependent variable, and *HEIGHT* and other continuous variables in the data set as explanatory variables. Provide an interpretation of the coefficients and perform t tests on them.

3.4 Multicollinearity

In the previous section, in the context of a model with two explanatory variables, it was seen that the higher is the correlation between the explanatory variables, the larger are the population variances of the distributions of their coefficients, and the greater is the risk of obtaining erratic estimates of the coefficients. If the correlation causes the regression model to become unsatisfactory in this respect, it is said to be suffering from **multicollinearity**.

A high correlation does not necessarily lead to poor estimates. If all the other factors determining the variances of the regression coefficients are helpful, that is, if the number of observations and the mean square deviations of the explanatory variables are large, and the variance of the disturbance term small, you may well obtain good estimates after all. Multicollinearity therefore must be caused by a *combination* of a high correlation and one or more of the other factors being unhelpful. And it is a matter of *degree*, not kind. Any regression will suffer from it to some extent, unless all the explanatory variables are uncorrelated. You only start to talk about it when you think that it is affecting the regression results seriously.

It is an especially common problem in time series regressions, that is, where the data consist of a series of observations on the variables over a number of time periods. If two or more of the explanatory variables have a strong time trend, they will be highly correlated and this condition may give rise to multicollinearity.

It should be noted that the presence of multicollinearity does not mean that the model is misspecified. Accordingly, the regression coefficients remain unbiased and the standard errors remain valid. The standard errors will be larger than they would have been in the absence of multicollinearity, warning you that the regression estimates are unreliable.

We will consider first the case of exact multicollinearity where the explanatory variables are perfectly correlated. Suppose that the true relationship is

$$Y = 2 + 3X_2 + X_3 + u. \tag{3.38}$$

Suppose that there is a linear relationship between X_2 and X_3:

$$X_3 = 2X_2 - 1, \tag{3.39}$$

and suppose that X_2 increases by one unit in each observation. X_3 will increase by 2 units, and Y by approximately 5 units, for example as shown in Table 3.6.

Looking at the data, you could come to any of the following conclusions:

1. the correct one, that Y is determined by (3.38),

2. that X_3 is irrelevant and Y is determined by the relationship

$$Y = 1 + 5X_2 + u, \tag{3.40}$$

3. that X_2 is irrelevant and Y is determined by the relationship

$$Y = 3.5 + 2.5X_3 + u. \tag{3.41}$$

In fact these are not the only possibilities. Any relationship that is a weighted average of (3.40) and (3.41) would also fit the data. For example, (3.38) may be regarded as such a weighted average, being (3.40) multiplied by 0.6 plus (3.41) multiplied by 0.4.

In such a situation it is impossible for regression analysis, or any other technique for that matter, to distinguish between these possibilities. You would not even be able to calculate the regression coefficients because both the numerator

Table 3.6

X_2	X_3	Y	Change in X_2	Change in X_3	Approximate change in Y
10	19	$51 + u_1$	1	2	5
11	21	$56 + u_2$	1	2	5
12	23	$61 + u_3$	1	2	5
13	25	$66 + u_4$	1	2	5
14	27	$71 + u_5$	1	2	5
15	29	$76 + u_6$	1	2	5

and the denominator of the regression coefficients would collapse to zero. This will be demonstrated with the general two-variable case. Suppose

$$Y = \beta_1 + \beta_2 X_2 + \beta_3 X_3 + u \tag{3.42}$$

and

$$X_3 = \lambda + \mu X_2. \tag{3.43}$$

First note that, given (3.43),

$$\left(X_{3i} - \overline{X}_3\right) = \left([\lambda + \mu X_{2i}] - [\lambda + \mu \overline{X}_2]\right) = \mu\left(X_{2i} - \overline{X}_2\right). \tag{3.44}$$

Hence

$$\sum_{i=1}^{n}(X_{3i} - \overline{X}_3)^2 = \mu^2 \sum_{i=1}^{n}(X_{2i} - \overline{X}_2)^2 \tag{3.45}$$

$$\sum_{i=1}^{n}(X_{3i} - \overline{X}_3)(Y_i - \overline{Y}) = \mu \sum_{i=1}^{n}(X_{2i} - \overline{X}_2)(Y_i - \overline{Y}) \tag{3.46}$$

$$\sum_{i=1}^{n}(X_{2i} - \overline{X}_2)(X_{3i} - \overline{X}_3) = \mu \sum_{i=1}^{n}(X_{2i} - \overline{X}_2)^2. \tag{3.47}$$

Substituting for X_3 in (3.11), one obtains

$$b_2 = \frac{\begin{array}{c}\sum_{i=1}^{n}(X_{2i} - \overline{X}_2)(Y_i - \overline{Y})\sum_{i=1}^{n}(X_{3i} - \overline{X}_3)^2 \\ -\sum_{i=1}^{n}(X_{3i} - \overline{X}_3)(Y_i - \overline{Y})\sum_{i=1}^{n}(X_{2i} - \overline{X}_2)(X_{3i} - \overline{X}_3)\end{array}}{\sum_{i=1}^{n}(X_{2i} - \overline{X}_2)^2 \sum_{i=1}^{n}(X_{3i} - \overline{X}_3)^2 - \left(\sum_{i=1}^{n}(X_{2i} - \overline{X}_2)(X_{3i} - \overline{X}_3)\right)^2}$$

$$= \frac{\begin{array}{c}\sum_{i=1}^{n}(X_{2i} - \overline{X}_2)(Y_i - \overline{Y})\left(\mu^2\sum_{i=1}^{n}(X_{2i} - \overline{X}_2)^2\right) \\ -\left(\mu\sum_{i=1}^{n}(X_{2i} - \overline{X}_2)(Y_i - \overline{Y})\right)\left(\mu\sum_{i=1}^{n}(X_{2i} - \overline{X}_2)^2\right)\end{array}}{\sum_{i=1}^{n}(X_{2i} - \overline{X}_2)^2\left(\mu^2\sum_{i=1}^{n}(X_{2i} - \overline{X}_2)^2\right) - \left(\mu\sum_{i=1}^{n}(X_{2i} - \overline{X}_2)^2\right)^2}$$

$$= \frac{0}{0}. \tag{3.48}$$

It is unusual for there to be an exact relationship between the explanatory variables in a regression. When this occurs, it is typically because there is a logical

Table 3.7

```
. reg EARNINGS S EXP EXPSQ

      Source        SS         df         MS              Number of obs =     540
---------------------------------------------             F(3,536)      =   45.57
       Model  22762.4472        3     7587.48241          Prob > F      =  0.0000
    Residual  89247.7839      536     166.507059          R-squared     =  0.2032
---------------------------------------------             Adj R-squared =  0.1988
       Total  112010.231      539     207.811189          Root MSE      =  12.904


    EARNINGS      Coef.   Std. Err.           t    P>|t|   [95% Conf.  Interval]
-----------------------------------------------------------------------------------
           S   2.754372   .2417286       11.39    0.000     2.279521   3.229224
         EXP  -.2353907    .665197       -0.35    0.724    -1.542103   1.071322
       EXPSQ   .0267843   .0219115        1.22    0.222    -.0162586    .0698272
       _cons  -22.21964   5.514827       -4.03    0.000    -33.05297  -11.38632
-----------------------------------------------------------------------------------

. cor EXP EXPSQ
   (obs = 540)

                  EXP       EXPSQ
-------------------------------------------
         EXP   1.0000
       EXPSQ   0.9812      1.0000
```

error in the specification. An example is provided by Exercise 3.13. However, it often happens that there is an approximate relationship.

For example, when relating earnings to schooling and work experience, it if often reasonable to suppose that the effect of work experience is subject to diminishing returns. A standard specification that allows for this is

$$EARNINGS = \beta_1 + \beta_2 S + \beta_3 EXP + \beta_4 EXPSQ + u \qquad (3.49)$$

where $EXPSQ$ is the square of EXP. According to the hypothesis of diminishing returns, β_4 should be negative. Table 3.7 gives the results of such a regression using $EAEF$ Data Set 21.

The regression results indicate that an extra year of schooling increases hourly earnings by $2.75. This is much the same as in the specification without $EXPSQ$, shown in Table 3.1. The standard error is also little changed and the coefficient remains highly significant.

By contrast the results for the experience part of the model are very different. The high correlation between EXP and $EXPSQ$, 0.9812, has given rise to the problem of multicollinearity. One consequence is that the coefficients of the affected variables become erratic, reflecting the difficulty in discriminating between their individual effects. In this case, the coefficient of EXP, which had been positive, as one would expect, and highly significant before the introduction of $EXPSQ$, has actually become negative. A second consequence is that the standard errors increase, providing a warning of the imprecision of the point estimates. In this case the standard error of the coefficient of EXP has increased from 0.1285 to 0.6652. Both EXP and $EXPSQ$ have low t statistics and we are unable to tell whether $EXPSQ$ belongs in the specification.

Multicollinearity in models with more than two explanatory variables

The foregoing discussion of multicollinearity was restricted to the case where there are two explanatory variables. In models with a greater number of explanatory variables, multicollinearity may be caused by an approximate linear relationship among them. It may be difficult to discriminate between the effects of one variable and those of a linear combination of the remainder. In the model with two explanatory variables, an approximate linear relationship automatically means a high correlation, but when there are three or more, this is not necessarily the case. A linear relationship does not inevitably imply high pairwise correlations between any of the variables. The effects of multicollinearity are the same as in the case with two explanatory variables, and, as in that case, the problem may not be serious if the population variance of the disturbance term is small, the number of observations large, and the mean square deviations of the explanatory variables large.

What can you do about multicollinearity?

The various ways of trying to alleviate multicollinearity fall into two categories: direct attempts to improve the four conditions responsible for the reliability of the regression estimates, and indirect methods.

First, you may try to reduce σ_u^2. The disturbance term is the joint effect of all the variables influencing Y that you have not included explicitly in the regression equation. If you can think of an important variable that you have omitted, and is therefore contributing to u, you will reduce the population variance of the disturbance term if you add it to the regression equation.

By way of illustration, we will take the earnings function discussed in the previous section, where there is a high correlation between EXP, years of work experience, and its square $EXPSQ$. We now add two new variables that are often found to be determinants of earnings: $MALE$, sex of respondent, and $ASVABC$, the composite score on the cognitive tests in the Armed Services Vocational Aptitude Battery. $MALE$ is a qualitative variable and the treatment of such variables will be explained in Chapter 5.

The results for the enlarged model specification are shown in Table 3.8. Both of the new variables have high t statistics and as a consequence the estimate of σ_u^2 falls from 166.51 to 155.53 (see the calculation of the residual sum of squares divided by the number of degrees of freedom in the top left quarter of the regression output). However, the joint contribution of the new variables to the explanatory power of the model is small, despite being highly significant, and as a consequence the problem of multicollinearity remains. The coefficient of EXP is still negative and the reduction in the standard errors of the coefficients of EXP and $EXPSQ$ is small. Note that the standard error of the coefficient of S has actually increased. This is attributable to the correlation of 0.58 between

Table 3.8

```
. reg EARNINGS S EXP EXPSQ MALE ASVABC

    Source       SS         df       MS                  Number of obs =    540
----------------------------------------------           F(5,534)      =  37.24
     Model   28957.3532      5    5791.47063              Prob > F      = 0.0000
  Residual   83052.8779    534    155.529734              R-squared     = 0.2585
----------------------------------------------           Adj R-squared = 0.2516
     Total   112010.231    539    207.811189              Root MSE      = 12.471


------------------------------------------------------------------------------
  EARNINGS       Coef.   Std. Err.        t    P>|t|     [95% Conf. Interval]
------------------------------------------------------------------------------
         S    2.031419    .296218      6.86    0.000     1.449524    2.613315
       EXP   -.0816828    .6441767    -0.13    0.899    -1.347114    1.183748
     EXPSQ    .0130223    .021334      0.61    0.542    -.0288866    .0549311
      MALE    5.762358   1.104734      5.22    0.000     3.592201    7.932515
    ASVABC    .2447687    .0714294     3.43    0.001     .1044516    .3850858
     _cons   -26.18541   5.452032     -4.80    0.000    -36.89547  -15.47535
------------------------------------------------------------------------------
```

S and *ASVABC*. This is a common problem with this approach to attempting to reduce the problem of multicollinearity. If the new variables are linearly related to one or more of the variables already in the equation, their inclusion may make the problem of multicollinearity worse.

The next factor to consider is *n*, the number of observations. If you are working with cross-sectional data (individuals, households, enterprises, etc.) and you are undertaking a survey, you could increase the size of the sample by negotiating a bigger budget. Alternatively, you could make a fixed budget go further by using a technique known as clustering. You divide the country geographically into localities. For example, the National Longitudinal Survey of Youth, from which the *EAEF* data are drawn, divides the country into counties, independent cities and standard metropolitan statistical areas. You select a number of localities randomly, perhaps using stratified random sampling to make sure that metropolitan, other urban and rural areas are properly represented. You then confine the survey to the localities selected. This reduces the travel time of the fieldworkers, allowing them to interview a greater number of respondents.

If you are working with time series data, you may be able to increase the sample by working with shorter time intervals for the data, for example quarterly or even monthly data instead of annual data. This is such an obvious thing to do that most researchers working with time series almost automatically use quarterly data, if they are available, instead of annual data, even if there does not appear to be a problem of multicollinearity, simply to minimize the population variances of the regression coefficients. There are, however, potential problems. You may introduce, or aggravate, autocorrelation (see Chapter 12), but this can be neutralized. Also you may introduce, or aggravate, measurement error bias (see Chapter 8) if the quarterly data are less accurately measured than the corresponding annual data. This problem is not so easily overcome, but it may be a minor one.

Table 3.9

```
. reg EARNINGS S EXP EXPSQ MALE ASVABC

   Source       SS          df        MS              Number of obs =    2714
                                                       F(5,2708)     = 183.99
    Model   161795.573        5    32359.1147          Prob > F      =  0.0000
 Residual   476277.268     2708    175.877869          R-squared     =  0.2536
                                                       Adj R-squared =  0.2522
    Total   638072.841     2713    235.190874          Root MSE      =  13.262

 EARNINGS      Coef.   Std. Err.         t    P>|t|     [95% Conf. Interval]

        S    2.312461    .135428     17.08    0.000     2.046909    2.578014
      EXP   -.3270651    .308231     -1.06    0.289    -.9314569    .2773268
    EXPSQ     .023743   .0101558      2.34    0.019     .0038291    .0436569
     MALE    5.947206   .5221755     11.39    0.000     4.923303    6.971108
   ASVABC    .2086846   .0336869      6.19    0.00      .1426301    .2747392
    _cons   -27.40462   2.579435    -10.62    0.000    -32.46248  -22.34676
```

Table 3.9 shows the result of running the regression with all 2,714 observations in the *EAEF* data set. Comparing this result with that using Data Set 21, we see that the standard errors are much smaller, as expected. As a consequence, the *t* statistics of *S* and the new variables are higher. However, the correlation between *EXP* and *EXPSQ* is just as high as in the smaller sample and the increase in the sample size has not been large enough to have any impact on the problem of multicollinearity. The coefficients of *EXP* and *EXPSQ* both still have unexpected signs since we expect the coefficient of *EXP* to be positive and that of *EXPSQ* to be negative, reflecting diminishing returns. The coefficient of *EXPSQ* has a rather large *t* statistic, which is a matter of concern. We could assume that this has occurred as a matter of chance. Alternatively, it might be an indication that the model is misspecified. As we will see in the next and subsequent chapters, there are good reasons for supposing that the dependent variable in an earnings function should be the logarithm of earnings, rather than earnings in linear form.

A third possible way of reducing the problem of multicollinearity might be to increase the mean square deviation of the explanatory variables. This is possible only at the design stage of a survey. For example, if you were planning a household survey with the aim of investigating how expenditure patterns vary with income, you should make sure that the sample included relatively rich and relatively poor households as well as middle-income households by stratifying the sample. (For a discussion of sampling theory and techniques, see, for example, Moser and Kalton, 1985, or Fowler, 1993.)

The fourth direct method is the most direct of all. If you are still at the design stage of a survey, you should do your best to obtain a sample where the explanatory variables are less related (more easily said than done, of course).

Next, indirect methods. If the correlated variables are similar conceptually, it may be reasonable to combine them into some overall index. That is precisely what has been done with the three cognitive variables in the Armed Services

Vocational Aptitude Battery. *ASVABC* has been calculated as a weighted average of *ASVAB02* (arithmetic reasoning), *ASVAB03* (word knowledge), and *ASVAB04* (paragraph comprehension). The three components are highly correlated and by combining them rather than using them individually one avoids a potential problem of multicollinearity. *ASVAB02* has been given twice the weight of the other two components so that numerical and verbal elements are equally represented, but this decision is merely a subjective judgment about what seems sensible.

Another possible solution to the problem of multicollinearity is to drop some of the correlated variables if they have insignificant coefficients. However, there is always a risk that such variables do truly belong in the model and that multicollinearity is causing their coefficients to be insignificant. Dropping variables that belong in the model may give rise to omitted variable bias (see Chapter 6).

A further way of dealing with the problem of multicollinearity is to use extraneous information, if available, concerning the coefficient of one of the variables. For example, suppose that one is relating aggregate demand for a category of consumer expenditure, Y, to aggregate disposable personal income, X, and a price index for the category, P.

$$Y = \beta_1 + \beta_2 X + \beta_3 P + u. \tag{3.50}$$

To fit a model of this type you would use time series data. If X and P possess strong time trends and are therefore highly correlated, which is often the case with time series variables, multicollinearity is likely to be a problem. Suppose, however, that you also have cross-sectional data on Y and X derived from a separate household survey. These variables will be denoted Y' and X' to indicate that the data are household data, not aggregate data. Assuming that all the households in the survey were paying roughly the same price for the commodity, one would fit the simple regression

$$\hat{Y}' = b_1' + b_2' X'. \tag{3.51}$$

Now substitute b_2' for β_2 in the time series model,

$$Y = \beta_1 + b_2' X + \beta_3 P + u, \tag{3.52}$$

subtract $b_2' X$ from both sides,

$$Y - b_2' X = \beta_1 + \beta_3 P + u \tag{3.53}$$

and regress $Z = Y - b_2' X$ on price. This is a simple regression, so multicollinearity has been eliminated.

There are, however, two possible problems with this technique. First, the estimate of β_3 in (3.53) depends on the accuracy of the estimate of b_2', and this of course is subject to sampling error. Second, you are assuming that the income coefficient has the same meaning in time series and cross-sectional contexts, and this may not be the case. For many commodities the short-run and long-run effects of changes in income may differ because expenditure patterns are subject to inertia. A change in income can affect expenditure both directly, by altering the budget constraint, and indirectly, through causing a change in lifestyle, and the indirect effect is much slower than the direct one. As a first approximation, it is commonly argued that time series regressions, particularly those using short sample periods, estimate short-run effects while cross-sectional regressions estimate long-run ones. For a discussion of this and related issues, see Kuh and Meyer (1957).

Last, but by no means least, is the use of a theoretical **restriction**, which is defined as a hypothetical relationship among the parameters of a regression model. It will be explained using an educational attainment model as an example. Suppose that we hypothesize that years of schooling, S, depends on $ASVABC$, and the years of schooling of the respondent's mother and father, SM and SF, respectively:

$$S = \beta_1 + \beta_2 ASVABC + \beta_3 SM + \beta_4 SF + u. \qquad (3.54)$$

Fitting the model using *EAEF* Data Set 21, we obtain the output shown in Table 3.10.

The regression coefficients imply that S increases by 0.13 years for every one-point increase in $ASVABC$, by 0.05 years for every extra year of schooling of the mother and by 0.11 years for every extra year of schooling of the father. Mother's education is generally held to be at least as important as father's education for educational attainment, so the relatively low coefficient of SM is unexpected. It is also surprising that the coefficient is not significant, even at the 5 percent level, using a one-sided test. However assortive mating leads to a high correlation between SM and SF and the regression appears to be suffering from multicollinearity.

Suppose that we hypothesize that mother's and father's education are equally important. We can then impose the restriction $\beta_3 = \beta_4$. This allows us to write

Table 3.10

```
. reg S ASVABC SM SF

    Source        SS          df         MS              Number of obs =     540
                                                         F(3,536)      = 104.30
    Model    1181.36981        3     393.789935          Prob > F      = 0.0000
  Residual   2023.61353      536     3.77539837          R-squared     = 0.3686
                                                         Adj R-squared = 0.3651
    Total    3204.98333      539     5.94616574          Root MSE      = 1.943

         S      Coef.     Std. Err.         t    P>|t|    [95% Conf. Interval]

    ASVABC   .1257087     .0098533      12.76    0.000    .1063528    .1450646
        SM   .0492424     .0390901       1.26    0.208   -.027546    .1260309
        SF   .1076825     .0309522       3.48    0.001    .04688     .1684851
     _cons   5.370631     .4882155      11.00    0.000    4.41158    6.329681
```

Table 3.11

```
. gen SP = SM + SF
. reg S ASVABC SP

    Source      SS          df        MS              Number of obs =     540
-------------------------------------------           F(2,537)      =  156.04
    Model   1177.98338       2     588.991689          Prob > F      =  0.0000
 Residual   2026.99996     537     3.77467403          R-squared     =  0.3675
-------------------------------------------           Adj R-squared =  0.3652
    Total   3204.98333     539     5.94616574          Root MSE      =  1.9429

-----------------------------------------------------------------------------
        S      Coef.    Std. Err.         t   P>|t|    [95% Conf. Interval]
-----------------------------------------------------------------------------
   ASVABC   .1253106    .0098434      12.73   0.000    .1059743    .1446469
       SP   .0828368    .0164247       5.04   0.000    .0505722    .1151014
    _cons    5.29617    .4817972      10.99   0.000    4.349731    6.242608
```

the equation as

$$S = \beta_1 + \beta_2 ASVABC + \beta_3(SM + SF) + u. \tag{3.55}$$

Defining SP to be the sum of SM and SF, the equation may be rewritten with $ASVABC$ and SP as the explanatory variables:

$$S = \beta_1 + \beta_2 ASVABC + \beta_3 SP + u. \tag{3.56}$$

Fitting the model using *EAEF* Data Set 21, we obtain the output shown in Table 3.11. The estimate of β_3 is now 0.083. Not surprisingly, this is a compromise between the coefficients of SM and SF in the previous specification. The standard error of SP is much smaller than those of SM and SF, indicating that the use of the restriction has led to a gain in efficiency, and as a consequence the t statistic is very high. Thus the problem of multicollinearity has been eliminated. However, it is possible that the restriction may not be valid. We should test it. We shall see how to do this in Chapter 6.

Exercises

3.11 Using your *EAEF* data set, regress S on SM, SF, $ASVAB02$, $ASVAB03$, and $ASVAB04$, the three components of the $ASVABC$ composite score. Compare the coefficients and their standard errors with those of $ASVABC$ in a regression of S on SM, SF, and $ASVABC$. Calculate correlation coefficients for the three $ASVAB$ components.

3.12 Investigate the determinants of family size by regressing $SIBLINGS$ on SM and SF using your *EAEF* data set. SM and SF are likely to be highly correlated (find the correlation in your data set) and the regression may be subject to multi-collinearity. Introduce the restriction that the theoretical coefficients of SM and SF are equal and run the regression a second time, replacing SM and SF by their sum, SP. Evaluate the regression results.

3.13* A researcher investigating the determinants of the demand for public transport in a certain city has the following data for 100 residents for the previous calendar year: expenditure on public transport, E, measured in dollars; number of days worked, W; and number of days not worked, NW. By definition NW is equal to $365 - W$. He attempts to fit the following model:

$$E = \beta_1 + \beta_2 W + \beta_3 NW + u.$$

Explain why he is unable to fit this equation. (Give both intuitive and technical explanations.) How might he resolve the problem?

3.14 Work experience is generally found to be an important determinant of earnings. If a direct measure is lacking in a data set, it is standard practice to use potential work experience, PWE, defined by

$$PWE = AGE - S - 5$$

as a proxy. This is the maximum number of years since the completion of full-time education, assuming that an individual enters first grade at the age of six. Using your EAEF data set, first regress EARNINGS on S and PWE, and then run the regression a second time adding AGE as well. Comment on the regression results.

3.5 Goodness of fit: R^2

As in simple regression analysis, the coefficient of determination, R^2, measures the proportion of the variation in Y explained by the regression and is defined equivalently by

$$R^2 = \frac{\sum_{i=1}^{n} \left(\hat{Y}_i - \overline{Y}\right)^2}{\sum_{i=1}^{n} \left(Y_i - \overline{Y}\right)^2} \tag{3.57}$$

by

$$R^2 = 1 - \frac{\sum_{i=1}^{n} e_i^2}{\sum_{i=1}^{n} \left(Y_i - \overline{Y}\right)^2} \tag{3.58}$$

or by the square of the correlation coefficient for Y and $\hat{Y}$. It can never decrease, and generally will increase, if you add another variable to a regression equation, provided that you retain all the previous explanatory variables. To see this, suppose that you regress Y on X_2 and X_3 and fit the equation

$$\hat{Y}_i = b_1 + b_2 X_{2i} + b_3 X_{3i}. \tag{3.59}$$

Next suppose that you regress Y on X_2 only and the result is

$$\hat{Y}_i = b_1^* + b_2^* X_{2i}. \tag{3.60}$$

This can be rewritten

$$\hat{Y}_i = b_1^* + b_2^* X_{2i} + 0 X_{3i}. \tag{3.61}$$

Comparing (3.59) and (3.61), the coefficients in the former have been determined freely by the OLS technique using the data for $Y, X_2,$ and X_3 to give the best possible fit. In (3.61), however, the coefficient of X has arbitrarily been set at zero, and the fit will be suboptimal unless, by coincidence, b_3 happens to be zero, in which case the fit will be the same. (b_1^* will then be equal to b_1, and b_2^* will be equal to b_2). Hence, in general, the level of R^2 will be higher in (3.59) than in (3.61), and it cannot be lower. Of course, if the new variable does not genuinely belong in the equation, the increase in R^2 is likely to be negligible.

You might think that, because R^2 measures the proportion of the variation jointly explained by the explanatory variables, it should be possible to deduce the individual contribution of each explanatory variable and thus obtain a measure of its relative importance. At least it would be very convenient if one could. Unfortunately, such a decomposition is impossible if the explanatory variables are correlated because their explanatory power will overlap. The problem will be discussed further in Section 6.2.

F tests

We saw in Section 2.11 that we could perform an F test of the explanatory power of the simple regression model

$$Y_i = \beta_1 + \beta_2 X_i + u_i \tag{3.62}$$

the null hypothesis being $H_0: \beta_2 = 0$ and the alternative being $H_1: \beta_2 \neq 0$. The null hypothesis was the same as that for a t test on the slope coefficient and it turned out that the F test was equivalent to a (two-sided) t test. However, in the case of the multiple regression model the tests have different roles. The t tests test the significance of the coefficient of each variable individually, while the F test tests their joint explanatory power. The null hypothesis, which we hope to reject, is that the model has no explanatory power. The model will have no explanatory power if it turns out that Y is unrelated to any of the explanatory variables. Mathematically, therefore, if the model is

$$Y_i = \beta_1 + \beta_2 X_{2i} + \cdots + \beta_k X_{ki} + u_i, \tag{3.63}$$

the null hypothesis for the F test is that all the slope coefficients $\beta_2, \ldots, \beta_k$ are zero:

$$H_0: \beta_2 = \cdots = \beta_k = 0. \tag{3.64}$$

The alternative hypothesis H_1 is that at least one of the slope coefficients $\beta_2, \ldots, \beta_k$ is different from zero. The F statistic is defined as

$$F(k-1, n-k) = \frac{ESS/(k-1)}{RSS/(n-k)} \tag{3.65}$$

and the test is performed by comparing this with the critical level of F in the column corresponding to $k-1$ degrees of freedom and the row corresponding to $n-k$ degrees of freedom in the appropriate part of Table A.3 in Appendix A.

This F statistic may also be expressed in terms of R^2 by dividing both the numerator and denominator of (3.65) by TSS, the total sum of squares, and noting that ESS/TSS is R^2 and RSS/TSS is $(1 - R^2)$:

$$F(k-1, n-k) = \frac{R^2/(k-1)}{(1-R^2)/(n-k)}. \tag{3.66}$$

Example

The educational attainment model will be used as an illustration. We will suppose that S depends on $ASVABC$, SM, and SF:

$$S = \beta_1 + \beta_2 ASVABC + \beta_3 SM + \beta_4 SF + u. \tag{3.67}$$

The null hypothesis for the F test of goodness of fit is that all three slope coefficients are equal to zero:

$$H_0: \beta_2 = \beta_3 = \beta_4 = 0. \tag{3.68}$$

The alternative hypothesis is that at least one of them is nonzero. The regression output using $EAEF$ Data Set 21 is shown in Table 3.12.

In this example, $k-1$, the number of explanatory variables, is equal to 3 and $n-k$, the number of degrees of freedom, is equal to 536. The numerator of the F statistic is the explained sum of squares divided by $k-1$. In the Stata output these numbers, 1181.4 and 3, respectively, are given in the Model row. The denominator is the residual sum of squares divided by the number of degrees of freedom remaining, 2023.6 and 536, respectively. Hence the F statistic is

$$F(3, 536) = \frac{1181.4/3}{2023.6/536} = 104.3 \tag{3.69}$$

as in the printed output. All serious regression applications compute this F statistic for you as part of the diagnostics in the regression output.

The critical value for $F(3,536)$ is not given in the F tables, but we know it must be lower than $F(3,500)$, which is given. At the 0.1 percent level, this is 5.51.

Table 3.12

```
. reg S ASVABC SM SF

    Source        SS           df         MS              Number of obs =    540
------------------------------------------------          F(3,536)      = 104.30
     Model    1181.36981        3     393.789935           Prob > F      = 0.0000
  Residual    2023.61353      536     3.77539837           R-squared     = 0.3686
------------------------------------------------          Adj R-squared = 0.3651
     Total    3204.98333      539     5.94616574           Root MSE      =  1.943

-----------------------------------------------------------------------------------
        S        Coef.     Std. Err.          t    P>|t|     [95% Conf.  Interval]
-----------------------------------------------------------------------------------
    ASVABC    .1257087     .0098533        12.76    0.000     .1063528   .1450646
        SM    .0492424     .0390901         1.26    0.208    -.027546    .1260309
        SF    .1076825     .0309522         3.48    0.001      .04688    .1684851
     _cons    5.370631     .4882155        11.00    0.000     4.41158    6.329681
```

Hence we reject H_0 at that significance level. This result could have been anticipated because both *ASVABC* and *SF* have highly significant t statistics. So we knew in advance that both β_2 and β_3 were nonzero.

In general, the F statistic will be significant if any t statistic is. In principle, however, it might not be. Suppose that you ran a nonsense regression with 40 explanatory variables, none being a true determinant of the dependent variable. Then the F statistic should be low enough for H_0 not to be rejected. However, if you are performing t tests on the slope coefficients at the 5 percent level, with a 5 percent chance of a Type I error, on average 2 of the 40 variables could be expected to have 'significant' coefficients.

On the other hand it can easily happen that the F statistic is significant while the t statistics are not. Suppose you have a multiple regression model that is correctly specified and R^2 is high. You would be likely to have a highly significant F statistic. However, if the explanatory variables are highly correlated and the model is subject to severe multicollinearity, the standard errors of the slope coefficients could all be so large that none of the t statistics is significant. In this situation you would know that your model has high explanatory power, but you are not in a position to pinpoint the contributions made by the explanatory variables individually.

Further analysis of variance

Besides testing the equation as a whole, you can use an F test to see whether or not the joint marginal contribution of a group of variables is significant. Suppose that you first fit the model

$$Y = \beta_1 + \beta_2 X_2 + \cdots + \beta_k X_k + u, \tag{3.70}$$

with explained sum of squares ESS_k. Next you add $m - k$ variables and fit the model

$$Y = \beta_1 + \beta_2 X_2 + \cdots + \beta_k X_k + \beta_{k+1} X_{k+1} + \cdots + \beta_m X_m + u, \tag{3.71}$$

with explained sum of squares ESS_m. You have then explained an additional sum of squares equal to $ESS_m - ESS_k$ using up an additional $m - k$ degrees of freedom, and you want to see whether the increase is greater than is likely to have arisen by chance.

Again an F test is used and the appropriate F statistic may be expressed in verbal terms as

$$F = \frac{\text{improvement in fit/extra degrees of freedom used up}}{\text{residual sum of squares remaining/degrees of freedom remaining}}. \quad (3.72)$$

Since RSS_m, the unexplained sum of squares in the second model, is equal to $TSS - ESS_m$, and RSS_k, the residual sum of squares in the first model, is equal to $TSS - ESS_k$, the improvement in the fit when the extra variables are added, $ESS_m - ESS_k$, is equal to $RSS_k - RSS_m$. Hence the appropriate F statistic is

$$F(m - k, n - m) = \frac{(RSS_k - RSS_m)/(m - k)}{RSS_m/(n - m)}. \quad (3.73)$$

Under the null hypothesis that the additional variables contribute nothing to the equation

$$H_0: \beta_{k+1} = \beta_{k+2} = \cdots = \beta_m = 0 \quad (3.74)$$

this F statistic is distributed with $m - k$ and $n - m$ degrees of freedom. The upper half of Table 3.13 gives the analysis of variance for the explanatory power of the original $k - 1$ variables. The lower half gives it for the joint marginal contribution of the new variables.

Table 3.13 Analysis of variance, original variables and a group of additional variables

	Sum of squares	Degrees of freedom	Sum of squares divided by degrees of freedom	F statistic
Explained by original variables	ESS_k	$k - 1$	$ESS_k/(k - 1)$	
				$\dfrac{ESS_k/(k - 1)}{RSS_k/(n - k)}$
Residual	$RSS_k = TSS - ESS_k$	$n - k$	$RSS_k/(n - k)$	
Explained by new variables	$ESS_m - ESS_k$ $= RSS_k - RSS_m$	$m - k$	$(RSS_k - RSS_m)/(m - k)$	
				$\dfrac{(RSS_k - RSS_m)/(m - k)}{RSS_m/(n - m)}$
Residual	$RSS_m = TSS - ESS_m$	$n - m$	$RSS_m/(n - m)$	

Table 3.14

```
. reg S ASVABC

    Source         SS           df        MS              Number of obs =     540
-------------------------------------------------          F(1,538)      = 274.19
    Model    1081.97059          1   1081.97059            Prob > F      = 0.0000
 Residual    2123.01275        538   3.94612035            R-squared     = 0.3376
-------------------------------------------------          Adj R-squared = 0.3364
    Total    3204.98333        539   5.94616574            Root MSE      = 1.9865

-----------------------------------------------------------------------------------
        S      Coef.    Std. Err.         t    P>|t|    [95% Conf.  Interval]
-----------------------------------------------------------------------------------
   ASVABC   .148084    .0089431        16.56   0.000    .1305165    .1656516
    _cons  6.066225    .4672261        12.98   0.000    5.148413    6.984036
-----------------------------------------------------------------------------------
```

Table 3.15

```
. reg S ASVABC SM SF

    Source         SS           df        MS              Number of obs =     540
-------------------------------------------------          F(3,536)      = 104.30
    Model   1181.36981          3   393.789935            Prob > F      = 0.0000
 Residual   2023.61353        536   3.77539837            R-squared     = 0.3686
-------------------------------------------------          Adj R-squared = 0.3651
    Total   3204.98333        539   5.94616574            Root MSE      = 1.943

-----------------------------------------------------------------------------------
        S      Coef.    Std. Err.         t    P>|t|    [95% Conf.  Interval]
-----------------------------------------------------------------------------------
   ASVABC  .1257087    .0098533        12.76   0.000    .1063528    .1450646
       SM  .0492424    .0390901         1.26   0.208   -.027546    .1260309
       SF  .1076825    .0309522         3.48   0.001    .04688     .1684851
    _cons  5.370631    .4882155        11.00   0.000    4.41158    6.329681
-----------------------------------------------------------------------------------
```

Example

We will illustrate the test with the educational attainment example. Table 3.14 shows the output from a regression of S on $ASVABC$ using $EAEF$ Data Set 21. We make a note of the residual sum of squares, 2123.0.

Now we add a group of two variables, the years of schooling of each parent, with the output shown in Table 3.15. Do the two new variables jointly make a significant contribution to the explanatory power of the model? Well, we can see that a t test would show that SF has a highly significant coefficient, but we will perform the F test anyway. We make a note of RSS, 2023.6.

The improvement in the fit on adding the parental schooling variables is the reduction in the residual sum of squares, $2123.0 - 2023.6$. The cost is two degrees of freedom because two additional parameters have been estimated. The residual sum of squares remaining unexplained after adding SM and SF is 2023.6. The number of degrees of freedom remaining after adding the new variables is $540 - 4 = 536$.

$$F(2, 536) = \frac{(2123.0 - 2023.6)/2}{2023.6/536} = 13.16. \qquad (3.75)$$

Table 3.16

```
. reg S ASVABC SM

    Source       SS          df        MS              Number of obs =    540
------------------------------------------             F(2,537)      =147.36
    Model    1135.67473        2    567.837363          Prob > F      =0.0000
 Residual    2069.30861      537    3.85346109          R-squared     =0.3543
------------------------------------------             Adj R-squared =0.3519
    Total    3204.98333      539    5.94616574          Root MSE      = 1.963

---------------------------------------------------------------------------
        S      Coef.   Std. Err.           t    P>|t|   [95% Conf. Interval]
---------------------------------------------------------------------------
   ASVABC   .1328069   .0097389       13.64    0.000    .1136758    .151938
       SM   .1235071   .0330837        3.73    0.000    .0585178   .1884963
    _cons   5.420733   .4930224       10.99    0.000    4.452244   6.389222
```

Thus the F statistic is 13.16. The critical value of $F(2,500)$ at the 0.1 percent level is 7.00. The critical value of $F(2,536)$ must be lower, so we reject H_0 and conclude that the parental education variables do have significant joint explanatory power.

Relationship between *F* statistic and *t* statistic

Suppose that you are considering the following alternative model specifications:

$$Y = \beta_1 + \beta_2 X_2 + \cdots + \beta_{k-1} X_{k-1} + u \qquad (3.76)$$

$$Y = \beta_1 + \beta_2 X_2 + \cdots + \beta_{k-1} X_{k-1} + \beta_k X_k + u \qquad (3.77)$$

the only difference being the addition of X_k as an explanatory variable in (3.77). You now have two ways to test whether X_k belongs in the model. You could perform a t test on its coefficient when (3.77) is fitted. Alternatively, you could perform an F test of the type just discussed, treating X_k as a 'group' of just one variable, to test its marginal explanatory power. For the F test the null hypothesis will be $H_0: \beta_k = 0$, since only X_k has been added and this is the same null hypothesis as that for the t test. Thus it might appear that there is a risk that the outcomes of the two tests might conflict with each other.

Fortunately, this is impossible, since it can be shown that the F statistic for this test must be equal to the square of the t statistic and that the critical value of F is equal to the square of the critical value of t (two-sided test). This result means that the t test of the coefficient of a variable is in effect a test of its marginal explanatory power, *after all the other variables have been included in the equation*.

If the variable is correlated with one or more of the other variables, its marginal explanatory power may be quite low, even if it genuinely belongs in the model. If all the variables are correlated, it is possible for all of them to have low marginal explanatory power and for none of the t tests to be significant, even though the F test for their joint explanatory power is highly significant. If this is the case, the model is said to be suffering from the problem of multicollinearity discussed earlier in this chapter.

No proof of the equivalence will be offered here, but it will be illustrated with the educational attainment model. In the first regression it has been hypothesized that S depends on $ASVABC$ and SM. In the second, it has been hypothesized that it depends on SF as well.

Comparing Tables 3.15 and 3.16, the improvement on adding SF is the reduction in the residual sum of squares, $2069.3 - 2023.6$. The cost is just the single degree of freedom lost when estimating the coefficient of SF. The residual sum of squares remaining after adding SF is 2023.6. The number of degrees of freedom remaining after adding SF is $540 - 4 = 536$. Hence the F statistic is 12.10:

$$F(1, 536) = \frac{(2069.3 - 2023.6)/1}{2023.6/536} = 12.10. \tag{3.78}$$

The critical value of F at the 0.1 percent significance level with 500 degrees of freedom is 10.96. The critical value with 536 degrees of freedom must be lower, so we reject H_0 at the 0.1 percent level. The t statistic for the coefficient of SF in the regression with both SM and SF is 3.48. The critical value of t at the 0.1 percent level with 500 degrees of freedom is 3.31. The critical value with 536 degrees of freedom must be lower, so we also reject H_0 with the t test. The square of 3.48 is 12.11, equal to the F statistic, except for rounding error, and the square of 3.31 is 10.96, equal to the critical value of $F(1,500)$. Hence the conclusions of the two tests must coincide.

'Adjusted' R^2

If you look at regression output, you will almost certainly find near the R^2 statistic something called the **'adjusted'** R^2. Sometimes it is called the 'corrected' R^2. 'Corrected' makes it sound as if it is better than the ordinary one, but this is debatable.

As was noted earlier in this section, R^2 cannot fall, and generally increases, if you add another variable to a regression equation. The adjusted R^2, usually denoted $\overline{R}^2$, attempts to compensate for this automatic upward shift by imposing a penalty for increasing the number of explanatory variables. It is defined as

$$\overline{R}^2 = 1 - (1 - R^2)\frac{n-1}{n-k} = \frac{n-1}{n-k}R^2 - \frac{k-1}{n-k}$$

$$= R^2 - \frac{k-1}{n-k}(1 - R^2) \tag{3.79}$$

where $k-1$ is the number of explanatory variables. As k increases, $(k-1)/(n-k)$ increases, and so the negative adjustment to R^2 increases.

It can be shown that the addition of a new variable to a regression will cause $\overline{R}^2$ to rise if and only if the absolute value of its t statistic is greater than 1.

Hence a rise in $\overline{R}^2$ when a new variable is added does not necessarily mean that its coefficient is significantly different from zero. It therefore does not follow, as is sometimes suggested, that a rise in $\overline{R}^2$ implies that the specification of an equation has improved.

This is one reason why $\overline{R}^2$ is not widely used as a diagnostic statistic. Another is the decrease in attention paid to R^2 itself. At one time there was a tendency for applied econometricians to regard R^2 as a key indicator of the success of model specification. In practice, however, as will be seen in the following chapters, even a very badly specified regression model may yield a high R^2, and recognition of this fact has led to the demotion of R^2 in importance. It is now regarded as just one of a whole set of diagnostic statistics that should be examined when evaluating a regression model. Consequently, there is little to be gained by fine tuning it with a 'correction' of dubious value.

Key terms

adjusted R^2

Frisch–Waugh–Lovell theorem

multicollinearity

multiple regression analysis

restriction

Exercises

3.15 Using your *EAEF* data set, fit an educational attainment function, regressing *S* on *ASVABC*, *SM*, and *SF*. Calculate the *F* statistic using R^2 and perform a test of the explanatory power of the equation as a whole.

3.16 Fit an educational attainment function using the specification in Exercise 3.15, adding the ASVAB speed test scores *ASVAB05* and *ASVAB06*. Perform an *F* test of the joint explanatory power of *ASVAB05* and *ASVAB06*, using the results of this regression and that in Exercise 3.15.

3.17 Fit an educational attainment function, regressing *S* on *ASVABC*, *SM*, *SF*, and *ASVAB05*. Perform an *F* test of the explanatory power of *ASVAB06*, using the results of this regression and that in Exercise 3.16. Verify that it leads to the same conclusion as a two-sided *t* test.

3.18* The researcher in Exercise 3.13 decides to divide the number of days not worked into the number of days not worked because of illness, *I*, and the number of days not worked for other reasons, *O*. The mean value of *I* in the sample is

2.1 and the mean value of O is 120.2. He fits the regression (standard errors in parentheses):

$$\hat{E} = -9.6 + 2.10W + 0.45O \qquad R^2 = 0.72.$$
$$\phantom{\hat{E} = -9.6 } (8.3) \quad (1.98) \quad (1.77)$$

Perform t tests on the regression coefficients and an F test on the goodness of fit of the equation. Explain why the t tests and the F test have different outcomes.

4 Transformations of Variables

Nonlinear relationships are more plausible than linear ones for many economic processes. In this chapter we will first define what is meant by linear regression analysis and then show how some apparently nonlinear relationships can be fitted by it. We will next see what can be done when linear methods cannot be used. The chapter ends with an exposition of a technique for discriminating statistically between linear and nonlinear relationships.

4.1 Basic procedure

One of the limitations of linear regression analysis is implicit in its very name, in that it can be used to fit only linear equations where every explanatory term, except the constant, is written in the form of a coefficient multiplied by variable:

$$Y = \beta_1 + \beta_2 X_2 + \beta_3 X_3 + \beta_4 X_4. \tag{4.1}$$

Equations such as

$$Y = \beta_1 + \frac{\beta_2}{X} \tag{4.2}$$

and

$$Y = \beta_1 X^{\beta_2} \tag{4.3}$$

are nonlinear.

However, both (4.2) and (4.3) have been suggested as suitable forms for Engel curves, the relationship between the demand for a particular commodity, Y, and income, X. Given data on Y and X, how could one estimate the parameters β_1 and β_2 in these equations?

Actually, in both cases, with a little preparation one can use linear regression analysis after all. First, note that (4.1) is linear in two senses. The right side is **linear in variables** because the variables are included exactly as defined, rather than as functions. It therefore consists of a weighted sum of the variables, the parameters being the weights. The right side is also **linear in parameters** since it consists of a weighted sum of these as well, the X variables being the weights this time.

For the purpose of linear regression analysis, only the second type of linearity is important. Nonlinearity in the variables can always be sidestepped by using appropriate definitions. For example, suppose that the relationship were of the form

$$Y = \beta_1 + \beta_2 X_2^2 + \beta_3 \sqrt{X_3} + \beta_4 \log X_4 + \cdots. \tag{4.4}$$

By defining $Z_2 = X_2^2, Z_3 = \sqrt{X_3}, Z_4 = \log X_4$, etc., the relationship can be rewritten

$$Y = \beta_1 + \beta_2 Z_2 + \beta_3 Z_3 + \beta_4 Z_4 + \cdots \tag{4.5}$$

and it is now linear in variables as well as in parameters. This type of transformation is only cosmetic, and you will usually see the regression equation presented with the variables written in their nonlinear form. This avoids the need for explanation and extra notation.

On the other hand an equation such as (4.3) is nonlinear in both parameters and variables and cannot be handled by a mere redefinition. (Do not be tempted to think that you can make it linear by defining $Z = X^{\beta_2}$ and replacing X^{β_2} with Z; since you do not know β_2, you have no way of calculating sample data for Z.) We will discuss the problem of fitting relationships that are nonlinear in parameters in the next section.

In the case of (4.2), however, all we have to do is to define $Z = 1/X$. Equation (4.2) now becomes

$$Y = \beta_1 + \beta_2 Z \tag{4.6}$$

and this is linear, so you regress Y on Z. The constant term in the regression will be an estimate of β_1 and the coefficient of Z will be an estimate of β_2.

Example

Suppose that you are investigating the relationship between annual consumption of bananas and annual income, and you have the observations shown in Table 4.1 for 10 households (ignore Z for the time being).

These observations are plotted in Figure 4.1, together with the line obtained by regressing Y on X (standard errors in parentheses):

$$\hat{Y} = 4.62 + 0.84X \quad R^2 = 0.69. \tag{4.7}$$
$$\quad (1.26) \ (0.20)$$

Now, if you look at Figure 4.1, you will see that the regression line does not fit the observations very well, despite the fact that the coefficient of income is

Table 4.1

Household	Bananas (lbs) Y	Income ($10,000) X	Z
1	1.71	1	1.000
2	6.88	2	0.500
3	8.25	3	0.333
4	9.52	4	0.250
5	9.81	5	0.200
6	11.43	6	0.167
7	11.09	7	0.143
8	10.87	8	0.125
9	12.15	9	0.111
10	10.94	10	0.100

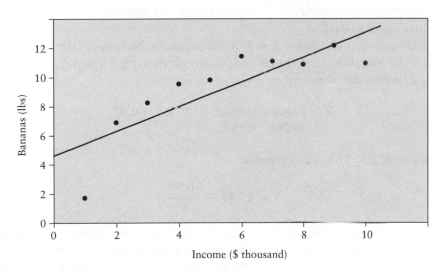

Figure 4.1 Regression of expenditure on bananas on income

significantly different from zero at the 1 percent level. Quite obviously, the observations lie on a curve, while the regression equation is of course a straight line. In this case, it is easy to see that the functional relationship between Y and X has been misspecified. In the case of multiple regression analysis, nonlinearity might be detected using the graphical technique described in Section 3.2. Alternatively, an examination of the residuals may be sufficient to indicate that something is wrong. In this case the residuals are as shown in Table 4.2.

The residuals ought to be randomly positive or negative, large or small. Instead, they start out being negative, cross to being positive, reach a maximum, fall again, and cross back to being negative: very suspicious indeed.

Table 4.2

Household	Y	$\hat{Y}$	e	Household	Y	$\hat{Y}$	e
1	1.71	5.46	−3.75	6	11.43	9.69	1.74
2	6.88	6.31	0.57	7	11.09	10.53	0.55
3	8.25	7.15	1.10	8	10.87	11.38	−0.51
4	9.52	8.00	1.52	9	12.15	12.22	−0.07
5	9.81	8.84	0.97	10	10.94	13.07	−2.13

The values of Y and X in this example were generated using the Monte Carlo technique, the true relationship being

$$Y = 12 - \frac{10}{X} + \text{disturbance term}, \tag{4.8}$$

X taking the numbers from 1 to 10 and the values of the disturbance term being obtained using normally distributed random numbers with zero mean and variance equal to 0.25.

If we realize this and define $Z = 1/X$, this equation becomes of the linear form (4.6). Z for each household has already been calculated in Table 4.1. Regressing Y on Z, we obtain (standard errors in parentheses)

$$\hat{Y} = 12.48 - 10.99Z \qquad R^2 = 0.97. \tag{4.9}$$
$$(0.26) \quad (0.65)$$

Substituting $Z = 1/X$, this becomes

$$\hat{Y} = 12.48 - \frac{10.99}{X}. \tag{4.10}$$

In view of the excellent fit obtained with (4.9), it is not surprising that (4.10) is close to the true equation (4.8). The regression relationship, together with the observations on Y, X, and Z, is shown in Figures 4.2 and 4.3. The improvement in the fit, as measured by R^2, is clear from a comparison of Figures 4.1 and 4.3.

4.2 Logarithmic transformations

Next we will tackle functions such as (4.3), which are nonlinear in parameters as well as variables:

$$Y = \beta_1 X^{\beta_2}. \tag{4.11}$$

When you see such a function, you can immediately say that the elasticity of Y with respect to X is constant and equal to β_2. This is easily demonstrated.

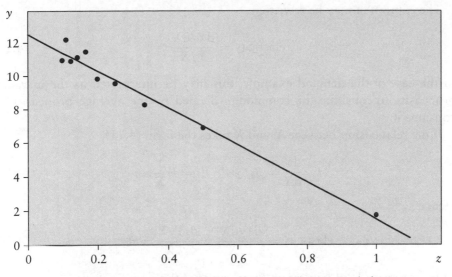

Figure 4.2 Regression of expenditure on bananas on the reciprocal of income

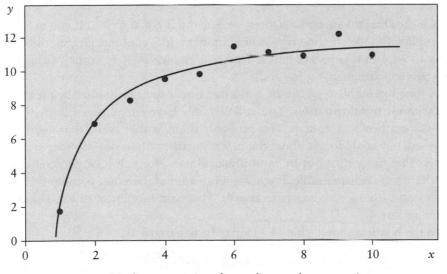

Figure 4.3 Nonlinear regression of expenditure on bananas on income

Regardless of the mathematical relationship connecting Y and X, or the definitions of Y and X, the elasticity of Y with respect to X is defined to be the proportional change in Y for a given proportional change in X:

$$\text{elasticity} = \frac{dY/Y}{dX/X}. \tag{4.12}$$

Thus, for example, if Y is demand and X is income, the expression defines the income elasticity of demand for the commodity in question.

The expression may be rewritten

$$\text{elasticity} = \frac{dY/dX}{Y/X}. \tag{4.13}$$

In the case of the demand example, this may be interpreted as the marginal propensity to consume the commodity divided by the average propensity to consume it.

If the relationship between Y and X takes the form (4.11),

$$\frac{dY}{dX} = \beta_1\beta_2 X^{\beta_2-1} = \beta_2 \frac{Y}{X}. \tag{4.14}$$

Hence

$$\text{elasticity} = \frac{dY/dX}{Y/X} = \frac{\beta_2 Y/X}{Y/X} = \beta_2. \tag{4.15}$$

Thus, for example, if you see an Engel curve of the form

$$Y = 0.01 X^{0.3} \tag{4.16}$$

this means that the income elasticity of demand is equal to 0.3. If you are trying to explain this to someone who is not familiar with economic jargon, the easiest way to explain it is to say that a 1 percent change in X (income) will cause a 0.3 percent change in Y (demand).

A function of this type can be converted into a linear equation by means of a **logarithmic transformation**. You will certainly have encountered logarithms in a basic mathematics course. You probably thought that when that course was finished, you could forget about them, writing them off as one of those academic topics that never turn out to be of practical use. No such luck. In econometric work they are indispensable. If you are unsure about their use, you should review your notes from that basic math course. The main properties of logarithms are given in Box 4.1.

In the box it is shown that (4.11) may be linearized as

$$\log Y = \log\beta_1 + \beta_2 \log X. \tag{4.17}$$

This is known as a **logarithmic model** or, alternatively, a **loglinear model**, referring to the fact that it is linear in logarithms. If we write $Y' = \log Y$, $Z = \log X$, and $\beta_1' = \log\beta_1$, the equation may be rewritten

$$Y' = \beta_1' + \beta_2 Z. \tag{4.18}$$

The regression procedure is now as follows. First calculate Y' and Z for each observation, taking the logarithms of the original data. Your regression application will almost certainly do this for you, given the appropriate instructions. Second, regress Y' on Z. The coefficient of Z will be a direct estimate of β_2.

BOX 4.1   Use of logarithms

First, some basic rules:

1. If $Y = XZ$, $\log Y = \log X + \log Z$
2. If $Y = X/Z$, $\log Y = \log X - \log Z$
3. If $Y = X^n$, $\log Y = n \log X$.

These rules can be combined to transform more complicated expressions. For example, take equation (5.11): if $Y = \beta_1 X^{\beta_2}$,

$$\log Y = \log \beta_1 + \log X^{\beta_2} \quad \text{using rule 1}$$
$$= \log \beta_1 + \beta_2 \log X \quad \text{using rule 3.}$$

Thus far we have not specified whether we are taking logarithms to base e or to base 10. Throughout this text we shall be using e as the base, and so we shall be using what are known as 'natural' logarithms. This is standard in econometrics. Purists sometimes write ln instead of log to emphasize that they are working with natural logarithms, but this is now unnecessary. Nobody uses logarithms to base 10 any more. They were tabulated in the dreaded log tables that were universally employed for multiplying or dividing large numbers until the early 1970s. When the pocket calculator was invented, they became redundant. They are not missed. With e as base, we can state another rule:

4. If $Y = e^X$, $\log Y = X$.

e^X, also sometimes written exp(X), is familiarly known as the antilog of X. One can say that $\log e^X$ is the log of the antilog of X, and since log and antilog cancel out, it is not surprising that $\log e^X$ turns out just to be X. Using rule 2 above, $\log e^X = X \log e = X$ since $\log e$ to base e is 1.

The constant term will be an estimate of β_1', that is, of $\log \beta_1$. To obtain an estimate of β_1, you have to take the antilog, that is, calculate $\exp(\beta_1')$.

Example: Engel curve

Figure 4.4 plots annual household expenditure on food eaten at home, *FDHO*, and total annual household expenditure, both measured in dollars, for 869 representative households in the United States in 1995, the data being taken from the Consumer Expenditure Survey.

When analysing household expenditure data, it is usual to relate types of expenditure to total household expenditure rather than income, the reason being that the relationship with expenditure tends to be more stable than that with income. The outputs from linear and logarithmic regressions are shown in Tables 4.3 and 4.4.

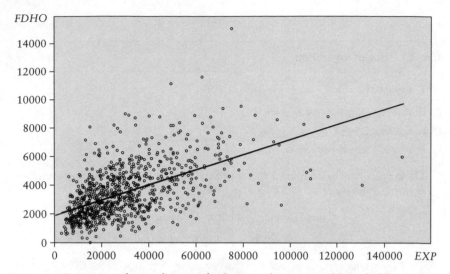

Figure 4.4 Regression of expenditure on food eaten at home on total household expenditure

Table 4.3

```
.reg FDHO EXP

   Source       SS           df        MS              Number of obs =     869
---------------------------------------------         F(1,867)      =  381.47
   Model    915843574         1      915843574         Prob > F      =  0.0000
Residual    2.0815e+09       867     2400831.16         R-squared     =  0.3055
---------------------------------------------         Adj R-squared =  0.3047
   Total    2.9974e+09       868     3453184.55         Root MSE      =  1549.5


------------------------------------------------------------------------------
    FDHO       Coef.    Std. Err.        t    P>|t|    [95% Conf.  Interval]
------------------------------------------------------------------------------
     EXP    .0528427    .0027055     19.531   0.000    .0475325    .0581529
   _cons    1916.143    96.54591     19.847   0.000    1726.652    2105.634
```

Table 4.4

```
.g LGFDHO = ln(FDHO)
.g LGEXP = ln(EXP)
.reg LGFDHO LGEXP

   Source       SS           df        MS              Number of obs =     868
---------------------------------------------         F(1,866)      =  396.06
   Model    84.4161692        1     84.4161692         Prob > F      =  0.0000
Residual    184.579612       866    .213140429         R-squared     =  0.3138
---------------------------------------------         Adj R-squared =  0.3130
   Total    268.995781       867    .310260416         Root MSE      =  .46167


------------------------------------------------------------------------------
  LGFDHO      Coef.   Std. Err.         t    P>|t|    [95% Conf.  Interval]
------------------------------------------------------------------------------
   LGEXP    .4800417   .0241212     19.901   0.000    .4326988    .5273846
   _cons    3.166271   .244297      12.961   0.000    2.686787    3.645754
```

The linear regression indicates that 5.3 cents out of the marginal dollar are spent on food eaten at home. Interpretation of the intercept is problematic because literally it implies that $1,916 would be spent on food eaten at home even if total expenditure were zero.

The logarithmic regression, shown in Figure 4.5, indicates that the elasticity of expenditure on food eaten at home with respect to total household expenditure is 0.48. Is this figure plausible? Yes, because food eaten at home is a necessity rather than a luxury, so one would expect the elasticity to be less than 1. The intercept has no economic meaning. Figure 4.6 plots the logarithmic regression line in the original diagram. While there is not much difference between the

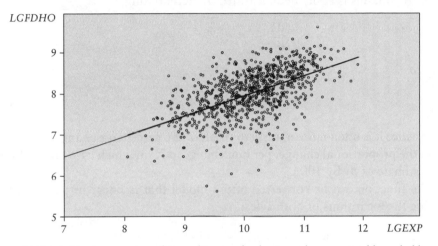

Figure 4.5 Logarithmic regression of expenditure on food eaten at home on total household expenditure

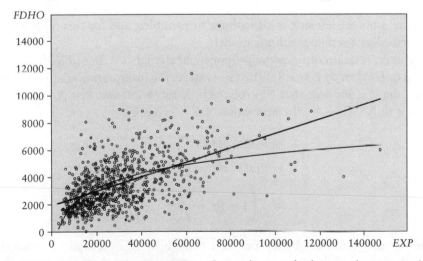

Figure 4.6 Linear and logarithmic regressions of expenditure on food eaten at home on total household expenditure

regression lines over the middle part of the range of observations, it is clear that the logarithmic regression gives a better fit for very low and very high levels of household expenditure.

Semilogarithmic models

Another common functional form is given by equation (4.19):

$$Y = \beta_1 e^{\beta_2 X}. \tag{4.19}$$

Here β_2 should be interpreted as the proportional change in Y per *unit* change in X. Again, this is easily demonstrated. Differentiating,

$$\frac{dY}{dX} = \beta_1 \beta_2 e^{\beta_2 X} = \beta_2 Y. \tag{4.20}$$

Hence

$$\frac{dY/dX}{Y} = \beta_2. \tag{4.21}$$

In practice it is often more natural to speak of the percentage change in Y, rather than the proportional change, per unit change in X, in which case one multiplies the estimate of β_2 by 100.

The function can be converted into a model that is linear in parameters by taking the logarithms of both sides:

$$\begin{aligned} \log Y = \log \beta_1 e^{\beta_2 X} &= \log \beta_1 + \log e^{\beta_2 X} \\ &= \log \beta_1 + \beta_2 X \log e \\ &= \log \beta_1 + \beta_2 X. \end{aligned} \tag{4.22}$$

Note that only the left side is logarithmic in variables, and for this reason (4.22) is described as a semilogarithmic model.

The interpretation of β_2 as the proportional change in Y per *unit* change in X is valid only when β_2 is small. When β_2 is large, the interpretation may be a little more complex. Suppose that Y is related to X by (4.19) and that X increases by one unit to X'. Then Y', the new value of Y is given by

$$\begin{aligned} Y' = \beta_1 e^{\beta_2 X'} &= \beta_1 e^{\beta_2 (X+1)} \\ &= \beta_1 e^{\beta_2 X} e^{\beta_2} = Y e^{\beta_2} \\ &= Y \left(1 + \beta_2 + \frac{\beta_2^2}{2!} + \cdots \right). \end{aligned} \tag{4.23}$$

Thus the proportional change per unit change in X is actually greater than β_2. However, if β_2 is small (say, less than 0.1), β_2^2 and further terms will be very small and can be neglected. In that case, the right side of the equation simplifies to $Y(1 + \beta_2)$ and the original marginal interpretation of β_2 still applies.

Example: semilogarithmic earnings function

For fitting earnings functions, the semilogarithmic model is generally considered to be superior to the linear model. We will start with the simplest possible version:

$$EARNINGS = \beta_1 e^{\beta_2 S}, \qquad (4.24)$$

where $EARNINGS$ is hourly earnings, measured in dollars, and S is years of schooling. After taking logarithms, the model becomes

$$LGEARN = \beta_1' + \beta_2 S \qquad (4.25)$$

where $LGEARN$ is the natural logarithm of $EARNINGS$ and β_1' is the logarithm of β_1.

The model was fitted using $EAEF$ Data Set 21, with the output shown in Table 4.5. The coefficient of S indicates that every extra year of schooling increases earnings by a proportion 0.110, that is, 11.0 percent, as a first approximation. Strictly speaking, a whole extra year of schooling is not marginal, so it would be more accurate to calculate $e^{0.110}$, which is 1.116. Thus a more accurate interpretation is that an extra year of schooling raises earnings by 11.6 percent.

The scatter diagram for the semilogarithmic regression is shown in Figure 4.7. For the purpose of comparison, it is plotted together with the linear regression in a plot with the untransformed variables in Figure 4.8. The two regression lines do not differ greatly in their overall fit, but the semilogarithmic specification has the advantages of not predicting negative earnings for individuals with low levels of schooling and of allowing the increase in earnings per year of schooling to increase with schooling.

Table 4.5

```
.reg LGEARN S

      Source        SS         df        MS              Number of obs =     540
                                                          F(1,538)      =  140.05
      Model    38.5643833        1    38.5643833          Prob > F      =  0.0000
   Residual    148.14326       538    .275359219          R-squared     =  0.2065
                                                          Adj R-squared =  0.2051
      Total    186.707643      539    .34639637           Root MSE      =  .52475


     LGEARN       Coef.   Std. Err.           t    P>|t|    [95% Conf. Interval]

          S    .1096934   .0092691        11.83    0.000    .0914853    .1279014
      _cons    1.292241   .1287252        10.04    0.000    1.039376    1.545107
```

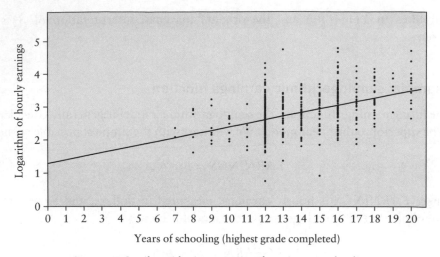

Figure 4.7 Semilogarithmic regression of earnings on schooling

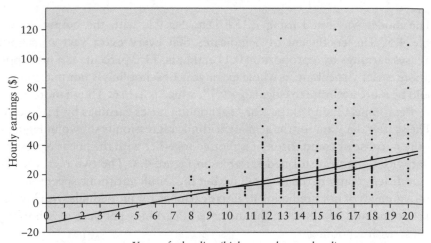

Figure 4.8 Linear and semilogarithmic regressions of earnings on schooling

Exercises

Note: For all of these exercises, you should discuss the plausibility of the estimated coefficients.

4.1 Download the *CES* data set from the website (see Appendix B) and fit linear and logarithmic regressions for your commodity on *EXP*, total household expenditure, excluding observations with zero expenditure on your commodity. Interpret the regressions and perform appropriate tests.

4.2 Repeat the logarithmic regression in Exercise 4.1, adding the logarithm of the size of the household as an additional explanatory variable. Interpret the results and perform appropriate tests.

4.3 What is the relationship between weight and height? Using your *EAEF* data set, regress the (natural) logarithm of *WEIGHT85* on the logarithm of *HEIGHT*. Interpret the regression results and perform appropriate tests.

4.4 Using your *EAEF* data set, regress the logarithm of earnings on *S* and *EXP*. Interpret the regression results and perform appropriate tests.

4.5* Download from the website (see Appendix B) the OECD data set on employment growth rates and GDP growth rates tabulated in Exercise 1.1, plot a scatter diagram and investigate whether a nonlinear specification might be superior to a linear one.

4.3　The disturbance term

Thus far, nothing has been said about how the disturbance term is affected by these transformations. Indeed, in the discussion above it has been left out altogether.

The fundamental requirement is that the disturbance term should appear in the transformed equation as an additive term $(+u)$ that satisfies the regression model conditions. If it does not, the least squares regression coefficients will not have the usual properties, and the tests will be invalid.

For example, it is highly desirable that (4.6) should be of the form

$$Y = \beta_1 + \beta_2 Z + u \tag{4.26}$$

when we take the random effect into account. Working backwards, this implies that the original (untransformed) equation should be of the form

$$Y = \beta_1 + \frac{\beta_2}{X} + u. \tag{4.27}$$

In this particular case, if it is true that in the original equation the disturbance term is additive and satisfies the regression model conditions, it will also be true in the transformed equation. No problem here.

What happens when we start off with a model such as

$$Y = \beta_1 X_2^{\beta_2}. \tag{4.28}$$

As we have seen, the regression model, after linearization by taking logarithms, is

$$\log Y = \log \beta_1 + \beta_2 \log X + u \tag{4.29}$$

when the disturbance term is included. Working back to the original equation, this implies that (4.13) should be rewritten

$$Y = \beta_1 X_2^{\beta_2} v \tag{4.30}$$

where v and u are related by $\log v = u$. Hence to obtain an additive disturbance term in the regression equation for this model, we must start with a multiplicative disturbance term in the original equation.

The disturbance term v modifies $\beta_1 X_2^{\beta_2}$ by increasing it or reducing it by a random *proportion*, rather than by a random amount. Note that $u = 0$ when $\log v = 0$, which occurs when $v = 1$. The random factor will be zero in the estimating equation (4.28) if v happens to be equal to 1. This makes sense, since if v is equal to 1 it is not modifying $\beta_1 X_2^{\beta_2}$ at all.

For the t tests and the F tests to be valid, u must be normally distributed. This means that $\log v$ must be normally distributed, which will occur only if v is lognormally distributed.

What would happen if we assumed that the disturbance term in the original equation was additive, instead of multiplicative?

$$Y = \beta_1 X_2^{\beta_2} + u. \tag{4.31}$$

The answer is that when you take logarithms, there is no mathematical way of simplifying $\log\left(\beta_1 X_2^{\beta_2} + u\right)$. The transformation does not lead to a linearization. You would have to use a nonlinear regression technique, for example, of the type discussed in the next section.

Example

The central limit theorem suggests that the disturbance term should have a normal distribution. It can be demonstrated that if the disturbance term has a normal distribution, so also will the residuals, provided that the regression equation is correctly specified. An examination of the distribution of the residuals thus provides indirect evidence of the adequacy of the specification of a regression model. Figure 4.9 shows the residuals from linear and semilogarithmic regressions of *EARNINGS* on *S* using *EAEF* Data Set 21, standardized so that they have standard deviation equal to 1, for comparison. The distribution of the residuals from the linear specification is right skewed, while that for the residuals from the semilogarithmic specification is much closer to a normal distribution. This suggests that the semilogarithmic specification is preferable.

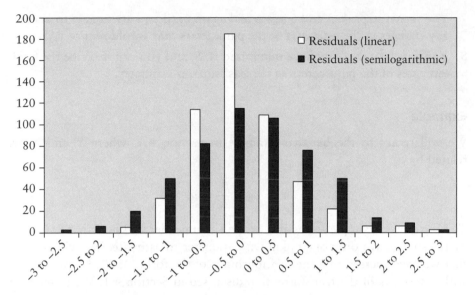

Figure 4.9 Standardized residuals from earnings function regressions

4.4 Nonlinear regression

Suppose you believe that a variable Y depends on a variable X according to the relationship

$$Y = \beta_1 + \beta_2 X^{\beta_3} + u, \tag{4.32}$$

and you wish to obtain estimates of β_1, β_2, and β_3 given data on Y and X. There is no way of transforming (4.32) to obtain a linear relationship, and so it is not possible to apply the usual regression procedure.

Nevertheless, one can still use the principle of minimizing the sum of the squares of the residuals to obtain estimates of the parameters. We will describe a simple **nonlinear regression algorithm** that uses the principle. It consists of a series of repeated steps:

1. You start by guessing plausible values for the parameters.

2. You calculate the predicted values of Y from the data on X, using these values of the parameters.

3. You calculate the residual for each observation in the sample, and hence RSS, the sum of the squares of the residuals.

4. You then make small changes in one or more of your estimates of the parameters.

5. You calculate the new predicted values of Y, residuals, and RSS.

6. If RSS is smaller than before, your new estimates of the parameters are better than the old ones and you take them as your new starting point.

7. You repeat steps 4, 5 and 6 again and again until you are unable to make any changes in the estimates of the parameters that would reduce *RSS*.

8. You conclude that you have minimized *RSS*, and you can describe the final estimates of the parameters as the least squares estimates.

Example

We will return to the bananas example in Section 4.1, where Y and X are related by

$$Y = \beta_1 + \frac{\beta_2}{X} + u. \tag{4.33}$$

To keep things as simple as possible, we will assume that we know that β_1 is equal to 12, so we have only one unknown parameter to estimate. We will suppose that we have guessed that the relationship is of the form (4.33), but we are too witless to think of the transformation discussed in Section 4.1. We instead use nonlinear regression.

Figure 4.10 shows the value of *RSS* that would result from any choice of b_2, given the values of Y and X in Table 4.1. Suppose we started off with a guess of -6.0 for b_2. Our provisional equation would be

$$Y = 12 - \frac{6}{X}. \tag{4.34}$$

We would calculate the predicted values of Y and the residuals, and from the latter calculate a value of 29.17 for *RSS*.

Next we try $b_2 = -7$. *RSS* is now 18.08, which is lower. We are going in the right direction. So we next try $b_2 = -8$. *RSS* is 10.08. We keep going. Putting

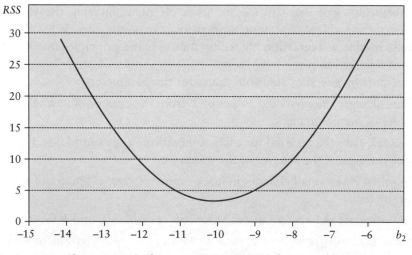

Figure 4.10 Nonlinear regression, *RSS* as a function of b_2

Table 4.6

b_2	RSS	b_2	RSS	b_2	RSS	b_2	RSS
−6	29.17	−10.8	4.19	−10.1	3.38	−10.06	3.384
−7	18.08	−10.7	3.98	−10.0	3.393	−10.07	3.384
−8	10.08	−10.6	3.80	−10.01	3.391	−10.08	3.383
−9	5.19	−10.5	3.66	−10.02	3.389	−10.09	3.384
−10	3.39	−10.4	3.54	−10.03	3.387		
−11	4.70	−10.3	3.46	−10.04	3.386.		
−10.9	4.43	−10.2	3.41	−10.05	3.385		

$b_2 = -9$, RSS is 5.19. Putting $b_2 = -10$, RSS is 3.39. Putting $b_2 = -11$, RSS is 4.70.

Clearly with $b_2 = -11$ we have overshot, because RSS has started rising again. We start moving backwards, but with smaller steps, say 0.1, trying −10.9, −10.8, etc. We keep moving backwards until we overshoot again, and then start moving forwards, with even smaller steps, say 0.01. Each time we overshoot, we reverse direction, cutting the size of the step. We continue doing this until we have achieved the desired accuracy in the calculation of the estimate of β_2. Table 4.6 shows the steps in this example.

The process shown in Table 4.6 was terminated after 25 iterations, by which time it is clear that the estimate, to two decimal places, is −10.08. Obviously, greater precision would have been obtained by continuing the iterative process further.

Note that the estimate is not exactly the same as the estimate obtained in equation (4.9), which was −10.99. In principle the two sets of results should be identical, because both are minimizing the sum of the squares of the residuals. The discrepancy is caused by the fact that we have cheated slightly in the nonlinear case. We have assumed that β_1 is equal to its true value, 12, instead of estimating it. If we had really failed to spot the transformation that allows us to use linear regression analysis, we would have had to use a nonlinear technique hunting for the best values of b_1 and b_2 simultaneously, and the final values of b_1 and b_2 would have been 12.48 and −10.99, respectively, as in equation (4.9).

In practice, the algorithms used for minimizing the residual sum of squares in a nonlinear model are mathematically far more sophisticated than the simple trial-and-error method described above. Nevertheless, until fairly recently a major problem with the fitting of nonlinear regressions was that it was very slow compared with linear regression, especially when there were several parameters to be estimated, and the high computing cost discouraged the use of nonlinear regression. This has changed as the speed and power of computers have increased. As a consequence, more interest is being taken in the technique and some regression applications now incorporate user-friendly nonlinear regression features.

4.5 Comparing linear and logarithmic specifications

The possibility of fitting nonlinear models, either by means of a linearizing transformation or by the use of a nonlinear regression algorithm, greatly increases the flexibility of regression analysis, but it also makes model specification more complex. You have to ask yourself whether you should start off with a linear relationship or a nonlinear one, and if the latter, what kind.

A graphical inspection, using the Frisch–Waugh–Lovell technique described in Section 3.2 in the case of multiple regression analysis, might help you decide. In the illustration in Section 4.1, it was obvious that the relationship was nonlinear, and it should not have taken much effort to discover that an equation of the form (4.2) would give a good fit. Usually, however, the issue is not so clear-cut. It often happens that several different nonlinear forms might approximately fit the observations if they lie on a curve.

When considering alternative models with the same specification of the dependent variable, the selection procedure is straightforward. The most sensible thing to do is to run regressions based on alternative plausible functions and choose the function that explains the greatest proportion of the variation in the dependent variable. If two or more functions are more or less equally good, you should present the results of each. Looking again at the illustration in Section 4.1, you can see that the linear function explained 69 percent of the variation in Y, whereas the hyperbolic function (4.2) explained 97 percent. In this instance we have no hesitation in choosing the latter.

However, when alternative models employ different functional forms for the dependent variable, the problem of model selection becomes more complicated because you cannot make direct comparisons of R^2 or the sum of the squares of the residuals. In particular—and this is the most common example of the problem—you cannot compare these statistics for linear and logarithmic dependent variable specifications.

For example, in Section 1.6, the linear regression of earnings on schooling has an R^2 of 0.173, and RSS is 92,689. For the semilogarithmic version in Section 4.2, the corresponding figures are 0.207 and 148. RSS is much smaller for the logarithmic version, but this means nothing at all. The values of $LGEARN$ are much smaller than those of $EARNINGS$, so it is hardly surprising that the residuals are also much smaller. Admittedly R^2 is unit-free, but it is referring to different concepts in the two equations. In one equation it is measuring the proportion of the variation in earnings explained by the regression, and in the other it is measuring the proportion of the variation in the logarithm of earnings explained. If R^2 is much greater for one model than for the other, you would probably be justified in selecting it without further fuss. But if R^2 is similar for the two models, simple eyeballing will not do.

One procedure under these circumstances, based on Box and Cox (1964), is to scale the observations on Y so that the residual sums of squares in the linear and logarithmic models are rendered directly comparable. The procedure has the following steps:

1. You calculate the geometric mean of the values of Y in the sample. This is equal to the exponential of the mean of $\log Y$, so it is easy to calculate:

$$e^{\frac{1}{n}\sum \log Y_i} = e^{\frac{1}{n}\log(Y_1 \times \cdots \times Y_n)} = e^{\log(Y_1 \times \cdots \times Y_n)^{\frac{1}{n}}}$$

$$= (Y_1 \times \cdots \times Y_n)^{\frac{1}{n}}. \tag{4.35}$$

2. You scale the observations on Y by dividing by this figure. So

$$Y_i^* = Y_i / \text{geometric mean of } Y, \tag{4.36}$$

where Y_i^* is the scaled value in observation i.

3. You then regress the linear model using Y^* instead of Y as the dependent variable, and the logarithmic model using $\log Y^*$ instead of $\log Y$, but otherwise leaving the models unchanged. The residual sums of squares of the two regressions are now comparable, and the model with the lower sum provides the better fit.

Table 4.7

```
.gen EARNSTAR = EARNINGS/16.3135
.gen LGEARNST = ln(EARNSTAR)
.reg EARNSTAR S EXP
```

Source	SS	df	MS			Number of obs =	540
						F(2,537) =	67.54
Model	84.5963381	2	42.298169			Prob > F =	0.0000
Residual	336.288615	537	.626235783			R-squared =	0.2010
						Adj R-squared =	0.1980
Total	420.884953	539	.780862622			Root MSE =	.79135

EARNSTAR	Coef.	Std. Err.	t	P>|t|	[95% Conf.	Interval]
S	.1641662	.0143225	11.46	0.000	.1360312	.1923011
EXP	.0344765	.0078777	4.38	0.000	.0190015	.0499515
_cons	−1.623503	.2619003	−6.20	0.000	−2.137977	−1.109028

```
.reg LGEARNST S EXP
```

Source	SS	df	MS			Number of obs =	540
						F(2,537) =	100.86
Model	50.9842589	2	25.4921295			Prob > F =	0.0000
Residual	135.72339	537	.252743742			R-squared =	0.2731
						Adj R-squared =	0.2704
Total	186.707649	539	.346396379			Root MSE =	.50274

LGEARNST	Coef.	Std. Err.	t	P>|t|	[95% Conf.	Interval]
S	.1235911	.0090989	13.58	0.000	.1057173	.141465
EXP	.0350826	.0050046	7.01	0.000	.0252515	.0449137
_cons	2.282673	.1663823	−13.72	0.000	−2.609513	−1.955833

Note that the scaled regressions are solely for deciding which model you prefer. You should *not* pay any attention to their coefficients, only to their residual sums of squares. You obtain the coefficients by fitting the unscaled version of the preferred model.

Example

The comparison will be made for the alternative specifications of the earnings function. The mean value of *LGEARN* is 2.7920. The scaling factor is therefore $\exp(2.7920) = 16.3135$. Table 4.7 begins with commands for generating *EARNSTAR*, the scaled version of *EARNINGS*, and its logarithm, *LGEARNST*. *EARNSTAR* is then regressed on *S* and *EXP*. The residual sum of squares is 336.29. The corresponding regression of *LGEARNST* on *S* and *EXP* follows. The residual sum of squares is 135.72. Hence in this case the semilogarithmic specification appears to provide the better fit.

Key terms

elasticity

linear in parameters

linear in variables

logarithmic model

logarithmic transformation

loglinear model

nonlinear regression algorithm

semilogarithmic model

Exercises

4.6 Using your *EAEF* data set, evaluate whether the dependent variable of an earnings function should be linear or logarithmic. Calculate the geometric mean of *EARNINGS* by taking the exponential of the mean of *LGEARN*. Define *EARNSTAR* by dividing *EARNINGS* by this quantity and calculate *LGEARNST* as its logarithm. Regress *EARNSTAR* and *LGEARNST* on *S* and *EXP* and compare the residual sums of squares.

4.7 Evaluate whether a linear or logarithmic specification of the dependent variable is preferable for the expenditure function for your commodity in the CES data set. *Note*: Drop households reporting no expenditure on your commodity.

5 Dummy Variables

It frequently happens that some of the factors that you would like to introduce into a regression model are qualitative in nature and therefore not measurable in numerical terms. Some examples are the following.

1. You are investigating the relationship between schooling and earnings, and you have both males and females in your sample. You would like to see if the sex of the respondent makes a difference.

2. You are investigating the relationship between income and expenditure in Belgium, and your sample includes both Flemish-speaking and French-speaking households. You would like to find out whether the ethnic difference is relevant.

3. You have data on the growth rate of GDP per capita and foreign aid per capita for a sample of developing countries, of which some are democracies and some are not. You would like to investigate whether the impact of foreign aid on growth is affected by the type of government.

In each of these examples, one solution would be to run separate regressions for the two categories and see if the coefficients are different. Alternatively, you could run a single regression using all the observations together, measuring the effect of the qualitative factor with what is known as a **dummy variable**. This has the two important advantages of providing a simple way of testing whether the effect of the qualitative factor is significant and, provided that certain assumptions are valid, making the regression estimates more efficient.

5.1 Illustration of the use of a dummy variable

We will illustrate the use of a dummy variable with a series of regressions investigating how the cost of running a secondary school varies with the number of students and the type of school. We will take as our starting point the model

$$COST = \beta_1 + \beta_2 N + u, \qquad (5.1)$$

where $COST$ is the annual recurrent expenditure incurred by a school and N is the number of students attending it. Fitting a regression to a sample of 74 secondary schools in Shanghai in the mid-1980s (for further information, see Appendix B), the Stata output is as shown in Table 5.1.

Table 5.1

```
.reg COST N
    Source        SS          df          MS              Number of obs =       74
                                                          F(1,72)       =    46.82
     Model    5.7974e+11       1      5.7974e+11          Prob > F      =   0.0000
                                                          R-squared     =   0.3940
  Residual    8.9160e+11      72      1.2383e+10          Adj R-squared =   0.3856
     Total    1.4713e+12      73      2.0155e+10          Root MSE      = 1.1e+05

      COST      Coef.    Std. Err.        t     P>|t|    [95% Conf.   Interval]

         N   339.0432    49.55144     6.842     0.000     240.2642    437.8222
     _cons    23953.3    27167.96     0.882     0.381    -30205.04    78111.65
```

The regression equation is thus (standard errors in parentheses)

$$\widehat{COST} = 24{,}000 + 339N \qquad R^2 = 0.39 \tag{5.2}$$
$$(27{,}000) \quad (50)$$

the cost being measured in yuan, one yuan being worth about 20 cents US at the time of the survey. The equation implies that the marginal cost per student is 339 yuan and that the annual overhead cost (administration and maintenance) is 24,000 yuan.

This is just the starting point. Next we will investigate the impact of the type of school on the cost. Occupational schools aim to provide skills for specific occupations and they tend to be relatively expensive to run because they need to maintain specialized workshops. We could model this by having two equations

$$COST = \beta_1 + \beta_2 N + u \tag{5.3}$$

and

$$COST = \beta_1' + \beta_2 N + u \tag{5.4}$$

the first equation relating to regular schools and the second to the occupational schools. Effectively, we are hypothesizing that the annual overhead cost is different for the two types of school, but the marginal cost is the same. The marginal cost assumption is not very plausible and we will relax it in due course. Let us define δ to be the difference in the intercepts: $\delta = \beta_1' - \beta_1$. Then $\beta_1' = \beta_1 + \delta$ and we can rewrite the cost function for occupational schools as

$$COST = \beta_1 + \delta + \beta_2 N + u. \tag{5.5}$$

The model is illustrated in Figure 5.1. The two lines show the relationship between the cost and the number of students, neglecting the disturbance term. The line for the occupational schools is the same as that for the regular schools, except that it has been shifted up by an amount δ.

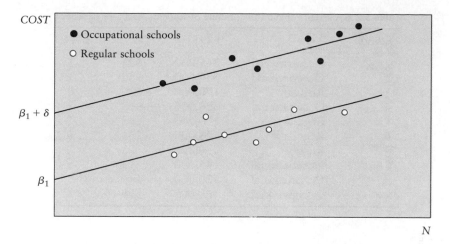

Figure 5.1 Cost functions for regular and occupational schools

The object of the present exercise is to estimate this unknown shift factor. To do this, we rewrite the model as

$$COST = \beta_1 + \delta OCC + \beta_2 N + u \qquad (5.6)$$

where OCC is a dummy variable, an artificial variable with two possible values, 0 and 1. If OCC is equal to 0, the cost function becomes (5.3), that for regular schools. If OCC is equal to 1, the cost function becomes (5.5), that for occupational schools. Hence, instead of two separate regressions for the different types of school, we can run just one regression using the whole sample. Using the whole sample in a single regression will reduce the population variances of the coefficients, and this should be reflected by smaller standard errors. We will also obtain a single estimate of β_2, instead of two separate ones that are likely to conflict. The price we have to pay is that we have to assume that β_2 is the same for both subsamples. We will relax this assumption in due course.

Data for the first 10 schools in the sample are shown in Table 5.2. Note how OCC varies with the type of school. Multiple regression is used to regress $COST$ on N and OCC. OCC is treated exactly like an ordinary variable, even though it consists only of 0s and 1s.

The Stata output in Table 5.3 gives the results of the regression, using the full sample of 74 schools. In equation form, we have (standard errors in parentheses)

$$\widehat{COST} = -34,000 + 133,000OCC + 331N \qquad R^2 = 0.62. \qquad (5.7)$$
$$(24,000) \quad (21,000) \qquad (40)$$

Table 5.2 Recurrent expenditure, number of students, and type of school

School	Type	COST	N	OCC
1	Occupational	345,000	623	1
2	Occupational	537,000	653	1
3	Regular	170,000	400	0
4	Occupational	526,000	663	1
5	Regular	100,000	563	0
6	Regular	28,000	236	0
7	Regular	160,000	307	0
8	Occupational	45,000	173	1
9	Occupational	120,000	146	1
10	Occupational	61,000	99	1

Table 5.3

```
.reg COST N OCC

    Source       SS         df       MS              Number of obs =      74
---------------------------------------------        F(2,71)       =   56.86
    Model    9.0582e+11      2    4.5291e+11          Prob > F      =  0.0000
 Residual    5.6553e+11     71    7.9652e+09          R-squared     =  0.6156
---------------------------------------------        Adj R-squared =  0.6048
    Total    1.4713e+12     73    2.0155e+10          Root MSE      =   89248

------------------------------------------------------------------------------
    COST      Coef.    Std. Err.       t    P>|t|    [95% Conf. Interval]
------------------------------------------------------------------------------
       N     331.4493   39.75844     8.337   0.000    252.1732    410.7254
     OCC     133259.1   20827.59     6.398   0.000    91730.06    174788.1
   _cons   -33612.55   23573.47    -1.426   0.158   -80616.71    13391.61
------------------------------------------------------------------------------
```

Putting OCC equal to 0 and 1, respectively, we can obtain the implicit cost functions for the two types of school:

$$\textit{Regular schools:} \qquad \widehat{COST} = -34,000 + 331N \qquad (5.8)$$

$$\textit{Occupational schools:} \quad \widehat{COST} = -34,000 + 133,000 + 331N$$

$$= 99,000 + 331N. \qquad (5.9)$$

The regression implies that the marginal cost per student per year is 331 yuan and that the annual overhead cost of a regular school is $-34,000$ yuan. Obviously having a negative intercept does not make any sense at all and it suggests that the model is misspecified in some way. We will come back to this later. The coefficient of the dummy variable, 133,000, is an estimate of the extra annual overhead cost of an occupational school. The marginal cost of an occupational school is the same as that for a regular school—it must be, given the model specification. Figure 5.2 shows the data and the cost functions derived from the regression results.

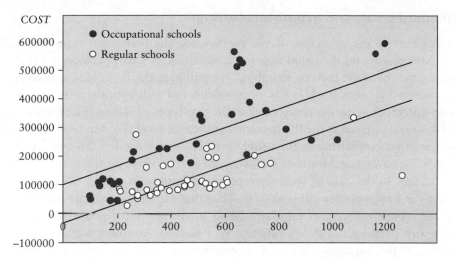

Figure 5.2 Cost functions for regular and occupational schools in Shanghai

---

BOX 5.1   Interpretation of dummy variable coefficients in logarithmic and semilogarithmic regressions

Suppose that the regression model is

$$\log Y = \beta_1 + \beta_2 \log X + \delta D + u$$

where D is a dummy variable and δ is its coefficient. Rewriting the model as

$$Y = e^{\beta_1 + \beta_2 \log X + \delta D + u} = e^{\beta_1} e^{\log X^{\beta_2}} e^{\delta D} e^u = e^{\beta_1} X^{\beta_2} e^{\delta D} e^u$$

it can be seen that the term $e^{\delta D}$ multiplies Y by e^0 when $D = 0$ for the reference category and e^δ when $D = 1$ for the other category. e^0 is of course 1, so the dummy variable has no effect on the reference category. For the other category where $D = 1$, the dummy variable multiplies Y by e^δ. If δ is small, e^δ is approximately equal to $(1 + \delta)$, implying that Y is a proportion δ greater for the other category than for the reference category. If δ is not small, the proportional difference is $(e^\delta - 1)$.

A semilogarithmic model

$$\log Y = \beta_1 + \beta_2 X + \delta D + u$$

can be rewritten

$$Y = e^{\beta_1 + \beta_2 X + \delta D + u} = e^{\beta_1} e^{\beta_2 X} e^{\delta D} e^u$$

The effect of the dummy variable and the interpretation of its coefficient are the same as in the logarithmic model.

Standard errors and hypothesis testing

In addition to the estimates of the coefficients, the regression results include standard errors and the usual diagnostic statistics. We will perform a t test on the coefficient of the dummy variable. Our null hypothesis is $H_0: \delta = 0$ and our alternative hypothesis is $H_1: \delta \neq 0$. In words, our null hypothesis is that there is no difference in the overhead costs of the two types of school. The t statistic is 6.40, so it is rejected at the 0.1 percent significance level. We can perform t tests on the other coefficients in the usual way. The t statistic for the coefficient of N is 8.34, so we conclude that the marginal cost is (very) significantly different from zero. In the case of the intercept, the t statistic is -1.43, so we do not reject the null hypothesis $H_0: \beta_1 = 0$. Thus one explanation of the nonsensical negative overhead cost of regular schools might be that they do not actually have any overheads and our estimate is a random number. A more realistic version of this hypothesis is that β_1 is positive but small (as you can see, the 95 percent confidence interval includes positive values) and the disturbance term is responsible for the negative estimate. As already noted, a further possibility is that the model is misspecified in some way.

Exercises

5.1 Does the sex of an individual affect educational attainment? Using your *EAEF* data set, regress S on *ASVABC*, *SM*, *SF* and *MALE*, a dummy variable that is 1 for male respondents and 0 for female ones. Interpret the coefficients and perform t tests. Is there any evidence that the educational attainment of males is different from that of females?

5.2* The Stata output shows the result of regressing weight on height, first with a linear specification, then with a logarithmic one, including a dummy variable *MALE*, defined as in Exercise 5.1, in both cases. Give an interpretation of the equations and perform appropriate statistical tests. See Box 5.1 for a guide to the interpretation of dummy variable coefficients in logarithmic regressions.

```
. reg WEIGHT85 HEIGHT MALE

      Source        SS          df        MS              Number of obs =     540
-----------------------------------------------           F(2,537)      =  191.56
       Model    273040.775       2    136520.388          Prob > F      =  0.0000
    Residual    382702.973      537    712.668479          R-squared     =  0.4164
-----------------------------------------------           Adj R-squared =  0.4142
       Total    655743.748      539    1216.59322          Root MSE      =  26.696

-------------------------------------------------------------------------------
    WEIGHT85      Coef.    Std. Err.       t      P>|t|     [95% Conf. Interval]
-------------------------------------------------------------------------------
      HEIGHT    4.006225   .3971644     10.09    0.000     3.226039    4.786412
        MALE    13.7615    3.363568      4.09    0.000     7.154131   20.36886
       _cons   -121.2502   25.70087     -4.72    0.000    -171.7367  -70.76363
-------------------------------------------------------------------------------
```

```
.reg LGWEIGHT LGHEIGHT MALE

   Source  |      SS        df       MS              Number of obs =     540
-----------+------------------------------           F(2,537)      =  224.03
    Model  | 11.3390838      2   5.66954189           Prob > F      =  0.0000
 Residual  | 13.5897932    537   .025306877           R-squared     =  0.4549
-----------+------------------------------           Adj R-squared =  0.4528
    Total  |  24.928877    539   .046250236           Root MSE      = .15908

------------------------------------------------------------------------------
 LGWEIGHT  |     Coef.   Std. Err.       t     P>|t|    [95% Conf. Interval]
-----------+------------------------------------------------------------------
 LGHEIGHT  |  1.675851   .1581459     10.60    0.000     1.36519    1.986511
     MALE  |  .0975722   .0199191      4.90    0.000    .0584432    .1367012
    _cons  | -2.077515   .6590635     -3.15    0.002   -3.372173    -.782856
------------------------------------------------------------------------------
```

5.3 Using your *EAEF* data set, regress *LGEARN* on *S*, *EXP*, and *MALE*. Interpret the coefficients and perform *t* tests. See Box 5.1 for a guide to the interpretation of dummy variable coefficients in semilogarithmic regressions.

5.2 Extension to more than two categories and to multiple sets of dummy variables

In the previous section we used a dummy variable to differentiate between regular and occupational schools when fitting a cost function. In fact there are two types of regular secondary school in Shanghai. There are general schools, which provide the usual academic education, and vocational schools. As their name implies, the vocational schools are meant to impart occupational skills as well as give an academic education. However, the vocational component of the curriculum is typically quite small and the schools are similar to the general schools. Often they are just general schools with a couple of workshops added. Likewise, there are two types of occupational school. There are technical schools training technicians and skilled workers' schools training craftsmen.

Thus now the qualitative variable has four categories and we need to develop a more elaborate set of dummy variables. The standard procedure is to choose one category as the reference category to which the basic equation applies, and then to define dummy variables for each of the other categories. In general it is good practice to select the dominant or most normal category, if there is one, as the reference category. In the Shanghai sample it is sensible to choose the general schools. They are the most numerous and the other schools are variations of them.

Accordingly we will define dummy variables for the other three types. *TECH* will be the dummy variable for the technical schools: *TECH* is equal to 1 if the observation relates to a technical school, 0 otherwise. Similarly we will define dummy variables *WORKER* and *VOC* for the skilled workers' schools and the

Table 5.4 Recurrent expenditure, number of students, and type of school

School	Type	COST	N	TECH	WORKER	VOC
1	Technical	345,000	623	1	0	0
2	Technical	537,000	653	1	0	0
3	General	170,000	400	0	0	0
4	Skilled workers'	526,000	663	0	1	0
5	General	100,000	563	0	0	0
6	Vocational	28,000	236	0	0	1
7	Vocational	160,000	307	0	0	1
8	Technical	45,000	173	1	0	0
9	Technical	120,000	146	1	0	0
10	Skilled workers'	61,000	99	0	1	0

Table 5.5

```
.reg COST N TECH WORKER VOC

    Source        SS         df        MS              Number of obs =      74
------------------------------------------------       F(4,69)      =   29.63
     Model   9.2996e+11       4    2.3249e+11          Prob > F     =  0.0000
  Residual   5.4138e+11      69    7.8461e+09          R-squared    =  0.6320
------------------------------------------------       Adj R-squared =  0.6107
     Total   1.4713e+12      73    2.0155e+10          Root MSE     =  88578
------------------------------------------------------------------------------
      COST      Coef.    Std. Err.        t    P>|t|    [95% Conf. Interval]
------------------------------------------------------------------------------
         N    342.6335    40.2195      8.519   0.000    262.3978    422.8692
      TECH    154110.9   26760.41      5.759   0.000    100725.3    207496.4
    WORKER    143362.4    27852.8      5.147   0.000    87797.57    198927.2
       VOC    53228.64   31061.65      1.714   0.091   -8737.646    115194.9
     _cons   -54893.09   26673.08     -2.058   0.043   -108104.4   -1681.748
```

vocational schools. The regression model is now

$$COST = \beta_1 + \delta_T TECH + \delta_W WORKER + \delta_V VOC + \beta_2 N + u \qquad (5.10)$$

where δ_T, δ_W, and δ_V are coefficients that represent the extra overhead costs of the technical, skilled workers', and vocational schools, relative to the cost of a general school. Note that you do not include a dummy variable for the reference category, and that is the reason why the reference category is often described as the **omitted category**. Note that we do not make any prior assumption about the size, or even the sign, of the δ coefficients. They will be estimated from the sample data.

Table 5.4 gives the data for the first 10 of the 74 schools. Note how the values of the dummy variables *TECH*, *WORKER*, and *VOC* are determined by the type of school in each observation.

The Stata output in Table 5.5 gives the regression results for this model. In equation form, we have (standard errors in parentheses)

$$\widehat{COST} = -55{,}000 + 154{,}000 TECH + 143{,}000 WORKER$$
$$\qquad (27{,}000) \quad (27{,}000) \qquad\qquad (28{,}000)$$

$$+ 53{,}000 VOC + 343 N \qquad R^2 = 0.63. \qquad\qquad (5.11)$$
$$\quad (31{,}000) \qquad\quad (40)$$

The coefficient of N indicates that the marginal cost per student per year is 343 yuan. The constant indicates that the annual overhead cost of a general academic school is $-55{,}000$ yuan per year. Obviously this is nonsense and indicates that something is wrong with the model. The coefficients of $TECH$, $WORKER$, and VOC indicate that the overhead costs of technical, skilled workers', and vocational schools are 154,000 yuan, 143,000 yuan, and 53,000 yuan greater than the cost of a general school.

From this equation we can obtain the implicit cost functions for the four types of school. First, putting the three dummy variables equal to 0, we obtain the cost function for general schools:

General schools: $\qquad\qquad \widehat{COST} = -55{,}000 + 343N.$ $\qquad\qquad$ (5.12)

Next, putting $TECH$ equal to 1 and $WORKER$ and VOC to 0, we obtain the cost function for technical schools:

Technical schools: $\quad \widehat{COST} = -55{,}000 + 154{,}000 + 343N$
$$= 99{,}000 + 343N. \qquad\qquad (5.13)$$

And similarly we obtain the cost functions for skilled workers' and vocational schools:

Skilled workers' schools: $\quad \widehat{COST} = -55{,}000 + 143{,}000 + 343N$
$$= 88{,}000 + 343N \qquad\qquad (5.14)$$

Vocational schools: $\quad \widehat{COST} = -55{,}000 + 53{,}000 + 343N$
$$= -2{,}000 + 343N. \qquad\qquad (5.15)$$

Note that in each case the annual marginal cost per student is estimated at 343 yuan. The model specification assumes that this figure does not differ according to type of school. The four cost functions are illustrated in Figure 5.3.

We can perform t tests on the coefficients in the usual way. The t statistic for N is 8.52, so the marginal cost is (very) significantly different from zero, as we would expect. The t statistic for the technical school dummy is 5.76, indicating that the annual overhead cost of a technical school is (very) significantly greater than that of a general school, again as expected. Similarly for skilled workers'

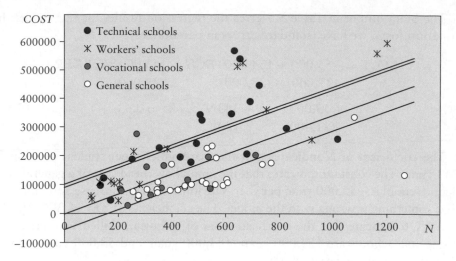

Figure 5.3 Cost functions for four types of school in Shanghai

schools, the t statistic being 5.15. In the case of vocational schools, however, the t statistic is only 1.71, indicating that the overhead cost of such a school is not significantly greater than that of a general school. This is not surprising, given that the vocational schools are not much different from the general schools. Note that the null hypotheses for the tests on the coefficients of the dummy variables are that the overhead costs of the other schools are not different from the overhead cost of a general school.

Joint explanatory power of a group of dummy variables

Finally, we will perform an F test of the joint explanatory power of the dummy variables as a group. The null hypothesis is H_0: $\delta_T = \delta_W = \delta_V = 0$. The alternative hypothesis H_1 is that at least one δ is different from zero. The residual sum of squares in the specification including the dummy variables is 5.41×10^{11}. (In the Stata output, it appears as 5.4138e+11. The e+11 means that the coefficient should be multiplied by 10^{11}.) The residual sum of squares in the original specification excluding the dummy variables was 8.92×10^{11} (see Section 5.1). The reduction in RSS when we include the dummies is therefore $(8.92 - 5.41) \times 10^{11}$. We will check whether this reduction is significant with the usual F test.

The numerator in the F ratio is the reduction in RSS divided by the cost, which is the three degrees of freedom given up when we estimate three additional coefficients (the coefficients of the dummies). The denominator is RSS for the specification including the dummy variables, divided by the number of degrees of freedom remaining after they have been added. The F ratio is therefore given by

$$F(3,69) = \frac{(8.9160 \times 10^{11} - 5.4138 \times 10^{11})/3}{5.4138 \times 10^{11}/69} = \frac{1.1674}{0.07846} = 14.9. \quad (5.16)$$

Note that the ratios were calculated to four significant figures. This will ensure that the F statistic will be correct to three significant figures. The critical value of $F(3, 69)$ will be a little below 6.17, the critical value for $F(3, 60)$ at the 0.1 percent significance level, so we can reject H_0 at this level. This is only to be expected because t tests showed that δ_T and δ_W were both significantly different from zero, and it is rare (but not impossible) for the F test not to reject H_0 when one or more coefficients are significant.

The dummy variable trap

What would happen if you included a dummy variable for the reference category? There would be two consequences. First, were it possible to compute regression coefficients, you would not be able to give them an interpretation. The coefficient b_1 is a basic estimate of the intercept, and the coefficients of the dummies are the estimates of the increase in the intercept from this basic level, but now there is no definition of what is basic, so the interpretation collapses. The other consequence is that the numerical procedure for calculating the regression coefficients will break down and the computer will simply send you an error message (or possibly, in sophisticated applications, drop one of the dummies for you). Suppose that there are m dummy categories and you define dummy variables $D_1, \ldots, D_m$. Then, in observation i, $\sum D_{ji} = 1$ because one of the dummy variables will be equal to 1 and all the others will be equal to 0. But the intercept β_1 is really the product of the parameter β_1 and a special variable whose value is 1 in all observations (see Box 3.1). Hence, for all observations, the sum of the dummy variables is equal to this special variable, and one has an exact linear relationship among the variables in the regression model. This is known as the **dummy variable trap**. As a consequence, the model is subject to a special case of exact multicollinearity, making it impossible to compute regression coefficients.

Change of reference category

The skilled workers' schools are considerably less academic than the others, even the technical schools. Suppose that we wish to investigate whether their costs are significantly different from the others. The easiest way to do this is to make them the reference category (omitted category). Then the coefficients of the dummy variables become estimates of the differences between the overhead costs of the other types of school and those of the skilled workers' schools. Since skilled workers' schools are now the reference category, we need a dummy variable, which will be called GEN, for the general academic schools. The model becomes

$$COST = \beta_1 + \delta_T TECH + \delta_V VOC + \delta_G GEN + \beta_2 N + u \qquad (5.17)$$

where δ_T, δ_V, and δ_G are the extra costs of technical, vocational, and general schools relative to skilled workers' schools. The data table for the first 10 schools is now as shown in Table 5.6. The Stata output is shown in Table 5.7.

The regression equation is therefore (standard errors in parentheses)

$$\widehat{COST} = 88,000 + 11,000TECH - 143,000GEN - 90,000VOC$$
$$(29,000) \quad (30,000) \qquad (28,000) \qquad (34,000)$$

$$+ 343N \qquad R^2 = 0.63. \qquad (5.18)$$
$$(40)$$

Table 5.6 Recurrent expenditure, enrolments and type of school

School	Type	COST	N	TECH	GEN	VOC
1	Technical	345,000	623	1	0	0
2	Technical	537,000	653	1	0	0
3	General	170,000	400	0	1	0
4	Skilled workers'	526,000	663	0	0	0
5	General	100,000	563	0	1	0
6	Vocational	28,000	236	0	0	1
7	Vocational	160,000	307	0	0	1
8	Technical	45,000	173	1	0	0
9	Technical	120,000	146	1	0	0
10	Skilled workers'	61,000	99	0	0	0

Table 5.7

```
.reg COST N TECH VOC GEN

   Source       SS          df        MS              Number of obs  =       74
                                                       F(4,69)        =    29.63
    Model    9.2996e+11      4     2.3249e+11          Prob > F       =   0.0000
                                                       R-squared      =   0.6320
 Residual    5.4138e+11     69     7.8461e+09
                                                       Adj R-squared  =   0.6107
    Total    1.4713e+12     73     2.0155e+10          Root MSE       =    88578


     COST      Coef.    Std. Err.        t     P>|t|    [95% Conf.    Interval]

        N    342.6335    40.2195      8.519    0.000     262.3978     422.8692
     TECH   10748.51    30524.87      0.352    0.726     -50146.93     71643.95
      VOC   -90133.74   33984.22     -2.652    0.010     -157930.4    -22337.07
      GEN   -143362.4   27852.8      -5.147    0.000     -198927.2    -87797.57
    _cons   88469.29    28849.56      3.067    0.003      30916.01     146022.6
```

From this equation we can again obtain the implicit cost functions for the four types of school. Putting all the dummy variables equal to 0, we obtain the cost function for skilled workers' schools:

$$\text{Skilled workers' schools:} \qquad \widehat{COST} = 88{,}000 + 343N. \qquad (5.19)$$

Then, putting *TECH*, *WORKER*, and *GEN* equal to 1 and the other two to 0, we derive the cost functions for the other types of school:

$$\text{Technical schools:} \qquad \widehat{COST} = 88{,}000 + 11{,}000 + 343N$$
$$= 99{,}000 + 343N \qquad (5.20)$$

$$\text{Vocational schools:} \qquad \widehat{COST} = 88{,}000 - 90{,}000 + 343N$$
$$= -2{,}000 + 343N \qquad (5.21)$$

$$\text{General schools:} \qquad \widehat{COST} = 88{,}000 - 143{,}000 + 343N$$
$$= -55{,}000 + 343N. \qquad (5.22)$$

Note that these equations are identical to those obtained when general schools were the reference category. The choice of omitted category does not affect the substance of the regression results. The only components that change are the standard errors and the interpretation of the t tests. R^2, the coefficients of the other variables, the t statistics for the other variables, and the F statistic for the equation as a whole do not alter. And of course the diagram representing the four cost functions is the same as before.

Multiple sets of dummy variables

It may happen that you wish to include more than one set of dummy variables in your regression equation. This is especially common when working with cross-sectional data, when you may have gathered data on a number of qualitative as well as quantitative characteristics. There is no problem in extending the use of dummy variables in this way, provided that the framework is defined clearly.

We will illustrate the procedure using the school cost data. Many of the occupational schools and some of the regular schools are residential. We will investigate the extra cost of running a residential school, controlling for number of students and type of school. To do this, we introduce a dummy variable, *RES*, which is equal to 1 for residential schools and 0 for the others. For the sake of simplicity we will revert to the occupational/regular classification of school type. The model now becomes

$$COST = \beta_1 + \delta OCC + \varepsilon RES + \beta_2 N + u \qquad (5.23)$$

where ε is the extra cost of a residential school. The reference category now has two dimensions, one for each qualitative characteristic. In this case it is a nonresidential ($RES = 0$), regular ($OCC = 0$) school. Table 5.8 presents the data for the first 10 schools in the sample. The second, fourth and seventh are residential schools and so RES is set equal to 1, while for the others it is 0.

The Stata regression results are shown in Table 5.9. The regression equation is therefore (standard errors in parentheses)

$$\widehat{COST} = -29{,}000 + 110{,}000 OCC + 58{,}000 RES + 322N$$
$$\quad\quad (23{,}000) \quad (24{,}000) \quad\quad (31{,}000) \quad\quad (39)$$
$$R^2 = 0.63. \quad\quad\quad\quad\quad\quad\quad\quad\quad\quad\quad (5.24)$$

Table 5.8 Recurrent expenditure, number of students, school type and whether residential

School	Type	COST	N	OCC	RES
1	Occupational, nonresidential	345,000	623	1	0
2	Occupational, residential	537,000	653	1	1
3	Regular, nonresidential	170,000	400	0	0
4	Occupational, residential	526,000	663	1	1
5	Regular, nonresidential	100,000	563	0	0
6	Regular, nonresidential	28,000	236	0	0
7	Regular, residential	160,000	307	0	1
8	Occupational, nonresidential	45,000	173	1	0
9	Occupational, nonresidential	120,000	146	1	0
10	Occupational, nonresidential	61,000	99	1	0

Table 5.9

```
.reg COST N OCC RES

      Source        SS          df        MS              Number of obs  =       74
                                                          F(3,70)        =    40.43
       Model    9.3297e+11       3     3.1099e+11         Prob > F       =   0.0000
                                                          R-squared      =   0.6341
    Residual    5.3838e+11      70     7.6911e+09         Adj R-squared  =   0.6184
                                                          Root MSE       =    87699
       Total    1.4713e+12      73     2.0155e+10


        COST      Coef.      Std. Err.        t      P>|t|     [95% Conf.   Interval]

           N    321.833     39.40225       8.168    0.000     243.2477     400.4183
         OCC   109564.6     24039.58       4.558    0.000     61619.15       157510
         RES   57909.01     30821.31       1.879    0.064    -3562.137     119380.2
       _cons  -29045.27     23291.54      -1.247    0.217    -75498.78     17408.25
```

Using the four combinations of *OCC* and *RES*, one may obtain the following subequations:

Regular, nonresidential: $\widehat{COST} = -29{,}000 + 322N$ (5.25)

Occupational, nonresidential: $\widehat{COST} = -29{,}000 + 110{,}000 + 322N$
$$= 81{,}000 + 322N \qquad (5.26)$$

Regular, residential: $\widehat{COST} = -29{,}000 + 58{,}000 + 322N$
$$= 29{,}000 + 322N \qquad (5.27)$$

Occupational, residential: $\widehat{COST} = -29{,}000 + 110{,}000 + 58{,}000$
$$+ 322N = 139{,}000 + 322N. \qquad (5.28)$$

The cost functions are illustrated in Figure 5.4. Note that the model incorporates the (plausible) assumption that the extra cost of a residential school is the same for regular and occupational schools.

The *t* statistic for the residential dummy is only 1.88. However, we can perform a one-sided test because it is reasonable to exclude the possibility that residential schools cost less to run than nonresidential ones, and so we can reject the null hypothesis of no difference in the costs at the 5 percent level.

The procedure may be generalized, with no limit on the number of qualitative characteristics in the model or the number of categories defined for each characteristic.

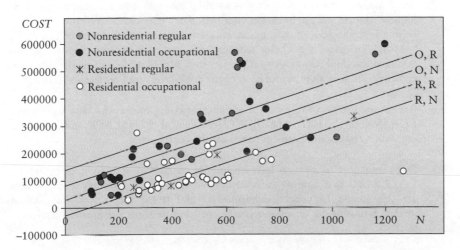

Figure 5.4 Cost functions for residential and nonresidential schools in Shanghai

Exercises

5.4 Does ethnicity affect educational attainment? In your *EAEF* data set you will find the following ethnic dummy variables:

ETHHISP   1 if hispanic, 0 otherwise
ETHBLACK   1 if black, 0 otherwise
ETHWHITE   1 if not hispanic or black, 0 otherwise.

Regress *S* on *ASVABC, MALE, SM, SF, ETHBLACK* and *ETHHISP*. (In this specification *ETHWHITE* has been chosen as the reference category, and so it is omitted.) Interpret the regression results and perform *t* tests on the coefficients.

5.5*

```
.reg LGEARN EDUCPROF EDUCMAST EDUCPHD EDUCBA

EDUCAA EDUCDO EXP MALE
```

Source	SS	df	MS		Number of obs	=	540
					F(8,531)	=	29.64
Model	57.6389757	8	7.20487196		Prob > F	=	0.0000
Residual	129.068668	531	.243067171		R-squared	=	0.3087
					Adj R-squared	=	0.2983
Total	186.707643	539	.34639637		Root MSE	=	.49302

LGEARN	Coef.	Std. Err.	t	P>|t|	[95% Conf.	Interval]
EDUCPROF	1.59193	.2498069	6.37	0.000	1.101199	2.082661
EDUCPHD	.3089521	.4943698	0.62	0.532	-.6622084	1.280113
EDUCMAST	.6280672	.0993222	6.32	0.000	.4329546	.8231798
EDUCBA	.5053643	.0561215	9.00	0.000	.3951168	.6156118
EDUCAA	.170838	.0765684	2.23	0.026	.0204238	.3212522
EDUCDO	-.2527803	.08179	-3.09	0.002	-.413452	-.0921085
EXP	.0230536	.0050845	4.53	0.000	.0130654	.0330419
MALE	.2755451	.0437642	6.30	0.000	.189573	.3615173
_cons	2.125885	.0915997	23.21	0.000	1.945943	2.305828

The Stata output shows the result of a semilogarithmic regression of earnings on highest educational qualification obtained, work experience, and the sex of the respondent, the educational qualifications being a professional degree, a PhD, a Master's degree, a Bachelor's degree, an Associate of Arts degree, and no qualification (high school drop-out). The high school diploma was the reference category. Provide an interpretation of the coefficients and perform *t* tests.

5.6 Are earnings subject to ethnic discrimination? Using your *EAEF* data set, regress *LGEARN* on *S, EXP, MALE, ETHHISP,* and *ETHBLACK*. Interpret the regression results and perform *t* tests on the coefficients.

5.7 Does belonging to a union have an impact on earnings? In the output below, *COLLBARG* is a dummy variable defined to be 1 for workers whose wages are determined by collective bargaining and 0 for the others. Provide an interpretation of the regression coefficients and perform appropriate statistical tests.

```
.reg LGEARN S EXP MALE COLLBARG

   Source        SS         df        MS              Number of obs =      540
------------------------------------------------              F(4,535)      =    64.84
   Model    60.9620285      4    15.2405071           Prob > F      =   0.0000
  Residual  125.745615     535    .235038532          R-squared     =   0.3265
------------------------------------------------              Adj R-squared =   0.3215
   Total    186.707643     539     .34639637          Root MSE      =   .48481

------------------------------------------------------------------------------
   LGEARN      Coef.    Std. Err.       t     P>|t|    [95% Conf. Interval]
------------------------------------------------------------------------------
        S     .1194004    .008798    13.57    0.000    .1021175    .1366832
      EXP     .0274958   .0049647     5.54    0.000    .0177431    .0372484
     MALE      .269056   .0429286     6.27    0.000    .1847267    .3533853
 COLLBARG     .0790935   .0536727     1.47    0.141   -.0263416    .1845287
    _cons     .5455149   .1606062     3.40    0.001    .2300187    .8610111
```

5.8 Evaluate whether the ethnicity dummies as a group have significant explanatory power for educational attainment by comparing the residual sums of squares in the regressions in Exercises 5.1 and 5.4.

5.9 Evaluate whether the ethnicity dummies as a group have significant explanatory power for earnings by comparing the residual sums of squares in the regressions in Exercises 5.3 and 5.6.

5.10 Repeat Exercise 5.4 making *ETHBLACK* the reference category. Evaluate the impact on the interpretation of the coefficients and the statistical tests.

5.11 Repeat Exercise 5.6 making *ETHBLACK* the reference category. Evaluate the impact on the interpretation of the coefficients and the statistical tests.

5.12 Repeat Exercise 5.3 including *FEMALE* as well as *MALE*. Regress *LGEARN* on *S*, *EXP*, *MALE*, and *FEMALE*. Discuss the regression results.

5.3 Slope dummy variables

We have so far assumed that the qualitative variables we have introduced into the regression model are responsible only for shifts in the intercept of the regression line. We have implicitly assumed that the slope of the regression line is the same for each category of the qualitative variables. This is not necessarily a plausible assumption, and we will now see how to relax it, and test it, using the device known as a slope dummy variable (also sometimes known as an interactive dummy variable).

To illustrate this, we will return to the school cost example. The assumption that the marginal cost per student is the same for occupational and regular schools is unrealistic because occupational schools incur expenditure on training materials related to the number of students and the staff–student ratio has to be

Table 5.10 Recurrent expenditure, number of students, and type of school

School	Type	COST	N	OCC	NOCC
1	Occupational	345,000	623	1	623
2	Occupational	537,000	653	1	653
3	Regular	170,000	400	0	0
4	Occupational	526,000	663	1	663
5	Regular	100,000	563	0	0
6	Regular	28,000	236	0	0
7	Regular	160,000	307	0	0
8	Occupational	45,000	173	1	173
9	Occupational	120,000	146	1	146
10	Occupational	61,000	99	1	99

higher in occupational schools because workshop groups cannot be, or at least should not be, as large as academic classes. We can relax the assumption by introducing the **slope dummy variable**, $NOCC$, defined as the product of N and OCC:

$$COST = \beta_1 + \delta OCC + \beta_2 N + \lambda NOCC + u. \tag{5.29}$$

If this is rewritten

$$COST = \beta_1 + \delta OCC + (\beta_2 + \lambda OCC)N + u, \tag{5.30}$$

it can be seen that the effect of the slope dummy variable is to allow the coefficient of N for occupational schools to be λ greater than that for regular schools. If OCC is 0, so is $NOCC$ and the equation becomes

$$COST = \beta_1 + \beta_2 N + u. \tag{5.31}$$

If OCC is 1, $NOCC$ is equal to N and the equation becomes

$$COST = \beta_1 + \delta + (\beta_2 + \lambda)N + u. \tag{5.32}$$

λ is thus the incremental marginal cost associated with occupational schools, in the same way that δ is the incremental overhead cost associated with them. Table 5.10 gives the data for the first 10 schools in the sample.

From the Stata output in Table 5.11 we obtain the regression equation (standard errors in parentheses)

$$\widehat{COST} = 51,000 - 4,000 OCC + 152N + 284 NOCC \quad R^2 = 0.68. \tag{5.33}$$
$$\phantom{\widehat{COST} = }(31,000) \ (41,000) (60) (76)$$

Putting OCC, and hence $NOCC$, equal to 0, we get the cost function for a regular school. We estimate that the annual overhead cost is 51,000 yuan and the annual marginal cost per student is 152 yuan:

$$Regular \ schools: \quad \widehat{COST} = 51,000 + 152N. \tag{5.34}$$

Table 5.11

```
. g NOCC = N*OCC

.reg COST N OCC NOCC

   Source        SS         df        MS              Number of obs  =      74
------------------------------------------            F(3,70)        =   49.64
    Model    1.0009e+12     3    3.3363e+11           Prob > F       =  0.0000
                                                      R-squared      =  0.6803
 Residual    4.7045e+11    70    6.7207e+09           Adj R-squared  =  0.6666
------------------------------------------            Root MSE       =   81980
    Total    1.4713e+12    73    2.0155e+10

---------------------------------------------------------------------------------
    COST       Coef.   Std. Err.         t    P>|t|   [95% Conf. Interval]
---------------------------------------------------------------------------------
       N    152.2982   60.01932     2.537    0.013    32.59349     272.003
     OCC   -3501.177   41085.46    -0.085    0.932   -85443.55    78441.19
    NOCC    284.4786   75.63211     3.761    0.000    133.6351    435.3221
   _cons    51475.25   31314.84     1.644    0.105   -10980.24    113930.7
```

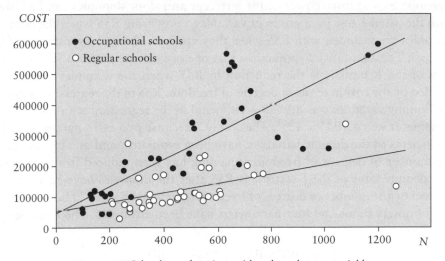

Figure 5.5 School cost functions with a slope dummy variable

Putting OCC equal to 1, and hence $NOCC$ equal to N, we estimate that the annual overhead cost of an occupational school is 47,000 yuan and the annual marginal cost per student is 436 yuan:

$$\textit{Occupational schools:} \quad \widehat{COST} = 51,000 - 4,000 + 152N + 284N$$
$$= 47,000 + 436N. \quad (5.35)$$

The two cost functions are shown in Figure 5.5. You can see that they fit the data much better than before and that the real difference is in the marginal cost, not the overhead cost. We can now see why we had a nonsensical negative estimate of the overhead cost of a regular school in previous specifications. The assumption of the same marginal cost led to an estimate of the marginal cost that was a compromise between the marginal costs of occupational and regular schools. The cost function for regular schools was too steep and as a consequence the intercept was underestimated, actually becoming negative and indicating that something must be wrong with the specification of the model.

We can perform t tests as usual. The t statistic for the coefficient of $NOCC$ is 3.76, so the marginal cost per student in an occupational school is significantly higher than that in a regular school. The coefficient of OCC is now negative, suggesting that the overhead cost of an occupational school is actually lower than that of a regular school. This is unlikely. However, the t statistic is only -0.09, so we do not reject the null hypothesis that the overhead costs of the two types of school are the same.

Joint explanatory power of the intercept and slope dummy variables

The joint explanatory power of the intercept and slope dummies can be tested with the usual F test for a group of variables, comparing RSS when the dummy variables are included with RSS when they are not. The null hypothesis is H_0: $\delta=\lambda=0$. The alternative hypothesis is that one or both are nonzero. The numerator of the F statistic is the reduction in RSS when the dummies are added, divided by the cost in terms of degrees of freedom. RSS in the regression without the dummy variables was 8.9160×10^{11}, and in the regression with the dummy variables it was 4.7045×10^{11}. The cost is 2 because two extra parameters, the coefficients of the dummy variables, have been estimated, and as a consequence the number of degrees of freedom remaining has been reduced from 72 to 70. The denominator of the F statistic is RSS after the dummies have been added, divided by the number of degrees of freedom remaining. This is 70 because there are 74 observations and four parameters have been estimated. The F statistic is therefore

$$F(2, 70) = \frac{(8.9160 \times 10^{11} - 4.7045 \times 10^{11})/2}{4.7045 \times 10^{11}/70} = 31.3. \qquad (5.36)$$

The critical value of $F(2, 70)$ at the 0.1 percent significance level is 7.64, so we come to the conclusion that the null hypothesis should be rejected. This is not a surprise because we know from the t tests that λ is significantly different from zero.

Exercises

5.13 Is the effect of the $ASVABC$ score on educational attainment different for males and females? Using your $EAEF$ data set, define a slope dummy variable $MALEASVC$ as the product of $MALE$ and $ASVABC$:

$$MALEASVC = MALE^*ASVABC.$$

Regress *S* on *ASVABC*, *SM*, *SF*, *ETHBLACK*, *ETHHISP*, *MALE*, and *MALEASVC*, interpret the equation and perform appropriate statistical tests.

5.14 Is the effect of education on earnings different for members of a union? In the output below, *COLLBARG* is a dummy variable defined to be 1 for workers whose wages are determined by collective bargaining and 0 for the others. *SBARG* is a slope dummy variable defined as the product of *S* and *COLLBARG*. Provide an interpretation of the regression coefficients, comparing them with those in Exercise 5.7, and perform appropriate statistical tests.

```
.g SBARG=S*COLLBARG

.reg LGEARN S EXP MALE COLLBARG SBARG

    Source        SS         df        MS              Number of obs =      540
------------------------------------------              F(5,534)      =    52.06
    Model     61.1824375      5     12.2364875          Prob > F      =   0.0000
                                                        R-squared     =   0.3277
 Residual     125.525206    534    .235065928           Adj R-squared =   0.3214
------------------------------------------              Root MSE      =  .48484
    Total     186.707643    539    .34639637

------------------------------------------------------------------------------
   LGEARN       Coef.    Std. Err.       t    P>|t|     [95% Conf. Interval]
------------------------------------------------------------------------------
        S     .1234328    .0097343    12.68   0.000     .1043107     .142555
      EXP     .0272315    .0049725     5.48   0.000     .0174635    .0369995
     MALE     .2658057    .0430621     6.17   0.000     .1812137    .3503977
 COLLBARG     .3669224    .3020525     1.21   0.225    -.2264344    .9602792
    SBARG    -.0209955    .0216024     0.97   0.333    -.0635887    .0215977
    _cons     .4964114    .1684306     2.95   0.003     .1655436    .8272792
------------------------------------------------------------------------------
```

5.15 Is the effect of education on earnings different for males and females? Using your *EAEF* data set, define a slope dummy variable *MALES* as the product of *MALE* and *S*:

$$MALES = MALE*S.$$

Regress *LGEARN* on *S*, *EXP*, *ETHBLACK*, *ETHHISP*, *MALE*, and *MALES*, interpret the equation and perform appropriate statistical tests.

5.16 Are there ethnic variations in the effect of the sex of a respondent on educational attainment? A special case of a slope dummy variable is the interactive dummy variable defined as the product of two dummy variables. Using your *EAEF* data set, define interactive dummy variables *MALEBLAC* and *MALEHISP* as the product of *MALE* and *ETHBLACK*, and of *MALE* and *ETHHISP*, respectively:

$$MALEBLAC = MALE*ETHBLACK$$

$$MALEHISP = MALE*ETHHISP.$$

Regress *S* on *ASVABC*, *SM*, *SF*, *MALE*, *ETHBLACK*, *ETHHISP*, *MALEBLAC* and *MALEHISP*. Interpret the regression results and perform appropriate statistical tests.

5.4 **The Chow test**

It sometimes happens that your sample of observations consists of two or more subsamples, and you are uncertain about whether you should run one combined regression or separate regressions for each subsample. Actually, in practice the choice is not usually as stark as this, because there may be some scope for combining the subsamples, using appropriate dummy and slope dummy variables to relax the assumption that all the coefficients must be the same for each subsample. This is a point to which we shall return.

Suppose that we have a sample consisting of two subsamples and that you are wondering whether to combine them in a pooled regression, P, or to run separate regressions, A and B. We will denote the residual sums of squares for the subsample regressions RSS_A and RSS_B. We will denote RSS_A^P and RSS_B^P the sum of the squares of the residuals in the pooled regression for the observations belonging to the two subsamples. Since the subsample regressions minimize RSS for their observations, they must fit them at least as well as, and generally better than, the pooled regression. Thus $RSS_A \leq RSS_A^P$ and $RSS_B \leq RSS_B^P$, and so $(RSS_A + RSS_B) \leq RSS_P$, where RSS_P, the total sum of the squares of the residuals in the pooled regression, is equal to the sum of RSS_A^P and RSS_B^P.

Equality between RSS_P and $(RSS_A + RSS_B)$ will occur only when the regression coefficients for the pooled and subsample regressions coincide. In general, there will be an improvement $(RSS_P - RSS_A - RSS_B)$ when the sample is split up. There is a price to pay, in that k extra degrees of freedom are used up, since instead of k parameters for the pooled regression we now have to estimate k for each subsample, making $2k$ in all. After breaking up the sample, we are still left with $(RSS_A + RSS_B)$ (unexplained) sum of squares of the residuals, and we have $n - 2k$ degrees of freedom remaining.

We are now in a position to see whether the improvement in fit when we split the sample is significant, performing an F test known as the **Chow test** (Chow, 1960). We use the F statistic

$$F(k, n - 2k)$$

$$= \frac{\text{improvement in fit/extra degrees of freedom used up}}{\text{residual sum of squares remaining/degrees of freedom remaining}}$$

$$= \frac{(RSS_P - RSS_A - RSS_B)/k}{(RSS_A + RSS_B)/(n - 2k)} \tag{5.37}$$

which is distributed with k and $n - 2k$ degrees of freedom under the null hypothesis of no significant improvement in fit.

We will illustrate the Chow test with reference to the school cost function data, making a simple distinction between regular and occupational schools.

Table 5.12

```
.reg COST N if OCC == 0

    Source        SS          df        MS              Number of obs =       40
                                                        F(1,38)       =    13.53
    Model     4.3273e+10       1     4.3273e+10         Prob > F      =   0.0007
                                                        R-squared     =   0.2626
 Residual     1.2150e+11      38     3.1973e+09
                                                        Adj R-squared =   0.2432
    Total     1.6477e+11      39     4.2249e+09         Root MSE      =    56545


    COST      Coef.   Std. Err.      t    P>|t|           [95% Conf. Interval]

       N   152.2982   41.39782    3.679   0.001          68.49275     236.1037
   _cons   51475.25   21599.14    2.383   0.022          7750.064     95200.43



.reg COST N if OCC == 1

    Source        SS          df        MS              Number of obs =       34
                                                        F(1,32)       =    55.52
    Model     6.0538e+11       1     6.0538e+11         Prob > F      =   0.0000
 Residual     3.4895e+11      32     1.0905e+10         R-squared     =   0.6344
                                                        Adj R-squared =   0.6229
    Total     9.5433e+11      33     2.8919e+10         Root MSE      =  1.0e+05


    COST      Coef.   Std. Err.      t    P>|t|           [95% Conf. Interval]

       N   436.7769   58.62085    7.451   0.000          317.3701     556.1036
   _cons   47974.07   33879.03    1.416   0.166         -21035.26     116983.4
```

We need to run three regressions. In the first we regress $COST$ on N using the whole sample of 74 schools. We have already done this in Section 5.1. This is the pooled regression. We make a note of RSS for it, 8.9160×10^{11}. In the second and third we run the same regression for the two subsamples of regular and occupational schools separately and again make a note of RSS. The output for the subsample regressions is shown in Table 5.12 and the regression lines are shown in Figure 5.6.

RSS is 1.2150×10^{11} for the regular schools and 3.4895×10^{11} for the occupational schools. The total RSS from the subsample regressions is therefore 4.7045×10^{11}. It must be lower than RSS for the pooled regression. To see if it is significantly lower, we perform the Chow test. The numerator of the F statistic is the improvement in fit on splitting the sample, $(8.9160 - 4.7045) \times 10^{11}$, divided by the cost in terms of degrees of freedom. The latter is equal to two because we have had to estimate two intercepts and two slope coefficients, instead of only one of each. The denominator is the joint RSS remaining after splitting the sample, 4.7045×10^{11}, divided by the joint number of degrees of freedom remaining. The latter is equal to 70 since there are 74 observations and we have used up four degrees of freedom estimating two parameters in each equation.

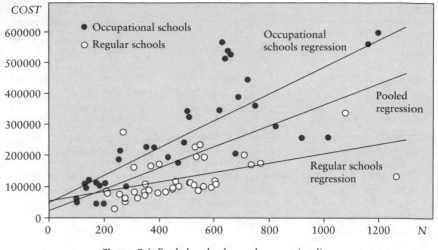

Figure 5.6 Pooled and subsample regression lines

When we calculate the F statistic the 10^{11} factors cancel out and we have

$$F(2, 70) = \frac{(8.9160 - 4.7045) \times 10^{11}/2}{4.7045 \times 10^{11}/70} = 31.3. \qquad (5.38)$$

The critical value of $F(2, 70)$ at the 0.1 percent significance level is 7.64, so we come to the conclusion that there is a significant improvement in the fit on splitting the sample and that we should not use the pooled regression.

Relationship between the Chow test and the *F* test of the explanatory power of a set of dummy variables

In this chapter we have used both dummy variables and a Chow test to investigate whether there are significant differences in a regression model for different categories of a qualitative characteristic. Could the two approaches have led to different conclusions? The answer is no, provided that a full set of dummy variables for the qualitative characteristic has been included in the regression model, a full set being defined as an intercept dummy, assuming that there is an intercept in the model, and a slope dummy for each of the other variables. The Chow test is then equivalent to an F test of the explanatory power of the dummy variables as a group.

To simplify the discussion, we will suppose that there are only two categories of the qualitative characteristic, as in the example of the cost functions for regular and occupational schools. Suppose that you start with the basic specification with no dummy variables. The regression equation will be that of the pooled regression in the Chow test, with every coefficient a compromise for the two categories of the qualitative variable. If you then add a full set of dummy variables, the intercept and the slope coefficients can be different for the two categories. The basic coefficients will be chosen so as to minimize the sum of the squares of the residuals relating to the reference category, and the intercept dummy and slope dummy coefficients will be chosen so as to minimize the sum of the squares of the residuals for the other category. Effectively, the outcome of the estimation of the coefficients is the same as if you had run separate regressions for the two categories.

In the school cost function example, the implicit cost functions for regular and occupational schools with a full set of dummy variables (in this case just an intercept dummy and a slope dummy for N), shown in Figure 5.5, are identical to the cost functions for the subsample regressions in the Chow test, shown in Figure 5.6. It follows that the improvement in the fit, as measured by the reduction in the residual sum of squares, when one adds the dummy variables to the basic specification is identical to the improvement in fit on splitting the sample and running subsample regressions. The cost, in terms of degrees of freedom, is also the same. In the dummy variable approach you have to add an intercept dummy and a slope dummy for each variable, so the cost is k if there are $k-1$ variables in the model. In the Chow test, the cost is also k because you have to estimate $2k$ parameters instead of k when you split the sample. Thus the numerator of the F statistic is the same for both tests. The denominator is also the same because in both cases it is the residual sum of squares for the subsample regressions divided by $n-2k$. In the case of the Chow test, $2k$ degrees of freedom are used up when fitting the separate regressions. In the case of the dummy variable group test, k degrees of freedom are used up when estimating the original intercept and slope coefficients, and a further k degrees of freedom are used up estimating the intercept dummy and the slope dummy coefficients.

What are the advantages and disadvantages of the two approaches? The Chow test is quick. You just run the three regressions and compute the test statistic. But it does not tell you how the functions differ, if they do. The dummy variable approach involves more preparation because you have to define a dummy variable for the intercept and for each slope coefficient. However, it is more informative because you can perform t tests on the individual dummy coefficients and they may indicate where the functions differ, if they do.

Key terms

Chow test	omitted category
dummy variable	reference category
dummy variable trap	slope dummy variable

Exercises

5.17 Are educational attainment functions different for males and females? Using your *EAEF* data set, regress *S* on *ASVABC*, *ETHBLACK*, *ETHHISP*, *SM*, and *SF* (do not include *MALE*). Repeat the regression using only the male respondents. Repeat it again using only the female respondents. Perform a Chow test.

5.18 Are earnings functions different for males and females? Using your *EAEF* data set, regress *LGEARN* on *S*, *EXP*, *ETHBLACK*, and *ETHHISP* (do not include *MALE*). Repeat the regression using only the male respondents. Repeat it again using only the female respondents. Perform a Chow test.

5.19 Are there differences in male and female educational attainment functions? This question has been answered by Exercise 5.17 but nevertheless it is instructive to investigate the issue using the dummy variable approach. Using your *EAEF* data set, define the following slope dummies combining *MALE* with the parental education variables:

$$MALESM = MALE*SM$$

$$MALESF = MALE*SF$$

and regress *S* on *ETHBLACK*, *ETHHISP*, *ASVABC*, *SM*, *SF*, *MALE*, *MALE-BLAC*, *MALEHISP*(defined in Exercise 5.15), *MALEASVC* (defined in Exercise 5.12), *MALESM*, and *MALESF*. Next regress *S* on *ETHBLACK*, *ETHHISP*, *ASVABC*, *SM*, and *SF* only. Perform an *F* test of the joint explanatory power of *MALE* and the slope dummy variables as a group (verify that the *F* statistic is the same as in Exercise 5.17) and perform *t* tests on the coefficients of the slope dummy variables in the first regression.

5.20 Where are the differences in male and female earnings functions? Using your *EAEF* data set, regress *LGEARN* on *S*, *EXP*, *ETHBLACK*, *ETHHISP*, *MALE*, *MALES*, *MALEEXP*, *MALEBLAC*, and *MALEHISP*. Next regress *LGEARN* on *S*, *EXP*, *ETHBLACK*, and *ETHHISP* only. Calculate the correlation matrix for *MALE* and the slope dummies. Perform an *F* test of the joint explanatory power of *MALE* and the slope dummies (verify that the *F* statistic is the same as in Exercise 5.18) and perform *t* tests on the coefficients of the dummy variables. *MALEEXP* should be defined as the product of *MALE* and *EXP*.

6 Specification of Regression Variables: A Preliminary Skirmish

What are the consequences of including in the regression model a variable that should not be there? What are the consequences of leaving out a variable that should be included? What happens if you have difficulty finding data on a variable and use a proxy instead? This chapter is a preliminary skirmish with these issues in the sense that it focuses on the consequences of variable misspecification, rather than on procedures for model selection, a much more complex subject that is left to later in the text. The chapter concludes by showing how simple restrictions on the parameters can be tested.

6.1 Model specification

The construction of an economic model involves the specification of the relationships that constitute it, the specification of the variables that participate in each relationship, and the mathematical function representing each relationship. The last element was discussed in Chapter 4. In this chapter, we will consider the second element, and we will continue to assume that the model consists of just one equation. We will discuss the application of regression analysis to models consisting of systems of simultaneous relationships in Chapter 9.

If we know exactly which explanatory variables ought to be included in the equation when we undertake regression analysis, our task is limited to calculating estimates of their coefficients, confidence intervals for these estimates, and so on. In practice, however, we can never be sure that we have specified the equation correctly. Economic theory ought to provide a guide, but theory is never perfect. Without being aware of it, we might be including some variables that ought not to be in the model, and we might be leaving out others that ought to be included.

The properties of the regression estimates of the coefficients depend crucially on the validity of the specification of the model. The consequences of misspecification of the variables in a relationship are summarized in Table 6.1.

1. If you leave out a variable that ought to be included, the regression estimates are in general (but not always) biased. The standard errors of the coefficients and the corresponding t tests are in general invalid.

Table 6.1 Consequences of variable specification

		True model	
		$Y = \beta_1 + \beta_2 X_2 + u$	$Y = \beta_1 + \beta_2 X_2 + \beta_3 X_3 + u$
Fitted model	$\hat{Y} = b_1 + b_2 X_2$	Correct specification, no problems	Coefficients are biased (in general). Standard errors are invalid
	$\hat{Y} = b_1 + b_2 X_2 + b_3 X_3$	Coefficients are unbiased (in general) but inefficient. Standard errors are valid (in general).	Correct specification, no problems

2. If you include a variable that ought not to be in the equation, the regression coefficients are in general (but not always) inefficient but not biased. The standard errors are in general valid but, because the regression estimation is inefficient, they will be needlessly large.

We will begin by discussing these two cases and then come to some broader issues of model specification.

6.2 The effect of omitting a variable that ought to be included

The problem of bias

Suppose that the dependent variable Y depends on two variables X_2 and X_3 according to a relationship

$$Y = \beta_1 + \beta_2 X_2 + \beta_3 X_3 + u, \tag{6.1}$$

but you are unaware of the importance of X_3. Thinking that the model should be

$$Y = \beta_1 + \beta_2 X_2 + u, \tag{6.2}$$

you use regression analysis to fit

$$\hat{Y} = b_1 + b_2 X_2, \tag{6.3}$$

and you calculate b_2 using the expression

$$b_2 = \frac{\sum_{i=1}^{n} \left(X_i - \overline{X} \right)\left(Y_i - \overline{Y} \right)}{\sum_{i=1}^{n} \left(X_i - \overline{X} \right)^2} \tag{6.4}$$

instead of the correct expression for a regression with two explanatory variables. By definition, b_2 is an unbiased estimator of β_2 if and only if $E(b_2)$ is equal to β_2. In fact, if (6.1) is true,

$$E\left[\frac{\sum_{i=1}^{n}\left(X_{2i}-\overline{X}_2\right)\left(Y_i-\overline{Y}\right)}{\sum_{i=1}^{n}\left(X_{2i}-\overline{X}_2\right)^2}\right] = \beta_2 + \beta_3\frac{\sum_{i=1}^{n}\left(X_{2i}-\overline{X}_2\right)\left(X_{3i}-\overline{X}_3\right)}{\sum_{i=1}^{n}\left(X_{2i}-\overline{X}_2\right)^2} \qquad (6.5)$$

and b_2 is then described as being subject to **omitted variable bias**. We shall give first an intuitive explanation of (6.5) and then a formal proof.

If X_3 is omitted from the regression model, X_2 will appear to have a double effect, as illustrated in Figure 6.1. It will have a direct effect and also a proxy effect when it mimics the effect of X_3. The apparent indirect effect of X_2 on Y depends on two factors: the apparent ability of X_2 to mimic X_3, and the effect of X_3 on Y.

The apparent ability of X_2 to explain X_3 is determined by the slope coefficient h in the pseudo-regression

$$\hat{X}_3 = g + hX_2. \qquad (6.6)$$

h of course is given by the usual simple regression formula

$$h = \frac{\sum_{i=1}^{n}\left(X_{2i}-\overline{X}_2\right)\left(X_{3i}-\overline{X}_3\right)}{\sum_{i=1}^{n}\left(X_{2i}-\overline{X}_2\right)^2}. \qquad (6.7)$$

The effect of X_3 on Y is β_3, so the mimic effect via X_3 may be written $\beta_3\left[\left(\sum\left(X_{2i}-\overline{X}_2\right)\left(X_{3i}-\overline{X}_3\right)\right)\Big/\sum\left(X_{2i}-\overline{X}_2\right)^2\right]$.

The direct effect of X_2 on Y is β_2, and hence when Y is regressed on X_2, omitting X_3, the coefficient of X_2 is given by

$$\beta_2 + \beta_3\frac{\sum_{i=1}^{n}\left(X_{2i}-\overline{X}_2\right)\left(X_{3i}-\overline{X}_3\right)}{\sum_{i=1}^{n}\left(X_{2i}-\overline{X}_2\right)^2} + \text{sampling error.} \qquad (6.8)$$

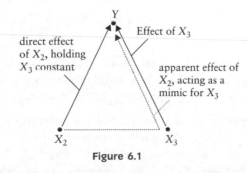

Figure 6.1

Provided that X_2 and X_3 are nonstochastic, the expected value of the coefficient will be the sum of the first two terms. The presence of the second term implies that in general the expected value of the coefficient will be different from the true value β_2 and therefore biased.

The formal proof of (6.5) is straightforward. We begin by making a theoretical expansion of the estimator b_2, replacing Y_i and $\overline{Y}$ using (6.1):

$$b_2 = \frac{\sum\limits_{i=1}^{n} \left(X_{2i} - \overline{X}_2 \right)\left(Y_i - \overline{Y} \right)}{\sum\limits_{i=1}^{n} \left(X_{2i} - \overline{X}_2 \right)^2}$$

$$= \frac{\sum\limits_{i=1}^{n} \left(X_{2i} - \overline{X}_2 \right)\left(\left[\beta_1 + \beta_2 X_{2i} + \beta_3 X_{3i} + u_i \right] - \left[\beta_1 + \beta_2 \overline{X}_2 + \beta_3 \overline{X}_3 + \overline{u} \right] \right)}{\sum\limits_{i=1}^{n} \left(X_{2i} - \overline{X}_2 \right)^2}$$

$$= \frac{\beta_2 \sum\limits_{i=1}^{n} \left(X_{2i} - \overline{X}_2 \right)^2 + \beta_3 \sum\limits_{i=1}^{n} \left(X_{2i} - \overline{X}_2 \right)\left(X_{3i} - \overline{X}_3 \right) + \sum\limits_{i=1}^{n} \left(X_{2i} - \overline{X}_2 \right)\left(u_i - \overline{u} \right)}{\sum\limits_{i=1}^{n} \left(X_{2i} - \overline{X}_2 \right)^2}$$

$$= \beta_2 + \beta_3 \frac{\sum\limits_{i=1}^{n} \left(X_{2i} - \overline{X}_2 \right)\left(X_{3i} - \overline{X}_3 \right)}{\sum\limits_{i=1}^{n} \left(X_{2i} - \overline{X}_2 \right)^2} + \frac{\sum\limits_{i=1}^{n} \left(X_{2i} - \overline{X}_2 \right)\left(u_i - \overline{u} \right)}{\sum\limits_{i=1}^{n} \left(X_{2i} - \overline{X}_2 \right)^2}. \tag{6.9}$$

Provided that X_2 and X_3 are nonstochastic, the first two terms are unaffected when we take expectations and the third is zero. Hence we obtain (6.5). Since $\sum \left(X_{2i} - \overline{X}_2 \right)^2$ must be positive (except in the case where X_2 is constant in all observations, in which case it would not be possible to run a regression), the direction of the bias will depend on the signs of β_3 and $\sum \left(X_{2i} - \overline{X}_2 \right)\left(X_{3i} - \overline{X}_3 \right)$. We note that the latter is the numerator of the sample correlation between X_2 and X_3, $r_{X_2 X_3}$:

$$r_{X_2 X_3} = \frac{\sum\limits_{i=1}^{n} \left(X_{2i} - \overline{X}_2 \right)\left(X_{3i} - \overline{X}_3 \right)}{\sqrt{\sum\limits_{i=1}^{n} \left(X_{2i} - \overline{X}_2 \right)^2 \sum\limits_{i=1}^{n} \left(X_{3i} - \overline{X}_3 \right)^2}}. \tag{6.10}$$

The denominator of the correlation coefficient must be positive (unless it is zero, in which case it would not be possible to run a regression). Hence the sign of $\sum \left(X_{2i} - \overline{X}_2 \right)\left(X_{3i} - \overline{X}_3 \right)$ is the same as that of the correlation coefficient.

For example, if β_3 is positive and the correlation is positive, the bias will be positive and b_2 will tend to overestimate β_2. There is, however, one exceptional case where b_2 is unbiased after all. That is when the sample correlation between X_2 and X_3 happens to be exactly zero. This would occur if $\sum \left(X_{2i} - \overline{X}_2\right)\left(X_{3i} - \overline{X}_3\right)$ is zero, and then the bias term disappears. Indeed, the regression coefficient obtained using simple regression will be exactly the same as if you had used a properly specified multiple regression. Of course, the bias term would also be zero if β_3 were zero, but then the model is not misspecified.

Invalidation of the statistical tests

Another serious consequence of omitting a variable that ought to be included in the regression is that the standard errors of the coefficients and the test statistics are in general invalidated. This means of course that you are not in principle able to test any hypotheses with your regression results.

Example

The problem of omitted variable bias will first be illustrated with the educational attainment function using *EAEF* Data Set 21. For the present purposes, it will be assumed that the true model is

$$S = \beta_1 + \beta_2 ASVABC + \beta_3 SM + u, \tag{6.11}$$

although obviously this is a great oversimplification. The first part of the regression output in Table 6.2 shows the result of this regression. The second and third parts of the output then show the effects of omitting *SM* and *ASVABC*, respectively.

When *SM* is omitted,

$$E\left(b_2\right) = \beta_2 + \beta_3 \frac{\sum\limits_{i=1}^{n}\left(ASVABC - \overline{ASVABC}\right)\left(SM - \overline{SM}\right)}{\sum\limits_{i=1}^{n}\left(ASVABC - \overline{ASVABC}\right)^2}. \tag{6.12}$$

The correlation between *ASVABC* and *SM* is positive (0.42). Therefore the numerator of the bias term is positive. The denominator must be positive (unless equal to zero, in which case it would not be possible to perform the regression). It is reasonable to assume that β_3 is positive, and the fact that its estimate in the first regression is indeed positive and highly significant provides overwhelming corroborative evidence. One would therefore anticipate that the coefficient of *ASVABC* will be upwards biased when *SM* is omitted, and you can see that it is indeed higher. Not all of the difference should be attributed to bias. Part of it may be attributable to the effects of the disturbance term, which could go either way.

Table 6.2

```
.reg S ASVABC SM

  Source        SS         df        MS              Number of obs =      540
--------------------------------------------         F(2,537)      =   147.36
   Model    1135.67473      2     567.837363          Prob > F      =   0.0000
                                                      R-squared     =   0.3543
Residual    2069.30861     537    3.85346109          Adj R-squared =   0.3519
--------------------------------------------         Root MSE      =    1.963
   Total    3204.98333     539    5.94616574

--------------------------------------------------------------------------------
       S      Coef.    Std. Err.      t    P>|t|        [95% Conf. Interval]
--------------------------------------------------------------------------------
  ASVABC   .1328069    .0097389    13.64   0.000        .1136758     .151938
      SM   .1235071    .0330837     3.73   0.000        .0585178    .1884963
   _cons   5.420733    .4930224    10.99   0.000        4.452244    6.389222
--------------------------------------------------------------------------------

.reg S ASVABC

  Source        SS         df        MS              Number of obs =      540
--------------------------------------------         F(1,538)      =   274.19
   Model    1081.97059      1     1081.97059          Prob > F      =   0.0000
                                                      R-squared     =   0.3376
Residual    2123.01275     538    3.94612035          Adj R-squared =   0.3364
--------------------------------------------         Root MSE      =   1.9865
   Total    3204.98333     539    5.94616574

--------------------------------------------------------------------------------
       S      Coef.    Std. Err.      t    P>|t|        [95% Conf. Interval]
--------------------------------------------------------------------------------
  ASVABC    .148084    .0089431    16.56   0.000        .1305165    .1656516
   _cons   6.066225    .4672261    12.98   0.000        5.148413    6.984036
--------------------------------------------------------------------------------

.reg S SM

  Source        SS         df        MS              Number of obs =      540
--------------------------------------------         F(1,538)      =    80.93
   Model    419.086251      1     419.086251          Prob > F      =   0.0000
                                                      R-squared     =   0.1308
Residual    2785.89708     538    5.17824736          Adj R-squared =   0.1291
--------------------------------------------         Root MSE      =   2.2756
   Total    3204.98333     539    5.94616574

--------------------------------------------------------------------------------
       S      Coef.    Std. Err.      t    P>|t|        [95% Conf. Interval]
--------------------------------------------------------------------------------
      SM   .3130793    .0348012     9.00   0.000        .2447165    .3814422
   _cons  10.04688    .4147121    24.23   0.000        9.232226    10.86153
--------------------------------------------------------------------------------
```

Similarly, when *ASVABC* is omitted,

$$E(b_3) = \beta_3 + \beta_2 \frac{\sum_{i=1}^{n}\left(ASVABC - \overline{ASVABC}\right)\left(SM - \overline{SM}\right)}{\sum_{i=1}^{n}\left(SM - \overline{SM}\right)^2}. \tag{6.13}$$

Since β_2 is also likely to be positive, the coefficient of *SM* in the third regression should be upwards biased. The estimate in the third regression is indeed higher than that in the first.

In this example, the omission of one explanatory variable causes the coefficient of the other to be overestimated. However, the bias could just as easily be negative. The sign of the bias depends on the sign of the true coefficient of the omitted variable and on the sign of the correlation between the included and omitted variables, and these will depend on the nature of the model being investigated.

It should be emphasized that the analysis above applies only to the case where the true model is a multiple regression model with two explanatory variables. When there are more explanatory variables, it may be difficult to predict the impact of omitted variable bias mathematically. Nevertheless, it may be possible to conclude that the estimates of the coefficients of some of the variables may have been inflated or deflated by the bias.

R^2 in the presence of omitted variable bias

In Section 3.5 it was asserted that in general it is impossible to determine the contribution to R^2 of each explanatory variable in multiple regression analysis, and we are now in a position to see why.

We will discuss the issue first with reference to the educational attainment model above. In the regression of S on $ASVABC$ alone, R^2 was 0.34. In the regression on SM alone, it was 0.13. Does this mean that $ASVABC$ explains 34 percent of the variation in S, and SM 13 percent? No, because this would imply that together they would explain 47 percent of the variation, and this conflicts with the finding in the multiple regression that their joint explanatory power is 0.35.

The explanation is that in the simple regression of S on $ASVABC$, $ASVABC$ is acting partly as a variable in its own right and partly as a proxy for the missing SM, as in Figure 6.1. R^2 for that regression therefore reflects the combined explanatory power of $ASVABC$ in both of these roles, and not just its direct explanatory power. Hence 0.34 overestimates the latter.

Similarly, in the simple regression of S on SM, SM is acting partly as a proxy for the missing $ASVABC$, and the level of R^2 in that regression reflects the combined explanatory power of SM in both those roles, and not just its direct explanatory power.

In this example, the explanatory power of the two variables overlapped, with the consequence that R^2 in the multiple regression was less than the sum of R^2 in the individual simple regressions. However, it is also possible for R^2 in the multiple regression to be greater than the sum of R^2 in the individual simple regressions, as is shown in the regression output in Table 6.3 for an earnings function model. It is assumed that the true model is

$$LGEARN = \beta_1 + \beta_2 S + \beta_3 EXP + u. \tag{6.14}$$

Table 6.3

```
.reg LGEARN S EXP

   Source        SS         df        MS              Number of obs  =      540
--------------------------------------------          F(2,537)       =   100.86
    Model    50.9842581       2    25.492129          Prob > F       =   0.0000
                                                      R-squared      =   0.2731
 Residual    135.723385      537   .252743734         Adj R-squared  =   0.2704
--------------------------------------------          Root MSE       =  .50274
    Total    186.707643      539   .34639637

-------------------------------------------------------------------------------
   LGEARN      Coef.    Std. Err.        t    P>|t|      [95% Conf. Interval]
-------------------------------------------------------------------------------
        S    .1235911   .0090989     13.58    0.000      .1057173    .141465
      EXP    .0350826   .0050046      7.01    0.000      .0252515   .0449137
    _cons    .5093196   .1663823      3.06    0.002      .1824796   .8361596
-------------------------------------------------------------------------------

.reg LGEARN S

   Source        SS         df        MS              Number of obs  =      540
--------------------------------------------          F(1,538)       =   140.05
    Model    38.5643833       1    38.5643833         Prob > F       =   0.0000
                                                      R-squared      =   0.2065
 Residual    148.14326       538   .275359219         Adj R-squared  =   0.2051
--------------------------------------------          Root MSE       =  .52475
    Total    186.707643      539   .34639637

-------------------------------------------------------------------------------
   LGEARN      Coef.    Std. Err.        t    P>|t|      [95% Conf. Interval]
-------------------------------------------------------------------------------
        S    .1096934   .0092691     11.83    0.000      .0914853   .1279014
    _cons   1.292241    .1287252     10.04    0.000     1.039376   1.545107
-------------------------------------------------------------------------------

.reg LGEARN EXP

   Source        SS         df        MS              Number of obs  =      540
--------------------------------------------          F(1,538)       =    12.84
    Model    4.35309315       1    4.35309315         Prob > F       =   0.0004
                                                      R-squared      =   0.0233
 Residual    182.35455       538   .338948978         Adj R-squared  =   0.0215
--------------------------------------------          Root MSE       =  .58219
    Total    186.707643      539   .34639637

-------------------------------------------------------------------------------
   LGEARN      Coef.    Std. Err.        t    P>|t|      [95% Conf. Interval]
-------------------------------------------------------------------------------
      EXP    .0202708   .0056564      3.58    0.000      .0091595    .031382
    _cons   2.44941     .0988233     24.79    0.000     2.255284   2.643537
-------------------------------------------------------------------------------
```

The first part of the regression output in Table 6.3 shows the result of fitting (6.14), and the second and third parts show the results of omitting, first *EXP*, and then *S*. R^2 in the multiple regression is 0.27, while it is 0.21 and 0.02 in the simple regressions, the sum being 0.23. As in the previous example, it can be assumed that both β_2 and β_3 are positive. However, *S* and *EXP* are negatively correlated, so in this case the coefficients of *S* and *EXP* in the second and third regressions may be expected to be biased downwards. As a consequence, the apparent explanatory power of *S* and *EXP* in the simple regressions is underestimated.

Exercises

6.1   Using your *EAEF* data set, regress *S* (1) on *ASVABC* and *SM*, (2) on *ASVABC* only, and (3) on *SM* only. Calculate the correlation between *ASVABC* and *SM*. Compare the coefficients of *ASVABC* in regressions (1) and (2). Give both mathematical and intuitive explanations of direction of the change. Also compare the coefficients of *SM* in regressions (1) and (3) and explain the direction of the change.

6.2   Using your *EAEF* data set, regress *LGEARN* (1) on *S* and *EXP*, (2) on *S* only, and (3) on *EXP* only. Calculate the correlation between *S* and *EXP*. Compare the coefficients of *S* in regressions (1) and (2). Give both mathematical and intuitive explanations of the direction of the change. Also compare the coefficients of *EXP* in regressions (1) and (3) and explain the direction of the change.

6.3   Using your *EAEF* data set, regress *LGEARN* (1) on *S*, *EXP*, *MALE*, *ETHHISP* and *ETHBLACK*, and (2) on *S*, *EXP*, *MALE*, *ETHHISP*, *ETHBLACK*, and *ASVABC*. Calculate the correlation coefficients for the explanatory variables and discuss the differences in the regression results. (A detailed mathematical analysis is not expected.)

6.4*   The table gives the results of multiple and simple regressions of *LGFDHO*, the logarithm of annual household expenditure on food eaten at home, on *LGEXP*, the logarithm of total annual household expenditure, and *LGSIZE*, the logarithm of the number of persons in the household, using a sample of 868 households in the 1995 Consumer Expenditure Survey. The correlation coefficient for *LGEXP* and *LGSIZE* was 0.45. Explain the variations in the regression coefficients.

	(1)	(2)	(3)
LGEXP	0.29	0.48	—
	(0.02)	(0.02)	
LGSIZE	0.49	—	0.63
	(0.03)		(0.02)
constant	4.72	3.17	7.50
	(0.22)	(0.24)	(0.02)
R^2	0.52	0.31	0.42

6.5   Suppose that Y is determined by X_2 and X_3 according to the relationship

$$Y = \beta_1 + \beta_2 X_2 + \beta_3 X_3 + u,$$

and that the correlation between X_2 and X_3, and hence $\sum \left(X_{2i} - \overline{X}_2\right)\left(X_{3i} - \overline{X}_3\right)$, is zero. Use this to simplify the multiple regression coefficient b_2 given by

$$b_2 = \frac{\sum\limits_{i=1}^{n} \left(X_{2i} - \overline{X}_2\right)\left(Y_i - \overline{Y}\right) \sum\limits_{i=1}^{n} \left(X_{3i} - \overline{X}_3\right)^2 - \sum\limits_{i=1}^{n} \left(X_{3i} - \overline{X}_3\right)\left(Y_i - \overline{Y}\right) \sum\limits_{i=1}^{n} \left(X_{2i} - \overline{X}_2\right)\left(X_{3i} - \overline{X}_3\right)}{\sum\limits_{i=1}^{n} \left(X_{2i} - \overline{X}_2\right)^2 \sum\limits_{i=1}^{n} \left(X_{3i} - \overline{X}_3\right)^2 - \left(\sum\limits_{i=1}^{n} \left(X_{2i} - \overline{X}_2\right)\left(X_{3i} - \overline{X}_3\right)\right)^2}$$

and show that it reduces to the simple regression expression. What are the implications for the specification of the regression equation?

6.6 In a Monte Carlo experiment, a variable Y was generated as a linear function of two variables X_2 and X_3:

$$Y = 10.0 + 10.0X_2 + 0.5X_3 + u$$

where X_2 was the sequence of integers $1, 2, \ldots, 30$, X_3 was generated from X_2 by adding random numbers, and u was a disturbance term with a normal distribution with mean zero and variance 10,000. The correlation between X_2 and X_3 was 0.95. The table shows the result of fitting the following regressions for 10 samples:

$$\text{Model A} \quad \hat{Y} = b_1 + b_2X_2 + b_3X_3$$

$$\text{Model B} \quad \hat{Y} = b_1 + b_2X_2.$$

Comment on all aspects of the regression results, giving full explanations of what you observe.

	Model A					Model B		
Sample	b_2	s.e.(b_2)	b_3	s.e.(b_3)	R^2	b_2	s.e.(b_2)	R^2
1	10.68	6.05	0.60	5.76	0.5800	11.28	1.82	0.5799
2	7.52	7.11	3.74	6.77	0.5018	11.26	2.14	0.4961
3	7.26	6.58	2.93	6.26	0.4907	10.20	1.98	0.4865
4	11.47	8.60	0.23	8.18	0.4239	11.70	2.58	0.4239
5	13.07	6.07	−3.04	5.78	0.5232	10.03	1.83	0.5183
6	16.74	6.63	−4.01	6.32	0.5966	12.73	2.00	0.5906
7	15.70	7.50	−4.80	7.14	0.4614	10.90	2.27	0.4523
8	8.01	8.10	1.50	7.71	0.3542	9.51	2.43	0.3533
9	1.08	6.78	9.52	6.45	0.5133	10.61	2.11	0.4740
10	13.09	7.58	−0.87	7.21	0.5084	12.22	2.27	0.5081

6.3 The effect of including a variable that ought not to be included

Suppose that the true model is

$$Y = \beta_1 + \beta_2X_2 + u \tag{6.15}$$

and you think it is

$$Y = \beta_1 + \beta_2X_2 + \beta_3X_3 + u, \tag{6.16}$$

and you estimate b_2 using

$$b_2 = \frac{\sum\limits_{i=1}^{n}\left(X_{2i}-\overline{X}_2\right)\left(Y_i-\overline{Y}\right)\sum\limits_{i=1}^{n}\left(X_{3i}-\overline{X}_3\right)^2 - \sum\limits_{i=1}^{n}\left(X_{3i}-\overline{X}_3\right)\left(Y_i-\overline{Y}\right)\sum\limits_{i=1}^{n}\left(X_{2i}-\overline{X}_2\right)\left(X_{3i}-\overline{X}_3\right)}{\sum\limits_{i=1}^{n}\left(X_{2i}-\overline{X}_2\right)^2\sum\limits_{i=1}^{n}\left(X_{3i}-\overline{X}_3\right)^2 - \left(\sum\limits_{i=1}^{n}\left(X_{2i}-\overline{X}_2\right)\left(X_{3i}-\overline{X}_3\right)\right)^2} \tag{6.17}$$

instead of

$$b_2 = \frac{\sum\limits_{i=1}^{n}\left(X_i-\overline{X}\right)\left(Y_i-\overline{Y}\right)}{\sum\limits_{i=1}^{n}\left(X_i-\overline{X}\right)^2}. \tag{6.18}$$

In general there is no problem of bias if you include a **redundant variable** in the model, even though b_2 has been calculated incorrectly. $E(b_2)$ will still be equal to β_2, but in general b_2 will be an inefficient estimator. It will be more erratic, in the sense of having a larger variance about β_2, than if it had been calculated correctly. This is illustrated in Figure 6.2.

There is a simple intuitive explanation. The true model may be rewritten

$$Y = \beta_1 + \beta_2 X_2 + 0X_3 + u. \tag{6.19}$$

So if you regress Y on X_2 and X_3, b_2 will be an unbiased estimator of β_2 and b_3 will be an unbiased estimator of zero, provided that the regression model conditions are satisfied. Effectively, you are discovering for yourself that $\beta_3 = 0$. If you

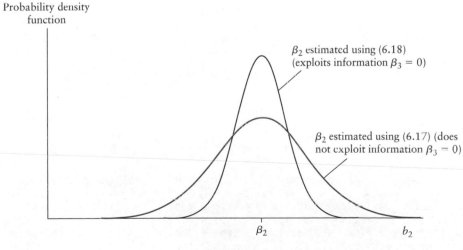

Probability density function

β_2 estimated using (6.18) (exploits information $\beta_3 = 0$)

β_2 estimated using (6.17) (does not exploit information $\beta_3 = 0$)

β_2 b_2

Figure 6.2

realized beforehand that $\beta_3 = 0$, you would be able to exploit this information to exclude X_3 and use simple regression, which in this context is more efficient.

The loss of efficiency caused by including X_3 when it ought not to be included depends on the correlation between X_2 and X_3. Compare the expressions for the variances of b_2 using simple and multiple regression in Table 6.4. The variance will in general be larger in the case of multiple regression, and the difference will be the greater the closer the correlation coefficient is to plus or minus 1. The one exception to the loss of efficiency occurs when the correlation coefficient happens to be exactly equal to zero. In that case the estimator b_2 for multiple regression is identical to that for simple regression. See Exercise 6.5.

Table 6.4

Simple regression	Multiple regression
$\sigma_{b_2}^2 = \dfrac{\sigma_u^2}{\sum\limits_{i=1}^{n}\left(X_{2i}-\overline{X}_2\right)^2}$	$\sigma_{b_2}^2 = \dfrac{\sigma_u^2}{\sum\limits_{i=1}^{n}\left(X_{2i}-\overline{X}_2\right)^2}\,\dfrac{1}{\left(1-r_{X_2X_3}^2\right)}$

Table 6.5

```
.reg LGFDHO LGEXP LGSIZE

   Source        SS          df        MS              Number of obs  =      868
----------------------------------------               F(2,865)       =   460.92
    Model    138.776549       2    69.3882747          Prob > F        =   0.0000
                                                       R-squared       =   0.5159
 Residual    130.219231     865    .150542464          Adj R-squared   =   0.5148
----------------------------------------               Root MSE        =     .388
    Total    268.995781     867    .310260416

----------------------------------------------------------------------------------
   LGFDHO      Coef.   Std. Err.        t    P>|t|       [95% Conf. Interval]
----------------------------------------------------------------------------------
    LGEXP    .2866813   .0226824   12.639   0.000       .2421622    .3312003
   LGSIZE    .4854698   .0255476   19.003   0.000       .4353272    .5356124
    _cons   4.720269    .2209996   21.359   0.000      4.286511    5.154027
----------------------------------------------------------------------------------

.reg LGFDHO LGEXP LGSIZE LGHOUS

   Source        SS          df        MS              Number of obs  =      868
----------------------------------------               F(3,864)       =   307.22
    Model    138.841976       3    46.2806586          Prob > F        =   0.0000
                                                       R-squared       =   0.5161
 Residual    130.153805     864    .150640978          Adj R-squared   =   0.5145
----------------------------------------               Root MSE        =   .38812
    Total    268.995781     867    .310260416

----------------------------------------------------------------------------------
   LGFDHO      Coef.   Std. Err.        t    P>|t|       [95% Conf. Interval]
----------------------------------------------------------------------------------
    LGEXP    .2673552   .0370782    7.211   0.000       1945813     .340129
   LGSIZE    .4868228   .0256383   18.988   0.000       .4365021    .5371434
   LGHOUS    .0229611   .0348408    0.659   0.510      -.0454214    .0913436
    _cons   4.708772    .2217592   21.234   0.000      4.273522    5.144022
----------------------------------------------------------------------------------
```

Example

The regression output in Table 6.5 shows the results of regressions of *LGFDHO*, the logarithm of annual household expenditure on food eaten at home, on *LGEXP*, the logarithm of total annual household expenditure, and *LGSIZE*, the logarithm of the number of persons in the household, using a sample of 868 households in the 1995 Consumer Expenditure Survey. In the second regression, *LGHOUS*, the logarithm of annual expenditure on housing services, has been added. It is safe to assume that *LGHOUS* is an irrelevant variable and, not surprisingly, its coefficient is not significantly different from zero. It is, however, highly correlated with *LGEXP* (correlation coefficient 0.81), and also, to a lesser extent, with *LGSIZE* (correlation coefficient 0.33). Its inclusion does not cause the coefficients of those variables to be biased but it does increase their standard errors, particularly that of *LGEXP*, as you would expect, given the loss of efficiency.

Exercises

6.7* A social scientist thinks that the level of activity in the shadow economy, Y, depends either positively on the level of the tax burden, X, or negatively on the level of government expenditure to discourage shadow economy activity, Z. Y might also depend on both X and Z. International cross-sectional data on Y, X, and Z, all measured in US\$ million, are obtained for a sample of 30 industrialized countries and a second sample of 30 developing countries. The social scientist regresses (1) log Y on both log X and log Z, (2) log Y on log X alone, and (3) log Y on log Z alone, for each sample, with the following results (standard errors in parentheses):

	Industrialized countries			Developing countries		
	(1)	(2)	(3)	(1)	(2)	(3)
log X	0.699	0.201	—	0.806	0.727	—
	(0.154)	(0.112)		(0.137)	(0.090)	
log Z	−0.646	—	−0.053	−0.091	—	0.427
	(0.162)		(0.124)	(0.117)		(0.116)
constant	−1.137	−1.065	1.230	−1.122	1.024	2.824
	(0.863)	(1.069)	(0.896)	(0.873)	(0.858)	(0.835)
R^2	0.44	0.10	0.01	0.71	0.70	0.33

X was positively correlated with Z in both samples. Having carried out the appropriate statistical tests, write a short report advising the social scientist how to interpret these results.

6.8 Using your *EAEF* data set, regress *LGEARN* on S, *EXP*, *ASVABC*, *MALE*, *ETHHISP* and *ETHBLACK*. Repeat the regression, adding *SIBLINGS*. Calculate the correlations between *SIBLINGS* and the other explanatory variables. Compare the results of the two regressions.

6.4 Proxy variables

It frequently happens that you are unable to obtain data on a variable that you would like to include in a regression equation. Some variables, such as socioeconomic status and quality of education, are so vaguely defined that it may be impossible even in principle to measure them. Others might be measurable, but require so much time and energy that in practice they have to be abandoned. Sometimes you are frustrated because you are using survey data collected by someone else, and an important variable (from your point of view) has been omitted.

Whatever the reason, it is usually a good idea to use a **proxy variable** to stand in for the missing variable, rather than leave it out entirely. For socioeconomic status, you might use income as a substitute, if data on it are available. For quality of education, you might use the staff–student ratio or expenditure per student. For a variable omitted in a survey, you will have to look at the data actually collected to see if there is a suitable substitute.

There are two good reasons for trying to find a proxy. First, if you simply leave the variable out, your regression is likely to suffer from omitted variable bias of the type described in Section 6.2, and the statistical tests will be invalidated. Second, the results from your proxy regression may indirectly shed light on the influence of the missing variable.

Suppose that the true model is

$$Y = \beta_1 + \beta_2 X_2 + \beta_3 X_3 + \cdots + \beta_k X_k + u. \tag{6.20}$$

Suppose that we have no data for X_2, but another variable Z is an **ideal proxy** for it in the sense that there exists an exact linear relationship between X_2 and Z:

$$X_2 = \lambda + \mu Z \tag{6.21}$$

λ and μ being fixed, but unknown, constants. (Note that if λ and μ were known, we could calculate X_2 from Z, and so there would be no need to use Z as a proxy. Note further that we cannot estimate λ and μ by regression analysis, because to do that we need data on X_2.)

Substituting for X_2 from (6.21) into (6.20), the model may be rewritten

$$Y = \beta_1 + \beta_2(\lambda + \mu Z) + \beta_3 X_3 + \cdots + \beta_k X_k + u$$
$$= \beta_1 + \beta_2\lambda + \beta_2\mu Z + \beta_3 X_3 + \cdots + \beta_k X_k + u. \tag{6.22}$$

The model is now formally specified correctly in terms of observable variables, and if we fit it, the following results will obtain:

1. The coefficients of $X_3, \ldots, X_k$, their standard errors, and their t statistics will be the same as if X_2 had been used instead of Z.
2. R^2 will be the same as if X_2 had been used instead of Z.

3. The coefficient of Z will be an estimate of $\beta_2\mu$ and so it will not be possible to obtain an estimate of β_2, unless you are able to guess the value of μ.

4. However, the t statistic for Z will be the same as that which would have been obtained for X_2, and so you are able to assess the significance of X_2, even though you are not able to estimate its coefficient.

5. It will not be possible to obtain an estimate of β_1, since the intercept is now $(\beta_1 + \beta_2\lambda)$, but usually the intercept is of secondary interest, anyway.

With regard to the third point, suppose that you are investigating migration from country A to country B and you are using the (very naïve) model

$$M = \beta_1 + \beta_2 W + u \tag{6.23}$$

where M is the rate of migration of a certain type of worker from A to B, and W is the ratio of the wage rate in B to the wage rate in A. The higher the relative wage rate, you think the higher is migration. But suppose that you only have data on GDP per capita, not wages. You might define a proxy variable G that is the ratio of GDP in B to GDP in A.

In this case it might be reasonable to assume, as a first approximation, that relative wages are proportional to relative GDP. If that were true, one could write (6.21) with $\lambda = 0$ and $\mu = 1$. In this case the coefficient of relative GDP would yield a direct estimate of the coefficient of relative wages. Since variables in regression analysis are frequently defined in relative terms, this special case actually has quite a wide application.

In this discussion we have assumed that Z is an ideal proxy for X_2, and the validity of all the foregoing results depends on this condition. In practice it is unusual to find a proxy that is exactly linearly related to the missing variable, but if the relationship is close the results will hold approximately. A major problem is posed by the fact that there is never any means of testing whether the condition is or is not approximated satisfactorily. One has to justify the use of the proxy subjectively.

Example

The main determinants of educational attainment appear to be the cognitive ability of an individual and the support and motivation provided by the family background. The NLSY data set is exceptional in that cognitive ability measures are available for virtually all the respondents, the data being obtained when the Department of Defense, needing to re-norm the Armed Services Vocational Aptitude Battery scores, sponsored the administration of the tests. However, there are no data that bear directly on support and motivation provided by the family background. This factor is difficult to define and probably has several dimensions. Accordingly, it is unlikely that a single proxy could do justice to it. The

Table 6.6

```
.reg S ASVABC

    Source        SS         df        MS              Number of obs  =      540
---------------------------------------------            F(1,538)     =   274.19
    Model    1081.97059      1    1081.97059            Prob > F       =   0.0000
 Residual    2123.01275    538    3.94612035            R-squared      =   0.3376
---------------------------------------------            Adj R-squared =   0.3364
    Total    3204.98333    539    5.94616574            Root MSE       =   1.9865

---------------------------------------------------------------------------------
        S     Coef.    Std. Err.       t    P>|t|       [95% Conf. Interval]
---------------------------------------------------------------------------------
   ASVABC   .148084     .0089431    16.56   0.000       .1305165    .1656516
    _cons  6.066225     .4672261    12.98   0.000       5.148413    6.984036
---------------------------------------------------------------------------------
.reg S ASVABC SM SF LIBRARY SIBLINGS

    Source        SS         df        MS              Number of obs  =      540
---------------------------------------------            F(5,534)     =    63.21
    Model    1191.57546      5    238.315093            Prob > F       =   0.0000
 Residual    2013.40787    534    3.77042672            R-squared      =   0.3718
---------------------------------------------            Adj R-squared =   0.3659
    Total    3204.98333    539    5.94616574            Root MSE       =   1.9418

---------------------------------------------------------------------------------
        S     Coef.    Std. Err.       t    P>|t|       [95% Conf. Interval]
---------------------------------------------------------------------------------
   ASVABC  .1245327     .0099875    12.47   0.000       .104913     .1441523
       SM  .0388414      .039969     0.97   0.332      -.0396743    .1173571
       SF  .1035001     .0311842     3.32   0.001       .0422413    .1647588
  LIBRARY -.0355224     .2134634    -0.17   0.868      -.4548534    .3838086
 SIBLINGS -.0665348     .0408795    -1.63   0.104      -.1468392    .0137696
    _cons  5.846517     .5681221    10.29   0.000       4.730489    6.962546
```

NLSY data set includes data on parental educational attainment and the number of siblings of the respondent, both of which could be used as proxies, the rationale for the latter being that parents who are ambitious for their children tend to limit the family size in order to concentrate resources. The data set also contains three dummy variables specifically intended to capture family background effects: whether anyone in the family possessed a library card, whether anyone in the family bought magazines, and whether anyone in the family bought newspapers, when the respondent was aged 14. However the explanatory power of these variables appears to be very limited.

The regression output in Table 6.6 shows the results of regressing S on $ASVABC$ only and on $ASVABC$, parental education, number of siblings, and the library card dummy variable. $ASVABC$ is positively correlated with SM, SF, and $LIBRARY$ (correlation coefficients 0.38, 0.42 and 0.22, respectively), and negatively correlated with $SIBLINGS$ (correlation coefficient -0.19). Its coefficient is therefore unambiguously biased upwards in the first regression. However, there may still be an element of bias in the second, given the weakness of the proxy variables.

Unintentional proxies

It sometimes happens that you use a proxy without realizing it. You think that Y depends upon Z, but in reality it depends upon X.

If the correlation between Z and X is low, the results will be poor, so you may realize that something is wrong but, if the correlation is good, the results may appear to be satisfactory (R^2 up to the anticipated level, etc.) and you may remain blissfully unaware that the relationship is false.

Does this matter? Well, it depends on why you are running the regression in the first place. If the purpose of fitting the regression line is to predict future values of Y, the use of a proxy will not matter much, provided of course that the correlation remains high and was not a statistical fluke in the sample period. However, if your intention is to use the explanatory variable as a policy instrument for influencing the dependent variable, the consequences could be serious. Unless there happens to be a functional connection between the proxy and the true explanatory variable, manipulating the proxy will have no effect on the dependent variable. If the motive for your regression is scientific curiosity, the outcome is equally unsatisfactory.

Unintentional proxies are especially common in time series analysis, particularly in macroeconomic models. If the true explanatory variable is subject to a time trend, you will probably get a good fit if you substitute (intentionally or otherwise) any other variable with a time trend. Even if you relate changes in your dependent variable to changes in your explanatory variable, you are likely to get similar results whether you are using the correct explanatory variable or a proxy, since macroeconomic variables tend to change in concert in periods of economic expansion or recession.

Exercises

6.9 Is potential work experience a satisfactory proxy for actual work experience? Length of work experience is generally found to be an important determinant of earnings. Many data sets do not contain this variable. To avoid the problem of omitted variable bias, a standard practice is to use PWE, potential years of work experience, as a proxy. PWE is defined as AGE, less age at completion of full-time education (years of schooling plus 5, assuming that schooling begins at the age of 6):

$$PWE = AGE - S - 5.$$

Using your $EAEF$ data set, regress $LGEARN$ (1) on S, $ASVABC$, $MALE$, $ETHBLACK$, $ETHHISP$, (2) on S, $ASVABC$, $MALE$, $ETHBLACK$, $ETHHISP$, and PWE and (3) on S, $ASVABC$, $MALE$, $ETHBLACK$, $ETHHISP$, and EXP. Compare the results and evaluate whether PWE would have been a satisfactory proxy for EXP if data for EXP had not been available.

Variation: *PWE* is not likely to be a satisfactory proxy for work experience for females because it does not take into account time spent not working while rearing children. Investigate this by running the three regressions for the male and female subsamples separately. You must drop the *MALE* dummy from the specification (explain why).

6.10* A researcher has data on output per worker, Y, and capital per worker, K, both measured in thousands of dollars, for 50 firms in the textiles industry in 2005. She hypothesizes that output per worker depends on capital per worker and perhaps also the technological sophistication of the firm, *TECH*:

$$Y = \beta_1 + \beta_2 K + \beta_3 TECH + u$$

where u is a disturbance term. She is unable to measure *TECH* and decides to use expenditure per worker on research and development in 2005, *R&D*, as a proxy for it. She fits the following regressions (standard errors in parentheses):

$$\hat{Y} = 1.02 + 0.32K \qquad R^2 = 0.749$$
$$\phantom{\hat{Y} = }(0.45)\ (0.04)$$

$$\hat{Y} = 0.34 + 0.29K + 0.05R\&D \qquad R^2 = 0.750.$$
$$\phantom{\hat{Y} = }(0.61)\ (0.22)\ \ \ (0.15)$$

The correlation coefficient for K and $R\&D$ was 0.92. Discuss these regression results

1. assuming that Y does depend on both K and *TECH*,

2. assuming that Y depends only on K.

6.5   Testing a linear restriction

In Section 3.4 it was demonstrated that you may be able to alleviate a problem of multicollinearity in a regression model if you believe that there exists a linear relationship between its parameters. By exploiting the information about the relationship, you will make the regression estimates more efficient. Even if the original model was not subject to multicollinearity, the gain in efficiency may yield a welcome improvement in the precision of the estimates, as reflected by their standard errors.

The example discussed in Section 3.4 was an educational attainment model with S as the dependent variable and *ASVABC*, *SM*, and *SF* as explanatory variables. The regression output is shown in Table 6.7.

Somewhat surprisingly, the coefficient of *SM* is not significant, even at the 5 percent level, using a one-sided test. However assortive mating leads to a high correlation between *SM* and *SF* and the regression appeared to be suffering from multicollinearity.

We then hypothesized that mother's and father's education are equally important for educational attainment, allowing us to impose the restriction $\beta_3 = \beta_4$ and rewrite the equation as

$$S = \beta_1 + \beta_2 ASVABC + \beta_3(SM + SF) + u$$
$$= \beta_1 + \beta_2 ASVABC + \beta_3 SP + u \qquad (6.24)$$

where *SP* is the sum of *SM* and *SF*. The regression output from this specification is shown in Table 6.8.

The standard error of *SP* is much smaller than those of *SM* and *SF*, indicating that the use of the restriction has led to a gain in efficiency, and as a consequence

Table 6.7

```
.reg S ASVABC SM SF

  Source         SS          df       MS            Number of obs  =     540
                                                    F(3,536)       =  104.30
  Model     1181.36981        3   393.789935         Prob > F       =  0.0000
                                                     R-squared      =  0.3686
  Residual  2023.61353      536   3.77539837         Adj R-squared  =  0.3651
                                                     Root MSE       =   1.943
  Total     3204.98333      539   5.94616574

       S      Coef.    Std. Err.       t    P>|t|      [95% Conf. Interval]

  ASVABC   .1257087    .0098533    12.76   0.000      .1063528    .1450646
      SM   .0492424    .0390901     1.26   0.208     -.027546    .1260309
      SF   .1076825    .0309522     3.48   0.001       .04688    .1684851
   _cons   5.370631    .4882155    11.00   0.000      4.41158    6.329681
```

Table 6.8

```
.g SP = SM + SF

.reg S ASVABC SP

  Source         SS          df       MS            Number of obs  =     540
                                                    F(2,537)       =  156.04
  Model     1177.98338        2   588.991689         Prob > F       =  0.0000
                                                     R-squared      =  0.3675
  Residual  2026.99996      537   3.77467403         Adj R-squared  =  0.3652
                                                     Root MSE       =  1.9429
  Total     3204.98333      539   5.94616574

       S      Coef.    Std. Err.       t    P>|t|      [95% Conf. Interval]

  ASVABC   .1253106    .0098434    12.73   0.000      .1059743    .1446469
      SP   .0828368    .0164247     5.04   0.000      .0505722    .1151014
   _cons    5.29617    .4817972    10.99   0.000      4.349731    6.242608
```

the t statistic is very high. Thus the problem of multicollinearity has been eliminated. However, we are obliged to test the validity of the restriction, and there are two equivalent procedures.

Before we do this, we should make a distinction between **linear restrictions** and **nonlinear restrictions**. In a linear restriction such as $\beta_2 = \beta_3$ or $\beta_2 + \beta_3 = 1$, the parameters conform to a simple linear equation. In a nonlinear restriction, such as $\beta_2 = \beta_3\beta_4$, they do not. The procedures described here are for linear restrictions only. We shall encounter nonlinear restrictions and tests for them in later chapters.

F test of a restriction

One procedure is to perform an **F test of a linear restriction**. We run the regression in both the restricted and the unrestricted forms and denote the sum of the squares of the residuals RSS_R for the restricted model and RSS_U for the unrestricted model. Since the imposition of the restriction makes it more difficult to fit the regression equation to the data, RSS_R cannot be less than RSS_U and will in general be greater. We would like to test whether the improvement in the fit on going from the restricted to the unrestricted model is significant. If it is, the restriction should be rejected.

For this purpose we can use an F test whose structure is the same as that described in Section 3.5:

$$F = \frac{\text{improvement in fit/extra degrees of freedom used up}}{\text{residual sum of squares remaining/degrees of freedom remaining}}.$$

(6.25)

In this case the improvement on going from the restricted to the unrestricted model is $(RSS_R - RSS_U)$, one extra degree of freedom is used up in the unrestricted model (because there is one more parameter to estimate), and the residual sum of squares remaining after the shift from the restricted to the unrestricted model is RSS_U. Hence the F statistic in this case is

$$F(1, n-k) = \frac{RSS_R - RSS_U}{RSS_U/(n-k)},$$

(6.26)

where k is the number of parameters in the unrestricted model. It is distributed with 1 and $n-k$ degrees of freedom under the null hypothesis that the restriction is valid. The first argument for the distribution of the F statistic is 1 because we are testing just one restriction. If we were simultaneously testing several restrictions, it would be equal to the number of restrictions being tested. The second argument is the number of degrees of freedom in the unrestricted model.

In the case of the educational attainment function, the null hypothesis was H_0: $\beta_3 = \beta_4$, where β_3 is the coefficient of SM and β_4 is the coefficient of SF. The residual sum of squares was 2027.00 in the restricted model and 2023.61 in the unrestricted model. Hence the F statistic is

$$F(1, n - k) = \frac{2027.00 - 2023.61}{2023.61/536} = 0.90. \qquad (6.27)$$

Since the F statistic is less than 1, it is not significant at any significance level and we do not reject the null hypothesis that the coefficients of SM and SF are equal.

t test of a restriction

The other procedure is to perform a t test of a linear restriction. This involves writing down the model for the restricted model and adding the term that would convert it back to the unrestricted model. The test evaluates whether this additional term is needed. To find the conversion term, we write the restricted model of the model under the unrestricted model and subtract:

$$S = \beta_1 + \beta_2 ASVABC + \beta_3 SM + \beta_4 SF + u \qquad (6.28)$$

$$S = \beta_1 + \beta_2 ASVABC + \beta_3 SP + u \qquad (6.29)$$

$$0 = \beta_3 SM + \beta_4 SF - \beta_3 SP$$

$$= \beta_3 SM + \beta_4 SF - \beta_3 (SM + SF)$$

$$= (\beta_4 - \beta_3) SF. \qquad (6.30)$$

If we add this term to the restricted model we obtain a re-parameterized version of the unrestricted model:

$$S = \beta_1 + \beta_2 ASVABC + \beta_3 SP + (\beta_4 - \beta_3) SF + u. \qquad (6.31)$$

We investigate whether the conversion term is needed.

The null hypothesis, $H_0: \beta_4 - \beta_3 = 0$, is that the coefficient of the conversion term is zero, and the alternative hypothesis is that it is different from zero. Of course the null hypothesis is that the restriction is valid. If it is valid, the conversion term is not needed, and the restricted model is an adequate representation of the data.

Table 6.9 presents the corresponding regression for the educational attainment example. We see that the coefficient of SF is not significantly different from zero, indicating that the term is not needed and that the restricted model is an adequate representation of the data.

Why is the t test approach equivalent to that of the F test? The F test tests the improvement in fit when you go from the restricted model to the unrestricted model. This is accomplished by adding the conversion term, but, as we know, an F test on the improvement in fit when you add an extra term is equivalent to the t test on the coefficient of that term (see Section 3.5).

Table 6.9

```
.reg S ASVABC SP SF

   Source        SS         df       MS              Number of obs =     540
------------------------------------------           F(3,536)       =  104.30
   Model     1181.36981      3    393.789935          Prob > F       =  0.0000
Residual     2023.61353    536    3.77539837          R-squared      =  0.3686
------------------------------------------           Adj R-squared  =  0.3651
   Total     3204.98333    539    5.94616574          Root MSE       =   1.943

------------------------------------------------------------------------------
       S      Coef.   Std. Err.      t    P>|t|        [95% Conf. Interval]
------------------------------------------------------------------------------
   ASVABC   .1257087   .0098533   12.76   0.000       .1063528    .1450646
       SP   .0492424   .0390901    1.26   0.208      -.027546     .1260309
       SF   .0584401   .0617051    0.95   0.344      -.0627734    .1796536
    _cons   5.370631   .4882155   11.00   0.000       4.41158     6.329681
```

Exercises

6.11 Is previous work experience as valuable as experience with the current employer? Using your *EAEF* data set, first regress *LGEARN* on *S*, *EXP*, *MALE*, *ETHBLACK*, and *ETHHISP*. Then define

$$PREVEXP = EXP - TENURE.$$

The variable *TENURE* in your data set is the number of years spent working with the current employer. Regress *LGEARN* on *S*, *PREVEXP*, *TENURE*, *MALE*, *ETHBLACK*, and *ETHHISP*. The estimates of the coefficients of *PREVEXP* and *TENURE* will be different. This raises the issue of whether the difference is due to random factors or whether the coefficients are significantly different. Set up the null hypothesis H_0: $\delta_1 = \delta_2$, where δ_1 is the coefficient of *PREVEXP* and δ_2 is the coefficient of *TENURE*. Explain why the regression with *EXP* is the correct specification if H_0 is true, while the regression with *PREVEXP* and *TENURE* should be used if H_0 is false. Perform an *F* test of the restriction using *RSS* for the two regressions. Do this for the combined sample and also for males and females separately.

6.12 Using your *EAEF* data set, regress *LGEARN* on *S*, *EXP*, *MALE*, *ETHBLACK*, *ETHHISP*, and *TENURE*. Demonstrate that a *t* test on the coefficient of *TENURE* is a test of the restriction described in Exercise 6.11. Verify that the same result is obtained. Do this for the combined sample and also for males and females separately.

6.13* The first regression shows the result of regressing *LGFDHO*, the logarithm of annual household expenditure on food eaten at home, on *LGEXP*, the logarithm of total annual household expenditure, and *LGSIZE*, the logarithm of the number of persons in the household, using a sample of 868 house-holds in the 1995 Consumer Expenditure Survey. In the second regression, *LGFDHOPC*, the logarithm of food expenditure per capita (*FDHO/SIZE*), is regressed on *LGEXPPC*, the logarithm of total expenditure per capita (*EXP/SIZE*). In the third regression *LGFDHOPC* is regressed on *LGEXPPC* and *LGSIZE*.

```
.reg LGFDHO LGEXP LGSIZE

  Source       SS         df        MS              Number of obs =     868
---------------------------------------------       F(2,865)      = 460.92
   Model    138.776549     2    69.3882747          Prob > F      =  0.0000
 Residual   130.219231    865   .150542464          R-squared     =  0.5159
---------------------------------------------       Adj R-squared =  0.5148
   Total    268.995781    867   .310260416          Root MSE      =   .388
-------------------------------------------------------------------------------
  LGFDHO     Coef.    Std. Err.       t     P>|t|   [95% Conf.  Interval]
-------------------------------------------------------------------------------
   LGEXP    .2866813   .0226824    12.639   0.000    .2421622    .3312003
  LGSIZE    .4854698   .0255476    19.003   0.000    .4353272    .5356124
   _cons   4.720269    .2209996    21.359   0.000   4.286511    5.154027
-------------------------------------------------------------------------------


.reg LGFDHOPC LGEXPPC

  Source       SS         df        MS              Number of obs =     868
---------------------------------------------       F(1,866)      = 313.04
   Model    51.4364364     1    51.4364364          Prob > F      =  0.0000
                                                    R-squared     =  0.2655
 Residual   142.293973    866   .164311747          Adj R-squared =  0.2647
---------------------------------------------       Root MSE      =  .40535
   Total     193.73041    867   .223449146
-------------------------------------------------------------------------------
 LGFDHOPC    Coef.    Std. Err.       t     P>|t|   [95% Conf.  Interval]
-------------------------------------------------------------------------------
 LGEXPPC     .376283   .0212674    17.693   0.000    .3345414    .4180246
  _ cons    3.700667   .1978925    18.700   0.000   3.312262    4.089072
-------------------------------------------------------------------------------


.reg LGFDHOPC LGEXPPC LGSIZE

  Source       SS         df        MS              Number of obs =     868
---------------------------------------------       F(2,865)      = 210.94
   Model    63.5111811     2    31.7555905          Prob > F      =  0.0000
                                                    R-squared     =  0.3278
 Residual   130.219229    865   .150542461          Adj R-squared =  0.3263
---------------------------------------------       Root MSE      =   .388
   Total     193.73041    867   .223449146
-------------------------------------------------------------------------------
 LGFDHOPC    Coef.    Std. Err.       t     P>|t|   [95% Conf.  Interval]
-------------------------------------------------------------------------------
 LGEXPPC    .2866813   .0226824    12.639   0.000    .2421622    .3312004
  LGSIZE   -.2278489   .0254412    -8.956   0.000   -.2777826   -.1779152
   _cons   4.720269    .2209996    21.359   0.000   4.286511    5.154027
-------------------------------------------------------------------------------
```

1. Explain why the second model is a restricted version of the first, stating the restriction.

2. Perform an F test of the restriction.

3. Perform a t test of the restriction.

4. Summarize your conclusions from the analysis of the regression results.

6.14 In his classic article (Nerlove, 1963), Nerlove derives the following cost function for electricity generation:

$$C = \beta_1 Y^{\beta_2} P_1^{\gamma_1} P_2^{\gamma_2} P_3^{\gamma_3} v,$$

where C is total production cost, Y is output (measured in kilowatt hours), P_1 is the price of labor input, P_2 is the price of capital input, P_3 is the price of fuel (all measured in appropriate units), and v is a disturbance term. Theoretically, the sum of the price elasticities should be 1:

$$\gamma_1 + \gamma_2 + \gamma_3 = 1$$

and hence the cost function may be rewritten

$$\frac{C}{P_3} = \beta_1 Y^{\beta_2} \left(\frac{P_1}{P_3}\right)^{\gamma_1} \left(\frac{P_2}{P_3}\right)^{\gamma_2} v.$$

The two versions of the cost function are fitted to the 29 medium-sized firms in Nerlove's sample, with the following results (standard errors in parentheses):

$$\widehat{\log C} = -4.93 + 0.94 \log Y + 0.31 \log P_1 - 0.26 \log P_2 + 0.44 \log P_3$$
$$\quad\;\;(1.62)\;(0.11)\qquad(0.23)\qquad\quad(0.29)\qquad\quad(0.07)$$
$$RSS = 0.336$$

$$\widehat{\log \frac{C}{P_3}} = -6.55 + 0.91 \log Y + 0.51 \log \frac{P_1}{P_3} + 0.09 \log \frac{P_2}{P_3} \quad RSS = 0.364.$$
$$\qquad\;(0.16)\;(0.11)\qquad\;\;(0.23)\qquad\quad(0.19)$$

Compare the regression results for the two equations and perform a test of the validity of the restriction.

6.6   Getting the most out of your residuals

There are two ways of looking at the residuals obtained after fitting a regression equation to a set of data. If you are pessimistic and passive, you will simply see them as evidence of failure. The bigger the residuals, the worse is your fit, and the smaller is R^2. The whole object of the exercise is to fit the regression equation in such a way as to minimize the sum of the squares of the residuals. However, if you are enterprising, you will also see the residuals as a potentially fertile source of new ideas, perhaps even new hypotheses. They offer both a challenge and constructive criticism. The challenge is that providing the stimulus for most scientific research: evidence of the need to find a better explanation of the facts. The constructive criticism comes in because the residuals, taken individually, indicate when and where and by how much the existing model is failing to fit the facts.

Taking advantage of this constructive criticism requires patience on the part of the researcher. If the sample is small enough, you should look for **outliers**, observations with large positive or negative residuals, and try to hypothesize explanations for them. Some regression applications actually identify outliers for you, as part of the regression diagnostics. Some of the outliers may be caused by special factors specific to the observations in question. These are not of much use to the theorist. Other factors, however, may appear to be associated with the residuals in several observations. As soon as you detect a regularity of this kind, you have the makings of progress. The next step is to find a sensible way of quantifying the factor and of including it in the model.

Key terms

F test of a restriction	outlier
ideal proxy	proxy variable
linear restriction	redundant variable
nonlinear restriction	t test of a restriction
omitted variable bias	

7 Heteroscedasticity

Medicine is traditionally divided into the three branches of anatomy, physiology, and pathology—what a body is made of, how it works, and what can go wrong with it. It is time to start discussing the pathology of least squares regression analysis. The properties of the estimators of the regression coefficients depend on the properties of the disturbance term in the regression model. In this and following chapters we shall be looking at some of the problems that arise when the regression model assumptions listed in Section 2.2 are not satisfied.

7.1 Heteroscedasticity and its implications

Assumption A.4 in Section 2.2 states that the variance of the disturbance term in each observation should be constant. This sounds peculiar and needs a bit of explanation. The disturbance term in each observation has only *one* value, so what can be meant by its 'variance'?

What we are talking about is its *potential* distribution *before* the sample is generated. When we write the model

$$Y = \beta_1 + \beta_2 X + u, \tag{7.1}$$

Assumptions A.3 and A.4 state that the disturbance terms $u_1, \ldots, u_n$ in the n observations are drawn from probability distributions that have zero mean and the same variance. The *actual* values of the disturbance term in the sample will sometimes be positive, sometimes negative, sometimes relatively far from zero, sometimes relatively close, but there will be no reason to anticipate a particularly erratic value in any given observation. To put it another way, the probability of u reaching a given positive (or negative) value will be the same in all observations. This condition is known as homoscedasticity, which means 'same dispersion'.

Figure 7.1 provides an illustration of homoscedasticity. To keep the diagram simple, the sample contains only five observations. Let us start with the first observation, where X has the value X_1. If there were no disturbance term in the model, the observation would be represented by the circle vertically above X_1 on the line $Y = \beta_1 + \beta_2 X$. The effect of the disturbance term is to shift the observation upwards or downwards vertically. The *potential* distribution of the

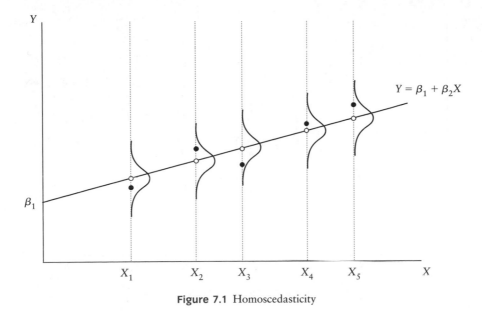

Figure 7.1 Homoscedasticity

disturbance term, before the observation has been generated, is shown by the normal distribution above and below the circle. The actual value of the disturbance term for this observation turned out to be negative, the observation being represented by the solid marker. The potential distribution of the disturbance term, and the actual outcome, are shown in a similar way for the other four observations.

Although homoscedasticity is often taken for granted in regression analysis, in some contexts it may be more reasonable to suppose that the potential distribution of the disturbance term is different for different observations in the sample. This is illustrated in Figure 7.2, where the variance of the potential distribution of the disturbance term is increasing as X increases. This does not mean that the disturbance term will *necessarily* have a particularly large (positive or negative) value in an observation where X is large, but it does mean that the *probability* of having an erratic value will be relatively high. This is an example of **heteroscedasticity**, which means 'differing dispersion'. Mathematically, homoscedasticity and heteroscedasticity may be defined:

Homoscedasticity: $\sigma_{u_i}^2 = \sigma_u^2$, same for all observations
Heteroscedasticity: $\sigma_{u_i}^2$ not the same for all observations.

Figure 7.3 illustrates how a typical scatter diagram would look if Y were an increasing function of X and the heteroscedasticity were of the type shown in Figure 7.2. You can see that, although the observations are not necessarily further away from the nonstochastic component of the relationship, represented by the line $Y = \beta_1 + \beta_2 X$, there is a tendency for their dispersion to increase as X increases. (You should be warned that heteroscedasticity is not necessarily of

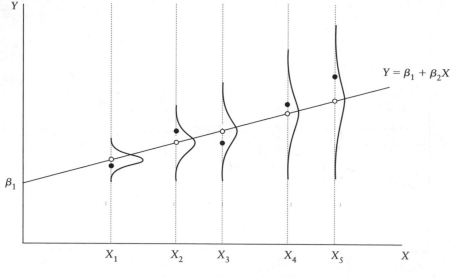

Figure 7.2 Heteroscedasticity

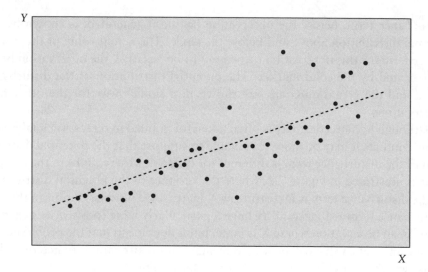

Figure 7.3 Model with a heteroscedastic disturbance term

the type shown in Figures 7.2 and 7.3. The term refers to any case in which the variance of the probability distribution of the disturbance term is not the same in all observations.)

Why does heteroscedasticity matter? This particular regression model assumption does not appear to have been used anywhere in the analysis so far, so it might seem almost irrelevant. In particular, the proofs of the unbiasedness of the OLS regression coefficients did not use this assumption.

There are two reasons. The first concerns the variances of the regression coefficients. You want these to be as small as possible so that, in a probabilistic sense, you have maximum precision. If there is no heteroscedasticity, and if the other regression model assumptions are satisfied, the OLS regression coefficients have the lowest variances of all the unbiased estimators that are linear functions of the observations of Y. If heteroscedasticity is present, the OLS estimators are inefficient because you could, at least in principle, find other estimators that have smaller variances and are still unbiased.

The second, equally important, reason is that the estimators of the standard errors of the regression coefficients will be wrong. They are computed on the assumption that the distribution of the disturbance term is homoscedastic. If this is not the case, they are biased, and as a consequence the t tests, and also the usual F tests, are invalid. It is quite likely that the standard errors will be underestimated, so the t statistics will be overestimated and you will have a misleading impression of the precision of your regression coefficients. You may be led to believe that a coefficient is significantly different from zero, at a given significance level, when in fact it is not.

The inefficiency property can be explained intuitively quite easily. Suppose that heteroscedasticity of the type displayed in Figures 7.2 and 7.3 is present. An observation where the potential distribution of the disturbance term has a small standard deviation, like the first observation in Figure 7.2, will tend to lie close to the line $Y = \beta_1 + \beta_2 X$ and hence will be a good guide to the location of the line. By contrast, an observation where the potential distribution has a large standard deviation, like that for the fifth observation in Figure 7.2, will be an unreliable guide to the location of the line. OLS does not discriminate between the quality of the observations, giving equal weight to each, irrespective of whether they are good or poor guides to the location of the line. It follows that if we can find a way of giving more weight to the high-quality observations and less to the unreliable ones, we are likely to obtain a better fit. In other words, our estimators of β_1 and β_2 will be more efficient. We shall see how to do this below.

Possible causes of heteroscedasticity

Heteroscedasticity is likely to be a problem when the values of the variables in the sample vary substantially in different observations. If the true relationship is given by $Y = \beta_1 + \beta_2 X + u$, it may well be the case that the variations in the omitted variables and the measurement errors that are jointly responsible for the disturbance term will be relatively small when Y and X are small and large when they are large, economic variables tending to move in size together.

For example, suppose that you are using the simple regression model to investigate the relationship between value added in manufacturing, $MANU$, and gross domestic product, GDP, in cross-country data, and that you have collected the sample of observations given in Table 7.1 and plotted in Figure 7.4.

Table 7.1 Manufacturing value added, GDP, and population for a sample of countries, 1994

Country	MANU	GDP	POP	MANU/POP	GDP/POP
Belgium	44517	232006	10.093	4411	22987
Canada	112617	547203	29.109	3869	18798
Chile	13096	50919	13.994	936	3639
Denmark	25927	151266	5.207	4979	29050
Finland	21581	97624	5.085	4244	19199
France	256316	1330998	57.856	4430	23005
Greece	9392	98861	10.413	902	9494
Hong Kong	11758	130823	6.044	1945	21645
Hungary	7227	41506	10.162	711	4084
Ireland	17572	52662	3.536	4970	14893
Israel	11349	74121	5.362	2117	13823
Italy	145013	1016286	57.177	2536	17774
Korea, S.	161318	380820	44.501	3625	8558
Kuwait	2797	24848	1.754	1595	14167
Malaysia	18874	72505	19.695	958	3681
Mexico	55073	420788	89.564	615	4698
Netherlands	48595	334286	15.382	3159	21732
Norway	13484	122926	4.314	3126	28495
Portugal	17025	87352	9.824	1733	8892
Singapore	20648	71039	3.268	6318	21738
Slovakia	2720	13746	5.325	511	2581
Slovenia	4520	14386	1.925	2348	7473
Spain	80104	483652	39.577	2024	12221
Sweden	34806	198432	8.751	3977	22675
Switzerland	57503	261388	7.104	8094	36794
Syria	3317	44753	13.840	240	3234
Turkey	31115	135961	59.903	519	2270
UK	244397	1024609	58.005	4213	17664

Source: UNIDO Yearbook 1997
Note: MANU and GDP are measured in US$ million. POP is measured in million.
MANU/POP and GDP/POP are measured in US$.

Manufacturing output tends to account for 15 to 25 percent of GDP, variations being caused by comparative advantage and historical economic development. The sample includes small economies such as Slovenia and Slovakia as well as large ones such as France, the UK, and Italy. Clearly, when GDP is large, a 1 percent variation will make a great deal more difference, in absolute terms, than when it is small.

South Korea and Mexico are both countries with relatively large GDP. The manufacturing sector is relatively important in South Korea, so its observation is far above the trend line. The opposite was the case for Mexico, at least in 1994. Singapore and Greece are another pair of countries with relatively large and small manufacturing sectors. However, because the GDP of both countries is small, their variations from the trend relationship are also small.

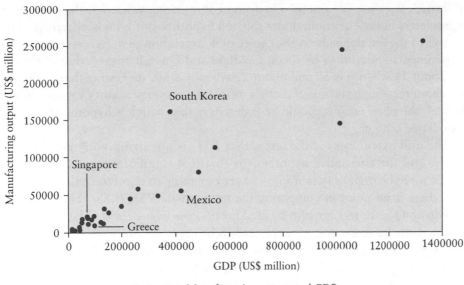

Figure 7.4 Manufacturing output and GDP

7.2 **Detection of heteroscedasticity**

In principle there is no limit to the possible different types of heteroscedasticity and accordingly a large number of different tests appropriate for different circumstances have been proposed. They fall into two categories: those that depend on a prior assumption concerning the nature of the heteroscedasticity, and those that do not. We will confine our attention to one of each: the Goldfeld–Quandt test, and the White test.

The Goldfeld–Quandt test

Perhaps the most common formal test for heteroscedasticity is the Goldfeld–Quandt test (Goldfeld and Quandt, 1965). It assumes that σ_{u_i}, the standard deviation of the probability distribution of the disturbance term in observation i, is proportional to the size of X_i. It also assumes that the disturbance term is normally distributed and satisfies the other regression model assumptions.

The n observations in the sample are ordered by the magnitude of X and separate regressions are run for the first n' and for the last n' observations, the middle $(n - 2n')$ observations being dropped entirely. If heteroscedasticity is present, and if the assumption concerning its nature is true, the variance of u in the last n' observations will be greater than that in the first n', and this will be reflected in the residual sums of squares in the two subregressions. Denoting these by RSS_1 and RSS_2 for the subregressions with the first n' and the last n' observations, respectively, the ratio RSS_2/RSS_1 will be distributed as an

F statistic with $(n' - k)$ and $(n' - k)$ degrees of freedom, where k is the number of parameters in the equation, under the null hypothesis of homoscedasticity. The power of the test depends on the choice of n' in relation to n. As a result of some experiments undertaken by them, Goldfeld and Quandt suggest that n' should be about 11 when n is 30 and about 22 when n is 60, suggesting that n' should be about three eighths of n. If there is more than one explanatory variable in the model, the observations should be ordered by that which is hypothesized to be associated with σ_i.

The null hypothesis for the test is that RSS_2 is not significantly greater than RSS_1, and the alternative hypothesis is that it is significantly greater. If RSS_2 turns out to be *smaller* than RSS_1, you are not going to reject the null hypothesis and there is no point in computing the test statistic RSS_2/RSS_1. However, the Goldfeld–Quandt test can also be used for the case where the standard deviation of the disturbance term is hypothesized to be inversely proportional to X_i. The procedure is the same as before, but the test statistic is now RSS_1/RSS_2, and it will again be distributed as an F statistic with $(n' - k)$ and $(n' - k)$ degrees of freedom under the null hypothesis of homoscedasticity.

In the case of the data in Table 7.1, OLS regressions were run using the observations for the 11 countries with smallest GDP and for the 11 countries with largest GDP. The residual sum of squares in the first regression was 157×10^6, and in the second it was $13,518 \times 10^6$. The ratio RSS_2/RSS_1 was therefore 86.1. The critical value of $F(9, 9)$ at the 0.1 percent level is 10.1, and the null hypothesis of homoscedasticity was therefore rejected.

The White test

The White test for heteroscedasticity (White, 1980) looks more generally for evidence of an association between the variance of the disturbance term and the regressors. Since the variance of the disturbance term in observation i is unobservable, the squared residual for that observation is used as a proxy. The test consists of regressing the squared residuals on the explanatory variables in the model, their squares, and their cross-products, omitting any duplicative variables. (For example, the square of a dummy variable would be duplicative since its values are the same as those of the dummy variable.) The test statistic is nR^2, using R^2 from this regression. Under the null hypothesis of no association, it is distributed as a chi-squared statistic with degrees of freedom equal to the number of regressors, including the constant, minus one, in large samples.

In the case of the data in Table 7.1, the squared residuals were regressed on *GDP*, its square, and a constant. R^2 was 0.2114 and n was 28. The test statistic was therefore 5.92. The critical value of chi-squared with two degrees of freedom is 5.99 at the 5 percent level and so the null hypothesis of homoscedasticity is not rejected.

Why has the White test failed to detect heteroscedasticity when the Goldfeld–Quandt test concluded that it was present at a high level of significance? One reason is that it is a large-sample test, and the sample is actually quite small. A second is that it tends to have low power—a price that one has to pay for its generality. These problems can be exacerbated by a loss of degrees of freedom if there are many explanatory variables in the original model. In the present example, there was only one explanatory variable, and so only three degrees of freedom were absorbed when fitting the squared residuals regression. If there had been four explanatory variables, 15 degrees of freedom would have been absorbed in the squared residuals regression: five for the constant and the variables, another four for the squares of the variables, and a further six for the cross-product terms, leaving only 13 degrees of freedom in this case for the regression.

Exercises

7.1 The table gives data on government recurrent expenditure, G, investment, I, gross domestic product, Y, and population, P, for 30 countries in 1997 (source: 1999 International Monetary Fund *Yearbook*). G, I, and Y are measured in US\$ billion and P in million. A researcher investigating whether government expenditure tends to crowd out investment fits the regression (standard errors in parentheses):

$$\hat{I} = 18.10 - 1.07G + 0.36Y \qquad R^2 = 0.99.$$
$$\phantom{\hat{I} = }(7.79)\ (0.14)\quad (0.02)$$

Country	I	G	Y	P	Country	I	G	Y	P
Australia	94.5	75.5	407.9	18.5	Netherlands	73.0	49.9	360.5	15.6
Austria	46.0	39.2	206.0	8.1	New Zealand	12.9	9.9	65.1	3.8
Canada	119.3	125.1	631.2	30.3	Norway	35.3	30.9	153.4	4.4
Czech Republic	16.0	10.5	52.0	10.3	Philippines	20.1	10.7	82.2	78.5
Denmark	34.2	42.9	169.3	5.3	Poland	28.7	23.4	135.6	38.7
Finland	20.2	25.0	121.5	5.1	Portugal	25.6	19.9	102.1	9.8
France	255.9	347.2	1409.2	58.6	Russia	84.7	94.0	436.0	147.1
Germany	422.5	406.7	2102.7	82.1	Singapore	35.6	9.0	95.9	3.7
Greece	24.0	17.7	119.9	10.5	Spain	109.5	86.0	532.0	39.3
Iceland	1.4	1.5	7.5	0.3	Sweden	31.2	58.8	227.8	8.9
Ireland	14.3	10.1	73.2	3.7	Switzerland	50.2	38.7	256.0	7.1
Italy	190.8	189.7	1145.4	57.5	Thailand	48.1	15.0	153.9	60.6
Japan	1105.9	376.3	3901.3	126.1	Turkey	50.2	23.3	189.1	62.5
Korea	154.9	49.3	442.5	46.0	UK	210.1	230.7	1256.0	58.2
Malaysia	41.6	10.8	97.3	21.0	USA	1517.7	1244.1	8110.9	267.9

She sorts the observations by increasing size of Y and runs the regression again for the 11 countries with smallest Y and the 11 countries with largest Y. *RSS* for these regressions is 321 and 28101, respectively. Perform a Goldfeld–Quandt test for heteroscedasticity.

7.2 The researcher saves the residuals from the full-sample regression in Exercise 7.1 and regresses their squares on G, Y, their squares, and their product. R^2 is 0.9878. Perform a White test for heteroscedasticity.

7.3 Fit an earnings function using your *EAEF* data set, taking *EARNINGS* as the dependent variable and S, *EXP*, and *MALE* as the explanatory variables, and perform a Goldfeld–Quandt test for heteroscedasticity in the S dimension. Remember to sort the observations by S first.

7.4 Fit an earnings function using your *EAEF* data set, using the same specification as in Exercise 7.3 and perform a White test for heterscedasticity.

7.5* The following regressions were fitted using the Shanghai school cost data introduced in Section 5.1 (standard errors in parentheses):

$$\widehat{COST} = 24,000 + 339N \qquad R^2 = 0.39$$
$$\phantom{\widehat{COST} = }(27,000) \quad (50)$$

$$\widehat{COST} = 51,000 - 4,000OCC + 152N + 284NOCC \qquad R^2 = 0.68.$$
$$\phantom{\widehat{COST} = }(31,000) \quad (41,000) \qquad (60) \qquad (76)$$

where *COST* is the annual cost of running a school, N is the number of students, *OCC* is a dummy variable defined to be 0 for regular schools and 1 for occupational schools, and *NOCC* is a slope dummy variable defined as the product of N and *OCC*. There are 74 schools in the sample. With the data sorted by N, the regressions are fitted again for the 26 smallest and 26 largest schools, the residual sum of squares being as shown in the table.

	26 smallest	26 largest
First regression	7.8×10^{10}	54.4×10^{10}
Second regression	6.7×10^{10}	13.8×10^{10}

Perform a Goldfeld–Quandt test for heteroscedasticity for the two models and, with reference to Figure 5.5, explain why the problem of heteroscedasticity is less severe in the second model.

7.6* The file educ.dta on the website contains international cross-sectional data on aggregate expenditure on education, *EDUC*, gross domestic product, *GDP*, and population, *POP*, for a sample of 38 countries in 1997. *EDUC* and *GDP* are measured in US\$ million and *POP* is measured in thousands. See Appendix B for further information. Download the data set, plot a scatter diagram of *EDUC* on *GDP*, and comment on whether the data set appears to be subject to heteroscedasticity. Sort the data set by *GDP* and perform a Goldfeld–Quandt test for heteroscedasticity, running regressions using the subsamples of 14 countries with the smallest and greatest *GDP*.

7.3   What can you do about heteroscedasticity?

Suppose that the true relationship is

$$Y_i = \beta_1 + \beta_2 X_i + u_i. \tag{7.2}$$

Let the standard deviation of the disturbance term in observation i be σ_{u_i}. If you happened to know σ_{u_i} for each observation, you could eliminate the heteroscedasticity by dividing each observation by its value of σ. The model becomes

$$\frac{Y_i}{\sigma_{u_i}} = \beta_1 \frac{1}{\sigma_{u_i}} + \beta_2 \frac{X_i}{\sigma_{u_i}} + \frac{u_i}{\sigma_{u_i}}. \tag{7.3}$$

The disturbance term u_i/σ_{u_i} is homoscedastic because the population variance of $\dfrac{u_i}{\sigma_{u_i}}$ is

$$E\left\{ \left(\frac{u_i}{\sigma_{u_i}} \right)^2 \right\} = \frac{1}{\sigma_{u_i}^2} E(u_i^2) = \frac{1}{\sigma_{u_i}^2} \sigma_{u_i}^2 = 1. \tag{7.4}$$

Therefore, every observation will have a disturbance term drawn from a distribution with population variance 1, and the model will be homoscedastic. The revised model may be rewritten

$$Y_i' = \beta_1 H_i + \beta_2 X_i' + u_i', \tag{7.5}$$

where $Y_i' = Y_i/\sigma_{u_i}$, $X_i' = X_i/\sigma_{u_i}$, H is a new variable whose value in observation i is $1/\sigma_{u_i}$, and $u_i' = u_i/\sigma_{u_i}$. Note that there should not be a constant term in the equation. By regressing Y' on H and X', you will obtain efficient estimates of β_1 and β_2 with unbiased standard errors.

A mathematical demonstration that the revised model will yield more efficient estimates than the original one is beyond the scope of this text, but it is easy to give an intuitive explanation. Those observations with the smallest values of σ_{u_i} will be the most useful for locating the true relationship between Y and X because they will tend to have the smallest disturbance terms. We are taking advantage of this fact by performing what is sometimes called a **weighted regression**. The fact that observation i is given weight $1/\sigma_{u_i}$ automatically means that the better its quality, the greater the weight that it receives.

The snag with this procedure is that it is most unlikely that you will know the actual values of the σ_{u_i}. However, if you can think of something that is proportional to it in each observation, and divide the equation by that, this will work just as well.

Suppose that you can think of such a variable, which we shall call Z, and it is reasonable to suppose that σ_{u_i} is proportional to Z_i:

$$\sigma_{u_i} = \lambda Z_i \tag{7.6}$$

for some constant, λ. If we divide the original equation through by Z, we have

$$\frac{Y_i}{Z_i} = \beta_1 \frac{1}{Z_i} + \beta_2 \frac{X_i}{Z_i} + \frac{u_i}{Z_i}. \tag{7.7}$$

The model is now homoscedastic because the population variance of $\frac{u_i}{Z_i}$ is

$$E\left\{\left(\frac{u_i}{Z_i}\right)^2\right\} = \frac{1}{Z_i^2} E(u_i^2) = \frac{1}{Z_i^2} \sigma_{u_i}^2 = \frac{\lambda^2 Z_i^2}{Z_i^2} = \lambda^2. \tag{7.8}$$

We do not need to know the value of λ, and indeed in general will not know it. It is enough that it should be constant for all observations.

In particular, it may be reasonable to suppose that σ_{u_i} is roughly proportional to X_i, as in the Goldfeld–Quandt test. If you then divide each observation by its value of X, the model becomes

$$\frac{Y_i}{X_i} = \beta_1 \frac{1}{X_i} + \beta_2 + \frac{u_i}{X_i}, \tag{7.9}$$

and, with a little bit of luck, the new disturbance term u_i/X_i will have constant variance. You now regress Y/X on $1/X$, including a constant term in the regression. The coefficient of $1/X$ will be an efficient estimate of β_1 and the constant will be an efficient estimate of β_2. In the case of the manufacturing output example in the previous section, the dependent variable would be manufacturing output as a proportion of GDP, and the explanatory variable would be the reciprocal of GDP.

Sometimes there may be more than one variable that might be used for scaling the equation. In the case of the manufacturing output example, an alternative candidate would be the size of the population of the country, POP. Dividing the original model through by POP, one obtains

$$\frac{Y_i}{POP_i} = \beta_1 \frac{1}{POP_i} + \beta_2 \frac{X_i}{POP_i} + \frac{u_i}{POP_i}, \tag{7.10}$$

and again one hopes that the disturbance term, u_i/POP_i, will have constant variance across observations. Thus now one is regressing manufacturing output per capita on GDP per capita and the reciprocal of the size of the population, this time without a constant term.

Examples

In the previous section it was found that a linear regression of $MANU$ on GDP using the data in Table 7.1 and the model

$$MANU = \beta_1 + \beta_2 GDP + u \tag{7.11}$$

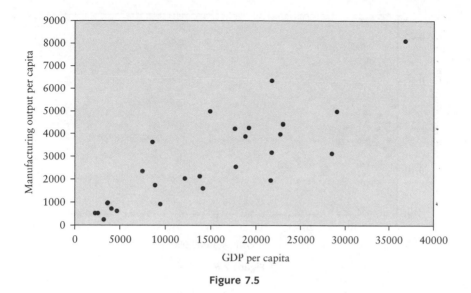

Figure 7.5

was subject to severe heteroscedasticity. One possible remedy might be to scale the observations by population, the model becoming

$$\frac{MANU}{POP} = \beta_1 \frac{1}{POP} + \beta_2 \frac{GDP}{POP} + \frac{u}{POP}. \tag{7.12}$$

Figure 7.5 provides a plot of $MANU/POP$ on GDP/POP. Despite scaling, the plot still looks heteroscedastic. When (7.12) is fitted using the 11 countries with smallest GDP per capita and the 11 countries with the greatest, the residual sums of squares are 5,378,000 and 17,362,000. The ratio, and hence the F statistic, is 3.23. If the subsamples are small, it is possible to obtain high ratios under the null hypothesis of homoscedasticity. In this case, the null hypothesis is just rejected at the 5 percent level, the critical value of $F(9, 9)$ being 3.18.

Figure 7.6 shows the result of scaling through by GDP itself, manufacturing as a share of GDP being plotted against the reciprocal of GDP. In this case the residual sums of squares for the subsamples are 0.065 and 0.070, and so finally we have a model where the null hypothesis of homoscedasticity is not rejected.

We will compare the regression results for the unscaled model and the two scaled models, summarized in equations (7.13)–(7.15) (standard errors in parentheses):

$$\widehat{MANU} = 604 + 0.194GDP \qquad R^2 = 0.89 \tag{7.13}$$
$$\phantom{\widehat{MANU} = } (5,700) \ (0.013)$$

$$\frac{\widehat{MANU}}{POP} = 612\frac{1}{POP} + 0.182\frac{GDP}{POP} \qquad R^2 = 0.70 \tag{7.14}$$
$$\phantom{\frac{\widehat{MANU}}{POP} = } (1,370) \qquad (0.016)$$

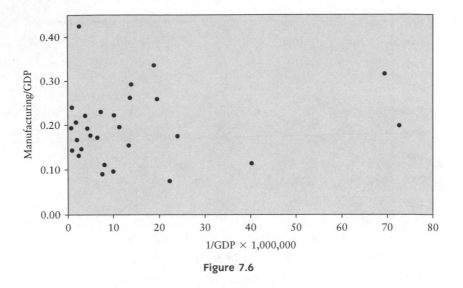

Figure 7.6

$$\frac{\widehat{MANU}}{GDP} = 0.189 + 533\frac{1}{GDP} \quad R^2 = 0.02. \tag{7.15}$$
$$\quad\quad\quad (0.019) \quad (841)$$

First, note that the estimate of the coefficient of GDP is much the same in the three regressions: 0.194, 0.182, and 0.189 (remember that it becomes the intercept when scaling through by the X variable). One would not expect dramatic shifts since heteroscedasticity does not give rise to bias. The estimator in the third estimate should have the smallest variance and therefore ought to have a tendency to be the most accurate. Perhaps surprisingly, its standard error is the largest, but then the standard errors in the first two regressions should be disregarded because they are invalidated by the heteroscedasticity.

In this model the intercept does not have any sensible economic interpretation. In any case its estimate in the third equation, where it has become the coefficient of $1/GDP$, is not significantly different from zero. The only apparent problem with the third model is that R^2 is very low. We will return to this in the next subsection.

Nonlinear models

Heteroscedasticity, or perhaps apparent heteroscedasticity, may be a consequence of misspecifying the model mathematically. Suppose that the true model is nonlinear, for example

$$Y = \beta_1 X^{\beta_2} v \tag{7.16}$$

with (for sake of argument) β_1 and β_2 positive so that Y is an increasing function of X. The multiplicative disturbance term v has the effect of increasing or reducing Y by a random proportion. Suppose that the probability distribution of v is

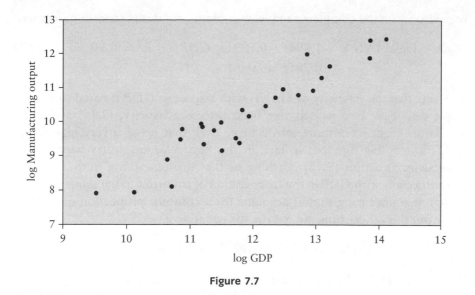

Figure 7.7

the same for all observations. This implies, for example, that the probability of a 5 percent increase or decrease in Y due to its effects is just the same when X is small as when X is large. However, in absolute terms a 5 percent increase has a larger effect on Y when X is large than when X is small. If Y is plotted against X, the scatter of observations will therefore tend to be more widely dispersed about the true relationship as X increases, and a linear regression of Y on X may therefore exhibit heteroscedasticity.

The solution, of course, is to run a logarithmic regression instead:

$$\log Y = \log \beta_1 + \beta_2 \log X + \log v. \tag{7.17}$$

Not only would this be a more appropriate mathematical specification, but it makes the regression model homoscedastic. $\log v$ now affects the dependent variable, $\log Y$, additively, so the absolute size of its effect is independent of the magnitude of $\log X$.

Figure 7.7 shows the logarithm of manufacturing output plotted against the logarithm of GDP using the data in Table 7.1. At first sight at least, the plot does not appear to exhibit heteroscedasticity. Logarithmic regressions using the subsamples of 11 countries with smallest and greatest GDP yield residual sums of squares 2.14 and 1.04, respectively. In this case the conventional Goldfeld–Quandt test is superfluous. Since the second RSS is *smaller* than the first, it cannot be significantly *greater*. However the Goldfeld–Quandt test can also be used to test for heteroscedasticity where the standard deviation of the distribution of the disturbance term is inversely proportional to the size of the X variable. The F statistic is the same, with RSS_1 and RSS_2 interchanged. In the present case the F statistic if 2.06, which is lower than the critical value of F at the 5 percent level, and we do not reject the null hypothesis of homoscedasticity. Running the regression with the complete sample, we obtain (standard errors in parentheses)

$$\log \widehat{MANU} = -1.694 + 0.999 \log GDP \qquad R^2 = 0.90 \qquad (7.18)$$
$$\qquad\qquad\quad (0.785) \quad (0.066)$$

implying that the elasticity of $MANU$ with respect to GDP is equal to 1.

We now have two models free from heteroscedasticity, (7.15) and (7.18). The latter might seem more satisfactory, given that it has a very high R^2 and (7.15) a very low one, but in fact, in this particular case, they happen to be equivalent. Equation (7.18) is telling us that manufacturing output increases proportionally with GDP in the cross-section of countries in the sample. In other words, manufacturing output accounts for a constant proportion of GDP. To work out this proportion, we rewrite the equation as

$$\widehat{MANU} = e^{-1.694} GDP^{0.999} = 0.184 GDP^{0.999}. \qquad (7.19)$$

Equation (7.15) is telling us that the ratio $MANU/GDP$ is effectively a constant, since the $1/GDP$ term appears to be redundant, and that the constant is 0.189. Hence in substance the interpretations coincide.

White's heteroscedasticity-consistent standard errors

Heteroscedasticity causes OLS standard errors to be biased in finite samples. However, it can be demonstrated that they are nevertheless consistent, provided that their variances are distributed independently of the regressors. Even if a White test demonstrates that this is not the case, it is still possible to obtain consistent estimators. We saw in Section 2.3 that the slope coefficient in a simple OLS regression could be decomposed as

$$b_2^{OLS} = \beta_2 + \sum_{i=1}^{n} a_i u_i \qquad (7.20)$$

where

$$a_i = \frac{(X_i - \overline{X})}{\sum\limits_{j=1}^{n} (X_j - \overline{X})^2} \qquad (7.21)$$

and we saw in Box 2.3 in Section 2.6 that the variance of the estimator is given by

$$\sigma_{b_2^{OLS}}^2 = \sum_{i=1}^{n} a_i^2 E\left(u_i^2\right) = \sum_{i=1}^{n} a_i^2 \sigma_{u_i}^2 \qquad (7.22)$$

if u_i is distributed independently of u_j for $j \neq i$. White (1980) demonstrates that a consistent estimator of $\sigma_{b_2^{OLS}}^2$ is obtained if the squared residual in observation i is used as an estimator of $\sigma_{u_i}^2$. Taking the square root, one obtains a **heteroscedasticity-consistent standard error**. Thus in a situation where heteroscedasticity is suspected, but there is not enough information to identify its nature other than it is of the type detected by a White test, it is possible to overcome the problem of biased standard errors, at least in large samples, and the t tests and F tests are asymptotically valid. Two points need to be kept in mind, however. One is that, although the White estimator is consistent, it may not perform well in finite samples (MacKinnon and White, 1985). The other is that the estimators of the coefficients are unaffected by the procedure and so they remain inefficient.

To illustrate the use of heteroscedasticity-consistent standard errors, the regression of *MANU* on *GDP* in (7.17) was repeated with the 'robust' option available in Stata. The point estimates of the coefficients were exactly the same and so their inefficiency is not alleviated. However the standard error of the coefficient of *GDP* rose from 0.13 to 0.18, indicating that it was underestimated in the original OLS regression.

How serious are the consequences of heteroscedasticity?

This will depend on the nature of the heteroscedasticity and there are no general rules. In the case of the heteroscedasticity depicted in Figure 7.3, where the standard deviation of the disturbance term is proportional to X, the population variance of the OLS estimator of the slope coefficient is approximately double that of the estimator using equation (7.9), where the heteroscedasticity has been eliminated by dividing through by X. Further, the standard errors of the OLS estimators are underestimated, giving a misleading impression of the precision of the OLS coefficients.

Key terms

Goldfeld–Quandt test	homoscedasticity
heteroscedasticity	weighted regression
heteroscedasticity-consistent standard error	White test

Exercises

7.7 The researcher mentioned in Exercise 7.1 runs the following regressions as alternative specifications of the model (standard errors in parentheses):

$$\frac{\hat{I}}{P} = -0.03\,\frac{1}{P} - 0.69\,\frac{G}{P} + 0.34\,\frac{Y}{P} \qquad R^2 = 0.97 \qquad (1)$$
$$\quad\;\;(0.28)\quad\;(0.16)\quad\;\;(0.03)$$

$$\frac{\hat{I}}{Y} = 0.39 + 0.03\,\frac{1}{Y} - 0.93\,\frac{G}{Y} \qquad R^2 = 0.78 \qquad (2)$$
$$\;\;(0.04)\;\;(0.42)\quad\;\;(0.22)$$

$$\log\widehat{I} = -2.44 - 0.63\log G + 1.60\log Y \qquad R^2 = 0.98. \qquad (3)$$
$$\quad\;\;(0.26)\;\;(0.12)\qquad\;\;(0.12)$$

In each case the regression is run again for the subsamples of observations with the 11 smallest and 11 greatest values of the sorting variable, after sorting by Y/P, G/Y, and $\log Y$, respectively. The residual sums of squares are as shown in the table.

	11 smallest	11 largest
(1)	1.43	12.63
(2)	0.0223	0.0155
(3)	0.573	0.155

Perform a Goldfeld–Quandt test for each model specification and discuss the merits of each specification. Is there evidence that investment is an inverse function of government expenditure?

7.8 Using your *EAEF* data set, repeat Exercises 7.3 and 7.4 with *LGEARN* as the dependent variable. Is there evidence that this is a preferable specification?

7.9* Repeat Exercise 7.6, using the Goldfeld–Quandt test to investigate whether scaling by population or by *GDP*, or whether running the regression in logarithmic form, would eliminate the heteroscedasticity. Compare the results of regressions using the entire sample and the alternative specifications.

7.10*It was reported above that the heteroscedasticity-consistent estimate of the standard error of the coefficient of *GDP* in equation (7.13) was 0.18. Explain why the corresponding standard error in equation (7.15) ought to be lower and comment on the fact that it is not.

8 Stochastic Regressors and Measurement Errors

So far we have been exploring the regression model within the framework of Model A, in terms of the model classification in Section 2.1, where we assume that the regressors—the explanatory variables—in the regression model are nonstochastic. This means that they do not have random components and that their values in the sample are fixed. Nonstochastic regressors are actually unusual in regression analysis. The reason for making the nonstochasticity assumption has been the technical one of simplifying the analysis of the properties of the regression estimators. We will now progress to Model B and the case of **stochastic regressors**, where the values of the regressors are assumed to be drawn randomly from defined populations. This is a much more realistic framework for regressions with cross-sectional data.

8.1 Assumptions for models with stochastic regressors

We will begin by re-stating the regression model assumptions and then review the properties of the modified model.

B.1 *The model is linear in parameters and correctly specified.*
This is the same as Assumption A.1.

B.2 *The values of the regressors are drawn randomly from fixed populations.*
The values of the regressors in the observations in the sample are drawn randomly from fixed populations with finite means and finite nonzero population variances. Note that we do *not* assume that the regressors are independent of each other. On the contrary, we allow their populations to have joint probability distributions and as a consequence their sample values may be correlated.

B.3 *There does not exist an exact linear relationship among the regressors.*
This is the counterpart of Assumption A.2. Note that if there is a constant in the model, the assumption includes a requirement that there be some variation in each of the regressors. Strictly speaking, this is a population assumption. However, as a practical matter, it must also be satisfied by the data in a sample. Otherwise there would be exact multicollinearity and it would be impossible to obtain estimates of the parameters of the model.

B.4 *The disturbance term has zero expectation.*

$$E(u_i) = 0 \quad \text{for all } i. \tag{8.1}$$

This is the same as Assumption A.3.

B.5 *The disturbance term is homoscedastic.*

$$\sigma_{u_i}^2 = \sigma_u^2 \quad \text{for all } i. \tag{8.2}$$

This is the same as Assumption A.4.

B.6 *The values of the disturbance term have independent distributions.*

$$u_i \text{ is distributed independently of } u_{i'} \quad \text{for all } i' \neq i. \tag{8.3}$$

This is the same as Assumption A.5.

B.7 *The disturbance term is distributed independently of the regressors.*

$$u_i \text{ is distributed independently of } X_{ji'} \quad \text{for all } i' \text{ and all } j. \tag{8.4}$$

This is a new assumption. In Model A, the fact that the regressors had fixed nonstochastic values meant that it was impossible for there to be a distributional relationship between them and the disturbance term. Now that they have random components, the possibility arises. We will see that a violation of the assumption has adverse consequences for the properties of the regression coefficients. Note that the assumption, as stated, means that u_i is distributed independently of the value of every regressor in every observation, not just observation i. In practice, with cross-sectional data it is usually reasonable to suppose that u_i is distributed independently of $X_{ji'}$ for all $i' \neq i$ and so the assumption reduces to u_i being distributed independently of X_{ji}. It can be weakened as follows:

B.7′ *The disturbance term has zero conditional expectation.*

$$E(u_i | \text{values of all the regressors in all observations}) = 0. \tag{8.5}$$

Again, in practice with cross-sectional data it is usually reasonable to suppose that it is sufficient to condition on the values of the regressors in observation i only.

B.8 *The disturbance term has a normal distribution.*

As with Model A, we need this assumption when we perform tests.

Assumption B.5 and the consequences of its violation have been discussed in the previous chapter. A discussion of Assumption B.6 will be deferred until we come to time series data in Chapter 11. As noted in Chapter 2, Assumption B.4 can be made to be true if we assume that any systematic component of the disturbance term is included in the intercept in the regression model. Note that if we make Assumption B.7′ instead of Assumption B.7, Assumption B.4 is redundant anyway. Under Assumption B.7′, the expectation of u_i, conditional on the specific values of the regressors in the sample, is zero. Since the values of the regressors are generated randomly (Assumption B.2), it follows that the expectation of u_i is zero for *any* values of the regressors, and hence it is zero unconditionally.

8.2 Finite sample properties of the OLS regression estimators

We will start by reviewing the properties of the OLS regression coefficients in our new framework. We will focus on the simple regression model

$$Y_i = \beta_1 + \beta_2 X_i + u_i. \tag{8.6}$$

We have seen in Chapter 2 that the OLS estimator of the slope coefficient can be decomposed as follows:

$$b_2 = \frac{\sum\limits_{i=1}^{n} \left(X_i - \overline{X}\right)\left(Y_i - \overline{Y}\right)}{\sum\limits_{i=1}^{n}\left(X_i - \overline{X}\right)^2} = \beta_2 + \sum\limits_{i=1}^{n} a_i u_i \tag{8.7}$$

where

$$a_i = \frac{\left(X_i - \overline{X}\right)}{\sum\limits_{j=1}^{n}\left(X_j - \overline{X}\right)^2}. \tag{8.8}$$

Hence

$$E\left(b_2^{\text{OLS}}\right) = \beta_2 + E\left(\sum a_i u_i\right) = \beta_2 + \sum E(a_i u_i). \tag{8.9}$$

In Model A, where the values of X were nonstochastic, and hence a_i was nonstochastic, we could rewrite $E(a_i u_i)$ as $a_i E(u_i)$, which is zero under Assumption A.3. We cannot do that here because the values of X in the observations are stochastic. Instead we appeal to Assumption B.7. If u_i is distributed independently of every value of X in the sample, it is distributed independently of a_i. Now if X and u are independent, we can make use of the decomposition

$$E\{f(X)g(u)\} = E\{f(X)\}\,E\{g(u)\} \tag{8.10}$$

for any functions $f(X)$ and $g(u)$ (see the Review chapter). Put $f(X) = a_i$ and $g(u) = u_i$ and we have

$$E(a_i u_i) = E(a_i)E(u_i) = 0. \tag{8.11}$$

This allows us to rewrite (8.9) as

$$E\left(b_2^{\text{OLS}}\right) = \beta_2 + \sum E(a_i)E(u_i). \qquad (8.12)$$

With $E(u_i)$ equal to zero under Assumption B.4, it would appear that the second term on the right side of the equation is equal to zero and hence that we have proved unbiasedness. However, we also need to be sure that $E(a_i)$ exists. For this we need Assumption B.3, which in a simple regression model reduces to the requirement that there be some variation in X. Strictly speaking, the assumption relates to the population from which X is drawn. Now even if there is variation in X in the population, it is conceivable that we might be unlucky and draw a sample with constant values. However, if this is the case, it is not possible to compute the OLS regression coefficients anyway. Thus we can say that the OLS estimators will be unbiased, if it is possible to compute them in the first place. See Box 8.1 for a similarly conditional proof of unbiasedness under the weaker Assumption B.7′.

BOX 8.1   Proof of the unbiasedness of the estimator of the slope coefficient in a simple regression model under Assumption B.7′

Writing the values of X in the sample as $\{X_1, \ldots, X_n\}$,

$$E\left(b_2^{\text{OLS}} \,|\, \{X_1, \ldots, X_n\}\right) = \beta_2 + E\left(\sum_{i=1}^{n} a_i u_i \,|\, \{X_1, \ldots, X_n\}\right)$$

$$= \beta_2 + \sum_{i=1}^{n} E\left(a_i u_i \,|\, \{X_1, \ldots, X_n\}\right).$$

Since a_i is a function of the X_i, it may be taken out of the expectation. Hence

$$E\left(b_2^{\text{OLS}} \,|\, \{X_1, \ldots, X_n\}\right) = \beta_2 + \sum_{i=1}^{n} a_i E\left(u_i \,|\, \{X_1, \ldots, X_n\}\right) = \beta_2$$

since

$$E\left(u_i \,|\, \{X_1, \ldots, X_n\}\right) = 0$$

under Assumption B.7′. Thus the estimator of the slope coefficient is unbiased, conditional on the actual values of X in the sample. But under Assumption B.2, this is true for any values of X, and hence the estimator is unbiased unconditionally. However, we do need the a_i to be defined, and for this we require Assumption B.3, which we need also to be able to compute the OLS coefficients. Hence, as with Assumption B.7, we conclude that the OLS estimators will be unbiased, if it is possible to compute the coefficients in the first place.

Precision and efficiency

Provided that they are regarded as being conditional on the sample values of the regressor(s), the expressions for the variances of the regression coefficients for the simple regression model in Chapter 2 and the multiple regression model with two regressors in Chapter 3 remain valid. Likewise the Gauss–Markov theorem remains valid in this conditional sense.

8.3 Asymptotic properties of the OLS regression estimators

We did not investigate the asymptotic properties of the regression estimators—their properties as the sample size becomes large—within the framework of Model A. Before discussing the reasons for this, we might ask why we should ever be interested in the asymptotic properties of estimators when in practice we have only finite samples.

The main reason is that the expected value rules are weak tools and generally do not allow us to investigate the properties of the regression estimators when the regression model becomes complex. By contrast, the plim rules are robust and often do allow us to predict what would happen if the sample became large. Even though in practice we normally have finite samples, rather than large ones, asymptotic results can be helpful indirectly. Other things being equal, we should prefer consistent estimators to inconsistent ones. A consistent estimator may be biased in finite samples, but often the bias is not serious. (Of course, on this latter point, one would need to undertake a suitable Monte Carlo experiment.) On the other hand, if an estimator is biased in large samples, it follows that it will also be biased in finite ones. Note the qualifying 'other things being equal'. We might prefer an inconsistent estimator to a consistent one after all if the element of bias is small and if the consistent estimator had a larger variance.

We have not needed to concern ourselves with these issues so far because we have been working within the framework of Model A where the regressors are assumed to be nonstochastic. This assumption has allowed us to obtain results using the expected value rules whenever we needed to do so. Indeed, this was the reason that we have been using Model A so far. It is also doubtful if we could have investigated these issues, even if we had so wished. This is because we need to be able to describe how the distribution of the regressors behaves as the sample size becomes large, and Model A is silent on this score. In Model A we assert that the regressors are nonstochastic, but we have no explanation of how their values are generated.

Now that we have moved to Model B, and the regression model has become more complex, asymptotics will become an important part of our analysis. And with Model B we do have a story to tell with regard to the regressors or, to put it more formally, a **data generation process**, if only a simple one. We are assuming that for each regressor the sample values are drawn randomly from a defined population. As a consequence, the sample distribution will increasingly resemble the population distribution as the sample size becomes large.

Consistency

We have seen that, for any finite sample of size n, the OLS slope coefficient in a simple regression model may be decomposed as

$$b_2 = \frac{\sum_{i=1}^{n}\left(X_i - \overline{X}\right)\left(Y_i - \overline{Y}\right)}{\sum_{i=1}^{n}\left(X_i - \overline{X}\right)^2}$$

$$= \beta_2 + \frac{\sum_{i=1}^{n}\left(X_i - \overline{X}\right)(u_i - \bar{u})}{\sum_{i=1}^{n}\left(X_i - \overline{X}\right)^2} = \beta_2 + \sum_{i=1}^{n} a_i u_i \qquad (8.13)$$

where a_i is defined in (8.8). What can we say about plim b_2, its limiting value as n becomes large? To use the plim rules, we have to organize the right side of the relationship so that it consists of constants or elements that have limits as n becomes large. In the present case, we focus on the second part of the equation. Neither $\sum\left(X_i - \overline{X}\right)(u_i - \bar{u})$ nor $\sum\left(X_i - \overline{X}\right)^2$ has a limit. In general both will increase indefinitely with n. However, if we rewrite the relationship as

$$b_2 = \beta_2 + \frac{\frac{1}{n}\sum_{i=1}^{n}\left(X_i - \overline{X}\right)(u_i - \bar{u})}{\frac{1}{n}\sum_{i=1}^{n}\left(X_i - \overline{X}\right)^2} \qquad (8.14)$$

we obtain what we need. As the sample size becomes large, the numerator of the quotient will converge on σ_{Xu}, the population covariance between X and u, and the denominator will converge on σ_X^2, the population variance of X. The former is zero by virtue of Assumption B.7 and the second is nonzero by virtue of Assumption B.3, so we have

$$\text{plim } b_2 = \beta_2 + \frac{\text{plim}\frac{1}{n}\sum_{i=1}^{n}\left(X_i - \overline{X}\right)(u_i - \bar{u})}{\text{plim}\frac{1}{n}\sum_{i=1}^{n}\left(X_i - \overline{X}\right)^2}$$

$$= \beta_2 + \frac{\sigma_{Xu}}{\sigma_X^2} = \beta_2 + \frac{0}{\sigma_X^2} = \beta_2 \qquad (8.15)$$

and we have shown that b_2 is a consistent estimator of β_2.

Asymptotic normality of the regression coefficients

We have shown that, provided that the regression model assumptions are valid, the OLS regression coefficients in the simple regression model can be decomposed into their true values and error terms that are a linear combination of the values of the disturbance terms in the sample. This decomposition generalizes to multiple regression analysis. It follows that if Assumption B.8, which states that the disturbance term should have a normal distribution, is valid, the regression coefficients will also have normal distributions. This follows from the fact that a sum of normal distributions is itself a normal distribution. This allows us to perform t tests and F tests in the usual way. The justification for Assumption B.8 is that it is reasonable to suppose that the disturbance term is jointly generated by a number of minor random factors, and a central limit theorem states that the combination of these factors should approximately have a normal distribution, even if the individual factors do not.

What happens if we have reason to believe that Assumption B.8 is not valid? The central limit theorem comes into the frame a second time. Since the random component of a regression coefficient is a linear combination of the values of the disturbance term in the sample, by virtue of the central limit theorem the combination will have an approximately normal distribution, even if the individual values of the disturbance term do not, provided that the sample is large enough.

Exercise

8.1 Demonstrate that $b_1 = \overline{Y} - b_2\overline{X}$ is a consistent estimator of β_1 in the simple regression model. (You may take as given that b_2 is a consistent estimator of β_2.)

8.4 The consequences of measurement errors

We have seen that progressing from Model A to Model B does not lead to any major change in the way that we view the regression model and its properties, provided that the regression model assumptions are satisfied. Assumption B.7, that the disturbance term be distributed independently of the regressors (or alternatively its weaker Assumption B.7′), is particularly important. We will now examine the consequences of its failure in two contexts: measurement error in the rest of this chapter, and simultaneous equations estimation in the next.

It frequently happens in economics that, when you are investigating a relationship, the variables involved have not been measured precisely. For example, most macroeconomic variables, such as gross domestic product, are estimated via sample surveys and the numbers are just approximations. Microeconomic surveys often contain errors caused by the respondent not remembering properly or not understanding a question correctly. However, survey errors are not the only source of inaccuracy. It sometimes happens that you have defined a variable in your model in a certain way, but the available data correspond to a slightly different concept. Friedman's critique of the conventional consumption function, discussed in Section 8.5, is a celebrated case of this.

Measurement errors in the explanatory variable(s)

Let us suppose that a variable Y depends on a variable Z according to the relationship

$$Y_i = \beta_1 + \beta_2 Z_i + v_i \tag{8.16}$$

where v is a disturbance term with mean zero and variance σ_v^2, distributed independently of Z. We shall suppose that Z cannot be measured absolutely accurately, and we shall use X to denote its measured value. In observation i, X_i is equal to the true value, Z_i, plus the **measurement error**, w_i:

$$X_i = Z_i + w_i. \tag{8.17}$$

We shall suppose that w has mean zero and variance σ_w^2, that Z has population variance σ_Z^2, and that w is distributed independently of Z and v.

Substituting from (8.17) into (8.16), we obtain

$$Y_i = \beta_1 + \beta_2(X_i - w_i) + v_i = \beta_1 + \beta_2 X_i + v_i - \beta_2 w_i. \tag{8.18}$$

This equation has two random components, the original disturbance term v and the measurement error (multiplied by $-\beta_2$). Together they form a composite disturbance term, which we shall call u:

$$u_i = v_i - \beta_2 w_i. \tag{8.19}$$

Equation (8.18) may then be written as

$$Y_i = \beta_1 + \beta_2 X_i + u_i. \tag{8.20}$$

You have your data on Y (which, for the time being, we shall assume has been measured accurately) and X, and you unsuspectingly regress Y on X. However, by virtue of (8.17) and (8.19), both X_i and u_i depend on w_i. Because they have a component in common, Assumption B.7 is violated and as a consequence b_2 is an inconsistent estimator of β_2. We will demonstrate this.

As usual, the regression coefficient b_2 is given by

$$b_2 = \frac{\sum_{i=1}^{n}\left(X_i - \overline{X}\right)\left(Y_i - \overline{Y}\right)}{\sum_{i=1}^{n}\left(X_i - \overline{X}\right)^2} = \beta_2 + \frac{\sum_{i=1}^{n}\left(X_i - \overline{X}\right)(u_i - \bar{u})}{\sum_{i=1}^{n}\left(X_i - \overline{X}\right)^2}. \tag{8.21}$$

Since X and u are not distributed independently of each other, there is no simple way of summarizing how the error term behaves in finite samples. We cannot even obtain an expression for its expected value. Rewriting it as $\sum a_i u_i$ with the a_i as defined in (8.8), does not help. $E\left(\sum a_i u_i\right) = \sum E(a_i u_i)$ cannot be decomposed as $\sum E(a_i) E(u_i)$ because the a_i are not independent of the u_i. The most we can do is to predict how the error term would behave if the sample were very large. As they stand, neither the numerator nor the denominator of the error term tends to a limit as the sample becomes large. However, if we divide both of them by n, this problem is overcome, since it can be shown that

$$\text{plim}\left(\frac{1}{n}\sum_{i=1}^{n}\left(X_i - \overline{X}\right)(u_i - \bar{u})\right) = \text{cov}(X, u) \tag{8.22}$$

and

$$\text{plim}\left(\frac{1}{n}\sum_{i=1}^{n}\left(X_i - \overline{X}\right)^2\right) = \text{var}(X). \tag{8.23}$$

Hence

$$\text{plim}\, b_2 = \beta_2 + \frac{\text{cov}(X, u)}{\text{var}(X)}. \tag{8.24}$$

We can analyze the error term in more detail by looking at the components of X and u. To do this, we will use the rules for manipulating population covariances and variances summarized in Section R.4 of the Review chapter. We will start with the numerator of the error term:

$$\text{cov}(X, u) = \text{cov}((Z + w), (v - \beta_2 w))$$
$$= \text{cov}(Z, v) + \text{cov}(w, v) + \text{cov}(Z, -\beta_2 w) + \text{cov}(w, -\beta_2 w). \tag{8.25}$$

We will assume that the disturbance term v in the original model satisfies the regression model assumptions and is therefore distributed independently of Z. We will also assume that the measurement error w is distributed independently of Z and v. If this is the case, the first three covariances on the right side of the equation are zero. However the last covariance is $\beta_2 \text{var}(w)$. Hence

$$\text{cov}(X, u) = -\beta_2 \text{var}(w) = -\beta_2 \sigma_w^2. \tag{8.26}$$

Next, take the denominator:

$$\text{var}(X) = \text{var}(Z + w) = \text{var}(Z) + \text{var}(w) + 2\text{cov}(Z, w) = \sigma_Z^2 + \sigma_w^2 \tag{8.27}$$

since we are assuming $\text{cov}(Z, w) = 0$.
Hence

$$\text{plim}\, b_2 = \beta_2 + \frac{\text{plim}\frac{1}{n}\sum_{i=1}^{n}\left(X_i - \overline{X}\right)(u_i - \bar{u})}{\text{plim}\frac{1}{n}\sum_{i=1}^{n}\left(X_i - \overline{X}\right)^2} = \beta_2 - \frac{\beta_2 \sigma_w^2}{\sigma_Z^2 + \sigma_w^2}. \tag{8.28}$$

Thus we have shown that in large samples b_2 is subject to **measurement error bias** that causes the coefficient to be underestimated in absolute size (the bias is negative if β_2 is positive and positive if β_2 is negative).

We have assumed that w is distributed independently of v and Z. The first assumption is usually plausible because in general there is no reason for any measurement error in an explanatory variable to be correlated with the disturbance term. However, we may have to relax the second assumption. If we do, b_2 remains inconsistent, but the expression for the bias becomes more complex. See Exercise 8.5.

The implications of (8.28) are fairly obvious. The bigger the population variance of the measurement error, relative to the population variance of Z, the bigger will be the bias. For example, if σ_w^2 were equal to $0.25\sigma_Z^2$, the bias would be

$$-\frac{0.25\sigma_Z^2}{1.25\sigma_Z^2}\beta_2 \tag{8.29}$$

which is $-0.2\beta_2$. Even if the sample were very large, your estimate would tend to be 20 percent below the true value if β_2 were positive, and 20 percent above it if β_2 were negative.

Figure 8.1 illustrates how measurement errors give rise to biased regression coefficients, using the model represented by (8.16) and (8.17). The circles represent the observations on Z and Y, the values of Y being generated by a process of type (8.16), the true relationship being given by the dashed line. The solid markers represent the observations on X and Y, the measurement error in each case causing a horizontal shift marked by a dotted line. Positive measurement errors tend to cause the observations to lie under the true relationship, and negative ones tend to cause the observations to lie above it. This causes the scatter of

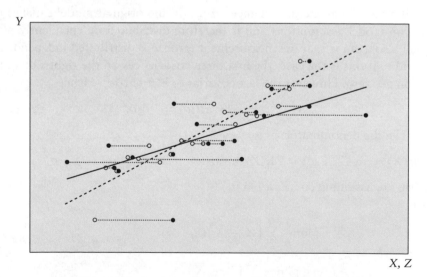

Figure 8.1 Effect of errors of measurement of the explanatory variable

observations on X and Y to look flatter than that for Z and Y and the best-fitting regression line will tend to underestimate the slope of the true relationship. The greater the variance of the measurement error relative to that of Z, the greater will be the flattening effect and the worse will be the bias.

Imperfect proxy variables

In Chapter 6 it was shown that, if we are unable to obtain data on one of the explanatory variables in a regression model and we run the regression without it, the coefficients of the other variables will in general be biased and their standard errors will be invalid. However, in Section 6.4 we saw that if we are able to find a perfect proxy for the missing variable, that is, another variable that has an exact linear relationship with it, and use that in its place in the regression, most of the regression results will be saved. Thus, the coefficients of the other variables will not be biased, their standard errors and associated t tests will be valid, and R^2 will be the same as if we had been able to include the unmeasurable variable directly. We will not be able to obtain an estimate of the coefficient of the latter, but the t statistic for the proxy variable will be the same as the t statistic for the unmeasurable variable.

Unfortunately, it is unusual to find a perfect proxy. Generally the best that you can hope for is a proxy that is approximately linearly related to the missing variable. The consequences of using an **imperfect proxy** instead of a perfect one are parallel to those of using a variable subject to measurement error instead of one that is free from it. It will cause the regression coefficients to be biased, the standard errors to be invalid, and so on, after all.

You may nevertheless justify the use of a proxy if you have reason to believe that the degree of imperfection is not so great as to cause the bias to be serious and the standard errors to be misleading. Since there is normally no way of testing whether the degree of imperfection is great or small, the case for using a proxy has to be made on subjective grounds in the context of the model.

Measurement errors in the dependent variable

Measurement errors in the dependent variable do not matter as much. In practice they can be thought of as contributing to the disturbance term. They are undesirable, because anything that increases the noise in the model will tend to make the regression estimates less accurate, but they will not cause the regression estimates to be biased.

Let the true value of the dependent variable be Q, and the true relationship be

$$Q_i = \beta_1 + \beta_2 X_i + v_i, \tag{8.30}$$

where v is a disturbance term. If Y_i is the measured value of the dependent variable in observation i, and r_i is the measurement error,

$$Y_i = Q_i + r_i. \tag{8.31}$$

Hence the relationship between the observed value of the dependent variable and X is given by

$$Y_i - r_i = \beta_1 + \beta_2 X_i + v_i, \tag{8.32}$$

which may be rewritten

$$Y_i = \beta_1 + \beta_2 X_i + u_i, \tag{8.33}$$

where u is the composite disturbance term $(v + r)$.

The only difference from the usual model is that the disturbance term in (8.33) has two components: the original disturbance term and the error in measuring Y. The important thing is that the explanatory variable X has not been affected. Hence OLS still yields unbiased estimates provided that X is nonstochastic or that it is distributed independently of v and r. The population variance of the slope coefficient will be given by

$$\sigma_{b_2}^2 = \frac{\sigma_u^2}{\sum\limits_{i=1}^{n} \left(X_i - \overline{X} \right)^2} = \frac{\sigma_v^2 + \sigma_r^2}{\sum\limits_{i=1}^{n} \left(X_i - \overline{X} \right)^2} \tag{8.34}$$

and so will be greater than it would have been in the absence of measurement error, reducing the precision of the estimator. The standard errors remain valid but will be larger than they would have been in the absence of the measurement error, reflecting the loss of precision.

Exercises

8.2 In a certain industry, firms relate their stocks of finished goods, Y, to their expected annual sales, X^e, according to a linear relationship

$$Y = \beta_1 + \beta_2 X^e.$$

Actual sales, X, differ from expected sales by a random quantity u, that is distributed with zero mean and constant variance:

$$X = X^e + u$$

where u is distributed independently of X^e. An investigator has data on Y and X (but not on X^e) for a cross-section of firms in the industry. Describe the problems that would be encountered if OLS were used to estimate β_1 and β_2, regressing Y on X.

8.3 In a similar industry, firms relate their *intended* stocks of finished goods, Y^*, to their expected annual sales, X^e, according to a linear relationship

$$Y^* = \beta_1 + \beta_2 X^e.$$

Actual sales, X, differ from expected sales by a random quantity u, which is distributed with zero mean and constant variance:

$$X = X^e + u$$

where u is distributed independently of X^e. Since unexpected sales lead to a reduction in stocks, actual stocks are given by

$$Y = Y^* - u.$$

An investigator has data on Y and X (but not on Y^* or X^e) for a cross-section of firms in the industry. Describe analytically the problems that would be encountered if OLS were used to estimate β_1 and β_2, regressing Y on X. [*Note:* You are warned that the standard expression for measurement error bias is not valid in this case.]

8.4* A variable Q is determined by the model

$$Q = \beta_1 + \beta_2 X + v,$$

where X is a variable and v is a disturbance term that satisfies the regression model conditions. The dependent variable is subject to measurement error and is measured as Y where

$$Y = Q + r$$

and r is the measurement error, distributed independently of v. Describe analytically the consequences of using OLS to fit this model if

1. the expected value of r is not equal to zero (but r is distributed independently of Q),

2. r is not distributed independently of Q (but its expected value is zero).

8.5* A variable Y is determined by the model

$$Y = \beta_1 + \beta_2 Z + v,$$

where Z is a variable and v is a disturbance term that satisfies the regression model conditions. The explanatory variable is subject to measurement error and is measured as X where

$$X = Z + w$$

and w is the measurement error, distributed independently of v. Describe analytically the consequences of using OLS to fit this model if

1. the expected value of w is not equal to zero (but w is distributed independently of Z),

2. w is not distributed independently of Z (but its expected value is zero).

8.6* A researcher investigating the shadow economy using international cross-sectional data for 25 countries hypothesizes that consumer expenditure on shadow goods and services, Q, is related to total consumer expenditure, Z, by the relationship

$$Q = \beta_1 + \beta_2 Z + v$$

where v is a disturbance term that satisfies the regression model conditions. Q is part of Z and any error in the estimation of Q affects the estimate of Z by the same amount. Hence

$$Y_i = Q_i + w_i$$

and

$$X_i = Z_i + w_i$$

where Y_i is the estimated value of Q_i, X_i is the estimated value of Z_i, and w_i is the measurement error affecting both variables in observation i. It is assumed that the expected value of w is zero and that v and w are distributed independently of Z and of each other.

1. Derive an expression for the large-sample bias in the estimate of β_2 when OLS is used to regress Y on X, and determine its sign if this is possible. [*Note:* You are warned that the standard expression for measurement error bias is not valid in this case.]

2. In a Monte Carlo experiment based on the model above, the true relationship between Q and Z is

$$Q = 2.0 + 0.2Z.$$

A sample of 25 observations is generated using the integers $1, 2, \ldots, 25$ as data for Z. The variance of Z is 52.0. A normally distributed random variable with mean 0 and variance 25 is used to generate the values of the measurement error in the dependent and explanatory variables. The results with 10 samples are summarized in the table. Comment on the results, stating whether or not they support your theoretical analysis.

Sample	b_1	s.e.(b_1)	b_2	s.e.(b_2)	R^2
1	−0.85	1.09	0.42	0.07	0.61
2	−0.37	1.45	0.36	0.10	0.36
3	−2.85	0.88	0.49	0.06	0.75
4	−2.21	1.59	0.54	0.10	0.57
5	−1.08	1.43	0.47	0.09	0.55
6	−1.32	1.39	0.51	0.08	0.64
7	−3.12	1.12	0.54	0.07	0.71
8	−0.64	0.95	0.45	0.06	0.74
9	0.57	0.89	0.38	0.05	0.69
10	−0.54	1.26	0.40	0.08	0.50

3. The graph plots the points (Q, Z) and (Y, X) for the first sample, with each (Q, Z) point linked to the corresponding (Y, X) point. Comment on this graph, given your answers to parts (1) and (2).

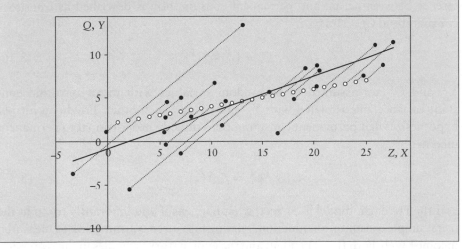

<hr>

8.5   **Friedman's critique of the conventional consumption function**

Now we come to the most celebrated application of measurement error analysis in the whole of economic theory: Friedman's critique of the use of OLS to fit a consumption function (Friedman, 1957). We discuss here Friedman's analysis of the problem and in Section 11.3 we will discuss his solution.

In Friedman's **permanent income hypothesis** model, the consumption of individual (or household) i is related, not to actual (measured) current income Y_i, but to **permanent income**, which will be denoted Y_i^P. Permanent income is to be thought of as a medium-term notion of income: the amount that the individual can more or less depend on for the foreseeable future, taking into account possible fluctuations. It is subjectively determined by recent experience and by expectations about the future, and because it is subjective it cannot be measured directly. Actual income at any moment may be higher or lower than permanent income depending on the influence of short-run random factors. The difference between actual and permanent income caused by these factors is described as **transitory income**, Y_i^T. Thus

$$Y_i = Y_i^P + Y_i^T. \tag{8.35}$$

In the same way, Friedman makes a distinction between actual consumption, C_i, and **permanent consumption**, C_i^P. Permanent consumption is the level of consumption justified by the level of permanent income. Actual consumption may differ from it as special, unforeseen circumstances arise (unanticipated medical bills, for example) or as a consequence of impulse purchases. The difference between actual and permanent consumption is described as **transitory consumption**, C_i^T. Thus

$$C_i = C_i^P + C_i^T. \tag{8.36}$$

Y_i^T and C_i^T are assumed to be random variables with mean zero and constant variance, uncorrelated with Y_i^P and C_i^P and each other. Friedman further hypothesizes that permanent consumption is directly proportional to permanent income:

$$C_i^P = \beta_2 Y_i^P. \tag{8.37}$$

If the Friedman model is correct, what happens if you ignorantly try to fit the usual simple consumption function, relating measured consumption to measured income? Well, both the dependent and the explanatory variables in the regression

$$\hat{C}_i = b_1 + b_2 Y_i \tag{8.38}$$

have been measured inappropriately, C_i^T and Y_i^T being the measurement errors. In terms of the previous section,

$$Z_i = Y_i^P, \quad w_i = Y_i^T, \quad Q_i = C_i^P, \quad r_i = C_i^T. \tag{8.39}$$

As we saw in that section, the only effect of the measurement error in the dependent variable is to increase the variance of the disturbance term. The use of the wrong income concept is more serious. It causes the estimate of β_2 to be inconsistent. From (8.28), we can see that in large samples

$$\text{plim } b_2 = \beta_2 - \frac{\sigma_{YT}^2}{\sigma_{YP}^2 + \sigma_{YT}^2} \beta_2 \tag{8.40}$$

where σ_{YT}^2 is the population variance of Y^T and σ_{YP}^2 is the population variance of Y^P. It implies that, even in large samples, the apparent marginal propensity to consume (your estimate b_2) will be lower than the value of β_2 in the true relationship (8.37). The size of the bias depends on the ratio of the variance of transitory income to that of permanent income. It will be highest for those occupations whose earnings are most subject to fluctuations. An obvious example is farming. Friedman's model predicts that, even if farmers have the same β_2 as the rest of the population, an OLS estimate of their marginal propensity to consume will be relatively low, and this is consistent with the facts (Friedman, 1957, pp. 57 ff.).

An illustration

The Friedman analysis will be illustrated with a Monte Carlo experiment. It was supposed that a sample of 20 individuals had permanent incomes 2000, 2100, 2200, ..., 3900. It was also assumed that each individual had transitory income equal to 200 times a random number drawn from a normal population with zero mean and unit variance. Measured income for each individual was the sum of permanent and transitory income. It was assumed that the true value of β_2 was 0.9, so that permanent consumption was 0.9 times the corresponding permanent income. There was no provision for a transitory component for consumption, so measured consumption was equal to permanent consumption. When measured consumption was regressed on measured income, the result was (standard errors in parentheses)

$$\hat{C} = 443 + 0.75Y \quad R^2 = 0.89. \tag{8.41}$$
$$\phantom{\hat{C} = 4}(179) \ (0.06)$$

As anticipated, the estimated marginal propensity to consume is below the true value. Indeed, if you construct a 95 percent confidence interval using the regression results, the true value lies outside it and would therefore be rejected at the 5 percent significance level. With 18 degrees of freedom, the critical level of t is 2.10, so the confidence interval would be calculated as

$$0.75 - 2.10 \times 0.06 \le \beta_2 \le 0.75 + 2.10 \times 0.06 \tag{8.42}$$

that is,

$$0.62 \le \beta_2 \le 0.88. \tag{8.43}$$

Therefore you would make a Type I error. Actually, the presence of measurement errors makes the standard error of Y, and hence the confidence interval, invalid. A further side effect is that the constant term, which ought to have been zero since there was no intercept in the model, appears to be significantly positive at the 5 percent level. The experiment was repeated nine further times and the results are summarized in Table 8.1, set A.

b_2 clearly gives a downwards biased estimate of the marginal propensity to consume. It is lower than the true value of 0.90 in nine of the 10 samples. We will check whether the results support the analysis leading to equation (8.40). In this example $\sigma_{Y^T}^2$ is 40,000, since Y^T has standard deviation 200. We will assume that in large samples Y^P takes the values 2,000, 2,100, ..., 3,900 with equal probability, and hence that $\sigma_{Y^P}^2$ is the variance of these numbers, which is 332,500. Hence in large samples β_2 would be underestimated by an amount

$$\frac{\sigma_{Y^T}^2}{\sigma_{Y^P}^2 + \sigma_{Y^T}^2}\beta_2 = \frac{40,000}{332,500 + 40,000} \times 0.90 = 0.11 \times 0.90 = 0.10. \tag{8.44}$$

Table 8.1 Experiments with measurement error

Sample	Experiment A				Experiment B			
	b_1	s.e.(b_1)	b_2	s.e.(b_2)	b_1	s.e.(b_1)	b_2	s.e.(b_2)
1	443	179	0.75	0.06	1001	251	0.56	0.08
2	152	222	0.83	0.07	755	357	0.62	0.11
3	101	222	0.89	0.08	756	376	0.68	0.13
4	195	179	0.83	0.06	668	290	0.66	0.09
5	319	116	0.78	0.04	675	179	0.64	0.06
6	371	200	0.78	0.07	982	289	0.57	0.10
7	426	161	0.74	0.05	918	229	0.56	0.07
8	−146	275	0.93	0.09	625	504	0.66	0.16
9	467	128	0.74	0.04	918	181	0.58	0.06
10	258	153	0.80	0.05	679	243	0.65	0.08

It should be stressed that this is valid only for large samples, and that we are not entitled to say anything about how b_2 behaves in small samples. However, in this case we can see that it does in fact provide a good guide. Looking at the estimates of b_2 in the 10 samples, we see that they appear to be randomly distributed about 0.80, instead of 0.90, and that there is thus a downwards bias of about 0.10.

A consequence of the underestimation of β_2 is that β_1 is overestimated, appearing to be positive even though its true value is zero. Indeed in four cases a t test would indicate that it is significantly different from zero at the 5 percent significance level. However, in these conditions the t tests are invalid because the standard errors, and hence the t statistics, are estimated wrongly if Assumption B.7 is violated.

What would happen if we increased the variance of Y^T, keeping everything else the same? In set B in Table 8.1 the original random numbers were multiplied by 400 instead of 200, so $\sigma_{Y^T}^2$ is now 160,000 instead of 40,000. The error term in expression (8.40) is now equal to 160,000/(332,500 + 160,000), which is 0.32, so we would anticipate that b_2 would tend to $(0.9 - 0.32 \times 0.9)$, which is 0.61, in large samples. Again, we see that this is a good guide to the actual distribution of b_2, even though each sample has only 20 observations. As should be predicted, the estimates of β_1 are even greater than in set A.

Policy implications

There are two separate and opposite implications for the multiplier. First, if Friedman is right, a regression of actual consumption on actual income will yield an underestimate of the marginal propensity to consume and hence an underestimate of the multiplier. In the illustration in the previous section, the true value of β_2 was 0.90, so the true value of the multiplier was 10. But in set A the estimate of β_2 was tending to 0.80, implying a multiplier of only 5. In set B, it would have been lower still. The estimate of β_2 was tending to 0.61, giving a multiplier of 2.6.

If the government underestimates the multiplier, it will underestimate the effects of fiscal policy. For example, an increase in government expenditure intended to reduce unemployment may in fact lead to an excessive increase in effective demand and an increase in the rate of inflation.

The second implication is that the multiplier applies only to that part of a change in income that is perceived as permanent, because (according to Friedman) consumption depends only on permanent income. Thus, if the increase in government expenditure is thought to be temporary, it will not affect consumption at all (as a first approximation), and the multiplier associated with it will be 1.

These remarks must however be qualified by a consideration of the form in which individuals hold their savings. We have implicitly assumed so far that they take them in the form of financial assets (bank deposits, bonds, and so on). However, in the Friedman model, expenditure on consumer durables is considered to be a form of saving. An increase in transitory income will not be spent on ordinary consumer goods, but it may be partly saved in the form of purchases of consumer durables, and the increase in the demand for these will give rise to a multiplier effect. The multiplier for transitory income may not be so low after all.

Exercises

8.7 In a certain economy the variance of transitory income is 0.5 that of permanent income, the propensity to consume nondurables out of permanent income is 0.6, and there is no expenditure on durables. What would be the value of the multiplier derived from a naïve regression of consumption on income, and what would be the true value?

8.8 In his definition of permanent consumption, Friedman includes the consumption of services provided by durables. Purchases of durables are classified as a form of saving. In an economy similar to that in Exercise 8.7, the variance of transitory income is 0.5 that of permanent income, the propensity to consume nondurables out of permanent income is 0.6, and half of current saving (actual income minus expenditure on nondurables) takes the form of expenditure on durables. What would be the value of the multiplier derived from a naïve regression of consumption on income, and what would be the true value?

8.6 Instrumental variables

What can be done about measurement errors? If the measurement errors are due to inaccuracy in the recording of the data, not much. If they arise because the variable being measured is conceptually different from the true variable in the relationship, the obvious answer is to attempt to obtain more appropriate data. Often, however, this is not possible. In the case of Friedman's permanent income hypothesis, there is no way of obtaining data directly on permanent income since it is a subjective concept. Sometimes the problem can be sidestepped. Friedman's own approach will be discussed in Section 11.3. Another technique, known as **instrumental variables estimation**, or **IV**, will be discussed here. IV is a major variation on OLS and it will be of great importance when we come to the fitting of models comprising several simultaneous equations.

Essentially IV consists of semi-replacing a defective explanatory variable with one that is not correlated with the disturbance term. The discussion will be confined to the simple regression case

$$Y_i = \beta_1 + \beta_2 X_i + u_i \tag{8.45}$$

and we shall suppose that for some reason X_i has a random component that is not distributed independently of u_i. A straightforward OLS regression of Y on X would then lead to inconsistent estimates of the parameters.

Suppose, however, that we can think of another variable Z that is correlated with X but not correlated with u. The instrumental variables estimator of β_2 with Z used as an **instrumental variable**, or **instrument**, is defined as

$$b_2^{IV} = \frac{\sum\limits_{i=1}^{n}\left(Z_i - \overline{Z}\right)\left(Y_i - \overline{Y}\right)}{\sum\limits_{i=1}^{n}\left(Z_i - \overline{Z}\right)\left(X_i - \overline{X}\right)}. \tag{8.46}$$

We shall show that it is consistent, provided that σ_{ZX}, the population covariance of Z and X, is nonzero.

Before doing this, it is instructive to compare b_2^{IV} with the OLS estimator, which will be denoted b_2^{OLS}:

$$b_2^{OLS} = \frac{\sum\limits_{i=1}^{n}\left(X_i - \overline{X}\right)\left(Y_i - \overline{Y}\right)}{\sum\limits_{i=1}^{n}\left(X_i - \overline{X}\right)^2} = \frac{\sum\limits_{i=1}^{n}\left(X_i - \overline{X}\right)\left(Y_i - \overline{Y}\right)}{\sum\limits_{i=1}^{n}\left(X_i - \overline{X}\right)\left(X_i - \overline{X}\right)}. \tag{8.47}$$

The IV estimator, in simple regression analysis, is obtained by substituting the instrument Z for the X in the numerator and for one X factor (but not both) in the denominator.

Substituting for Y from (8.45), we can expand the expression for b_2^{IV}:

$$b_2^{IV} = \frac{\sum\limits_{i=1}^{n}\left(Z_i - \overline{Z}\right)\left([\beta_1 + \beta_2 X_i + u_i] - [\beta_1 + \beta_2 \overline{X} + \bar{u}]\right)}{\sum\limits_{i=1}^{n}\left(Z_i - \overline{Z}\right)\left(X_i - \overline{X}\right)}$$

$$= \frac{\sum\limits_{i=1}^{n} \left(\beta_2 \left(Z_i - \overline{Z} \right) \left(X_i - \overline{X} \right) + \left(Z_i - \overline{Z} \right) (u_i - \bar{u}) \right)}{\sum\limits_{i=1}^{n} \left(Z_i - \overline{Z} \right) \left(X_i - \overline{X} \right)}$$

$$= \beta_2 + \frac{\sum\limits_{i=1}^{n} \left(Z_i - \overline{Z} \right) (u_i - \bar{u})}{\sum\limits_{i=1}^{n} \left(Z_i - \overline{Z} \right) \left(X_i - \overline{X} \right)}. \qquad (8.48)$$

We can see therefore that the instrumental variable estimator is equal to the true value plus an error term. In large samples, the error term will vanish. Dividing the numerator and the denominator of the error term by n so that they both have limits when we take plims,

$$\text{plim } b_2^{IV} = \beta_2 + \frac{\text{plim } \frac{1}{n} \sum\limits_{i=1}^{n} \left(Z_i - \overline{Z} \right) (u_i - \bar{u})}{\text{plim} \frac{1}{n} \sum\limits_{i=1}^{n} \left(Z_i - \overline{Z} \right) \left(X_i - \overline{X} \right)}$$

$$= \beta_2 + \frac{\sigma_{Zu}}{\sigma_{ZX}} = \beta_2 + \frac{0}{\sigma_{ZX}} = \beta_2 \qquad (8.49)$$

provided that we are correct in supposing that Z is distributed independently of u and so $\sigma_{Zu} = 0$. Hence in large samples b_2^{IV} will tend to the true value β_2.

Nothing much can be said about the distribution of b_2^{IV} in small samples, but as n increases, the distribution will converge on a normal one with mean β_2 and variance $\sigma_{b_2^{IV}}^2$ given by

$$\sigma_{b_2^{IV}}^2 = \frac{\sigma_u^2}{\sum\limits_{i=1}^{n} \left(X_i - \overline{X} \right)^2} \times \frac{1}{r_{XZ}^2} \qquad (8.50)$$

where r_{XZ} is the correlation between X and Z.

Compare this with the variance of the OLS estimator:

$$\sigma_{b_2^{OLS}}^2 = \frac{\sigma_u^2}{\sum\limits_{i=1}^{n} \left(X_i - \overline{X} \right)^2}. \qquad (8.51)$$

The difference is that the variance of b_2^{IV} is multiplied by the factor $1/r_{XZ}^2$. The greater the correlation between X and Z, the smaller will be this factor, and hence the smaller will be the variance of b_2^{IV}.

We are now in a position to state the three requirements of an instrument:

1. It should be correlated with the variable being instrumented, and the higher the correlation, the better, provided that the second requirement is satisfied.

2. It should not be correlated with the disturbance term. If it is stochastic, its random component should be distributed independently of the disturbance term. Otherwise plim $\frac{1}{n}\sum\left(Z_i - \overline{Z}\right)(u_i - \bar{u})$ in (8.49) will not be zero. Thus it would not be desirable to use an instrument that is perfectly correlated with X, even if you could find one, because then it would automatically be correlated with u as well and you would still obtain inconsistent estimates.

3. It should not be an explanatory variable in its own right.

What should you do if you cannot find an instrumental variable highly correlated with X? Well, you may wish to stick with OLS after all. If, for example, your criterion for selecting an estimator is its mean square error, you may find that the OLS estimator is preferable to an IV estimator, despite the bias, because its variance is smaller.

Example: Use of IV to fit the Friedman consumption function

The pioneering use of IV in the context of the Friedman permanent income hypothesis is Liviatan (1963). Liviatan had data on the consumption and income of the same 883 households for two consecutive years. We will denote consumption and income in the first year C_1 and Y_1, and in the second year C_2 and Y_2.

Liviatan observed that if Friedman's theory is correct, Y_2 can act as an instrument for Y_1. Obviously it is likely to be highly correlated with Y_1, so the first requirement of a good instrument is satisfied. If the transitory component of measured income is uncorrelated from one year to the next, as hypothesized by Friedman, Y_2 will be uncorrelated with the disturbance term in the relationship between C_1 and Y_1, and so the second condition is satisfied. Finally, C_1 is likely to be related to Y_1 rather than Y_2, so the third condition is satisfied. The instrumental variable estimator is then given by

$$b_2^{\text{IV}} = \frac{\sum\limits_{i=1}^{n}\left(Y_{2i} - \overline{Y}_2\right)\left(C_{1i} - \overline{C}_1\right)}{\sum\limits_{i=1}^{n}\left(Y_{2i} - \overline{Y}_2\right)\left(Y_{1i} - \overline{Y}_1\right)}. \tag{8.52}$$

Alternatively, one could use C_2 as an instrument for Y_1. It will be highly correlated with Y_2, and therefore with Y_1, and also not correlated with the disturbance term in the relationship between C_1 and Y_1 if, as Friedman hypothesized, the transitory components of consumption are uncorrelated.

Similarly, one could run regressions using the data for year 2, using Y_1 and C_1 as instruments for Y_2. Liviatan tried all four combinations, separating his sample into employees and self-employed. He found that four of the estimates of the marginal propensity to consume were significantly greater than those obtained by straightforward OLS at the 1 percent level; one was significantly greater at the 5 percent level, and in the other three cases the difference was not significant, evidence that on the whole corroborates the permanent income hypothesis.

However, the marginal propensity to consume was generally not as high as the average propensity; therefore, his results did not support the hypothesis of a unit elasticity of consumption with respect to permanent income, which is implicit in equation (8.37).

Example: Use of IV to fit an earnings function

In some data sets up to 10 percent of the variance of measured years of schooling is thought to be attributable to measurement error. Accordingly, the coefficient of schooling in an earnings function may be underestimated. The regression output in Table 8.2 gives first the output from an OLS regression of the logarithm of hourly earnings on years of schooling and work experience, and then the output from an IV regression with mother's years of schooling used as an instrument for years of schooling. SM is likely to be a suitable instrument because it is correlated with S, unlikely to be correlated with the disturbance term, and unlikely to be a direct determinant of earnings.

Table 8.2

```
.reg LGEARN S EXP

    Source        SS         df        MS            Number of obs  =      540
                                                     F(2,537)       =   100.86
    Model    50.9842581      2     25.492129         Prob>F         =   0.0000
 Residual   135.723385     537    .252743734         R-squared      =   0.2731
                                                     Adj R-squared  =   0.2704
    Total   186.707643     539     .34639637         Root MSE       =   .50274


   LGEARN       Coef.   Std. Err.       t    P>|t|   [95% Conf. Interval]

        S    .1235911   .0090989    13.58   0.000    .1057173   .141465
      EXP    .0350826   .0050046     7.01   0.000    .0252515   .0449137
    _cons    .5093196   .1663823     3.06   0.002    .1824796   .8361596


.ivreg LGEARN EXP (S = SM)
Instrumental variables (2SLS) regression

    Source        SS         df        MS            Number of obs  =      540
                                                     F(2,537)       =    28.38
    Model   46.9446075      2     23.4723038         Prob>F         =   0.0000
 Residual  139.763036     537    .260266361         R-squared      =   0.2514
                                                     Adj R-squared  =   0.2486
    Total  186.707643     539     .34639637         Root MSE       =   .51016


   LGEARN       Coef.   Std. Err.       t    P>|t|   [95% Conf. Interval]

        S    .1599676   .0252801     6.33   0.000    .1103076   .2096277
      EXP    .0394422   .0058092     6.79   0.000    .0280306   .0508537
    _cons  -.0617062   .4061769    -0.15   0.879   -.8595966   .7361841

Instrumented: S
Instruments: EXP SM
```

The coefficient of schooling is larger in the IV regression, suggesting that measurement error may have led to a downwards bias in its coefficient in the OLS regression. However, note that its standard error is much larger than in the OLS regression. This is because the correlation between S and SM, 0.36, is not very high. It is possible that the difference in the OLS and IV estimates of the coefficient may be due to chance. We will improve the IV estimation by drawing on a group of family background variables, instead of just SM, to instrument for S, and then we will perform a formal test of the difference in the coefficients.

First, however, some practical notes. The example used here is a multiple regression model, and you should be aware that the expressions for IV coefficients in a multiple regression model are more complex than those in a simple regression model, in the same way that OLS multiple regression coefficients are more complex than OLS simple regression coefficients. However, the expressions are straightforward in a treatment using matrix algebra. A facility for performing IV regressions is a standard feature of all regression applications. A typical procedure is to state the variables for the regression in the usual way and append a list of non-instrumented variables and instrument(s) in parentheses. The output in Table 8.2 used version 8 of Stata, which departs from this convention in two ways. The command for IV regressions is different from that for OLS regressions ('**ivreg**' instead of '**reg**'), and the list of variables in parentheses is in the form of an equation with the instrumented variable(s) to the left of the = sign and the instruments to the right of it.

Multiple instruments

Father's years of schooling, number of siblings, and possession of a library card are other factors that may be associated with years of schooling of the respondent but are not likely to be direct determinants of earnings. Thus we have four potential instruments for S and, for reasons that will be explained in the next chapter, IV estimation is more efficient if they are used as a group rather than individually. To do this, you include all of them in the list of instruments in the regression command. The corresponding regression output is shown in Table 8.3.

The smaller standard error indicates that there has been a gain in efficiency, but it is still much larger than that for the original OLS regression and it is possible that the difference in the OLS and IV estimates of the coefficient of S is purely random. We will perform a formal test.

The Durbin–Wu–Hausman specification test

Most economic data are subject to some element of measurement error and a recurring issue, as in the present case, is whether it is potentially serious enough

Table 8.3

```
.iverg LGEARN EXP (S = SM SF SIBLINGS LIBRARY)
Instrumental variables (2SLS) regression

   Source        SS         df           MS          Number of obs  =      540
--------------------------------------------------   F(2,537)       =    37.11
   Model     46.331893       2       23.1659465       Prob>F         =   0.0000
   Residual  140.37575      537        .261407356     R-squared      =   0.2482
--------------------------------------------------   Adj R-squared  =   0.2454
   Total     186.707643     539        .34639637      Root MSE       =   .51128


-------------------------------------------------------------------------------
   LGEARN        Coef.     Std. Err.       t     P>|t|      [95% Conf.  Interval]
-------------------------------------------------------------------------------
        S       .162629    .0214328      7.59    0.000      .1205266   .2047313
      EXP       .0397611   .0055922      7.11    0.000      .0287758   .507464
    _cons      -.1034832   .3474573     -0.30    0.766     -.7860253   .5790588
-------------------------------------------------------------------------------

Instrumented: S
Instruments: EXP SM
```

to require the use of IV instead of OLS to fit a model. It has been shown that if measurement error is serious, OLS estimates will be inconsistent and IV is to be preferred. However, if there is no measurement error, both OLS and IV will be consistent and OLS will be preferred because it is more efficient. The **Durbin–Wu–Hausman (DWH) specification test** (sometimes described as the Hausman test: the standard reference is Hausman (1978), but Durbin (1954) and Wu (1973) made important contributions to its development) can be used in this context to discriminate between the two possibilities. We will assume that the regression model is given by

$$Y = \beta_1 + \beta_2 X_2 + \cdots + \beta_k X_k + u \tag{8.53}$$

where one or more of the explanatory variables are potentially subject to measurement error. Under the null hypothesis that there is no measurement error, the OLS and IV coefficients will not be systematically different. The test statistic is based on the differences between the OLS and IV coefficients (all of them, not just those of the variables potentially subject to measurement error). Under the null hypothesis of no significant difference it has a chi-squared distribution with degrees of freedom in principle equal to the number of coefficients being compared. In practice, for technical reasons, the actual number of degrees of freedom may be smaller. The regression application should compute the number for you. The computation of the test statistic is too complex to be described here and you would be well advised to employ a regression application such as Stata or EViews that will do it for you.

Table 8.4 gives the Stata output from performing the test for the earnings function example. The first part of the table gives the output from the IV regression of the logarithm of earnings on work experience, *ASVABC*, dummy variables

Table 8.4

```
.ivreg LGEARN EXP ASVABC MALE ETHBLACK ETHHISP
  (S = SM SF SIBLINGS LIBRARY)
Instrumental variables (2SLS) regression
```

Source	SS	df	MS		
Model	64.4915831	6	10.7485972	Number of obs =	540
Residual	122.21606	533	.229298424	F(6,533) =	37.85
				Prob > F =	0.0000
				R-squared =	0.3454
Total	186.707643	539	.34639637	Adj R-squared =	0.3380
				Root MSE =	.47885

LGEARN	Coef.	Std. Err.	t	P>|t|	[95% Conf.	Interval]
S	.111379	.0476886	2.34	0.020	.0176984	.2050596
EXP	.0258798	.0081187	3.19	0.002	.0099313	.0418284
ASVABC	.0092263	.007991	1.15	0.249	−.0064714	.024924
MALE	.2619787	.0429283	6.10	0.000	.1776492	.3463082
ETHBLACK	−.0121846	.0822942	−0.15	0.882	−.1738454	.1494763
ETHHISP	.0457639	.0955115	0.48	0.632	−.1418612	.2333891
_cons	.2258512	.3887468	0.58	0.562	−.5378125	.989515

```
Instrumented: S
Instruments: EXP ASVABC MALE ETHBLACK ETHHISP SM SF SIBLINGS LIBRARY
```

```
.estimates store EARNIV

.reg LGEARN S EXP ASVABC MALE ETHBLACK ETHHISP
```

Source	SS	df	MS		
Model	65.490707	6	10.9151178	Number of obs =	540
Residual	121.216936	533	.227423895	F(6,533) =	47.99
				Prob > F =	0.0000
				R-squared =	0.3508
Total	186.707643	539	.34639637	Adj R-squared =	0.3435
				Root MSE =	.47689

LGEARN	Coef.	Std. Err.	t	P>|t|	[95% Conf.	Interval]
S	.0883257	.0109987	8.03	0.000	.0667196	.1099318
EXP	.0227131	.0050095	4.53	0.000	.0128724	.0325538
ASVABC	.0129274	.0028834	4.48	0.000	.0072633	.0185916
MALE	.2652878	.042235	6.28	0.000	.1823203	.3482552
ETHBLACK	.0077265	.0715863	0.11	0.914	−.1328994	.1483524
ETHHISP	.0536544	.0937966	0.57	0.568	−.1306019	.2379107
_cons	.4002952	.1663149	2.41	0.016	.0735821	.7270083

for male sex and black and hispanic ethnicity, and years of schooling. Years of schooling is instrumented with multiple instruments: mother's and father's years of schooling, number of siblings, and a dummy variable equal to 1 if anyone in the family possessed a library card, 0 otherwise, when the respondent was 14. The IV regression is followed by the command 'estimates store name1' where 'name1' is a name identifying this regression. In this case the IV regression has been named 'EARNIV'. Next comes the output from the corresponding OLS regression, followed by the command 'estimates store name2' where 'name2' is a name

Table 8.4 (*Continued*)

```
.estimates store EARNOLS

.hausman EARNIV EARNOLS, constant
             — Coefficients —
                                                        sqrt(diag
              (b)          (B)          (b—B)          (V_b — V_B))
            EARNIV       EARNOLS       Difference          S.E.
-----------------------------------------------------------------
       S    .111379      .0883257      .0230533          .0464029
     EXP    .0258798     .0227131      .0031667          .0063889
  ASVABC    .0092263     .0129274     —.0037011          .0074527
    MALE    .2619787     .2652878     —.0033091          .0076842
ETHBLACK   —.0121846     .0077265     —.019911           .0405924
 ETHHISP    .0457639     .0536544     —.0078904          .018018
   _cons    .2258512     .4002952     —.174444           .3513736
-----------------------------------------------------------------
 b = consistent under Ho and Ha; obtained from ivreg
 B = inconsistent under Ha, efficient under Ho;
     obtained from regress

Test: Ho: difference in coefficients not systematic
chi2(7) = (b—B)'[(V_b—V_B) (—1)](b—B)
        = 0.25
Prob > chi2 = 0.9999
```

identifying the OLS regression. It has been called 'EARNOLS'. The command for performing the DWH test is 'hausman name1 name2, constant'—in our case, 'hausman EARNIV EARNOLS, constant'. The qualifier ', constant' should be omitted if for some reason the constant has different meanings in the two regressions being compared. In the present case it has the same (uninteresting) meaning in both regressions, so it is included.

The top half of the output for the DWH test reproduces the IV coefficients in the column headed (b) and the OLS coefficients in that headed (B). The bottom half confirms that there are seven degrees of freedom and computes the chi-squared statistic. This is 0.25, lower than 14.07, the critical value of chi-squared at the 5 percent significance level with seven degrees of freedom, and so we do not reject the null hypothesis of no difference in the OLS and IV estimates. We infer that it is safe to use OLS rather than IV, and we are happy to do so because the OLS standard errors, particularly those of the coefficients of S, EXP, and $ASVABC$, are smaller than their IV counterparts. This is likely to be the correct conclusion. The schooling histories are recorded in great detail in the NLSY data set and accordingly measurement error is almost certainly minimal.

The DWH test can be used in any comparison of OLS and IV estimators where both are consistent, but OLS more efficient, under a null hypothesis, and OLS is inconsistent under the alternative hypothesis. We will encounter another application in the next chapter. With the usage of the test becoming more common, a facility for performing it is now a standard feature of regression applications.

Key terms

Durbin–Wu–Hausman (DWH) test	measurement error bias
imperfect proxy variable	permanent consumption
instrument	permanent income
instrumental variable	permanent income hypothesis
instrumental variable estimation (IV)	transitory consumption
measurement error	transitory income

Exercises

8.9 In Exercise 8.2, the amount of labor, L, employed by the firms is also a linear function of expected sales:

$$L = \delta_1 + \delta_2 X^e.$$

Explain how this relationship might be exploited by the investigator to counter the problem of measurement error bias.

8.10* It is possible that the *ASVABC* test score is a poor measure of the kind of ability relevant for earnings. Accordingly, perform an OLS regression of the logarithm of hourly earnings on years of schooling, work experience, and *ASVABC* using your *EAEF* data set and an IV regression using *SM*, *SF*, *SIBLINGS*, and *LIBRARY* as instruments for *ASVABC*. Perform a Durbin–Wu–Hausman test to evaluate whether *ASVABC* appears to be subject to measurement error.

8.11* What is the difference between an instrumental variable and a proxy variable (as described in Section 6.4)? When would you use one and when would you use the other?

9 Simultaneous Equations Estimation

If you employ OLS to estimate the parameters of an equation that is embedded in a simultaneous equations model, it is likely that the estimates will be biased and inconsistent and that the statistical tests will be invalid. This is demonstrated in the first part of this chapter. The second part discusses how these problems may be overcome by using instrumental variables estimation.

9.1 Simultaneous equations models: structural and reduced form equations

When we progressed from Model A to Model B in Chapter 8, replacing the assumption that the explanatory variables are nonstochastic by the more realistic assumption for cross-sectional data that their sample values are randomly drawn from defined populations, it was noted that Assumption B.7 was particularly important. This stated that the disturbance term be distributed independently of the explanatory variables. Subsequently in that chapter we saw that measurement errors in the explanatory variables would cause the assumption to be violated and that as a consequence OLS estimators would be inconsistent. However, measurement error is not the only possible reason why that assumption may be violated. **Simultaneous equations bias** is another, and it is best explained with an example.

Suppose that you are investigating the determinants of price inflation and wage inflation. We will start with a very simple model that supposes that p, the annual rate of growth of prices, is related to w, the annual rate of growth of wages, it being hypothesized that increases in wage costs force prices upwards:

$$p = \beta_1 + \beta_2 w + u_p. \tag{9.1}$$

At the same time w is related to p and U, the rate of unemployment, workers protecting their real wages by demanding increases in wages as prices rise, but their ability to do so being the weaker, the higher the rate of unemployment ($\alpha_3 < 0$):

$$w = \alpha_1 + \alpha_2 p + \alpha_3 U + u_w \tag{9.2}$$

where u_p and u_w are disturbance terms.

By its very specification, this simultaneous equations model involves a certain amount of circularity: w determines p in the first equation, and in turn p helps to determine w in the second. To cut through the circularity we need to make a distinction between **endogenous** and **exogenous** variables. Endo- and exo- are Greek prefixes that mean within and outside, respectively. Endogenous variables are variables whose values are determined by the interaction of the relationships in the model. Exogenous ones are those whose values are determined externally. Thus in the present case p and w are both endogenous and U is exogenous. The exogenous variables and the disturbance terms ultimately determine the values of the endogenous variables, once one has cut through the circularity. The mathematical relationships expressing the endogenous variables in terms of the exogenous variables and disturbance terms are known as the **reduced form equations**. The original equations that we wrote down when specifying the model are described as the **structural equations**. We will derive the reduced form equations for p and w. To obtain that for p, we take the structural equation for p and substitute for w from the second equation:

$$p = \beta_1 + \beta_2 w + u_p$$
$$= \beta_1 + \beta_2(\alpha_1 + \alpha_2 p + \alpha_3 U + u_w) + u_p. \qquad (9.3)$$

Hence

$$(1 - \alpha_2\beta_2)p = \beta_1 + \alpha_1\beta_2 + \alpha_3\beta_2 U + u_p + \beta_2 u_w \qquad (9.4)$$

and so

$$p = \frac{\beta_1 + \alpha_1\beta_2 + \alpha_3\beta_2 U + u_p + \beta_2 u_w}{1 - \alpha_2\beta_2}. \qquad (9.5)$$

Similarly, we obtain the reduced form equation for w:

$$w = \alpha_1 + \alpha_2 p + \alpha_3 U + u_w$$
$$= \alpha_1 + \alpha_2(\beta_1 + \beta_2 w + u_p) + \alpha_3 U + u_w. \qquad (9.6)$$

Hence

$$(1 - \alpha_2\beta_2)w = \alpha_1 + \alpha_2\beta_1 + \alpha_3 U + u_w + \alpha_2 u_p \qquad (9.7)$$

and so

$$w = \frac{\alpha_1 + \alpha_2\beta_1 + \alpha_3 U + u_w + \alpha_2 u_p}{1 - \alpha_2\beta_2}. \qquad (9.8)$$

Exercise

9.1* A simple macroeconomic model consists of a consumption function and an income identity:

$$C = \beta_1 + \beta_2 Y + u$$
$$Y = C + I,$$

where C is aggregate consumption, I is aggregate investment, Y is aggregate income, and u is a disturbance term. On the assumption that I is exogenous, derive the reduced form equations for C and Y.

9.2 Simultaneous equations bias

In many (but by no means all) simultaneous equations models, the reduced form equations express the endogenous variables in terms of all the exogenous variables and all the disturbance terms. You can see that this is the case with the price inflation/wage inflation model. In this model, there is only one exogenous variable, U. w depends on it directly; p does not depend on it directly but does so indirectly because it is determined by w. Similarly, both p and w depend on u_p, p directly and w indirectly. And both depend on u_w, w directly and p indirectly.

The dependence of w on u_p means that OLS would yield inconsistent estimates if used to fit equation (9.1), the structural equation for p. w is a stochastic regressor and its random component is not distributed independently of the disturbance term u_p. Similarly, the dependence of p on u_w means that OLS would yield inconsistent estimates if used to fit (9.2). Since (9.1) is a simple regression equation, it is easy to analyze the large-sample bias in the OLS estimator of β_2 and we will do so. After writing down the expression for b_2^{OLS}, the first step, as usual, is to substitute for p. Here we have to make a decision. We now have two equations for p, the structural equation (9.1) and the reduced form equation (9.5). Ultimately it does not matter which we use, but the algebra is a little more straightforward if we use the structural equation because the expression for b_2^{OLS} decomposes immediately into the true value and the error term. We can then concentrate on the error term:

$$b_2^{OLS} = \frac{\sum_{i=1}^{n} (p_i - \bar{p})(w_i - \bar{w})}{\sum_{i=1}^{n} (w_i - \bar{w})^2}$$

$$= \frac{\sum_{i=1}^{n} ([\beta_1 + \beta_2 w_i + u_{pi}] - [\beta_1 + \beta_2 \bar{w} + \bar{u}_p])(w_i - \bar{w})}{\sum_{i=1}^{n} (w_i - \bar{w})^2}$$

$$= \frac{\sum\limits_{i=1}^{n} \left(\beta_2 \left(w_i - \overline{w}\right)\left(w_i - \overline{w}\right) + \left(u_{pi} - \overline{u}_p\right)\left(w_i - \overline{w}\right)\right)}{\sum\limits_{i=1}^{n} \left(w_i - \overline{w}\right)^2}$$

$$= \beta_2 + \frac{\sum\limits_{i=1}^{n} \left(u_{pi} - \overline{u}_p\right)\left(w_i - \overline{w}\right)}{\sum\limits_{i=1}^{n} \left(w_i - \overline{w}\right)^2}. \tag{9.9}$$

The error term is a nonlinear function of both u_p and u_w (remember that w depends on both) and it is not possible to obtain an analytical expression for its expected value. Instead we will investigate its probability limit, using the rule that the probability limit of a ratio is equal to the probability limit of the numerator divided by the probability limit of the denominator, provided that both exist. As written in (9.9) neither the numerator nor the denominator have probability limits. However, it can be shown that if we divide both of them by n, they will tend to the population covariance of u_p and w, and the population variance of w, respectively:

$$\text{plim } b_2^{\text{OLS}} = \beta_2 + \frac{\text{plim } \dfrac{1}{n} \sum\limits_{i=1}^{n} \left(u_{pi} - \overline{u}_p\right)\left(w_i - \overline{w}\right)}{\text{plim } \dfrac{1}{n} \sum\limits_{i=1}^{n} \left(w_i - \overline{w}\right)^2}$$

$$= \beta_2 + \frac{\text{cov}\left(u_p, w\right)}{\text{var}\left(w\right)}. \tag{9.10}$$

We will first focus on cov(u_p, w). We need to substitute for w and again have two choices, the structural equation (9.2) and the reduced form equation (9.8). We choose (9.8) because (9.2) would reintroduce p and we would find ourselves going round in circles:

$$\text{cov}(u_p, w) = \text{cov}\left(u_p, \frac{1}{1 - \alpha_2\beta_2}\left(\alpha_1 + \alpha_2\beta_1 + \alpha_3 U + u_w + \alpha_2 u_p\right)\right)$$

$$= \frac{1}{1 - \alpha_2\beta_2}\left(\begin{array}{c}\text{cov}\left(u_p, [\alpha_1 + \alpha_2\beta_1]\right) + \alpha_3\text{cov}\left(u_p, U\right) \\ + \text{cov}\left(u_p, u_w\right) + \alpha_2\text{cov}\left(u_p, u_p\right)\end{array}\right). \tag{9.11}$$

cov(u_p, $[\alpha_1 + \alpha_2\beta_1]$) $= 0$ because $[\alpha_1 + \alpha_2\beta_1]$ is a constant. cov(u_p, U) $= 0$ if U is truly exogenous, as we have assumed. cov(u_p, u_w) $= 0$ provided that the disturbance terms in the structural equations are independent. But cov(u_p, u_p) is nonzero because it is var(u_p). Hence

$$\text{cov}(u_p, w) = \frac{\alpha_2}{1 - \alpha_2\beta_2}\,\text{var}\left(u_p\right) = \frac{\alpha_2\sigma_{u_p}^2}{1 - \alpha_2\beta_2}. \tag{9.12}$$

Now for var(w):

$$\text{var}(w) = \text{var}\left(\frac{\alpha_1 + \alpha_2\beta_1}{1 - \alpha_2\beta_2} + \frac{\alpha_3 U + u_w + \alpha_2 u_p}{1 - \alpha_2\beta_2}\right)$$

$$= \text{var}\left(\frac{\alpha_3 U + u_w + \alpha_2 u_p}{1 - \alpha_2\beta_2}\right) \tag{9.13}$$

since $\dfrac{\alpha_1 + \alpha_2\beta_1}{1 - \alpha_2\beta_2}$ is an additive constant. So

$$\text{var}(w) = \frac{1}{(1 - \alpha_2\beta_2)^2}\left(\begin{array}{c} \text{var}(\alpha_3 U) + \text{var}(u_w) + \text{var}(\alpha_2 u_p) \\ +2\text{cov}(\alpha_3 U, u_w) + 2\text{cov}(\alpha_3 U, \alpha_2 u_p) \\ +2\text{cov}(u_w, \alpha_2 u_p) \end{array}\right). \tag{9.14}$$

Now if U, u_p and u_w are independently distributed, the three covariance terms are equal to zero. Hence

$$\text{var}(w) = \frac{1}{(1 - \alpha_2\beta_2)^2}\left(\alpha_3^2 \text{var}(U) + \text{var}(u_w) + \alpha_2^2 \text{var}(u_p)\right)$$

$$= \frac{1}{(1 - \alpha_2\beta_2)^2}\left(\alpha_3^2\sigma_U^2 + \sigma_{u_w}^2 + \alpha_2^2\sigma_{u_p}^2\right). \tag{9.15}$$

Thus

$$\text{plim}\, b_2^{\text{OLS}} = \beta_2 + (1 - \alpha_2\beta_2)\frac{\alpha_2\sigma_{u_p}^2}{\alpha_3^2\sigma_U^2 + \sigma_{u_w}^2 + \alpha_2^2\sigma_{u_p}^2} \tag{9.16}$$

and so b_2^{OLS} is an inconsistent estimator of β_2.

The direction of simultaneous equations bias depends on the structure of the model being fitted. Can one say anything about it in this case? Variances are always positive, if not zero, and α_2 should be positive, so it depends on the sign of $(1 - \alpha_2\beta_2)$. Looking at the reduced form equation (9.8), it is reasonable to suppose that w will be negatively influenced by U. Since it is also reasonable to suppose that α_3 is negative, one may infer that $(1 - \alpha_2\beta_2)$ is positive. Actually, this is a condition for equilibrium in this model. Consider the effect of a change ΔU in U. In view of (9.2), its immediate effect is to change w, in the opposite direction, by an amount $\alpha_3\Delta U$. Looking at (9.1), this in turn changes p by an amount $\alpha_3\beta_2\Delta U$. Returning to (9.2), this causes a secondary change in w of $\alpha_2\alpha_3\beta_2\Delta U$, and hence, returning to (9.1), a secondary change in p equal to $\alpha_2\alpha_3\beta_2^2\Delta U$. Returning again to (9.2), this causes a further change in w equal to $\alpha_2^2\alpha_3\beta_2^2\Delta U$. The total change in w, after taking account of all secondary effects, will therefore be

$$\Delta w = (1 + \alpha_2\beta_2 + \alpha_2^2\beta_2^2 + \alpha_2^3\beta_2^3 + \cdots)\alpha_3\Delta U \tag{9.17}$$

and this will be finite only if $\alpha_2\beta_2 < 1$.

A Monte Carlo experiment

This section reports on a Monte Carlo experiment that investigates the performance of OLS and, later, IV when fitting the price inflation equation in the price inflation/wage inflation model. Numerical values were assigned to the parameters of the equations as follows:

$$p = 1.5 + 0.5w + u_p \tag{9.18}$$

$$w = 2.5 + 0.5p - 0.4U + u_w. \tag{9.19}$$

The sample size was 20, with U being assigned the values 2, 2.25, increasing by steps of 0.25 to 6.75. u_p was generated as a normal random variable with zero mean and unit variance, scaled by a factor 0.8. The disturbance term u_w is not responsible for the inconsistency of the regression coefficients when OLS is used to fit the price inflation equation and so, to keep things simple, it was suppressed. Using the expression derived above, plim b_2^{OLS} is equal to 0.99 when the price inflation equation is fitted with OLS. The results of 10 regressions, each using the same values of U, but different random numbers for u_p, are shown in Table 9.1.

It is evident that the estimates are heavily biased. Every estimate of the slope coefficient is above the true value of 0.5, and every estimate of the intercept is below the true value of 1.5. The mean of the slope coefficients is 0.96, not far from the theoretical plim for the OLS estimate. The standard errors are invalidated by the violation of the regression model assumption that the disturbance term be distributed independently of the explanatory variable.

Next the experiment was repeated with 1 million samples, again keeping the same values of U but generating different random numbers for u_p. The distribution of the OLS estimates of the slope coefficient is shown in Figure 9.1. Almost all the estimates of the slope coefficient are above the true value of 0.5, confirming the conclusion of the large-sample analysis that there is a positive bias. Moreover, since the mean of the distribution is 0.95, the plim (0.99) provides quite a good guide to the magnitude of the bias.

Table 9.1

Sample	a	s.e.(a)	b	s.e.(b)
1	0.36	0.39	1.11	0.22
2	0.45	0.38	1.06	0.17
3	0.65	0.27	0.94	0.12
4	0.41	0.39	0.98	0.19
5	0.92	0.46	0.77	0.22
6	0.26	0.35	1.09	0.16
7	0.31	0.39	1.00	0.19
8	1.06	0.38	0.82	0.16
9	−0.08	0.36	1.16	0.18
10	1.12	0.43	0.69	0.20

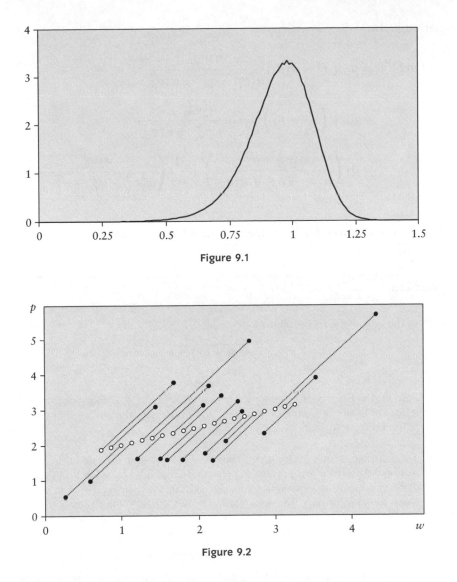

Figure 9.1

Figure 9.2

Figure 9.2 shows how the bias arises. The hollow circles show what the relationship between p and w would look like in the absence of the disturbance terms, for 20 observations. The disturbance term u_p alters the values of both p and w in each observation when it is introduced. As can be seen from the reduced form equations, it increases p by an amount $u_p/(1 - \alpha_2\beta_2)$ and w by an amount $\alpha_2 u_p/(1 - \alpha_2\beta_2)$. It follows that the shift is along a line with slope $1/\alpha_2$. The solid circles are the actual observations, after u_p has been introduced. The shift line has been drawn for each observation. As can be seen, the overall effect is to skew the pattern of observations, with the result that the OLS slope coefficient is a compromise between the slope of the true relationship, β_2, and the slope of the shift lines, $1/\alpha_2$. This can be demonstrated mathematically by rewriting equation (9.16):

$$\text{plim}\, b_2^{\text{OLS}} = \beta_2 + (1 - \alpha_2\beta_2)\frac{\alpha_2\sigma_{u_p}^2}{\alpha_3^2\sigma_U^2 + \sigma_{u_w}^2 + \alpha_2^2\sigma_{u_p}^2}$$

$$= \beta_2 + \left(\frac{1}{\alpha_2} - \beta_2\right)\frac{\alpha_2^2\sigma_{u_p}^2}{\alpha_3^2\sigma_U^2 + \sigma_{u_w}^2 + \alpha_2^2\sigma_{u_p}^2}$$

$$= \beta_2\left(\frac{\alpha_3^2\sigma_U^2 + \sigma_{u_w}^2}{\alpha_3^2\sigma_U^2 + \sigma_{u_w}^2 + \alpha_2^2\sigma_{u_p}^2}\right) + \frac{1}{\alpha_2}\left(\frac{\alpha_2^2\sigma_{u_p}^2}{\alpha_3^2\sigma_U^2 + \sigma_{u_w}^2 + \alpha_2^2\sigma_{u_p}^2}\right).$$

$$(9.20)$$

$\text{plim}\, b_2^{\text{OLS}}$ is thus a weighted average of β_2 and $1/\alpha_2$, the bias being proportional to the variance of u_p.

Exercises

9.2* In the simple macroeconomic model

$$C = \beta_1 + \beta_2 Y + u$$
$$Y = C + I$$

described in Exercise 9.1, demonstrate that OLS would yield inconsistent results if used to fit the consumption function, and investigate the direction of the bias in the slope coefficient.

9.3 A researcher is investigating the impact of advertising on sales using cross-sectional data from firms producing recreational goods. For each firm there are data on sales, S, and expenditure on advertising, A, both measured in suitable units, for a recent year. The researcher proposes the following model:

$$S = \beta_1 + \beta_2 A + u_S$$
$$A = \alpha_1 + \alpha_2 S + u_A$$

where u_S and u_A are disturbance terms. The first relationship reflects the positive effect of advertising on sales, and the second the fact that largest firms, as measured by sales, tend to spend most on advertising. Give a mathematical analysis of what would happen if the researcher tried to fit the model using OLS.

9.3   Instrumental variables estimation

As we saw in the discussion of measurement error, the instrumental variables approach may offer a solution to the problems caused by a violation of the regression model assumption that the disturbance term be distributed independently of the explanatory variables. In the present case, when we fit the structural equation for p, this condition is violated because w is not distributed independently of u_p. We need a variable that is correlated with w but not with u_p, and does not already appear in the equation in its own right. The reduced form equation for w gave us some bad news—it revealed that w was dependent on u_p. But it also gives us some good news—it shows that w is correlated with U, which is exogenous and thus independent of u_p. So we can fit the equation using U as an instrument for w. Using equation (8.46), the IV estimator of β_2 is given by

$$b_2^{IV} = \frac{\sum\limits_{i=1}^{n} \left(U_i - \overline{U}\right)\left(p_i - \overline{p}\right)}{\sum\limits_{i=1}^{n} \left(U_i - \overline{U}\right)\left(w_i - \overline{w}\right)}. \qquad (9.21)$$

We will demonstrate that it is consistent. Substituting from the structural equation for p,

$$b_2^{IV} = \frac{\sum\limits_{i=1}^{n} \left(U_i - \overline{U}\right)\left([\beta_1 + \beta_2 w_i + u_{pi}] - [\beta_1 + \beta_2 \overline{w} + \overline{u}_p]\right)}{\sum\limits_{i=1}^{n} \left(U_i - \overline{U}\right)\left(w_i - \overline{w}\right)}$$

$$= \frac{\sum\limits_{i=1}^{n} \beta_2\left(U_i - \overline{U}\right)\left(w_i - \overline{w}\right) + \left(U_i - \overline{U}\right)\left(u_{pi} - \overline{u}_p\right)}{\sum\limits_{i=1}^{n} \left(U_i - \overline{U}\right)\left(w_i - \overline{w}\right)}$$

$$= \beta_2 + \frac{\sum\limits_{i=1}^{n} \left(U_i - \overline{U}\right)\left(u_{pi} - \overline{u}_p\right)}{\sum\limits_{i=1}^{n} \left(U_i - \overline{U}\right)\left(w_i - \overline{w}\right)}. \qquad (9.22)$$

We cannot take the expectation of the error term because it contains random quantities in the denominator as well as the numerator (remember that the reduced from equation for w_i shows that it is a function of both u_{pi} and u_{wi}). Instead we take plims:

$$\text{plim } b_2^{IV} = \beta_2 + \frac{\text{plim } \dfrac{1}{n} \sum\limits_{i=1}^{n} \left(U_i - \overline{U}\right)\left(u_{pi} - \overline{u}_p\right)}{\text{plim } \dfrac{1}{n} \sum\limits_{i=1}^{n} \left(U_i - \overline{U}\right)\left(w_i - \overline{w}\right)}$$

$$= \beta_2 + \frac{\text{cov}\left(U, u_p\right)}{\text{cov}\left(U, w\right)} = \beta_2 + \frac{0}{\text{cov}\left(U, w\right)} = \beta_2. \qquad (9.23)$$

Note that we had to divide both the numerator and the denominator of the error term by n in order for them to have probability limits. $\text{cov}(U, u_p) = 0$ because U is exogenous and therefore distributed independently of u_p. $\text{cov}(U, w)$ is nonzero because U is a determinant of w. Hence the instrumental variable estimator is a consistent estimate of β_2.

Table 9.2 shows the results when IV is used to fit the model described in Section 9.2. In contrast to the OLS estimates, the IV estimates are distributed around the true values, the mean of the estimates of the slope coefficient (true value 0.5) being 0.37 and of those of the intercept (true value 1.5) being 1.69. There is no point in comparing the standard errors using the two approaches. Those for OLS may appear to be slightly smaller, but the simultaneous equations bias renders them invalid. The standard errors of the IV estimates are valid only for large samples, but they may be approximately valid in finite samples.

Table 9.2

	OLS				IV			
Sample	b_1	s.e.(b_1)	b_2	s.e.(b_2)	b_1	s.e.(b_1)	b_2	s.e.(b_2)
1	0.36	0.39	1.11	0.22	2.33	0.97	0.16	0.45
2	0.45	0.38	1.06	0.17	1.53	0.57	0.53	0.26
3	0.65	0.27	0.94	0.12	1.13	0.32	0.70	0.15
4	0.41	0.39	0.98	0.19	1.55	0.59	0.37	0.30
5	0.92	0.46	0.77	0.22	2.31	0.71	0.06	0.35
6	0.26	0.35	1.09	0.16	1.24	0.52	0.59	0.25
7	0.31	0.39	1.00	0.19	1.52	0.62	0.33	0.32
8	1.06	0.38	0.82	0.16	1.95	0.51	0.41	0.22
9	−0.08	0.36	1.16	0.18	1.11	0.62	0.45	0.33
10	1.12	0.43	0.69	0.20	2.26	0.61	0.13	0.29

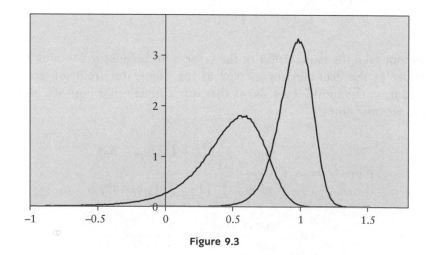

Figure 9.3

The experiment was repeated with 1 million samples, keeping the same values of U but generating different random numbers for u_p. The distribution of the OLS and IV estimates of the slope coefficient is shown in Figure 9.3. The mean of the IV estimates is 0.46. It should be remembered that the IV estimator is consistent, meaning that it will tend to the true value in large samples, but there is no claim that it is unbiased in finite samples. In this example, it turned out to be biased downwards, at least for sample size 20, but the bias is quite small and certainly it is much smaller than the upwards bias in the OLS estimates. The standard deviation of the IV estimates is 0.26. The standard errors of the IV estimates in Table 9.2 do appear to be distributed around this figure.

In this example, IV definitely gave better results than OLS, but that outcome was not inevitable. The variance of an IV estimator will in general be greater than that of a corresponding OLS estimator. If the instrument is weak, in the sense of not being highly correlated with the variable for which it is acting, the IV variance may be much greater. So if the bias in the OLS estimator is small, it is possible that OLS might yield superior estimates according to a criterion such as the mean square error that allows a trade-off between bias and variance.

Underidentification

If OLS were used to fit the wage inflation equation

$$w = \alpha_1 + \alpha_2 p + \alpha_3 U + u_w \tag{9.24}$$

the estimates would be subject to simultaneous equations bias caused by the (indirect) dependence of p on u_w. However, in this case it is not possible to use the instrumental variables approach to obtain consistent estimates, and the relationship is said to be **underidentified**. The only determinant of p, apart from the disturbance terms, is U, and it is already in the model in its own right. An attempt to use it as an instrument for p would lead to a form of exact multicollinearity and it would be impossible to obtain estimates of the parameters. Using the expression in Box 9.1, we would have

$$a_2^{IV} = \frac{\sum_{i=1}^{n}\left(Z_i - \overline{Z}\right)(w_i - \overline{w})\sum_{i=1}^{n}\left(U_i - \overline{U}\right)^2 - \sum_{i=1}^{n}\left(U_i - \overline{U}\right)(w_i - \overline{w})\sum_{i=1}^{n}\left(Z_i - \overline{Z}\right)\left(U_i - \overline{U}\right)}{\sum_{i=1}^{n}\left(Z_i - \overline{Z}\right)(p_i - \overline{p})\sum_{i=1}^{n}\left(U_i - \overline{U}\right)^2 - \sum_{i=1}^{n}(p_i - \overline{p})\left(U_i - \overline{U}\right)\sum_{i=1}^{n}\left(Z_i - \overline{Z}\right)\left(U_i - \overline{U}\right)}$$

$$
\begin{aligned}
&\sum_{i=1}^{n}\left(U_i - \overline{U}\right)(w_i - \overline{w}) \sum_{i=1}^{n}\left(U_i - \overline{U}\right)^2 \\
&\quad - \sum_{i=1}^{n}\left(U_i - \overline{U}\right)(w_i - \overline{w}) \sum_{i=1}^{n}\left(U_i - \overline{U}\right)\left(U_i - \overline{U}\right) \\
= \; &\frac{}{\sum_{i=1}^{n}\left(U_i - \overline{U}\right)\left(p_i - \overline{p}\right) \sum_{i=1}^{n}\left(U_i - \overline{U}\right)^2} \\
&\quad - \sum_{i=1}^{n}\left(p_i - \overline{p}\right)\left(U_i - \overline{U}\right) \sum_{i=1}^{n}\left(U_i - \overline{U}\right)\left(U_i - \overline{U}\right)
\end{aligned}
\tag{9.25}
$$

and the numerator and denominator both reduce to zero.

However, suppose that the rate of price inflation were hypothesized to be determined by the rate of growth of the money supply, m, as well as the rate of growth of wages, and that m were assumed to be exogenous:

$$
p = \beta_1 + \beta_2 w + \beta_3 m + u_p. \tag{9.26}
$$

The reduced form equations become

$$
p = \frac{\beta_1 + \alpha_1 \beta_2 + \alpha_3 \beta_2 U + \beta_3 m + u_p + \beta_2 u_w}{1 - \alpha_2 \beta_2} \tag{9.27}
$$

$$
w = \frac{\alpha_1 + \alpha_2 \beta_1 + \alpha_3 U + \alpha_2 \beta_3 m + u_w + \alpha_2 u_p}{1 - \alpha_2 \beta_2}. \tag{9.28}
$$

U may be used as an instrument for w in the price inflation equation, as before, and m can be used as an instrument for p in the wage inflation equation because

---

BOX 9.1   Instrumental variables estimation in a model with two explanatory variables

Suppose that the true model is

$$
Y = \beta_1 + \beta_2 X_2 + \beta_3 X_3 + u,
$$

that X_2 is not distributed independently of u, and that Z is being used as an instrument for X_2. Then the IV estimator of β_2 is given by

$$
b_2^{IV} = \frac{\sum_{i=1}^{n}\left(Z_i - \overline{Z}\right)\left(Y_i - \overline{Y}\right)\sum_{i=1}^{n}\left(X_{3i} - \overline{X}_3\right)^2 - \sum_{i=1}^{n}\left(X_{3i} - \overline{X}_3\right)\left(Y_i - \overline{Y}\right)\sum_{i=1}^{n}\left(Z_i - \overline{Z}\right)\left(X_{3i} - \overline{X}_3\right)}{\sum_{i=1}^{n}\left(Z_i - \overline{Z}\right)\left(X_{2i} - \overline{X}_2\right)\sum_{i=1}^{n}\left(X_{3i} - \overline{X}_3\right)^2 - \sum_{i=1}^{n}\left(X_{2i} - \overline{X}_2\right)\left(X_{3i} - \overline{X}_3\right)\sum_{i=1}^{n}\left(Z_i - \overline{Z}\right)\left(X_{3i} - \overline{X}_3\right)}.
$$

The IV estimator of β_3 is the same, with the subscripts 2 and 3 interchanged.

it satisfies the three conditions required of an instrument. It is correlated with p, by virtue of being a determinant; it is not correlated with the disturbance term, by virtue of being assumed to be exogenous; and it is not already in the structural equation in its own right. Both structural equations are now said to be exactly identified, **exact identification** meaning that the number of exogenous variables available as instruments (that is, not already in the equation in their own right) is equal to the number of endogenous variables requiring instruments.

Overidentification

Next consider the model

$$p = \beta_1 + \beta_2 w + u_p \tag{9.29}$$

$$w = \alpha_1 + \alpha_2 p + \alpha_3 U + \alpha_4 x + u_w \tag{9.30}$$

where x is the rate of growth of productivity. The corresponding reduced form equations are

$$p = \frac{\beta_1 + \alpha_1 \beta_2 + \alpha_3 \beta_2 U + \alpha_4 \beta_2 x + u_p + \beta_2 u_w}{1 - \alpha_2 \beta_2} \tag{9.31}$$

$$w = \frac{\alpha_1 + \alpha_2 \beta_1 + \alpha_3 U + \alpha_4 x + u_w + \alpha_2 u_p}{1 - \alpha_2 \beta_2}. \tag{9.32}$$

The wage inflation equation is underidentified because there is no exogenous variable available to act as an instrument for p. p is correlated with both U and x, but both these variables appear in the wage equation in their own right.

However, the price inflation equation is now said to be **overidentified** because we have two potential instruments for w. We could use U as an instrument for w, as before:

$$b_2^{IV} = \frac{\sum\limits_{i=1}^{n} \left(U_i - \overline{U} \right) (p_i - \overline{p})}{\sum\limits_{i=1}^{n} \left(U_i - \overline{U} \right) (w_i - \overline{w})}. \tag{9.33}$$

Alternatively, we could use x as an instrument:

$$b_2^{IV} = \frac{\sum\limits_{i=1}^{n} (x_i - \overline{x})(p_i - \overline{p})}{\sum\limits_{i=1}^{n} (x_i - \overline{x})(w_i - \overline{w})}. \tag{9.34}$$

Both are consistent estimators, so they would converge to the true value, and therefore to each other, as the sample size became large, but for finite samples they would give different estimates. Suppose that you had to choose between them (you do not, as we will see). Which would you choose? The population variance of the first is given by

$$\sigma^2_{b_2^{\mathrm{IV}}} = \frac{\sigma^2_{u_p}}{\sum\limits_{i=1}^{n} (w_i - \overline{w})^2} \times \frac{1}{r^2_{w,U}}. \tag{9.35}$$

The population variance of the second estimator is given by a similar expression with the correlation coefficient replaced by that between w and x. We want the population variance to be as small as possible, so we would choose the instrument with the higher correlation coefficient.

Two-stage least squares

In practice, rather than choose between the instruments in this situation, we would construct a linear function of them and use that instead. The main reason for this is that in general a linear function, with suitably chosen weights, will be more efficient than either instrument individually. A secondary consideration is that using a linear function eliminates the problem of conflicting estimates. Let the linear function be Z, where

$$Z = h_1 + h_2 U + h_3 x. \tag{9.36}$$

How do we choose the h coefficients? Very straightforward. Using OLS, regress w on U and x, save the fitted values, and call the saved variable Z:

$$Z = \hat{w} = h_1 + h_2 U + h_3 x. \tag{9.37}$$

The fitted values are automatically linear functions of U and x and the h coefficients will have been chosen in such a way as to maximize the correlation between the fitted values and w. As we saw in Chapter 1, OLS yields estimates that are optimal according to three mutually equivalent criteria: minimizing the sum of the squares of the residuals, maximizing R^2, and (the criterion that is relevant here) maximizing the correlation between the actual and the fitted values. This is the first stage of the **two-stage least squares (TSLS)** estimator. The second stage is the calculation of the estimate of β_2 using Z as an instrument:

$$b_2^{\mathrm{TSLS}} = \frac{\sum\limits_{i=1}^{n} (Z_i - \overline{Z})(p_i - \overline{p})}{\sum\limits_{i=1}^{n} (Z_i - \overline{Z})(w_i - \overline{w})} = \frac{\sum\limits_{i=1}^{n} (\hat{w}_i - \overline{\hat{w}})(p_i - \overline{p})}{\sum\limits_{i=1}^{n} (\hat{w}_i - \overline{\hat{w}})(w_i - \overline{w})}. \tag{9.38}$$

The population variance of b_2^{TSLS} is given by

$$\sigma^2_{b_2^{\mathrm{TSLS}}} = \frac{\sigma^2_{u_p}}{\sum\limits_{i=1}^{n} (w_i - \overline{w})^2} \times \frac{1}{r^2_{w,\hat{w}}} \tag{9.39}$$

and in general this will be smaller than the population variances of the IV estimators using U or x because the correlation coefficient will be higher.

The order condition for identification

We have observed that in general an equation will be identified if there are enough exogenous variables not appearing in it to act as instruments for the endogenous variables that do appear in it. In a fully specified model, there will be as many equations as there are endogenous variables. Let us suppose that there are G of each. The maximum number of endogenous variables that can appear on the right side of an equation is $G - 1$ (the other is the dependent variable of that equation). In such a case, we would need at least $G - 1$ exogenous variables not appearing in the equation to have enough instruments.

Suppose, however, that j endogenous variables are also missing from the equation. We would then need only $G - 1 - j$ instruments, so only $G - 1 - j$ exogenous variables would have to be missing from the equation. The total number of variables missing, however, remains the same: j endogenous variables and $G - 1 - j$ exogenous variables make a total of $G - 1$.

Thus we come to the general conclusion that an equation in a simultaneous equations model is likely to be identified if $G - 1$ or more variables are missing from it. If exactly $G - 1$ are missing, it is likely to be exactly identified, and if more than $G - 1$ are missing, it is likely to be overidentified, calling for the use of TSLS.

This is known as the **order condition for identification**. It must be stressed that this is a necessary condition for identification but not a sufficient one. There are cases, which we will not discuss here, in which an equation is in fact underidentified even if the order condition is satisfied.

Unobserved heterogeneity

In the examples above, simultaneous equations bias and instrumental variables estimation were discussed in the context of fully specified multi-equation models. However, it is common to find these issues discussed in the context of a single-equation model, where the equation is implicitly embedded in a simultaneous equations model where the other relationships are unspecified. For example, in the case of the earnings function

$$LGEARN = \beta_1 + \beta_2 S + \cdots + u, \tag{9.40}$$

it is often asserted that '**unobserved heterogeneity**' will cause the OLS estimate of β_2 to be biased. In this case unobserved heterogeneity refers to unobserved variations in the characteristics of the respondents, such as ambition and various types of intelligence and ability, that influence both educational attainment and earnings. Because they are unobserved, their influence on earnings is captured

Table 9.3

	OLS	IV
Coefficient of S	0.073	0.140
Standard error	0.004	0.055

by the disturbance term, and thus S and u are positively correlated. As a consequence, the OLS estimate of β_2 will be subject to a positive bias. If this is the case, S needs to be instrumented with a suitable instrument.

However, it requires ingenuity to find a credible instrument, for most factors affecting educational attainment are also likely to affect earnings. One such example is the use of proximity to a four-year college by Card (1995), who argued that this could have a positive effect on educational attainment but was unlikely to be a determinant of earnings.

Table 9.3 presents the results of OLS and IV regressions using a sample of 3,010 males derived from the National Longitudinal Survey of Young Men, a panel study that was a precursor to the NLSY. The earnings data relate to 1976. The regressions included personal, family, and regional characteristics not shown. As can be seen, using college proximity to instrument for educational attainment does make a difference—but it is in a direction opposite to that expected, for if the OLS estimate is upwards biased, the IV estimate ought to be smaller, not larger. Measurement error in S, which would cause a downwards bias in the OLS estimate, could account for part of the perverse effect, but not all of it. Card sought an explanation in terms of a higher-than-average return to education for those with relatively poorly-educated parents, combined with a higher responsiveness of educational attainment to college proximity for such respondents. However, although educational attainment is positively correlated with college proximity, the correlation is weak and accordingly the standard error of the IV estimate large. It is thus possible that the apparent increase occurred as a matter of chance and that a Durbin–Wu–Hausman test would have shown that the OLS and IV estimates were not significantly different.

Durbin–Wu–Hausman test

In Chapter 8 it was shown that measurement error causes a violation of the regression model assumption that the disturbance term be distributed independently of the regressors, and that one can use the **Durbin–Wu–Hausman test**, which compares the OLS and IV coefficients, to test for suspected measurement error. The test can be used in the same way more broadly for suspected violations of this regression model assumption and in particular for violations caused by simultaneous equations bias. To illustrate this, we will return to the Monte Carlo experiment described above. The regression output in Table 9.4 shows the result of performing the test for the first of the 10 replications of the experiment summarized in Table 9.2.

Table 9.4

```
. ivreg p (w=U)
Instrumental variables (2SLS) regression
```

Source	SS	df	MS		Number of obs =	20
					F(1,18) =	0.13
Model	5.39052472	1	5.39052472		Prob > F =	0.7207
Residual	28.1781361	18	1.565452		R-squared =	0.1606
					Adj R-squared =	0.1139
Total	33.5686608	19	1.76677162		Root MSE =	1.2512

p	Coef.	Std. Err.	t	P>|t|	[95% Conf.	Interval]
w	.1619431	.4459005	0.36	0.721	−.7748591	1.098745
_cons	2.328433	.9699764	2.40	0.027	.2905882	4.366278

```
Instrumented: w
Instruments: U
```

```
. estimates store regiv

. reg p w
```

Source	SS	df	MS		Number of obs =	20
					F(1,18) =	26.16
Model	19.8854938	1	19.8854938		Prob > F =	0.0001
Residual	13.683167	18	.760175945		R-squared =	0.5924
					Adj R-squared =	0.5697
Total	33.5686608	19	1.76677162		Root MSE =	.87188

p	Coef.	Std. Err.	t	P>|t|	[95% Conf.	Interval]
w	1.107448	.2165271	5.11	0.000	.6525417	1.562355
_cons	.3590688	.4913327	0.73	0.474	−.673183	1.391321

```
. estimates store regols

. hausman regiv regols, constant
```

	Coefficients			
	(b)	(B)	(b−B)	sqrt(diag(V_b−V_B))
	regiv	regols	Difference	S.E.
w	.1619431	1.107448	−.9455052	.389799
_cons	2.328433	.3590688	1.969364	.8363291

```
                        b = consistent under Ho and Ha; obtained from ivreg
         B = inconsistent under Ha, efficient under Ho; obtained from regress

  Test: Ho: difference in coefficients not systematic

              chi2(2) = (b−B)' [(V_b−V_B)(−1)](b−B)
                      =        5.88
           Prob > chi2 =       0.0528
```

Under the null hypothesis that there is no simultaneous equations bias, both OLS and IV will be consistent estimators, but OLS will be more efficient. Under the alternative hypothesis, OLS will be inconsistent. As can be seen from the output, the chi-squared statistic summarizing the differences in the coefficients is 5.88. In principle there should be two degrees of freedom because we are comparing two parameters. This is confirmed by the output. The critical value of chi-squared with two degrees of freedom at the 5 percent level is 5.99, and hence we just fail to reject the null hypothesis at this significance level. This is a surprise since the Monte Carlo experiment involved a simultaneous equations model designed to demonstrate that OLS would yield inconsistent estimates. The failure to reject the null hypothesis in this case is an example of Type II error, probably attributable to the small size of the sample and the imprecision of the estimates.

BOX 9.2   Indirect least squares

Indirect least squares (ILS), an alternative procedure for obtaining consistent estimates of parameters in a simultaneous equations model, is no longer used in practice but it retains some pedagogical interest. Returning to the price inflation/wage inflation model

$$p = \beta_1 + \beta_2 w + u_p$$

$$w = \alpha_1 + \alpha_2 p + \alpha_3 U + u_w,$$

the reduced form equations for p and w were

$$p = \frac{\beta_1 + \alpha_1 \beta_2 + \alpha_3 \beta_2 U + u_p + \beta_2 u_w}{1 - \alpha_2 \beta_2}$$

$$w = \frac{\alpha_1 + \alpha_2 \beta_1 + \alpha_3 U + u_w + \alpha_2 u_p}{1 - \alpha_2 \beta_2}.$$

On the assumption that U is exogenous, it is independent of u_p and u_w and so OLS will give unbiased estimates of the parameters of the equations. The parameters of these equations are of course functions of the parameters of the structural equations, but it may be possible to derive estimates of the structural parameters from them. For example, using the data for the first replication of the Monte Carlo experiment, the fitted reduced form equations are

$$\hat{p} = 2.9741 - 0.0705 U$$

$$\hat{w} = 3.9871 - 0.4352 U.$$

Hence, linking the numerical estimates to the theoretical coefficients, one has four equations

$$\frac{b_1 + a_1 b_2}{1 - a_2 b_2} = 2.9741 \qquad \frac{a_3 b_2}{1 - a_2 b_2} = -0.0705$$

$$\frac{a_1 + a_2 b_1}{1 - a_2 b_2} = 3.9871 \qquad \frac{a_3}{1 - a_2 b_2} = -0.4352$$

Substituting the fourth equation into the second, one has $-0.4352b_2 = -0.0705$, and so $b_2 = 0.1620$. Further, since

$$\frac{b_1 + a_1 b_2}{1 - a_2 b_2} - b_2 \frac{a_1 + a_2 b_1}{1 - a_2 b_2} = b_1$$

one has $b_1 = 2.9741 - 0.1620 \times 3.9871 = 2.3282$. There is no way of deriving estimates of the three remaining parameters. Indeed, since we had four equations in five unknowns, we were lucky to pin down two of the parameters. Since we have obtained (unique) estimates of the parameters of the structural price equation, that equation is said to be exactly identified, while the structural wage equation is said to be underidentified.

Next consider the model

$$p = \beta_1 + \beta_2 w + u_p$$

$$w = \alpha_1 + \alpha_2 p + \alpha_3 U + \alpha_4 x + u_w$$

where x is the rate of growth of productivity. The corresponding reduced form equations are

$$p = \frac{\beta_1 + \alpha_1 \beta_2 + \alpha_3 \beta_2 U + \alpha_4 \beta_2 x + u_p + \beta_2 u_w}{1 - \alpha_2 \beta_2}$$

$$w = \frac{\alpha_1 + \alpha_2 \beta_1 + \alpha_3 U + \alpha_4 x + u_w + \alpha_2 u_p}{1 - \alpha_2 \beta_2}.$$

Suppose that when these are fitted we obtain, in abstract form,

$$\hat{p} = B_1 + B_2 U + B_3 x$$

$$\hat{w} = A_1 + A_2 U + A_3 x$$

where the B_i and the A_i are numerical regression coefficients. Linking these numerical coefficients to their theoretical counterparts, we obtain six equations in six unknowns:

$$\frac{b_1 + a_1 b_2}{1 - a_2 b_2} = B_1 \qquad \frac{a_3 b_2}{1 - a_2 b_2} = B_2 \qquad \frac{a_4 b_2}{1 - a_2 b_2} = B_3$$

$$\frac{a_1 + a_2 b_1}{1 - a_2 b_2} = A_1 \qquad \frac{a_3}{1 - a_2 b_2} = A_2 \qquad \frac{a_4}{1 - a_2 b_2} = A_3.$$

Substituting the fifth equation into the second, we have $A_2 b_2 = B_2$, and so B_2/A_2 provides an estimate of β_2. However, substituting the sixth equation into the third, we have $A_3 b_2 = B_3$, and so B_3/A_3 also provides an estimate of β_2. Thus we have more than one way of obtaining an estimate and the model is said to be overidentified. This is the counterpart of having alternative instruments in IV estimation. The estimates would both be consistent, and so in large samples they would converge to the true value, but in finite samples they would differ. One would also be able to obtain conflicting estimates of α. However, it would not be possible to obtain estimates of the remaining parameters and the wage equation is said to be underidentified.

ILS has no advantages over IV and has the disadvantage of requiring more computation. If an equation is underidentified for IV, it is underidentified for ILS; if it exactly identified, IV and ILS yield identical estimates; if it is overidentified, ILS yields conflicting estimates, a problem that is resolved with IV by using TSLS.

Key terms

Durbin–Wu–Hausman (DWH) test	overidentification
endogenous variable	reduced form equation
exact identification	simultaneous equations bias
exogenous variable	structural equation
identification	two-stage least squares (TSLS)
indirect least squares	underidentification
order condition for identification	unobserved heterogeneity

Exercises

9.4* The table gives consumption per capita, C, gross investment per capita, I, and gross domestic product per capita, Y, all measured in US\$, for 33 countries in 1998. The output from an OLS regression of C on Y, and an IV regression using I as an instrument for Y, are shown. Comment on the differences in the results.

	C	I	Y		C	I	Y
Australia	15024	4749	19461	South Korea	4596	1448	6829
Austria	19813	6787	26104	Luxembourg	26400	9767	42650
Belgium	18367	5174	24522	Malaysia	1683	873	3268
Canada	15786	4017	20085	Mexico	3359	1056	4328
China–PR	446	293	768	Netherlands	17558	4865	24086
China–HK	17067	7262	24452	New Zealand	11236	2658	13992
Denmark	25199	6947	32769	Norway	23415	9221	32933
Finland	17991	4741	24952	Pakistan	389	79	463
France	19178	4622	24587	Philippines	760	176	868
Germany	20058	5716	26219	Portugal	8579	2644	9976
Greece	9991	2460	11551	Spain	11255	3415	14052
Iceland	25294	6706	30622	Sweden	20687	4487	26866
India	291	84	385	Switzerland	27648	7815	36864
Indonesia	351	216	613	Thailand	1226	479	1997
Ireland	13045	4791	20132	UK	19743	4316	23844
Italy	16134	4075	20580	USA	26387	6540	32377
Japan	21478	7923	30124				

```
. reg C Y

    Source |      SS          df          MS              Number of obs =        33
-------------+------------------------------              F(1,31)       =   1331.29
     Model | 2.5686e+09       1     2.5686e+09            Prob > F      =    0.0000
  Residual | 59810749.2      31     1929379.01            R-squared     =    0.9772
-------------+------------------------------              Adj R-squared =    0.9765
     Total | 2.6284e+09      32     82136829.4            Root MSE      =      1389

-------------------------------------------------------------------------------------
        C |     Coef.    Std. Err.       t    P>|t|       [95% Conf. Interval]
-------------------------------------------------------------------------------------
        Y |  .7303066    .0200156     36.49   0.000       .6894845     .7711287
    _cons |  379.4871    443.6764      0.86   0.399      -525.397     1284.371
-------------------------------------------------------------------------------------

. ivreg C (Y = I)

Instrumental variables (2SLS) regression

    Source |      SS          df          MS              Number of obs =        33
-------------+------------------------------              F(1,31)       =   1192.18
     Model | 2.5679e+09       1     2.5679e+09            Prob > F      =    0.0000
  Residual | 60494538.1      31     1951436.71            R-squared     =    0.9770
-------------+------------------------------              Adj R-squared =    0.9762
     Total | 2.6284e+09      32     82136829.4            Root MSE      =    1396.9

-------------------------------------------------------------------------------------
        C |     Coef.    Std. Err.       t    P>|t|       [95% Conf. Interval]
-------------------------------------------------------------------------------------
        Y |  .7183909    .0208061     34.53   0.000       .6759566     .7608252
    _cons |  600.946     456.7973      1.32   0.198      -330.6982    1532.59
-------------------------------------------------------------------------------------

Instrumented: Y
Instruments:  I
```

9.5 The researcher in Exercise 9.3 discovers that last year's advertising budget, $A(-1)$, is also an important determinant of A, so that the model is

$$S = \beta_1 + \beta_2 A + u_S$$
$$A = \alpha_1 + \alpha_2 S + \alpha_3 A(-1) + u_A.$$

Explain how this information could be used to obtain a consistent estimator of β_2, and prove that it is consistent.

9.6 Suppose that $A(-1)$ in Exercise 9.5 also has an influence on S. How would this affect the fitting of the model?

9.7 The researcher in Exercise 9.3 finds out that the average price of the product, P, and last year's sales, $S(-1)$, are important determinants of S, so that the model is

$$S = \beta_1 + \beta_2 A + \beta_3 P + \beta_4 S(-1) + u_S$$
$$A = \alpha_1 + \alpha_2 S + u_A.$$

How would this affect the fitting of the model?

9.8 In principle $ASVABC$ might be a positive function of S, in which case the educational attainment model should have two equations:

$$S = \beta_1 + \beta_2 ASVABC + \beta_3 SM + u_S$$
$$ASVABC = \alpha_1 + \alpha_2 S + u_A.$$

Using your *EAEF* data set, fit the second equation, first using OLS, second using instrumental variables estimation with SM as an instrument. Demonstrate that in principle IV should yield consistent estimates. Investigate analytically the likely direction of the bias in the slope coefficient in the OLS regression, and check whether a comparison of the OLS and IV estimates confirms your analysis.

9.9 The output from a Durbin–Wu–Hausman test using the regressions in Exercise 9.4 is shown. 'CGIV' and 'CGOLS' are the names given to the IV and OLS regressions, respectively. Perform the test and state whether or not it supports your discussion in Exercise 9.4.

```
. hausman CGIV CGOLS, constant

        ——Coefficients——
             (b)          (B)         (b−B)      sqrt(diag(V_b−V_B))
            CGIV         CGOLS      Difference          S.E.
-------------------------------------------------------------------
        Y  .7183909     .7303066    −.0119157        .0056807
    _cons  600.946      379.4871    221.4589         108.6968
-------------------------------------------------------------------
                b = consistent under Ho and Ha; obtained from ivreg
     B = inconsistent under Ha, efficient under Ho; obtained from regress

   Test: Ho: difference in coefficients not systematic

            chi2(1) = (b−B)′ [(V_b−V_B)(−1)](b−B)
                    =           4.15
          Prob>chi2 =          0.0416
```

10 Binary Choice and Limited Dependent Variable Models, and Maximum Likelihood Estimation

Economists are often interested in the factors behind the decision-making of individuals or enterprises. Examples are:

- Why do some people go to college while others do not?
- Why do some women enter the labor force while others do not?
- Why do some people buy houses while others rent?
- Why do some people migrate while others stay put?

The models that have been developed are known as **binary choice** or **qualitative response models** with the outcome, which we will denote Y, being assigned a value of 1 if the event occurs and 0 otherwise. Models with more than two possible outcomes have been developed, but we will restrict our attention to binary choice. The linear probability model apart, binary choice models are fitted using maximum likelihood estimation. The chapter ends with an introduction to this topic.

10.1 The linear probability model

The simplest binary choice model is the linear probability model where, as the name implies, the probability of the event occurring, p, is assumed to be a linear function of a set of explanatory variable(s):

$$p_i = p(Y_i = 1) = \beta_1 + \beta_2 X_i. \qquad (10.1)$$

Graphically, the relationship is as shown in Figure 10.1, if there is just one explanatory variable. Of course p is unobservable. One has data only on the outcome, Y. In the linear probability model this is used as a dummy variable for the dependent variable.

As an illustration, we investigate the factors influencing graduating from high school. We will define a variable $GRAD$ that is equal to 1 for those individuals who graduated, and 0 for those who dropped out, and we will regress it on $ASVABC$, the composite cognitive ability test score. The regression output in Table 10.1 shows the result of fitting this linear probability model, using *EAEF* Data Set 21.

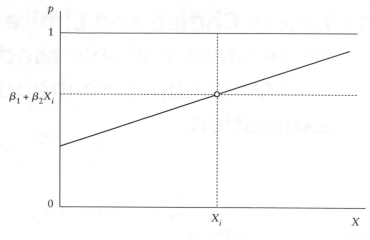

Figure 10.1 Linear probability model

Table 10.1

```
. reg GRAD ASVABC

    Source        SS           df         MS              Number of obs   =       540
--------------------------------------------              F(1,538)        =     49.59
     Model     2.46607893       1      2.46607893          Prob > F        =    0.0000
  Residual    26.7542914      538      .049729166          R-squared       =    0.0844
--------------------------------------------              Adj R-squared   =    0.0827
     Total    29.2203704      539      .05421219           Root MSE        =      .223

--------------------------------------------------------------------------------------
      GRAD        Coef.    Std. Err.        t       P>|t|      [95% Conf.  Interval]
--------------------------------------------------------------------------------------
    ASVABC     .0070697    .0010039        7.04     0.000      .0050976    .0090419
     _cons     .5794711    .0524502       11.05     0.000      .4764387    .6825035
```

The regression result suggests that the probability of graduating from high school increases by a proportion 0.007, that is, 0.7 percent, for every point increase in the $ASVABC$ score. $ASVABC$ is scaled so that it has mean 50 and standard deviation 10, so a one-standard deviation increase in the score would increase the probability of graduating by 7 percent. The intercept implies that if $ASVABC$ were zero, the probability of graduating would be 58 percent. However, the $ASVABC$ score is scaled in such a way as to make its minimum about 20, and accordingly it is doubtful whether the interpretation should be taken at face value.

Unfortunately, the linear probability model has some serious defects. First, there are problems with the disturbance term. As usual, the value of the dependent variable Y_i in observation i has a deterministic component and a random component. The deterministic component depends on X_i and the parameters and is the expected value of Y_i given X_i, $E(Y_i \mid X_i)$. The random component is the disturbance term:

$$Y_i = E(Y_i \mid X_i) + u_i. \tag{10.2}$$

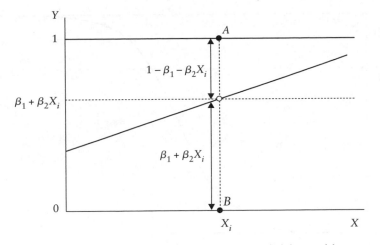

Figure 10.2 Disturbance term in the linear probability model

It is simple to compute $E(Y_i | X_i)$, the expected value of Y_i given X_i, because Y can take only two values. It is 1 with probability p_i and 0 with probability $(1 - p_i)$:

$$E(Y_i | X_i) = 1 \times p_i + 0 \times (1 - p_i) = p_i = \beta_1 + \beta_2 X_i. \qquad (10.3)$$

The expected value in observation i is therefore $\beta_1 + \beta_2 X_i$. This means that we can rewrite the model as

$$Y_i = \beta_1 + \beta_2 X_i + u_i. \qquad (10.4)$$

The probability function is thus also the deterministic component of the relationship between Y and X. It follows that, for the outcome variable Y_i to be equal to 1, as represented by the point A in Figure 10.2, the disturbance term must be equal to $(1 - \beta_1 - \beta_2 X_i)$. For the outcome to be 0, as represented by the point B, the disturbance term must be $(-\beta_1 - \beta_2 X_i)$. Thus the distribution of the disturbance term consists of just two specific values. It is not even continuous, never mind normal. This means that the standard errors and the usual test statistics are invalidated. For good measure, the two possible values of the disturbance term change with X, so the distribution is heteroscedastic as well. It can be shown that the population variance of u_i is $(\beta_1 + \beta_2 X_i)(1 - \beta_1 - \beta_2 X_i)$, and this varies with X_i.

Another problem is that the predicted probability may be greater than 1 or less than 0 for extreme values of X. In the example of graduating from high school, the regression equation predicts a probability greater than 1 for the 176 respondents with $ASVABC$ scores greater than 56.

The first problem is dealt with by fitting the model with a technique known as maximum likelihood estimation, described in Section 10.6, instead of least squares. The second problem involves elaborating the model as follows. Define

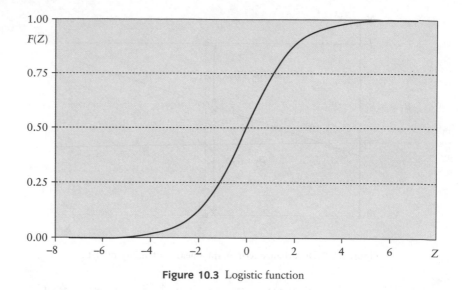

Figure 10.3 Logistic function

a variable Z that is a linear function of the explanatory variables. In the present case, since we have only one explanatory variable, this function is

$$Z_i = \beta_1 + \beta_2 X_i. \tag{10.5}$$

Next, suppose that p is a sigmoid (S-shaped) function of Z, for example as shown in Figure 10.3. Below a certain value of Z, there is very little chance of the individual graduating from high school. Above a certain value, the individual is almost certain to graduate. In between, the probability is sensitive to the value of Z.

This deals with the problem of nonsense probability estimates, but then there is the question of what should be the precise mathematical form of this function. There is no definitive answer to this. The two most popular forms are the logistic function, which is used in logit estimation, and the cumulative normal distribution, which is used in probit estimation. According to one of the leading authorities on the subject, Amemiya (1981), both give satisfactory results most of the time and neither has any particular advantage. We will start with the former.

10.2 Logit analysis

In the **logit model** one hypothesizes that the probability of the occurrence of the event is determined by the function

$$p_i = F(Z_i) = \frac{1}{1 + e^{-Z_i}}. \tag{10.6}$$

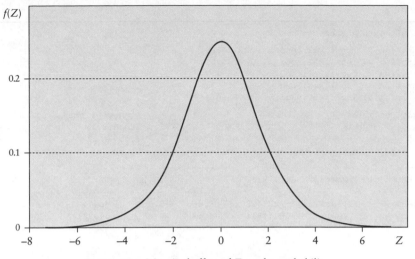

Figure 10.4 Marginal effect of Z on the probability

This is the function shown in Figure 10.3. As Z tends to infinity, e^{-Z} tends to 0 and p has a limiting upper bound of 1. As Z tends to minus infinity, e^{-Z} tends to infinity and p has a limiting lower bound of 0. Hence there is no possibility of getting predictions of the probability being greater than 1 or less than 0.

The marginal effect of Z on the probability, which will be denoted $f(Z)$, is given by the derivative of this function with respect to Z:

$$f(Z) = \frac{dp}{dZ} = \frac{e^{-Z}}{\left(1 + e^{-Z}\right)^2}. \tag{10.7}$$

The function is shown in Figure 10.4. You can see that the effect of changes in Z on the probability is very small for large positive or large negative values of Z, and that the sensitivity of the probability to changes in Z is greatest at the midpoint value of 0.

In the case of the example of graduating from high school, the function is

$$p_i = \frac{1}{1 + e^{-\beta_1 - \beta_2 ASVABC_i}}. \tag{10.8}$$

If we fit the model, we get the output shown in Table 10.2.

The model is fitted by maximum likelihood estimation and, as the output in Table 10.2 indicates, this uses an iterative process to estimate the parameters. How should one interpret the coefficients? To calculate the marginal effect of $ASVABC$ on p we need to calculate $dp/dASVABC$. You could calculate the differential directly, but the best way to do this, especially if Z is a function of more than one variable, is to break it up into two stages. p is a function of Z, and Z is a function of $ASVABC$, so

$$\frac{dp}{dASVABC} = \frac{dp}{dZ} \frac{dZ}{dASVABC} = f(Z)\,\beta_2 \tag{10.9}$$

Table 10.2

```
. logit GRAD ASVABC

Iteration 0: log likelihood = −118.67769
Iteration 1: log likelihood = −104.45292
Iteration 2: log likelihood = −97.135677
Iteration 3: log likelihood = −96.887294
Iteration 4: log likelihood = −96.886017

Logit estimates                              Number of obs   =       540
                                             LR chi2(1)      =     43.58
                                             Prob > chi2     =    0.0000
Log likelihood = −96.886017                  Pseudo R2       =    0.1836
-------------------------------------------------------------------------
    GRAD        Coef.     Std. Err.      z      P>|z|    [95% Conf.   Interval]
-------------------------------------------------------------------------
  ASVABC      .1313626     .022428     5.86    0.000    .0874045    .1753206
   _cons    −3.240218     .9444844    −3.43    0.001   −5.091373   −1.389063
```

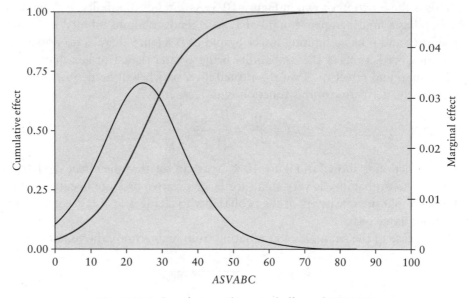

Figure 10.5 Cumulative and marginal effects of *ASVABC*

where $f(Z)$ is as defined in (10.7). The probability of graduating from high school, and the marginal effect, are plotted as functions of *ASVABC* in Figure 10.5.

How can you summarize the effect of the *ASVABC* score on the probability of graduating? The usual method is to calculate the marginal effect at the mean value of the explanatory variables. In this sample the mean value of *ASVABC* was 51.36. For this value, Z is equal to 3.5085 and e^{-Z} is equal to 0.0299. Using this, $f(Z)$ is 0.0282 and the marginal effect is 0.0037:

$$f(Z)\beta_2 = \frac{e^{-Z}}{(1+e^{-Z})^2}\beta_2 = \frac{0.0299}{(1.0299)^2} \times 0.1314 = 0.0037. \tag{10.10}$$

In other words, at the sample mean, a one-point increase in *ASVABC* increases the probability of going to college by 0.4 percent. This is a very small amount and the reason is that, for those with the mean *ASVABC*, the estimated probability of graduating is already so high that an increase in *ASVABC* can make little difference:

$$p = \frac{1}{1+e^{-Z}} = \frac{1}{1+0.0299} = 0.9709. \tag{10.11}$$

See also Figure 10.5. Of course we could calculate the marginal effect for other values of *ASVABC* if we wished and in this particular case it may be of interest to evaluate it for low *ASVABC*, where individuals are at greater risk of not graduating. For example, when *ASVABC* is 30, Z is 0.7018, e^{-Z} is 0.4957, $f(Z)$ is 0.2216, and the marginal effect is 0.0291, or 2.9 percent. It is much higher because an individual with such a low score has only a 67 percent chance of graduating and an increase in *ASVABC* can make a substantial difference.

Generalization to more than one explanatory variable

Logit analysis is easily extended to the case where there is more than one explanatory variable. Suppose that we decide to relate graduating from high school to *ASVABC*, *SM*, the number of years of schooling of the mother, *SF*, the number of years of schooling of the father, and a dummy variable *MALE* that is equal to 1 for males, 0 for females. The Z variable becomes

$$Z = \beta_1 + \beta_2 ASVABC + \beta_3 SM + \beta_4 SF + \beta_5 MALE. \tag{10.12}$$

The corresponding regression output (with iteration messages deleted) is shown in Table 10.3.

The mean values of *ASVABC*, *SM*, *SF*, and *MALE* were as shown in Table 10.4, and hence the value of Z at the mean was 3.5143. From this one obtains 0.0298 for e^{-Z} and 0.0281 for $f(Z)$. The table shows the marginal effects, calculated by multiplying $f(Z)$ by the estimates of the coefficients of the logit regression.

According to the computations, a one-point increase in the *ASVABC* score increases the probability of graduating from high school by 0.4 percent, and being male increases it by the same amount. Variations in parental education appear to have negligible effects. From the regression output it can be seen that

Table 10.3

```
. logit GRAD ASVABC SM SF MALE

Logit estimates                                    Number of obs   =      540
                                                   LR chi2(4)      =    43.75
                                                   Prob > chi2     =   0.0000
Log likelihood = -96.804844                        Pseudo R2       =   0.1843

---------------------------------------------------------------------------
    GRAD      Coef.    Std. Err.      z      P>|z|    [95% Conf.    Interval]
---------------------------------------------------------------------------
   ASVABC   .1329127   .0245718     5.41    0.000    .0847528     .1810726
      SM   -.023178    .0868122    -0.27    0.789   -.1933267     .1469708
      SF    .0122663   .0718876     0.17    0.865   -.1286307     .1531634
    MALE    .1279654   .3989345     0.32    0.748   -.6539318     .9098627
   _cons   -3.252373   1.065524    -3.05    0.002   -5.340761    -1.163985
```

Table 10.4 Logit estimation, dependent variable GRAD

Variable	Mean	b	Mean $\times b$	$f(Z)$	$bf(Z)$
ASVABC	51.36	0.1329	6.8257	0.0281	0.0037
SM	11.58	−0.0231	−0.2687	0.0281	−0.0007
SF	11.84	0.0123	0.1456	0.0281	0.0003
MALE	0.50	0.1280	0.0640	0.0281	0.0036
constant	1.000	−3.2524	−3.2524		
Total			3.5143		

the effect of *ASVABC* was significant at the 0.1 percent level but the effects of the other variables were insignificant.

Goodness of fit and statistical tests

There is no measure of goodness of fit equivalent to R^2 in maximum likelihood estimation. In default, numerous measures have been proposed for comparing alternative model specifications. Denoting the actual outcome in observation i as Y_i, with $Y_i = 1$ if the event occurs and 0 if it does not, and denoting the predicted probability of the event occurring $\hat{p}_i$, the measures include the following:

- the number of outcomes correctly predicted, taking the prediction in observation i as 1 if $\hat{p}_i$ is greater than 0.5 and 0 if it is less;
- the sum of the squared residuals $\sum \left(Y_i - \hat{p}_i \right)^2$;
- the correlation between the outcomes and predicted probabilities, $r_{Y_i \hat{p}_i}$;
- the pseudo-R^2 in the logit output, explained in Section 10.6.

Each of these measures has its shortcomings and Amemiya (1981) recommends considering more than one and comparing the results.

Nevertheless, the standard significance tests are similar to those for the standard regression model. The significance of an individual coefficient can be evaluated via its t statistic. However, since the standard error is valid only asymptotically (in large samples), the same goes for the t statistic, and since the t distribution converges on the normal distribution in large samples, the critical values of the latter should be used. This is emphasized in Stata by replacing 't' by 'z' in the output. The counterpart of the F test of the explanatory power of the model (H_0: all the slope coefficients are zero, H_1: at least one is nonzero) is a chi-squared test with the chi-squared statistic in the logit output distributed under H_0 with degrees of freedom equal to the number of explanatory variables. Details are provided in Section 10.6.

Exercises

10.1 What are the factors influencing going to college? Using your *EAEF* data set, define a binary variable *COLLEGE* to be equal to 1 if $S > 12$ and 0 otherwise. Regress *COLLEGE* on *ASVABC*, *SM*, *SF*, and *MALE* (1) using ordinary least squares, and (2) using logit analysis. Calculate the marginal effects in the logit analysis and compare them with those obtained using OLS.

10.2* A researcher, using a sample of 2,868 individuals from the NLSY, is investigating how the probability of a respondent obtaining a bachelor's degree from a four-year college is related to the respondent's score on *ASVABC*. 26.7 percent of the respondents earned bachelor's degrees. *ASVABC* ranged from 22 to 65, with mean value 50.2, and most scores were in the range 40 to 60. Defining a variable *BACH* to be equal to 1 if the respondent has a bachelor's degree (or higher degree) and 0 otherwise, the researcher fitted the OLS regression (standard errors in parentheses)

$$\widehat{BACH} = -0.864 + 0.023 ASVABC \quad R^2 = 0.21.$$
$$\phantom{\widehat{BACH} = }(0.042) \ (0.001)$$

The researcher also fitted the following logit regression:

$$\hat{Z} = -11.103 + 0.189 \ ASVABC$$
$$\phantom{\hat{Z} = }(0.487) \ (0.009)$$

where Z is the variable in the logit function. Using this regression, the probability and marginal effect functions are shown in the diagram.

(a) Give an interpretation of the OLS regression. and explain why OLS is not a satisfactory estimation method for this kind of model.

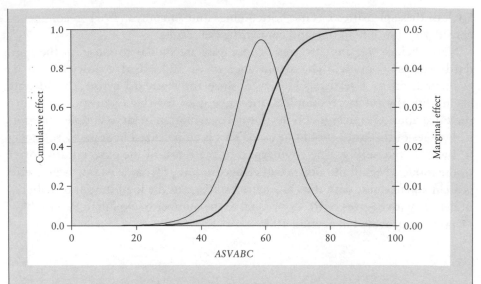

(b) With reference to the diagram, discuss the variation of the marginal effect of the *ASVABC* score implicit in the logit regression and compare it with that in the OLS regression.

(c) Sketch the probability and marginal effect diagrams for the OLS regression and compare them with those for the logit regression. In your discussion, make use of the information in the first paragraph of this question.

10.3   Probit analysis

The **probit model** provides an alternative approach to binary choice. It uses the cumulative standardized normal distribution to model the sigmoid relationship $F(Z)$. (A standardized normal distribution is one with zero mean and unit variance). As with the logit model, you start by defining a variable Z that is a linear function of the variables that determine the probability:

$$Z = \beta_1 + \beta_2 X_2 + \cdots + \beta_k X_k. \tag{10.13}$$

$F(Z)$, the cumulative standardized normal distribution, gives the probability of the event occurring for any value of Z:

$$p_i = F(Z_i). \tag{10.14}$$

Maximum likelihood analysis is used to obtain estimates of the parameters. The marginal effect of X_i is $\partial p / \partial X_i$ which, as in the case of logit analysis, is best computed as

$$\frac{\partial p}{\partial X_i} = \frac{dp}{dZ}\frac{\partial Z}{\partial X_i} = f(Z)\,\beta_i. \tag{10.15}$$

Now since $F(Z)$ is the cumulative standardized normal distribution, $f(Z)$, its derivative, is just the standardized normal distribution itself:

$$f(Z) = \frac{1}{\sqrt{2\pi}}e^{-\frac{1}{2}Z^2}. \tag{10.16}$$

Figure 10.6 plots $F(Z)$ and $f(Z)$ for probit analysis. As with logit analysis, the marginal effect of any variable is not constant. It depends on the value of $f(Z)$, which in turn depends on the values of each of the explanatory variables. To obtain a summary statistic for the marginal effect, the usual procedure is parallel to that used in logit analysis. You calculate Z for the mean values of the explanatory variables. Next you calculate $f(Z)$, as in (10.16). Then you calculate $f(Z)\beta_i$ to obtain the marginal effect of X_i.

This will be illustrated with the example of graduating from high school, using the same specification as in the logit regression. The regression output, with iteration messages deleted, is shown in Table 10.5.

The computation of the marginal effects at the sample means is shown in Table 10.6. Z is 1.8814 when evaluated at the mean values of the variables and $f(Z)$ is 0.0680. The estimates of the marginal effects are virtually the same as those obtained using logit analysis. Generally logit and probit analysis yield similar marginal effects. However, the shapes of the tails of the logit and probit

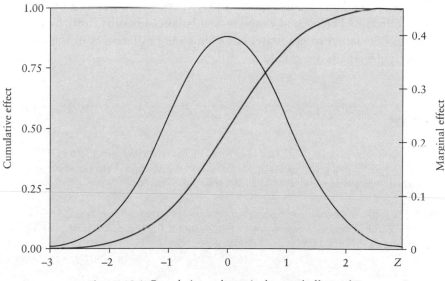

Figure 10.6 Cumulative and marginal normal effects of Z.

Table 10.5

```
. probit GRAD ASVABC SM SF MALE

Probit estimates                          Number of obs =      540
                                          LR chi2(4)    =    44.11
                                          Prob > chi2   =   0.0000
Log likelihood = −96.624926               Pseudo R2     =   0.1858
---------------------------------------------------------------------
    GRAD      Coef.   Std. Err.     z    P>|z|     [95% Conf. Interval]
---------------------------------------------------------------------
   ASVABC   .0648442   .0120378   5.39   0.000     .0412505   .0884379
      SM  −.0081163   .0440399  −0.18   0.854    −.094433    .0782004
      SF   .0056041   .0359557   0.16   0.876    −.0648677   .0760759
    MALE   .0630588   .1988279   0.32   0.751    −.3266368   .4527544
   _cons  −1.450787   .5470608  −2.65   0.008    −2.523006  −.3785673
```

Table 10.6 Probit estimation, dependent variable *GRAD*

Variable	Mean	b	Mean $\times$ b	$f(Z)$	$bf(Z)$
ASVABC	51.36	0.0648	3.3281	0.0680	0.0044
SM	11.58	−0.0081	−0.0938	0.0680	−0.0006
SF	11.84	0.0056	0.0663	0.0680	0.0004
MALE	0.50	0.0631	0.0316	0.0680	0.0043
constant	1.00	−1.4508	−1.4508		
Total			1.8814		

distributions are different and so logit and probit can give different results if the sample is unbalanced, with most of the outcomes similar and only a small minority different. The present example is unbalanced because only 6 percent of the respondents failed to graduate, but even so the differences in the estimates of the marginal effects are small.

Exercises

10.3 Regress the variable *COLLEGE* defined in Exercise 10.1 on *ASVABC*, *MALE*, *SM* and *SF* using probit analysis. Calculate the marginal effects and compare them with those obtained using OLS and logit analysis.

10.4* The following probit regression, with iteration messages deleted, was fitted using 2,726 observations on females in the National Longitudinal Survey of Youth using the *LFP94* data set described in Appendix B. The data are for 1994, when the respondents were aged 29 to 36 and many of them were raising young families.

```
. probit WORKING S AGE CHILDL06 CHILDL16 MARRIED ETHBLACK
ETHHISP if MALE == 0

Probit estimates                        Number of obs   =     2726
                                        LR chi2(7)      =   165.08
                                        Prob > chi2     =   0.0000
Log likelihood = −1403.0835             Pseudo R2       =   0.0556

-----------------------------------------------------------------------
  WORKING      Coef.   Std. Err.      z     P>|z|    [95% Conf.  Interval]
-----------------------------------------------------------------------
        S     .0892571  .0120629    7.399   0.000    .0656143      .1129
      AGE    −.0438511   .012478   −3.514   0.000   −.0683076   .0193946
 CHILDL06    −.5841503  .0744923   −7.842   0.000   −.7301525  −.4381482
 CHILDL16    −.1359097  .0792359   −1.715   0.086   −.2912092   .0193897
  MARRIED    −.0076543  .0631618   −0.121   0.904   −.1314492   .1161407
 ETHBLACK    −.2780887   .081101   −3.429   0.001   −.4370436  −.1191337
  ETHHISP    −.0191608  .1055466   −0.182   0.856   −.2260284   .1877068
    _cons      .673472  .2712267    2.483   0.013    .1418775   1.205066
-----------------------------------------------------------------------
```

WORKING is a binary variable equal to 1 if the respondent was working in 1994, 0 otherwise. *CHILDL06* is a dummy variable equal to 1 if there was a child aged less than 6 in the household, 0 otherwise. *CHILDL16* is a dummy variable equal to 1 if there was a child aged less than 16, but no child less than 6, in the household, 0 otherwise. *MARRIED* is equal to 1 if the respondent was married with spouse present, 0 otherwise. The remaining variables are as described in Appendix B. The mean values of the variables are given in the output from the sum command:

```
. sum WORKING S AGE CHILDL06 CHILDL16 MARRIED ETHBLACK
ETHHISP if MALE == 0

  Variable      Obs       Mean     Std. Dev.    Min     Max
-----------------------------------------------------------------
   WORKING     2726    .7652238    .4239366      0       1
         S     2726    13.30998    2.444771      0      20
       AGE     2726    17.64637    2.24083      14      22
  CHILDL06     2726    .3991196    .4898073      0       1
  CHILDL16     2726    .3180484    .4658038      0       1
   MARRIED     2726    .6228907    .4847510      0       1
  ETHBLACK     2726    .1305943    .3370179      0       1
   ETHHISP     2726    .0722671    .2589771      0       1
-----------------------------------------------------------------
```

Calculate the marginal effects and discuss whether they are plausible.

10.4 Censored regressions: tobit analysis

Suppose that one hypothesizes the relationship

$$Y^* = \beta_1 + \beta_2 X + u, \qquad (10.17)$$

with the dependent variable subject to either a lower bound Y_L or an upper bound Y_U. In the case of a lower bound, the model can be characterized as

$$Y^* = \beta_1 + \beta_2 X + u$$
$$Y = Y^* \quad \text{for } Y^* > Y_L,$$
$$Y = Y_L \quad \text{for } Y^* \le Y_L \tag{10.18}$$

and similarly for a model with an upper bound. Such a model is known as a censored regression model because Y^* is unobserved for $Y^* < Y_L$ or $Y^* > Y_U$. It is effectively a hybrid between a standard regression model and a binary choice model, and OLS would yield inconsistent estimates if used to fit it.

To see this, consider the relationship illustrated in Figure 10.7, a one-shot Monte Carlo experiment where the true relationship is

$$Y = -40 + 1.2X + u, \tag{10.19}$$

the data for X are the integers from 11 to 60, and u is a normally distributed random variable with mean zero and variance 100. If Y were unconstrained, the observations would be as shown in Figure 10.7. However, we will suppose that Y is constrained to be non-negative, in which case the observations will be as shown in Figure 10.8. For such a sample, it is obvious that an OLS regression that included those observations with Y constrained to be zero would yield inconsistent estimates, with the estimator of the slope downwards biased and that of the intercept upwards biased.

The remedy, you might think, would be to use only the subsample of unconstrained observations, but even then the OLS estimators would be biased. An

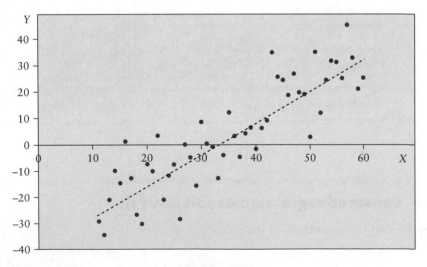

Figure 10.7

observation i will appear in the subsample only if $Y_i > 0$, that is, if

$$-40 + 1.2X_i + u_i > 0. \qquad (10.20)$$

This requires

$$u_i > 40 - 1.2X_i \qquad (10.21)$$

and so u_i must have the truncated distribution shown in Figure 10.9. In this example, the expected value of u_i must be positive and a negative function of X_i. Since u_i is negatively correlated with X_i, the regression model condition that

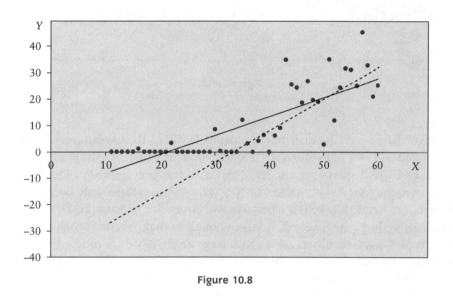

Figure 10.8

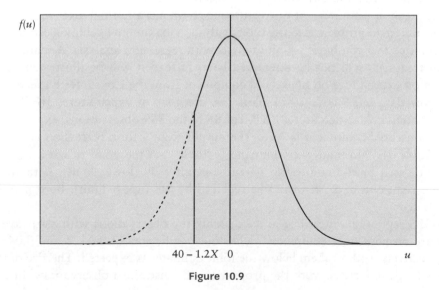

Figure 10.9

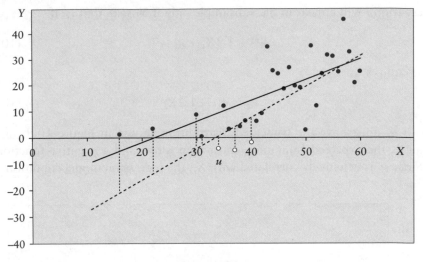

Figure 10.10

the disturbance term be distributed independently of the explanatory variables is violated and as a consequence OLS will yield inconsistent estimates.

Figure 10.10 displays the impact of this correlation graphically. The observations with the four lowest values of X appear in the sample only because their disturbance terms (marked) are positive and large enough to make Y positive. In addition, in the range where X is large enough to make the nonstochastic component of Y positive, observations with large negative values of the disturbance term are dropped. Three such observations, marked as circles, are shown in the figure. Both of these effects cause the intercept to tend to be overestimated, and the slope to be underestimated, in an OLS regression.

If it can be assumed that the disturbance term has a normal distribution, one solution to the problem is to use tobit analysis, a maximum likelihood estimation technique that combines probit analysis with regression analysis. A mathematical treatment will not be attempted here. Instead it will be illustrated using data on expenditure on household equipment from the Consumer Expenditure Survey data set. Figure 10.11 plots this category of expenditure, HEQ, and total household expenditure, EXP. For 86 of the 869 observations, expenditure on household equipment is zero. The output from a tobit regression is shown in Table 10.7. In Stata the command is 'tobit' and the point of left-censoring is indicated by the number in parentheses after 'll' (lower limit). If the data were right-censored, 'll' would be replaced by 'ul' (upper limit). Both may be included.

OLS regressions including and excluding the observations with zero expenditure on household equipment yield slope coefficients of 0.0472 and 0.0468, respectively, both of them below the tobit estimate, as expected. The size of the bias tends to increase with the proportion of constrained observations. In this

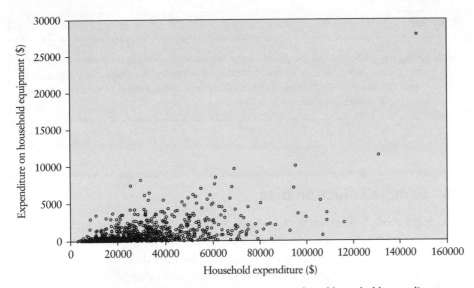

Figure 10.11 Expenditure on household equipment and total household expenditure

Table 10.7

```
. tobit HEQ EXP, ll(0)

Tobit Estimates                          Number of obs    =      869
                                         chi2(1)          =   315.41
                                         Prob > chi2      =   0.0000
Log Likelihood = -6911.0175              Pseudo R2        =   0.0223
-------------------------------------------------------------------------
   HEQ      Coef.    Std. Err.       t    P>|t|     [95% Conf.   Interval]
-------------------------------------------------------------------------
   EXP   .0520828    .0027023   19.273   0.000      .0467789   .0573866
 _cons  -661.8156    97.95977   -6.756   0.000     -854.0813  -469.5499
-------------------------------------------------------------------------
   _se   1521.896    38.6333            (Ancillary parameter)
-------------------------------------------------------------------------
Obs. summary:          86 left-censored observations at HEQ <= 0
                      783 uncensored observations
```

case only 10 percent are constrained, and hence the difference between the tobit and OLS estimates is small.

Tobit regression yields inconsistent estimates if the disturbance term does not have a normal distribution or if it is subject to heteroscedasticity (Amemiya, 1984). Judging by the plot in Figure 10.11, the observations in the example are subject to heteroscedasticity and it may be preferable to use expenditure on household equipment as a proportion of total expenditure as the dependent variable, in the same way that in his seminal study, which investigated expenditure on consumer durables, Tobin (1958) used expenditure on durables as a proportion of disposable personal income.

Exercise

10.5 Using the *CES* data set, perform a tobit regression of expenditure on your commodity on total household expenditure, and compare the slope coefficient with those obtained in OLS regressions including and excluding observations with zero expenditure on your commodity.

10.5 Sample selection bias

In the tobit model, whether or not an observation falls into the regression category ($Y > Y_L$ or $Y < Y_U$) or the constrained category ($Y = Y_L$ or $Y = Y_U$) depends entirely on the values of the regressors and the disturbance term. However, it may well be that participation in the regression category may depend on factors other than those in the regression model, in which case a more general model specification with an explicit two-stage process may be required. The first stage, participation in the regression category, or being constrained, depends on the net benefit of participating, B^*, a latent (unobservable) variable that depends on a set of $m - 1$ variables Q_j and a random term ε:

$$B_i^* = \delta_1 + \sum_{j=2}^{m} \delta_j Q_{ji} + \varepsilon_i. \tag{10.22}$$

The second stage, the regression model, is parallel to that for the tobit model:

$$Y_i^* = \beta_1 + \sum_{j=2}^{k} \beta_j X_{ji} + u_i$$

$$Y_i = Y_i^* \qquad \text{for } B_i^* > 0,$$

$$Y_i \text{ is not observed} \quad \text{for } B_i^* \leq 0. \tag{10.23}$$

For an observation in the sample,

$$E\left(u_i \,|\, B_i^* > 0\right) = E\left(u_i \,|\, \varepsilon_i > -\delta_1 - \sum_{j=2}^{m} \delta_j Q_{ji}\right). \tag{10.24}$$

If ε_i and u_i are distributed independently, $E\left(u_i \,|\, \varepsilon_i > -\delta_1 - \sum \delta_j Q_{ji}\right)$ reduces to the unconditional $E(u_i)$ and the selection process does not interfere with the regression model. However, if ε_i and u_i are correlated, $E(u_i)$ will be nonzero and problems parallel to those in the tobit model arise, with the consequence

BOX 10.1   The Heckman two-step procedure

The problem of selection bias arises because the expected value of u is nonzero for observations in the selected category if u and ε are correlated. It can be shown that, for these observations,

$$
E\left(u_i \,\middle|\, \varepsilon_i > -\delta_1 - \sum_{j=2}^{m} \delta_j Q_{ji}\right) = \frac{\sigma_{u\varepsilon}}{\sigma_\varepsilon} \lambda_i
$$

where $\sigma_{u\varepsilon}$ is the population covariance of u and ε, σ_ε is the standard deviation of ε, and λ_i, the inverse of Mills' ratio, is given by

$$
\lambda_i = \frac{f(v_i)}{F(v_i)}
$$

where

$$
v_i = \frac{\varepsilon_i}{\sigma_\varepsilon} = \frac{-\delta_1 - \sum\limits_{j=2}^{m} \delta_j Q_{ji}}{\sigma_\varepsilon}
$$

and the functions f and F are as defined in the section on probit analysis: $f(v_i)$ is the density function for ε normalized by its standard deviation and $F(v_i)$ is the probability of B_i^* being positive. It follows that

$$
E\left(Y_i \,\middle|\, \varepsilon_i > -\delta_1 - \sum_{j=2}^{m} \delta_j Q_{ji}\right) = E\left(\beta_1 + \sum_{j=2}^{k} \beta_j X_{ji} + u_i \,\middle|\, \varepsilon_i > -\delta_1 - \sum_{j=2}^{m} \delta_j Q_{ji}\right)
$$

$$
= \beta_1 + \sum_{j=2}^{k} \beta_j X_{ji} + \frac{\sigma_{u\varepsilon}}{\sigma_\varepsilon} \lambda_i.
$$

The sample selection bias arising in a regression of Y on the X variables using only the selected observations can therefore be regarded as a form of omitted variable bias, with λ the omitted variable. However, since its components depend only on the selection process, λ can be estimated from the results of probit analysis of selection (the first step). If it is included as an explanatory variable in the regression of Y on the X variables, least squares will then yield consistent estimates.

As Heckman (1976) acknowledges, the procedure was first employed by Gronau (1974), but it is known as the Heckman two-step procedure in recognition of its development by Heckman into an everyday working tool, its attraction being that it is computationally far simpler than maximum likelihood estimation of the joint model. However, with the improvement in computing speeds and the development of appropriate procedures in regression applications, maximum likelihood estimation of the joint model is no more burdensome than the two-step procedure and it has the advantage of being more efficient.

that OLS estimates are inconsistent and are described as being subject to **sample selection bias** (see Box 10.1 on the Heckman two-step procedure). If it can be assumed that ε_i and u_i are jointly normally distributed with correlation ρ, the model may be fitted by maximum likelihood estimation, with null hypothesis of no selection bias H_0: $\rho = 0$. The Q and X variables may overlap, identification requiring in practice that at least one Q variable is not also an X variable.

The procedure will be illustrated by fitting an earnings function for females on the lines of Gronau (1974), the earliest study of this type, using the *LFP94* subsample from the NLSY data set described in Exercise 10.4. *CHILDL06* is a dummy variable equal to 1 if there was a child aged less than 6 in the household, 0 otherwise. *CHILDL16* is a dummy variable equal to 1 if there was a child aged less than 16, but no child less than 6, in the household, 0 otherwise. *MARRIED* is equal to 1 if the respondent was married with spouse present, 0 otherwise. The other variables have the same definitions as in the *EAEF* data sets. The Stata command for this type of regression is 'heckman' and as usual it is followed by the dependent variable and the explanatory variables and qualifier, if any (here the sample is restricted to females). The variables in parentheses after 'select' are those hypothesized to influence whether the dependent variable is observed. In this example the dependent variable is observed for the 2,021 females who were working in 1994 and is missing for the remaining 640 who were not working. Seven iteration messages have been deleted from the output shown in Table 10.8.

First we will check whether there is evidence of selection bias, that is, that $\rho \neq 0$. For technical reasons, ρ is estimated indirectly through atanh $\rho = \frac{1}{2} \log \left(\frac{1+\rho}{1-\rho} \right)$, but the null hypothesis H_0: atanh $\rho = 0$ is equivalent to H_0: $\rho = 0$. atanh ρ is denoted 'athrho' in the output and, with an asymptotic t statistic of 10.92, the null hypothesis is rejected. A second test of the same null hypothesis that can be performed by comparing likelihood ratios is described in Section 10.6.

The regression results indicate that schooling and the *ASVABC* score have highly significant effects on earnings, that schooling has a positive effect on the probability of working, and that age, having a child aged less than 6, and being black have negative effects. The probit coefficients are different from those reported in Exercise 10.4, the reason being that, in a model of this type, probit analysis in isolation yields inefficient estimates.

It is instructive to compare the regression results with those from an OLS regression not correcting for selection bias. The results, shown in Table 10.9, are in fact quite similar, despite the presence of selection bias. The main difference is in the coefficient of *ETHBLACK*. The probit regression indicates that black females are significantly less likely to work than whites, controlling for other characteristics. If this is the case, black females, controlling for other characteristics, may require higher wage offers to be willing to work. This would reduce the apparent earnings discrimination against them, accounting for the

Table 10.8

```
. heckman LGEARN S ASVABC ETHBLACK ETHHISP if MALE==0, select (S AGE
CHILDL06 > CHILDL16 MARRIED ETHBLACK ETHHISP)
Iteration 0: log likelihood = −2683.5848 (not concave)
...
Iteration 8: log likelihood = −2668.8105
```

Heckman selection model				Number of obs =	2661	
(regression model with sample selection)				Censored obs =	640	
				Uncensored obs =	2021	
				Wald chi2(4)	= 714.73	
Log likelihood = −2668.81				Prob > chi2	= 0.0000	

	Coef.	Std. Err.	z	P>|z|	[95% Conf.	Interval]
LGEARN						
S	.095949	.0056438	17.001	0.000	.0848874	.1070106
ASVABC	.0110391	.0014658	7.531	0.000	.0081663	.0139119
ETHBLACK	−.066425	.0381626	−1.741	0.082	−.1412223	.0083722
ETHHISP	.0744607	.0450095	1.654	0.098	−.0137563	.1626777
_cons	4.901626	.0768254	63.802	0.000	4.751051	5.052202
select						
S	.1041415	.0119836	8.690	0.000	.0806541	.1276288
AGE	−.0357225	.011105	−3.217	0.001	−.0574879	−.0139572
CHILDL06	−.3982738	.0703418	−5.662	0.000	−.5361412	−.2604064
CHILDL16	.0254818	.0709693	0.359	0.720	−.1136155	.164579
MARRIED	.0121171	.0546561	0.222	0.825	−.0950069	.1192412
ETHBLACK	−.2941378	.0787339	−3.736	0.000	−.4484535	−.1398222
ETHHISP	−.0178776	.1034237	−0.173	0.863	−.2205043	.1848292
_cons	.1682515	.2606523	0.646	0.519	−.3426176	.6791206
/athrho	1.01804	.0932533	10.917	0.000	.8352669	1.200813
/lnsigma	−.6349788	.0247858	−25.619	0.000	−.6835582	−.5863994
rho	.769067	.0380973			.683294	.8339024
sigma	.5299467	.0131352			.5048176	.5563268
lambda	.4075645	.02867			.3513724	.4637567

```
LR test of indep. eqns. (rho = 0): chi2(1) = 32.90 Prob > chi2 = 0.0000
```

Table 10.9

```
. reg LGEARN S ASVABC ETHBLACK ETHHISP if MALE==0
```

Source	SS	df	MS	Number of obs	=	2021
				F(4,2016)	=	168.55
Model	143.231149	4	35.8077873	Prob > F	=	0.0000
Residual	428.301239	2016	.212451012	R-squared	=	0.2506
				Adj R-squared	=	0.2491
Total	571.532389	2020	.282936826	Root MSE	=	.46092

LGEARN	Coef.	Std. Err.	t	P>|t|	[95% Conf.	Interval]
S	.0807836	.005244	15.405	0.000	.0704994	.091067
ASVABC	.0117377	.0014886	7.885	0.000	.0088184	.014657
ETHBLACK	−.0148782	.0356868	−0.417	0.677	−.0848649	.0551086
ETHHISP	.0802266	.041333	1.941	0.052	−.0008333	.1612865
_cons	5.223712	.0703534	74.250	0.000	5.085739	5.361685

smaller negative coefficient in the OLS regression. The other difference in the results is that the schooling coefficient in the OLS regression is 0.081, a little lower than that in the selection bias model, indicating that selection bias leads to a modest underestimate of the effect of education on female earnings.

One of the problems with the selection bias model is that it is often difficult to find variables that belong to the selection process but not the main regression. Having a child aged less than 6 is an excellent variable because it clearly affects the willingness to work of a female but not her earning power while working, and for this reason the example discussed here is very popular in expositions of the model.

One final point, made by Heckman (1976): if a selection variable is illegitimately included in a least squares regression, it may appear to have a significant effect. In the present case, if *CHILDL06* is included in the earnings function, it has a *positive* coefficient significant at the 5 percent level. The explanation would appear to be that females with young children tend to require an especially attractive wage offer, given their education and other endowments, to be induced to work.

Exercises

10.6 Does sample selection bias affect the OLS estimate of the return to college education? Using your *EAEF* data set, investigate whether there is evidence that selection bias affects the least squares estimate of the returns to college education. Define $COLLYEAR = S - 12$ if $S > 12$, 0 otherwise, and $LGEARNCL = LGEARN$ if $COLLYEAR > 0$, missing otherwise. Use the heckman procedure to regress *LGEARNCL* on *COLLYEAR*, *EXP*, *ASVABC*, *MALE*, *ETHBLACK*, and *ETHHISP*, with *ASVABC*, *SM*, *SF*, and *SIBLINGS* being used to determine whether the respondent attended college. Run the equivalent regression using least squares. Comment on your findings.

10.7* Show that the tobit model may be regarded as a special case of a selection bias model.

10.8 Investigate whether having a child aged less than 6 is likely to be an especially powerful deterrent to working if the mother is unmarried by downloading the *LFP* data set from the website and repeating the regressions in this section adding an interactive dummy variable *MARL06* defined as the product of *MARRIED* and *CHILDL06* to the selection part of the model. See Appendix B for further information relating to the data set.

10.6   An introduction to maximum likelihood estimation

Suppose that a random variable X has a normal distribution with unknown mean μ and standard deviation σ. For the time being we will assume that we know that σ is equal to 1. We will relax this assumption later. You have a sample of two observations, values 4 and 6, and you wish to obtain an estimate of μ. The common sense answer is 5, and we have seen that this is scientifically respectable as well since the sample mean is the least squares estimator and as such it is an unbiased and efficient estimator of the population mean, provided the regression model assumptions are valid.

However, we have seen that in practice in econometrics the assumptions are often not satisfied and as a consequence least squares estimators lose one or more of their desirable properties. We have seen that in some circumstances they may be inconsistent and we have been concerned to develop alternative estimators that are consistent. Typically we are not able to analyze the finite sample properties of these estimators and we just hope that the estimators are well behaved.

Once we are dealing with consistent estimators, there is no guarantee that those based on the least squares criterion of goodness of fit are optimal. Indeed it can be shown that, under certain assumptions, a different approach, **maximum likelihood estimation**, will yield estimators that, besides being consistent, are asymptotically efficient (efficient in large samples).

To return to the numerical example, suppose for a moment that the true value of μ is 3.5. The probability density function of the normal distribution is given by

$$f(X) = \frac{1}{\sigma\sqrt{2\pi}} e^{-\frac{1}{2}\left(\frac{X-\mu}{\sigma}\right)^2}. \tag{10.25}$$

Figure 10.12 shows the distribution of X conditional on $\mu = 3.5$ and $\sigma = 1$. In particular, the probability density is 0.3521 when $X = 4$ and 0.0175 when $X = 6$. The joint probability density for the two observations is the product, 0.0062.

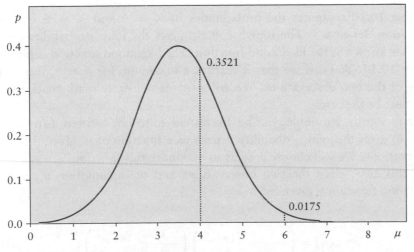

Figure 10.12 Probability densities at $X_1 = 4$ and $X_2 = 6$ conditional on $\mu = 3.5$

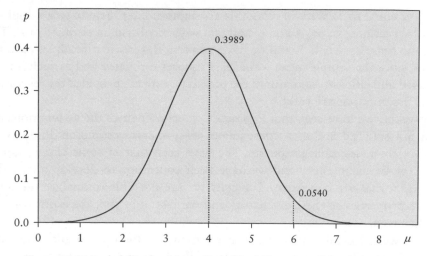

Figure 10.13 Probability densities at $X_1 = 4$ and $X_2 = 6$ conditional on $\mu = 4.0$

Now suppose that the true value of μ is 4. Figure 10.13 shows the distribution of X conditional on this value. The probability density is 0.3989 when $X = 4$ and 0.0540 when $X = 6$. The joint probability density for the two observations is now 0.0215. We conclude that the probability of getting values 4 and 6 for the two observations would be three times as great if μ were 4 than it would be if μ were 3.5. In that sense, $\mu = 4$ is more likely than $\mu = 3.5$. If we had to choose between these estimates, we should therefore choose 4. Of course we do not have to choose between them. According to the maximum likelihood principle, we should consider all possible values of μ and select the one that gives the observations the greatest joint probability density.

Table 10.10 computes the probabilities of $X = 4$ and $X = 6$ for values of μ from 3.5 to 6.5. The fourth column gives the joint probability density, which is known as the **likelihood function**. The likelihood function is plotted in Figure 10.14. You can see that it reaches a maximum for $\mu = 5$, the average value of the two observations. We will now demonstrate mathematically that this must be the case.

First, a little terminology. The likelihood function, written $L(\mu \mid X_1 = 4, X_2 = 6)$ gives the joint probability density as a function of μ, given the sample observations. We will choose μ so as to maximize this function.

In this case, given the two observations and the assumption $\sigma = 1$, the likelihood function is given by

$$L(\mu) = \left(\frac{1}{\sqrt{2\pi}} e^{-\frac{1}{2}(4-\mu)^2} \right) \left(\frac{1}{\sqrt{2\pi}} e^{-\frac{1}{2}(6-\mu)^2} \right). \qquad (10.26)$$

Table 10.10

μ	$p(4\|\mu)$	$p(6\|\mu)$	L	$\log L$
3.5	0.3521	0.0175	0.0062	−5.0879
4.0	0.3989	0.0540	0.0215	−3.8379
4.5	0.3521	0.1295	0.0456	−3.0879
4.6	0.3332	0.1497	0.0499	−2.9979
4.7	0.3123	0.1714	0.0535	−2.9279
4.8	0.2897	0.1942	0.0563	−2.8779
4.9	0.2661	0.2179	0.0580	−2.8479
5.0	0.2420	0.2420	0.0585	−2.8379
5.1	0.2179	0.2661	0.0580	−2.8479
5.2	0.1942	0.2897	0.0563	−2.8779
5.3	0.1714	0.3123	0.0535	−2.9279
5.4	0.1497	0.3332	0.0499	−2.9979
5.5	0.1295	0.3521	0.0456	−3.0879
6.0	0.0540	0.3989	0.0215	−3.8379
6.5	0.0175	0.3521	0.0062	−5.0879

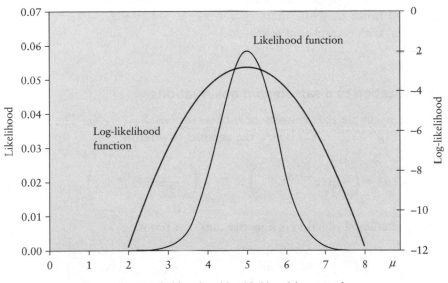

Figure 10.14 Likelihood and log-likelihood functions for μ

We will now differentiate this with respect to μ and set the result equal to zero to obtain the first order condition for a maximum. We will then differentiate a second time to check the second order condition. Well, actually we won't. Even with only two observations in the sample, this would be laborious, and when we generalize to n observations it would be very messy. We will use a trick to simplify the proceedings. The **log-likelihood**, log L, is a monotonically increasing function of L. So the value of μ that maximizes L also maximizes $\log L$, and vice versa. $\log L$ is much easier to work with, since

$$
\begin{aligned}
\log L &= \log \left[\left(\frac{1}{\sqrt{2\pi}} e^{-\frac{1}{2}(4-\mu)^2} \right) \left(\frac{1}{\sqrt{2\pi}} e^{-\frac{1}{2}(6-\mu)^2} \right) \right] \\
&= \log \left(\frac{1}{\sqrt{2\pi}} e^{-\frac{1}{2}(4-\mu)^2} \right) + \log \left(\frac{1}{\sqrt{2\pi}} e^{-\frac{1}{2}(6-\mu)^2} \right) \\
&= \log \left(\frac{1}{\sqrt{2\pi}} \right) - \frac{1}{2}(4-\mu)^2 + \log \left(\frac{1}{\sqrt{2\pi}} \right) - \frac{1}{2}(6-\mu)^2.
\end{aligned}
\tag{10.27}
$$

The maximum likelihood estimator, which we will denote $\hat{\mu}$, is the value of μ that maximizes this function, given the data for X. It is given by the first order condition

$$
\frac{d \log L}{d\mu} = (4 - \hat{\mu}) + (6 - \hat{\mu}) = 0.
\tag{10.28}
$$

Thus $\hat{\mu} = 5$. The second derivative is -2, so this gives a maximum value for $\log L$, and hence L. [Note that $-\frac{1}{2}(a - \mu)^2 = -\frac{1}{2}a^2 + a\mu - \frac{1}{2}\mu^2$. Hence the differential with respect to μ is $(a - \mu)$.]

Generalization to a sample of n observations

Consider a sample that consists of n observations $X_1, \ldots, X_n$. The likelihood function $L(\mu \mid X_1, \ldots, X_n)$ is now the product of n terms:

$$
L(\mu) = \left(\frac{1}{\sqrt{2\pi}} e^{-\frac{1}{2}(X_1-\mu)^2} \right) \times \cdots \times \left(\frac{1}{\sqrt{2\pi}} e^{-\frac{1}{2}(X_n-\mu)^2} \right).
\tag{10.29}
$$

The log-likelihood function is now the sum of n terms:

$$
\begin{aligned}
\log L &= \log \left(\frac{1}{\sqrt{2\pi}} e^{-\frac{1}{2}(X_1-\mu)^2} \right) + \cdots + \log \left(\frac{1}{\sqrt{2\pi}} e^{-\frac{1}{2}(X_n-\mu)^2} \right) \\
&= \log \left(\frac{1}{\sqrt{2\pi}} \right) - \frac{1}{2}(X_1 - \mu)^2 + \cdots + \log \left(\frac{1}{\sqrt{2\pi}} \right) - \frac{1}{2}(X_n - \mu)^2.
\end{aligned}
\tag{10.30}
$$

Hence the maximum likelihood estimator of μ is given by

$$
\frac{d \log L}{d\mu} = (X_1 - \hat{\mu}) + \cdots + (X_n - \hat{\mu}) = 0.
\tag{10.31}
$$

Thus

$$\sum_{i=1}^{n} X_i - n\hat{\mu} = 0 \qquad\qquad (10.32)$$

and the maximum likelihood estimator of μ is the sample mean. Note that the second derivative is $-n$, confirming that the log-likelihood has been maximized.

Generalization to the case where σ is unknown

We will now relax the assumption that σ is equal to 1 and accept that in practice it would be unknown, like μ. We will investigate the determination of its maximum likelihood graphically using the two-observation example and then generalize to a sample of n observations.

Figure 10.15 shows the probability distribution for X conditional on μ being equal to 5 and σ being equal to 2. The probability density at $X_1 = 4$ and $X_2 = 6$ is 0.1760 and the joint density 0.0310. Clearly we would obtain higher densities, and higher joint density, if the distribution had smaller variance. If we try σ equal to 0.5, we obtain the distribution shown in Figure 10.16. Here the individual densities are 0.1080 and the joint density 0.0117. Clearly we have made the distribution too narrow, for X_1 and X_2 are now in its tails with even lower density than before.

Figure 10.17 plots the joint density as a function of σ. We can see that it is maximized when σ is equal to 1, and this is therefore the maximum likelihood estimate, provided that we have been correct in assuming that the maximum likelihood estimate of μ is 5.

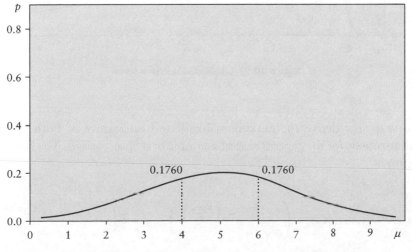

Figure 10.15 Probability densities at $X_1 = 4$ and $X_2 = 6$ conditional on $\sigma = 2$

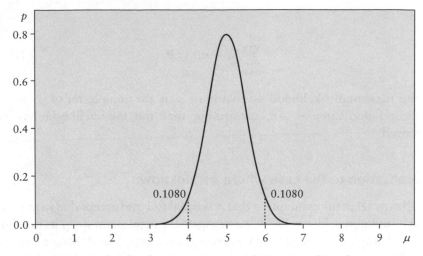

Figure 10.16 Probability densities at $X_1 = 4$ and $X_2 = 6$ conditional on $\sigma = 0.5$

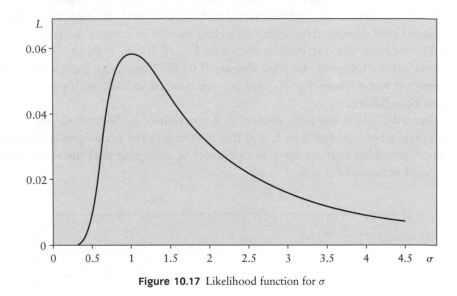

Figure 10.17 Likelihood function for σ

We will now derive the maximum likelihood estimators of both μ and σ simultaneously, for the general case of a sample of n observations. The likelihood function is

$$L(\mu, \sigma | X_1, \ldots, X_n) = \left(\frac{1}{\sigma \sqrt{2\pi}} e^{-\frac{1}{2}\left(\frac{X_1 - \mu}{\sigma}\right)^2} \right) \times \cdots \times \left(\frac{1}{\sigma \sqrt{2\pi}} e^{-\frac{1}{2}\left(\frac{X_n - \mu}{\sigma}\right)^2} \right)$$

$$(10.33)$$

and so the log-likelihood function is

$$
\log L = \log \left[\left(\frac{1}{\sigma\sqrt{2\pi}} e^{-\frac{1}{2}\left(\frac{X_1-\mu}{\sigma}\right)^2} \right) \times \cdots \times \left(\frac{1}{\sigma\sqrt{2\pi}} e^{-\frac{1}{2}\left(\frac{X_n-\mu}{\sigma}\right)^2} \right) \right]
$$

$$
= \log \left(\frac{1}{\sigma\sqrt{2\pi}} e^{-\frac{1}{2}\left(\frac{X_1-\mu}{\sigma}\right)^2} \right) + \cdots + \log \left(\frac{1}{\sigma\sqrt{2\pi}} e^{-\frac{1}{2}\left(\frac{X_n-\mu}{\sigma}\right)^2} \right)
$$

$$
= n \log \left(\frac{1}{\sigma\sqrt{2\pi}} \right) - \frac{1}{2}\left(\frac{X_1-\mu}{\sigma}\right)^2 - \cdots - \frac{1}{2}\left(\frac{X_n-\mu}{\sigma}\right)^2
$$

$$
= n \log \frac{1}{\sigma} + n \log \frac{1}{\sqrt{2\pi}} + \frac{1}{\sigma^2}\left(-\frac{1}{2}(X_1-\mu)^2 - \cdots - \frac{1}{2}(X_n-\mu)^2 \right).
$$

$$(10.34)$$

The partial derivative of this with respect to μ is

$$
\frac{\partial \log L}{\partial \mu} = \frac{1}{\sigma^2}\left[(X_1-\mu) + \cdots + (X_n-\mu) \right]. \tag{10.35}
$$

Setting this equal to zero, one finds that the maximum likelihood estimator of μ is the sample mean, as before. The partial derivative with respect to σ is

$$
-\frac{n}{\sigma} + \frac{1}{\sigma^3}\sum_{i=1}^{n}(X_i-\mu)^2. \tag{10.36}
$$

Substituting its maximum likelihood estimator for μ, and putting the expression equal to zero, we obtain

$$
\hat{\sigma}^2 = \frac{1}{n}\sum_{i=1}^{n}(X_i-X)^2. \tag{10.37}
$$

Note that this is actually biased downwards in finite samples, the unbiased estimator being given by the same expression with n replaced by $n-1$. However, it is asymptotically more efficient using the mean square error criterion, its smaller variance more than compensating for the bias. The bias in any case attenuates as the sample size becomes large.

Application to the simple regression model

Suppose that Y_i depends on X_i according to the simple relationship

$$
Y_i = \beta_1 + \beta_2 X_i + u_i. \tag{10.38}
$$

Potentially, before the observations are generated, Y_i has a distribution around $(\beta_1 + \beta_2 X_i)$, according to the value of the disturbance term. We will assume that the disturbance term is normally distributed with mean zero and standard deviation σ, so

$$f(u) = \frac{1}{\sigma\sqrt{2\pi}}e^{-\frac{1}{2}\left(\frac{u}{\sigma}\right)^2}. \tag{10.39}$$

The probability that Y will take a specific value Y_i in observation i is determined by the probability that u_i is equal to $(Y_i - \beta_1 - \beta_2 X_i)$. Given (10.39), the probability density is

$$\frac{1}{\sigma\sqrt{2\pi}}e^{-\frac{1}{2}\left(\frac{Y_i-\beta_1-\beta_2 X_i}{\sigma}\right)^2}. \tag{10.40}$$

The joint probability density function for the observations in the sample is the product of the terms for each observation. Taking the observations as given, and treating the unknown parameters as variables, we say that the likelihood function for β_1, β_2 and σ is given by

$$L(\beta_1, \beta_2, \sigma | Y_1, \ldots, Y_n) = \left(\frac{1}{\sigma\sqrt{2\pi}}e^{-\frac{1}{2}\left(\frac{Y_1-\beta_1-\beta_2 X_1}{\sigma}\right)^2}\right)$$

$$\times \cdots \times \left(\frac{1}{\sigma\sqrt{2\pi}}e^{-\frac{1}{2}\left(\frac{Y_n-\beta_1-\beta_2 X_n}{\sigma}\right)^2}\right). \tag{10.41}$$

The log-likelihood function is thus given by

$$\log L = n\log\left(\frac{1}{\sigma\sqrt{2\pi}}\right) - \frac{1}{2\sigma^2}\left[(Y_1 - \beta_1 - \beta_2 X_1)^2 + \cdots + (Y_n - \beta_1 - \beta_2 X_n)^2\right]. \tag{10.42}$$

The values of β_1 and β_2 that maximize this function are exactly the same as those obtained using the least squares principle. However, the estimate of σ is slightly different.

Goodness of fit and statistical tests

As noted in the discussion of logit analysis, there is no measure of goodness of fit equivalent to R^2 in maximum likelihood estimation. The pseudo-R^2 seen in some regression output, including that of Stata, compares its log-likelihood, log L, with the log-likelihood that would have been obtained with only the intercept in the regression, log L_0. A likelihood, being a joint probability, must lie between

0 and 1, and as a consequence a log-likelihood must be negative. The pseudo-R^2 is the proportion by which $\log L$ is smaller, in absolute size, than $\log L_0$:

$$\text{pseudo-}R^2 = 1 - \frac{\log L}{\log L_0}. \tag{10.43}$$

While it has a minimum value of 0, its maximum value must be less than 1 and unlike R^2 it does not have a natural interpretation. However, variations in the likelihood, like variations in the residual sum of squares in a standard regression, can be used as a basis for tests. In particular, the explanatory power of the model can be tested via the likelihood ratio statistic

$$2 \log \frac{L}{L_0} = 2(\log L - \log L_0). \tag{10.44}$$

This is distributed as a chi-squared statistic with $k-1$ degrees of freedom, where $k-1$ is the number of explanatory variables, under the null hypothesis that the coefficients of the variables are all jointly equal to zero. Further, the validity of a restriction can be tested by comparing the constrained and unconstrained likelihoods, in the same way that it can be tested by comparing the constrained and unconstrained residual sum of squares in a least squares regression model. For example, the null hypothesis H_0: $\rho = 0$ in the selection bias model can be tested by comparing the unconstrained likelihood L_U with the likelihood L_R when the model is fitted assuming that u and ε are distributed independently. Under the null hypothesis H_0: $\rho = 0$, the test statistic $2 \log \frac{L_U}{L_R}$ is distributed as a chi-squared statistic with one degree of freedom. In the sample selection example in Section 10.5, the test statistic, 32.90, appears in the last line of the output and the null hypothesis is rejected, the critical value of $\chi^2(1)$ being 10.83 at the 0.1 percent level.

As was noted in Section 10.2, the significance of an individual coefficient can be evaluated via its asymptotic t statistic, so-called because the standard error is valid only in large samples. Since the t distribution converges on the normal distribution in large samples, the critical values of the latter should be used.

Key terms

binary choice model	maximum likelihood estimation
likelihood function	probit model
likelihood ratio statistic	qualitative response model
linear probability model	sample selection bias
logit model	tobit model
log-likelihood	

Exercises

10.9* An event is hypothesized to occur with probability p. In a sample of n observations, it occurred m times. Demonstrate that the maximum likelihood estimator of p is m/n.

10.10* In Exercise 10.4, $\log L_0 = -1485.62$. Compute the pseudo-R^2 and confirm that it is equal to that reported in the output.

10.11* In Exercise 10.4, compute the likelihood ratio statistic $2(\log L - \log L_0)$, confirm that it is equal to that reported in the output, and perform the likelihood ratio test.

11 Models Using Time Series Data

Hitherto the analysis has been confined to cross-sectional data within the framework of Model A and then, more realistically, Model B. We now switch to time series data and the framework of Model C. A major difference between Model C and Model B lies in the characterization of the data generation process (DGP), the explanation that we give concerning the way the observations come into being. In Model B the DGP was very simple: observations were generated randomly and independently. As a consequence, the ordering of the observations in the sample was arbitrary. In Model C the time dimension imposes a natural ordering. To emphasize this, the observations will be indexed using t rather than i, and the number of observations in a sample will be denoted T rather than n. The ordering in itself would make no difference if the observations on the regressors were generated randomly from a fixed population. However, this is not the case, on two counts.

First, the observations on X form a sequence $\{X_1, \ldots, X_T\}$ that is a subset of a potentially infinite sequence $\{X_{-\infty}, \ldots, X_0, X_1, \ldots, X_T, X_{T+1}, \ldots, X_\infty\}$. It is described as a **realization** of the data generation process for the period $t = 1, \ldots, T$. Conceptually this is different from a random sampling of observations from a fixed population. Second, many regressors in time series models exhibit what is known as persistence, the DGP being characterized by evolution through time and successive observations being correlated.

These differences will cause the properties of the regression model in turn to be different from those of Model B. The properties of course depend on the regression model assumptions, and we will need to restate them for time series regressions. However, rather than do this in abstract, we will defer the task until the next chapter. To understand the assumptions, it is advantageous to have some familiarity with time series regressions. Accordingly, this chapter will look at some models involving simple dynamics, and the restatement of the regression assumptions will be deferred to Chapter 12.

11.1 Static models

Much of the analysis will be illustrated with a core data set for fitting demand functions. The Demand Functions data set is drawn from national accounts data published by the US Bureau of the Census and consists of annual aggregate data on 20 different categories of consumer expenditure for the period 1959–2003, along with data on disposable personal income, *DPI*, and price index numbers for the 20 categories. A detailed description is provided in Appendix B, with information on how to download the data set from the website. Two of the categories, *FOOD* and *HOUS* (consumer expenditure on food and housing services, respectively) are used as examples in the text and exercises. The other categories are intended for practical work by a small group of students, each student working with a different category, starting with a simple regression specification and gradually developing a more sophisticated one. We will start with a very simple specification for the demand equation for housing services, regressing consumer expenditure on this category, *HOUS*, on *DPI* and a price index for housing, *PRELHOUS*:

$$HOUS_t = \beta_1 + \beta_2 DPI_t + \beta_3 PRELHOUS_t + u_t. \qquad (11.1)$$

HOUS and *DPI* are measured in $ billion at 2000 constant prices. *PRELHOUS* is an index constructed by dividing the nominal price deflator for housing, *PHOUS*, by the price deflator for total personal expenditure, *PTPE*, and multiplying by 100. *PRELHOUS* thus is a real or relative price index that keeps track of whether housing is becoming more or less expensive relative to other types of expenditure. It is plotted in Figure 11.1, which shows that the relative price declined by about 10 percent from the early 1960s to the late 1970s and since then has been rising slowly. A straightforward linear regression using EViews gives the output shown in Table 11.1.

The regression implies that an increase of $1 billion in disposable personal income leads to an increase of $0.15 billion in expenditure on housing. In other words, out of the marginal dollar, 15 cents is spent on housing. Is this a plausible

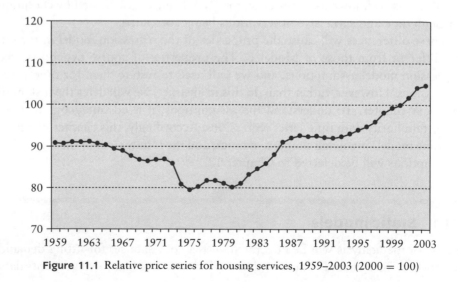

Figure 11.1 Relative price series for housing services, 1959–2003 (2000 = 100)

figure? It is a bit difficult to tell, but certainly housing is the largest category of consumer expenditure and one would expect a substantial coefficient. Note that we are talking about housing services, and not investment in housing. Housing services is the value of the services provided by the existing housing stock. In the case of rented housing, rents are taken as a measure of the value of the services. In the case of owner-occupied housing and housing rented at a subsidized rate, imputed rents, that is, the market rents the housing could command, are used instead. The coefficient of *PRELHOUS* implies that a one-point increase in the price index leads to a reduction of $3.83 billion in expenditure on housing. The constant term literally indicates the amount that would be spent on housing if *DPI* and *PRELHOUS* were both zero, but obviously any such interpretation is nonsense. If the observations referred to households, there might be some that had no income and yet purchased housing services and other essentials with transfer payments, but here we are talking about aggregate data for the whole of the United States and that kind of interpretation is not sensible.

It is common to hypothesize that a constant elasticity function of the type

$$HOUS = \beta_1 DPI^{\beta_2} PRELHOUS^{\beta_3} \nu \qquad (11.2)$$

is mathematically more appropriate for demand functions. Linearizing it by taking logarithms, one obtains

$$LGHOUS = \beta_1' + \beta_2 LGDPI + \beta_3 LGPRHOUS + u, \qquad (11.3)$$

where *LGHOUS*, *LGDPI* and *LGPRHOUS* are the (natural) logarithms of *HOUS*, *DPI* and *PRELHOUS*, respectively, *u* is the natural logarithm of the

Table 11.1

```
Dependent Variable: HOUS
Method: Least Squares
Sample: 1959 2003
Included observations: 45
```

Variable	Coefficient	Std. Error	t-Statistic	Prob.
C	334.6657	37.26625	8.980396	0.0000
DPI	0.150925	0.001665	90.65785	0.0000
PRELHOUS	−3.834387	0.460490	−8.326764	0.0000

R-squared	0.996722	Mean dependent var	630.2830
Adjusted R-squared	0.996566	S.D. dependent var	249.2620
S.E. of regression	14.60740	Akaike info criteri	8.265274
Sum squared resid	8961.801	Schwarz criterion	8.385719
Log likelihood	−182.9687	F-statistic	6385.025
Durbin-Watson stat	0.337638	Prob(F-statistic)	0.000000

Table 11.2

```
Dependent Variable: LGHOUS
Method: Least Squares
Sample: 1959 2003
Included observations: 45
-----------------------------------------------------------------
     Variable     Coefficient     Std. Error     t-Statistic     Prob.
-----------------------------------------------------------------
            C       0.005625       0.167903       0.033501       0.9734
        LGDPI       1.031918       0.006649     155.1976         0.0000
      LGPRHOUS     -0.483421       0.041780     -11.57056        0.0000
-----------------------------------------------------------------
R-squared           0.998583     Mean dependent var      6.359334
Adjusted R-squared  0.998515     S.D. dependent var      0.437527
S.E. of regression  0.016859     Akaike info criter     -5.263574
Sum squared resid   0.011937     Schwarz criterion      -5.143130
Log likelihood    121.4304       F-statistic         14797.05
Durbin-Watson stat  0.633113     Prob(F-statistic)       0.000000
```

disturbance term v, β_1' is the logarithm of β_1, and β_2 and β_3 are income and price elasticities. The regression result is shown in Table 11.2.

The coefficients of *LGDPI* and *LGPRHOUS* are direct estimates of the income and price elasticities. Is 1.03 a plausible income elasticity? Probably. It is conventional to classify consumer expenditure into normal goods and inferior goods, types of expenditure whose income elasticities are positive and negative, respectively, and to subdivide normal goods into necessities and luxuries, types of expenditure whose income elasticities are less than 1 and greater than 1. Housing is obviously a necessity, so you might expect the elasticity to be positive but less than 1. However, it also has a luxury element, since people spend more on better quality housing as their income rises. Overall, the elasticity seems to work out at about 1, so the present estimate seems reasonable.

Exercises

11.1 The results of linear and logarithmic regressions of consumer expenditure on food, *FOOD*, on *DPI* and a relative price index series for food, *PRELFOOD*, using the Demand Functions data set, are shown. Provide an economic interpretation of the coefficients and perform appropriate statistical tests.

$$\widehat{FOOD} = 139.4 + 0.053\,DPI + 0.536\,PRELFOOD \quad R^2 = 0.987$$
$$\quad\quad\;\; (43.2)\;\;(0.001)\quad\quad(0.372)$$

$$\widehat{LGFOOD} = 2.24 + 0.50\,LGDPI - 0.07\,LGPRFOOD \quad R^2 = 0.992.$$
$$\quad\quad\;\; (0.39)\;\;(0.01)\quad\quad\quad(0.07)$$

11.2 Download the Demand Functions data set from the website (see Appendix B). You should choose, or be assigned by your instructor, one category of expenditure, and it may be helpful to simplify the data set by deleting the expenditure and price variables relating to the other categories. Construct a relative price index series for your category by dividing its nominal price series by *PTPE*, the price series for total consumer expenditure, and multiplying by 100. Plot the series and try to explain why it has changed over the time period.

11.3 Regress your category of expenditure on *DPI* and the relative price index series constructed in Exercise 11.2. Give an economic interpretation of the regression coefficients and perform appropriate statistical tests.

11.4 Regress the logarithm of expenditure on your category on *LGDPI* and the logarithm of the relative price series. Give an economic interpretation of the regression coefficients and perform appropriate statistical tests.

11.5 Sometimes a time trend is included in a regression as an explanatory variable, acting as a proxy for some gradual change not associated with income or price. Changing tastes might be an example. However, in the present case the addition of a time trend might give rise to a problem of multicollinearity because it will be highly correlated with the income series and perhaps also the price series. Calculate the correlations between the *TIME* variable in the data set, *LGDPI*, and the logarithm of expenditure on your category. Regress the logarithm of expenditure on your category on *LGDPI*, the logarithm of the relative price series, and *TIME* (not the logarithm of *TIME*). Provide an interpretation of the regression coefficients, perform appropriate statistical tests, and compare the regression results with those of the same regression without *TIME*.

11.2 Dynamic models

Next, we will introduce some simple dynamics. One might suppose that some types of consumer expenditure are largely determined by current income and price, but this is not so for a category such as housing that is subject to substantial inertia. We will consider specifications in which expenditure on housing depends on lagged values of income and price and we will attempt to determine the **lag structure**, that is, the sizes of the coefficients of the current and lagged values of the explanatory variables. A variable X lagged one time period has values that are simply the previous values of X, and it is conventionally referred to as $X(-1)$. Generalizing, a variable lagged s time periods has the X values s periods previously, and is denoted $X(-s)$. Major regression applications adopt this convention and for these there is no need to define lagged variables separately. Table 11.3 shows the data for $LGDPI$, $LGDPI(-1)$ and $LGDPI(-2)$. Note that obviously there is a very high correlation between $LGDPI$, $LGDPI(-1)$ and $LGDPI(-2)$, and this is going to cause problems.

Table 11.3 Current and lagged values of the logarithm of disposable personal income

Year	LGDPI	LGDPI(−1)	LGDPI(−2)
1959	7.4474	–	–
1960	7.4729	7.4474	–
1961	7.5062	7.4729	7.4474
1962	7.5539	7.5062	7.4729
1963	7.5904	7.5539	7.5062
1964	7.6605	7.5904	7.5539
1965	7.7202	7.6605	7.5904
......	......	......	......
......	......	......	......
1996	8.7129	8.6837	8.6563
1997	8.7476	8.7129	8.6837
1998	8.8045	8.7476	8.7129
1999	8.8337	8.8045	8.7476
2000	8.8810	8.8337	8.8045
2001	8.9002	8.8810	8.8337
2002	8.9306	8.9002	8.8810
2003	8.9534	8.9306	8.9002

Table 11.4 Alternative dynamic specifications, expenditure on housing services

Variable	(1)	(2)	(3)	(4)	(5)
LGDPI	1.03	–	–	0.33	0.29
	(0.01)			(0.15)	(0.14)
LGDPI(−1)	–	1.01	–	0.68	0.22
		(0.01)		(0.15)	(0.20)
LGDPI(−2)	–	–	0.98	–	0.49
			(0.01)		(0.13)
LGPRHOUS	−0.48	–	–	−0.09	−0.28
	(0.04)			(0.17)	(0.17)
LGPRHOUS(−1)	–	−0.43	–	−0.36	0.23
		(0.04)		(0.17)	(0.30)
LGPRHOUS(−2)	–	–	−0.38	–	−0.38
			(0.04)		(0.18)
R^2	0.999	0.999	0.999	0.999	0.999

The first column of Table 11.4 presents the results of a logarithmic regression using current income and price. The second and third columns show the results of regressing expenditure on housing on income and price lagged one and two time periods, respectively. It is reasonable to hypothesize that expenditure on a category of consumer expenditure might depend on both current and lagged income and price. The fourth column shows the results of a regression using current income and price and the same variables lagged one time period. The fifth column adds the same variables lagged two time periods, as well.

The first three regressions are almost identical. This is because $LGDPI$, $LGDPI(-1)$ and $LGDPI(-2)$ are very highly correlated. The last two regressions display the classic symptoms of multicollinearity. The point estimates are unstable and the standard errors become much larger when current and lagged values of income and price are simultaneously included as regressors. We may be able to obtain precise estimates of the long-run elasticities with respect to income and price (see Box 11.1), but multicollinearity is preventing us from discriminating between their current and lagged effects. For a type of expenditure such as housing, where one might expect long lags, simply adding lags to a static model is unlikely to help us determine the lag structure.

A common solution to the problem of multicollinearity is to hypothesize that the dynamic process has a **parsimonious lag structure**, that is, a lag structure that can be characterized with few parameters. One of the most popular lag structures is the Koyck distribution, which assumes that the coefficients of the explanatory variables have geometrically declining weights. We will look at two such models, the adaptive expectations model and the partial adjustment model.

BOX 11.1   Re-parameterizing a dynamic model to determine long-run effects

Suppose that you have a regression model

$$Y_t = \beta_1 + \beta_2 X_t + \beta_3 X_{t-1} + \beta_4 X_{t-2} + u_t.$$

As we have seen, multicollinearity may prevent us from obtaining precise estimates of β_2, β_3, and β_4. Nevertheless, it may be possible to demonstrate that the estimate of the long-run effect of X on Y is stable. In equilibrium, we would have

$$\overline{Y} = \beta_1 + \beta_2 \overline{X} + \beta_3 \overline{X} + \beta_4 \overline{X} = \beta_1 + (\beta_2 + \beta_3 + \beta_4)\overline{X}$$

where $\overline{Y}$ and $\overline{X}$ are the equilibrium values of Y and X. Hence $(\beta_2 + \beta_3 + \beta_4)$ is a measure of the long-run effect of X. We can calculate this quantity from the point estimates of β_2, β_3, and β_4 in the original specification, but we would not have an estimate of its standard error. To estimate the standard error, rewrite the model as

$$Y_t = \beta_1 + (\beta_2 + \beta_3 + \beta_4)X_t - \beta_3(X_t - X_{t-1}) - \beta_4(X_t - X_{t-2}) + u_t.$$

The point estimate of the coefficient of X_t will be the sum of the point estimates of β_2, β_3, and β_4 in the original specification and we now have its standard error. Since X_t may well not be highly correlated with $(X_t - X_{t-1})$ or $(X_t - X_{t-2})$, there may not be a problem of multicollinearity and so the standard error may be relatively small.

When the model in column (5) of Table 11.4 is rewritten in this way and fitted, the coefficient of $LGDPI_t$ is 1.00 with standard error 0.01 and the coefficient of $LGPRHOUS_t$ is -0.41 with standard error 0.01. As expected, the standard errors are much lower than those of the individual coefficients in the original specification.

> **Exercises**
>
> **11.6** Give an economic interpretation of the coefficients of $LGDPI$, $LGDPI(-1)$, and $LGDPI(-2)$, in column 5 of Table 11.4.
>
> **11.7** To allow for the possibility that expenditure on your category is partly subject to a one-period lag, regress the logarithm of expenditure on your commodity on $LGDPI$, the logarithm of your relative price series, and those two variables lagged one period. Repeat the experiment adding $LGDPI(-2)$ and the logarithm of the price series lagged two periods. Compare the regression results, paying attention to the changes in the regression coefficients and their standard errors.

11.3 The adaptive expectations model

The applied economist using time series data frequently needs to model expectations. This can be an important and difficult task. In macroeconomics, for example, investment, saving, and the demand for assets are all sensitive to expectations about the future. Unfortunately, there is no satisfactory way of measuring expectations directly for macroeconomic purposes. Consequently, macroeconomic models tend not to give particularly accurate forecasts, and this makes economic management difficult.

If expectations cannot be observed directly, some indirect technique may be used instead. The **adaptive expectations model** is one such solution. It involves a simple learning process in which, in each time period, the actual value of the variable is compared with the value that had been expected. If the actual value is greater, the expected value is adjusted upwards for the next period. If it is lower, the expected value is adjusted downwards. The size of the adjustment is hypothesized to be proportional to the discrepancy between the actual and expected value.

If X is the variable in question, and X_t^e is the value expected in time period t given the information available at time period $t - 1$,

$$X_{t+1}^e - X_t^e = \lambda(X_t - X_t^e) \quad (0 \le \lambda \le 1). \tag{11.4}$$

This can be rewritten as

$$X_{t+1}^e = \lambda X_t + (1 - \lambda)X_t^e, \quad (0 \le \lambda \le 1). \tag{11.5}$$

which states that the expected value of X in the next time period is a weighted average of the actual value of X in the current time period and the value that had been expected. The larger the value of λ, the quicker the expected value adjusts to previous actual outcomes.

For example, suppose that you hypothesize that a dependent variable, Y_t, is related to the expected value of the explanatory variable, X, in year $t + 1$, X_{t+1}^e:

$$Y_t = \beta_1 + \beta_2 X_{t+1}^e + u_t. \tag{11.6}$$

Equation (11.6) expresses Y_t in terms of X_{t+1}^e, which is unobservable and must somehow be replaced by observable variables, that is, by actual current and lagged values of X, and perhaps lagged values of Y. We start by substituting for X_{t+1}^e using (11.5):

$$Y_t = \beta_1 + \beta_2 \left(\lambda X_t + (1 - \lambda) X_t^e \right) + u_t$$
$$= \beta_1 + \beta_2 \lambda X_t + \beta_2 (1 - \lambda) X_t^e + u_t. \tag{11.7}$$

Of course we still have unobservable variable X_t^e as an explanatory variable, but if (11.5) is true for time period t, it is also true for time period $t - 1$:

$$X_t^e = \lambda X_{t-1} + (1 - \lambda) X_{t-1}^e. \tag{11.8}$$

Substituting for X_t^e in (11.7), we now have

$$Y_t = \beta_1 + \beta_2 \lambda X_t + \beta_2 \lambda (1 - \lambda) X_{t-1} + \beta_2 (1 - \lambda)^2 X_{t-1}^e + u_t. \tag{11.9}$$

After lagging and substituting s times, the expression becomes

$$Y_t = \beta_1 + \beta_2 \lambda X_t + \beta_2 \lambda (1 - \lambda) X_{t-1} + \beta_2 \lambda (1 - \lambda)^2 X_{t-2} + \cdots$$
$$+ \beta_2 \lambda (1 - \lambda)^{s-1} X_{t-s+1} + \beta_2 (1 - \lambda)^s X_{t-s+1}^e + u_t. \tag{11.10}$$

Now it is reasonable to suppose that λ lies between 0 and 1, in which case $1 - \lambda$ will also lie between 0 and 1. Thus $(1 - \lambda)^s$ becomes progressively smaller as s increases. Eventually there will be a point where the term $\beta_2 (1 - \lambda)^s X_{t-s+1}^e$ is so small that it can be neglected and we have a model in which all the variables are observable.

A lag structure with geometrically declining weights, such as this one, is described as having a **Koyck distribution**. As can be seen from (11.10), it is highly parsimonious in terms of its parameterization, requiring only one parameter more than the static version. Since it is nonlinear in the parameters, OLS should not be used to fit it, for two reasons. First, multicollinearity would almost certainly make the estimates of the coefficients so erratic that they would be worthless—it is precisely this problem that caused us to search for another way of specifying a lag structure. Second, the point estimates of the coefficients would yield conflicting estimates of the parameters. For example, suppose that the fitted relationship began

$$\hat{Y}_t = 101 + 0.60 X_t + 0.45 X_{t-1} + 0.20 X_{t-2} + \cdots. \tag{11.11}$$

Relating the theoretical coefficients of the current and lagged values of X in (11.10) to the estimates in (11.11), one has $b_2 l = 0.60$, $b_2 l(1 - l) = 0.45$, and

$b_2 l(1 - l)^2 = 0.20$. From the first two you could infer that b_2 was equal to 2.40 and l was equal to 0.25—but these values would conflict with the third equation and indeed with the equations for all the remaining coefficients in the regression.

Instead, a nonlinear estimation technique should be used. Most major regression applications have facilities for performing nonlinear regressions built into them. If your application does not, you could fit the model using a **grid search**. It is worth describing this technique, despite the fact that it is obsolete, because it makes it clear that the problem of multicollinearity has been solved. We rewrite (11.10) as two equations:

$$Y_t = \beta_1 + \beta_2 Z_t + u_t \tag{11.12}$$

$$Z_t = \lambda X_t + \lambda(1 - \lambda)X_{t-1} + \lambda(1 - \lambda)^2 X_{t-2} + \lambda(1 - \lambda)^3 X_{t-3} + \cdots. \tag{11.13}$$

The values of Z_t depend of course on the value of λ. You construct ten versions of the Z_t variable using the following values for λ: $0.1, 0.2, 0.3, \ldots, 1.0$ and fit (11.12) with each of them. The version with the lowest residual sum of squares is by definition the least squares solution. Note that the regressions involve a regression of Y on the different versions of Z in a simple regression equation and so the problem of multicollinearity has been completely eliminated.

Table 11.5 shows the parameter estimates and residual sums of squares for a grid search where the dependent variable was the logarithm of housing services and the explanatory variables were the logarithms of *DPI* and the relative price series for housing. Eight lagged values were used. You can see that the optimal value of λ is about 0.2, and that the income elasticity is about 1.12 and the price elasticity about -0.44. If we want a more precise estimate of λ, we can continue the grid search with steps of 0.01 over the range from 0.1 to 0.3. If we do this, we find that λ is equal to 0.21, with income elasticity 1.11 and the price elasticity unchanged. Note that the implicit income coefficient for X_{t-8}, $\beta_2 \lambda(1 - \lambda)^8$, was $1.11 \times 0.21 \times 0.79^8 = 0.0354$. Perhaps it would have been better to use a few more lags. The problem is that the weights are

Table 11.5 Logarithmic regression of expenditure on housing services on disposable personal income and a relative price index, assuming an adaptive expectations model, fitted using a grid search

λ	b_2	s.e.(b_2)	b_3	s.e.(b_3)	RSS
0.1	1.55	0.01	−0.54	0.05	0.002107
0.2	1.12	0.01	−0.44	0.03	0.001901
0.3	1.03	0.01	−0.45	0.03	0.002063
0.4	1.02	0.01	−0.49	0.03	0.002533
0.5	1.03	0.01	−0.52	0.03	0.003190
0.6	1.04	0.01	−0.55	0.04	0.003935
0.7	1.05	0.01	−0.57	0.04	0.004719
0.8	1.06	0.01	−0.59	0.05	0.005531
0.9	1.06	0.01	−0.60	0.05	0.006377
1.0	1.07	0.01	−0.61	0.05	0.007263

declining slowly in this case because the speed of adjustment, λ, is small and so $1 - \lambda$ is large.

Dynamics in the adaptive expectations model

As you can see from (11.10), X_t, the current value of X, has coefficient $\beta_2\lambda$ in the equation for Y_t. This is the short-run or impact effect of X on Y. At time t, the terms involving lagged values of X are already determined and hence effectively form part of the intercept in the short-run relationship. However, we can also derive a long-run relationship between Y and X by seeing how the equilibrium value of Y would be related to the equilibrium value of X, if equilibrium were ever achieved. Denoting equilibrium Y and X by $\overline{Y}$ and $\overline{X}$, respectively, then in equilibrium $Y_t = \overline{Y}$ and $X_t = X_{t-1} = X_{t-2} = \cdots = \overline{X}$. Substituting into (11.10), one has

$$
\begin{aligned}
\overline{Y} &= \beta_1 + \beta_2\lambda\overline{X} + \beta_2\lambda(1-\lambda)\overline{X} + \beta_2\lambda(1-\lambda)^2\overline{X} + \cdots \\
&= \beta_1 + \beta_2\overline{X}[\lambda + \lambda(1-\lambda) + \lambda(1-\lambda)^2 + \cdots] \\
&= \beta_1 + \beta_2\overline{X}.
\end{aligned}
\tag{11.14}
$$

To see the last step, write

$$
S = \lambda + \lambda(1-\lambda) + \lambda(1-\lambda)^2 + \cdots .
\tag{11.15}
$$

Then

$$
(1-\lambda)S = \lambda(1-\lambda) + \lambda(1-\lambda)^2 + \lambda(1-\lambda)^3 + \cdots .
\tag{11.16}
$$

Subtracting (11.16) from (11.15),

$$
S - (1-\lambda)S = \lambda
\tag{11.17}
$$

and hence S is equal to 1. Thus the long-run effect of X on Y is given by β_2.

An alternative way of exploring the dynamics of an adaptive expectations model is to perform what is known as a **Koyck transformation**. This allows us to express the dependent variable in terms of a finite number of observable variables: the current values of the explanatory variable(s) and the dependent variable itself, lagged one time period. We start again with the original equations and combine them to obtain (11.20):

$$
Y_t = \beta_1 + \beta_2 X^e_{t+1} + u_t
\tag{11.18}
$$

$$
X^e_{t+1} = \lambda X_t + (1-\lambda)X^e_t
\tag{11.19}
$$

$$
\begin{aligned}
Y_t &= \beta_1 + \beta_2\left(\lambda X_t + (1-\lambda)X^e_t\right) + u_t \\
&= \beta_1 + \beta_2\lambda X_t + \beta_2(1-\lambda)X^e_t + u_t.
\end{aligned}
\tag{11.20}
$$

Now if (11.18) is true for time t, it is also true for time $t - 1$:

$$
Y_{t-1} = \beta_1 + \beta_2 X^e_t + u_{t-1}.
\tag{11.21}
$$

Hence

$$\beta_2 X_t^e = Y_{t-1} - \beta_1 - u_{t-1}. \tag{11.22}$$

Substituting this into (11.20), we now have

$$
\begin{aligned}
Y_t &= \beta_1 + \beta_2 \lambda X_t + (1 - \lambda)(Y_{t-1} - \beta_1 - u_{t-1}) + u_t \\
&= \beta_1 \lambda + (1 - \lambda)Y_{t-1} + \beta_2 \lambda X_t + u_t - (1 - \lambda)u_{t-1}.
\end{aligned} \tag{11.23}
$$

As before, the short-run coefficient of X is $\beta_2 \lambda$, the effective intercept for the relationship being $\beta_1 \lambda + (1 - \lambda)Y_{t-1}$ at time t. In equilibrium, the relationship implies

$$\overline{Y} = \beta_1 \lambda + (1 - \lambda)\overline{Y} + \beta_2 \lambda \overline{X} \tag{11.24}$$

and so

$$\overline{Y} = \beta_1 + \beta_2 \overline{X}. \tag{11.25}$$

Hence again we obtain the result that β_2 gives the long-run effect of X on Y.

We will investigate the relationship between the short-run and long-run dynamics graphically. We will suppose, for convenience, that β_2 is positive and that X increases with time, and we will neglect the effect of the disturbance term. At time t, Y_t is given by (11.23). Y_{t-1} has already been determined, so the term $(1 - \lambda)Y_{t-1}$ is fixed. The equation thus gives the short-run relationship between Y_t and X_t. $[\beta_1 \lambda + (1 - \lambda)Y_{t-1}]$ is effectively the intercept and $\beta_2 \lambda$ is the slope coefficient. When we come to time $t + 1$, Y_{t+1} is given by

$$Y_{t+1} = \beta_1 \lambda + \beta_2 \lambda X_{t+1} + (1 - \lambda)Y_t \tag{11.26}$$

and the effective intercept is now $[\beta_1 \lambda + (1 - \lambda)Y_t]$. Since X is increasing, Y is increasing, so the intercept is larger than that for Y_t and the short-run relationship has shifted upwards. The slope is the same as before, $\beta_2 \lambda$. Thus two factors are responsible for the growth of Y: the direct effect of the increase in X, and the gradual upward shift of the short-run relationship. Figure 11.2 shows the outcomes for time t as far as time $t+4$. You can see that the long-run relationship is steeper than the short-run one.

Example: Friedman's permanent income hypothesis

Without doubt the most celebrated application of the adaptive expectations model is Friedman's use of it when fitting an aggregate consumption function using time series data and his **permanent income hypothesis**. In the early years after the Second World War, econometricians working with macroeconomic data were puzzled by the fact that the long-run average propensity to consume seemed to be roughly constant, despite the marginal propensity to consume being much lower. A model in which current consumption was a function of current income

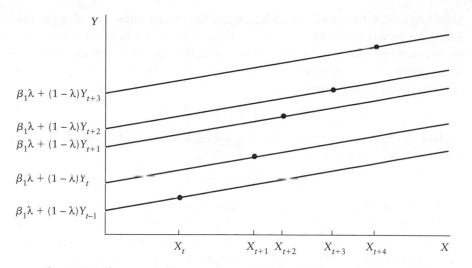

$\beta_1\lambda + (1-\lambda)Y_{t+3}$

$\beta_1\lambda + (1-\lambda)Y_{t+2}$
$\beta_1\lambda + (1-\lambda)Y_{t+1}$

$\beta_1\lambda + (1-\lambda)Y_t$

$\beta_1\lambda + (1-\lambda)Y_{t-1}$

Figure 11.2 Short-run and long-run dynamics in the adaptive expectations model

could not explain this phenomenon and was therefore clearly too simplistic. Several more sophisticated models that could explain this apparent contradiction were developed, notably Friedman's permanent income hypothesis, Brown's habit persistence model (discussed in the next section), Duesenberry's relative income hypothesis and the Modigliani–Ando–Brumberg life cycle model.

Under the permanent income hypothesis, permanent consumption, C_t^P, is proportional to permanent income, Y_t^P:

$$C_t^P = \beta_2 Y_t^P. \tag{11.27}$$

Actual consumption, C_t, and actual income, Y_t, also contain transitory components, C_t^T and Y_t^T respectively:

$$C_t = C_t^P + C_t^T \tag{11.28}$$

$$Y_t = Y_t^P + Y_t^T. \tag{11.29}$$

It is assumed, at least as a first approximation, that the transitory components of consumption and income have expected value zero and are distributed independently of their permanent counterparts and of each other. Substituting for C_t^P in (11.27) using (11.28) one has

$$C_t = \beta_2 Y_t^P + C_t^T. \tag{11.30}$$

We thus obtain a relationship between actual consumption and permanent income in which C_t^T plays the role of a disturbance term, previously lacking in the model.

Earlier, when we discussed the permanent income hypothesis in the context of cross-sectional data, the observations related to households. When Friedman fitted the model, he actually used aggregate time series data. To solve the problem that permanent income is unobservable, he hypothesized that it was subject to an adaptive expectations process in which the notion of permanent income was updated by a proportion of the difference between actual income and the previous period's permanent income:

$$Y_t^P - Y_{t-1}^P = \lambda(Y_t - Y_{t-1}^P). \tag{11.31}$$

Hence permanent income at time t is a weighted average of actual income at time t and permanent income at time $t - 1$:

$$Y_t^P = \lambda Y_t + (1 - \lambda)Y_{t-1}^P. \tag{11.32}$$

Friedman used (11.32) to relate permanent income to current and lagged values of income. Of course it cannot be used directly to measure permanent income in year t because we do not know λ and we have no way of measuring Y_{t-1}^P. We can solve the second difficulty by noting that, if (11.32) holds for time t, it also holds for time $t - 1$:

$$Y_{t-1}^P = \lambda Y_{t-1} + (1 - \lambda)Y_{t-2}^P. \tag{11.33}$$

Substituting this into (11.32), we obtain

$$Y_t^P = \lambda Y_t + \lambda(1 - \lambda)Y_{t-1} + (1 - \lambda)^2 Y_{t-2}^P. \tag{11.34}$$

This includes the unmeasurable term Y_{t-2}^P, but we can deal with it by lagging (11.32) two periods and substituting, thus obtaining Y_t^P in terms of Y_t, Y_{t-1}, Y_{t-2} and Y_{t-3}^P. Continuing this process indefinitely, we can write Y_t^P as a weighted sum of current and past measured income:

$$Y_t^P = \lambda Y_t + \lambda(1 - \lambda)Y_{t-1} + \lambda(1 - \lambda)^2 Y_{t-2} + \lambda(1 - \lambda)^3 Y_{t-3} + \cdots. \tag{11.35}$$

Provided that λ lies between 0 and 1, a reasonable assumption, $(1 - \lambda)^s$ is a decreasing function of s and eventually the weights attached to the lagged values of Y become so small that they can be neglected.

This still leaves us with the problem of estimating λ. Friedman's solution was to use a grid search, calculating the permanent income time series for a range of values of λ between 0 and 1, and regressing consumption on each permanent income series. He then chose that value of λ that produced the series for Y^P that gave him the best fit. Effectively, of course, he was fitting the nonlinear model

$$C_t = \beta_2 \lambda Y_t + \beta_2 \lambda(1 - \lambda)Y_{t-1} + \beta_2 \lambda(1 - \lambda)^2 Y_{t-2} + \cdots + C_t^T. \tag{11.36}$$

The dynamic properties of the model are as illustrated in Figure 11.2. Mathematically they are best analyzed by performing the Koyck transformation on the model. This could be done on the lines of equations (11.21) – (11.23), or by lagging (11.36) one period and multiplying through by $1 - \lambda$:

$$(1 - \lambda)C_{t-1} = \beta_2 \lambda(1 - \lambda)Y_{t-1} + \beta_2 \lambda(1 - \lambda)^2 Y_{t-2} + \beta_2 \lambda(1 - \lambda)^3 Y_{t-3}$$

$$+ \cdots + (1 - \lambda)C_{t-1}^T. \tag{11.37}$$

Subtracting (11.37) from (11.36), one has

$$C_t - (1 - \lambda)C_{t-1} = \beta_2 \lambda Y_t + C_t^T - (1 - \lambda)C_{t-1}^T \qquad (11.38)$$

and so

$$C_t = \beta_2 \lambda Y_t + (1 - \lambda)C_{t-1} + C_t^T - (1 - \lambda)C_{t-1}^T. \qquad (11.39)$$

The short-run marginal propensity to consume is $\beta_2 \lambda$ and the long-run propensity is β_2. Since λ is less than 1, the model is able to reconcile a low short-run marginal propensity to consume with a higher long-run average propensity.

Exercise

11.8* The output shows the result of fitting the model

$$LGFOOD = \beta_1 + \beta_2 \lambda LGDPI + \beta_2 \lambda(1 - \lambda)LGDPI(-1)$$
$$+ \beta_2 \lambda(1 - \lambda)^2 LGDPI(-2) + \beta_3 LGPRFOOD + u$$

using the data on expenditure on food in the Demand Functions data set. *LGFOOD* and *LGPRFOOD* are the logarithms of expenditure on food and the relative price index series for food. C(1), C(2), C(3), and C(4) are estimates of β_1, β_2, λ, and β_3, respectively. Explain how the regression equation could be interpreted as an adaptive expectations model and discuss the dynamics implicit in it, both short-run and long-run. Should the specification have included further lagged values of *LGDPI*?

```
Dependent Variable: LGFOOD
Method: Least Squares
Sample(adjusted): 1962 2003
Included observations: 42 after adjusting endpoints
Convergence achieved after 25 iterations
LGFOOD=C(1)+C(2)*C(3)*LGDPI +C(2)*C(3)*
        (1-C(3))*LGDPI(-1)+C(2)*C(3)*(1-C(3))^2*
        LGDPI(-2)+C(2)*C(3)*(1-C(3))^3*
        LGDPI(-3)+C(4)*LGPRFOOD
```

	Coefficient	Std. Error	t-Statistic	Prob.
C(1)	2.339513	0.468550	4.993091	0.0000
C(2)	0.496425	0.012264	40.47818	0.0000
C(3)	0.915046	0.442851	2.066264	0.0457
C(4)	-0.089681	0.083250	-1.077247	0.2882

R-squared	0.989621	Mean dependent var	6.049936
Adjusted R-squared	0.988802	S.D. dependent var	0.201706
S.E. of regression	0.021345	Akaike info criter	-4.765636
Sum squared resid	0.017313	Schwarz criterion	-4.600143
Log likelihood	104.0784	Durbin-Watson stat	0.449978

11.4 The partial adjustment model

In the partial adjustment model it is assumed that the right side of the equation determines the 'desired' (or 'target') value, Y_t^*, of the dependent variable, rather than the actual value, Y_t:

$$Y_t^* = \beta_1 + \beta_2 X_t + u_t. \tag{11.40}$$

It is then assumed that the actual increase in the dependent variable, $Y_t - Y_{t-1}$, is proportional to the discrepancy between the desired value and the previous value, $Y_t^* - Y_{t-1}$:

$$Y_t - Y_{t-1} = \lambda(Y_t^* - Y_{t-1}) \quad (0 \le \lambda \le 1). \tag{11.41}$$

This may be rewritten

$$Y_t = \lambda Y_t^* + (1 - \lambda)Y_{t-1} \tag{11.42}$$

so it can be seen that Y_t is a weighted average of the current desired value and the previous actual value. The higher is the value of λ, the more rapid is the adjustment process. If λ is equal to 1, Y_t is equal to Y_t^* and there is full adjustment in one period. At the other extreme, if λ is equal to 0, Y_t does not adjust at all.

Substituting for Y_t^* from the target relationship, one obtains

$$Y_t = \lambda(\beta_1 + \beta_2 X_t + u_t) + (1 - \lambda)Y_{t-1}$$
$$= \beta_1\lambda + \beta_2\lambda X_t + (1 - \lambda)Y_{t-1} + \lambda u_t. \tag{11.43}$$

Thus the parameters β_1, β_2, and λ of the model can be estimated by regressing Y_t on X_t and Y_{t-1}. The model relates Y to the current value of X and the lagged value of itself, and so has the same structure as the Koyck-transformed version of the adaptive expectations model. It follows that its dynamics are exactly the same. The coefficient of Y_{t-1} yields an estimate of $1 - \lambda$ and hence of λ, the speed of adjustment. The coefficient of X_t gives the short-run effect of X on Y and also, when divided by the estimate of λ, the long-run effect.

Example: Brown's habit persistence model of aggregate consumption

The first attempts by econometricians to fit an aggregate consumption function naturally used the simple static model

$$C_t = \beta_1 + \beta_2 Y_t + u_t. \tag{11.44}$$

With estimates of β_2 well below 1, this model implied that the average propensity to consume should fall. Nevertheless, long-run data showed no tendency for this to happen. Consequently, macroeconomists started looking for more elaborate models that could reconcile these apparently contradictory facts. Friedman's permanent income hypothesis was one such model. Another was Brown's habit persistence model (Brown, 1952). In this model, desired consumption C_t^* was related to wage income, W_t, and nonwage income, NW_t:

$$C_t^* = \beta_1 + \beta_2 W_t + \beta_3 NW_t + \delta A + u_t. \tag{11.45}$$

Brown used aggregate data for Canada for the years 1926–49, omitting the war years 1942–45, A being a dummy variable equal to 0 for the pre-war period and 1 for the post-war period. The division of income into wage income and nonwage income follows the observation of Michael Kalecki that the marginal propensity to consume out of wage income was likely to be much higher than that out of nonwage income, for two reasons. First, nonwage income tends to be received by relatively rich households with higher savings rates than poorer ones. Second, in a market economy, much nonwage income originates as company profits, and companies normally pass on only part of their profits as dividends to shareholders, retaining the remainder for investment in the business.

Because households are slow to adapt their spending patterns in response to changes in income, Brown hypothesized a partial adjustment process for actual consumption:

$$C_t - C_{t-1} = \lambda(C_t^* - C_{t-1}). \tag{11.46}$$

From this one obtains current consumption as the weighted average of desired consumption and consumption in the previous time period:

$$C_t = \lambda C_t^* + (1 - \lambda)C_{t-1}. \tag{11.47}$$

Substituting for C_t^* from (11.45), one then has an equation in observable variables:

$$\begin{aligned} C_t &= \lambda(\beta_1 + \beta_2 W_t + \beta_3 NW_t + \delta A + u_t) + (1 - \lambda)C_{t-1} \\ &= \beta_1\lambda + \beta_2\lambda W_t + \beta_3\lambda NW_t + (1 - \lambda)C_{t-1} + \lambda\delta A + \lambda u_t. \end{aligned} \tag{11.48}$$

Fitting the model with a simultaneous equations technique, Brown obtained (t statistics in parentheses)

$$\hat{C}_t = 0.90 + 0.61 W_t + 0.28 NW_t + 0.22 C_{t-1} + 0.69 A. \tag{11.49}$$
$$\quad\ (4.8)\quad (7.4)\qquad (4.2)\qquad\ (2.8)\qquad\ (4.8)$$

The variables were all measured in Canadian $ billion at constant prices of the 1935–39 period. From the regression one obtains short-run marginal propensities to consume of 0.61 and 0.28 for wage income and nonwage income, respectively. The coefficient of C_{t-1} indicates that 0.78 of the discrepancy between desired and actual consumption is eliminated in one year. Dividing the short-run marginal propensities by the speed of adjustment, one obtains long-run propensities to consume of 0.78 and 0.36 for wage income and nonwage income, respectively.

Comparison of the Friedman and Brown models

Despite the fact that their theoretical frameworks are completely different, one being concerned with the future and expectations, the other with the past and inertia, the Friedman model, in its Koyck-transformed form (11.39), and the habit persistence model (11.48) are virtually identical. They both incorporate short-run and long-run propensities to consume and a speed of adjustment. The only difference in the variable specification is that the Brown model divides income into wage income and nonwage income. This is a useful refinement that should be applied to the Friedman model as well. Indeed, it is now a standard feature of empirical models. The Friedman model does not have an intercept, but that is a minor empirical detail. The disturbance term in the Friedman model is different from that in the Brown model, and its structure may cause problems, but as will be seen in the next chapter, that is likewise not an important difference. This is an example of the problem of observationally equivalent theories, where two or more theories can be used to fit the same data set in the same way and there is no possibility of discriminating between them.

Exercises

11.9 Expenditure on housing services, *HOUS*, was regressed on *DPI*, the relative price index for housing, *PRELHOUS*, and the lagged value of *HOUS*, *HOUS*(–1), for the period 1959–2003 for the United States using the Demand Functions data set. The regression was repeated in logarithmic form, *LGHOUS* being regressed on *LGDPI*, *LGPRHOUS*, and *LGHOUS*(–1), with the results shown. Give an interpretation of the regression coefficients, paying attention to the dynamics implicit in the model.

$$\widehat{HOUS} = 75.35 + 0.03\,DPI - 0.75\,PRELHOUS + 0.81\,HOUS(-1)$$
$$(17.78)\ (0.01)\qquad (0.22)\qquad\qquad (0.04)\quad R^2 = 0.9997$$

$$\widehat{LGHOUS} = 0.07 + 0.28\,LGDPI - 0.12\,LGPRHOUS + 0.71\,LGHOUS(-1)$$
$$(0.06)\ (0.05)\qquad (0.03)\qquad\qquad (0.04)\quad R^2 = 0.9998.$$

11.10 Perform regressions parallel to those reported in Exercise 11.9 for your category of expenditure in the Demand Functions data set. Give an interpretation of the regression coefficients, paying attention to the dynamics implicit in the model.

11.11* How would you test Kalecki's assertion concerning the coefficients of wage and nonwage income, if you had access to Brown's data set?

11.12* In his classic study *Distributed Lags and Investment Analysis* (1954), Koyck investigated the relationship between investment in railcars and the volume of freight carried on the US railroads using data for the period 1884–1939. Assuming that the desired stock of railcars in year t depended on the volume of freight in year $t-1$ and year $t-2$ and a time trend, and assuming that investment in railcars was subject to a partial adjustment process, he fitted the following regression equation using OLS (standard errors and constant term not reported):

$$\hat{I}_t = 0.077\,F_{t-1} + 0.017\,F_{t-2} - 0.0033t - 0.110K_{t-1} \quad R^2 = 0.85.$$

Provide an interpretation of the equation and describe the dynamic process implied by it. (*Note*: It is best to substitute $K_t - K_{t-1}$ for I_t in the regression and treat it as a dynamic relationship determining K_t.)

11.5 Prediction

Suppose that you have fitted a model

$$Y_t = \beta_1 + \beta_2 X_t + u_t \tag{11.50}$$

to a sample of T time series observations ($t = 1, \ldots, T$):

$$\hat{Y}_t = b_1 + b_2 X_t. \tag{11.51}$$

Define the post-sample period to be $T + 1, \ldots, T + P$. Given any post-sample period value of X, say X_{T+p}, you are now in a position to predict the corresponding value of Y:

$$\hat{Y}_{T+p} = b_1 + b_2 X_{T+p}. \tag{11.52}$$

There are two reasons why such predictions may be important to you. First, you may be one of those econometricians whose business it is to peer into the economic future. Some econometricians are concerned with teasing out economic relationships with the aim of improving our understanding of how the economy works, but for others this is only a means to the more practical objective of trying to anticipate what will happen. In most countries, macroeconomic forecasting has a particularly high profile, teams of econometricians being employed by the Ministry of Finance or other branches of government, private financial institutions, universities and research institutes, and their predictions are actively used for framing public policy, for commenting on it, or for business purposes. When they are published in the press, they typically attract far more attention than most other forms of economic analysis, both on account of their subject matter and because, unlike most other forms of economic analysis, they are easily understood by the ordinary citizen. Even the most innumerate and non-technically minded person can have a good understanding of what is meant by estimates of the future levels of unemployment, inflation, etc.

There is, however, a second use of econometric prediction, one that has made it of concern to econometricians, irrespective of whether they are involved in forecasting. It provides a method of evaluating the robustness of a regression model that is more searching than the diagnostic statistics that have been used so far.

Before we go any further, we will have to clarify what we mean by *prediction*. Unfortunately, in the econometric literature this term can have several slightly different meanings, according to the status of X_{T+p} in (11.52). We will differentiate between **ex post predictions** and **forecasts**. This classification corresponds to what seems to be the most common usage, but the terminology is not standard.

Ex post predictions

We will describe $\hat{Y}_{T+p}$ as an ex post prediction if X_{T+p} is known. How can this be the case? In general, econometricians make use of all available data, to maximize the sample size and hence minimize the population variances of their estimators, so X_T will simply be the most recent recorded value of X available at the time of running the regression. Nevertheless, there are two circumstances when X_{T+p} will be known as well: when you have waited p or more periods after running the regression, and when you have deliberately terminated the sample period early so that you have a few of the most recent observations left over. The reason for doing this, as we shall see in the next section, is to enable you to evaluate the predictive accuracy of the model without having to wait.

For example, referring again to the price inflation/wage inflation model of equation (3.39), suppose that we had fitted the equation

$$\hat{p} = 1.0 + 0.80w \tag{11.53}$$

where p and w are the percentage annual rates of price inflation and wage inflation, respectively, using time series data for some sample period. Suppose that we know that the rate of wage inflation was 6 percent in some prediction period year. Then we can say that the ex post prediction of the rate of price inflation is 5.8 percent. We should, of course, be able to compare it immediately with the actual rate of price inflation for that year, and hence we can evaluate the prediction error, which is just the difference between actual outcome and the predicted value. In general, if Y_{T+p} is the actual outcome, and $\hat{Y}_{T+p}$ the predicted value, the forecast error is defined as f_{T+p} where

$$f_{T+p} = Y_{T+p} - \hat{Y}_{T+p}. \tag{11.54}$$

Why is there a prediction error? For two reasons. First, $\hat{Y}_{T+p}$ has been calculated using the parameter estimates, b_1 and b_2, instead of the true values.

And second, $\hat{Y}_{T+p}$ cannot take account of the disturbance term u_{T+p}, which is a component of Y_{T+p}. In the discussion that follows, we shall assume that the data include $T + P$ observations on the variables, the first T (the sample period) being used to fit the regression and the last P (the prediction period or prediction interval) being used to check predictive accuracy.

Example

Suppose that when we fitted the demand function for housing using the Demand Functions data set, we had only used the first 41 observations in the sample, that is, the observations for 1959–99, reserving the last four observations for checking predictions. The fitted equation for 1959–99 is (standard errors in parentheses)

$$\widehat{LGHOUS} = -0.30 + 1.04LGDPI - 0.42LGPRHOUS \quad R^2 = 0.998.$$
$$\quad\quad (0.19) \ (0.01) \quad\quad\quad (0.05) \quad\quad\quad\quad\quad\quad (11.55)$$

The predicted values of $LGHOUS$ for the period 2000–03, using the equation and the actual values of disposable personal income and the relative price of housing services for those years, are shown in Table 11.6, together with the actual outcomes and the prediction errors. The predictions, like the basic data, are in logarithmic form. For convenience, Table 11.6 also shows the absolute values, derived from the logarithmic values, expressed in US\$ billion at 2000 prices.

We can see that in this case the predicted value of expenditure on housing services exceeds the actual value by between 2.2 percent and 4.2 percent. Is this predictive performance satisfactory? We shall see in the next section.

Forecasts

If you are willing to predict a particular value of Y_{T+p}, without knowing the actual value of X_{T+p}, you are said to be making a forecast, at least in the terminology of this text. The macroeconomic divinations published in the press are usually forecasts in this sense. Policymakers, and indeed the general public, are not much interested in two-handed economists (ones who say 'on the one hand

Table 11.6 Actual and predicted expenditure on housing services, 2000–2003

Year	Logarithms			Absolute equivalent		
	LGHOUS	$\widehat{LGHOUS}$	Error	HOUS	$\widehat{HOUS}$	Error
2000	6.914	6.956	−0.042	1006	1049	−43
2001	6.941	6.968	−0.027	1034	1063	−29
2002	6.968	6.990	−0.022	1062	1086	−24
2003	6.981	7.012	−0.030	1076	1109	−33

this ... but if ... then on the other hand that ...'). They want the best possible single-point estimates, perhaps with some indication of the likely margin of error, often not even that. Forecasts are less accurate than predictions because they are subject to an additional source of error, the error in the prediction of X_{T+p}. Obviously, those making forecasts normally attempt to minimize the additional error by forecasting future values of X as carefully as possible, in some instances constructing a separate model for it, in others bringing the equation determining Y and the equation determining X together, usually with other relationships as well, in a simultaneous equations model of the type discussed in Chapter 9.

Properties of least squares predictors

In the discussion that follows, we will be concerned with predictions rather than forecasts, the reason being that we are in a position to make statements about the properties of the regression coefficients and the disturbance term, but not about X if its values are not known. First, there is some good news. If Y_{T+p} is generated by the same process as the sample period values of Y (that is, according to equation (11.50) with u_{T+p} conforming to the regression model assumptions), and if we make our prediction $\hat{Y}_{T+p}$ using equation (11.52), the prediction error f_{T+p} will have zero mean and minimum variance.

The first property is easily demonstrated:

$$
\begin{aligned}
E\left(f_{T+p}\right) &= E\left(Y_{T+p}\right) - E\left(\hat{Y}_{T+p}\right) \\
&= E\left(\beta_1 + \beta_2 X_{T+p} + u_{T+p}\right) - E\left(b_1 + b_2 X_{T+p}\right) \\
&= \beta_1 + \beta_2 X_{T+p} + E\left(u_{T+p}\right) - E\left(b_1\right) - X_{T+p}E\left(b_2\right) \\
&= \beta_1 + \beta_2 X_{T+p} - \beta_1 - \beta_2 X_{T+p} = 0 \qquad (11.56)
\end{aligned}
$$

since $E(b_1) = \beta_1$, $E(b_2) = \beta_2$, and $E(u_{T+p}) = 0$. We will not attempt to prove the minimum variance property (for a proof, see Johnston and Dinardo, 1997). Both of these properties carry over to the general case of multiple regression analysis.

In the simple regression case, the population variance of f_{T+p} is given by

$$
\sigma^2_{f_{T+p}} = \left\{ 1 + \frac{1}{T} + \frac{\left(X_{T+p} - \overline{X}\right)^2}{\sum\limits_{t=1}^{T}\left(X_t - \overline{X}\right)^2} \right\} \sigma^2_u \qquad (11.57)
$$

where $\overline{X}$ and $\sum\left(X_t - \overline{X}\right)^2$ are the sample period mean and sum of squared deviations of X. Unsurprisingly, this implies that, the further is the value of X from its sample mean, the larger will be the population variance of the prediction error. It also implies, again unsurprisingly, that, the larger is the sample, the smaller will be the population variance of the prediction error, with a lower limit of σ_u^2. As the sample becomes large, b_1 and b_2 will tend to their true values (provided that the regression model assumptions are valid), so the only source of error in the prediction will be u_{T+p}, and by definition this has population variance σ_u^2.

Confidence intervals for predictions

We can obtain the standard error of the prediction error by replacing σ_u^2 in (11.57) by s_u^2 and taking the square root. Then $(Y_{T+p} - \hat{Y}_{T+p})$/standard error follows a t distribution with the number of degrees of freedom when fitting the equation in the sample period, $T - k$. Hence we can derive a confidence interval for the actual outcome, Y_{T+p}:

$$\hat{Y}_{T+p} - t_{\text{crit}} \times \text{s.e.} < Y_{T+p} < \hat{Y}_{T+p} + t_{\text{crit}} \times \text{s.e.} \qquad (11.58)$$

where t_{crit} is the critical level of t, given the significance level selected and the number of degrees of freedom, and s.e. is the standard error of the prediction. Figure 11.3 depicts in general terms the relationship between the confidence interval for prediction and the value of the explanatory variable.

In multiple regressions, the counterpart to (11.57) is much more complicated and is best handled with matrix algebra. Fortunately, there is a simple trick that you can use to get the computer to calculate the standard errors for you. Let the sample period be denoted $1, \ldots, T$ and the prediction period $T + 1, \ldots, T + P$. You run the regression for the sample and prediction periods combined, adding a (different) dummy variable to each of the prediction period observations. This means adding to the model a set of dummy variables $D_{T+1}, \ldots, D_{T+P}$, where D_{T+p} is defined to be 0 for every observation except observation $T + p$, for which it is 1. It can be shown (Salkever, 1976; Dufour, 1980) that the estimates of the nondummy coefficients and their standard errors will be exactly the same

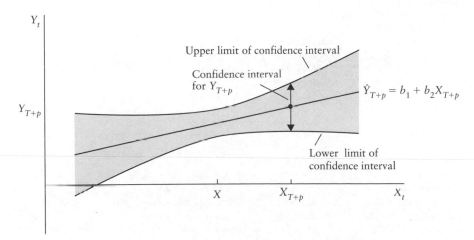

Figure 11.3 Confidence interval for a projection

as in the regression confined to the sample period only. The computer uses the dummy variables to obtain a perfect fit in each observation in the prediction period, and it does this by setting the coefficient of the dummy variable equal to the prediction error as defined above. The standard error of this coefficient is equal to the standard error of the prediction error.

Example

The output in Table 11.7 shows the result of a logarithmic regression of housing services on income and relative price with dummy variables $D00$–$D03$ for the years 2000–03. The coefficients of the dummy variables give the forecast errors presented in Table 11.6. The predicted logarithm of expenditure on housing services in 2000 in Table 11.6 was 6.956. From the output in Table 11.7 we see that the standard error of the prediction error for that year was 0.017. With 38 degrees of freedom, the critical value of t at the 5 percent significance level is 2.024, so we obtain the following 95 percent confidence interval for the prediction for that year:

$$6.956 - 2.024 \times 0.017 < Y < 6.956 + 2.024 \times 0.017 \qquad (11.59)$$

that is,

$$6.922 < Y < 6.990. \qquad (11.60)$$

The confidence interval does not include the actual outcome, 6.914, and thus, for that year at least, the prediction was unsatisfactory. An obvious reason is

Table 11.7

```
Dependent Variable: LGHOUS
Method: Least Squares
Sample: 1959 2003
Included observations: 45
```

Variable	Coefficient	Std. Error	t-Statistic	Prob.
C	−0.298460	0.194922	−1.531173	0.1340
LGDPI	1.036576	0.006497	159.5366	0.0000
LGPRHOUS	−0.423765	0.045451	−9.323628	0.0000
D00	−0.041629	0.017210	−2.418867	0.0205
D01	−0.027473	0.017436	−1.575655	0.1234
D02	−0.022256	0.017788	−1.251167	0.2185
D03	−0.030428	0.017893	−1.700556	0.0972

R-squared	0.998852	Mean dependent var		6.359334
Adjusted R-squared	0.998670	S.D. dependent var		0.437527
S.E. of regression	0.015955	Akaike info criter		−5.296084
Sum squared resid	0.009673	Schwarz criterion		−5.015048
Log likelihood	126.1619	F-statistic		5508.485
Durbin-Watson stat	0.802456	Prob(F-statistic)		0.000000

that we have used a very simple static model for housing services. As we shall see in the next chapter, a dynamic one would be preferable.

Exercise

11.13 Use the Salkever indirect method to compute forecasts and their standard errors for the logarithmic demand function for your category of expenditure. Add dummy variables to the last four observations and hence obtain the prediction errors for these years, given a regression based on the first 41 observations. Subtract these from the actual outcomes to obtain the forecasts. Derive a confidence interval for the forecast for 2003.

11.6 Stability tests

Stability tests of a regression model are tests designed to evaluate whether the performance of a model in a prediction period is compatible with its performance in the sample period used to fit it. There are two principles on which stability tests can be constructed. One approach is to focus on the predictive performance of the model; the other is to evaluate whether there is any evidence of shifts in the parameters in the prediction period.

The Chow test of predictive failure

In the previous section we saw that we could compute the prediction errors by adding a set of dummy variables to the prediction period observations. It is natural to test whether the prediction errors are significantly different from zero, and we can do this with an F test of the joint explanatory power of the dummy variables. Combining the sample and prediction period observations, we run the regression first without the dummy variables and then with them included. Let the residual sum of squares be denoted RSS_{T+P} and RSS_{T+P}^D, the subscript indicating the number of observations in the regression and the superscript D indicating the inclusion of the dummy variables. We then see whether the improvement in the fit on adding the dummy variables is significant, using the F test presented in Section 3.5. The improvement is $(RSS_{T+P} - RSS_{T+P}^D)$; the number of dummy variables is P; the residual sum of squares after adding the dummy variables is RSS_{T+P}^D; and the number of degrees of freedom remaining is the number of observations in the combined sample, $T + P$, less the number of parameters estimated, $k + P$. The test statistic is therefore

$$F(P, T - k) = \frac{\left(RSS_{T+P} - RSS_{T+P}^D\right)/P}{RSS_{T+P}^D/(T - k)}.$$

(11.61)

In practice, you do not even have to run the regression with the dummy variables to perform the test, because RSS_{T+P}^{D} is identical to RSS_T, the sum of the squares of the residuals in the regression limited to the sample period. The fit for this regression is exactly the same as the fit for the first T observations in the dummy variable regression, which means that the residuals are the same. And there are no residuals in the last P observations of the dummy variable regression because the inclusion of an observation-specific dummy in each observation guarantees a perfect fit in those observations. Hence RSS_{T+P}^{D} is exactly the same as RSS_T, and the F statistic can be written

$$F(P, T - k) = \frac{\left(RSS_{T+P} - RSS_T\right)/P}{RSS_T/(T - k)}. \tag{11.62}$$

The test is usually known as the **Chow test of predictive failure**, after its originator, but the interpretation given here is later (Pesaran, Smith, and Yeo, 1985).

Example

The housing services expenditure function was fitted first for the period 1959–99, giving $RSS_T = 0.009673$, and then for the period 1959–2003, giving $RSS_{T+P} = 0.011937$. The F statistic is therefore

$$F(4,38) = \frac{(0.011937 - 0.009673)/4}{0.009673/38} = 2.22. \tag{11.63}$$

The null hypothesis is that the coefficients of the dummy variables are all equal to zero. The critical value of $F(4,38)$ at the 5 percent level is 2.62. Hence there is no significant difference between the sample period and prediction period fits and so we do not reject the hypothesis that the model is stable.

F test of coefficient stability

If there are sufficient observations in the prediction period, you can perform a Chow test on the lines of that discussed in Chapter 5 to evaluate whether the coefficients in the sample period and prediction period appear to be significantly different. To perform the test, you run the regression for the sample and prediction periods separately, and then for the two periods combined, and see whether sample period/prediction period division results in a significant improvement in fit compared with that obtained with the combined regression. If it does, this is evidence that the coefficients are unstable.

Example

In the case of the housing services expenditure function, with the observations for 1959–99 being used as the sample period and those for 2000–03 as the prediction period, the sums of the squares of the residuals for the sample period, prediction period, and combination were 0.009673, 0.000012, and 0.011937, respectively. Running separate regressions for the two subperiods costs three degrees of freedom, and the number of degrees of freedom remaining after estimating six parameters (constant twice, coefficient of $LGDPI$ twice, and coefficient of $LGPRHOUS$ twice) is 39. Hence we obtain the following F statistic, which is distributed with 3 and 39 degrees of freedom:

$$F(3,39) = \frac{(0.011937 - [0.009673 + 0.000012])/3}{(0.009673 + 0.000012)/39} = 3.02. \qquad (11.64)$$

The critical value of $F(3,39)$ at the 5 percent significance level is 2.84 and hence we conclude that there is some evidence of coefficient instability. At the 1 percent level the critical value is 4.31. It is thus possible for the Chow test of predictive failure and the F test of coefficient stability to come to different conclusions. However, even in this case they are not far apart. The predictive failure test was nearly significant at the 5 percent level, and the coefficient stability test was only narrowly significant at that level.

Key terms

adaptive expectations model	Koyck distribution
Chow test of predictive failure	Koyck transformation
data generation process	lag structure
ex post prediction	parsimonious lag structure
forecast	partial adjustment model
grid search	permanent income hypothesis
habit persistence model	realization

Exercises

11.14 Fit the logarithmic form of your demand function for your category of expenditure for the periods 1959–99 and 1959–2003 and perform the Chow test of predictive failure.

11.15 Fit your demand function to the data for 1959–2003, 1959–99 and 2000–03 and perform the F test of coefficient stability.

12 Properties of Regression Models with Time Series Data

Chapter 11 introduced some basic concepts relating to time series regressions. We now need to consider the properties of the regression estimators. We will start by stating the regression model assumptions appropriate for Model C. The rest of this chapter will focus on two of the assumptions that are particularly important for time series regressions and that are often violated.

12.1 Assumptions for regressions with time series data

Assumptions C.1, C.3, C.4, and C.5, and the consequences of their violations are the same as those for Model B and they will not be discussed further here.

    C.1 *The model is linear in parameters and correctly specified.*

    C.2 *The time series for the regressors are weakly persistent.*

This assumption replaces the Model B assumption that the values of the regressors in the observations in the sample are drawn randomly from fixed populations. That assumption is wholly unrealistic in a time series setting because the values of many time series variables are correlated, often strongly so, from one time period to the next. A discussion of the meaning of 'weakly persistent' and the importance of this assumption leads us to relatively advanced technical issues and will be deferred to Chapter 13.

    C.3 *There does not exist an exact linear relationship among the regressors in the sample.*

    C.4 *The disturbance term has zero expectation.*

$$E(u_t) = 0 \quad \text{for all } t. \tag{12.1}$$

    C.5 *The disturbance term is homoscedastic.*

$$\sigma_{u_t}^2 = \sigma_u^2 \quad \text{for all } t. \tag{12.2}$$

    C.6 *The values of the disturbance term have independent distributions.*

$$u_t \text{ is distributed independently of } u_{t'} \text{ for } t' \neq t. \tag{12.3}$$

This assumption is rarely an issue with cross-sectional data. When observations are generated randomly, there is no reason to suppose that there should be any connection between the value of the disturbance term in one observation and its value in any other. However with time series data it often happens that the value of the disturbance term in one observation is correlated with its value in the next. The reasons for this and its consequences are discussed in Sections 12.3–12.5.

C.7 *The disturbance term is distributed independently of the regressors.*

u_t is distributed independently of $X_{jt'}$ for all t' (including t) and j.   (12.4)

We have already seen, in the context of cross-sectional data, how violations of this assumption can lead to inconsistent estimates (measurement error bias in Chapter 8 and simultaneous equations bias in Chapter 9). This assumption is of even greater practical importance in the context of time series regressions and will be discussed in the next section. As with Assumption B.7, the assumption can be expressed in the weaker form of a conditional expectation:

C.7' *The disturbance term has zero conditional expectation.*

$E(u_t \mid$ values of all the regressors in all observations $) = 0$.   (12.5)

C.8 *The disturbance term has a normal distribution.*

12.2 The assumption of the independence of the disturbance term and the regressors

Assumption C.7, like its counterpart B.7 in Model B, is required for the unbiasedness of the OLS regression coefficients. For example, we know that for the simple regression model

$$Y_t = \beta_1 + \beta_2 X_t + u_t \tag{12.6}$$

with $t = 1, \ldots, T$, the OLS slope coefficient can be decomposed as

$$b_2^{OLS} = \beta_2 + \sum_{t=1}^{T} a_t u_t \tag{12.7}$$

where

$$a_t = \frac{X_t - \overline{X}}{\sum\limits_{s=1}^{T} \left(X_s - \overline{X} \right)^2}. \tag{12.8}$$

Hence

$$E\left(b_2^{\text{OLS}}\right) = E\left(\beta_2 + \sum_{t=1}^{T} a_t u_t\right) = \beta_2 + \sum_{t=1}^{T} E\left(a_t u_t\right) = \beta_2 + \sum_{t=1}^{T} E\left(a_t\right) E\left(u_t\right)$$

$$= \beta_2 + \sum_{t=1}^{T} E\left(a_t\right) \times 0 = \beta_2. \tag{12.9}$$

Note that we use Assumption C.7 in the decomposition $E\left(a_t u_t\right) = E\left(a_t\right) E\left(u_t\right)$. For the decomposition to be valid, u_t must be distributed independently of a_t, and since a_t depends on all of the observations on X in the sample, this means that u_t must be distributed independently of all of the observations on X, not just X_t. For the purposes of our discussion it is convenient to break down Assumption C.7 into two components:

1. the disturbance term in any observation is distributed independently of the values of the regressors in the same observation, and
2. the disturbance term in any observation is distributed independently of the values of the regressors in the other observations.

For cross-sectional regressions, part (2) is seldom an issue. Since the observations are generated randomly there is almost never any reason to suppose that the disturbance term in one observation is not independent of the values of the regressors in the other observations. Hence unbiasedness really depends on part (1). Of course, this might fail, as we saw with measurement errors in the regressors and with simultaneous equations estimation.

With time series regression, part (2) becomes a major concern. Consider, for example, a model with a lagged dependent variable:

$$Y_t = \beta_1 + \beta_2 X_t + \beta_3 Y_{t-1} + u_t. \tag{12.10}$$

This is precisely the model that we have explored in Chapter 11 in the context of partial adjustment and adaptive expectations. Suppose that u_t is well behaved in the sense that it is distributed independently of X_t and Y_{t-1} and hence there is no violation of part (1) of Assumption C.7. In the next observation,

$$Y_{t+1} = \beta_1 + \beta_2 X_{t+1} + \beta_3 Y_t + u_{t+1}. \tag{12.11}$$

For this observation u_t is correlated with the regressor Y_t, violating part (2) of the assumption. In fact u_t will be correlated with every value of Y from time t onwards.

The following model was used to illustrate finite-sample bias in a model with a lagged dependent variable. The true model was

$$Y_t = 10 + 0.5X_t + 0.8Y_{t-1} + u_t \tag{12.12}$$

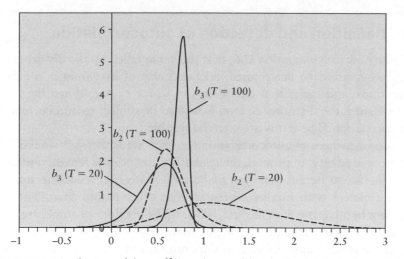

Figure 12.1 Distributions of the coefficients in a model with a lagged dependent variable

with X_t being assigned the values $1, 2, \ldots, T$ for sample size T. The values of the disturbance term were drawn independently from a normal distribution with zero mean and unit variance. Figure 12.1 shows the distributions of b_2 (dashed lines) and b_3 (solid lines) for sample sizes 20 and 100, for 1 million samples in each case. For sample size 20, b_3 was severely downwards biased, the mean of its distribution being 0.50. b_2 was severe upwards biased, its mean being 1.26. When the sample size was increased to 100, the biases became smaller, the means of the distributions being 0.74 and 0.64, respectively. Increasing the sample size further, the simulation demonstrated that the estimators were consistent, the biases disappearing and the distributions collapsing to spikes at the true values.

Consider next the two-equation model

$$Y_t = \beta_1 + \beta_2 X_{t-1} + u_t \tag{12.13}$$

$$X_t = \alpha_1 + \alpha_2 Y_{t-1} + v_t. \tag{12.14}$$

Neither equation possesses a lagged dependent variable as a regressor. However u_t is a determinant of Y_t, and hence of X_{t+1}. This means that u_t is correlated with the X regressor in (12.13) in the observations for Y_{t+2}, $Y_{t+4}, \ldots$ etc. Again, part (2) of Assumption C.7 is violated and the OLS estimators will be biased.

Since interactions and lags are common in economic models using time series data, the problem of biased coefficients should be taken as the working hypothesis, the rule rather than the exception. Fortunately, part (2) of Assumption C.7 is not required for consistency. Part (1) is a necessary condition. If it is violated, the regression coefficients will be inconsistent. However, it is not a sufficient condition for consistency because it is possible that the regression estimators may not tend to finite limits as the sample size becomes large. This is a relatively technical issue that will be discussed in Chapter 13.

12.3   Definition and detection of autocorrelation

We come now to Assumption C.6, that the value taken by the disturbance term in any observation be determined independently of its values in all the other observations, and hence that $cov(u_t, u_{t'}) = 0$, for $t' \neq t$. When the condition is not satisfied, the disturbance term is said to be subject to **autocorrelation**, or **serial correlation**. The terms are interchangeable.

The consequences of autocorrelation for OLS are somewhat similar to those of heteroscedasticity. In general, the regression coefficients remain unbiased, but OLS is inefficient because one can find an alternative regression technique that yields estimators with smaller variances. The other main consequence, which should not be mixed up with the first, is that in the presence of autocorrelation the standard errors are estimated wrongly, often being biased downwards. Finally, although in general autocorrelation does not cause OLS estimates to be biased, there is an important special case where it does.

Possible causes of autocorrelation

Autocorrelation normally occurs only in regression analysis using time series data. The disturbance term in a regression equation picks up the influence of those variables affecting the dependent variable that have not been included in the regression equation. If the value of u in any observation is to be independent of its value in the previous one, the value of any variable hidden in u must be uncorrelated with its value at the time of the previous observation.

Persistence of the effects of excluded variables is probably the most frequent cause of **positive autocorrelation**, the most common type in economic analysis. In Figure 12.2, Y depends on X and a number of minor variables not included explicitly in the specification. The disturbance term in the model is generated by the combined effects of these excluded variables. In the first observation, the excluded variables have a net positive effect and the disturbance term is positive. If the excluded variables change slowly, their positive effect will persist and the disturbance term will remain positive. Eventually the balance will change and the net effect of the excluded variables becomes negative. Now the persistence effect works the other way and the disturbance term remains negative for a few observations. The duration and amplitude of each positive and negative sequence are essentially random, but overall there will be a tendency for positive values of the disturbance term to be followed by positive ones and for negative values to be followed by negative ones.

One important point to note is that autocorrelation is on the whole more likely to be a problem, the shorter the interval between observations. Obviously, the longer the interval, the less likely are the effects of the excluded variables to persist from one observation to the next.

In principle, one may also encounter **negative autocorrelation**. This occurs when the correlation between successive values of the disturbance term is

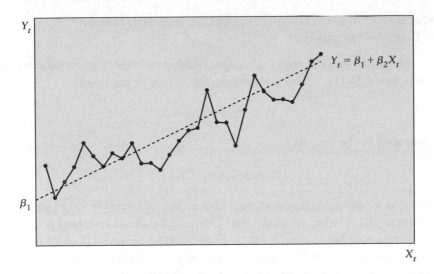

Figure 12.2 Positive autocorrelation

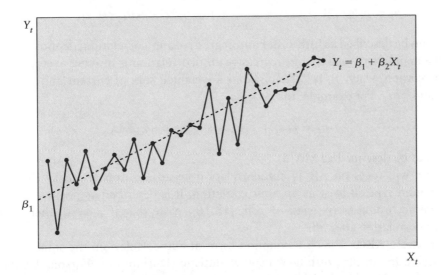

Figure 12.3 Negative autocorrelation

negative. A positive value in one observation is more likely to be followed by a negative value than a positive value in the next, and vice versa, the scatter diagram looking like Figure 12.3. A line joining successive observations to one another would cross the line relating Y to X with greater frequency than one would expect if the values of the disturbance term were independent of each other. Economic examples of negative autocorrelation are relatively uncommon, but sometimes it is induced by manipulations used to transform the original specification of a model into a form suitable for regression analysis.

Detection of first-order autoregressive autocorrelation: the Durbin–Watson test

We will mostly be concerned with first-order **autoregressive autocorrelation**, often denoted AR(1), where the disturbance term u in the model

$$Y_t = \beta_1 + \beta_2 X_t + u_t \tag{12.15}$$

is generated by the process

$$u_t = \rho u_{t-1} + \varepsilon_t, \tag{12.16}$$

where ε_t is a random variable whose value in any observation is independent of its value in all the other observations. This type of autocorrelation is described as autoregressive because u_t is being determined by lagged values of itself plus the fresh element of randomness ε_t, sometimes described as an innovation. It is described as first-order because u_t depends only on u_{t-1} and the innovation. A process of the type

$$u_t = \rho_1 u_{t-1} + \rho_2 u_{t-2} + \rho_3 u_{t-3} + \rho_4 u_{t-4} + \rho_5 u_{t-5} + \varepsilon_t, \tag{12.17}$$

would be described as fifth-order autoregressive autocorrelation, denoted AR(5). The main alternative to autoregressive autocorrelation is **moving average autocorrelation**, where u_t is determined as a weighted sum of current and previous values of ε_t. For example, the process

$$u_t = \lambda_0 \varepsilon_t + \lambda_1 \varepsilon_{t-1} + \lambda_2 \varepsilon_{t-2} + \lambda_3 \varepsilon_{t-3} \tag{12.18}$$

would be described as MA(3).

We will focus on AR(1) autocorrelation because it appears to be the most common type, at least as an approximation. It is described as positive or negative according to the sign of ρ in (12.16). Note that if $\rho = 0$, there is no autocorrelation after all.

Because AR(1) is such a common form of autocorrelation, the standard test statistic for it, the **Durbin–Watson d statistic** (Durbin and Watson, 1950), is usually included in the basic diagnostic statistics printed out with the regression results. It is calculated from the residuals using the expression

$$d = \frac{\sum\limits_{t=2}^{T} (e_t - e_{t-1})^2}{\sum\limits_{t=1}^{T} e_t^2}. \tag{12.19}$$

It can be shown (see Appendix 12.1) that in large samples

$$d \to 2 - 2\rho. \tag{12.20}$$

If there is no autocorrelation present, $\rho = 0$ and d should be close to 2. If there is positive autocorrelation, d will tend to be less than 2. If there is negative autocorrelation, it will tend to be greater than 2. The **Durbin–Watson test** assumes that ρ lies in the interval $-1 < \rho < 1$ and hence that d lies between 4 and 0.

The null hypothesis for the test is that $\rho = 0$. Of course, even if H_0 is true, d will not be exactly equal to 2, except by freak chance. However, a value of d much lower than 2 leaves you with two choices. One is to assume that H_0 is true and that the low value of d has arisen as a matter of chance. The other is that the disturbance term is subject to positive autocorrelation. As usual, the choice is made by establishing a critical value d_{crit} below which d would not sink, say, more than 5 percent of the time. If d were below d_{crit}, you would then reject H_0 at the 5 percent significance level.

The critical value of d at any significance level depends, as you might expect, on the number of explanatory variables in the regression equation and the number of observations in the sample. Unfortunately, it also depends on the particular values taken by the explanatory variables. Thus it is not possible to construct a table giving the exact critical values for all possible samples, as one can with the t test and the F test, but it is possible to calculate upper and lower *limits* for the critical value of d. Those for positive autocorrelation are usually denoted d_U and d_L.

Figure 12.4 represents the situation schematically, with the arrow indicating the critical level of d, which will be denoted d_{crit}. If you knew the exact value of d_{crit}, you could compare the d statistic for your regression with it. If $d > d_{crit}$, you would fail to reject the null hypothesis of no autocorrelation. If $d < d_{crit}$, you would reject the null hypothesis and conclude that there is evidence of positive autocorrelation.

However, all you know is that d_{crit} lies somewhere between d_L and d_U. This leaves you with three possible outcomes for the test.

1. d is less than d_L. In this case, it must be lower than d_{crit}, so you would reject the null hypothesis and conclude that positive autocorrelation is present.

2. d is greater than d_U. In this case, d must be greater than d_{crit}, so you would fail to reject the null hypothesis.

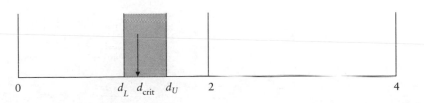

| 0 | d_L d_{crit} d_U | 2 | 4 |

Figure 12.4 Durbin–Watson test for autocorrelation, showing the zone of indeterminacy in the case of suspected positive autocorrelation

3. d lies between d_L and d_U. In this case, d might be greater or less than d_{crit}. You do not know which, so you cannot tell whether you should reject or not reject the null hypothesis.

In cases (1) and (2), the Durbin–Watson test gives you a definite answer, but in case (3) you are left in a zone of indecision, and there is nothing that you can do about it.

Table A.5 at the end of this text gives d_L and d_U cross-classified by number of explanatory variables and number of observations, for the 5 percent and 1 percent significance levels, for the case of positive AR(1) autocorrelation. You can see the zone of indecision between d_L and d_U decreases as the sample size increases. Testing for negative autocorrelation follows a similar pattern, with the zone containing the critical value symmetrically located to the right of 2. Since negative autocorrelation is relatively uncommon, you are expected to calculate the limits of the zone yourself from the figures for positive autocorrelation for the corresponding number of explanatory variables and number of observations. This is easy enough to do. As is illustrated in Figure 12.5, $4 - d_U$ gives the lower limit, below which you fail to reject the null hypothesis of no autocorrelation, and $4 - d_L$ gives the upper one, above which you conclude that there is evidence of negative autocorrelation.

It should be noted that a low d statistic does not necessarily mean that the model is subject to AR(1) autocorrelation. It will be low whenever there is a pattern of positive residuals tending to be followed by positive ones and negative ones by negative ones, and this could be caused by model misspecification. In particular, it is often caused by the omission of an important variable from the model, and it may happen if the regression is using an inappropriate mathematical function. We will discuss these cases of apparent autocorrelation below.

Example

The output shown in Table 12.1 gives the result of a logarithmic regression of housing services on disposable personal income and the relative price of housing services. The Durbin–Watson statistic is 0.63. For $H_0: \rho = 0$ and $H_1: \rho \neq 0$, d_L is 1.24 for a 1 percent significance test (2 explanatory variables, 45 observations). We would therefore reject H_0.

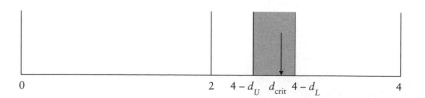

Figure 12.5 Durbin–Watson test for autocorrelation, showing the zone of indeterminacy in the case of suspected negative autocorrelation

Table 12.1

```
Dependent Variable: LGHOUS
Method: Least Squares
Sample: 1959 2003
Included observations: 45
```

Variable	Coefficient	Std. Error	t-Statistic	Prob.
C	0.005625	0.167903	0.033501	0.9734
LGDPI	1.031918	0.006649	155.1976	0.0000
LGPRHOUS	−0.483421	0.041780	-11.57056	0.0000

R-squared	0.998583	Mean dependent var	6.359334
Adjusted R-squared	0.998515	S.D. dependent var	0.437527
S.E. of regression	0.016859	Akaike info criter	−5.263574
Sum squared resid	0.011937	Schwarz criterion	−5.143130
Log likelihood	121.4304	F-statistic	14797.05
Durbin-Watson stat	0.633113	Prob (F-statistic)	0.000000

Exercises

12.1 Examine the Durbin–Watson statistic for the logarithmic demand function that you fitted in Exercise 11.4. Is there evidence of autocorrelation? If so, what are the implications for the statistical tests you performed?

12.2 If your regression application allows you to graph or print the residuals from a regression, do this in the case of your logarithmic demand function. Does an inspection of the residuals corroborate the presence (or absence) of autocorrelation indicated by the Durbin–Watson statistic?

12.4   What can you do about autocorrelation?

We will consider only the case of AR(1) autocorrelation. It has received the most attention in the literature because it is intuitively plausible and there is seldom sufficient evidence to make it worthwhile considering more complicated models. If the observations are taken quarterly or monthly, however, other models may be more suitable, but we will not investigate them here.

AR(1) autocorrelation can be eliminated by a simple manipulation of the model. Suppose that the model is

$$Y_t = \beta_1 + \beta_2 X_t + u_t \tag{12.21}$$

with u_t generated by the process

$$u_t = \rho u_{t-1} + \varepsilon_t. \tag{12.22}$$

If we lag equation (12.21) by one time period and multiply by ρ, we have

$$\rho Y_{t-1} = \beta_1 \rho + \beta_2 \rho X_{t-1} + \rho u_{t-1}. \qquad (12.23)$$

Now subtract (12.23) from (12.21):

$$Y_t - \rho Y_{t-1} = \beta_1 (1 - \rho) + \beta_2 X_t - \beta_2 \rho X_{t-1} + u_t - \rho u_{t-1}. \qquad (12.24)$$

Hence

$$Y_t = \beta_1 (1 - \rho) + \rho Y_{t-1} + \beta_2 X_t - \beta_2 \rho X_{t-1} + \varepsilon_t. \qquad (12.25)$$

The model is now free from autocorrelation because the disturbance term has been reduced to the innovation ε_t. In the case of the more general multiple regression model

$$Y_t = \beta_1 + \beta_2 X_{2t} + \cdots + \beta_k X_{kt} + u_t, \qquad (12.26)$$

with u_t following an AR(1) process, we follow the same procedure. We lag the equation and multiply it by ρ:

$$\rho Y_{t-1} = \beta_1 \rho + \beta_2 \rho X_{2,t-1} + \cdots + \beta_k \rho X_{k,t-1} + \rho u_{t-1}. \qquad (12.27)$$

Subtracting (12.27) from (12.26) and rearranging, we again derive a model free from autocorrelation:

$$Y_t = \beta_1 (1 - \rho) + \rho Y_{t-1} + \beta_2 X_{2t} - \beta_2 \rho X_{2,t-1} + \cdots + \beta_k X_{kt} - \beta_k \rho X_{k,t-1} + \varepsilon_t. \qquad (12.28)$$

Note that the model incorporates the nonlinear restriction that the coefficient of the lagged value of each X variable is equal to minus the product of the coefficients of its current value and Y_{t-1}. This means that you should not use OLS to fit it. If you did, there would be no guarantee that the coefficients would conform to the theoretical restrictions. Thus one has to use some nonlinear estimation procedure instead. The most common are nonlinear least squares, on the lines discussed in Chapter 4, and maximum likelihood estimation.

Example

The output in Table 12.2 shows the result of a logarithmic regression of housing services on disposable personal income and the relative price of housing services, using the nonlinear specification represented by equation (12.28). The model is

$$LGHOUS_t = \beta_1 (1 - \rho) + \rho LGHOUS_{t-1} + \beta_2 LGDPI_t - \beta_2 \rho LGDPI_{t-1}$$
$$+ \beta_3 LGPRHOUS_t - \beta_3 \rho LGPRHOUS_{t-1} + \varepsilon_t. \qquad (12.29)$$

The nonlinear equation is reproduced as part of the regression output. C(1), C(2), C(3), and C(4) are estimates of β_1, ρ, β_2, and β_3, respectively. The fitted equation is therefore

$$\widehat{LGHOUS} = C(1)[1 - C(2)] + C(2)LGHOUS(-1)$$
$$+ C(3)LGDPI - C(2)C(3)LGDPI(-1)$$
$$+ C(4)LGPRHOUS - C(2)C(4)LGPRHOUS(-1). \quad (12.30)$$

You can see that the estimate of ρ is high, 0.72, suggesting that there was severe autocorrelation in the original specification. The estimates of the income and price elasticities are similar to those in the OLS regression. This is what we would expect. Autocorrelation does not cause OLS estimates to be biased, but the AR(1) estimates will in principle be more efficient and therefore should tend to be more accurate.

Table 12.2

```
Dependent Variable: LGHOUS
Method: Least Squares
Sample(adjusted): 1960 2003
Included observations: 44 after adjusting endpoints
Convergence achieved after 12 iterations
LGHOUS=C(1)*(1-C(2))+C(2)*LGHOUS(-1)+C(3)*LGDPI-C(2)*C(3)*
          LGDPI(-1)+C(4)*LGPRHOUS-C(2)*C(4)*LGPRHOUS(-1)
```

	Coefficient	Std. Error	t-Statistic	Prob.
C(1)	0.154815	0.354990	0.436111	0.6651
C(2)	0.719102	0.115689	6.215838	0.0000
C(3)	1.011295	0.021830	46.32636	0.0000
C(4)	−0.478070	0.091594	−5.219434	0.0000

R-squared	0.999205	Mean dependent var	6.379059
Adjusted R-squared	0.999145	S.D. dependent var	0.421861
S.E. of regression	0.012333	Akaike info criter	−5.866567
Sum squared resid	0.006084	Schwarz criterion	−5.704368
Log likelihood	133.0645	Durbin-Watson stat	1.901082

```
Dependent Variable: LGHOUS
Method: Least Squares
Sample(adjusted): 1960 2003
Included observations: 44 after adjusting endpoints
Convergence achieved after 9 iterations
```

Variable	Coefficient	Std. Error	t-Statistic	Prob.
C	0.154815	0.354989	0.436111	0.6651
LGDPI	1.011295	0.021830	46.32642	0.0000
LGPRHOUS	−0.478070	0.091594	−5.219437	0.0000
AR(1)	0.719102	0.115689	6.215836	0.0000

R-squared	0.999205	Mean dependent var	6.379059
Adjusted R-squared	0.999145	S.D. dependent var	0.421861
S.E. of regression	0.012333	Akaike info criter	−5.866567
Sum squared resid	0.006084	Schwarz criterion	−5.704368
Log likelihood	133.0645	F-statistic	16757.24
Durbin-Watson stat	1.901081	Prob(F-statistic)	0.000000

Inverted AR Roots	.72	

We have noted that most regression applications designed for time series analysis include the Durbin–Watson statistic as a standard component of the output. In the same way, they usually have a built-in option for fitting models where the disturbance term has an AR(1) specification, making it unnecessary to use a nonlinear equation such as (12.30) to spell out the structure of the model. In the case of EViews, adding AR(1) to the list of regressors converts the specification from OLS to that appropriate for AR(1) autocorrelation. Early regression applications tended to use the Cochrane–Orcutt iterative procedure described in Box 12.1. It effectively enables the nonlinear AR(1) model to be fitted using linear regression analysis, a major benefit when computers were still in their infancy and nonlinear estimation was so time-consuming that it was avoided if possible. Now that nonlinear regression is a standard feature of major regression applications, the Cochrane–Orcutt iterative procedure is mainly of historical interest and most applications designed for time series analysis offer alternative methods.

BOX 12.1   The Cochrane–Orcutt iterative procedure for eliminating AR(1) autocorrelation

---

The starting point for the **Cochrane–Orcutt iterative procedure** is equation (12.24), which may be rewritten

$$\tilde{Y}_t = \beta_1' + \beta_2 \tilde{X}_t + \varepsilon_t$$

where $\tilde{Y}_t = Y_t - \rho Y_{t-1}$, $\tilde{X}_t = X_t - \rho X_{t-1}$, and $\beta_1' = \beta_1(1 - \rho)$. If you knew the value of ρ, all you would have to do would be to calculate $\tilde{Y}_t$ and $\tilde{X}_t$ from the data on Y and X, and perform a simple regression of $\tilde{Y}_t$ on $\tilde{X}_t$. The coefficient of $\tilde{X}_t$ would be a direct estimate of β_2, and the intercept could be used to derive an estimate of β_1. Of course, you do not know ρ and it has to be estimated, along with the other parameters of the model. The Cochrane–Orcutt iterative procedure does this by assuming that if the disturbance term follows an AR(1) process, the residuals will do so as well (approximately), and hence a regression of e_t on e_{t-1} will yield an estimate of ρ. The procedure involves the following steps:

1. Y is regressed on X with the original, untransformed data.
2. The residuals are calculated.
3. e_t is regressed on e_{t-1} to obtain an estimate of ρ.
4. $\tilde{Y}_t$ and $\tilde{X}_t$ are calculated using this estimate of ρ and the equation at the top of the box is fitted. The coefficient of $\tilde{X}_t$ provides a revised estimate of β_2 and the estimate of β_1' yields a revised estimate of β_1.
5. The residuals are recalculated and the process returns to step 3.

The process alternates between revising the estimates of β_1 and β_2, and revising the estimate of ρ, until convergence is obtained, that is, until the estimates at the end of the latest cycle are the same as the estimates at the end of the previous one, to a prespecified number of decimal places.

The output for the logarithmic demand function for housing using the AR(1) short-cut is also shown in Table 12.2. You can see that the regression results are identical to those for the explicit nonlinear specification. Note that the coefficient of AR(1) is the estimate of ρ, and corresponds to C(2) in the previous regression.

Exercise

12.3 Perform a logarithmic regression of expenditure on your commodity on income and relative price, first using OLS and then using the option for AR(1) regression. Compare the coefficients and standard errors of the two regressions and comment.

12.5 Autocorrelation with a lagged dependent variable

Suppose that you have a model in which the dependent variable, lagged one time period, is used as one of the explanatory variables (for example, a partial adjustment model). When this is the case, autocorrelation is likely to cause OLS to yield inconsistent estimates.

For example, suppose the model is of the form

$$Y_t = \beta_1 + \beta_2 X_t + \beta_3 Y_{t-1} + u_t. \tag{12.31}$$

If there were no autocorrelation, OLS would yield consistent estimates. Strictly speaking, the use of the lagged dependent variable will make OLS estimates subject to some element of bias in finite samples, as shown in Section 12.2, but in practice this bias is not considered serious and is ignored. However, if the disturbance term is subject to autocorrelation, the situation is entirely different. We will investigate the case where u_t is subject to AR(1) autocorrelation

$$u_t = \rho u_{t-1} + \varepsilon_t. \tag{12.32}$$

Then the model may be rewritten

$$Y_t = \beta_1 + \beta_2 X_t + \beta_3 Y_{t-1} + \rho u_{t-1} + \varepsilon_t. \tag{12.33}$$

Lagging (12.31) one period, we see that

$$Y_{t-1} = \beta_1 + \beta_2 X_{t-1} + \beta_3 Y_{t-2} + u_{t-1}. \tag{12.34}$$

Hence in (12.33) we have a violation of part (1) of Assumption C.7. One of the explanatory variables, Y_{t-1}, is partly determined by u_{t-1}, which is also a component of the disturbance term. As a consequence, OLS will yield inconsistent estimates. It is not hard to obtain an analytical expression for the large-sample bias, but it is laborious and it will not be attempted here.

Detection of autocorrelation with a lagged dependent variable

As Durbin and Watson noted in their original article, the Durbin–Watson d statistic is invalid when the regression equation includes a lagged dependent variable. It tends to be biased towards 2, increasing the risk of a Type II error. In this case one may use the **Durbin h statistic** (Durbin, 1970), which is also computed from the residuals, to perform a **Durbin h test**. The h statistic is defined as

$$h = \hat{\rho} \sqrt{\frac{n}{1 - ns^2_{b_{Y(-1)}}}} \tag{12.35}$$

where $\hat{\rho}$ is an estimate of ρ in the AR(1) process, $s^2_{b_{Y(-1)}}$ is an estimate of the variance of the coefficient of the lagged dependent variable Y_{t-1}, and n is the number of observations in the regression. Note that n will usually be one less than the number of observations in the sample because the first observation is lost when the equation is fitted. There are various ways in which one might estimate ρ but, since this test is valid only for large samples, it does not matter which you use. The most convenient is to take advantage of the large-sample relationship between d and ρ:

$$d \to 2 - 2\rho. \tag{12.36}$$

From this one estimates ρ as $(1 - \frac{1}{2}d)$. The estimate of the variance of the coefficient of the lagged dependent variable is obtained by squaring its standard error. Thus h can be calculated from the usual regression results. In large samples, h is distributed as $N(0,1)$, that is, as a normal variable with zero mean and unit variance, under the null hypothesis of no autocorrelation. The hypothesis of no autocorrelation can therefore be rejected at the 5 percent significance level if the absolute value of h is greater than 1.96, and at the 1 percent significance level if it is greater than 2.58, using two-sided tests and a large sample.

An occasional problem with this test is that the h statistic cannot be computed if $ns^2_{b_2}$ is greater than 1, which can happen if the sample size is not very large. An even worse problem occurs when $ns^2_{b_2}$ is near to, but less than, 1. In such a situation the h statistic could be enormous, without there being any problem of autocorrelation. For this reason, it is a good idea to keep an eye on the d statistic as well, despite the fact that it is biased.

Example

The partial adjustment model leads to a specification with a lagged dependent variable. That for the logarithmic demand function for housing services was used as an exercise in Chapter 11. The output is reproduced in Table 12.3. The Durbin–Watson statistic is 1.8109. $(1 - \frac{1}{2}d) = 0.0945$ gives us an estimate of ρ. The standard error of the lagged dependent variable is 0.0444. Thus our

BOX 12.2   **Autocorrelation in the partial adjustment and adaptive expectations models**

The partial adjustment model

$$Y_t^* = \beta_1 + \beta_2 X_t + u_t$$

$$Y_t - Y_{t-1} = \lambda(Y_t^* - Y_{t-1}) \quad (0 \le \lambda \le 1)$$

leads to the regression specification

$$Y_t = \beta_1\lambda + \beta_2\lambda X_t + (1-\lambda)Y_{t-1} + \lambda u_t.$$

Hence the disturbance term in the fitted equation is a fixed multiple of that in the first equation and combining the first two equations to eliminate the unobservable Y_t^* will not have introduced any new complication. In particular, it will not have caused the disturbance term to be autocorrelated, if it is not autocorrelated in the first equation. By contrast, in the case of the adaptive expectations model,

$$Y_t = \beta_1 + \beta_2 X_{t+1}^e + u_t$$
$$X_{t+1}^e - X_t^e = \lambda(X_t - X_t^e)$$

the Koyck transformation would cause a problem. The fitted equation is then

$$Y_t = \beta_1\lambda + (1-\lambda)Y_{t-1} + \beta_2\lambda X_t + u_t - (1-\lambda)u_{t-1}$$

and the disturbance term is subject to moving average autocorrelation. We noted that we could not discriminate between the two models on the basis of the variable specification because they employ exactly the same variables. Could we instead use the properties of the disturbance term to discriminate between them? Could we regress Y_t on X_t and Y_{t-1}, test for autocorrelation, and conclude that the dynamics are attributable to a partial adjustment process if we do not find autocorrelation, and to an adaptive expectations process if we do?

Unfortunately, this does not work. If we do find autocorrelation, it could be that the true model is a partial adjustment process, and that the original disturbance term was autocorrelated. Similarly, the absence of autocorrelation does not rule out an adaptive expectations process. Suppose that the disturbance term u_t is subject to AR(1) autocorrelation:

$$u_t = \rho u_{t-1} + \varepsilon_t.$$

Then

$$u_t - (1-\lambda)u_{t-1} = \rho u_{t-1} + \varepsilon_t - (1-\lambda)u_{t-1} = \varepsilon_t - (1-\lambda-\rho)u_{t-1}.$$

Now it is reasonable to suppose that both λ and ρ will lie between 0 and 1, and hence it is possible that their sum might be close to 1. If this is the case, the disturbance term in the fitted model will be approximately equal to ε_t, and the AR(1) autocorrelation will have been neutralized by the Koyck transformation.

Table 12.3

```
Dependent Variable: LGHOUS
Method: Least Squares
Sample(adjusted): 1960 2003
Included observations: 44 after adjusting endpoints
```

Variable	Coefficient	Std. Error	t-Statistic	Prob.
C	0.073957	0.062915	1.175499	0.2467
LGDPI	0.282935	0.046912	6.031246	0.0000
LGPRHOUS	−0.116949	0.027383	−4.270880	0.0001
LGHOUS(−1)	0.707242	0.044405	15.92699	0.0000

R-squared	0.999795	Mean dependent var		6.379059
Adjusted R-squared	0.999780	S.D. dependent var		0.421861
S.E. of regression	0.006257	Akaike info criter		−7.223711
Sum squared resid	0.001566	Schwarz criterion		−7.061512
Log likelihood	162.9216	F-statistic		65141.75
Durbin–Watson stat	1.810958	Prob(F-statistic)		0.000000

estimate of the variance of its coefficient is 0.0020. There are 45 observations in the sample, but the first cannot be used and n is 44. Hence the h statistic is

$$h = 0.0945 \times \sqrt{\frac{44}{1 - 44 \times 0.0020}} = 0.66. \qquad (12.37)$$

This is below 1.96 and so, at the 5 percent significance level, we do not reject the null hypothesis of no autocorrelation (reminding ourselves of course, that this is a large-sample test and we have only 44 observations).

12.6   The common factor test

We now return to the ordinary AR(1) model to investigate it a little further. The nonlinear equation

$$Y_t = \beta_1(1 - \rho) + \rho Y_{t-1} + \beta_2 X_t - \beta_2 \rho X_{t-1} + \varepsilon_t, \qquad (12.38)$$

fitted on the hypothesis that the disturbance term is subject to AR(1) autocorrelation, is a restricted version of the more general ADL(1,1) model (autoregressive distributed lag, the first argument referring to the maximum lag in the Y variable and the second to the maximum lag in the X variable(s))

$$Y_t = \lambda_1 + \lambda_2 Y_{t-1} + \lambda_3 X_t + \lambda_4 X_{t-1} + \varepsilon_t, \qquad (12.39)$$

with the restriction

$$\lambda_4 = -\lambda_2\lambda_3. \tag{12.40}$$

The presence of this implicit restriction provides us with an opportunity to perform a test of the validity of the model specification known as the **common factor test**. The test helps us to discriminate between cases where the d statistic is low because the disturbance term is genuinely subject to an AR(1) process and cases where it is low for other reasons. The theory behind the test procedure will not be presented here (for a summary, see Hendry and Mizon, 1978), but you should note that the usual F test of a restriction is not appropriate because the restriction is nonlinear. Instead we calculate the statistic

$$n\log(RSS_R/RSS_U) \tag{12.41}$$

where n is the number of observations in the regression, RSS_R and RSS_U are the residual sums of squares from the restricted model (12.38) and the unrestricted model (12.39), and the logarithm is to base e. Remember that n will usually be one less than the number of observations in the sample because the first observation is lost when (12.38) and (12.39) are fitted. Strictly speaking, this is a large sample test. If the original model has only one explanatory variable, as in this case, the test statistic has a chi-squared distribution with one degree of freedom under the null hypothesis that the restriction is valid. As we saw in the previous section, if we had started with the more general model

$$Y_t = \beta_1 + \beta_2 X_{2t} + \cdots + \beta_k X_{kt} + u_t, \tag{12.42}$$

the restricted model would have been

$$Y_t = \beta_1(1-\rho) + \rho Y_{t-1} + \beta_2 X_{2t} - \beta_2\rho X_{2,t-1} + \cdots + \beta_k X_{kt} - \beta_k\rho X_{k,t-1} + \varepsilon_t. \tag{12.43}$$

There are now $k-1$ restrictions because the model imposes the restriction that the coefficient of the lagged value of each explanatory variable is equal to minus the coefficient of its current value multiplied by the coefficient of the lagged dependent variable Y_{t-1}. Under the null hypothesis that the restrictions are valid, the test statistic has a chi-squared distribution with $k-1$ degrees of freedom.

If the null hypothesis is not rejected, we conclude that the AR(1) model is an adequate specification of the data. If it is rejected, we have to work with the unrestricted ADL(1,1) model

$$Y_t = \lambda_1 + \lambda_2 Y_{t-1} + \lambda_3 X_{2t} + \lambda_4 X_{2,t-1} + \cdots + \lambda_{2k-1} X_{kt} + \lambda_{2k} X_{k,t-1} + \varepsilon_t,$$

$$(12.44)$$

including the lagged value of Y and the lagged values of all the explanatory variables as regressors. The problem of multicollinearity will often be encountered when fitting the unrestricted model, especially if there are several explanatory variables. Sometimes it can be alleviated by dropping those variables that do not have significant coefficients, but precisely because multicollinearity causes t statistics to be low, there is a risk that you will end up dropping variables that do genuinely belong in the model.

Two further points. First, if the null hypothesis is not rejected, the coefficient of Y_{t-1} may be interpreted as an estimate of ρ. If it is rejected, the whole of the AR(1) story is abandoned and the coefficient of Y_{t-1} in the unrestricted version does not have any special interpretation. Second, when fitting the restricted version using the specification appropriate for AR(1) autocorrelation, the coefficients of the lagged explanatory variables are not reported. If for some reason you need them, you could calculate them easily yourself, as minus the product of the coefficient of Y_{t-1} and the coefficients of the corresponding current explanatory variables. The fact that the lagged variables, other than Y_{t-1}, do not appear explicitly in the regression output does not mean that they have not been included. They have.

Example

The output for the AR(1) regression for housing services has been shown in Table 12.2. The residual sum of squares was 0.006084. The unrestricted version of the model yields the output shown in Table 12.4.

Before we perform the common factor test, we should check that the unrestricted model is free from autocorrelation. Otherwise neither it nor the AR(1) model would be satisfactory specifications. The h statistic is given by

$$h = 0.1182 \times \sqrt{\frac{44}{1 - 44 \times 0.0034}} = 0.85. \qquad (12.45)$$

This is below 1.96 and so we do not reject the null hypothesis of no autocorrelation.

Next we will check whether the coefficients appear to satisfy the restrictions implicit in the AR(1) model. Minus the product of the lagged dependent variable and the income elasticity is $-0.7259 \times 0.2755 = -0.20$. The coefficient of lagged

Table 12.4

```
Dependent Variable: LGHOUS
Method: Least Squares
Sample(adjusted): 1960 2003
Included observations: 44 after adjusting endpoints
```

Variable	Coefficient	Std. Error	t-Statistic	Prob.
C	0.041458	0.065137	0.636465	0.5283
LGDPI	0.275527	0.067914	4.056970	0.0002
LGPRHOUS	−0.229086	0.075499	−.034269	0.0043
LGHOUS(−1)	0.725893	0.058485	12.41159	0.0000
LGDPI(−1)	−0.010625	0.086737	−0.122502	0.9031
LGPRHOUS(−1)	0.126270	0.084296	1.497928	0.1424

R-squared	0.999810	Mean dependent var		6.379059
Adjusted R-squared	0.999785	S.D. dependent var		0.421861
S.E. of regression	0.006189	Akaike info criter		−7.205830
Sum squared resid	0.001456	Schwarz criterion		−6.962531
Log likelihood	164.5282	F-statistic		39944.40
Durbin–Watson stat	1.763676	Prob(F-statistic)		0.000000

income is numerically much lower than this. Minus the product of the lagged dependent variable and the price elasticity is $-0.7259 \times -0.2291 = 0.17$, which is a little higher than the coefficient of lagged price. Hence the restriction for the price side of the model appears to be nearly satisfied, but that for the income side does not.

The common factor test confirms this preliminary observation. The residual sum of squares has fallen to 0.001456. The test statistic is $44 \times \log(0.006084/0.001456) = 62.92$. The critical value of chi-squared at the 0.1 percent level with two degrees of freedom is 13.82, so we reject the restrictions implicit in the AR(1) model and conclude that we should use the unrestricted ADL(1,1) model instead.

We note that the lagged income and price variables in the unrestricted model do not have significant coefficients, so we consider dropping them. If we are going to drop both of them, we have to satisfy ourselves that their joint explanatory power is not significant. *RSS* for the regression omitting them is 0.001566. The *F* statistic for the null hypothesis that both their coefficients are zero is

$$F(2,38) = \frac{(0.001566 - 0.001456)/2}{0.001456/38} = 1.44. \qquad (12.46)$$

The critical value of $F(2,38)$ at the 5 percent level is 3.24. Hence we conclude that we can drop the variables and we arrive at the partial adjustment model specification already considered above. As we saw, the *h* statistic is 0.66, and we conclude that this may be a satisfactory specification.

Exercises

12.4 A researcher has annual data on aggregate consumer expenditure on financial intermediaries, F_t, aggregate disposable personal income, X_t, and the relative price index for consumer expenditure on financial intermediaries, P_t, for the United States for the period 1959–2003 and fits the following logarithmic regressions (standard errors in parentheses; method of estimation as indicated):

	1: OLS	2: AR(1)	3: OLS	4: OLS
X	1.56	1.51	0.04	0.42
	(0.04)	(0.08)	(0.60)	(0.17)
P	−0.26	0.07	0.03	−0.10
	(0.21)	(0.21)	(0.20)	(0.15)
$F(-1)$	–	–	0.70	0.73
			(0.11)	(0.11)
$X(-1)$	–	–	0.43	–
			(0.61)	
$P(-1)$	–	–	−0.22	–
			(0.20)	
constant	−7.40	−8.53	−1.68	−1.80
	(0.77)	(1.04)	(1.02)	(1.01)
$\hat{\rho}$	–	0.70	–	–
		(0.11)		
R^2	0.984	0.991	0.993	0.992
RSS	0.317	0.164	0.138	0.144
d	0.65	1.87	1.68	1.78

Explain the relationship between the second and third specifications, perform a common factor test, and discuss the adequacy of each specification.

12.5 Perform a logarithmic regression of expenditure on your category of consumer expenditure on income and price using an AR(1) estimation technique. Perform a second regression with the same variables but adding the lagged variables as regressors and using OLS. With an h test, check that the second specification is not subject to autocorrelation.

Explain why the first regression is a restricted version of the second, stating the restrictions, and check whether the restrictions appear to be satisfied by the estimates of the coefficients of the second regression. Perform a common factor test. If the AR(1) model is rejected, and there are terms with insignificant coefficients in the second regression, investigate the consequences of dropping them.

12.6*

Year	Y	K	L	Year	Y	K	L
1899	100	100	100	1911	153	216	145
1900	101	107	105	1912	177	226	152

Table (*Continued*)

Year	Y	K	L	Year	Y	K	L
1901	112	114	110	1913	184	236	154
1902	122	122	118	1914	169	244	149
1903	124	131	123	1915	189	266	154
1904	122	138	116	1916	225	298	182
1905	143	149	125	1917	227	335	196
1906	152	163	133	1918	223	366	200
1907	151	176	138	1919	218	387	193
1908	126	185	121	1920	231	407	193
1909	155	198	140	1921	179	417	147
1910	159	208	144	1922	240	431	161

Source: Cobb and Douglas (1928)

The table gives the data used by Cobb and Douglas (1928) to fit the original Cobb–Douglas production function:

$$Y_t = \beta_1 K_t^{\beta_2} L_t^{\beta_3} v_t$$

Y_t, K_t, and L_t being index number series for real output, real capital input, and real labor input, respectively, for the manufacturing sector of the United States for the period 1899–1922 (1899 = 100). The model was linearized by taking logarithms of both sides and the following regressions were run (standard errors in parentheses; method of estimation as indicated):

	1: OLS	2: AR(1)	3: OLS
log K	0.23	0.22	0.18
	(0.06)	(0.07)	(0.56)
log L	0.81	0.86	1.03
	(0.15)	(0.16)	(0.15)
log Y(−1)	−	−	0.40
			(0.21)
log K(−1)	−	−	0.17
			(0.51)
log L(−1)	−	−	−1.01
			(0.25)
constant	−0.18	−0.35	1.04
	(0.43)	(0.51)	(0.41)
$\hat{\rho}$	−	0.19	−
		(0.25)	
R^2	0.96	0.96	0.98
RSS	0.0710	0.0697	0.0259
d	1.52	1.54	1.46

Evaluate the three regression specifications.

12.7 **Apparent autocorrelation**

As has been seen above, a positive correlation among the residuals from a regression, and a correspondingly low Durbin–Watson statistic, may be attributable to the omission of one or more lagged variables from the model specification, rather than to an autocorrelated disturbance term. We will describe this as **apparent autocorrelation**. Although the examples above relate to the omission of lagged variables, it could arise from the omission of any important variable from the regression specification.

Apparent autocorrelation can also arise from functional misspecification. For example, we saw in Section 4.1 that, if the true model is of the form

$$Y = \beta_1 + \frac{\beta_2}{X} + u \qquad (12.47)$$

and we execute a linear regression, we obtain the fit illustrated in Figure 4.1 and summarized in Table 4.2: a negative residual in the first observation, positive residuals in the next six, and negative residuals in the last three. In other words, there appears to be very strong positive autocorrelation. However, when the regression is of the form

$$\hat{Y} = b_1 + b_2 X' \qquad (12.48)$$

where X' is defined as $1/X$, not only does one obtain a much better fit but the autocorrelation disappears.

The most straightforward way of detecting autocorrelation caused by functional misspecification is to look at the residuals directly. This may give you some idea of the correct specification. The Durbin–Watson d statistic may also provide a signal, although of course a test based on it would be invalid since the disturbance term is not AR(1) and the use of an AR(1) specification would be inappropriate. In the case of the example just described, the Durbin–Watson statistic was 0.86, indicating that something was wrong with the specification.

Exercises

12.7* Using the 50 observations on two variables Y and X shown in the diagram, an investigator runs the following five regressions (standard errors in parentheses; estimation method as indicated; all variables as logarithms in the logarithmic regressions):

	1	2	3	4	5
	linear		logarithmic		
	OLS	AR(1)	OLS	AR(1)	OLS
X	0.178	0.223	2.468	2.471	1.280
	(0.008)	(0.027)	(0.029)	(0.033)	(0.800)
$Y(-1)$	–	–	–	–	0.092
					(0.145)
$X(-1)$	–	–	–	–	0.966
					(0.865)
$\hat{\rho}$	–	0.87	–	0.08	–
		(0.06)		(0.14)	
constant	−24.4	−39.7	−11.3	−11.4	−10.3
	(2.9)	(12.1)	(0.2)	(0.2)	(1.7)
R^2	0.903	0.970	0.993	0.993	0.993
RSS	6286	1932	1.084	1.070	1.020
d	0.35	3.03	1.82	2.04	2.08

Discuss each of the five regressions, stating, with reasons, which is your preferred specification.

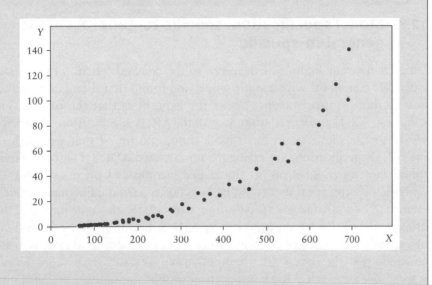

12.8*Using the data on food in the Demand Functions data set, the following regressions were run, each with the logarithm of food as the dependent variable: (1) an OLS regression on a time trend T defined to be 1 in 1959, 2 in 1960, etc.; (2) an AR(1) regression using the same specification; and (3) an OLS regression on T and the logarithm of food lagged one time period, with the results shown in the table (standard errors in parentheses):

	1: OLS	2: AR(1)	3: OLS
T	0.0168	0.0161	0.0019
	(0.0004)	(0.0015)	(0.0012)
$LGFOOD(-1)$	–	–	0.8797
			(0.0691)
constant	5.6356	5.6665	0.6960
	(0.0102)	(0.0537)	(0.3881)
$\hat{\rho}$	–	0.8797	–
		(0.0691)	
R^2	0.9776	0.9953	0.9953
RSS	0.0490	0.0095	0.0095
d	0.2103	1.1928	1.1928
h	–	–	3.01

Discuss why each regression specification appears to be unsatisfactory. Explain why it was not possible to perform a common factor test.

12.8   Model specification: specific-to-general versus general-to-specific

Let us review our findings with regard to the demand function for housing services. We started off with a static model and found that it had an unacceptably low Durbin–Watson statistic. Under the hypothesis that the relationship was subject to AR(1) autocorrelation, we ran the AR(1) specification. We then tested the restrictions implicit in this specification, and found that we had to reject the AR(1) specification, preferring the unrestricted ADL(1,1) model. Finally we found that we could drop off the lagged income and price variables, ending up with a specification that could be based on a partial adjustment model. This seemed to be a satisfactory specification, particularly given the nature of the type of expenditure, for we do expect there to be substantial inertia in the response of expenditure on housing services to changes in income and relative price. We conclude that the reason for the low Durbin–Watson statistic in the original static model was not AR(1) autocorrelation but the omission of an important regressor (the lagged dependent variable).

The research strategy that has implicitly been adopted can be summarized as follows:

1. On the basis of economic theory, experience, and intuition, formulate a provisional model.

2. Locate suitable data and fit the model.

3. Perform diagnostic checks.

4. If any of the checks reveal inadequacies, revise the specification of the model with the aim of eliminating them.

5. When the specification appears satisfactory, congratulate oneself on having completed the task and quit.

The danger with this strategy is that the reason that the final version of the model appears satisfactory is that you have massaged its specification to fit your particular data set, not that it really corresponds to the true model. The econometric literature is full of two types of indirect evidence that this happens frequently, particularly with models employing time series data, and particularly with models of macroeconomic relationships. It often happens that researchers investigating the same phenomenon with access to the same sources of data construct internally consistent but mutually incompatible models, and it often happens that models that survive sample period diagnostic checks exhibit miserable predictive performance. The literature on models of the determinants of aggregate investment is especially notorious in both respects. Further evidence, if any were needed, has been provided by experiments showing that it is not hard to set up nonsense models that survive the conventional checks (Peach and Webb, 1983). As a consequence, there is growing recognition of the fact that the tests eliminate only those models with the grossest misspecifications, and the survival of a model is no guarantee of its validity.

This is true even of the tests of predictive performance described in Chapter 11, where the models are subjected to an evaluation of their ability to fit fresh data. There are two problems with these tests. First, their power may be rather low. It is quite possible that a misspecified model will fit the prediction period observations well enough for the null hypothesis of model stability not to be rejected, especially if the prediction period is short. Lengthening the prediction period by shortening the sample period might help, but again there is a problem, particularly if the sample is not large. By shortening the sample period, you will increase the population variances of the estimates of the coefficients, so it will be more difficult to determine whether the prediction period relationship is significantly different from the sample period relationship.

The other problem with tests of predictive stability is the question of what the investigator does if the test is failed. Understandably, it is unusual for an investigator to quit at that point, acknowledging defeat. The natural course of action is to continue tinkering with the model until this test too is passed, but of course the test then has no more integrity than the sample period diagnostic checks.

This unsatisfactory state of affairs has generated interest in two interrelated topics: the possibility of eliminating some of the competing models by confronting them with each other, and the possibility of establishing a more systematic research strategy that might eliminate bad model-building in the first place.

Comparison of alternative models

The comparison of alternative models can involve much technical complexity and the present discussion will be limited to a very brief and partial outline of some of the issues involved. We will begin by making a distinction between nested and non-nested models. A model is said to be nested inside another if it can be obtained from it by imposing a number of restrictions. Two models are said to be non-nested if neither can be represented as a restricted version of the other. The restrictions may relate to any aspect of the specification of the model, but the present discussion will be limited to restrictions on the parameters of the explanatory variables in a single equation model. It will be illustrated with reference to the demand function for housing services, with the logarithm of expenditure written Y and the logarithms of the income and relative price variables written X_2 and X_3.

Three alternative dynamic specifications have been considered: the ADL(1,1) model including current and lagged values of all the variables and no parameter restrictions, which will be denoted A; the model that hypothesized that the disturbance term was subject to an AR(1) process (B); and the model with only one lagged variable, the lagged dependent variable (C). For good measure we will add the original static model (D).

$$\text{(A)} \quad Y_t = \lambda_1 + \lambda_2 Y_{t-1} + \lambda_3 X_{2t} + \lambda_4 X_{2,t-1} + \lambda_5 X_{3t} + \lambda_6 X_{3,t-1} + \varepsilon_t, \tag{12.49}$$

$$\text{(B)} \quad Y_t = \lambda_1(1 - \lambda_2) + \lambda_2 Y_{t-1} + \lambda_3 X_{2t} - \lambda_2 \lambda_3 X_{2,t-1} + \lambda_5 X_{3t}$$
$$- \lambda_2 \lambda_5 X_{3,t-1} + \varepsilon_t, \tag{12.50}$$

$$\text{(C)} \quad Y_t = \lambda_1 + \lambda_2 Y_{t-1} + \lambda_3 X_{2t} + \lambda_5 X_{3t} + \varepsilon_t, \tag{12.51}$$

$$\text{(D)} \quad Y_t = \lambda_1 + \lambda_3 X_{2t} + \lambda_5 X_{3t} + \varepsilon_t. \tag{12.52}$$

The ADL(1,1) model is the most general specification and the others are nested within it. For B to be a legitimate simplification, the common factor test should not lead to a rejection of the restrictions. For C to be a legitimate simplification, $H_0: \lambda_4 = \lambda_6 = 0$ should not be rejected. For D to be a legitimate simplification, $H_0: \lambda_2 = \lambda_4 = \lambda_6 = 0$ should not be rejected. The nesting structure is represented by Figure 12.6.

In the case of the demand function for housing, if we compare B with A, we find that the common factor restrictions implicit in B are rejected and so it is struck off our list of acceptable specifications. If we compare C with A, we find that it is a valid alternative because the estimated coefficients of lagged income and price variables are not significantly different from zero, either individually (via t tests on their coefficients) or jointly (via an F test of their joint explanatory

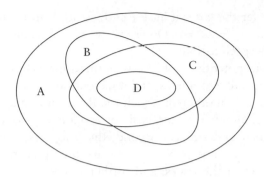

Figure 12.6 Nesting structure for specifications A, B, C, and D

power). Finally, D must be rejected because the restriction that the coefficient of Y_{t-1} is zero is rejected by a simple t test. (In the whole of this discussion, we have assumed that the test procedures are not substantially affected by the use of a lagged dependent variable as an explanatory variable. This is strictly true only if the sample is large.)

The example illustrates the potential both for success and for failure within a nested structure: success in that two of the four specifications are eliminated and failure in that some indeterminacy remains. Is there any reason for preferring A to C or vice versa? Some would argue that C should be preferred because it is more parsimonious in terms of parameters, requiring only four instead of six. It also has the advantage of lending itself to the intuitively appealing interpretation involving short-run and long-run dynamics discussed in Chapter 11. However, the efficiency/potential bias trade-off between including and excluding variables with insignificant coefficients discussed in Chapter 6 makes the answer unclear.

What should you do if the rival specifications are not nested? One possible procedure is to create a union specification embracing the two rivals as restricted versions and to see if any progress can be made by testing each against the union. For example, suppose that the rival specifications are

(E) $Y = \lambda_1 + \lambda_2 X_2 + \lambda_3 X_3 + \varepsilon_t,$ \hfill (12.53)

(F) $Y = \lambda_1 + \lambda_2 X_2 + \lambda_4 X_4 + \varepsilon_t.$ \hfill (12.54)

Then the union specification would be

(G) $Y = \lambda_1 + \lambda_2 X_2 + \lambda_3 X_3 + \lambda_4 X_4 + \varepsilon_t.$ \hfill (12.55)

We would then fit G, with the following possible outcomes: the estimate of λ_3 is significant, but that of λ_4 is not, so we would choose E; the estimate of λ_3 is not significant, but that of λ_4 is significant, so we would choose F; the estimates of both λ_3 and λ_4 are significant (a surprise outcome), in which case we would choose G; neither estimate is significant, in which case we could test G against the simple specification

(H) $Y = \lambda_1 + \lambda_2 X_2 + \varepsilon_t,$ \hfill (12.56)

and we might prefer the latter if an F test does not lead to the rejection of the null hypothesis H_0: $\lambda_3 = \lambda_4 = 0$. Otherwise we would be unable to discriminate between the three specifications.

There are various potential problems with this approach. First, the tests use G as the basis for the null hypotheses, and it may not be intuitively appealing. If E and F are constructed on different principles, their union may be so implausible that it could be eliminated on the basis of economic theory. The framework for the tests is then undermined. Second, the last possibility, indeterminacy, is likely to be the outcome if X_3 and X_4 are highly correlated. For a more extended discussion of the issues, and further references, see Kmenta (1986), pp. 595–598.

The general-to-specific approach to model specification

We have seen that, if we start with a simple model and elaborate it in response to diagnostic checks, there is a risk that we will end up with a false model that satisfies us because, by successive adjustments, we have made it appear to fit the sample period data, 'appear to fit' because the diagnostic tests are likely to be invalid if the model specification is incorrect. Would it not be better, as some writers urge, to adopt the opposite approach. Instead of attempting to develop a specific initial model into a more general one, using what has been described as the **specific-to-general approach** to model specification, should we not instead start with a fully general model and reduce it to a more focused one by successively imposing restrictions (after testing their validity)?

Of course the **general-to-specific approach** is preferable, at least in principle. The problem is that, in its pure form, it is often impracticable. If the sample size is limited, and the initial specification contains a large number of potential explanatory variables, multicollinearity may cause most or even all of them to have insignificant coefficients. This is especially likely to be a problem in time series models. In an extreme case, the number of variables may exceed the number of observations, and the model could not be fitted at all. Where the model may be fitted, the lack of significance of many of the coefficients may appear to give the investigator considerable freedom to choose which variables to drop. However, the final version of the model may be highly sensitive to this initial arbitrary decision. A variable that has an insignificant coefficient initially and is dropped might have had a significant coefficient in a cut-down version of the model, had it been retained. The conscientious application of the general-to-specific principle, if applied systematically, might require the exploration of an unmanageable number of possible model-reduction paths. Even if the number were small enough to be explored, the investigator may well be left with a large number of rival models, none of which is dominated by the others.

Therefore, some degree of compromise is normally essential, and of course there are no rules for this, any more than there are for the initial conception of a model in the first place. A weaker but more operational version of the approach is to guard against formulating an initial specification that imposes restrictions that might be rejected. However, it is probably fair to say that the ability to do this is one measure of the experience of an investigator, in which case the approach amounts to little more than an exhortation to be experienced. For a nontechnical discussion of the approach, replete with entertainingly caustic remarks about the shortcomings of specific-to-general model-building and an illustrative example by a leading advocate of the general-to-specific approach, see Hendry (1979).

Key terms

apparent autocorrelation	Durbin–Watson test
autocorrelation	general-to-specific approach
autoregressive autocorrelation	moving average autocorrelation
Cochrane–Orcutt iterative procedure	negative autocorrelation
common factor test	positive autocorrelation
Durbin h statistic	serial correlation
Durbin h test	specific-to-general approach
Durbin–Watson d statistic	

Exercises

12.9 A researcher is considering the following alternative regression models:

$$Y_t = \beta_1 + \beta_2 Y_{t-1} + \beta_3 X_t + \beta_4 X_{t-1} + u_t \tag{1}$$

$$\Delta Y_t = \gamma_1 + \gamma_2 \Delta X_t + v_t \tag{2}$$

$$Y_t = \delta_1 + \delta_2 X_t + w_t \tag{3}$$

where $\Delta Y_t = Y_t - Y_{t-1}, \Delta X_t = X_t - X_{t-1}$, and u_t, v_t, and w_t are disturbance terms.

(a) Show that models (2) and (3) are restricted versions of model (1), stating the restrictions.

(b) Explain the implications for the disturbance terms in (1) and (2) if (3) is the correct specification and w_t satisfies the regression model assumptions. What problems, if any, would be encountered if ordinary least squares were used to fit (1) and (2)?

12.10 Explain how your answer to Exercise 12.9 illustrates some of the methodological issues discussed in this section.

Appendix 12.1: Demonstration that the Durbin–Watson statistic approximates $2 - 2\rho$ in large samples

$$d = \frac{\sum_{t=2}^{T} (e_t - e_{t-1})^2}{\sum_{t=1}^{T} e_t^2} = \frac{\sum_{t=2}^{T} \left(e_t^2 - 2e_t e_{t-1} + e_{t-1}^2 \right)}{\sum_{t=1}^{T} e_t^2}$$

$$= \frac{\sum_{t=2}^{T} e_t^2}{\sum_{t=1}^{T} e_t^2} + \frac{\sum_{t=2}^{T} e_{t-1}^2}{\sum_{t=1}^{T} e_t^2} - 2\frac{\sum_{t=2}^{T} e_t e_{t-1}}{\sum_{t=1}^{T} e_t^2} \rightarrow 2 - 2\frac{\sum_{t=2}^{T} e_t e_{t-1}}{\sum_{t=1}^{T} e_t^2}$$

as the sample size becomes large because both $\dfrac{\sum_{t=2}^{T} e_t^2}{\sum_{t=1}^{T} e_t^2}$ and $\dfrac{\sum_{t=2}^{T} e_{t-1}^2}{\sum_{t=1}^{T} e_t^2}$ tend to 1.

Since $\dfrac{\sum_{t=2}^{T} e_t e_{t-1}}{\sum_{t=1}^{T} e_t^2}$ is an estimator of ρ, d tends to $2 - 2\rho$.

Introduction to Nonstationary Time Series

The purpose of this chapter is to provide a brief overview of the problems associated with the application of regression analysis to nonstationary time series. The chapter begins with an explanation of the concepts of stationarity and nonstationarity and a discussion of the consequences of nonstationarity for regression analysis. It continues with a description of methods of discriminating between stationary and nonstationary time series, and concludes with an outline of appropriate regression procedures. It should be stressed that the intention is to present these topics at a level appropriate to an introductory econometrics course and to demonstrate that more advanced study is required by those planning to work with time series data.

13.1 Stationarity and nonstationarity

Univariate time series

Much recent work on forecasting has focused on the fitting of univariate (single variable) processes of the type

$$X_t = \beta_1 + \beta_2 X_{t-1} + \cdots + \beta_{p+1} X_{t-p} + \varepsilon_t + \alpha_2 \varepsilon_{t-1} + \cdots + \alpha_{q+1} \varepsilon_{t-q} \quad (13.1)$$

where the variable is written as a linear function of previous values of itself and the error term. In this case the model is said to be an **ARMA**(p, q) **time series** because it is autoregressive of order p and the error term follows a moving average process of order q. From the point of view of a conventional econometrician, a time series model of this type appears primitive because it does not include any explanatory variables, other than lagged values of X itself. On the other hand, precisely because it is so simple, it allows one to focus on the representation of the dynamics of the process. The time series approach became established when it was shown that forecasts made with it were generally superior to those based on conventional econometric models (Box and Jenkins, 1970). We are not concerned with forecasting here, but time series analysis is useful for understanding the limitations of the classical regression model.

Stationary time series

We will begin by defining **stationarity** and **nonstationarity**. A time series X_t is said to be weakly stationary (the only type of stationarity to be considered here) if its expected value and population variance are independent of time and if the population covariance between its values at time t and $t + s$ depends on s but not on time. An example of a stationary time series is an AR(1) process

$$X_t = \beta_2 X_{t-1} + \varepsilon_t \tag{13.2}$$

with $-1 < \beta_2 < 1$, where ε_t is white noise (an innovation with zero mean and constant variance, not subject to autocorrelation). The stationarity of the series can easily be demonstrated. If equation (13.2) is valid for time period t, it is also valid for time period $t - 1$:

$$X_{t-1} = \beta_2 X_{t-2} + \varepsilon_{t-1}. \tag{13.3}$$

Substituting for X_{t-1} in equation (13.2), one has

$$X_t = \beta_2^2 X_{t-2} + \beta_2 \varepsilon_{t-1} + \varepsilon_t. \tag{13.4}$$

Continuing this process of lagging and substituting, one has

$$X_t = \beta_2^t X_0 + \beta_2^{t-1} \varepsilon_1 + \cdots + \beta_2 \varepsilon_{t-1} + \varepsilon_t. \tag{13.5}$$

The expected value of X_t is then given by

$$E(X_t) = \beta_2^t X_0 + \beta_2^{t-1} E(\varepsilon_1) + \cdots + \beta_2 E(\varepsilon_{t-1}) + E(\varepsilon_t). \tag{13.6}$$

For t large enough, $\beta_2^t X_0$ tends to zero. Each of the expectations is zero, so the expected value of X_t is zero and thus independent of t. (Strictly speaking, the term $\beta_2^t X_0$ causes the series to be only asymptotically stationary because it is a function of t. See Exercise 13.2 for a variation that is stationary for finite samples.)

The variance of X_t is given by the variance of $\beta_2^{t-1} \varepsilon_1 + \cdots + \beta_2 \varepsilon_{t-1} + \varepsilon_t$ since it is unaffected by the additive constant $\beta_2^t X_0$. Since ε_t is not autocorrelated, $\text{cov}(\varepsilon_t, \varepsilon_s) = 0$ $(t \neq s)$ and the variance of X_t is given by

$$\sigma_{X_t}^2 = \beta_2^{2t-2} \sigma_\varepsilon^2 + \cdots + \beta_2^2 \sigma_\varepsilon^2 + \sigma_\varepsilon^2$$

$$= \frac{1 - \beta_2^{2t}}{1 - \beta_2^2} \sigma_\varepsilon^2. \tag{13.7}$$

Since the term β_2^{2t} tends to zero as t becomes large, the variance is asymptotically independent of t, and so the second condition for stationarity is asymptotically satisfied. (Again, see Exercise 13.2 for a variation that is stationary in finite samples.)

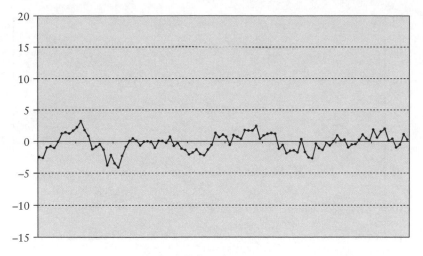

Figure 13.1 A stationary process

Similarly, it can be shown that the covariance of X_t and X_s, $t > s$, is equal to $\beta_2^{t-s}\sigma_\varepsilon^2/(1 - \beta_2^2)$. This depends on the difference between t and s but is independent of t itself. Figure 13.1 provides an example of this type of stationary process with $\beta_2 = 0.7$.

A slightly more general version of the autoregressive process is

$$X_t = \beta_1 + \beta_2 X_{t-1} + \varepsilon_t \tag{13.8}$$

where β_1 is a constant. By lagging and substituting as before, one obtains

$$X_t = \beta_2^t X_0 + (\beta_2^{t-1} + \cdots + \beta_2^2 + \beta_2 + 1)\beta_1 + \beta_2^{t-1}\varepsilon_1 + \cdots + \beta_2\varepsilon_{t-1} + \varepsilon_t. \tag{13.9}$$

Provided that β_2 is less than 1, the series remains (asymptotically) stationary, with expected value $\beta_1/(1 - \beta_2)$. The population variance of X_t and the population covariance of X_t and X_s are unaffected by the inclusion of β_1.

Nonstationary time series

In the previous examples, the condition $-1 < \beta_2 < 1$ was crucial for stationarity. If β_2 is equal to 1, the original series becomes

$$X_t = X_{t-1} + \varepsilon_t. \tag{13.10}$$

This is an example of a nonstationary process known as a **random walk**. If it starts at X_0 at time 0, its value at time t is given by

$$X_t = X_0 + \varepsilon_1 + \cdots + \varepsilon_t. \tag{13.11}$$

The key difference between this process and the corresponding AR(1) process (13.5) is that the contribution of each innovation, or shock, as it is sometimes

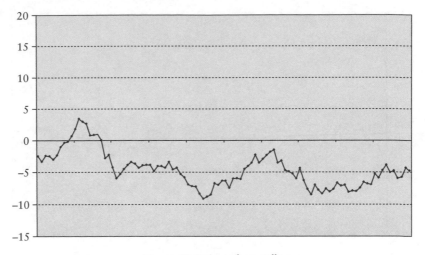

Figure 13.2 A random walk

described in this context, is permanently built into the time series. Because the series incorporates the sum of the shocks, it is said to be **integrated**. By contrast, when $\beta_2 < 1$, as in (13.5), the contribution of each shock to the series is exponentially attenuated and eventually becomes negligible.

In the case of a random walk, the expected value and population variance of X_t do not have unconditional meanings. If the expectations are taken at time 0, the expected value at any future time t is independent of t (it is always equal to X_0); but its variance is given by

$$\sigma_{X_t}^2 = \sigma_\varepsilon^2 + \cdots + \sigma_\varepsilon^2$$
$$= t\sigma_\varepsilon^2 \tag{13.12}$$

and so increases with time. Figure 13.2 provides an example of a random walk.

In the more general version of the autoregressive process with the constant β_1, the process becomes what is known as a **random walk with drift**, if β_2 equals 1:

$$X_t = \beta_1 + X_{t-1} + \varepsilon_t. \tag{13.13}$$

If the series starts at X_0 at time 0, X_t is given by

$$X_t = X_0 + \beta_1 t + \varepsilon_1 + \cdots + \varepsilon_t. \tag{13.14}$$

Now the expectation of X_t at time 0, $(X_0 + \beta_1 t)$, is also a function of t. Figure 13.3 provides an example of a random walk with drift.

Random walks are not the only type of nonstationary process. Another common example of a nonstationary time series is one possessing a time trend:

$$X_t = \beta_1 + \beta_2 t + \varepsilon_t. \tag{13.15}$$

This type of trend is sometimes described as a **deterministic trend**, to differentiate it from the trend found in a model of a random walk with drift. The expected

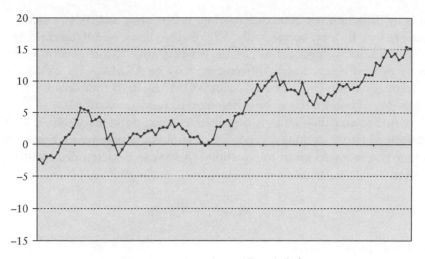

Figure 13.3 A random walk with drift

value of X_t at time t, $(\beta_1 + \beta_2 t)$, is not independent of t and so X_t is nonstationary. The population variance of X_t is not defined.

The key difference between a deterministic trend and a random walk with drift is that in the former, the series must keep coming back to the trend line. In any given observation, X_t will be displaced from the trend line by an amount ε_t, but apart from this transitory effect it must adhere to the trend line. By contrast, in a random walk with drift, the displacement from the underlying trend line at time t is the random walk $\sum \varepsilon_t$, plus the displacement at time 0. Since the displacement is a random walk, there is no reason why X_t should ever return to its trend line.

Difference-stationarity and trend-stationarity

In the discussion that follows, a distinction will be made between **difference-stationarity** and **trend-stationarity**. If a nonstationary process can be transformed into a stationary one by differencing, it is said to be difference-stationary. A random walk, with or without drift, is an example. If X_t is a random walk with drift, as in equation (13.13),

$$\Delta X_t = (X_t - X_{t-1}) = \beta_1 + \varepsilon_t. \qquad (13.16)$$

This is a stationary process with population mean β_1 and variance σ_ε^2, both independent of time. If a nonstationary time series can be transformed into a stationary process by differencing once, as in this case, it is described as integrated of order 1, or I(1). If a time series can be made stationary by differencing twice, it is known as I(2), and so on. To complete the picture, a stationary process, which by definition needs no differencing, is described as I(0). In practice most series are I(0), I(1), or, occasionally, I(2) (Box, Jenkins, and Reinsel, 1994).

The stochastic component in (13.16) is white noise. More generally, the stationary process reached after differencing may be ARMA(p, q), in which case the original series is characterized as an **ARIMA(p, d, q) time series**, where d is the number of times it has to be differenced to render it stationary.

A nonstationary time series is described as being trend-stationary if it can be transformed into a stationary process by extracting a time trend. For example, the very simple model given by equation (13.15) can be detrended by fitting the equation

$$\hat{X}_t = b_1 + b_2 t \tag{13.17}$$

and defining a new variable

$$\tilde{X}_t = X_t - \hat{X}_t = X_t - b_1 - b_2 t. \tag{13.18}$$

The new, detrended, variable is of course just the residuals from the regression of X on t.

The distinction between difference-stationarity and trend-stationarity is important for the analysis of time series. At one time it was conventional to assume that time series could be decomposed into trend and cyclical components, the former being determined by real factors, such as the growth of GDP, and the latter being determined by transitory factors, such as monetary policy. Typically the cyclical component was analyzed using detrended versions of the variables in the model. However, as Nelson and Plosser (1982) point out, this approach is inappropriate if the process is difference-stationary, for although detrending may remove any drift, it does not affect the increasing variance of the series, and so the detrended component remains nonstationary. Further, because it ignores the contribution of real shocks to economic fluctuations, the approach causes the role of transitory factors in the cycle to be overestimated.

Exercises

13.1* Demonstrate that the MA(1) process

$$X_t = \varepsilon_t + \alpha_2 \varepsilon_{t-1}$$

is stationary. Does the result generalize to higher-order MA processes?

13.2* Demonstrate that the AR(1) process (13.2), with $\beta_2 < 1$, is stationary for finite samples if X_0 is generated as a random variable with appropriate mean and variance.

13.2 Consequences of nonstationarity

There are two reasons for being wary of regressions using nonstationary time series. One is that the properties of the regression estimators are likely to be adversely affected. The second is that there is a heightened risk of spurious regressions. We will start with the first.

Requirements for consistency

In Section 12.2 we saw that Assumption C.7 had two components:

(1) the disturbance term in any observation is distributed independently of the values of the regressors in the same observation, and

(2) the disturbance term in any observation is distributed independently of the values of the regressors in the other observations.

We hope that part (1) is valid, because if it is not, OLS estimators are inconsistent and we have to resort to some other estimation technique such as instrumental variables. Even if it is valid, we are still likely to have a problem with part (2). It was argued in Section 12.2 that our working hypothesis is that part (2) is violated, given the lags and interactions that are commonly found in relationships using time series data. When part (2) is violated, OLS estimators are biased in finite samples. The best that we can hope for is that they are consistent. The two requirements for consistency are that the estimator should tend to a limit as the sample size becomes large, and that that limit should be the true value. If the model is correctly specified and we are able to decompose the regression estimator into the true value of the parameter and an error term, we need the distribution of the error term to collapse to a spike at zero as the sample size becomes large.

To put this in concrete terms, consider the simple regression model

$$Y_i = \beta_1 + \beta_2 X_i + u_i. \tag{13.19}$$

The OLS estimator may be decomposed as

$$b_2 = \frac{\sum\limits_{i=1}^{n}\left(X_i - \overline{X}\right)\left(Y_i - \overline{Y}\right)}{\sum\limits_{i=1}^{n}\left(X_i - \overline{X}\right)^2} = \beta_2 + \frac{\sum\limits_{i=1}^{n}\left(X_i - \overline{X}\right)(u_i - \overline{u})}{\sum\limits_{i=1}^{n}\left(X_i - \overline{X}\right)^2}$$

$$= \beta_2 + \frac{\dfrac{1}{n}\sum\limits_{i=1}^{n}\left(X_i - \overline{X}\right)(u_i - \overline{u})}{\dfrac{1}{n}\sum\limits_{i=1}^{n}\left(X_i - \overline{X}\right)^2}. \tag{13.20}$$

Now with cross-sectional data where the regressors are hypothesized to be drawn randomly from fixed populations, one can show that the limiting value of the numerator of the error term is $cov(X, u)$ and this is zero if Assumption B.7, the counterpart of Assumption C.7, is satisfied. One can also show that the denominator tends to $var(X)$ as the sample size becomes large and hence, provided that $var(X) \neq 0$, the error term as a whole tends to zero.

With time series data the situation is more complicated. The components of the error term will tend to finite limits only if Assumption C.2 is satisfied and the regressors are 'weakly persistent'. A precise definition of weak persistence leads us into technicalities that are beyond the scope of this text. (See, for example, Wooldridge, 1994). As a first approximation, we could use stationarity as a definition, and this criterion seems to be widely adopted in practice. However, it is possible in theory that regression estimators could be consistent in a model with nonstationary regressors, and it is also possible in theory that regression estimators might not be consistent even if the regressors are stationary.

Spurious regressions

In the case of a model where the nonstationarity of the time series is caused by them being subject to deterministic time trends, the risk of obtaining spurious results is evident. Suppose that a variable Y_t is regressed on a variable X_t, both of them possessing time trends but not being directly related. If the time trends give rise to a high sample correlation between the two variables, R^2 will be high because it is equal to the square of the correlation. Hence the F statistic and the t statistic for the coefficient of X_t will also be high, despite the fact that X_t is not a determinant of Y_t. A spurious regression of this type can be avoided by detrending the variables before performing the regression. Equivalently, in view of the Frisch–Waugh–Lovell theorem described in Section 3.2, it could be avoided by including a time trend in the regression model.

As Granger and Newbold (1974) demonstrated with a celebrated Monte Carlo experiment, spurious regressions can also arise in regressions using integrated time series, and even in regressions using stationary time series, if evidence of autocorrelation in the disturbance term is ignored. They fitted the model

$$Y_t = \beta_1 + \beta_2 X_t + u_t \tag{13.21}$$

where Y_t and X_t were independently generated random walks:

$$Y_t = Y_{t-1} + \zeta_t \tag{13.22}$$

$$X_t = X_{t-1} + v_t \tag{13.23}$$

where ζ_t and v_t were unrelated white noise processes. Obviously, a regression of one random walk on another ought not to yield significant results except as a matter of Type I error. Granger and Newbold generated 100 samples of pairs of random walks and so, using a 5 percent significance test, one would anticipate that Type I error would cause the slope coefficient to appear to be significantly different from zero about 5 times. However, they found that the slope coefficient had an apparently significant t statistic in 77 samples. Using a more cautious 1 percent test made very little difference. The null hypothesis of no relationship was rejected in 70 samples.

The reason for this finding is that (13.21) contains a double misspecification given that (13.22) is the DGP for Y_t. Not only has an irrelevant variable X_t been added, but also a relevant variable Y_{t-1} has been excluded. The omission has serious implications for the disturbance term. Under the null hypothesis H_0: $\beta_1 = \beta_2 = 0$, (13.21) becomes

$$Y_t = u_t. \tag{13.24}$$

This means that, under the null hypothesis, u_t is a random walk and as a consequence the standard errors and t statistics are invalidated. This is why Granger and Newbold found such a high incidence of Type I errors.

Y_t and X_t do not have to be random walks for this problem to occur. Suppose that they are generated as AR(1) stationary processes

$$Y_t = \alpha_2 Y_{t-1} + \zeta_t \tag{13.25}$$

$$X_t = \gamma_2 X_{t-1} + v_t \tag{13.26}$$

with $-1 < \alpha_2 < 1$ and $-1 < \gamma_2 < 1$. Again, under the null hypothesis H_0: $\beta_1 = \beta_2 = 0$, (13.21) reduces to (13.24), implying that u_t is subject to AR(1) autocorrelation. Again, regressions of Y_t on X_t yield an abnormal number of Type I errors, the incidence being higher the greater the value of α_2. The Granger–Newbold experiment with $\alpha_2 = \gamma_2 = 1$ may be seen as an extreme case. Evidence of misspecification is provided by the tendency of the Durbin–Watson statistic to be low.

Consider what happens if we take care of the disturbance term problem by including Y_{t-1} as an explanatory variable, fitting the model

$$Y_t = \beta_1 + \beta_2 X_t + \beta_3 Y_{t-1} + u_t. \tag{13.27}$$

This is now a valid model because there is no omitted variable. Of course there is still the redundant variable X_t, but as we know from Section 6.3, if the model is otherwise correctly specified, the inclusion of a redundant variable ought only to cause a loss of efficiency.

If Y_t and X_t are generated as autocorrelated stationary processes (13.25) and (13.26), we find that H_0: $\beta_2 = 0$ is still rejected more often than it should be as a matter of Type I error, for finite samples, but the over-rejection rate is much less than when we fitted the model without Y_{t-1} and disappears for large samples. The OLS estimator b_3 tends to β_3 and b_2 tends to zero as the sample size becomes large. The over-rejection of $H_0\colon \beta_2 = 0$ for finite samples is caused by the violation of part (2) of Assumption C.7.

However, if Y_t and X_t are generated as random walks, the incidence of Type I error remains above its proper level, even in large samples. Several studies have investigated the asymptotic properties of least squares estimators of the coefficients when the regressors are nonstationary. In particular, Phillips (1986) shows that the distribution of β_2 converges to a nondegenerate limiting distribution, not a spike, with the probability of an apparent Type I error increasing with the sample size. He also showed that these findings extend to stationary series with ρ close to 1 (Phillips, 1987). These and similar findings underline the importance of identifying nonstationary processes and developing appropriate regression models.

Exercises

13.3 Repeat Granger and Newbold's experiment, with 100 observations instead of 50. Construct two independent 100-observation random walks and regress one on the other. Does the t statistic on the slope coefficient appear to be significant using a 5 percent test? Repeat the experiment several times (at least 5 times; 10 would be better) and note the frequency of Type I errors.

13.4 Construct two independent 100-observation AR(1) processes with $\rho = 0.95$, and regress one on the other. Does the t statistic on the slope coefficient appear to be significant using a 5 percent test? Run the regression a second time using an AR(1) specification, and compare the results. Repeat the experiment several times (at least 5 times; 10 would be better) and note the frequency of Type I errors in the OLS and AR(1) specifications. Compare the results with those in Exercise 13.3.

13.5 Repeat Exercise 13.3 with a series of 10,000 observations, and compare the results with those of Exercise 13.3.

13.6 Repeat Exercise 13.4 with a series of 10,000 observations, and compare the results with those of Exercise 13.4.

13.7* Suppose that a series is generated as

$$X_t = \beta_2 X_{t-1} + \varepsilon_t$$

with β_2 is equal to $1 - \delta$, where δ is small. Demonstrate that, if δ is small enough that terms involving δ^2 may be neglected, the variance may be approximated as

$$\sigma_{X_t}^2 = ((1 - [2t - 2]\delta) + \cdots + (1 - 2\delta) + 1)\, \sigma_\varepsilon^2$$

$$= (1 - [t - 1]\delta)\, t \sigma_\varepsilon^2$$

and draw your conclusions concerning the properties of the time series.

13.3   **Detection of nonstationarity**

Unfortunately for econometricians working with time series data, many economic time series appear to be of the I(1) type. It is therefore important to assess whether a time series is nonstationary before attempting to use it in a regression model. Often it is evident from the inspection of a plot that a time series is subject to a secular upward or downward trend and is therefore nonstationary. In the case of a series such as the logarithm of *DPI*, shown in Figure 13.4, the only questions are whether the series is difference-stationary or trend-stationary, and if difference-stationary, the order of integration. Similarly, with strong upward trends attributable to rising per capita income and a growing population, all of the time series of the categories of consumer expenditure in the Demand Functions data set are clearly nonstationary. Some of the price series also exhibit nonstationarity. They are influenced by production costs that rise with increases in real wages and fall with increasing efficiency. In some cases one of these influences is dominant and responsible for a trend.

Correlograms

The **correlogram** is a tool used by time series analysts in the identification of the orders p, d, and q of a time series assumed to be ARIMA(p, d, q). The autocorrelation function of a series X_t gives the theoretical correlation between the value of a series at time t and its value at time $t + k$, for values of k from 1 to (typically) about 20, being defined as the series

$$\rho_k = \frac{E\left((X_t - \mu_X)(X_{t+k} - \mu_X)\right)}{\sqrt{E\left((X_t - \mu_X)^2 E\left((X_{t+k} - \mu_X)^2\right)\right)}} \quad \text{for } k = 1, \dots \quad (13.28)$$

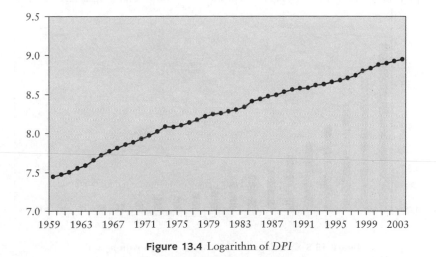

Figure 13.4 Logarithm of *DPI*

and the correlogram is its graphical representation. For example, the autocorrelation function for an AR(1) process $X_t = \beta_2 X_{t-1} + \varepsilon_t$ is

$$\rho_k = \beta_2^k, \tag{13.29}$$

the coefficients decreasing exponentially with the lag provided that $\beta_2 < 1$ and the process is stationary. The corresponding correlogram is shown in Figure 13.5 for β_2 equal to 0.8.

Higher-order stationary AR(p) processes may exhibit a more complex mixture of damped sine waves and damped exponentials, but they retain the feature that the weights eventually decline to zero.

By contrast, an MA(q) process has nonzero weights for only the first q lags and zero weights thereafter. In particular, the first autocorrelation coefficient for the MA(1) process

$$X_t = \varepsilon_t + \alpha_2 \varepsilon_{t-1} \tag{13.30}$$

is given by

$$\rho_1 = \frac{\alpha_2}{1 + \alpha_2^2} \tag{13.31}$$

and all subsequent autocorrelation coefficients are zero.

In the case of nonstationary processes, the theoretical autocorrelation coefficients are not defined but one may be able to obtain an expression for $E(r_k)$, the expected value of the sample autocorrelation coefficients, and for long time series, these coefficients decline slowly. For example, in the case of a random walk, the correlogram for a series with 200 observations is as shown in Figure 13.6 (Wichern, 1973).

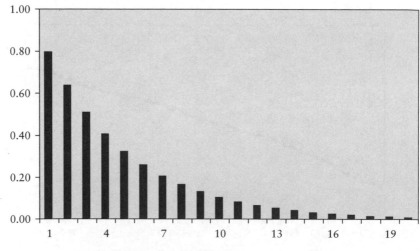

Figure 13.5 Correlogram of an AR(1) process with $\beta_2 = 0.8$

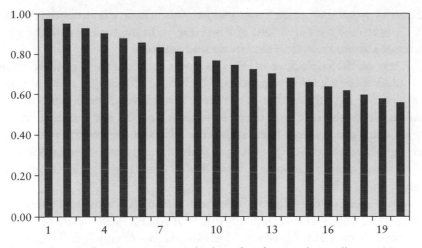

Figure 13.6 Correlogram (expected values of r_k) for a random walk, $n = 200$

Time series analysts exploit this fact in a two-stage procedure for identifying the orders of a series believed to be of the ARIMA(p, d, q) type. In the first stage, if the correlogram exhibits slowly declining coefficients, the series is differenced d times until the series exhibits a stationary pattern. Usually one differencing is sufficient, and at most two. The second stage is to inspect the correlogram of the differenced series and its partial correlogram, a related tool, to determine the orders p and q, a task whose complexity is limited by the fact that in practice most series are adequately represented by a process with the sum of p and q no greater than 2 (Box, Jenkins, and Reinsel, 1994).

There are, however, two problems with using correlograms to identify non-stationarity. One is that a correlogram such as that in Figure 13.6 could result from a stationary AR(1) process with a high value of β_2. The other is that the coefficients of a nonstationary process may decline quite rapidly if the series is not long. This is illustrated in Figure 13.7, which shows the expected values of r_k for a random walk when the series has only 50 observations.

Unit root tests

A more formal method of detecting nonstationarity is often described as testing for **unit roots**, for reasons that need not concern us here. The standard test, pioneered by Dickey and Fuller (1979), is based on the model

$$X_t = \beta_1 + \beta_2 X_{t-1} + \gamma t + \varepsilon_t. \tag{13.32}$$

Rewritten as

$$\wedge X_t = \beta_1 + (\beta_2 - 1)X_{t-1} + \gamma t + \varepsilon_t \tag{13.33}$$

where $\Delta X_t = X_t - X_{t-1}$, the series will be nonstationary if either the coefficient of X_{t-1} is zero or the coefficient of t is nonzero. In the former case the series is difference-stationary, and in the latter trend-stationary.

The test on the coefficient of X_{t-1} is one-sided because a positive value of β_2 would imply an explosive process, which normally can be ruled out. Under the alternative hypothesis that the process is stationary, the coefficient will be negative. Under the null hypothesis of nonstationarity, the t statistic does not have its usual distribution, even asymptotically, and the critical value, for any given significance level, is higher than that shown in the standard tables. For this reason, some authors denote it τ instead of t. Critical values for large samples are shown in Table 13.1.

A requirement of the Dickey–Fuller test is that the disturbance term in the model should not be autocorrelated. If it is, further lagged values of X_t should be included on the right side of equation (13.32). For example, if the disturbance term in (13.32) followed an AR(1) process, an appropriate specification would be

$$X_t = \beta_1 + \beta_2 X_{t-1} + \beta_3 X_{t-2} + \gamma t + \varepsilon_t \qquad (13.34)$$

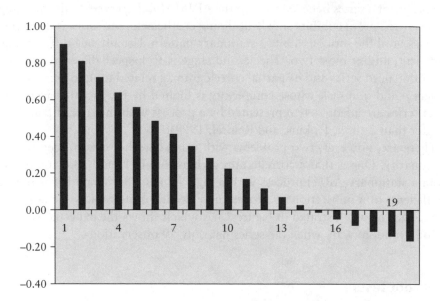

Figure 13.7 Correlogram (expected values of r_k) of a random walk, $n = 50$

Table 13.1 Asymptotic critical values of the ADF statistic

	5 percent	1 percent
No constant, no trend	−1.94	−2.56
Constant, no trend	−2.86	−3.43
Constant and trend	−3.41	−3.96

Source: Davidson and MacKinnon (1993)

where ε_t is white noise (see Exercise 13.8). It can be shown that in this case the process will be nonstationary if $\beta_2 + \beta_3 = 1$ or if γ is nonzero. Again, to test the first hypothesis, it is convenient to rewrite the equation as

$$\Delta X_t = \beta_1 + (\beta_2 + \beta_3 - 1)X_{t-1} - \beta_3 \Delta X_{t-1} + \gamma t + \varepsilon_t \qquad (13.35)$$

and test the null hypothesis that the coefficient of X_{t-1} is equal to zero. When one or more lagged differences in X_t are included on the right side of the model, the test is known as the **augmented Dickey–Fuller (ADF) test.**

It should be noted that in practice the test tends to have low power and a failure to reject the null hypothesis does not automatically mean that the series is nonstationary. In particular, as with the approach using correlograms, it is often impossible to distinguish between a nonstationary process and a highly autocorrelated stationary AR process.

Example

Figure 13.8 presents the sample correlogram for the logarithm of *DPI*. At first sight, the falling autocorrelation coefficients suggest a stationary AR(1) process with a high value of β_2. Although the theoretical correlogram for such a process, shown in Figure 13.5, looks a little different in that the coefficients decline exponentially to zero without becoming negative, a sample correlogram would have negative values similar to those in Figure 13.8. However, the correlogram in Figure 13.8 is also very similar to that for the finite nonstationary process shown in Figure 13.7.

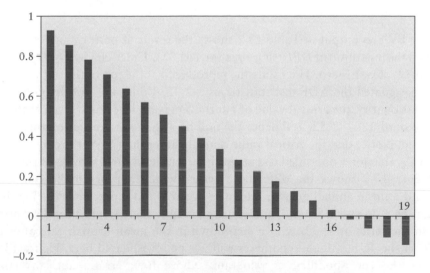

Figure 13.8 Sample correlogram for the logarithm of *DPI*

Table 13.2

```
               Augmented Dickey—Fuller Unit Root Test on LGDPI
-------------------------------------------------------------------------
Null Hypothesis: LGDPI has a unit root
Exogenous: Constant, Linear Trend
Lag Length: 1 (Fixed)
-------------------------------------------------------------------------
                                                    t-Statistic      Prob.
-------------------------------------------------------------------------
Augmented Dickey—Fuller test statistic              −2.322310       0.4134
Test critical values 1% level                       −4.186481
                     5% level                        −3.518090
                     10% level                       −3.189732
-------------------------------------------------------------------------
*MacKinnon (1996) one-sided p-values.

Augmented Dickey—Fuller Test Equation
Dependent Variable: D(LGDPI)
Method: Least Squares
Sample(adjusted): 1961 2003
Included observations: 43 after adjusting endpoints
-------------------------------------------------------------------------
    Variable      Coefficient    Std. Error    t-Statistic      Prob.
-------------------------------------------------------------------------
   LGDPI(−1)       −0.120908      0.052064      −2.322310       0.0255
  D(LGDPI(−1))      0.107910      0.147515       0.731520       0.4688
      C             0.947906      0.390441       2.427787       0.0199
 @TREND(1959)       0.003580      0.001737       2.061228       0.0460
-------------------------------------------------------------------------
R-squared             0.235301    Mean dependent var       0.034429
Adjusted R-squared    0.176478    S.D. dependent var       0.016525
S.E. of regression    0.014996    Akaike info criter      −5.473597
Sum squared resid     0.008771    Schwarz criterion       −5.309764
Log likelihood      121.6823      F-statistic              4.000157
Durbin—Watson stat    2.109986    Prob(F-statistic)        0.014147
```

The EViews output in Table 13.2 shows the result of performing a unit root test on the logarithm of *DPI* using equation (13.35). The coefficient of $LGDPI_{t-1}$ is -0.12, close to zero. The t statistic, reproduced at the top of the output where it is designated the ADF test statistic, is -2.32. Under the null hypothesis of nonstationarity, the critical value of t at the 5 percent level, also given at the top of the output, is -3.52, and hence the null hypothesis of nonstationarity is not rejected. Notice that the critical value is much larger than 1.69, the conventional critical value for a one-sided test at the 5 percent level for a sample of this size.

Figure 13.9 shows the differenced series, which appears to be stationary around a mean annual growth rate of between 2 and 3 percent. Possibly there might be a downward trend, and equally possibly there might be a discontinuity in the series at 1972, with a step down in the mean growth rate after the first oil shock, but these hypotheses will not be investigated here. Figure 13.10 shows the corresponding correlogram, whose low, erratic autocorrelation

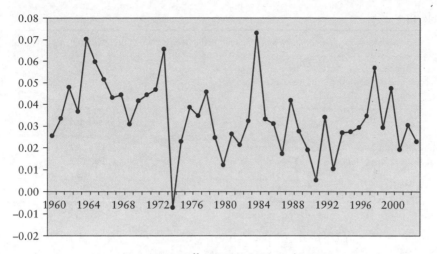

Figure 13.9 Differenced logarithm of *DPI*

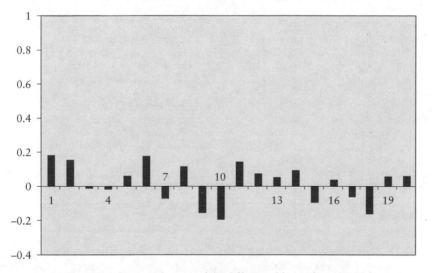

Figure 13.10 Correlogram of the differenced logarithm of *DPI*

coefficients provide support for the hypothesis that the differenced series is stationary.

The EViews output in Table 13.3 for a unit root test on the differenced series provides further support for this hypothesis. The coefficient of $\Delta LGDPI_{t-1}$ is -0.89, well below zero, and the t statistic is -4.13, allowing the null hypothesis of nonstationarity to be rejected at the 5 percent level (critical value -3.52) but not quite at the 1 percent level (critical value -4.19).

Table 13.3

```
               Augmented Dickey—Fuller Unit Root Test on DLGDPI
------------------------------------------------------------------------
Null Hypothesis: DLGDPI has a unit root
Exogenous: Constant, Linear Trend
Lag Length: 1 (Fixed)
------------------------------------------------------------------------

                                              t-Statistic       Prob.*
------------------------------------------------------------------------
Augmented Dickey—Fuller test statistic         -4.125167        0.0119
Test critical values 1% level                  -4.192337
                     5% level                  -3.520787
                    10% level                  -3.191277
------------------------------------------------------------------------

*MacKinnon (1996) one-sided p-values.

Augmented Dickey—Fuller Test Equation
Dependent Variable: D(DLGDPI)
Method: Least Squares
Sample(adjusted): 1962 2003
Included observations: 42 after adjusting endpoints
------------------------------------------------------------------------
   Variable         Coefficient     Std. Error     t-Statistic      Prob.
------------------------------------------------------------------------
  DLGDPI(-1)         -0.892399       0.216330       -4.125167       0.0002
 D(DLGDPI(-1))       -0.045015       0.158840       -0.283400       0.7784
      C               0.041368       0.011109        3.723927       0.0006
 @TREND(1959)        -0.000453       0.000225       -2.007941       0.0518
------------------------------------------------------------------------
R-squared            0.471341     Mean dependent var       -0.000249
Adjusted R-squared   0.429605     S.D. dependent var        0.021331
S.E. of regression   0.016110     Akaike info criter       -5.328341
Sum squared resid    0.009862     Schwarz criterion        -5.162848
Log likelihood       115.8952     F-statistic              11.29333
Durbin—Watson stat   1.975986     Prob(F-statistic)         0.000019
```

Exercises

13.8* Demonstrate that if the disturbance term in (13.32) is u_t, where u_t is generated by an AR(1) process, the appropriate specification for the augmented Dickey—Fuller test is given by equation (13.35).

13.9 Perform augmented Dickey—Fuller tests for difference-stationarity on the logarithms of expenditure on your commodity and the relative price series. Calculate the first differences and test these for difference-stationarity.

13.4 **Cointegration**

In general, a linear combination of two or more time series will be nonstationary if one or more of them is nonstationary, and the degree of integration of the combination will be equal to that of the most highly integrated individual series. Hence, for example, a linear combination of an I(1) series and an I(0) series will be I(1), that of two I(1) series will also be I(1), and that of an I(1) series and an I(2) series will be I(2).

However, if there is a long-run relationship between the time series, the outcome may be different. Consider, for example, Friedman's Permanent Income Hypothesis and the consumption function

$$C_t^P = \beta_2 Y_t^P v_t \tag{13.36}$$

where C_t^P and Y_t^P are permanent consumption and income, respectively, and v_t is a multiplicative disturbance term. In logarithms, the relationship becomes

$$\log C_t^P = \log \beta_2 + \log Y_t^P + u_t \tag{13.37}$$

where u_t is the logarithm of v_t. If the theory is correct, in the long run, ignoring short-run dynamics and the differences between the permanent and actual measures of the variables, consumption and income will grow at the same rate and the mean of the difference between their logarithms will be $\log \beta_2$. Figure 13.11 shows plots of the logarithms of aggregate disposable personal income, *DPI*, and aggregate personal consumer expenditure, *PCE*, (both left scale) and their difference (right scale) for the United States for the period 1959–2003. It can be seen that the gap between the two has been fairly stable, increasing a little in the first part of the period and declining a little thereafter. Thus, although the series for *DPI* and *PCE* are nonstationary, they appear to be wandering together. For this to be possible, u_t must be a stationary process, for if it were not, the two series could drift apart indefinitely, violating the theoretical relationship.

When two or more nonstationary time series are linked in such a way, they are said to be **cointegrated**. In this example, the slope coefficient of $\log Y^P$ in (13.37) is theoretically equal to 1, making it possible to inspect the divergence graphically in Figure 13.11. More generally, if there exists a relationship

$$Y_t = \beta_1 + \beta_2 X_{2t} + \cdots + \beta_k X_{kt} + u_t \tag{13.38}$$

between a set of variables $Y_t, X_{2t}, \ldots, X_{kt}$, the disturbance term u_t can be thought of as measuring the deviation between the components of the model:

$$u_t = Y_t - \beta_1 + \beta_2 X_{2t} - \cdots - \beta_k X_{kt}. \tag{13.39}$$

In the short run the divergence between the components will fluctuate, but if the model is genuinely correct there will be a limit to the divergence. Hence, although the time series are nonstationary, u_t will be stationary.

If there are more than two variables in the model, it is possible that there may be multiple cointegrating relationships, the maximum number in theory being equal to $k - 1$.

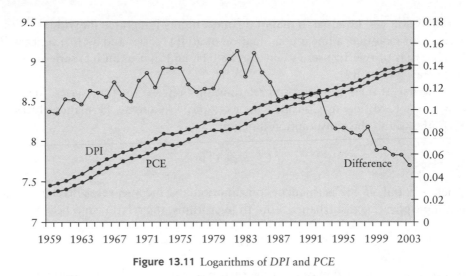

Figure 13.11 Logarithms of *DPI* and *PCE*

To test for cointegration, it is necessary to evaluate whether the disturbance term is a stationary process. In the case of the example of consumer expenditure and income, it is sufficient to perform a standard ADF unit root test on the difference between the two series. The results are shown in Table 13.4, with the difference between the logarithms being denoted Z. The ADF test statistic is -1.41, which is less than -3.52, the critical value at the 5 percent level under the null hypothesis of nonstationarity. This is a surprising result, for other studies have found the logarithms of consumer expenditure and income to be cointegrated (for example, Engle and Granger, 1987). Part of the problem is the low power of the test against an alternative hypothesis of u_t being a stationary process with high autocorrelation. The coefficient of the lagged residual is -0.11, suggesting (see equation 13.35) that the process is approximately AR(1) with autocorrelation 0.89, but the standard error is too large for the null hypothesis of nonstationarity to be rejected. It is likely that persistence in the way that consumers behave is responsible for this. As consumers become more savings conscious, as they seem to have done from 1959 to about 1984, the gap between the logarithms widens. As they become less savings conscious, as seems to be the case since 1984, it narrows. However, these changes evidently have long cycles, and so even over a period as long as 45 years it is difficult to discriminate between the hypothesis that the gap is a random walk and the alternative that it is stationary, with strong autocorrelation. However, a sufficiently long time series would show that the gap is stationary, for it is not possible for it to decrease indefinitely.

In the more general case of a model such as (13.38), where the cointegrating relationship has to be estimated, the test is an indirect one because it must be performed on the residuals from the regression, rather than on the disturbance term. In view of the fact that the least squares coefficients are chosen so as to minimize the sum of the squares of the residuals, the time series for the residuals

Table 13.4

Augmented Dickey—Fuller Unit Root Test on Z		

Null Hypothesis: Z has a unit root
Exogenous: Constant, Linear Trend
Lag Length: 1 (Fixed)

	t-Statistic	Prob.
Augmented Dickey—Fuller test statistic	−1.409037	0.8441
Test critical values 1% level	−4.186481	
5% level	−3.518090	
10% level	−3.189732	

*MacKinnon (1996) one-sided p-values.

Augmented Dickey—Fuller Test Equation
Dependent Variable: D(Z)
Method: Least Squares
Sample(adjusted): 1961 2003
Included observations: 43 after adjusting endpoints

Variable	Coefficient	Std. Error	t-Statistic	Prob.
Z(−1)	−0.114209	0.081055	−1.409037	0.1667
D(Z(−1))	−0.228610	0.154586	−1.478856	0.1472
C	0.020752	0.011302	1.036006	0.0740
@TREND(1959)	−0.000408	0.000151	−2.698052	0.0103

R-squared	0.191040	Mean dependent var	−0.001085
Adjusted R-squared	0.128812	S.D. dependent var	0.011007
S.E. of regression	0.010273	Akaike info criter	−6.230132
Sum squared resid	0.004116	Schwarz criterion	−6.066299
Log likelihood	137.9478	F-statistic	3.070017
Durbin—Watson stat	2.024272	Prob(F-statistic)	0.038931

will tend to appear more stationary than the underlying series for the disturbance term. To allow for this, the critical values for the test statistic are even higher than those for the standard test for nonstationarity of a time series. Asymptotic critical values for the case where the cointegrating relationship involves two variables are shown in Table 13.5. The test assumes that a constant has been included in the cointegrating relationship, and the critical values depend on whether a trend has been included as well.

In the case of a cointegrating relationship, least squares estimators can be shown to be superconsistent, in the sense that the parameter estimates approach their true values faster than they would in a regression involving cross-sectional or stationary time series data (Stock, 1987). In the latter case, the population variances of the estimators are of the order of $1/n$, where n is the number of observations in the sample or series, while in the case of a cointegrating relationship, the variances are of the order of $1/n^2$. An important consequence of this is that OLS may be used to fit a cointegrating relationship, even if it belongs to a

Table 13.5 Asymptotic critical values of the Dickey–Fuller statistic for a cointegrating relationship with two variables

	5 percent	1 percent
Constant, no trend	−3.34	−3.90
Constant and trend	−3.78	−4.32

Source: Davidson and MacKinnon (1993)

system of simultaneous relationships, for any simultaneous equations bias tends to zero asymptotically.

Example

A logarithmic regression of expenditure on food on *DPI* and the relative price of food was performed using the Demand Functions data set, the fitted equation being

$$\widehat{LGFOOD} = 2.24 + 0.50\ LGDPI - 0.07\ LGPRFOOD \quad R^2 = 0.992.$$
$$\quad\quad\quad (0.39)\ (0.01) \quad\quad\quad (0.07) \quad\quad\quad\quad\quad\quad\quad (13.40)$$

The residuals are shown in Figure 13.12. The pattern is mixed and it is not possible to say whether it looks stationary or nonstationary. The Engle–Granger statistic is −1.93, not significant even at the 5 percent level. The failure to reject the null hypothesis of nonstationarity suggests that the variables are not cointegrated. Nevertheless, the coefficient of the lagged residuals is −0.21, suggesting an AR(1) process with ρ equal to about 0.8. Thus, once again, the failure of the test to reject the null hypothesis of nonstationarity may merely reflect its low power against the alternative hypothesis that the disturbance term is a highly autocorrelated stationary process. Consequently, it is possible that the variables are in fact cointegrated.

Exercises

13.10 Generate a random walk and a stationary AR(1) series. Generate Y_t as one arbitrary linear combination and X_t as another. Test Y_t and X_t for a cointegrating relationship.

13.11 Run logarithmic regressions of expenditure on your commodity on disposable personal income and relative price, plot the residuals, and test for cointegration.

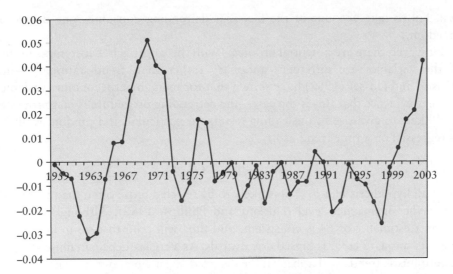

Figure 13.12 Residuals from a logarithmic regression of food on income and relative price

13.5 Fitting models with nonstationary time series

Much to the embarrassment of those constructing them, early macroeconomic models tended to produce poor forecasts, despite having excellent sample period fits. Often, indeed, the forecasts were no more accurate than those made by extrapolating simple linear trends (Nelson, 1973). There were two main reactions to this disappointing state of affairs. One was a resurgence of interest in the use of univariate time series for forecasting purposes, led by Box and Jenkins (1970). The other, of greater appeal to economists who did not wish to give up multivariate analysis, was to search for ways of constructing models that avoided the fitting of spurious relationships. We will briefly consider three of them: detrending the variables in a relationship, differencing the variables in a relationship, and constructing error correction models.

Detrending

As noted in Section 13.1, for models where the variables possess deterministic trends, the fitting of spurious relationships can be avoided by detrending the variables before use. This was a common procedure in early econometric analysis with time series data. Alternatively, and equivalently, one may include a time trend as a regressor in the model. By virtue of the Frisch–Waugh–Lovell theorem, the coefficients obtained with such a specification will be exactly the same as those obtained with a regression using detrended versions of the variables. (The standard errors will be marginally different. The specification with the time trend will calculate them correctly, while the specification with the detrended variables will fail to take account of the fact that detrending consumes one degree of freedom.)

However, there are potential problems with this approach. Most importantly, if the variables are difference-stationary rather than trend-stationary—and Nelson and Plosser (1982) have shown that for many macroeconomic variables there is evidence that this is the case—the detrending procedure is inappropriate and likely to give rise to misleading results. In particular, if a random walk X_t is regressed on a time trend as in

$$X_t = \beta_1 + \beta_2 t + \varepsilon_t \tag{13.41}$$

the null hypothesis H_0: $\beta_2 = 0$ is likely to be rejected more often than it should, given the significance level (Durlauf and Phillips, 1988). Although the least squares estimator of β_2 is consistent, and thus will tend to zero in large samples, its standard error is biased downwards. As a consequence, in finite samples deterministic trends will appear to be detected, even when not present.

Further, if a series is difference-stationary, the procedure does not make it stationary. In the case of a random walk, extracting a non-existent trend in the mean of the series can do nothing to alter the trend in its variance. As a consequence, the series remains nonstationary. In the case of a random walk with drift, the procedure can remove the drift, but again it does not remove the trend in the variance. In either case the problem of spurious regressions is not resolved, and for this reason detrending is now not usually considered to be an appropriate procedure.

Differencing

In early time series studies, if the disturbance term in a model

$$Y_t = \beta_1 + \beta_2 X_t + u_t \tag{13.42}$$

was believed to be subject to severe positive AR(1) autocorrelation $u_t = \rho u_{t-1} + \varepsilon_t$, a common rough-and-ready remedy was to regress the model in differences rather than levels:

$$\begin{aligned} \Delta Y_t &= \beta_2 \Delta X_t + \Delta u_t \\ &= \beta_2 \Delta X_t + (\rho - 1)u_{t-1} + \varepsilon_t. \end{aligned} \tag{13.43}$$

Of course differencing overcompensated for the autocorrelation, but if ρ was near 1, the resulting weak negative autocorrelation was held to be relatively innocuous. Unknown to practitioners of the time, the procedure is an effective antidote to spurious regressions, and was advocated as such by Granger and Newbold (1974). If both Y_t and X_t are unrelated I(1) processes, they are stationary in the differenced model and the absence of any relationship will be revealed.

A major shortcoming of differencing is that it precludes the investigation of a long-run relationship. In equilibrium $\Delta Y = \Delta X = 0$, and if one substitutes these values into (13.43) one obtains, not an equilibrium relationship, but an equation in which both sides are zero.

Error correction models

We have seen that a long-run relationship between two or more variables is given by a cointegrating relationship, if it exists. On its own, a cointegrating relationship sheds no light on short-run dynamics, but its very existence indicates that there must be some short-term forces that are responsible for keeping the relationship intact, and thus that it should be possible to construct a more comprehensive model that combines short-run and long-run dynamics. This is the objective of an **error correction model**.

For example, suppose that the relationship between two I(1) variables Y_t and X_t is characterized by the ADL(1,1) model considered in Section 12.6:

$$Y_t = \beta_1 + \beta_2 Y_{t-1} + \beta_3 X_t + \beta_4 X_{t-1} + \varepsilon_t. \tag{13.44}$$

In equilibrium,

$$\overline{Y} = \beta_1 + \beta_2 \overline{Y} + \beta_3 \overline{X} + \beta_4 \overline{X}. \tag{13.45}$$

Hence

$$\overline{Y} = \frac{\beta_1}{1 - \beta_2} + \frac{\beta_3 + \beta_4}{1 - \beta_2} X \tag{13.46}$$

and

$$Y_t = \frac{\beta_1}{1 - \beta_2} + \frac{\beta_3 + \beta_4}{1 - \beta_2} X_t \tag{13.47}$$

is the cointegrating relationship.

The ADL(1,1) relationship (13.44) may be rewritten to incorporate this relationship by subtracting Y_{t-1} from both sides, subtracting $\beta_3 X_{t-1}$ from the right side and adding it back again, and rearranging:

$$Y_t - Y_{t-1} = \beta_1 + (\beta_2 - 1) Y_{t-1} + \beta_3 X_t + \beta_4 X_{t-1} + \varepsilon_t$$

$$= \beta_1 + (\beta_2 - 1) Y_{t-1} + \beta_3 X_t - \beta_3 X_{t-1} + \beta_3 X_{t-1} + \beta_4 X_{t-1} + \varepsilon_t$$

$$= (\beta_2 - 1) \left(Y_{t-1} - \frac{\beta_1}{1 - \beta_2} - \frac{\beta_3 + \beta_4}{1 - \beta_2} X_{t-1} \right) + \beta_3 (X_t - X_{t-1}) + \varepsilon_t. \tag{13.48}$$

Hence we obtain the error correction model

$$\Delta Y_t = (\beta_2 - 1) \left(Y_{t-1} - \frac{\beta_1}{1 - \beta_2} - \frac{\beta_3 + \beta_4}{1 - \beta_2} X_{t-1} \right) + \beta_3 \Delta X_t + \varepsilon_t. \tag{13.49}$$

The model states that the change in Y in any period will be governed by the change in X and the discrepancy between Y_{t-1} and the value predicted by the cointegrating relationship. The latter term is denoted the error correction mechanism, the effect of the term being to reduce the discrepancy between Y_t and its cointegrating level and its size being proportional to the discrepancy.

The point of this rearrangement is that, although Y_t and X_t are both I(1), all of the terms ΔY_t, ΔX_t, and $\left(Y_{t-1} - \frac{\beta_1}{1-\beta_2} - \frac{\beta_3+\beta_4}{1-\beta_2}X_{t-1}\right)$ in (13.49) are I(0), the latter by virtue of being just the disturbance term in the cointegrating relationship, and hence the model may be fitted using least squares in the standard way.

Of course, the β parameters are not known and the cointegrating term is unobservable. One way of overcoming this problem, known as the Engle–Granger two-step procedure, is to use the values of the parameters estimated in the cointegrating regression to compute the cointegrating term. Engle and Granger (1987) demonstrate that asymptotically the estimators of the coefficients of (13.49) will have the same properties as if the true values had been used.

Example

The EViews output in Table 13.6 shows the results of fitting an error correction model for the demand function for food using the Engle–Granger two-step procedure, on the assumption that (13.40) is a cointegrating relationship. The coefficient of the cointegrating term, $ZFOOD(-1)$, indicates that about 15 percent of the disequilibrium divergence tends to be eliminated in one year.

Exercise

13.12 Fit an error correction model for your commodity, assuming that a cointegrating relationship has been found in Exercise 13.11.

Table 13.6

```
Dependent Variable: DLGFOOD
Method: Least Squares
Sample(adjusted): 1960 2003
Included observations: 44 after adjusting endpoints
```

Variable	Coefficient	Std. Error	t-Statistic	Prob.
ZFOOD(-1)	−0.148063	0.105268	−1.406533	0.1671
DLGDPI	0.493715	0.050948	9.690642	0.0000
DPFOOD	−0.353901	0.115387	−3.067086	0.0038

R-squared	0.343031	Mean dependent var	0.018243
Adjusted R-squared	0.310984	S.D. dependent var	0.015405
S.E. of regression	0.012787	Akaike info criter	−5.815054
Sum squared resid	0.006704	Schwarz criterion	−5.693405
Log likelihood	130.9312	Durbin–Watson stat	1.526946

13.6 Conclusion

This chapter has attempted to provide a brief and limited exposition of some of the concepts and issues that arise when regression analysis is applied to non-stationary time series. The treatment has been guided by the need to avoid complexity that would be inappropriate in an introductory econometrics course. For this reason there is no mention of some important mathematical tools, such as lag operators, or some major econometric topics, such as vector autoregression, and the discussion barely scratches at the surface of those topics that are included, sidestepping problems encountered in practice, such as the extent to which asymptotic analysis is relevant to analysis of finite samples. The chapter therefore does not pretend to provide a perspective or overview. Rather than attempting to provide tools for immediate use, the overriding objective has been to convince a reader intending to work with time series data that there is a need for further study at a higher level, and that further study would be worthwhile. For precisely because many of the problems have been recognized only relatively recently, much remains to be explored and the econometric analysis of time series is at the present time an especially exciting and challenging field.

Key terms

ARIMA(p, d, q) time series

ARMA(p, q) time series

augmented Dickey–Fuller (ADF) test

cointegrated time series

correlogram

deterministic trend

difference stationarity

error correction model

integrated time series

nonstationarity

random walk

random walk with drift

stationarity

trend stationarity

unit root

14 Introduction to Panel Data Models

14.1 Introduction

If the same units of observation in a cross-sectional sample are surveyed two or more times, the resulting observations are described as forming a **panel** or **longitudinal data set**. The National Longitudinal Survey of Youth that has provided data for many of the examples and exercises in this text is such a data set. The NLSY started with a baseline survey in 1979 and the same individuals have been reinterviewed many times since, annually until 1994 and biennially since then. However the unit of observation of a panel data set need not be individuals. It may be households, or enterprises, or geographical areas, or indeed any set of entities that retain their identities over time.

Because panel data have both cross-sectional and time series dimensions, the application of regression analysis to fit econometric models is more complex than that for simple cross-sectional data sets. Nevertheless, panel data sets are increasingly being used in applied work and the aim of this chapter is to provide a brief introduction. For comprehensive treatments see Hsiao (2003), Baltagi (2001), and Wooldridge (2002).

There are several reasons for the increasing interest in panel data sets. An important one is that their use may offer a solution to the problem of bias caused by unobserved heterogeneity, a common problem in the fitting of models with cross-sectional data sets. This will be discussed in the next section.

A second reason is that it may be possible to exploit panel data sets to reveal dynamics that are difficult to detect with cross-sectional data. For example, if one has cross-sectional data on a number of adults, it will be found that some are employed, some are unemployed, and the rest are economically inactive. For policy purposes, one would like to distinguish between frictional unemployment and long-term unemployment. Frictional unemployment is inevitable in a changing economy, but long-term unemployment can indicate a social problem that needs to be addressed. To design an effective policy to counter long-term unemployment, one needs to know the characteristics of those affected or at risk. In principle the necessary information might be captured with a cross-sectional survey using retrospective questions about past employment status, but in practice the scope for this is often very limited. The further back in the past one goes, the worse are the problems of a lack of records and fallible memories, and the greater becomes the problem of measurement error. Panel studies avoid this problem in that the need for recall is limited to the time interval since the previous interview, often no more than a year.

A third attraction of panel data sets is that they often have very large numbers of observations. If there are n units of observation and if the survey is undertaken in T time periods, there are potentially nT observations consisting of time series of length T on n parallel units. In the case of the NLSY, there were just over 6,000 individuals in the core sample. The survey has been conducted 19 times as of 2004, generating over 100,000 observations. Further, because it is expensive to establish and maintain them, such panel data sets tend to be well designed and rich in content.

A panel is described as **balanced** if there is an observation for every unit of observation for every time period, and as **unbalanced** if some observations are missing. The discussion that follows applies equally to both types. However, if one is using an unbalanced panel, one needs to take note of the possibility that the causes of missing observations are endogenous to the model. Equally, if a balanced panel has been created artificially by eliminating all units of observation with missing observations, the resulting data set may not be representative of its population.

Example of the use of a panel data set to investigate dynamics

In many studies of the determinants of earnings it has been found that married men earn significantly more than single men. One explanation is that marriage entails financial responsibilities—in particular, the rearing of children—that may encourage men to work harder or seek better paying jobs. Another is that certain unobserved qualities that are valued by employers are also valued by potential spouses and hence are conducive to getting married, and that the dummy variable for being married is acting as a proxy for these qualities. Other explanations have been proposed, but we will restrict attention to these two. With cross-sectional data it is difficult to discriminate between them. However, with panel data one can find out whether there is an uplift at the time of marriage or soon after, as would be predicted by the increased productivity hypothesis, or whether married men tend to earn more even before marriage, as would be predicted by the unobserved heterogeneity hypothesis.

In 1988 there were 1,538 NLSY males working 30 or more hours a week, not also in school, with no missing data. The respondents were divided into three categories: the 904 who were already married in 1988 (dummy variable $MARRIED = 1$); a further 212 who were single in 1988 but who married within the next four years (dummy variable $SOONMARR = 1$); and the remaining 422 who were single in 1988 and still single four years later (the omitted category). Divorced respondents were excluded from the sample. The following earnings function was fitted (standard errors in parentheses):

$$\widehat{LGEARN} = 0.163\ MARRIED + 0.096\ SOONMARR + \text{constant} + \text{controls}$$
$$\phantom{\widehat{LGEARN} =} (0.028) (0.037) \phantom{SOONMARR + \text{constant} +} R^2 = 0.27.$$

$$(14.1)$$

The controls included years of schooling, $ASVABC$ score, years of tenure with the current employer and its square, years of work experience and its square, age and its square, and dummy variables for ethnicity, region of residence, and living in an urban area.

The regression indicates that those who were married in 1988 earned 16.3 percent more than the reference category (strictly speaking, 17.7 percent, if the proportional increase is calculated properly as $e^{0.163} - 1$) and that the effect is highly significant. However, it is the coefficient of $SOONMARR$ that is of greater interest here. Under the null hypothesis that the marital effect is dynamic and marriage encourages men to earn more, the coefficient of $SOONMARR$ should be zero. The men in this category were still single as of 1988. The t statistic of the coefficient is 2.60 and so the coefficient is significantly different from zero at the 0.1 percent level, leading us to reject the null hypothesis at that level.

However, if the alternative hypothesis is true, the coefficient of $SOONMARR$ should be equal to that of $MARRIED$, but it is lower. To test whether it is significantly lower, the easiest method is to change the reference category to those who were married by 1988 and to introduce a new dummy variable $SINGLE$ that is equal to 1 if the respondent was single in 1988 and still single four years later. The omitted category is now those who were already married by 1988. The fitted regression is (standard errors in parentheses)

$$\widehat{LGEARN} = -0.163\ SINGLE - 0.066\ SOONMARR + \text{constant} + \text{controls}$$
$$\phantom{\widehat{LGEARN} =} (0.028) (0.034) \phantom{SOONMARR + \text{constant} +} R^2 = 0.27.$$

$$(14.2)$$

The coefficient of $SOONMARR$ now estimates the difference between the coefficients of those married by 1988 and those married within the next four years, and if the second hypothesis is true, it should be equal to zero. The t statistic is -1.93, so we (just) do not reject the second hypothesis at the 5 percent level. The evidence seems to provide greater support for the second hypothesis, but it is possible that neither hypothesis is correct on its own and the truth might reside in some compromise.

In the foregoing example, we used data only from the 1988 and 1992 rounds of the NLSY. In most applications using panel data it is normal to exploit the data from all the rounds, if only to maximize the number of observations in the sample. A standard specification is

$$Y_{it} = \beta_1 + \sum_{j=2}^{k} \beta_j X_{jit} + \sum_{p=1}^{s} \gamma_p Z_{pi} + \delta t + \varepsilon_{it} \qquad (14.3)$$

where Y is the dependent variable, the X_j are observed explanatory variables, and the Z_p are unobserved explanatory variables. The index i refers to the unit of observation, t refers to the time period, and j and p are used to differentiate between different observed and unobserved explanatory variables. ε_{it} is a disturbance term assumed to satisfy the usual regression model conditions. A trend term t has been introduced to allow for a shift of the intercept over time. If the implicit assumption of a constant rate of change seems too strong, the trend can be replaced by a set of dummy variables, one for each time period except the reference period.

The X_j variables are usually the variables of interest, while the Z_p variables are responsible for unobserved heterogeneity and as such constitute a nuisance component of the model. The following discussion will be confined to the (quite common) special case where it is reasonable to assume that the unobserved heterogeneity is unchanging and accordingly the Z_p variables do not need a time subscript. Because the Z_p variables are unobserved, there is no means of obtaining information about the $\sum \gamma_p Z_{pi}$ component of the model and it is convenient to rewrite (14.3) as

$$Y_{it} = \beta_1 + \sum_{j=2}^{k} \beta_j X_{jit} + \alpha_i + \delta t + \varepsilon_{it} \qquad (14.4)$$

where

$$\alpha_i = \sum_{p=1}^{s} \gamma_p Z_{pi}. \qquad (14.5)$$

α_i, known as the **unobserved effect,** represents the joint impact of the Z_{pi} on Y_i. Henceforward it will be convenient to refer to the unit of observation as an individual, and to the α_i as the individual-specific unobserved effect, but it should be borne in mind that the individual in question may actually be a household or an enterprise, etc. If α_i is correlated with any of the X_j variables, the regression estimates from a regression of Y on the X_j variables will be subject to unobserved heterogeneity bias. Even if the unobserved effect is not correlated with any of the explanatory variables, its presence will in general cause OLS to yield inefficient estimates and invalid standard errors. We will now consider ways of overcoming these problems.

First, however, note that if the X_j controls are so comprehensive that they capture all the relevant characteristics of the individual, there will be no relevant unobserved characteristics. In that case the α_i term may be dropped and a **pooled**

OLS regression may be used to fit the model, treating all the observations for all of the time periods as a single sample.

14.2 Fixed effects regressions

The two main approaches to the fitting of models using panel data are known as **fixed effects regressions**, discussed in this section, and **random effects regressions**, discussed in the next. Three versions of the fixed effects approach will be described. In the first two, the model is manipulated in such a way that the unobserved effect is eliminated.

Within-groups fixed effects

In the first version, the mean values of the variables in the observations on a given individual are calculated and subtracted from the data for that individual. In view of (14.4), one may write

$$\overline{Y}_i = \beta_1 + \sum_{j=2}^{k} \beta_j \overline{X}_{ij} + \delta \overline{t} + \alpha_i + \overline{\varepsilon}_{it}. \tag{14.6}$$

Subtracting this from (14.4), one obtains

$$Y_{it} - \overline{Y}_i = \sum_{j=2}^{k} \beta_j \left(X_{ijt} - \overline{X}_{ij} \right) + \delta (t - \overline{t}) + \varepsilon_{it} - \overline{\varepsilon}_i \tag{14.7}$$

and the unobserved effect disappears. This is known as the **within-groups regression** model because it is explaining the variations about the mean of the dependent variable in terms of the variations about the means of the explanatory variables for the group of observations relating to a given individual. The possibility of tackling unobserved heterogeneity bias in this way is a major attraction of panel data for researchers.

However, there are some prices to pay. First, the intercept β_1 and any X variable that remains constant for each individual will drop out of the model. The elimination of the intercept may not matter, but the loss of the unchanging explanatory variables may be frustrating. Suppose, for example, that one is fitting an earnings function to data for a sample of individuals who have completed their schooling, and that the schooling variable for individual i in period t is S_{it}. If the education of the individual is complete by the time of the first time period, S_{it} will be the same for all t for that individual and $S_{it} = \overline{S}_i$ for all t. Hence $(S_{it} - \overline{S}_i)$ is zero for all time periods. If all individuals have completed their schooling by the first time period, S_{it} will be zero for all i and t. One cannot include a variable whose values are all zero in a regression model. Thus if the object of the exercise were to obtain an estimate of the returns to schooling untainted by unobserved heterogeneity bias, one ends up with no estimate at all.

A second problem is the potential impact of the disturbance term. We saw in Chapter 3 that the precision of OLS estimates depends on the mean square deviations of the explanatory variables being large in comparison with the variance of the disturbance term. The analysis was in the context of the simple regression model, but it generalizes to multiple regression. The variation in $(X_j - \overline{X}_j)$ may well be much smaller than the variation in X_j. If this is the case, the impact of the disturbance term may be relatively large, giving rise to imprecise estimates. The situation is aggravated in the case of measurement error, since this will lead to bias, and the bias is the greater, the smaller the variation in the explanatory variable in comparison with the variance of the measurement error.

A third problem is that we lose a substantial number of degrees of freedom in the model when we manipulate the model to eliminate the unobserved effect: we lose one degree of freedom for every individual in the sample. If the panel is balanced, with nT observations in all, it may seem that there would be $nT - k$ degrees of freedom. However, in manipulating the model, the number of degrees of freedom is reduced by n, for reasons that will be explained later in this section. Hence the true number of degrees of freedom will be $n(T - 1) - k$. If T is small, the impact can be large. (Regression applications with a fixed effects regression facility will automatically make the adjustment to the degrees of freedom when implementing the within-groups method.)

First differences fixed effects

In a second version of the fixed effects approach, the first differences regression model, the unobserved effect is eliminated by subtracting the observation for the previous time period from the observation for the current time period, for all time periods. For individual i in time period t the model may be written

$$Y_{it} = \beta_1 + \sum_{j=2}^{k} \beta_j X_{ijt} + \delta t + \alpha_i + \varepsilon_{it}. \tag{14.8}$$

For the previous time period, the relationship is

$$Y_{it-1} = \beta_1 + \sum_{j=2}^{k} \beta_j X_{ijt-1} + \delta(t - 1) + \alpha_i + \varepsilon_{it-1}. \tag{14.9}$$

Subtracting (14.9) from (14.8), one obtains

$$\Delta Y_{it} = \sum_{j=2}^{k} \beta_j \Delta X_{ijt} + \delta + \varepsilon_{it} - \varepsilon_{it-1} \tag{14.10}$$

and again the unobserved heterogeneity has disappeared. However, the other problems remain. In particular, the intercept and any X variable that remains fixed for each individual will disappear from the model and n degrees of freedom are lost because the first observation for each individual is not defined. In addition, this type of differencing gives rise to autocorrelation if ε_{it} satisfies the regression model conditions. The error term for ΔY_{it} is $(\varepsilon_{it} - \varepsilon_{it-1})$. That for the previous observation is $(\varepsilon_{it-1} - \varepsilon_{it-2})$. Thus the two error terms both have a component ε_{it-1} with opposite signs and negative moving average autocorrelation has been induced. However, if ε_{it} is subject to autocorrelation:

$$\varepsilon_{it} = \rho \varepsilon_{it-1} + v_{it} \tag{14.11}$$

where v_{it} is a well behaved innovation, the moving average disturbance term is equal to $v_{it} - (1 - \rho)\varepsilon_{it-1}$. If the autocorrelation is severe, the $(1 - \rho)\varepsilon_{it-1}$ component could be small and so the first differences estimator could be preferable to the within-groups estimator.

Least squares dummy variable fixed effects

In the third version of the fixed effects approach, known as the **least squares dummy variable (LSDV) regression** model, the unobserved effect is brought explicitly into the model. If we define a set of dummy variables A_i, where A_i is equal to 1 in the case of an observation relating to individual i and 0 otherwise, the model can be rewritten

$$Y_{it} = \sum_{j=2}^{k} \beta_j X_{ijt} + \delta t + \sum_{i=1}^{n} \alpha_i A_i + \varepsilon_{it}. \tag{14.12}$$

Formally, the unobserved effect is now being treated as the coefficient of the individual-specific dummy variable, the $\alpha_i A_i$ term representing a fixed effect on the dependent variable Y_i for individual i (this accounts for the name given to the fixed effects approach). Having re-specified the model in this way, it can be fitted using OLS.

Note that if we include a dummy variable for every individual in the sample as well as an intercept, we will fall into the dummy variable trap described in Section 5.2. To avoid this, we could define one individual to be the reference category, so that β_1 is its intercept, and then treat the α_i as the shifts in the intercept for the other individuals. However, the choice of reference category is often arbitrary and accordingly the interpretation of the α_i in such a specification not particularly illuminating. Alternatively, we can drop the β_1 intercept and define dummy variables for all of the individuals, as has been done in (14.12). The α_i now become the intercepts for each of the individuals. Note that, in common with the first two versions of the fixed effects approach, the LSDV method requires panel data. With cross-sectional data, one would be defining a dummy variable for every observation, exhausting the degrees of freedom. The dummy variables on their own would give a perfect but meaningless fit.

If there are a large number of individuals, using the LSDV method directly is not a practical proposition, given the need for a large number of dummy

Table 14.1 Individual-specific dummy variables and an unchanging X variable

Individual	Time period	A_1	A_2	A_3	A_4	X_j
1	1	1	0	0	0	c_1
1	2	1	0	0	0	c_1
1	3	1	0	0	0	c_1
2	1	0	1	0	0	c_2
2	2	0	1	0	0	c_2
2	3	0	1	0	0	c_2
3	1	0	0	1	0	c_3
3	2	0	0	1	0	c_3
3	3	0	0	1	0	c_3
4	1	0	0	0	1	c_4
4	2	0	0	0	1	c_4
4	3	0	0	0	1	c_4

variables. However, it can be shown mathematically that the method is identical to the within-groups method. The only apparent difference is in the number of degrees of freedom. It is easy to see from (14.12) that there are $nT - k - n$ degrees of freedom if the panel is balanced. In the within-groups approach, it seemed at first that there were $nT - k$. However, n degrees of freedom are consumed in the manipulation that eliminates the α_i.

Given that it is equivalent to the within-groups approach, the LSDV method is subject to the same problems. In particular, we are unable to estimate coefficients for the X variables that are fixed for each individual. Suppose that X_{ij} is equal to c_i for all the observations for individual i. Then

$$X_j = \sum_{i=1}^{n} c_i A_i. \tag{14.13}$$

To see this, suppose that there are four individuals and three time periods, as in Table 14.1, and consider the observations for the first individual. X_j is equal to c_1 for each observation. A_1 is equal to 1. All the other A dummies are equal to 0. Hence both sides of the equation are equal to c_1. Similarly, both sides of the equation are equal to c_2 for the observations for individual 2, and similarly for individuals 3 and 4.

Thus there is an exact linear relationship linking X_j with the dummy variables and the model is subject to exact multicollinearity. Accordingly X_j cannot be included in the regression specification.

Example

To illustrate the use of a fixed effects model, we return to the example in Section 14.1 and use all the available data from 1980 to 1996, 20,343 observations in all. Table 14.2 shows the extra hourly earnings of married men and of men who are single but married within the next four years. The controls (not shown) are the

Table 14.2 Earnings premium for married and soon-to-be-married men, NLSY 1980–96

	OLS	Fixed effects		Random effects	
Married	0.184	0.106	–	0.134	–
	(0.007)	(0.012)		(0.010)	
Single, married	0.096	0.045	−0.061	0.060	−0.075
within 4 years	(0.009)	(0.010)	(0.008)	(0.009)	(0.007)
Single, not married	–	–	−0.106	–	−0.134
within 4 years			(0.012)		(0.010)
R^2	0.358	0.268	0.268	0.346	0.346
DWH test	–	–	–	205.8	205.8
n	20,343	20,343	20,343	20,343	20,343

same as in Section 14.1. The first column gives the estimates obtained by simply pooling the observations and using OLS with robust standard errors. The second column gives the fixed effects estimates, using the within-groups method, with single men as the reference category. The third gives the fixed effects estimates with married men as the reference category. The fourth and fifth give the random effects estimates, discussed in the next section.

The OLS estimates are very similar to those in the wage equation for 1988 discussed in Section 14.1. The fixed effects estimates are considerably lower, suggesting that the OLS estimates were inflated by unobserved heterogeneity. Nevertheless, the pattern is the same. Soon-to-be-married men earn significantly more than single men who stay single. However, if we fit the specification corresponding to equation (14.2), shown in the third column, we find that soon-to-be married men earn significantly less than married men. Hence both hypotheses relating to the marriage premium appear to be partly true.

14.3 Random effects regressions

As we saw in the previous section, when the variables of interest are constant for each individual, a fixed effects regression is not an effective tool because such variables cannot be included. In this section we will consider an alternative approach, known as a random effects regression that may, subject to two conditions, provide a solution to this problem.

The first condition is that it is possible to treat each of the unobserved Z_p variables as being drawn randomly from a given distribution. This may well be the case if the individual observations constitute a random sample from a given population as, for example, with the NLSY where the respondents were randomly drawn from the US population aged 14 to 21 in 1979. If this is the case, the α_i may be treated as random variables (hence the name of this approach) drawn from a given distribution and we may rewrite the model as

$$Y_{it} = \beta_1 + \sum_{j=2}^{k} \beta_j X_{jit} + \alpha_i + \delta t + \varepsilon_{it}$$

$$= \beta_1 + \sum_{j=2}^{k} \beta_j X_{jit} + \delta t + u_{it} \qquad (14.14)$$

where

$$u_{it} = \alpha_i + \varepsilon_{it}. \qquad (14.15)$$

We have thus dealt with the unobserved effect by subsuming it into the disturbance term.

The second condition is that the Z_p variables are distributed independently of all of the X_j variables. If this is not the case, α, and hence u, will not be uncorrelated with the X_j variables and the random effects estimation will be biased and inconsistent. We would have to use fixed effects estimation instead, even if the first condition seems to be satisfied.

If the two conditions are satisfied, we may use (14.14) as our regression specification, but there is a complication. u_{it} will be subject to a special form of autocorrelation and we will have to use an estimation technique that takes account of it.

First, we will check the other regression model conditions relating to the disturbance term. Given our assumption that ε_{it} satisfies the usual regression model conditions, we can see that u_{it} satisfies the condition that its expectation be zero, since

$$E(u_{it}) = E(\alpha_i + \varepsilon_{it}) = E(\alpha_i) + E(\varepsilon_{it}) = 0 \quad \text{for all } i \text{ and } t \qquad (14.16)$$

Here we are assuming without loss of generality that $E(\alpha_i) = 0$, any nonzero component being absorbed by the intercept, β_1. u_{it} will also satisfy the condition that it should have constant variance, since

$$\sigma_{u_{it}}^2 = \sigma_{\alpha_i + \varepsilon_{it}}^2 = \sigma_\alpha^2 + \sigma_\varepsilon^2 + 2\sigma_{\alpha\varepsilon} = \sigma_\alpha^2 + \sigma_\varepsilon^2 \quad \text{for all } i \text{ and } t. \qquad (14.17)$$

The $\sigma_{\alpha\varepsilon}$ term is zero on the assumption that α_i is distributed independently of ε_{it}. u_{it} will also satisfy the regression model condition that it be distributed independently of the values of X_j, since both α_i and ε_{it} are assumed to satisfy this condition.

However, there is a problem with the regression model condition that the value of u_{it} in any observation be generated independently of its value in all other observations. For all the observations relating to a given individual, α_i will have the same value, reflecting the unchanging unobserved characteristics of the individual. This is illustrated in Table 14.3 for the case where there are four individuals and three time periods.

Table 14.3 Example of disturbance term values in a random effects model

Individual	Time period	u
1	1	$\alpha_1 + \varepsilon_{11}$
1	2	$\alpha_1 + \varepsilon_{12}$
1	3	$\alpha_1 + \varepsilon_{13}$
2	1	$\alpha_2 + \varepsilon_{21}$
2	2	$\alpha_2 + \varepsilon_{22}$
2	3	$\alpha_2 + \varepsilon_{23}$
3	1	$\alpha_3 + \varepsilon_{31}$
3	2	$\alpha_3 + \varepsilon_{32}$
3	3	$\alpha_3 + \varepsilon_{33}$
4	1	$\alpha_4 + \varepsilon_{41}$
4	2	$\alpha_4 + \varepsilon_{42}$
4	3	$\alpha_4 + \varepsilon_{43}$

Since the disturbance terms for individual i have a common component α_i, they are correlated. For individual i in period t, the disturbance term is $(\alpha_i + \varepsilon_{it})$. For the same individual in any other period t' it is $(\alpha_i + \varepsilon_{it'})$. The population covariance between them is

$$\sigma_{u_{it},u_{it'}} = \sigma_{(\alpha_i+\varepsilon_{it}),(\alpha_i+\varepsilon_{it'})} = \sigma_{\alpha_i,\alpha_i} + \sigma_{\alpha_i,\varepsilon_{it'}} + \sigma_{\varepsilon_{it},\alpha_i} + \sigma_{\varepsilon_{it},\varepsilon_{it'}} = \sigma_\alpha^2. \qquad (14.18)$$

For observations relating to different individuals the problem does not arise because then the α components will be different and generated independently.

We have encountered a problem of the violation of this regression model condition once before, in the case of autocorrelated disturbance terms in a time series model. As in that case, OLS remains unbiased and consistent, but it is inefficient and the OLS standard errors are computed wrongly.

The solution then was to transform the model so that the transformed disturbance term satisfied the regression model condition, and a similar procedure is adopted in the present case. However, while the transformation in the case of autocorrelation was very straightforward, in the present case it is more complex. Known as feasible generalized least squares, its description requires the use of linear algebra and is therefore beyond the scope of this text. It yields consistent estimates of the coefficients and therefore depends on n being sufficiently large. For small n its properties are unknown.

Assessing the appropriateness of fixed effects and random effects estimation

When should you use fixed effects estimation rather than random effects estimation, or vice versa? In principle, random effects is more attractive because observed characteristics that remain constant for each individual are retained in the regression model. In fixed effects estimation, they have to be dropped.

Also, with random effects estimation we do not lose n degrees of freedom, as is the case with fixed effects.

However, if either of the preconditions for using random effects is violated, we should use fixed effects instead. One precondition is that the observations can be described as being drawn randomly from a given population. This is a reasonable assumption in the case of the NLSY because it was designed to be a random sample. By contrast, it would not be a reasonable assumption if the units of observation in the panel data set were countries and the sample consisted of those countries that are members of the Organization for Economic Cooperation and Development (OECD). These countries certainly cannot be considered to represent a random sample of the 200-odd sovereign states in the world.

The other precondition is that the unobserved effect be distributed independently of the X_j variables. How can we tell if this is the case? The standard procedure is yet another implementation of the **Durbin–Wu–Hausman** test used to help us choose between OLS and IV estimation in models where there is suspected measurement error (Section 8.5) or simultaneous equations endogeneity (Section 9.3). The null hypothesis is that the α_i are distributed independently of the X_j. If this is correct, both random effects and fixed effects are consistent, but fixed effects will be inefficient because, looking at it in its LSDV form, it involves estimating an unnecessary set of dummy variable coefficients. If the null hypothesis is false, the random effects estimates will be subject to unobserved heterogeneity bias and will therefore differ systematically from the fixed effects estimates.

As in its other applications, the DWH test determines whether the estimates of the coefficients, taken as a group, are significantly different in the two regressions. If any variables are dropped in the fixed effects regression, they are excluded from the test. Under the null hypothesis the test statistic has a chi-squared distribution. In principle this should have degrees of freedom equal to the number of slope coefficients being compared but, for technical reasons that require matrix algebra for an explanation, the actual number may be lower. A regression application that implements the test, such as Stata, should determine the actual number of degrees of freedom.

Example

The fixed effects estimates, using the within-groups approach, of the coefficients of married men and soon-to-be-married men in Table 14.2 are 0.106 and 0.045, respectively. The corresponding random effects estimates are considerably higher, 0.134 and 0.060, inviting the suspicion that they may be inflated by unobserved heterogeneity. The DWH test involves the comparison of 13 coefficients (those of *MARRIED*, *SOONMARR*, and 11 controls). Stata reports that there are in fact only 12 degrees of freedom. The test statistic is 205.8. With 12 degrees of freedom the critical value of chi-squared at the 0.1 percent level is 32.9, so we definitely conclude that we should be using fixed effects estimation.

Our findings are the same as in the simpler example in Section 14.1. They confirm that married men earn more than single men. Part of the differential appears to be attributable to the characteristics of married men, since men who are soon-to-marry but still single also enjoy an earnings premium. However, part of the marriage premium appears to be attributable to the effect of marriage itself, since married men earn significantly more than those who are soon-to-marry but still single.

Random effects or OLS?

Suppose that the DWH test indicates that we can use random effects rather than fixed effects. We should then consider whether there are any unobserved effects at all. It is just possible that the model has been so well specified that the disturbance term

$$u_{it} = \alpha_i + \varepsilon_{it} \tag{14.19}$$

consists of only the purely random component ε_{it} and there is no individual-specific α_i term. In this situation we should use pooled OLS, with two advantages. There is a gain in efficiency because we are not attempting to allow for non-existent within-groups autocorrelation, and we will be able to take advantage of the finite-sample properties of OLS, instead of having to rely on the asymptotic properties of random effects.

Various tests have been developed to detect the presence of random effects. The most common, implemented in some regression applications, is the Breusch–Pagan Lagrange multiplier test, the test statistic having a chi-squared distribution with one degree of freedom under the null hypothesis of no random effects. In the case of the marriage effect example the statistic is very high indeed, 20,007, but in this case it is meaningless because we are not able to use random effects estimation.

A note on the random effects and fixed effects terminology

It is generally agreed that random effects/fixed effects terminology can be misleading, but that it is too late to change it now. It is natural to think that random effects estimation should be used when the unobserved effect can be characterized as being drawn randomly from a given population and that fixed effects should be used when the unobserved effect is considered to be non-random. The second part of that statement is correct. However, the first part is correct only if the unobserved effect is distributed independently of the X_j variables. If it is not, fixed effects should be used instead to avoid the problem of unobserved heterogeneity bias. Figure 14.1 summarizes the decision-making process for fitting a model with panel data.

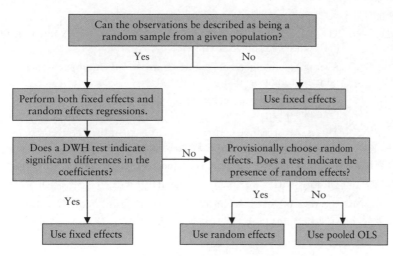

Figure 14.1 Choice of regression model for panel data

Key terms

balanced panel

Durbin–Wu–Hausman test

first differences regression

fixed effects

least squares dummy variable (LSDV) regression

longitudinal data set

panel data set

pooled OLS regression

random effects

unbalanced panel

unobserved effect

within-groups regression

14.1 Download the OECD2000 data set from the website. See Appendix B for details. The data set contains 32 variables:

ID   This is the country identification, with $1 = $ Australia, $2 = $ Austria, $3 = $ Belgium, $4 = $ Canada, $5 = $ Denmark, $6 = $ Finland, $7 = $ France, $8 = $ Germany, $9 = $ Greece, $10 = $ Iceland, $11 = $ Ireland, $12 = $ Italy, $13 = $ Japan, $14 = $ Korea, $15 = $ Luxembourg, $16 = $ Mexico, $17 = $ Netherlands, $18 = $ New Zealand, $19 = $ Norway, $20 = $ Portugal, $21 = $ Spain, $22 = $ Sweden, $23 = $ Switzerland, $24 = $ Turkey, $25 = $ United Kingdom, $26 = $ United States. Four countries that have recently joined the OECD, the Czech Republic, Hungary, Poland, and Slovakia, are excluded because their data do not go back far enough.

ID01–26   These are individual country dummy variables. For example, *ID09* is the dummy variable for Greece.

E   Average annual percentage rate of growth of employment for country i during time period t.

G   Average annual percentage rate of growth of GDP for country i during time period t.

TIME   There are three time periods, denoted 1, 2, and 3. They refer to average annual data for 1971–80, 1981–90, and 1991–2000.

TIME2   Dummy variable defined to be equal to 1 when $TIME = 2$, 0 otherwise.

TIME3   Dummy variable defined to be equal to 1 when $TIME = 3$, 0 otherwise.

Perform a pooled OLS regression of E on G. Regress E on G, *TIME2*, and *TIME3*. Perform appropriate statistical tests and give an interpretation of the regression results.

14.2 Using the OECD2000 data set, perform a (within-groups) fixed effects regression of E on G, *TIME2*, and *TIME3*. Perform appropriate statistical tests, give an interpretation of the regression coefficients, and comment on R^2.

14.3 Perform the corresponding LSDV regression, using OLS to regress E on G, *TIME2*, *TIME3*, and the country dummy variables (a) dropping the intercept, and (b) dropping one of the dummy variables. Perform appropriate statistical tests and give an interpretation of the coefficients in each case. Explain why either the intercept or one of the dummy variables must be dropped.

14.4 Perform a test for fixed effects in the OECD2000 regression by evaluating the explanatory power of the country dummy variables as a group.

14.5 Download the NLSY2000 data set from the website. See Appendix B for details. This contains the variables found in the *EAEF* data sets for the years 1980–94, 1996, 1998, and 2000 (there were no surveys in 1995, 1997, or 1999). Assuming that a random effects model is appropriate, investigate the apparent impact of unobserved heterogeneity on estimates of the coefficient of schooling by fitting the same earnings function, first using pooled OLS, then using random effects.

14.6 The *UNION* variable in the NLSY2000 data set is defined to be equal to 1 if the respondent was a member of a union in the year in question and 0 otherwise. Assuming that a random effects model is appropriate, add *UNION* to the earnings function specification and fit it using pooled OLS and random effects.

14.7 Using the NLSY2000 data set, perform a fixed effects regression of the earnings function specification used in Exercise 14.5 and compare the estimated coefficients with those obtained using OLS and random effects. Perform a Durbin–Wu–Hausman test to discriminate between random effects and fixed effects.

14.8 Using the NLSY2000 data set, perform a fixed effects regression of the earnings function specification used in Exercise 14.6 and compare the estimated coefficients with those obtained using OLS and random effects. Perform a Durbin–Wu–Hausman test to discriminate between random effects and fixed effects.

14.9 The within-groups version of the fixed effects regression model involved subtracting the group mean relationship

$$\overline{Y}_i = \beta_1 + \sum_{j=2}^{k} (\beta_j \overline{X}_{ij}) + \delta \overline{t} + \alpha_i + \overline{\varepsilon}_{it}$$

from the original specification in order to eliminate the individual-specific effect α_i. Regressions using the group mean relationship are described as between effects regressions. Explain why the between effects model is in general inappropriate for estimating the parameters of a model using panel data. (Consider the two cases where the α_i are correlated and uncorrelated with the X_j controls.)

APPENDIX A: Statistical Tables

Table A.1 Cumulative standardized normal distribution

$A(z)$ is the integral of the standardized normal distribution from $-\infty$ to z (in other words, the area under the curve to the left of z). It gives the probability of a normal random variable not being more than z standard deviations above its mean. Values of z of particular importance:

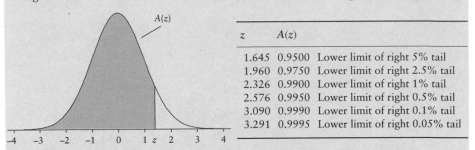

z	$A(z)$	
1.645	0.9500	Lower limit of right 5% tail
1.960	0.9750	Lower limit of right 2.5% tail
2.326	0.9900	Lower limit of right 1% tail
2.576	0.9950	Lower limit of right 0.5% tail
3.090	0.9990	Lower limit of right 0.1% tail
3.291	0.9995	Lower limit of right 0.05% tail

z	0.00	0.01	0.02	0.03	0.04	0.05	0.06	0.07	0.08	0.09
0.0	0.5000	0.5040	0.5080	0.5120	0.5160	0.5199	0.5239	0.5279	0.5319	0.5359
0.1	0.5398	0.5438	0.5478	0.5517	0.5557	0.5596	0.5636	0.5675	0.5714	0.5753
0.2	0.5793	0.5832	0.5871	0.5910	0.5948	0.5987	0.6026	0.6064	0.6103	0.6141
0.3	0.6179	0.6217	0.6255	0.6293	0.6331	0.6368	0.6406	0.6443	0.6480	0.6517
0.4	0.6554	0.6591	0.6628	0.6664	0.6700	0.6736	0.6772	0.6808	0.6844	0.6879
0.5	0.6915	0.6950	0.6985	0.7019	0.7054	0.7088	0.7123	0.7157	0.7190	0.7224
0.6	0.7257	0.7291	0.7324	0.7357	0.7389	0.7422	0.7454	0.7486	0.7517	0.7549
0.7	0.7580	0.7611	0.7642	0.7673	0.7704	0.7734	0.7764	0.7794	0.7823	0.7852
0.8	0.7881	0.7910	0.7939	0.7967	0.7995	0.8023	0.8051	0.8078	0.8106	0.8133
0.9	0.8159	0.8186	0.8212	0.8238	0.8264	0.8289	0.8315	0.8340	0.8365	0.8389
1.0	0.8413	0.8438	0.8461	0.8485	0.8508	0.8531	0.8554	0.8577	0.8599	0.8621
1.1	0.8643	0.8665	0.8686	0.8708	0.8729	0.8749	0.8770	0.8790	0.8810	0.8830
1.2	0.8849	0.8869	0.8888	0.8907	0.8925	0.8944	0.8962	0.8980	0.8997	0.9015
1.3	0.9032	0.9049	0.9066	0.9082	0.9099	0.9115	0.9131	0.9147	0.9162	0.9177
1.4	0.9192	0.9207	0.9222	0.9236	0.9251	0.9265	0.9279	0.9292	0.9306	0.9319
1.5	0.9332	0.9345	0.9357	0.9370	0.9382	0.9394	0.9406	0.9418	0.9429	0.9441
1.6	0.9452	0.9463	0.9474	0.9484	0.9495	0.9505	0.9515	0.9525	0.9535	0.9545
1.7	0.9554	0.9564	0.9573	0.9582	0.9591	0.9599	0.9608	0.9616	0.9625	0.9633
1.8	0.9641	0.9649	0.9656	0.9664	0.9671	0.9678	0.9686	0.9693	0.9699	0.9706
1.9	0.9713	0.9719	0.9726	0.9732	0.9738	0.9744	0.9750	0.9756	0.9761	0.9767
2.0	0.9772	0.9778	0.9783	0.9788	0.9793	0.9798	0.9803	0.9808	0.9812	0.9817
2.1	0.9821	0.9826	0.9830	0.9834	0.9838	0.9842	0.9846	0.9850	0.9854	0.9857

Table A.1 (*Continued*)

z	0.00	0.01	0.02	0.03	0.04	0.05	0.06	0.07	0.08	0.09
2.2	0.9861	0.9864	0.9868	0.9871	0.9875	0.9878	0.9881	0.9884	0.9887	0.9890
2.3	0.9893	0.9896	0.9898	0.9901	0.9904	0.9906	0.9909	0.9911	0.9913	0.9916
2.4	0.9918	0.9920	0.9922	0.9925	0.9927	0.9929	0.9931	0.9932	0.9934	0.9936
2.5	0.9938	0.9940	0.9941	0.9943	0.9945	0.9946	0.9948	0.9949	0.9951	0.9952
2.6	0.9953	0.9955	0.9956	0.9957	0.9959	0.9960	0.9961	0.9962	0.9963	0.9964
2.7	0.9965	0.9966	0.9967	0.9968	0.9969	0.9970	0.9971	0.9972	0.9973	0.9974
2.8	0.9974	0.9975	0.9976	0.9977	0.9977	0.9978	0.9979	0.9979	0.9980	0.9981
2.9	0.9981	0.9982	0.9982	0.9983	0.9984	0.9984	0.9985	0.9985	0.9986	0.9986
3.0	0.9987	0.9987	0.9987	0.9988	0.9988	0.9989	0.9989	0.9989	0.9990	0.9990
3.1	0.9990	0.9991	0.9991	0.9991	0.9992	0.9992	0.9992	0.9992	0.9993	0.9993
3.2	0.9993	0.9993	0.9994	0.9994	0.9994	0.9994	0.9994	0.9995	0.9995	0.9995
3.3	0.9995	0.9995	0.9995	0.9996	0.9996	0.9996	0.9996	0.9996	0.9996	0.9997
3.4	0.9997	0.9997	0.9997	0.9997	0.9997	0.9997	0.9997	0.9997	0.9997	0.9998
3.5	0.9998	0.9998	0.9998	0.9998	0.9998	0.9998	0.9998	0.9998	0.9998	0.9998
3.6	0.9998	0.9998	0.9999							

Tables A.2 and A.3 © C. Dougherty (2006). They may be reproduced subject to attribution.

Table A.2 t distribution: critical values of t

Degrees of freedom	Two-tailed test: One-tailed test:	Significance level					
		10% 5%	5% 2.5%	2% 1%	1% 0.5%	0.2% 0.1%	0.1% 0.05%
1		6.314	12.706	31.821	63.657	318.309	636.619
2		2.920	4.303	6.965	9.925	22.327	31.599
3		2.353	3.182	4.541	5.841	10.215	12.924
4		2.132	2.776	3.747	4.604	7.173	8.610
5		2.015	2.571	3.365	4.032	5.893	6.869
6		1.943	2.447	3.143	3.707	5.208	5.959
7		1.894	2.365	2.998	3.499	4.785	5.408
8		1.860	2.306	2.896	3.355	4.501	5.041
9		1.833	2.262	2.821	3.250	4.297	4.781
10		1.812	2.228	2.764	3.169	4.144	4.587
11		1.796	2.201	2.718	3.106	4.025	4.437
12		1.782	2.179	2.681	3.055	3.930	4.318
13		1.771	2.160	2.650	3.012	3.852	4.221
14		1.761	2.145	2.624	2.977	3.787	4.140
15		1.753	2.131	2.602	2.947	3.733	4.073
16		1.746	2.120	2.583	2.921	3.686	4.015
17		1.740	2.110	2.567	2.898	3.646	3.965
18		1.734	2.101	2.552	2.878	3.610	3.922
19		1.729	2.093	2.539	2.861	3.579	3.883
20		1.725	2.086	2.528	2.845	3.552	3.850
21		1.721	2.080	2.518	2.831	3.527	3.819
22		1.717	2.074	2.508	2.819	3.505	3.792
23		1.714	2.069	2.500	2.807	3.485	3.768
24		1.711	2.064	2.492	2.797	3.467	3.745
25		1.708	2.060	2.485	2.787	3.450	3.725

Table A.2 (*Continued*)

Degrees of freedom	Two-tailed test: One-tailed test:	Significance level					
		10% 5%	5% 2.5%	2% 1%	1% 0.5%	0.2% 0.1%	0.1% 0.05%
26		1.706	2.056	2.479	2.779	3.435	3.707
27		1.703	2.052	2.473	2.771	3.421	3.690
28		1.701	2.048	2.467	2.763	3.408	3.674
29		1.699	2.045	2.462	2.756	3.396	3.659
30		1.697	2.042	2.457	2.750	3.385	3.646
32		1.694	2.037	2.449	2.738	3.365	3.622
34		1.691	2.032	2.441	2.728	3.348	3.601
36		1.688	2.028	2.434	2.719	3.333	3.582
38		1.686	2.024	2.429	2.712	3.319	3.566
40		1.684	2.021	2.423	2.704	3.307	3.551
42		1.682	2.018	2.418	2.698	3.296	3.538
44		1.680	2.015	2.414	2.692	3.286	3.526
46		1.679	2.013	2.410	2.687	3.277	3.515
48		1.677	2.011	2.407	2.682	3.269	3.505
50		1.676	2.009	2.403	2.678	3.261	3.496
60		1.671	2.000	2.390	2.660	3.232	3.460
70		1.667	1.994	2.381	2.648	3.211	3.435
80		1.664	1.990	2.374	2.639	3.195	3.416
90		1.662	1.987	2.368	2.632	3.183	3.402
100		1.660	1.984	2.364	2.626	3.174	3.390
120		1.658	1.980	2.358	2.617	3.160	3.373
150		1.655	1.976	2.351	2.609	3.145	3.357
200		1.653	1.972	2.345	2.601	3.131	3.340
300		1.650	1.968	2.339	2.592	3.118	3.323
400		1.649	1.966	2.336	2.588	3.111	3.315
500		1.648	1.965	2.334	2.586	3.107	3.310
600		1.647	1.964	2.333	2.584	3.104	3.307
∞		1.645	1.960	2.326	2.576	3.090	3.291

Table A.3 F distribution: critical values of F (5% significance level)

v_1	1	2	3	4	5	6	7
v_2							
1	161.45	199.50	215.71	224.58	230.16	233.99	236.77
2	18.51	19.00	19.16	19.25	19.30	19.33	19.35
3	10.13	9.55	9.28	9.12	9.01	8.94	8.89
4	7.71	6.94	6.59	6.39	6.26	6.16	6.09
5	6.61	5.79	5.41	5.19	5.05	4.95	4.88
6	5.99	5.14	4.76	4.53	4.39	4.28	4.21
7	5.59	4.74	4.35	4.12	3.97	3.87	3.79
8	5.32	4.46	4.07	3.84	3.69	3.58	3.50
9	5.12	4.26	3.86	3.63	3.48	3.37	3.29
10	4.96	4.10	3.71	3.48	3.33	3.22	3.14
11	4.84	3.98	3.59	3.36	3.20	3.09	3.01
12	4.75	3.89	3.49	3.26	3.11	3.00	2.91
13	4.67	3.81	3.41	3.18	3.03	2.92	2.83
14	4.60	3.74	3.34	3.11	2.96	2.85	2.76
15	4.54	3.68	3.29	3.06	2.90	2.79	2.71
16	4.49	3.63	3.24	3.01	2.85	2.74	2.66
17	4.45	3.59	3.20	2.96	2.81	2.70	2.61
18	4.41	3.55	3.16	2.93	2.77	2.66	2.58
19	4.38	3.52	3.13	2.90	2.74	2.63	2.54
20	4.35	3.49	3.10	2.87	2.71	2.60	2.51
21	4.32	3.47	3.07	2.84	2.68	2.57	2.49
22	4.30	3.44	3.05	2.82	2.66	2.55	2.46
23	4.28	3.42	3.03	2.80	2.64	2.53	2.44
24	4.26	3.40	3.01	2.78	2.62	2.51	2.42
25	4.24	3.39	2.99	2.76	2.60	2.49	2.40
26	4.22	3.37	2.98	2.74	2.59	2.47	2.39
27	4.21	3.35	2.96	2.73	2.57	2.46	2.37
28	4.20	3.34	2.95	2.71	2.56	2.45	2.36
29	4.18	3.33	2.93	2.70	2.55	2.43	2.35
30	4.17	3.32	2.92	2.69	2.53	2.42	2.33
35	4.12	3.27	2.87	2.64	2.49	2.37	2.29
40	4.08	3.23	2.84	2.61	2.45	2.34	2.25
50	4.03	3.18	2.79	2.56	2.40	2.29	2.20
60	4.00	3.15	2.76	2.53	2.37	2.25	2.17
70	3.98	3.13	2.74	2.50	2.35	2.23	2.14
80	3.96	3.11	2.72	2.49	2.33	2.21	2.13
90	3.95	3.10	2.71	2.47	2.32	2.20	2.11
100	3.94	3.09	2.70	2.46	2.31	2.19	2.10
120	3.92	3.07	2.68	2.45	2.29	2.18	2.09
150	3.90	3.06	2.66	2.43	2.27	2.16	2.07
200	3.89	3.04	2.65	2.42	2.26	2.14	2.06
250	3.88	3.03	2.64	2.41	2.25	2.13	2.05
300	3.87	3.03	2.63	2.40	2.24	2.13	2.04
400	3.86	3.02	2.63	2.39	2.24	2.12	2.03
500	3.86	3.01	2.62	2.39	2.23	2.12	2.03
600	3.86	3.01	2.62	2.39	2.23	2.11	2.02
750	3.85	3.01	2.62	2.38	2.23	2.11	2.02
1000	3.85	3.00	2.61	2.38	2.22	2.11	2.02

Table A.3 (*Continued*)

v_1	8	9	10	12	14	16
v_2						
1	238.88	240.54	241.88	243.91	245.36	246.46
2	19.37	19.38	19.40	19.41	19.42	19.43
3	8.85	8.81	8.79	8.74	8.71	8.69
4	6.04	6.00	5.96	5.91	5.87	5.84
5	4.82	4.77	4.74	4.68	4.64	4.60
6	4.15	4.10	4.06	4.00	3.96	3.92
7	3.73	3.68	3.64	3.57	3.53	3.49
8	3.44	3.39	3.35	3.28	3.24	3.20
9	3.23	3.18	3.14	3.07	3.03	2.99
10	3.07	3.02	2.98	2.91	2.86	2.83
11	2.95	2.90	2.85	2.79	2.74	2.70
12	2.85	2.80	2.75	2.69	2.64	2.60
13	2.77	2.71	2.67	2.60	2.55	2.51
14	2.70	2.65	2.60	2.53	2.48	2.44
15	2.64	2.59	2.54	2.48	2.42	2.38
16	2.59	2.54	2.49	2.42	2.37	2.33
17	2.55	2.49	2.45	2.38	2.33	2.29
18	2.51	2.46	2.41	2.34	2.29	2.25
19	2.48	2.42	2.38	2.31	2.26	2.21
20	2.45	2.39	2.35	2.28	2.22	2.18
21	2.42	2.37	2.32	2.25	2.20	2.16
22	2.40	2.34	2.30	2.23	2.17	2.13
23	2.37	2.32	2.27	2.20	2.15	2.11
24	2.36	2.30	2.25	2.18	2.13	2.09
25	2.34	2.28	2.24	2.16	2.11	2.07
26	2.32	2.27	2.22	2.15	2.09	2.05
27	2.31	2.25	2.20	2.13	2.08	2.04
28	2.29	2.24	2.19	2.12	2.06	2.02
29	2.28	2.22	2.18	2.10	2.05	2.01
30	2.27	2.21	2.16	2.09	2.04	1.99
35	2.22	2.16	2.11	2.04	1.99	1.94
40	2.18	2.12	2.08	2.00	1.95	1.90
50	2.13	2.07	2.03	1.95	1.89	1.85
60	2.10	2.04	1.99	1.92	1.86	1.82
70	2.07	2.02	1.97	1.89	1.84	1.79
80	2.06	2.00	1.95	1.88	1.82	1.77
90	2.04	1.99	1.94	1.86	1.80	1.76
100	2.03	1.97	1.93	1.85	1.79	1.75
120	2.02	1.96	1.91	1.83	1.78	1.73
150	2.00	1.94	1.89	1.82	1.76	1.71
200	1.98	1.93	1.88	1.80	1.74	1.69
250	1.98	1.92	1.87	1.79	1.73	1.68
300	1.97	1.91	1.86	1.78	1.72	1.68
400	1.96	1.90	1.85	1.78	1.72	1.67
500	1.96	1.90	1.85	1.77	1.71	1.66
600	1.95	1.90	1.85	1.77	1.71	1.66
750	1.95	1.89	1.84	1.77	1.70	1.66
1000	1.95	1.89	1.84	1.76	1.70	1.65

Table A.3 (*Continued*)

v_1	18	20	25	30	35	40
v_2						
1	247.32	248.01	249.26	250.10	250.69	251.14
2	19.44	19.45	19.46	19.46	19.47	19.47
3	8.67	8.66	8.63	8.62	8.60	8.59
4	5.82	5.80	5.77	5.75	5.73	5.72
5	4.58	4.56	4.52	4.50	4.48	4.46
6	3.90	3.87	3.83	3.81	3.79	3.77
7	3.47	3.44	3.40	3.38	3.36	3.34
8	3.17	3.15	3.11	3.08	3.06	3.04
9	2.96	2.94	2.89	2.86	2.84	2.83
10	2.80	2.77	2.73	2.70	2.68	2.66
11	2.67	2.65	2.60	2.57	2.55	2.53
12	2.57	2.54	2.50	2.47	2.44	2.43
13	2.48	2.46	2.41	2.38	2.36	2.34
14	2.41	2.39	2.34	2.31	2.28	2.27
15	2.35	2.33	2.28	2.25	2.22	2.20
16	2.30	2.28	2.23	2.19	2.17	2.15
17	2.26	2.23	2.18	2.15	2.12	2.10
18	2.22	2.19	2.14	2.11	2.08	2.06
19	2.18	2.16	2.11	2.07	2.05	2.03
20	2.15	2.12	2.07	2.04	2.01	1.99
21	2.12	2.10	2.05	2.01	1.98	1.96
22	2.10	2.07	2.02	1.98	1.96	1.94
23	2.08	2.05	2.00	1.96	1.93	1.91
24	2.05	2.03	1.97	1.94	1.91	1.89
25	2.04	2.01	1.96	1.92	1.89	1.87
26	2.02	1.99	1.94	1.90	1.87	1.85
27	2.00	1.97	1.92	1.88	1.86	1.84
28	1.99	1.96	1.91	1.87	1.84	1.82
29	1.97	1.94	1.89	1.85	1.83	1.81
30	1.96	1.93	1.88	1.84	1.81	1.79
35	1.91	1.88	1.82	1.79	1.76	1.74
40	1.87	1.84	1.78	1.74	1.72	1.69
50	1.81	1.78	1.73	1.69	1.66	1.63
60	1.78	1.75	1.69	1.65	1.62	1.59
70	1.75	1.72	1.66	1.62	1.59	1.57
80	1.73	1.70	1.64	1.60	1.57	1.54
90	1.72	1.69	1.63	1.59	1.55	1.53
100	1.71	1.68	1.62	1.57	1.54	1.52
120	1.69	1.66	1.60	1.55	1.52	1.50
150	1.67	1.64	1.58	1.54	1.50	1.48
200	1.66	1.62	1.56	1.52	1.48	1.46
250	1.65	1.61	1.55	1.50	1.47	1.44
300	1.64	1.61	1.54	1.50	1.46	1.43
400	1.63	1.60	1.53	1.49	1.45	1.42
500	1.62	1.59	1.53	1.48	1.45	1.42
600	1.62	1.59	1.52	1.48	1.44	1.41
750	1.62	1.58	1.52	1.47	1.44	1.41
1000	1.61	1.58	1.52	1.47	1.43	1.41

Table A.3 (*Continued*)

v_1	50	60	75	100	150	200
v_2						
1	251.77	252.20	252.62	253.04	253.46	253.68
2	19.48	19.48	19.48	19.49	19.49	19.49
3	8.58	8.57	8.56	8.55	8.54	8.54
4	5.70	5.69	5.68	5.66	5.65	5.65
5	4.44	4.43	4.42	4.41	4.39	4.39
6	3.75	3.74	3.73	3.71	3.70	3.69
7	3.32	3.30	3.29	3.27	3.26	3.25
8	3.02	3.01	2.99	2.97	2.96	2.95
9	2.80	2.79	2.77	2.76	2.74	2.73
10	2.64	2.62	2.60	2.59	2.57	2.56
11	2.51	2.49	2.47	2.46	2.44	2.43
12	2.40	2.38	2.37	2.35	2.33	2.32
13	2.31	2.30	2.28	2.26	2.24	2.23
14	2.24	2.22	2.21	2.19	2.17	2.16
15	2.18	2.16	2.14	2.12	2.10	2.10
16	2.12	2.11	2.09	2.07	2.05	2.04
17	2.08	2.06	2.04	2.02	2.00	1.99
18	2.04	2.02	2.00	1.98	1.96	1.95
19	2.00	1.98	1.96	1.94	1.92	1.91
20	1.97	1.95	1.93	1.91	1.89	1.88
21	1.94	1.92	1.90	1.88	1.86	1.84
22	1.91	1.89	1.87	1.85	1.83	1.82
23	1.88	1.86	1.84	1.82	1.80	1.79
24	1.86	1.84	1.82	1.80	1.78	1.77
25	1.84	1.82	1.80	1.78	1.76	1.75
26	1.82	1.80	1.78	1.76	1.74	1.73
27	1.81	1.79	1.76	1.74	1.72	1.71
28	1.79	1.77	1.75	1.73	1.70	1.69
29	1.77	1.75	1.73	1.71	1.69	1.67
30	1.76	1.74	1.72	1.70	1.67	1.66
35	1.70	1.68	1.66	1.63	1.61	1.60
40	1.66	1.64	1.61	1.59	1.56	1.55
50	1.60	1.58	1.55	1.52	1.50	1.48
60	1.56	1.53	1.51	1.48	1.45	1.44
70	1.53	1.50	1.48	1.45	1.42	1.40
80	1.51	1.48	1.45	1.43	1.39	1.38
90	1.49	1.46	1.44	1.41	1.38	1.36
100	1.48	1.45	1.42	1.39	1.36	1.34
120	1.46	1.43	1.40	1.37	1.33	1.32
150	1.44	1.41	1.38	1.34	1.31	1.29
200	1.41	1.39	1.35	1.32	1.28	1.26
250	1.40	1.37	1.34	1.31	1.27	1.25
300	1.39	1.36	1.33	1.30	1.26	1.23
400	1.38	1.35	1.32	1.28	1.24	1.22
500	1.38	1.35	1.31	1.28	1.23	1.21
600	1.37	1.34	1.31	1.27	1.23	1.20
750	1.37	1.34	1.30	1.26	1.22	1.20
1000	1.36	1.33	1.30	1.26	1.22	1.19

Table A.3 F distribution: critical values of F (1% significance level)

v_1	1	2	3	4	5	6	7
v_2							
1	4052.18	4999.50	5403.35	5624.58	5763.65	5858.99	5928.36
2	98.50	99.00	99.17	99.25	99.30	99.33	99.36
3	34.12	30.82	29.46	28.71	28.24	27.91	27.67
4	21.20	18.00	16.69	15.98	15.52	15.21	14.98
5	16.26	13.27	12.06	11.39	10.97	10.67	10.46
6	13.75	10.92	9.78	9.15	8.75	8.47	8.26
7	12.25	9.55	8.45	7.85	7.46	7.19	6.99
8	11.26	8.65	7.59	7.01	6.63	6.37	6.18
9	10.56	8.02	6.99	6.42	6.06	5.80	5.61
10	10.04	7.56	6.55	5.99	5.64	5.39	5.20
11	9.65	7.21	6.22	5.67	5.32	5.07	4.89
12	9.33	6.93	5.95	5.41	5.06	4.82	4.64
13	9.07	6.70	5.74	5.21	4.86	4.62	4.44
14	8.86	6.51	5.56	5.04	4.69	4.46	4.28
15	8.68	6.36	5.42	4.89	4.56	4.32	4.14
16	8.53	6.23	5.29	4.77	4.44	4.20	4.03
17	8.40	6.11	5.18	4.67	4.34	4.10	3.93
18	8.29	6.01	5.09	4.58	4.25	4.01	3.84
19	8.18	5.93	5.01	4.50	4.17	3.94	3.77
20	8.10	5.85	4.94	4.43	4.10	3.87	3.70
21	8.02	5.78	4.87	4.37	4.04	3.81	3.64
22	7.95	5.72	4.82	4.31	3.99	3.76	3.59
23	7.88	5.66	4.76	4.26	3.94	3.71	3.54
24	7.82	5.61	4.72	4.22	3.90	3.67	3.50
25	7.77	5.57	4.68	4.18	3.85	3.63	3.46
26	7.72	5.53	4.64	4.14	3.82	3.59	3.42
27	7.68	5.49	4.60	4.11	3.78	3.56	3.39
28	7.64	5.45	4.57	4.07	3.75	3.53	3.36
29	7.60	5.42	4.54	4.04	3.73	3.50	3.33
30	7.56	5.39	4.51	4.02	3.70	3.47	3.30
35	7.42	5.27	4.40	3.91	3.59	3.37	3.20
40	7.31	5.18	4.31	3.83	3.51	3.29	3.12
50	7.17	5.06	4.20	3.72	3.41	3.19	3.02
60	7.08	4.98	4.13	3.65	3.34	3.12	2.95
70	7.01	4.92	4.07	3.60	3.29	3.07	2.91
80	6.96	4.88	4.04	3.56	3.26	3.04	2.87
90	6.93	4.85	4.01	3.53	3.23	3.01	2.84
100	6.90	4.82	3.98	3.51	3.21	2.99	2.82
120	6.85	4.79	3.95	3.48	3.17	2.96	2.79
150	6.81	4.75	3.91	3.45	3.14	2.92	2.76
200	6.76	4.71	3.88	3.41	3.11	2.89	2.73
250	6.74	4.69	3.86	3.40	3.09	2.87	2.71
300	6.72	4.68	3.85	3.38	3.08	2.86	2.70
400	6.70	4.66	3.83	3.37	3.06	2.85	2.68
500	6.69	4.65	3.82	3.36	3.05	2.84	2.68
600	6.68	4.64	3.81	3.35	3.05	2.83	2.67
750	6.67	4.63	3.81	3.34	3.04	2.83	2.66
1000	6.66	4.63	3.80	3.34	3.04	2.82	2.66

Table A.3 (*Continued*)

v_1	8	9	10	12	14	16
v_2						
1	5981.07	6022.47	6055.85	6106.32	6142.67	6170.10
2	99.37	99.39	99.40	99.42	99.43	99.44
3	27.49	27.35	27.23	27.05	26.92	26.83
4	14.80	14.66	14.55	14.37	14.25	14.15
5	10.29	10.16	10.05	9.89	9.77	9.68
6	8.10	7.98	7.87	7.72	7.60	7.52
7	6.84	6.72	6.62	6.47	6.36	6.28
8	6.03	5.91	5.81	5.67	5.56	5.48
9	5.47	5.35	5.26	5.11	5.01	4.92
10	5.06	4.94	4.85	4.71	4.60	4.52
11	4.74	4.63	4.54	4.40	4.29	4.21
12	4.50	4.39	4.30	4.16	4.05	3.97
13	4.30	4.19	4.10	3.96	3.86	3.78
14	4.14	4.03	3.94	3.80	3.70	3.62
15	4.00	3.89	3.80	3.67	3.56	3.49
16	3.89	3.78	3.69	3.55	3.45	3.37
17	3.79	3.68	3.59	3.46	3.35	3.27
18	3.71	3.60	3.51	3.37	3.27	3.19
19	3.63	3.52	3.43	3.30	3.19	3.12
20	3.56	3.46	3.37	3.23	3.13	3.05
21	3.51	3.40	3.31	3.17	3.07	2.99
22	3.45	3.35	3.26	3.12	3.02	2.94
23	3.41	3.30	3.21	3.07	2.97	2.89
24	3.36	3.26	3.17	3.03	2.93	2.85
25	3.32	3.22	3.13	2.99	2.89	2.81
26	3.29	3.18	3.09	2.96	2.86	2.78
27	3.26	3.15	3.06	2.93	2.82	2.75
28	3.23	3.12	3.03	2.90	2.79	2.72
29	3.20	3.09	3.00	2.87	2.77	2.69
30	3.17	3.07	2.98	2.84	2.74	2.66
35	3.07	2.96	2.88	2.74	2.64	2.56
40	2.99	2.89	2.80	2.66	2.56	2.48
50	2.89	2.78	2.70	2.56	2.46	2.38
60	2.82	2.72	2.63	2.50	2.39	2.31
70	2.78	2.67	2.59	2.45	2.35	2.27
80	2.74	2.64	2.55	2.42	2.31	2.23
90	2.72	2.61	2.52	2.39	2.29	2.21
100	2.69	2.59	2.50	2.37	2.27	2.19
120	2.66	2.56	2.47	2.34	2.23	2.15
150	2.63	2.53	2.44	2.31	2.20	2.12
200	2.60	2.50	2.41	2.27	2.17	2.09
250	2.58	2.48	2.39	2.26	2.15	2.07
300	2.57	2.47	2.38	2.24	2.14	2.06
400	2.56	2.45	2.37	2.23	2.13	2.05
500	2.55	2.44	2.36	2.22	2.12	2.04
600	2.54	2.44	2.35	2.21	2.11	2.03
750	2.53	2.43	2.34	2.21	2.11	2.02
1000	2.53	2.43	2.34	2.20	2.10	2.02

Table A.3 (*Continued*)

v_1	18	20	25	30	35	40
v_2						
1	6191.53	6208.73	6239.83	6260.65	6275.57	6286.78
2	99.44	99.45	99.46	99.47	99.47	99.47
3	26.75	26.69	26.58	26.50	26.45	26.41
4	14.08	14.02	13.91	13.84	13.79	13.75
5	9.61	9.55	9.45	9.38	9.33	9.29
6	7.45	7.40	7.30	7.23	7.18	7.14
7	6.21	6.16	6.06	5.99	5.94	5.91
8	5.41	5.36	5.26	5.20	5.15	5.12
9	4.86	4.81	4.71	4.65	4.60	4.57
10	4.46	4.41	4.31	4.25	4.20	4.17
11	4.15	4.10	4.01	3.94	3.89	3.86
12	3.91	3.86	3.76	3.70	3.65	3.62
13	3.72	3.66	3.57	3.51	3.46	3.43
14	3.56	3.51	3.41	3.35	3.30	3.27
15	3.42	3.37	3.28	3.21	3.17	3.13
16	3.31	3.26	3.16	3.10	3.05	3.02
17	3.21	3.16	3.07	3.00	2.96	2.92
18	3.13	3.08	2.98	2.92	2.87	2.84
19	3.05	3.00	2.91	2.84	2.80	2.76
20	2.99	2.94	2.84	2.78	2.73	2.69
21	2.93	2.88	2.79	2.72	2.67	2.64
22	2.88	2.83	2.73	2.67	2.62	2.58
23	2.83	2.78	2.69	2.62	2.57	2.54
24	2.79	2.74	2.64	2.58	2.53	2.49
25	2.75	2.70	2.60	2.54	2.49	2.45
26	2.72	2.66	2.57	2.50	2.45	2.42
27	2.68	2.63	2.54	2.47	2.42	2.38
28	2.65	2.60	2.51	2.44	2.39	2.35
29	2.63	2.57	2.48	2.41	2.36	2.33
30	2.60	2.55	2.45	2.39	2.34	2.30
35	2.50	2.44	2.35	2.28	2.23	2.19
40	2.42	2.37	2.27	2.20	2.15	2.11
50	2.32	2.27	2.17	2.10	2.05	2.01
60	2.25	2.20	2.10	2.03	1.98	1.94
70	2.20	2.15	2.05	1.98	1.93	1.89
80	2.17	2.12	2.01	1.94	1.89	1.85
90	2.14	2.09	1.99	1.92	1.86	1.82
100	2.12	2.07	1.97	1.89	1.84	1.80
120	2.09	2.03	1.93	1.86	1.81	1.76
150	2.06	2.00	1.90	1.83	1.77	1.73
200	2.03	1.97	1.87	1.79	1.74	1.69
250	2.01	1.95	1.85	1.77	1.72	1.67
300	1.99	1.94	1.84	1.76	1.70	1.66
400	1.98	1.92	1.82	1.75	1.69	1.64
500	1.97	1.92	1.81	1.74	1.68	1.63
600	1.96	1.91	1.80	1.73	1.67	1.63
750	1.96	1.90	1.80	1.72	1.66	1.62
1000	1.95	1.90	1.79	1.72	1.66	1.61

Table A.3 (*Continued*)

v_1	50	60	75	100	150	200
v_2						
1	6302.52	6313.03	6323.56	6334.11	6344.68	6349.97
2	99.48	99.48	99.49	99.49	99.49	99.49
3	26.35	26.32	26.28	26.24	26.20	26.18
4	13.69	13.65	13.61	13.58	13.54	13.52
5	9.24	9.20	9.17	9.13	9.09	9.08
6	7.09	7.06	7.02	6.99	6.95	6.93
7	5.86	5.82	5.79	5.75	5.72	5.70
8	5.07	5.03	5.00	4.96	4.93	4.91
9	4.52	4.48	4.45	4.41	4.38	4.36
10	4.12	4.08	4.05	4.01	3.98	3.96
11	3.81	3.78	3.74	3.71	3.67	3.66
12	3.57	3.54	3.50	3.47	3.43	3.41
13	3.38	3.34	3.31	3.27	3.24	3.22
14	3.22	3.18	3.15	3.11	3.08	3.06
15	3.08	3.05	3.01	2.98	2.94	2.92
16	2.97	2.93	2.90	2.86	2.83	2.81
17	2.87	2.83	2.80	2.76	2.73	2.71
18	2.78	2.75	2.71	2.68	2.64	2.62
19	2.71	2.67	2.64	2.60	2.57	2.55
20	2.64	2.61	2.57	2.54	2.50	2.48
21	2.58	2.55	2.51	2.48	2.44	2.42
22	2.53	2.50	2.46	2.42	2.38	2.36
23	2.48	2.45	2.41	2.37	2.34	2.32
24	2.44	2.40	2.37	2.33	2.29	2.27
25	2.40	2.36	2.33	2.29	2.25	2.23
26	2.36	2.33	2.29	2.25	2.21	2.19
27	2.33	2.29	2.26	2.22	2.18	2.16
28	2.30	2.26	2.23	2.19	2.15	2.13
29	2.27	2.23	2.20	2.16	2.12	2.10
30	2.25	2.21	2.17	2.13	2.09	2.07
35	2.14	2.10	2.06	2.02	1.98	1.96
40	2.06	2.02	1.98	1.94	1.90	1.87
50	1.95	1.91	1.87	1.82	1.78	1.76
60	1.88	1.84	1.79	1.75	1.70	1.68
70	1.83	1.78	1.74	1.70	1.65	1.62
80	1.79	1.75	1.70	1.65	1.61	1.58
90	1.76	1.72	1.67	1.62	1.57	1.55
100	1.74	1.69	1.65	1.60	1.55	1.52
120	1.70	1.66	1.61	1.56	1.51	1.48
150	1.66	1.62	1.57	1.52	1.46	1.43
200	1.63	1.58	1.53	1.48	1.42	1.39
250	1.61	1.56	1.51	1.46	1.40	1.36
300	1.59	1.55	1.50	1.44	1.38	1.35
400	1.58	1.53	1.48	1.42	1.36	1.32
500	1.57	1.52	1.47	1.41	1.34	1.31
600	1.56	1.51	1.46	1.40	1.34	1.30
750	1.55	1.50	1.45	1.39	1.33	1.29
1000	1.54	1.50	1.44	1.38	1.32	1.28

Table A.3 F distribution: critical values of F (0.1% significance level)

v_1	1	2	3	4	5	6	7
v_2							
1	4.05e05	5.00e05	5.40e05	5.62e05	5.76e05	5.86e05	5.93e05
2	998.50	999.00	999.17	999.25	999.30	999.33	999.36
3	167.03	148.50	141.11	137.10	134.58	132.85	131.58
4	74.14	61.25	56.18	53.44	51.71	50.53	49.66
5	47.18	37.12	33.20	31.09	29.75	28.83	28.16
6	35.51	27.00	23.70	21.92	20.80	20.03	19.46
7	29.25	21.69	18.77	17.20	16.21	15.52	15.02
8	25.41	18.49	15.83	14.39	13.48	12.86	12.40
9	22.86	16.39	13.90	12.56	11.71	11.13	10.70
10	21.04	14.91	12.55	11.28	10.48	9.93	9.52
11	19.69	13.81	11.56	10.35	9.58	9.05	8.66
12	18.64	12.97	10.80	9.63	8.89	8.38	8.00
13	17.82	12.31	10.21	9.07	8.35	7.86	7.49
14	17.14	11.78	9.73	8.62	7.92	7.44	7.08
15	16.59	11.34	9.34	8.25	7.57	7.09	6.74
16	16.12	10.97	9.01	7.94	7.27	6.80	6.46
17	15.72	10.66	8.73	7.68	7.02	6.56	6.22
18	15.38	10.39	8.49	7.46	6.81	6.35	6.02
19	15.08	10.16	8.28	7.27	6.62	6.18	5.85
20	14.82	9.95	8.10	7.10	6.46	6.02	5.69
21	14.59	9.77	7.94	6.95	6.32	5.88	5.56
22	14.38	9.61	7.80	6.81	6.19	5.76	5.44
23	14.20	9.47	7.67	6.70	6.08	5.65	5.33
24	14.03	9.34	7.55	6.59	5.98	5.55	5.23
25	13.88	9.22	7.45	6.49	5.89	5.46	5.15
26	13.74	9.12	7.36	6.41	5.80	5.38	5.07
27	13.61	9.02	7.27	6.33	5.73	5.31	5.00
28	13.50	8.93	7.19	6.25	5.66	5.24	4.93
29	13.39	8.85	7.12	6.19	5.59	5.18	4.87
30	13.29	8.77	7.05	6.12	5.53	5.12	4.82
35	12.90	8.47	6.79	5.88	5.30	4.89	4.59
40	12.61	8.25	6.59	5.70	5.13	4.73	4.44
50	12.22	7.96	6.34	5.46	4.90	4.51	4.22
60	11.97	7.77	6.17	5.31	4.76	4.37	4.09
70	11.80	7.64	6.06	5.20	4.66	4.28	3.99
80	11.67	7.54	5.97	5.12	4.58	4.20	3.92
90	11.57	7.47	5.91	5.06	4.53	4.15	3.87
100	11.50	7.41	5.86	5.02	4.48	4.11	3.83
120	11.38	7.32	5.78	4.95	4.42	4.04	3.77
150	11.27	7.24	5.71	4.88	4.35	3.98	3.71
200	11.15	7.15	5.63	4.81	4.29	3.92	3.65
250	11.09	7.10	5.59	4.77	4.25	3.88	3.61
300	11.04	7.07	5.56	4.75	4.22	3.86	3.59
400	10.99	7.03	5.53	4.71	4.19	3.83	3.56
500	10.96	7.00	5.51	4.69	4.18	3.81	3.54
600	10.94	6.99	5.49	4.68	4.16	3.80	3.53
750	10.91	6.97	5.48	4.67	4.15	3.79	3.52
1000	10.89	6.96	5.46	4.65	4.14	3.78	3.51

Table A.3 (*Continued*)

v_1	8	9	10	12	14	16
v_2						
1	5.98e05	6.02e05	6.06e05	6.11e05	6.14e05	6.17e05
2	999.37	999.39	999.40	999.42	999.43	999.44
3	130.62	129.86	129.25	128.32	127.64	127.14
4	49.00	48.47	48.05	47.41	46.95	46.60
5	27.65	27.24	26.92	26.42	26.06	25.78
6	19.03	18.69	18.41	17.99	17.68	17.45
7	14.63	14.33	14.08	13.71	13.43	13.23
8	12.05	11.77	11.54	11.19	10.94	10.75
9	10.37	10.11	9.89	9.57	9.33	9.15
10	9.20	8.96	8.75	8.45	8.22	8.05
11	8.35	8.12	7.92	7.63	7.41	7.24
12	7.71	7.48	7.29	7.00	6.79	6.63
13	7.21	6.98	6.80	6.52	6.31	6.16
14	6.80	6.58	6.40	6.13	5.93	5.78
15	6.47	6.26	6.08	5.81	5.62	5.46
16	6.19	5.98	5.81	5.55	5.35	5.20
17	5.96	5.75	5.58	5.32	5.13	4.99
18	5.76	5.56	5.39	5.13	4.94	4.80
19	5.59	5.39	5.22	4.97	4.78	4.64
20	5.44	5.24	5.08	4.82	4.64	4.49
21	5.31	5.11	4.95	4.70	4.51	4.37
22	5.19	4.99	4.83	4.58	4.40	4.26
23	5.09	4.89	4.73	4.48	4.30	4.16
24	4.99	4.80	4.64	4.39	4.21	4.07
25	4.91	4.71	4.56	4.31	4.13	3.99
26	4.83	4.64	4.48	4.24	4.06	3.92
27	4.76	4.57	4.41	4.17	3.99	3.86
28	4.69	4.50	4.35	4.11	3.93	3.80
29	4.64	4.45	4.29	4.05	3.88	3.74
30	4.58	4.39	4.24	4.00	3.82	3.69
35	4.36	4.18	4.03	3.79	3.62	3.48
40	4.21	4.02	3.87	3.64	3.47	3.34
50	4.00	3.82	3.67	3.44	3.27	3.41
60	3.86	3.69	3.54	3.32	3.15	3.02
70	3.77	3.60	3.45	3.23	3.06	2.93
80	3.70	3.53	3.39	3.16	3.00	2.87
90	3.65	3.48	3.34	3.11	2.95	2.82
100	3.61	3.44	3.30	3.07	2.91	2.78
120	3.55	3.38	3.24	3.02	2.85	2.72
150	3.49	3.32	3.18	2.96	2.80	2.67
200	3.43	3.26	3.12	2.90	2.74	2.61
250	3.40	3.23	3.09	2.87	2.71	2.58
300	3.38	3.21	3.07	2.85	2.69	2.56
400	3.35	3.18	3.04	2.82	2.66	2.53
500	3.33	3.16	3.02	2.81	2.64	2.52
600	3.32	3.15	3.01	2.80	2.63	2.51
750	3.31	3.14	3.00	2.78	2.62	2.49
1000	3.30	3.13	2.99	2.77	2.61	2.48

Table A.3 (*Continued*)

v_1	18	20	25	30	35	40
v_2						
1	6.19e05	6.21e05	6.24e05	6.26e05	6.28e05	6.29e05
2	999.44	999.45	999.46	999.47	999.47	999.47
3	126.74	126.42	125.84	125.45	125.17	124.96
4	46.32	46.10	45.70	45.43	45.23	45.09
5	25.57	25.39	25.08	24.87	24.72	24.60
6	17.27	17.12	16.85	16.67	16.54	16.44
7	13.06	12.93	12.69	12.53	12.41	12.33
8	10.60	10.48	10.26	10.11	10.00	9.92
9	9.01	8.90	8.69	8.55	8.46	8.37
10	7.91	7.80	7.60	7.47	7.37	7.30
11	7.11	7.01	6.81	6.68	6.59	6.52
12	6.51	6.40	6.22	6.09	6.00	5.93
13	6.03	5.93	5.75	5.63	5.54	5.47
14	5.66	5.56	5.38	5.25	5.17	5.10
15	5.35	5.25	5.07	4.95	4.86	4.80
16	5.09	4.99	4.82	4.70	4.61	4.54
17	4.87	4.78	4.60	4.48	4.40	4.33
18	4.68	4.59	4.42	4.30	4.22	4.15
19	4.52	4.43	4.26	4.14	4.06	3.99
20	4.38	4.29	4.12	4.00	3.92	3.86
21	4.26	4.17	4.00	3.88	3.80	3.74
22	4.15	4.06	3.89	3.78	3.70	3.63
23	4.05	3.96	3.79	3.68	3.60	3.53
24	3.96	3.87	3.71	3.59	3.51	3.45
25	3.88	3.79	3.63	3.52	3.43	3.37
26	3.81	3.72	3.56	3.44	3.36	3.30
27	3.75	3.66	3.49	3.38	3.30	3.23
28	3.69	3.60	3.43	3.32	3.24	3.18
29	3.63	3.54	3.38	3.27	3.18	3.12
30	3.58	3.49	3.33	3.22	3.13	3.07
35	3.38	3.29	3.13	3.02	2.93	2.87
40	3.23	3.14	2.98	2.87	2.79	2.73
50	3.04	2.95	2.79	2.68	2.60	2.53
60	2.91	2.83	2.67	2.55	2.47	2.41
70	2.83	2.74	2.58	2.47	2.39	2.32
80	2.76	2.68	2.52	2.41	2.32	2.26
90	2.71	2.63	2.47	2.36	2.27	2.21
100	2.68	2.59	2.43	2.32	2.24	2.17
120	2.62	2.53	2.37	2.26	2.18	2.11
150	2.56	2.48	2.32	2.21	2.12	2.06
200	2.51	2.42	2.26	2.15	2.07	2.00
250	2.48	2.39	2.23	2.12	2.03	1.97
300	2.46	2.37	2.21	2.10	2.01	1.94
400	2.43	2.34	2.18	2.07	1.98	1.92
500	2.41	2.33	2.17	2.05	1.97	1.90
600	2.40	2.32	2.16	2.04	1.96	1.89
750	2.39	2.31	2.15	2.03	1.95	1.88
1000	2.38	2.30	2.14	2.02	1.94	1.87

Table A.3 (*Continued*)

v_1	50	60	75	100	150	200
v_2						
1	6.30e05	6.31e05	6.32e05	6.33e05	6.35e05	6.35e05
2	999.48	999.48	999.49	999.49	999.49	999.49
3	124.66	124.47	124.27	124.07	123.87	123.77
4	44.88	44.75	44.61	44.47	44.33	44.26
5	24.44	24.33	24.22	24.12	24.01	23.95
6	16.31	16.21	16.12	16.03	15.93	15.89
7	12.20	12.12	12.04	11.95	11.87	11.82
8	9.80	9.73	9.65	9.57	9.49	9.45
9	8.26	8.19	8.11	8.04	7.96	7.93
10	7.19	7.12	7.05	6.98	6.91	6.87
11	6.42	6.35	6.28	6.21	6.14	6.10
12	5.83	5.76	5.70	5.63	5.56	5.52
13	5.37	5.30	5.24	5.17	5.10	5.07
14	5.00	4.94	4.87	4.81	4.74	4.71
15	4.70	4.64	4.57	4.51	4.44	4.41
16	4.45	4.39	4.32	4.26	4.19	4.16
17	4.24	4.18	4.11	4.05	3.98	3.95
18	4.06	4.00	3.93	3.87	3.80	3.77
19	3.90	3.84	3.78	3.71	3.65	3.61
20	3.77	3.70	3.64	3.58	3.51	3.48
21	3.64	3.58	3.52	3.46	3.39	3.36
22	3.54	3.48	3.41	3.35	3.28	3.25
23	3.44	3.38	3.32	3.25	3.19	3.16
24	3.36	3.29	3.23	3.17	3.10	3.07
25	3.28	3.22	3.15	3.09	3.03	2.99
26	3.21	3.15	3.08	3.02	2.95	2.92
27	3.14	3.08	3.02	2.96	2.89	2.86
28	3.09	3.02	2.96	2.90	2.83	2.80
29	3.03	2.97	2.91	2.84	2.78	2.74
30	2.98	2.92	2.86	2.79	2.73	2.69
35	2.78	2.72	2.66	2.59	2.52	2.49
40	2.64	2.57	2.51	2.44	2.38	2.34
50	2.44	2.38	2.31	2.25	2.18	2.14
60	2.32	2.25	2.19	2.12	2.05	2.01
70	2.23	2.16	2.10	2.03	1.95	1.92
80	2.16	2.10	2.03	1.96	1.89	1.85
90	2.11	2.05	1.98	1.91	1.83	1.79
100	2.08	2.01	1.94	1.87	1.79	1.75
120	2.02	1.95	1.88	1.81	1.73	1.68
150	1.96	1.89	1.82	1.74	1.66	1.62
200	1.90	1.83	1.76	1.68	1.60	1.55
250	1.87	1.80	1.72	1.65	1.56	1.51
300	1.85	1.78	1.70	1.62	1.53	1.48
400	1.82	1.75	1.67	1.59	1.50	1.45
500	1.80	1.73	1.65	1.57	1.48	1.43
600	1.79	1.72	1.64	1.56	1.46	1.41
750	1.78	1.71	1.63	1.55	1.45	1.40
1000	1.77	1.69	1.62	1.53	1.44	1.38

Table A.4 χ^2 (chi-squared) distribution: critical values of χ^2

Degrees of freedom	Significance level		
	5%	1%	0.1%
1	3.841	6.635	10.828
2	5.991	9.210	13.816
3	7.815	11.345	16.266
4	9.488	13.277	18.467
5	11.070	15.086	20.515
6	12.592	16.812	22.458
7	14.067	18.475	24.322
8	15.507	20.090	26.124
9	16.919	21.666	27.877
10	18.307	23.209	29.588
12	21.026	26.217	32.909
15	24.996	30.578	37.697
20	31.410	37.566	45.315
30	43.773	50.892	59.703

Table A.5 Durbin–Watson d statistic: d_L and d_U, 5% significance level

n	$k = 2$		$k = 3$		$k = 4$		$k = 5$		$k = 6$	
	d_L	d_U	d_L	d_U	d_L	d_U	d_L	d_U	d_L	d_U
15	1.08	1.36	0.95	1.54	0.82	1.75	0.69	1.97	0.56	2.21
16	1.10	1.37	0.98	1.54	0.86	1.73	0.74	1.93	0.62	2.15
17	1.13	1.38	1.02	1.54	0.90	1.71	0.78	1.90	0.67	2.10
18	1.16	1.39	1.05	1.53	0.93	1.69	0.82	1.87	0.71	2.06
19	1.18	1.40	1.08	1.53	0.97	1.68	0.86	1.85	0.75	2.02
20	1.20	1.41	1.10	1.54	1.00	1.68	0.90	1.83	0.79	1.99
21	1.22	1.42	1.13	1.54	1.03	1.67	0.93	1.81	0.83	1.96
22	1.24	1.43	1.15	1.54	1.05	1.66	0.96	1.80	0.86	1.94
23	1.26	1.44	1.17	1.54	1.08	1.66	0.99	1.79	0.90	1.92
24	1.27	1.45	1.19	1.55	1.10	1.66	1.01	1.78	0.93	1.90
25	1.29	1.45	1.21	1.55	1.12	1.66	1.04	1.77	0.95	1.89
26	1.30	1.46	1.22	1.55	1.14	1.65	1.06	1.76	0.98	1.88
27	1.32	1.47	1.24	1.56	1.16	1.65	1.08	1.76	1.01	1.86
28	1.33	1.48	1.26	1.56	1.18	1.65	1.10	1.75	1.03	1.85
29	1.34	1.48	1.27	1.56	1.20	1.65	1.12	1.74	1.05	1.84
30	1.35	1.49	1.28	1.57	1.21	1.65	1.14	1.74	1.07	1.83
31	1.36	1.50	1.30	1.57	1.23	1.65	1.16	1.74	1.09	1.83
32	1.37	1.50	1.31	1.57	1.24	1.65	1.18	1.73	1.11	1.82
33	1.38	1.51	1.32	1.58	1.26	1.65	1.19	1.73	1.13	1.81
34	1.39	1.51	1.33	1.58	1.27	1.65	1.21	1.73	1.15	1.81
35	1.40	1.52	1.34	1.58	1.28	1.65	1.22	1.73	1.16	1.80
36	1.41	1.52	1.35	1.59	1.29	1.65	1.24	1.73	1.18	1.80
37	1.42	1.53	1.36	1.59	1.31	1.66	1.25	1.72	1.19	1.80
38	1.43	1.54	1.37	1.59	1.32	1.66	1.26	1.72	1.21	1.79
39	1.43	1.54	1.38	1.60	1.33	1.66	1.27	1.72	1.22	1.79
40	1.44	1.54	1.39	1.60	1.34	1.66	1.29	1.72	1.23	1.79
45	1.48	1.57	1.43	1.62	1.38	1.67	1.34	1.72	1.29	1.78
50	1.50	1.59	1.46	1.63	1.42	1.67	1.38	1.72	1.34	1.77
55	1.53	1.60	1.49	1.64	1.45	1.68	1.41	1.72	1.38	1.77
60	1.55	1.62	1.51	1.65	1.48	1.69	1.44	1.73	1.41	1.77
65	1.57	1.63	1.54	1.66	1.50	1.70	1.47	1.73	1.44	1.77
70	1.58	1.64	1.55	1.67	1.52	1.70	1.49	1.74	1.46	1.77
75	1.60	1.65	1.57	1.68	1.54	1.71	1.51	1.74	1.49	1.77
80	1.61	1.66	1.59	1.69	1.56	1.72	1.53	1.74	1.51	1.77
85	1.62	1.67	1.60	1.70	1.57	1.72	1.55	1.75	1.52	1.77
90	1.63	1.68	1.61	1.70	1.59	1.73	1.57	1.75	1.54	1.78
95	1.64	1.69	1.62	1.71	1.60	1.73	1.58	1.75	1.56	1.78
100	1.65	1.69	1.63	1.72	1.61	1.74	1.59	1.76	1.57	1.78

n = number of observations; k = number of parameters.
Reprinted from Durbin and Watson (1951) with the kind permission of the Biometrika Trustees

Table A.5 Durbin–Watson d statistic: d_L and d_U, 1% significance level

n	$k = 2$		$k = 3$		$k = 4$		$k = 5$		$k = 6$	
	d_L	d_U	d_L	d_U	d_L	d_U	d_L	d_U	d_L	d_U
15	0.81	1.07	0.70	1.25	0.59	1.46	0.49	1.70	0.39	1.96
16	0.84	1.09	0.74	1.25	0.63	1.44	0.53	1.66	0.44	1.90
17	0.87	1.10	0.77	1.25	0.67	1.43	0.57	1.63	0.48	1.85
18	0.90	1.12	0.80	1.26	0.71	1.42	0.61	1.60	0.52	1.80
19	0.93	1.13	0.83	1.26	0.74	1.41	0.65	1.58	0.56	1.77
20	0.95	1.15	0.86	1.27	0.77	1.41	0.68	1.57	0.60	1.74
21	0.97	1.16	0.89	1.27	0.80	1.41	0.72	1.55	0.63	1.71
22	1.00	1.17	0.91	1.28	0.83	1.40	0.75	1.54	0.66	1.69
23	1.02	1.19	0.94	1.29	0.86	1.40	0.77	1.53	0.70	1.67
24	1.04	1.20	0.96	1.30	0.88	1.41	0.80	1.53	0.72	1.66
25	1.05	1.21	0.98	1.30	0.90	1.41	0.83	1.52	0.75	1.65
26	1.07	1.22	1.00	1.31	0.93	1.41	0.85	1.52	0.78	1.64
27	1.09	1.23	1.02	1.32	0.95	1.41	0.88	1.51	0.81	1.63
28	1.10	1.24	1.04	1.32	0.97	1.41	0.90	1.51	0.83	1.62
29	1.12	1.25	1.05	1.33	0.99	1.42	0.92	1.51	0.85	1.61
30	1.13	1.26	1.07	1.34	1.01	1.42	0.94	1.51	0.88	1.61
31	1.15	1.27	1.08	1.34	1.02	1.42	0.96	1.51	0.90	1.60
32	1.16	1.28	1.10	1.35	1.04	1.43	0.98	1.51	0.92	1.60
33	1.17	1.29	1.11	1.36	1.05	1.43	1.00	1.51	0.94	1.59
34	1.18	1.30	1.13	1.36	1.07	1.43	1.01	1.51	0.95	1.59
35	1.19	1.31	1.14	1.37	1.08	1.44	1.03	1.51	0.97	1.59
36	1.21	1.32	1.15	1.38	1.10	1.44	1.04	1.51	0.99	1.59
37	1.22	1.32	1.16	1.38	1.11	1.45	1.06	1.51	1.00	1.59
38	1.23	1.33	1.18	1.39	1.12	1.45	1.07	1.52	1.02	1.58
39	1.24	1.34	1.19	1.39	1.14	1.45	1.09	1.52	1.03	1.58
40	1.25	1.34	1.20	1.40	1.15	1.46	1.10	1.52	1.05	1.58
45	1.29	1.38	1.24	1.42	1.20	1.48	1.16	1.53	1.11	1.58
50	1.32	1.40	1.28	1.45	1.24	1.49	1.20	1.54	1.16	1.59
55	1.26	1.43	1.32	1.47	1.28	1.51	1.25	1.55	1.21	1.59
60	1.38	1.45	1.35	1.48	1.32	1.52	1.28	1.56	1.25	1.60
65	1.41	1.47	1.38	1.50	1.35	1.53	1.31	1.57	1.28	1.61
70	1.43	1.49	1.40	1.52	1.37	1.55	1.34	1.58	1.31	1.61
75	1.45	1.50	1.42	1.53	1.39	1.56	1.37	1.59	1.34	1.62
80	1.47	1.52	1.44	1.54	1.42	1.57	1.39	1.60	1.36	1.62
85	1.48	1.53	1.46	1.55	1.43	1.58	1.41	1.60	1.39	1.63
90	1.50	1.54	1.47	1.56	1.45	1.59	1.43	1.61	1.41	1.64
95	1.51	1.55	1.49	1.57	1.47	1.60	1.45	1.62	1.42	1.64
100	1.52	1.56	1.50	1.58	1.48	1.60	1.46	1.63	1.44	1.65

n = number of observations; k = number of parameters.

APPENDIX B: Data Sets

Seven data sets, downloadable from the website (http://www.oup.co/best.textbooks/dougherty 3e/, are intended to provide an opportunity for practical work. The two main ones are the *Educational Attainment and Earnings Functions (EAEF)* and the *Demand Functions (DF)* data sets. Both of these are accompanied by a long series of exercises that are intended to provide continuity in practical work as one progresses through the text. *EAEF* is a cross-sectional data set that provides exercises for most topics covered in Chapters 1–10 and *DF* is a time series data set with exercises for most topics in Chapters 11–13. Both of them are also used to provide examples in the text. The other five data sets are more specialized in nature and are intended for use on specific topics.

All the data sets are provided in Stata, EViews and ASCII formats. To download a data set, click on its name and follow the instructions in the dialogue box. A Stata format data set should be ready for use. At the present time, an EViews data set will need renaming. For example, the Demand Functions data set will download with filename demand_wf1.bin. It should have extension wf1, not bin, so rename it as demand.wf1. To do this, go to My Computer, browse until you find the downloaded file, click on File and then Rename. You will now be able to delete the .bin extension and replace _wf1 with .wf1. EViews will now recognize it.

In all of the regressions you should include a constant. Most regression packages automatically assume that a constant is included, unless specifically indicated otherwise. However some, including EViews, require you to specify a constant if you wish to include one.

Educational Attainment and Earnings Functions (*EAEF*)

In view of its relevance for social policy, it is not surprising that analysis of the closely related topics of the determinants of educational attainment and the determinants of earnings has long been a major application of econometrics. Particularly sensitive issues are those relating to differences in educational attainment and earnings attributable to ethnicity, sex, and genetic endowment, to interactions in the effects of these factors, and to changes through time. The data sets described here will allow you to explore some of these issues using a subset of a major US data-base, the National Longitudinal Survey of Youth 1979– (NLSY79).

NLSY79 is a panel survey with repeated interviews of a nationally representative sample of young males and females aged 14 to 21 in 1979. From 1979 to 1994 the interviews took place annually. Since 1994 they have been conducted at two-year intervals. The core sample originally consisted of 3,003 males and 3,108 females. In addition there are special supplementary samples (some now discontinued) of ethnic minorities, those in poverty, and those serving in the armed forces. Extensive background information was obtained in the base-year survey in 1979 and since then information has been updated each year on education, training, employment, marital status, fertility, health, child care and assets and income. In addition special sections have been added from time to time on other topics—for example, drug use. The surveys have been extremely detailed and the quality of the execution of the survey is very high. As a consequence NLSY79 is regarded as one of the most important data bases available to social scientists working with US data.

This cross-section data set is supplied in the form of 22 parallel subsets each consisting of 540 observations, 270 drawn randomly from the male respondents in the source data set and the same number drawn randomly from the female respondents. The first twenty data sets are intended for use by members of a workshop. At the beginning of the course, the workshop instructor should assign a different data set to each member of the workshop. If you are working on your own, choose any one of the 20. Data Set 21 is used in examples in the text. You can use it to replicate the examples if you so wish. Data Set 22 is intended for use by instructors.

Each subset contains the same variables and they provide an opportunity for a small group to work through the exercises together with some variation in the results. As the name suggests, most of the exercises involve the fitting of educational attainment functions and earnings functions, starting with simple regression analysis and developing more complex models as new topics are encountered in the cross-sectional part of the text, Chapters 1–10.

Each subset contains data for each respondent on the following variables (C indicates a continuous variable, D a dummy variable):

Personal variables

FEMALE	D	Sex of respondent (0 if male, 1 if female)
MALE	D	Sex of respondent (1 if male, 0 if female)

Ethnicity:

ETHBLACK	D	Black
ETHHISP	D	Hispanic
ETHWHITE	D	Non-black, non-hispanic
AGE	C	Age in 2002
S	C	Years of schooling (highest grade completed as of 2002)

Highest educational qualification:

EDUCPROF	D	Professional degree
EDUCPHD	D	Doctorate
EDUCMAST	D	Master's degree
EDUCBA	D	Bachelor's degree
EDUCAA	D	Associate's (two-year college) degree
EDUCHSD	D	High school diploma or equivalent
EDUCDO	D	High school drop-out

Marital status:

SINGLE	D	Single, never married
MARRIED	D	Married, spouse present
DIVORCED	D	Divorced or separated

Scaled score on a component of the ASVAB battery:

ASVAB02	C	Arithmetic reasoning
ASVAB03	C	Word knowledge
ASVAB04	C	Paragraph comprehension
ASVAB05	C	Numerical operations (speed test)
ASVAB06	C	Coding speed (speed test)
ASVABC	C	Composite of *ASVAB02* (with double weight), *ASVAB03* and *ASVAB04*

Faith:

FAITHN	D	None
FAITHC	D	Catholic

FAITHJ	D	Jewish
FAITHP	D	Protestant
FAITHO	D	Other
HEIGHT	C	Height, in inches, in 1985
WEIGHT85	C	Weight, in pounds, in 1985
WEIGHT02	C	Weight, in pounds, in 2002

Family background variables

SM	C	Years of schooling of respondent's mother
SF	C	Years of schooling of respondent's father
SIBLINGS	C	Number of siblings

Living at age 14:

L14TOWN	D	in a town or city
L14COUN	D	in the country, not on a farm
L14FARM	D	on a farm
LIBRARY	D	Member of family possessed a library card when respondent was 14
POV78	D	Family living in poverty in 1978

Work-related variables

EARNINGS	C	Current hourly earnings in $ reported at the 2002 interview
HOURS	C	Usual number of hours worked per week, 2002 interview
TENURE	C	Tenure (years) with current employer at the 2002 interview
EXP	C	Total out-of-school work experience (years) as of the 2002 interview.
COLLBARG	D	Pay set by collective bargaining, 2002

Category of employment:

CATGOV	D	Government
CATPRI	D	Private sector
CATSE	D	Self-employment
URBAN	D	Living in an urban area at 2002 interview

Living in 2002 in:

REGNC	D	North central census region
REGNE	D	North eastern
REGS	D	Southern
REGW	D	Western

Not all of the variables are used in the exercises suggested in the next section. You should feel free to experiment by trying alternative regression specifications with the extra variables.

The data set is intended for use with the following exercises in Chapters 1–10 in the text:

1.3, 1.4, 2.17, 2.18, 2.21, 2.25, 2.26, 2.28 (simple regression, *t* tests, and *F* tests)

3.2, 3.3, 3.4 3.7, 3.8, 3.11, 3.12, 3.14, 3.15, 3.16, 3.1 (multiple regression, tests, and multicollinearity)

4.3, 4.4 (logarithmic and semilogarithmic regressions)

5.1, 5.3, 5.4, 5.6, 5.8 5.9, 5.10, 5.11, 5.12, 5.13, 5.15, 5.16, 5.17, 5.18, 5.19, 5.20 (dummy variables)

6.1, 6.2, 6.3, 6.8, 6.9, 6.11, 6.12 (variable specification, proxy variables, and tests of restictions)

7.3, 7.4, 7.8 (heteroscedasticity)

8.10 (measurement error)

9.8 (simultaneous equations estimation)

10.1, 10.3, 10.6 (binary choice and sample selection)

Demand Functions (*DF*)

The data set is a subset of the National Income and Product Accounts published on a regular basis by the U.S. Bureau of the Census. The data are aggregate (for the whole of the United States) annual observations for the period 1959–2003 on income, 20 categories of consumer expenditure, and price index series for these categories. The intention is that the exercises should provide material for practical work for a small group of students working in parallel, each student working with a different category of expenditure.

The income and expenditure variables are all measured in $ billion at 2000 constant prices. The price index series are all based with 2000 = 100. The variables are as follows:

Income and population

DPI	Aggregate disposable personal income
TPE	Aggregate personal expenditure
POP	Population, measured in thousands

Expenditure on nondurables

CLOT	Clothing and shoes
FLOW	Flowers, seeds, and potted plants
FOOD	Food purchased for off-premise consumption (this category should not be assigned for practical work because it is used for examples in the text).
GASO	Gasoline and oil
MAGS	Magazines, newspapers, and sheet music
TOB	Tobacco products
TOYS	Nondurable toys and sport supplies

Expenditure on services

ADM	Admissions to specified spectator amusements
BUSI	Personal business
DENT	Dentists
DOC	Physicians
GAS	Gas
HOUS	Housing (this category should not be assigned for practical work because it is used for examples in the text).
LEGL	Legal services
MASS	Local transportation: mass transit systems
REL	Religious and welfare activities
TELE	Telephone and telegraph

Expenditure on durables

BOOK	Books and maps
FURN	Furniture
OPHT	Ophthalmic products

The nominal price index series for the categories of expenditure have the name of the category prefixed by *P*: *PFOOD, PHOUS*, etc. The data set includes the nominal price index for total personal expenditure, *PTPE*. In the regressions, economic theory (and common sense) suggests that one should use real price indices rather than nominal ones in regression analysis, where a real price index is defined relative to general inflation as measured by *PTPE*. For example, the real (or relative) price index for food, *PRELFOOD*, is defined as

$$PRELFOOD = 100 * (PFOOD/PTPE)$$

The data set also includes a trend variable *TIME* that is defined to be 1 for 1959, 2 for 1960, and so on.

You should choose, or be assigned by your instructor, one of the categories of expenditure listed above. In the exercises below you will develop a regression specification for this category, starting with a simple regression model and gradually improving it. If you are working with just one category of expenditure, it may be helpful to simplify the data set by deleting the expenditure and price variables relating to the other categories.

The data set is intended for use with the following exercises in Chapters 11–13 in the text:

11.2, 11.3, 11.4, 11.5, 11.7, 11.10, 11.13, 11.14, 11.5 (static models, dynamics, and predictions)

12.1, 12.2, 12.3, 12.5 (autocorrelation and the common factor test)

13.9, 13.11, 13.12 (unit root tests, cointegration, and the error correction model)

Consumer Expenditure Survey (*CES*)

This cross-sectional data set contains annual household expenditure on twenty-one categories of expenditure for 869 households in 1995. The suite of exercises provided for it is similar to that for *EAEF*, the data set being intended for extra practice for students out-of-class. Answers to all the exercises are provided in the *Study Guide*.

The data set has been derived from the Quarterly Interview Survey of the Consumer Expenditure Survey undertaken by the US Department of Labor, Bureau of Labor Statistics. The survey has a nationally representative sample of about 5,000 households, each household being interviewed five times, the first time to gather basic data about the household, and the other four times at quarterly intervals to gather data on expenditures. The households in the present data set entered the quarterly survey at the beginning of 1995 and the data give the total expenditure by category over the 1995 calendar year. The variables are as follows:

Household characteristics

SIZE	Number of persons in the household.
SIZEAM	Number of adult males (males older than 15) in the household.
SIZEAF	Number of adult females (females older than 15) in the household.
SIZEJM	Number of junior males (males aged 2 through 15) in the household.
SIZEJF	Number of junior females (females aged 2 through 15) in the household.
SIZEIN	Number of children aged less than 2 in the household.
REFAGE	Age of the reference person in the household (the individual who owns or rents the dwelling).
REFEDUC	Education of the reference person, coded as

    0 Never went to school
    1 Elementary school only(1–8 years)
    2 Some high school, but did not graduate
    3 High school graduate, no college
    4 Some college, but did not graduate
    5 College graduate
    6 Graduate school

REFRACE	Ethnicity of the reference person, coded as

    1 White
    2 Black
    3 American Indian, Aleut, Eskimo
    4 Asian or Pacific Islander
    5 Other

HHTENURE	Household tenure, coded as
	1 Owned with mortgage
	2 Owned without mortgage
	3 Owned, mortgage not reported
	4 Rented
	5 Occupied without payment of cash rent
	6 Student housing

Expenditure variables

EXP	Total household expenditure, including some items not listed as variables below.
FDHO	Food and nonalcoholic beverages consumed at home.
FDAW	Food and nonalcoholic beverages consumed away from home, excluding meals as pay in kind
HOUS	Housing, excluding expenditure on utilities, household operations, and household equipment. In the case of owned dwellings it comprises mortgage interest, property taxes, and the cost of maintenance, repairs, and insurance. In the case of rented dwellings, it consists of rent, including rent as pay in kind. *HOUS* also includes the recurrent costs of vacation houses, expenditure on lodging away from home, and the cost of school housing. Note that this category of expenditure does *not* include purchases of dwellings.
TELE	Telephone services.
DOM	Domestic services, such as condo housekeeping and management, gardening, and babysitting and child day care.
TEXT	Household textiles such as bathroom, bedroom, kitchen and dining room linens, curtains and cushions.
FURN	Furniture.
MAPP	Major household appliances, such as dishwashers, refrigerators, clothes washers, stoves and ovens, air conditioners, floor cleaning machines and sewing machines.
SAPP	Small appliances and miscellaneous housewares.
CLOT	Clothing
FOOT	Footwear
GASO	Gasoline and motor oil
TRIP	Public transportation on out-of-town trips.
LOCT	Local public transportation.
HEAL	Health care, comprising health insurance, medical services, prescription drugs, and medical supplies.
ENT	Entertainment, comprising fees and admissions, televisions, radios, and sound equipment, pets, toys, and playground equipment, and other related equipment and services.
FEES	Membership fees of recreational and health clubs, fees for participant sports, admission fees for movies, theatre, concerts, opera, and sporting events, and fees for recreational instruction.
TOYS	Toys, games, hobbies, playground equipment, and pets, including veterinarian expenses.
READ	Reading matter, such as newspapers, magazines, and books
EDUC	Education, such as tuition fees, school books, supplies and equipment for elementary school, high school, and college, and other types of school.
TOB	Tobacco products and supplies such as cigarettes, cigars, and pipe tobacco.

All the expenditure variables are measured in current dollars. If you are working with just one category of expenditure, it may be helpful to simplify the data set by deleting the expenditure variables relating to the other categories.

The data set is intended for use with the following exercises in the text:

4.1, 4.2, 4.7, and 10.5

A comprehensive set of exercises covering the same topics as the *EAEF* data set will be found in the *Study Guide*.

OECD employment and GDP growth rates (*OECD*)

This data set is provided for Exercise 4.5, an investigation into alternative nonlinear functional forms. An answer is provided in the *Study Guide*. The data set contains the average annual growth rate of various macroeconomic aggregates for the period 1988–1997 for 26 OECD countries. It has been compiled from various issues of OECD *Economic Outlook* over the period 1990–2000. Missing values have been coded –9999, except in the Stata data set, where the missing value code has been used. The variables are

WAGES	Average annual rate of growth of nominal wages
PRICES	Average annual rate of growth of prices
GDP	Average annual rate of growth of real GDP
EMPLOY	Average annual rate of growth of employment
MONEY1	Average annual rate of growth of money and quasi-money
MONEY2	Average annual rate of growth of money and quasi-money, alternative data compiled from individual country tables in the IMF *International Financial Statistics Yearbook 2000*.
UNEMPLOY	Average rate of unemployment

In regressions involving *EMPLOY*, the observation for Mexico should be excluded because the figure has been distorted by special circumstances. With the NAFTA agreement, US firms started moving their manufacturing plants to low-wage Mexico, recruiting workers many of whom had previously been employed in the informal sector. The official employment statistics, collected by social security, measure only employment in the formal sector and therefore grossly overestimate the net increase in employment. In 1997 alone, employment increased by 13.3 percent according to the official figures, clearly nonsensical. Over the whole period, the average employment growth rate was greater than the average GDP growth rate, also nonsensical.

School Costs (*SC*)

This cross-sectional data set provides data on annual recurrent expenditure, numbers of students, type of curriculum, and other characteristics for 74 schools in Shanghai. The intention is to provide an opportunity for using dummy variables, investigating how type of curriculum affects the cost function.

The data set is an extract taken by the author with permission from a series of annual surveys of 105 Shanghai secondary schools undertaken by Fujian University staff during the period 1981–1985 with the support of the World Bank. The data in this data set relate to 1985. It was a time of rapid expansion of secondary education, both in terms of the number of schools and in the enrollments of some. To guard against the possibility that enrolments and budgets might be in disequilibrium, the 24 schools with enrolments that had increased (or decreased) by more than one third over the previous year were excluded from the sample. Likewise seven schools with incomplete data were excluded, leaving 74 in the sample. The data on capital expenditure were very volatile and not susceptible to meaningful analysis. The recurrent cost data comprised staff costs, non-staff administrative expenditure, non-staff instructional expenditure, expenditure on books and expenditure on utilities. Maintenance expenditure was excluded because, like capital expenditure, it was very volatile and seemingly determined more by the availability of a budget rather than actual year-to-year need.

The variables are (C indicates a continuous variable, D a dummy variable):

COST	C	Annual recurrent cost, in yuan (worth about US$0.25 at the time)
N	C	Number of students enrolled
OCC	D	Occupational school (1 if technical or skilled workers' school, 0 if general or vocational school)
REGULAR	D	Regular school (1 if general or vocational school, 0 if technical or skilled workers' school)
TECH	D	Technical school (1 if technical school, 0 otherwise)
WORKER	D	Skilled workers' school (1 if skilled workers' school, 0 otherwise)
VOC	D	Vocational school (1 if vocational school, 0 otherwise)
GEN	D	General school (1 if general school, 0 otherwise)
RES	D	Residential school (1 if residential school, 0 otherwise)

Labor Force Participation (*LFP*)

This cross-section data set consists of data on labor force participation and background characteristics for 2,726 individuals in the US National Longitudinal Survey of Youth data set for 1994. See the *EAEF* entry above for a description of this survey. C indicates a continuous variable, D a dummy variable, T a coded variable.

Personal variables

AGE	C	Age in 1994
S	C	Years of schooling (highest grade completed as of 1994)
MALE	D	Sex of respondent (1 if male, 0 if female)

Ethnicity:

ETHBLACK	D	Black
ETHHISP	D	Hispanic

Scaled score on a component of the ASVAB battery:

ASVAB2	C	Arithmetic reasoning
ASVAB3	C	Word knowledge
ASVAB4	C	Paragraph comprehension
ASVABC	C	Composite of *ASVAB2* (with double weight), *ASVAB3* and *ASVAB4*
CHILDREN	C	Number of children in the household
YOUNGEST	C	Age of youngest child
CHILDL06	C	Presence of a child age < 6 in the household
CHILDL16	C	Presence of a child age < 16, but no child age < 6, in the household
MARISTAT	T	Marital status, coded as: 1 never married; 2 married, spouse present; 3 other
MARRIED	D	Married (*MARISTAT*=2)

Work-related variables

EARNINGS	C	Current hourly earnings in $ reported at 1994 interview
WORKING	D	Working (has recorded earnings)
EMPSTAT	T	Employment status, coded as: 1 employed; 2 unemployed; 3 out of the labor force

The data set is used for exercises in Chapter 10 on probit analysis (Exercise 10.4) and sample selection bias (Exercise 10.8).

Educational Expenditure (*EDUC*)

This data set contains cross-section data on aggregate expenditure on education, GDP, and population for a sample of 38 countries in 1997. It is provided for Exercises 7.6 and 7.9, an investigation into heteroscedasticity and measures to alleviate it. It contains three variables:

EDUC   Public recurrent expenditure on education (US$ million)
GDP   Gross domestic product (US$ million)
POP   Population (million)

Bibliography

Amemiya, Takeshi (1981). Qualitative response models: a survey. *Journal of Economic Literature* 19(4): 1483–1536

Amemiya, Takeshi (1984). Tobit models: a survey. *Journal of Econometrics* 24(1): 3–61

Baltagi, Badi H. (2001). *Econometric Analysis of Panel Data* (second edition). Chichester, England: Wiley

Box, George E.P., and David R. Cox (1964). An analysis of transformations. *Journal of the Royal Statistical Society Series B* 26(2): 211–243

Box, George E.P., and Gwilym M. Jenkins (1970). *Time Series Analysis: Forecasting and Control*. San Francisco: Holden Day

Box, George E.P., Gwilym M. Jenkins, and Gregory C. Reinsel (1994). *Time Series Analysis: Forecasting and Control* (third edition). Englewood Cliffs, NJ: Prentice-Hall

Brown, T.M. (1952). Habit persistence and lags in consumer behaviour. *Econometrica* 20(3): 355–371

Card, David (1995). Using geographic variation in college proximity to estimate the return to schooling. In Louis N. Christofides, E. Kenneth Grant, and Robert Swidinsky (editors), *Aspects of Labour Market Behaviour: Essays in Honour of John Vanderkamp*. Toronto: University of Toronto Press

Chow, Gregory C. (1960). Tests of equality between sets of coefficients in two linear regressions. *Econometrica* 28(3): 591–605

Cobb, Charles W., and Paul H. Douglas (1928). A theory of production. *American Economic Review* 18(1, Supplement): 139–165

Davidson, James E.H. (2000). *Econometric Theory*. Oxford: Blackwell

Davidson, Russell, and James G. MacKinnon (1993). *Estimation and Inference in Econometrics*. New York: Oxford University Press

Dickey, David A., and Wayne A. Fuller (1979). Distribution of the estimators for autoregressive time series with a unit root. *Journal of the American Statistical Association* 74(366): 427–431

Dufour, Jean-Marie (1980). Dummy variables and predictive tests for structural change. *Economics Letters* 6(3): 241–247

Durbin, James (1954). Errors in variables. *Review of the International Statistical Institute* 22(1): 23–32

Durbin, James (1970). Testing for serial correlation in least-squares regression when some of the regressors are lagged dependent variables. *Econometrica* 38(3): 410–421

Durbin, James, and G.S. Watson (1950). Testing for serial correlation in least-squares regression I. *Biometrika* 37(3–4): 409–428

Durlauf, Steven N., and Peter C.B. Phillips (1988). Trends versus random walks in time series analysis. *Econometrica* 56(6): 1333–1354

Engle, Robert F., and Clive W.J. Granger (1987). Co-integration and error correction representation, estimation, and testing. *Econometrica* 50(2): 251–276

Fowler, Floyd J. (1993). *Survey Research Methods* (second edition). Newbury Park, CA: Sage

Friedman, Milton (1957). *A Theory of the Consumption Function*. Princeton, NJ: Princeton University Press

Friedman, Milton (1959). The demand for money: some theoretical and empirical results. *Journal of Political Economy* 67(4): 327–351

Frisch, Ragnar, and Frederick V. Waugh (1933). Partial time regressions as compared with individual trends. *Econometrica* 1(4): 387–401

Goldfeld, Stephen M., and Richard E. Quandt (1965). Some tests for homoscedasticity. *Journal of the American Statistical Association* 60(310): 539–547

Granger, Clive W.J., and Paul Newbold (1974). Spurious regressions in econometrics. *Journal of Econometrics* 2(2): 111–120

Gronau, Reuben (1974). Wage comparisons—a selectivity bias. *Journal of Political Economy* 82(6): 1119–1155

Hausman, Jerry A. (1978). Specification tests in econometrics. *Econometrica* 46(6): 1251–1271

Heckman, James (1976). The common structure of statistical models of truncation, sample selection, and limited dependent variables and a simple estimator for such models. *Annals of Economic and Social Measurement* 5(4): 475–492

Hendry, David F. (1979). Predictive failure and econometric modelling in macroeconomics: the transactions demand for money. In Paul Ormerod (editor), *Modelling the Economy*. London: Heinemann

Hendry, David F., and Grayham E. Mizon (1978). Serial correlation as a convenient simplification, not a nuisance. *Economic Journal* 88(351): 549–563

Hsiao, Cheng (2003). *Analysis of Panel Data* (second edition). Cambridge: Cambridge University Press

Johnston, Jack and John Dinardo (1997). *Econometric Methods* (fourth edition). New York: McGraw-Hill

Kmenta, Jan (1986). *Elements of Econometrics* (second edition). New York: Macmillan

Koyck, Leendert M. (1954). *Distributed Lags and Investment Analysis*. Amsterdam: North-Holland

Kuh, Edwin, and John R. Meyer (1957). How extraneous are extraneous estimates? *Review of Economics and Statistics* 39(4): 380–393

Liviatan, Nissan (1963). Tests of the Permanent-Income Hypothesis based on a reinterview savings survey. In Carl Christ (editor), *Measurement in Economics*. Stanford, CA: Stanford University Press

Lovell, Michael C. (1963). Seasonal adjustment of economic time series. *Journal of the American Statistical Association* 58: 993–1010

MacKinnon, James G., and Halbert White (1985). Some heteroskedasticity-consistent covariance matrix estimators with improved finite sample properties. *Journal of Econometrics* 29(3): 305–325

Moser, Claus and Graham Kalton (1985). *Survey Methods in Social Investigation* (second edition). Aldershot: Gower

Nelson, Charles R. (1973). *Applied Time Series Analysis*. San Francisco: Holden Day

Nelson, Charles R., and Charles I. Plosser (1982). Trends and random walks in macroeconomic time series: some evidence and implications. *Journal of Monetary Economics* 10(2): 139–162

Nerlove, Marc (1963). Returns to scale in electricity supply. In Carl Christ (editor), *Measurement in Economics*. Stanford, CA: Stanford University Press

Peach, James T., and James L. Webb (1983). Randomly specified macroeconomic models: some implications for model selection. *Journal of Economic Issues* 17(3): 697–720

Pesaran, Hashem M., R.P. Smith, and Yeo J. Stephen (1985). Testing for structural stability and predictive failure: a review. *Manchester School* 53(3): 280–295

Phillips, Peter C.B. (1986). Understanding spurious regressions in econometrics. *Journal of Econometrics* 33(3): 311–340

Phillips, Peter C.B. (1987). Towards a unified asymptotic theory for autoregression. *Biometrika* 74(3): 535–547

Salkever, David S. (1976). The use of dummy variables to compute predictions, prediction errors and confidence intervals. *Journal of Econometrics* 4(4): 393–397

Stock, James H. (1987). Asymptotic properties of least squares estimators of cointegrating vectors. *Econometrica* 55(5): 1035–1056

Tobin, James (1958). Estimation of relationships for limited dependent variables. *Econometrica* 26(1): 24–36

Wichern, Dean W. (1973). The behaviour of the sample autocorrelation function for an integrated moving average process. *Biometrika* 60(2): 235–239

White, Halbert (1980). A heteroskedasticity-consistent covariance matrix estimator and a direct test for heteroskedasticity. *Econometrica* 48(4): 817–838

Wonnacott, Thomas H., and Ronald J. Wonnacott (1990). *Introductory Statistics for Business and Economics* (fourth edition). New York: Wiley

Wooldridge, Jeffrey M. (1994). Estimation and inference for dependent processes. In Robert F. Engle and Daniel F. McFadden (editors), *Handbook of Econometrics*, Volume 4. Amsterdam: North-Holland

Wooldridge, Jeffrey M. (2002). *Econometric Analysis of Cross Section and Panel Data*. Cambridge, MA: MIT Press

Wu, De-Min (1973). Alternative tests of independence between stochastic regressors and disturbances. *Econometrica* 41(4): 733–750

Author Index

Subject Index